P9-AOG-425

EVERYMAN,
I WILL GO WITH THEE,
AND BE THY GUIDE,
IN THY MOST NEED
TO GO BY THY SIDE

WILLIAM SHAKESPEARE

Tragedies

with an Introduction by Tony Tanner
General Editor – Sylvan Barnet

VOLUME 1

EVERYMAN'S LIBRARY

92

First included in Everyman's Library, 1906

These plays are published by arrangement with New American Library, a division of Penguin Books USA Inc.

Typography by Peter B. Willberg

ISBN 1-85715-092-9

A catalogue record for this book is available from the British Library

Published by David Campbell Publishers Ltd., 79 Berwick Street, London W1V 3PF

Distributed by Random House (UK) Ltd., 20 Vauxhall Bridge Road, London SW1V 2SA

CONTENTS

SHAKESPEARE: THE MAJOR TRAGEDIES

Blood hath been shed ere now, i' th' olden time,
Ere humane statute purged the gentle weal;
(*Macbeth*, III, iv, 77–8)

Western tragedy opens with a troubled and apprehensive watchman or guard on the roof of the palace of King Agamemnon, watching and waiting for news and signals concerning the outcome of the Greek war against Troy. He conveys a sense of unease and disquiet. Something, which he dare not, or will not, or cannot, articulate is wrong within the palace or 'house' for which he is the watchman. It is night-time and the atmosphere is ominous, full of dubiety and an incipient sense of festering secrets. The long drama of the *Oresteia* has begun. Some two thousand years later, *Hamlet*, the first indisputably great European tragedy since the time of the Greeks, will open in very much the same way – on 'A guard platform of the castle' (of Elsinore), at midnight, with a nervous, jittery guardsman – Barnado – asking apprehensive questions in the darkness, and revealing that, for unspecified reasons, he is 'sick at heart'. The similarity betokens no indebtedness of Shakespeare to Aeschylus (whose work he could not have known), but rather a profound similarity of apprehension as to what might constitute a source for tragic drama. Shakespeare does not start where Aeschylus left off: he starts where Aeschylus started. And the subject, which is to say the problem, which is to say the potentially – and actually – catastrophic issue which they both set out to explore in their plays – the drama they dramatized – centres on revenge.

The *Oresteia* is a trilogy and what the three plays dramatize is – to put it at its simplest – how do you effect the painful, difficult, but absolutely essential transition from the revenge code (vendetta) – blood will have blood, an eye for an eye – to the impersonalization and institutionalization of revenge by the setting up of courts of law (whereby, as we now say, the state has a monopoly of violence); just, exactly, the crucial transition described by Macbeth in the quotation at the start of this introduction. How – to put it starkly – do you, does the human race in whatever communal or aggregated form, 'legalize' murder. Or – to put it at its starkest – how does the group (house, tribe, city, state) handle, cope with, somehow control, the problem which, arguably, is THE problem for any community or would-be communality – the problem of violence.

René Girard has much to say about the problems the revenge code poses for the community in his book *Violence and the Sacred* (1977). 'Vengeance, then, is an interminable, infinitely repetitive process. Every time it turns up in some part of the community, it threatens to involve the whole social body. There is the risk that the act of vengeance will initiate a chain reaction whose consequences will quickly prove fatal to any society of modest size. The multiplication of reprisals instantaneously puts the very existence of a society in jeopardy, and that is why it is universally proscribed.' And, we might add, why Hamlet is thrown into such confusion when reprisal is very specifically prescribed for him. 'Vengeance is a vicious circle whose effect on primitive societies can only be surmised. For us the circle has been broken. We owe our good fortune to one of our social institutions above all: our judicial system, which serves to deflect the menace of vengeance.'

In a society in which a fully elaborated judicial system is not in place, Girard suggests, ritual sacrifice, by deflecting vengeance onto a surrogate victim, 'serves to protect the entire community from *its own violence*; it prompts the entire community to choose victims outside itself.' It thus serves to keep violence in check – which Girard sees as perhaps the profoundest need of any community. This is because violence is endlessly 'self-propagating'. At the same time, Girard reminds us that while it is essential to recognize and acknowledge the differences, both functional and mythical, between vengeance, sacrifice, and legal punishment, 'it is important to recognize their fundamental identity'. 'Murder most foul, as in the best it is' – as in the best revenge code, the best religion, the best legal system. With these words alone, the ghost of Hamlet's father renders the task he has set his son virtually impossible to execute. However the killing is ritualized or legalized, if we look hard enough 'we find ourselves face to face with the specter of reciprocal reprisal'. It is a disturbing sight. Nevertheless, using whatever sanctions, and they will usually be transcendental, a society must find a way of defining and justifying 'a violence that is holy, legal, and legitimate, successfully opposed to a violence that is unjust, illegal, and illegitimate'.

I think the problem of violence is central to tragedy and that, in some tentative sense, we can think of the tragic drama as a form of ritual sacrifice, and the tragic hero or protagonist who goes to his death as bearing some relationship to the figure of the scapegoat or surrogate victim. But, to emphasize what I take to be the importance of this matter, a final quotation from Girard. 'The mechanism of reciprocal violence can be described as a vicious circle. Once a community enters the circle, it is unable to extricate itself. We can define this circle in terms of vengeance and reprisals... In more general terms, the mimetic character of violence is so intense that once violence is installed in a community, it cannot burn itself out.' In the *Oresteia*, Aeschylus shows the House of Atreus to be hopelessly trapped within this vicious circle over generations. The question then becomes – how can the circle be broken? Who will take the first step out – and how?

*

When, in *The Libation Bearers*, the second play of the *Oresteia*, Orestes finally confronts his mother, Clytemnestra, and is about to kill her, she begs for pity from him as her son, reminding him that he drew milk from her breasts. And Orestes stops. There follows this exchange.[1]

Orestes. What shall I do, Pylades? Be shamed to kill my mother?
Pylades. What then becomes thereafter of the oracles
  declared by Loxias at Pytho? What of sworn oaths?
  Count all men hateful to you rather than the gods.
Orestes. I judge that you win. Your advice is good.

[1]. Aeschylus quotation from the translation by Greene and Lattimore, *Greek Tragedies*, University of Chicago Press, 1960.

This, I will make so bold as to say, is the most crucial moment in the whole trilogy – indeed, I will make bolder to say that it is a crucial moment in the emergence of western drama. Not just because with the authoritative pronouncement from Pylades we hear for the first time the voice of the famous 'third actor', marking a crucial further move away from the earlier choric-ritual form of tragedy. But, more importantly, because, in this brief moment, Orestes has introduced a break in the circle. He steps back from his ordained and premeditated act and, as it were, looks at it from the outside. He has opened up a gap in which, albeit briefly, reflection interrupts and defers action. He has, for that moment, stalled the imperatives of revenge and begun to raise matters of principle. It *is* terrible to kill your mother. 'What should I do?' It is the first time that question has been asked. Heretofore, wife killed husband, father killed daughter, uncle killed nephews, god killed offspring without any such reflective questioning or moment of ethical uncertainty. They may, like animals, have had to wait to leap, but they never, like Orestes, stopped to think. What Orestes has done is to introduce or insert a 'pause' in which he 'scans' his imminent deed (meaning, looks at it before performing it). I use these two words because they are absolutely central to Shakespearean tragedy as I hope will emerge. We could say that, what for Orestes is a very short 'pause' and a very brief 'scan', becomes in *Hamlet* almost the whole of the play. Because, between Aeschylus and Shakespeare, something has taken place which permanently changed the western mind – namely, Christianity, and more particularly for the Elizabethans, the Reformation.

*

The earliest Elizabethan attempts at tragedy were mainly revenge plays, with Seneca as the model. The most important of them before *Hamlet*, is *The Spanish Tragedy* (probably 1586–7) by Thomas Kyd. He is said to have written the lost play of *Hamlet* (sometime before 1589), but that play has vanished without any real trace and nothing can be proved.

There are certainly features of *The Spanish Tragedy* which can be seen as anticipating Shakespeare's play. There is a ghost demanding revenge. Hieronimo, called on to revenge the very brutal murder of his son, engages in soliloquies in which he goes over the problems of what he has to do. (At one point he quotes to himself 'Vengeance is mine saith the Lord', but he does it anyway.) Perhaps most crucially, he uses a play-within-the-play to effect his revenge. In this case literally, the supposed 'actors' step out and actually murder the guilty creatures sitting at *that* play. Hamlet's dramaturgy is a good deal more complicated.

But rather than these obvious similarities, I wish to draw attention to some lines spoken by Hieronimo, now seemingly, but perhaps only seemingly, mad (another anticipation of Hamlet):

> There is a path upon your left-hand side,
> That leadeth from a guilty conscience
> Unto a forest of distrust and fear,
> A darksome place and dangerous to pass:
> There shall you meet with melancholy thoughts,
> Whose baleful humours if you but uphold,
> It will conduct you to despair and death:
>
> (III, xi, 13–19)

What we have here is a landscape, as it were a topography, of a 'guilty conscience'. It would be too much to say that Christianity 'invented' conscience, but between the time of Augustine and Aquinas, the concept had been elaborated and expanded in an entirely new way. The Reformation served to give it even more centrality and prominence. The word seems to come into currency in English during the fourteenth century (the earliest usage cited by the OED is 1325), replacing the attractive Middle-English word 'inwit'. It is tempting but anachronistic to suggest that Orestes opened the gap of conscience in a world hitherto locked into a spiral of conscienceless action. The Greeks had much to say about guilt, but they had no word for 'conscience' and there is nothing like Hieronimo's speech in their drama. The Furies come from outside and are visibly there. Conscience – vast, frightening tracts of it – is all inside. As Brutus, Hamlet, and Macbeth will variously discover.

Here is a soliloquy by Brutus in *Julius Caesar* which is absolutely crucial in the evolution of Shakespearian tragedy:

> Since Cassius first did whet me against Caesar,
> I have not slept.
> Between the acting of a dreadful thing
> And the first motion, all the interim is
> Like a phantasma, or a hideous dream.
> The genius and the mortal instruments
> Are then in council, and the state of man,
> Like to a little kingdom, suffers then
> The nature of an insurrection.
>
> (II, i, 61–9)

Shakespearian tragedy takes place in and focuses on, exactly, the 'interim' between the first 'motion' (or prompting, or provocation, or incitement, or some stirring inclination) and 'the acting of a dreadful thing'. The 'motion' may be started by an ambiguous ghost (*Hamlet*), a scheming devil (*Othello*), or equivocating witches (*Macbeth*). The 'dreadful thing' is always murder – albeit in very different circumstances. The period in between is experienced by the protagonist as, in different ways, 'like a phantasma, or a hideous dream'. And that 'phantasma' is, among other things, the phantasmagoria of the conscience started, startled, into unprecedented activity. The experience takes all the tragic protagonists, in varying degrees, to the edge of madness. This period or 'interim' may be long or short. *Hamlet*, the longest and slowest of Shakespeare's tragedies, is almost all 'interim'. *Macbeth*, his shortest and fastest, concentrates on a man who, with increasing desperation, tries to shrink and indeed obliterate the 'interim'. These are the parameters of Shakespeare's major tragedies. And this is what they are about.

*

HAMLET

Why is *Hamlet* so long, and what do I mean by saying that it is nearly all 'interim'? It is, famously, a delaying play, a play about delay. Hamlet's procrastination, if that is what it is, has been endlessly discussed. At the simplest level there is the unassailable argument of 'no delay, no play', and certainly if Hamlet had hurried to dispatch Claudius as soon as the ghost had issued his imperative, or even if he had killed him when, by his own account, he might 'do it pat' shortly after the ambiguous success of his 'play', we would not have the 'play' we have. But mere dramaturgical expediency would not have made *Hamlet* the most famous and inexhaustible western tragedy of our modern era, and we must certainly enquire a bit more curiously than that. Here are some words from Claudius, inciting Laertes to revenge:

> That we would do
> We should do when we would, for this "would" changes,
> And hath abatements and delays as many
> As there are tongues, are hands, are accidents . . .
>
> (IV, vii, 118–21)

'Should' and 'would'; 'tongues' and 'hands'; intention and obligation; word and deed – the complex inter-relation and interaction between these things occupy much of the play. And 'accidents' turn out to be crucial. 'Abatements' covers weakenings and bluntings of resolve and general retardations, and these all contribute to the lengthening of the play. Once again, we are looking at the 'interim' between prompting or provocation – the 'first motion' – and performance – the 'dreadful deed'.

Let us just consider the matter of slowness and speed. When the ghost promises to tell Hamlet about his 'unnatural' murder (but is there such a thing as a *natural* murder?), Hamlet responds:

> Haste me to know't, that I, with wings as swift
> As meditation or the thoughts of love,
> May sweep to my revenge.
>
> (I, v, 29–31)

The analogies are startlingly but prophetically inapposite. As swift as *meditation*? It is precisely because Hamlet meditates so much – thinks 'too precisely on th'event', finds 'the native hue of resolution/Is sicklied o'er with the pale cast of thought' – that he can act so little. 'Sweep' to his revenge is very exactly the last thing he does. It is Claudius and his regime that move quickly. He and Gertrude married before the mourning for her husband was completed – as Hamlet comments:

> O, most *wicked speed*, to post
> With such dexterity to incestuous sheets.
>
> (I, ii, 156–7 – my italics)

When Claudius perceives that Hamlet is becoming distinctly dangerous, he dispatches him to England 'with fiery quickness'. Hamlet knows very well that Rosencrantz and Guildenstern are the bearers of some plot against him: 'they must sweep my way/ And marshal me to knavery' (III, iv, 205–6). Claudius and his gang are the 'sweepers' and work with 'wicked speed'. Hamlet's instincts – scholar that he is (i.e. given to the life contemplative) – are all the other way. When he is told about the ghost, but before he has heard his story, his reaction is – to do absolutely nothing:

> then sit still, my soul. Foul deeds will rise,
> Though all the earth o'erwhelm them, to men's eyes.
>
> (I, ii, 257–8)

Stillness is associated with virtue, as it was in the Elizabethan mind. As is made clear in the ghost's comment on his wife's hasty marriage to the brother who murdered him.

> But virtue, *as it never will be moved*,
> Though lewdness court it in a shape of heaven,
> So lust, though to a radiant angel linked,
> Will sate itself in a celestial bed
> And prey on garbage.
>
> (I, v, 53–7 – my italics)

The lustful are always on the move. How the meditative and would-be virtuous Hamlet can find an appropriate way to insert himself into, and to intervene in, a court, a society, for him a world, now given over to, taken over by, those who, to satisfy their appetites, act with 'fiery quickness' and 'wicked speed', is indeed the great prolonging problem of the play. No wonder there are 'abatements and delays'.

But before looking more carefully at this central problem, we might do well to consider another rather curious aspect of the play which certainly contributes to its length. In a word, there seem to be two of everything.[1] There are two kings (one dead, one alive); Hamlet has now two fathers (Claudius being now 'uncle-father'); there are two sons who have to avenge murdered fathers (Hamlet and Laertes – Fortinbras makes a third but I'll come back to that); Claudius sends two ambassadors to Norway – Cornelius and Voltimand; and there are his two tools, made almost comically indistinguishable – Rosencrantz and Guildenstern. The ghost appears to Hamlet twice; Laertes makes a double departure; Hamlet's play to catch the king is performed twice; Hamlet abuses two women; after the play he goes and speaks daggers to his mother and then, when it seems he has finished, he does it again.

But it is perhaps above all in the amazing language of the play that we most often encounter what seems like a compulsive doubling, as though Shakespeare will not use one word when he can think of two. I will run together a few examples: 'the sensible and true avouch of mine own eyes'; 'the gross and scope of my opinion'; 'this posthaste and romage in the land'; 'the extravagant and erring spirit'; 'the dead waste and middle of the night'; 'the perfume and suppliance of a minute'; 'the shot and danger of desire'; 'the pales and forts of reason'; 'the single and peculiar life'; 'the book and volume of my brain'; 'this encompassment and drift of question'; 'the flash and outbreak of a fiery mind'; 'the motive and cue for passion'; 'the hatch and the disclose'; 'the teeth and forehead of our faults'; 'the proof and bulwark against sense'; and so on.

This is not just Shakespeare exploring and exploiting the resources of the English language as he found it, as no one before (or since) had done – though it is gloriously that as well. On the one hand, Shakespeare continually confronts, or assails, us with strange couplings, unexpected conjunctions, at every turn, or in every speech. Either the pair is too similar –

[1]. On 'doubles' in Hamlet, see Frank Kermode's brilliant chapter, 'Cornelius and Voltemand', in *Forms of Attention*, University of Chicago Press, 1985.

Rosencrantz and Guildenstern, 'book and volume' – or so different that you would expect them to be kept separate, not, that is, in the same clause – or in the same bed: 'perfume and suppliance' – Gertrude and Claudius. One of the things that all these varyingly odd doublings serves to point up is that the central rottenness of this out-of-joint society is an incestuous relationship grounded in murder. Murder and incest are the most graphic and violent or lustful ways of annihilating the differences and annulling the separations and distinctions on which any society depends. 'More than kin, and less than kind' – these are Hamlet's first words; only one letter separates 'kin' and 'kind' – similar indeed, almost echoic. But the difference is also important. We must know 'kin' from 'kind' (though we should be kind to all our 'kind'). Through Claudius' incestuous marriage, Hamlet has become at once too closely 'related' to him, and more distant and antipathetically alienated from him. Kin and kind are merging or falling apart in all sorts of ways throughout the play. Kinship terms have become oxymoronically muddled – 'uncle-father and aunt-mother', 'my cousin and my son'; and the continuities effected by appropriate kinship relationships have been skewed off course – Claudius should not marry Gertrude, but he does; Hamlet should marry Ophelia but he does not (Ophelia is the most pathetic victim of this sick and perverted society). Something has gone wrong at the controlling centre. This feeling is only enhanced by what seems like the uncontrollable tendency towards redundancy and proliferation which, I have tried to suggest, characterizes the atmosphere of the play. I take it that a cancer is the uncontrollable multiplication of cells to the mortal detriment of the housing organism. As the imagery of the play constantly reminds us, the society in which Hamlet finds himself is very sick indeed – 'ulcerous', cancerous; and, among other things, the structure of the play enacts that condition.

In this polluted and poisoned atmosphere, Hamlet finds it very difficult to know, to decide, how to act. Or whether to act. Indeed, what, exactly, 'acting' is. A traditional avenger would have no problem. As we are reminded by the reactions and behaviour of Laertes when he returns to Denmark and finds that *his* father has been murdered. Nothing makes *him* hesitate and he has to be almost forcibly restrained from starting the killing immediately.

> Conscience and grace to the profoundest pit!
> I dare damnation . . .
> I'll be revenged
> Most thoroughly for my father.
>
> (IV, v, 132–6)

I'll come back to 'conscience'. The point is that Laertes is an almost unthinking adherent to the old revenge code. What would he do to Hamlet? – 'cut his throat i' th' church!' Claudius (of course) approves – 'Revenge should have no bounds.' But this points the way back to chaos and old night. As his effect on Denmark sufficiently indicates. According to a messenger:

> young Laertes, in a riotous head,
> O'erbears your officers. The rabble call him lord,
> And, as the world were now but to begin,
> Antiquity forgot, custom not known,
> The ratifiers and props of every word . . .
>
> (IV, v, 101–5)

This is the nightmare which Aeschylus dramatized, and René Girard outlined, in which 'mere anarchy' and unending violence are loosed upon the world which threatens to collapse back into its original confusion. Laertes portends atavism and regression (he becomes a willing agent in the devious and bloody plans of Claudius). Hamlet has evolved too much, or become too complicated, to revert to that kind of response.

There is another avenger whose behaviour Hamlet can compare with what he himself takes to be his own culpable and incomprehensible dilatoriness. When the Players arrive, Hamlet asks one of them to recite a speech from a play in which Aeneas recounts the details of the slaughter of Priam by Pyrrhus. Pyrrhus is about to kill Priam when the 'hideous' noise of the collapse of Troy 'takes prisoner Pyrrhus' ear' (we'll come back to ears), and he stops.

For lo, his sword,
Which was declining on the milky head
Of reverend Priam, seemed i'th'air to stick.
So as a painted tyrant Pyrrhus stood,
And like a neutral to his will and matter
Did nothing.
But as we often see, against some storm,
A silence in the heavens, the rack stand still,
The bold winds speechless, and the orb below
As hush as death, anon the dreadful thunder
Doth rend the region, so after Pyrrhus' *pause*,
A roused vengeance sets him new awork,
And never did the Cyclops' hammer fall
On Mars's armor, forged for proof eterne,
With less remorse than Pyrrhus' bleeding sword
Now falls on Priam.

(II, ii, 488–503 – my italics)

Hamlet himself is, at that moment, a 'neutral to his will and matter' (i.e. caught in a moment of suspended passivity between his intention and his task – between purpose and performance), and he too is doing nothing. But after a brief 'pause', Pyrrhus, with 'roused vengeance', sets remorselessly about his killing. But Hamlet's 'pause' lasts almost the whole play. Not because he is paralysed by possible 'remorse' – he detests Claudius, and he feels little remorse for killing Polonius and none for sending Rosencrantz and Guildenstern to their deaths. It is something else which is so extending the 'interim' between the 'first motion' and the 'dreadful deed'. 'The interim's mine,' he says, late in the play. He is referring to a specific period of time before the news of what has happened to Rosencrantz and Guildenstern will reach the Danish court. But, in a larger sense, he both creates and owns the 'interim' which is, effectively, the play.

Why is the 'interim' – which became the most influential drama in western Europe – so long? Although, like Orestes, he has no taste for the deed, Hamlet can kill allright – his claim 'Yet have I in me something dangerous' is amply borne out by the events. Yet it takes him the whole of the long play finally to close with Claudius. Macbeth will speak of 'the pauser, reason' (meaning that once you start thinking about a course of action, it 'gives you pause' as we say). Hamlet, the scholar, is much inclined to 'reason' about almost everything, so we can say that he has become, by nature, a 'pauser'. After his 'play' has disturbed the king, Hamlet comes across Claudius – praying. Not praying with any conviction, however, because as he says his 'guilt defeats my strong intent'. His next words are:

> And like a man to double business bound
> I stand in pause where I shall first begin,
> And both neglect.
>
> (III, iii, 41–3)

It is part of the atmosphere of the play, full of ricocheting analogies, that these words could have just as well been spoken by Hamlet, himself 'standing in pause'. But this seems a perfect opportunity to enact his too-long-deferred revenge.

> Now might I do it pat, now 'a is a-praying,
> And now I'll do't. And so 'a goes to heaven,
> And so am I revenged. *That would be scanned.*
> A villain kills my father, and for that
> I, his sole son, do this same villain send to heaven.
> Why, this is hire and salary, not revenge.
>
> (III, iii, 73–8 – my italics)

Scan – to look something over carefully. As he is a great 'pauser' so Hamlet is a great 'scanner' – the one directly because of the other. Orestes opened up a very small pause for a very short scan of the matricidal deed required of him. Hamlet opens up an immeasurably larger gap in which, indeed, he seems to scan everything, moving from the problematical aspects of revenge out to the position of man, and woman, in the universe. In Shakespeare's hands, the old revenge play opens up to the spaces of metaphysics. And one of the faculties or organs responsible for the unprecedented distension is – conscience. The word occurs seven times in the play. Hamlet concludes Act II with his plan: 'The play's the thing/Wherein I'll catch the conscience of the King.' Almost immediately after, in the next scene, when Polonius has quite innocently observed that 'with devotion's visage/And pious action we do sugar o'er/The devil himself', the King makes an aside:

> How smart a lash that speech doth give my conscience!
> The harlot's cheek, beautied with plast'ring art,
> Is not more ugly to the thing that helps it
> Than is my deed to my most painted word.
>
> (III, i, 50–53)

One of the poisonous effects of this festering guilty conscience at the centre of the realm is just this insidious separation of 'deeds' from 'painted words'. Very shortly after this, Hamlet gives this instruction to the Players: 'Suit the action to the word, the word to the action.' One of his own major problems is how somehow to effect a realignment of words and deeds. In the court of Claudius, saturated with intrigue, indirections, spying, this takes a long time.

But the 'conscience of the King' is something he wants and tries to keep 'plastered over'. There is Hamlet's 'conscience' as well, and this we see and hear at work, particularly in the great soliloquies. Shortly after the King's aside, in one of those soliloquies, Hamlet says:

> Thus conscience does make cowards of us all,
> And enterprises of great pitch and moment,
> With this regard their currents turn awry,
> And lose the name of action.
>
> (III, i, 83–8)

Specifically, he is talking about the fear of what might come after death, but we can from this generalize the 'pausing' power of 'conscience'. The word was drawing many senses into it during this period, and here we may say that it both includes the Christian sense of conscience, and the more inclusive faculty and disposition of introspection, reflection, self-consciousness. Hamlet is certainly no orthodox sort of a Christian. Having sent Rosencrantz and Guildenstern to their deaths, he says to Horatio – 'They are not near my conscience.' Perhaps we should briefly consider just what sort of a Christian Hamlet is, what sort of a 'conscience' he has ('the widest consciousness in literature' Henry James called it).

It is hard to date with any certainty the action of the play. Clearly it is an early Renaissance court of some kind. The Hamlet story itself goes back to ancient Norse legend and archaic traces of this origin find their way into Shakespeare's play.[1] When referring to his father, Hamlet invokes Hyperion, Jove, Mercury, Mars, and Hercules; the ancient Rome of Julius Caesar is also invoked more than once. It is as though he is drawing effortlessly on precedents and memories of an earlier heroic, pagan age. On the other hand, when he encounters the 'questionable shape' of the ghost (capable of answering, but also dubious), he draws on a quite different lexicon.

> Angels and ministers of grace defend us!
> Be thou a spirit of health or goblin damned,
> Bring with thee airs from heaven or blasts from hell ...
>
> (I, iv, 39–41)

When the ghost departs, Hamlet's first words are:

> O all you host of heaven! O earth! What else?
> And shall I couple hell?
>
> (I, v, 93–4)

And even up to the time he puts on his play he is entertaining this possibility – 'The spirit that I have seen/May be a devil.' Hamlet, at the start, has just returned from studying in Wittenberg (whither he wishes to return, but is forbidden). Wittenberg, of course, was where Luther nailed his famous *Theses* to the church door, thus effectively starting the Reformation in northern Europe. If he is not – detectably – a devout Protestant, nevertheless Hamlet's 'conscience', like his vocabulary, will be marked by Protestant thinking. For a Protestant, the Ghost would indeed have been regarded as a devil from hell (for a Catholic it could be a spirit from purgatory – the play seems to incline that way, but let us not get involved in fruitless speculations about Shakespeare's religious affiliations or allegiances). Perhaps more important, one of the main

[1]. In this compressed introduction I do not intend to go into Shakespeare's sources nor the ways he transformed them. The sources for the four tragedies in this volume are all most conveniently collected in Volume Seven of Geoffrey Bullough's majestic work – *Narrative and Dramatic Sources of Shakespeare*, Routledge and Kegan Paul, 1975.

contentions of the Reformation thinkers was that 'justification' (salvation) could only be by faith, and not, not *at all*, by works as the Catholics maintained. Our fates were 'predestined', so it was folly to think any human effort could influence the divine plan. Taken to an extreme, this belief could see all attempts at significant salvational or restorative or corrective or expiatory action as, at best, futile, and more probably sinful. This, surely, is the theology which, among other things, Hamlet has been studying. Yet he is, most imperiously, called on to *act*.

Act as a good hero and soldier (following the models of Hercules, Mars, Pyrrhus); or act, by desisting from action, like a good Protestant (attending to the voice of Wittenberg)? Here again, the instructions or orders from the Ghost compound rather than simplify the problem. His first demand seems straightforward enough – (referring to himself as Hamlet's father) 'Revenge his foul and most unnatural murder.' (I will return to the problem of what is, or should be, 'natural' – central to Shakespearian tragedy – and whether there could be such a thing as *natural* murder.) Here is the unambiguous old revenge code. But then:

> Murder most foul, as in the best it is,
> But this most foul, strange, and unnatural.
>
> I, v, 27–8)

The Ghost has lost his point, even while trying to make it. His 'but' tries to introduce a distinction, but fails to. If murder is always 'most foul' (as in the best it is), his murder cannot be somehow more 'most foul' than any other. By definition, there cannot be comparatives within a superlative. The repetition of the phrase reveals the impossibility of making distinctions. The Ghost bewails and condemns a 'most foul' deed – and orders Hamlet to commit one. No wonder Hamlet goes into a spin. But even more puzzling:

> But howsomever thou pursues this act,
> Taint not thy mind, nor let thy soul contrive
> Against thy mother aught. Leave her to heaven.
>
> (I, v, 84–6)

'Soul', 'heaven'? This does not sound like the old revenge

code. If that's the way it is, why not leave Claudius to heaven too? (As Horatio – also from Wittenberg – comments after the initial commotion caused by the appearance of the Ghost – 'Heaven will direct it.' But will it? Hard to be sure in this uncertain atmosphere. In the event, Hamlet becomes a secular kind of 'director' – he puts on a play.) Hamlet is to be a killer-avenger to the uncle-father, but a forbearing Christian to his mother-aunt. The point, simple enough perhaps but crucially generative for the play, is that Hamlet's mind, his 'conscience', becomes a meeting-place, a battlefield, a forcing house, a breeding ground, for the different codes, value systems, religions, cosmologies, which (with all due recognition of the prior influence of the Greek and Jewish traditions) formed the modern European mind – ancient heroism, Roman paganism, and Christian Reformation. And monarchial feudalism.

In a most interesting little book,[1] Carl Schmitt suggests that, rather than situating *Hamlet* between the Renaissance and the Baroque as Walter Benjamin does, we might more profitably see the play as coming (and dramatizing) somewhere between the 'barbaric' and the 'political'. He explains his terms. Summarizing and simplifying – the 'political' means the evolution and implementation of a state in which politics were separated from religion. On the continent in the early seventeenth century, this was happening (Machiavelli was a crucial influence). The 'barbaric' connotes a society still dominated by what Schmitt calls 'pre-statal forms': it is feudal, and religion and politics are still inter-involved. The sovereign state is a product of the divorce between religion and politics; what this meant, among other things, is that *power* is no longer mediated through (and thus sanctioned by) God. It becomes mundane. But when a society is still in the 'barbaric' stage, power is conceived as coming from (and thus sanctified and legitimated by) some trans-human source. As Schmitt sees it, the Stuarts remained unaware of the new movements on the

[1]. *Hamlet oder Hekuba*, Dusseldorf, 1956 – to my knowledge, not translated into English. I wish to thank Nadia Fusini for introducing me to this work and helping me with translating the contents, and for many helpful discussions concerning Shakespeare.

continent, and were unable to detach themselves from the feudal and religious Middle Ages. James I (of England), for instance, still believed in the concept of 'the divine right of kings' although it was already an anachronistic notion by his time and would soon be done away with. It is notable that the articulation of this doctrine in *Hamlet* is given to the supremely hypocritical Claudius – ('There's such divinity doth hedge a king' etc. – IV, v, 123–5). More, one feels by this time, of his desperate plastering over. The society or the world of *Hamlet* is still predominantly 'barbaric'. But it is sick, and falling to pieces.

It is not my intention to explore the contemporary historical background to Shakespeare's plays in this introduction. But Schmitt points out something so interesting, and probably constitutively crucial for the play, that I will summarize it here. He starts from the question of why the question of Gertrude's guilt and complicity in the murder of her husband is left unclear and unresolved. But she must not be touched. It is as though there is a taboo on dealing directly with the queen. Mary Stuart was married to Henry Lord Darnley who was assassinated by the Earl of Bothwell in February 1586. Very shortly after, in May of the same year, Mary married the assassin ('Thrift, thrift, Horatio'). It was a big scandal and the question of Mary's involvement in the murder was never settled. Perhaps needless to say, Protestants were convinced she instigated it. Queen Elizabeth died in 1603, the year of the first Quarto of *Hamlet*. This means that Shakespeare was writing his play when the question of the succession to Elizabeth was both unclear and increasingly pressing. Southampton and Essex supported James (Mary Stuart's son) for the succession, and Shakespeare and the Players supported them. Essex of course was executed (and his last words are said to be echoed in Horatio's farewell to the dying Hamlet), and Shakespeare and the Players temporarily had to leave London. James duly succeeded – Shakespeare and the Players came back to London. James was baptised a Catholic but brought up a Protestant – thus enabling him to succeed to the English throne (he also wrote a 'Demonology' in 1597 in which he discussed the question of the apparition of ghosts).

He also honoured his mother and would hear no suggestion that she was involved in the murder of his father. The parallels to Shakespeare's play are too obvious to need spelling out – Schmitt calls it 'the potent eruption of historical reality in the play'. It would also provide a specific reason for why Shakespeare had to be so circumspect in his handling of the Queen. Schmitt is suggesting that, among many many other things, the figure and situation of Hamlet contain lineaments and echoes of those of James I. And thus, Hamlet's bestowal of Denmark to Fortinbras – making a man from another country the legitimate successor – could be seen as, before James' coronation, an augury and a hope; and after the coronation, a gesture of homage. In this instance, the contribution of contemporary history seems to me to be both powerful and incontestable. Which only makes it the more remarkable that, perhaps more than any other work, it has come to be felt to be a play for all time.

To place *Hamlet* in a period still in some ways 'barbaric' and feudal can be illuminating in another way. Here are some words from Hegel concerning tragedy. 'The Greek heroes make their appearance in an epoch anterior to legal enactment . . . so that right and social order, law and ethical custom, emanate from them'; by contrast, modern man acts 'within the bounds already marked out for him by legislative enactments in the social order . . . he is only a member of a fixed order of society and appears as such limited in his range rather then the vital representative and individual embodiment of society itself.' There are lawyers referred to (very disparagingly) in *Hamlet*, but not much sign of a legal system and 'legislative enactment'.[1] There is nothing of what Hegel calls 'the legalized fabric of modern society'. Hence the traces of the archaic, the barbaric, the heroic ages in the play. 'The time is out of joint' and Hamlet himself has to 'set it right': there are no police and law-courts to do it for him. Claudius knows right from wrong, but he makes his own laws, which Hamlet is powerless to obstruct (though it is clear that he has been 'illegally' dispossessed); and Hamlet will spend the whole play

[1]. *Hegel on Tragedy*, Doubleday, New York, 1962; pp. 100, 109, 111.

trying to find ways to circumvent and frustrate, repeal and replace, the power-backed edicts of a usurping king. Who still – an ultimate mockery – claims his power is God-given.

As we learn from Ophelia's encomium-lament (III, i, 153 *et seq.*), Hamlet is admired and looked up to as a courtier, soldier, and scholar – 'Th' expectancy and rose of the fair state.' This is not, necessarily, an impossible trilogy of identities to maintain and roles to discharge (though I suppose there could be some friction between the impulses of the scholar and the soldier). But he is also, I have been trying to suggest, a rather more uneasy compound – a 'barbarian'-Christian. This is made clear even, or particularly, at his death. Horatio – fellow-Wittenbergian – bids farewell to the Christian: 'flights of angels sing thee to thy rest'. Fortinbras, the warrior, pays his respects to the man of Mars:

> Let four captains
> Bear Hamlet like a soldier to the stage,
> For he was likely, had he been put on,
> To have proved most royal; and for his passage
> The soldier's music and the rite of war
> Speak loudly for him.
>
> (V, ii, 397–401)

Songs of angels and soldier's music – can they be harmonized? Or did Hamlet live out a life of perpetual dissonance – and that is what we have been watching?[1] And what can action, acting, mean and be for a courtier-soldier-scholar-barbarian-Christian? Hamlet indeed has much to 'scan'.

Fortinbras orders the captains to bear Hamlet 'to the stage' because, 'had he been put on', he was likely to have proved most royal. But Hamlet is already *on* a stage, and *Hamlet* has just *been* 'put on' (these are effectively the closing lines). A stage on a stage; a play within a play – what is Shakespeare doing? When an audience is presented with people who are already actors acting as 'actors' in a play staged within a play,

[1]. On this, and indeed on the whole play, see Nigel Alexander's admirable book, *Poison, Play and Duel*, Routledge and Kegan Paul, 1971.

it sets up ripples of ontological unease. This has been called the Pirandello effect. For where, one begins to wonder, does the acting stop? Are we not *all*, in one sense or another, 'guilty creatures sitting at a play'? Given that the Globe Theatre was indeed taken to be an image of the 'great globe' itself, and its symbolic façade represented the traditional cosmos, the feeling of the world as stage must have been very strong for an Elizabethan audience.[1] Hamlet persuades Claudius to watch a play containing a 'Player King'. But, an unlegitimated usurper, Claudius, is also a 'player king' (so two of these, too). We see him performing, acting the king, in Act I, scene ii, in which, with what looks like authority, he issues orders, dispenses advice, grants requests in a manner which 'seems' authentically royal. It is, in fact, all 'show', and Claudius knows that, for his survival and success, the 'show' must go on. But Hamlet, from the very beginning, announces that he knows not '"seems"', and already has 'that within which passes show'. The trouble for Claudius will come from here – that we can anticipate. But it will not be easy. For in a court, a society, which seems saturated with 'seeming' and 'acting' of one kind or another, how establish or discover a more authentic mode of 'action'? And that, indeed, is what Hamlet and the play itself spend a good deal of time 'scanning' – simply, the problems and the meaning of 'action'.

In the graveyard scene (V, i), we see two clowns being very disrespectful of the dead. In this they are just like their so-called betters (cf. the treatment of Hamlet's father, Polonius, Ophelia) only somewhat coarser, or more direct. And one of them makes a most pertinent point, even while he seems to be mocking legal pedantry. They are discussing – *à propos* of the doubt hovering over Ophelia's death – suicide, and one of them says: 'For here lies the point: if I drown myself wittingly, it argues an act, and an act hath three branches – it is to act, to do, to perform (V, i, 10–12). It is Hamlet's problem and task to work out the relations between acting, doing, and perform-

[1]. See *The Idea of a Theatre* by Francis Fergusson, Doubleday, New York, 1955, pp. 128–30). The whole long section on *Hamlet* in this book is seminal and extremely important.

ing (but perhaps the distinctions are illusory?); to somehow recover or re-establish, to use his own phrase, 'the name of action'. When Claudius is trying to pray, after the play, he speaks with the clear-sightedness of a guilty conscience. In 'the corrupted currents of this world', he knows very well – from personal experience – that 'Offense's gilded hand may shove by justice' and that 'the wicked prize itself/Buys out the law.' The law is, as yet, helpless in the face of power, and is indeed too often easily purchasable by it.

> But 'tis not so above.
> There is no shuffling; there the action lies
> In his true nature
>
> (III, iii, 60–63)

Claudius presides over a 'shuffling' society; indeed he has created it. Trickery, spying, intrigue, lying and deception, everywhere. In this world, is it possible to find, or create, a place where 'action lies in his true nature' and thereby, we may infer, recovers its 'name'?

Hamlet contains a number of speeches alluding to, or describing, the fading of the will to act. I have quoted one by Claudius to Laertes concerning 'abatements and delays'. Here is part of another, by the Player King (the other one):

> But what we do determine oft we break
> Purpose is but the slave to memory...
>
> What to ourselves in passion we propose,
> The passion ending, doth the purpose lose...
>
> Our wills and fates do so contrary run
> That our devices still are overthrown;
> Our thoughts are ours, their ends none of our own.
>
> (III, ii, 194–5, 200–201, 217–20)

Claudius's 'devices' are massively 'overthrown' in the climactic conclusion to the play, and I will come to that. Here we may note the pointing to the difficulty of, as it were, binding together passion, purpose, and performance. And this indeed is Hamlet's problem. After he has listened to the recital of the actor who has worked himself up 'in a fiction, in a dream of passion' he goes on to wonder;

What would he do
Had he the motive and the cue for passion
That I have?

(II, ii, 570–72)

After Fortinbras and his army have passed him, on their way to fight, and very likely die, for a piece of worthless land and 'a fantasy and trick of fame', again he scans and ponders his inaction:

I do not know
Why yet I live to say, "This thing's to do,"
Sith I have cause, and will, and strength, and means
To do't.

(IV, iv, 43–6)

He has, then, the motive, the cue, the cause, the will, the strength, the means – yes, why *doesn't* he 'do't'?

At this point I want to return to his encounter with the Ghost. When he appeals to Hamlet to avenge him he says: 'If thou hast nature in thee, bear it not', and then proceeds to give Hamlet his directly contradictory imperatives – kill/do not kill – after he has already described his own murder as 'unnatural'. 'Nature' is perhaps the most ambiguous, or capacious, or problematical word in Shakespeare, and as we shall see, his tragedies time and again address themselves to the matter of what is nature, what is 'natural'? Here, the appeal to 'nature' can hardly help Hamlet. Will a 'natural' murder somehow avenge an 'unnatural' one? But is there such a thing? Aren't all murders 'most foul'? What I want to suggest is that the Ghost is effectively paralysing Hamlet even while goading him to action. Indeed, I would even say 'poisoning' him. Or rather, transmitting Claudius' poison to him. But to explain that I must turn to the matter of 'ears'.

The Ghost informs Hamlet that he was murdered by his brother who poured literal poison in his ear ('in the porches of my ear did pour/ The leprous distillment'). But before this is told to Hamlet and the audience, we have heard this:

And let us once again assail your ears,
That are so fortified against our story

(I, i, 31–2)

and this:

> Nor shall you do my ear that violence
> To make it truster of your own report
>
> (I, ii, 171–2)

and this:

> But this eternal blazon must not be
> To ears of flesh and blood
>
> (I, v, 21–2)

and this:

> So the whole ear of Denmark
> Is by a forged process of my death
> Rankly abused
>
> (I, v, 36–8).

And, after the Ghost's graphic account of the effect on his body of the 'leprous distillment', we will hear this:

> and with a hideous crash
> Takes prisoner Pyrrhus' ear
>
> (II, ii, 487–8)

and this:

> And I'll be placed, so please you, in the ear
> Of all their conference
>
> (III, i, 187–8)

and this:

> And wants not buzzers to infect his ear
> With pestilent speeches . . .
> Will nothing stick our person to arraign
> In ear and ear
>
> (IV, v, 90–91, 93–4)

– this from Claudius who, indeed, knows about infecting ears with pestilence.

And finally, though by no means exhaustively, this:

> I have words to speak in thine ear will make thee dumb
>
> (IV, vi, 25–6).

In *Othello*, Othello, explaining his 'enchantment' of Desdemona, says that she would come to listen to his exotic stories and 'with a greedy ear/Devour up my discourse' (I, ii, 148–9). Her father is sceptical: 'But words are words. I never yet did hear/That the bruised heart was pierced through the ear' (I, iii, 215–16). How wrong he is, the rest of the play will demonstrate as Iago sets about 'bruising' Othello's heart by 'abusing' his ear – 'I'll pour this pestilence into his ear' (II, ii, 356). Not, this time, a 'leprous distillment', but insinuations of Desdemona's sexual infidelity and promiscuity. Deadly poison comes in many forms. In *King Lear* Edmund, who can produce false 'evidence' as diabolically as Iago, promises to afford Gloucester 'auricular assurance' of Edgar's treachery, another 'poison' which Gloucester catastrophically believes (I shall return to the matter of 'evidence' in Shakespeare). Lady Macbeth, who has already resolved that her husband will murder the king, can hardly wait for Macbeth's return: 'Hie thee hither,/That I may pour my spirits in thine ear' (I, v, 26–7) – and poisonous and 'unnatural' 'spirits' they are too.

In bringing all these quotations from the tragedies together, I am hoping to make an important point without belabouring the obvious. We can be mistaken in what we see (bent sticks in water, etc.), and we can hallucinate; we may be incorrect about the exact nature of something we touch; we may err in identifying a taste or a smell. But in no other sense are we so vulnerable as in our hearing. This is because (and this is where I risk being too obvious) it is through the ear that language enters the body. This is how and where we can be most 'rankly abused' and variously 'poisoned'. We may like to invoke Freud's point that it is through the ear that we internalize 'the family's *sounds* or *sayings*, the spoken or secret discourses, going on prior to the subject's arrival, within which he must make his way'[1]. Or we may be content with Montaigne's contention that the ears 'are the most dangerous instruments we have to receive violent and sudden impressions to trouble and alter us'. In the middle, literally, of his first

[1]. See an interesting comment on this in *Disowning Knowledge* by Stanley Cavell, Cambridge University Press, 1987, p. 189, though his reading of *Hamlet*, insofar as I follow it, strikes me as wild.

really major tragedy (it happens almost exactly half way through, in the middle of Act III), the physical poisoning of the king's ear is re-enacted on the stage within the stage for all, if they are paying proper attention, to see – as if to make starkly visible what will everywhere else occur as an absolutely crucial metaphor. Crucial, because an abiding concern in the tragedies is – how and why do things (people, societies) go wrong? Where does the 'poison' come from? How does it spread? And what is the how and when of 'cure' or purgation? The Ghost, I want to suggest, 'poisons' Hamlet's ear with the truth of murder and incest – for there *are* truths which, to all intents and purposes, 'poison' the hearer. As the poison spreads to him, Hamlet is at once both enlightened and arrested – with the result that he must 'unpack my heart with words'. Macbeth compares the wounds of murdered Duncan to 'a breach in nature/For ruin's wasteful entrance'. How do ruin and waste – murder and poison – enter the world? What are the promptings, processes, and procedures of evil? And what – if anything – can be done about it? What are the chances – they may seem slim, they may turn out to be inexorable – of *re*paration, *re*stitution, *re*storation (as opposed to, simply, '*re*venge')? These are central concerns in all Shakespeare's tragedies, and of course they torment Hamlet's consciousness and conscience unrelentingly. With a vengeance, we might say. O cursed spite . . .

In the first scene of the play, the sentinel Francisco reports – 'Not a mouse stirring.' Hamlet says his play is called '*The Mousetrap*'. After the performance of that play, and after Claudius has thereby been 'frighted with false fire', the mice start stirring. And the rats, too. Hamlet thinks he has killed one behind the arras in the Queen's closet ('How now? A rat? Dead for a ducat . . .'), but it turns out to be Polonius, who could, I suppose, be described as one of Claudius' mice. But King Rat, or the rat-King, will prove harder to pin down, and pin through, though Hamlet will, finally, manage it. How he manages it may be said to be problematical. He can scarcely claim that he has recovered 'the name of action' since, arguably, he himself initiates nothing. Indeed, it could be said that he settles for *re*action over action. Perhaps he has arrived at another name for action, action in another key. Although at the conclusion of his last soliloquy (IV, iv) he had resolved – 'O, from this time forth,/My thoughts be bloody or be nothing worth', after his return from England – that is Act V – his mood, as everyone recognizes, has changed. No more 'whirling words', an end to 'antic disposition', self-tormenting soliloquies put behind him. His mood is more one of quiescence, acquiescence – this may be seen as religious resignation or stoic fatalism, or something of both. His language touches on various possibilities: 'There's a divinity that shapes our ends,/Rough-hew them how we will' – 'Why even in that was heaven ordinant' – 'There is special providence in the fall of a sparrow': divinity, heaven, providence – none of them capitalized. Hamlet thought his role was to be a 'scourge and minister', but he finds a larger wisdom (or you could say, he finds the best way of being both), in just capitulating to the more mysterious, ineluctable processes which he feels to be moving in and through the unfolding events – divinity? history? fate? undecidable; unknowable. His last words as he goes into the final, fatal, fateful, scene, are simply – 'Let be.' Shakespeare's incomparable dramatic poetry is never more piercing and powerful than when it delivers itself in staccato monosyllables.

In a characteristically original formulation, Walter Benjamin writes: 'Hamlet wants to breathe in the suffocating air of fate in one deep breath. He wants to die by some accident, and as the fateful stage-properties gather around him, as around their lord and master, the drama of fate flares up in the conclusion of this *Trauerspiel*, as something that is contained, but of course overcome in it.'[1] We may supplement this with a formulation by Philip Brockbank: 'the play turns itself about... At the start ... there is apparent order in the macrocosm and disorder in the microcosm. But at the play's end, the most memorable passages suggest quiescence and

[1]. *The Origin of German Tragic Drama*,)NLB, 1977 p. 137. This book contains many pregnant thoughts about *Hamlet*, though I do not think the play can be contained within the category of '*Trauerspiel*' (Mourning-play) in which Benjamin wishes to place it.

calm within the mind of Hamlet while the spectacle presents total confusion in the court of Claudius.'[1] As Brockbank goes on to say: 'Nothing in the play goes according to plan, but everything happens by significant accident when the time is ripe.' In almost his last speech, Horatio speaks:

> Of accidental judgments, casual slaughters,
> Of deaths put on by cunning and forced cause,
> And, in this upshot, purposes mistook
> Fall'n on th'inventors' heads.
>
> (V, ii, 383-6)

This certainly covers the havoc, error, the confusion and ritual perversions (sporting duels which are murders, celebratory refreshments which are poisoned) of the last scene – without Hamlet planning it, planning anything, a purgation of the realm is effected, a clean succession ensured, a kind of justice done. (As well as stabbing the king with the 'envenomed point' of the treacherous sword – the poison of Claudius' court is everywhere now – Hamlet makes him drink the poisoned drink he had prepared for Hamlet which contains an 'union' (pearl). His last words to Claudius are 'Drink off this potion. Is thy union here? Follow my mother.' By a dramatic pun, Hamlet is forcing Claudius to swallow the incestuous 'union' with his mother which is part of the originating poison of the play.) It would seem as if you cannot, finally, 'take arms against a sea of troubles', but rather have to let the ultimately cleansing tides of providence and history 'sweep' you along, sweep you through, sweep you off. John Holloway has a

[1]. *On Shakespeare*, Blackwell, 1989, p. 170. Anyone teaching English for over thirty years, as I have been doing, will inevitably have read a large number of books on Shakespeare, and I cannot hope to trace all my influences nor acknowledge all my debts. Where I can I have signalled specific sources. But I just single out the work of Philip Brockbank. This, alas posthumous, collection of his essays on Shakespeare I regard as indispensable reading and is an identifiable influence on what I have to say. But Philip Brockbank was also my supervisor when I was an undergraduate and I think I learned, perhaps not always consciously, more from his fine, complex, ironic humanism than from any subsequent influence.

helpful formulation: 'over and over in *Hamlet*, chance turns into a larger design, randomness becomes retribution'.[1] From the immediate, or contrived, bloody reprisals and mimetic violence of the revenge code, Shakespeare has moved to – 'Let be.' In the process, he has transformed primitive revenge drama into metaphysical tragedy of enduringly awesome spaciousness, resonance, and reverberation.

*

OTHELLO

Hamlet could not have recourse to law. Othello, by contrast, is involved – embroiled is perhaps a better word – in law and legalism effectively from start to finish. The whole lexicon of 'justice' pervades the play: arraignment and accusation; defence and pleading; testimony, evidence, and proof (crucial word); causes, vows, oaths; solicitors, imputations, and depositions – the law is, somehow, everywhere in the air. Since soldier Othello's discourse is – initially – almost entirely martial and exotic, he is bound to go astray in this fog of forensic terminology, and of course he disastrously does. The third scene sees him accused of bewitching and seducing Desdemona by her father, Brabantio, though we should note that this is not a formally constituted court of law but a sort of improvized hearing in front of the Duke of Venice which takes place, like much of the play, misleadingly at night. Improvized law, and finally the grossest perversion of 'justice', are to become major themes of the play.

We should also note that this scene has a double character or function. Othello is initially summoned to the Duke's council chamber because Venice has need of Othello – the great heroic warrior – against 'the general enemy Ottoman' who seems to be threatening to attack Cyprus (an important part of Venice's empire). Then Brabantio tries to use the occasion to indict Othello of criminal seduction and abduction. So Othello, in effectively his first appearance, is put in an

[1]. *The Story of the Night*, Routledge and Kegan Paul, 1961, p. 35. This is an interesting book on Shakespearian tragedy which should not be neglected.

ambiguous light – he is the military hero, essential to the defence of the state; but he might also be a sexual villain, racially un-Venetian and a deep threat to domestic order. On this occasion he is, of course, cleared of the 'crime' thanks to Desdemona's evidence. But at the end he will indeed appear in the dual role of soldier/criminal (Venetian/Turk), and play *all* the roles – accuser, penitent, judge, defendant, witness, jury and, finally, executioner – of himself, his Venetian part passing summary judgement on his Turkish part:

> And say besides that in Aleppo once,
> Where a malignant and a turbaned Turk
> Beat a Venetian and traduced the state
> I took by th'throat the circumcised dog
> And smote him – thus. [He stabs himself.]
>
> (V, ii, 347–51)

There are no Turks in the play, only people who more or less 'turn Turk': we are perhaps not very comfortable with the implied racialism, but it has to be recognized that, in terms of this play and the Venetian lexicon which necessarily dominates it, the name 'Turk' stood for the barbarian, the heathen, the feared and savage Other. Iago is Florentine, but when he says to Desdemona 'Nay, it is true, or else I am a Turk' (II, i, 112) we should recognize one of his bitter ironies – what he says is, crucially, *not* true, and he *is* – in the terms of the play – a 'Turk', and turns people into Turks. When he organizes the drunken chaos of Othello's first night in Cyprus, Othello storms out of his house, asking angrily 'From whence ariseth this? Are we turned Turks?' (II, iii, 168–9). The double answer, which of course he cannot know yet, is that it ariseth from Iago and *Othello himself* is about to 'turn Turk'. Iago is, exactly, the barbarian within – within Venice, finally within Othello.

I want to return to the third scene of the play, the improvized 'trial' of Othello. When Brabantio complains that his daughter has been 'abused, stol'n from me, and corrupted', the Duke promises him full recourse to, and support by, 'the bloody book of law' (I, iii, 67). It is a strange formulation. The *bloody* book of *law*? The bloody *book* of law? As I tried to suggest, 'law' was developed precisely to prevent bloodshed, at least as far as possible. Books (of rules and precedents) *instead* of blood; writing instead of fighting; law instead of private revenge; tribunals instead of murders; court-rooms instead of carnage. Of course, in its ultimate reaches the law *can* be 'bloody', but it is rather worrying to see law and blood thus conflated so early in the play, and by the ultimate source of authority in civilized Venice at that. It is, of course, unconsciously prophetic. In the course of the play law will drown in blood, or rather blood will take over law for its own bloody purposes. ''Sblood' is Iago's first word in the play (I, i, 3) and the word is often on his lips ('the blood and baseness of our natures' – I, iii, 332; 'lust of the blood' – I, iii, 339 etc.). Put very simply, what happens is that he transforms Othello – who as an important servant and protector of the state should be an instrument of law – into a man of blood, and introduces 'blood' into his mind and discourse until they are both awash with the word:

> My blood begins my safer guides to rule
>
> (II, iii, 205);

> O, blood, blood, blood!
>
> (III, iii, 451);

> Even so my bloody thoughts, with violent pace,
> Shall ne'er look back, ne'er ebb to humble love
>
> (III, iii, 457–8);

> I will be found most cunning in my patience;
> But (dost thou hear?) most bloody
>
> (IV, i, 91–2);

> Thy bed, lust-stain'd, shall with lust's blood be spotted
>
> (V, i, 36).

When he finally kills himself, Lodovico comments 'O bloody period!' (V, ii, 352). Given that the play is, among other things, about a constantly interrupted honeymoon in which the marriage is never properly consummated – or is consummated by murder (as we might say, the *wrong* form of 'dying'), and in which a good deal of the language traffics in sexuality – the increasing stress on blood, and the spilling or releasing of it, necessarily has an added specific resonance, glancing (without stating) at both menstruation and defloration. The crucial handkerchief which Desdemona drops and loses is, I will just note, 'spotted with strawberries' (III, iii, 432). Her marriage bed turns out to be her death-bed. 'O bloody period!'

Yet Othello manages to convince himself, or allows Iago to manage this managing, that he is, throughout, administering 'justice'. In Venice, the Duke is in charge of justice and, as we see, he dispenses it fairly. In the island outpost of Cyprus, Othello is the sole authority (with Iago the main manipulator), and 'justice' is increasingly, disastrously, perverted until, when Iago suggests that Othello should strangle Desdemona in her bed, Othello responds by saying with obvious pleasure – 'The justice of it pleases' (IV, i, 222). Of course, by now the manifest *in*justice of it appalls, and how Othello has so quickly arrived at this point of aberration constitutes the essence of the tragedy. The sensationally good soldier turns out to be a catastrophically bad judge. As things rapidly disintegrate into disorder and confusion in Cyprus (again at night – Iago works best in the dark), Othello thrashes around, interrogating, accusing, passing judgement, sentencing, in what becomes an increasingly ghastly black parody and simulation of proper judicial processes. What is happening is that the old blood-lust for revenge – for this, too, is a 'revenge' play though, as always with Shakespeare, with a difference – subverts and then appropriates established legal procedures until the eruption and outbreak of a kind of insane private violence can mask itself (at least, and indeed only, to itself) as the impersonal administration of the law. When Othello comes to kill Desdemona, he tries to turn the bedroom into a court-room – a final bit of improvized 'legality'. He talks of 'the cause, the cause' – a word which recurs throughout the play, first heard from the mouth of Brabantio complaining of the abduction of Desdemona – 'Mine's not an idle cause' (I, ii, 94). (In a curious way, Brabantio foreshadows Othello. And Emilia is in the right of it when she says to Desdemona – 'They are not ever jealous for the cause,/But jealous for they're jealous' (III, iv, 159–60). Othello likes the word – it is what justifies you in going to law

– but, in truth, he *has* no 'cause'.) Othello accuses Desdemona, warns her of 'perjury', acts as her confessor, passes judgement, then executes the sentence (V, ii). It is a kind of ultimate nightmare – pure blind, brutal barbarity acting as if it were the acme of civilized justice. Othello wants to think that what he is doing has the ritual dignity of 'a sacrifice' – in fact, he knows it is 'a murder' (V, ii, 65). (Robert Heilman describes the systematic degradation of justice in the play as moving through three stages from the opening scenes in Venice to the bedroom murder: 'Justice: the imitation of justice: the negation of justice. Private passion controlled by public form: private passion endeavouring to find public form: private passion triumphant over public form.')[1]

How does this come about? How is it that within two nights of his marrying Desdemona, Othello is so eager to kill her? (for it *is* only two nights, though I will come back to the strange time-scheme of the play). I will defer consideration of why Othello is even willing (eager?) to listen to the insinuating suggestions and calumnies concerning his new wife from his lowly standard-bearer. Once he allows even the possibility of Desdemona's infidelity to arise in his mind as an idea, he makes what is a fatal mistake in Shakespearian tragedy – he starts asking for the wrong sort of 'evidence' – in this way, 'ruin's wasteful entrance' is both enabled and assured. In this connection, it is worth concentrating on the word 'proof'. The word first occurs early in scene i when Iago is complaining to Roderigo that Othello did not promote him to be his 'lieutenant', although 'his eyes had seen the proof' of his valuable service (I, i, 25). Whether or not this is Iago's prime motive in plotting against Othello is undecidable, perhaps irrelevant. But Iago will dangle another kind of 'proof' in front of Othello's eyes which will drive him mad. Othello might have been warned by the sensible words of the Duke in response to Brabantio's wild accusations against Othello – 'To vouch this is no proof' (I, iii, 107), but in the event he will be persuaded

[1]. *Magic in the Web*, University of Kentucky Press, 1956, pp. 134–5. This remains one of the most sensitive and suggestive explorations of the play.

by less even than vouching. In Act III, scene iii, in the course of which Othello – within the space of some four hundred lines – allows himself to be persuaded of Desdemona's promiscuity and infidelity and dedicates himself to 'a capable and wide revenge' (456), the notion of 'proof' becomes crucial. The word occurs a number of times and I want to bring some instances together.

> No, Iago;
> I'll see before I doubt; when I doubt, prove;
> And on the proof there is no more but this:
> Away at once with love or jealousy!
>
> (189–92)

Iago has just warned him of the misery experienced by the jealous lover 'who dotes, yet doubts' (170) and he is about to convert Othello from a doter into a doubter with terrifying speed. Soon Othello is musing 'If I do prove her haggard ...' (259 – i.e. a trained hawk which has gone wild again). Of course, Iago has nothing resembling 'proof'; indeed he has no 'evidence' against Desdemona at all. Indeed he cunningly seems to warn Othello against believing in what he calls his 'scattering and unsure observance' (III, iii, 151). But when Emilia gives Iago the precious handkerchief which Desdemona has dropped, Iago knows he has all he needs.

> Trifles light as air
> Are to the jealous confirmations strong
> As proofs of holy writ. This may do something.
>
> (319–21)

It does everything. Soon Othello is saying:

> Villain, be sure thou prove my love a whore!
> Be sure of it; give me the ocular proof ...
> Make me to see't; or at the least so prove it ...
> I'll have some proof.
>
> (356–7, 361, 383)

Ocular proof – of what? What kind of proof does he think he is after? What kind of proof could it be? As Iago very reasonably says – would you 'grossly gape on?/Behold her topped?' (392–3). People make love on their own in guarded privacy –

'It is impossible you should see this' (399). What Iago offers instead is 'imputation and strong circumstances/Which lead directly to the door of truth' (III, iii, 403–4). But only *to* the door – which is why we are suspicious of what we call merely 'circumstantial evidence'. But by this time, Othello can hardly wait to push through the door so misleadingly pointed out for him by Iago. And what you *can* see is, for example, a handkerchief – almost the only prop and accessory which Iago needs for his suggestive theatricals. What you *cannot* see is – fidelity. As Iago very exactly phrases it (often diabolically speaking truths he knows will not be registered):

> Her honor is an essence that's not seen;
> They have it very oft that have it not.
> But for the handkerchief –
>
> (IV, i, 16–18)

Here is the play in little. You cannot *see* essences, in any empirical way – love, trust, honour, loyalty etc., there is no '*ocular* proof' for these. (As the Bible perfectly states: 'Now faith is the sustance of things hoped for, the *evidence of things not seen*' (Hebrews II, – my italics). Othello has lost, misplaced, his 'faith'.) But for the handkerchief... Othello has entirely lost his hold on and apprehension of and belief and trust in 'essences' and handed himself and his vision (ocular not spiritual) over to the management and direction of a master of manipulable appearances. Here is 'vision' gone wrong indeed. No wonder most of the play takes place at night.

Problems involved in proper seeing – coming to see the true, the real – are often central to tragedy in which the process of arriving at true vision is often shown to be both horrendously difficult and fiercely resisted (Othello's period of true vision at the end lasts, arguably, for about thirty lines). In this play there are problems from the start. There is, for example, great uncertainty about the Turkish fleet. How many ships do they have? Which island are they heading for? One Senator suspects trickery and deception – ''Tis a pageant to keep us in false gaze' (I, iii, 19). A storm takes care of the Turkish fleet, but as the action shifts to the relatively domestic setting of a peace-time garrison, we may say Iago keeps Othello (who could have handled Turks and fleets) in 'false gaze' with his 'pageants'. Iago is always directing Othello to mark this, behold that, look there, take note, see – and all the time he is, of course, blinding him. A vital play on words indicates how closely the two activities might appear. At the start, Othello promises that marriage will not interfere with his soldiering; there will never, he is sure, come a time 'when light-winged toys/Of feathered Cupid seel with wanton dullness/My speculative and officed instrument' (I, iii, 263–5). He is right. He is not in any danger from Cupid. But Iago will 'seel' his 'speculative instrument' more lethally than any Eros. When he is turning Othello into a doubter, Iago reminds him that Desdemona deceived her father: 'She that so young could give out such a seeming/To seel her father's eyes up close as oak' (III, iii, 209–10).

Iago is a master of that slight shift which makes, literally, a world of difference – he can almost effortlessly transform doting into doubting; he can make 'seeling' feel like 'seeing'. Indeed, he can run seeing and seeling and seeming all together to the confusion of all and the destruction of some. Lodovico's last words to Iago, pointing to the corpses on the bed, are: 'This is thy work. The object poisons sight' (V, ii, 360). That is the triumph of evil and one of the phenomena which tragedy is most involved in exploring – the poisoning of sight.

*

We must take Desdemona to be of the essence, essential – one who 'in th'essential vesture of creation/Does tire the ingener' (II, i, 64–5). In this connection I wish to draw together three other words which play an important role in the play – 'soul', 'jewel' (and other precious stones), and 'reputation' (or 'good name'). The word 'soul' occurs some thirty times – in a play which Iago attempts to dominate with a strongly physical, corporeal, material discourse. Othello himself refers to 'my perfect soul' (I, ii, 30) and 'mine eternal soul' (III, iii, 358), and there must be some question as to what extent he might have lost that soul in having, as it were, switched his trust (faith) from the essential Desdemona (she is much connected with 'soul') to the rankly material Iago. There are literal jewels, which Roderigo wants given to Desdemona and which Iago steals; and the metaphoric jewel, Desdemona herself. Her father calls her his 'jewel' (I, ii, 193) which, as far as he is concerned, Othello has stolen. Othello himself, after he has robbed himself of Desdemona, compares her to 'one entire and perfect chyrsolite' (V, ii, 142) and realizes he has thrown 'a pearl away/Richer than all his tribe' (V, ii, 343–4). She, effectively, was his jewel-soul. Now this, in one of Iago's devastatingly truthful utterances with which he confuses Othello:

> Good name in man and woman, dear my lord,
> Is the immediate jewel of their souls.
> Who steals my purse steals trash; 'tis something, nothing;
> 'Twas mine, 'tis his, and has been slave to thousands;
> But he that filches from me my good name
> Robs me of that which not enriches him
> And makes me poor indeed.
>
> (III, iii, 155–61)

Now Iago is supremely a 'purse' man ('put money in thy purse') as he is also the 'filcher' of jewels, and of 'good names' (Cassio's, Desdemona's). Perhaps he even manages to steal Othello's 'soul'. But what he says is a crucial truth of the play. 'Good name', 'reputation', like honour, like the soul, is an 'essence that's not seen'. And like them, it belongs to the realm of lasting values (thus a 'jewel') as opposed to the contingent world of the market in which prices rise and fall and purses endlessly circulate. Cassio realizes this when he falls into disgrace (engineered by Iago). He laments to Iago: 'Reputation, reputation! O, I have lost my reputation! I have lost the immortal part of myself, and what remains is bestial. My reputation, Iago, my reputation' (II, iii, 261–4).

He thus equates 'reputation' with 'soul' – more usually known as 'the immortal part'. Iago, on this occasion, is concerned to scotch and deride any such ideas. 'As I am an honest man, I had thought you had received some bodily wound. There is more sense in that than in reputation. Reputation is an idle and most false imposition oft got without merit and lost without deserving' (II, iii, 265–9). This is also true, another kind of truth. This is the truth of Iago who only believes in the body as in 'sense' (physical sensation), in that part of us which Cassio regards as 'bestial'. But no matter how vulnerable, how seemingly underminable, it is shown to be, the realm of 'soul' and 'reputation', imaged by jewels, must be registered as a reality which is ultimately – but *only* ultimately and after much destruction – out of Iago's reach. This is borne out by a most suggestive detail. Iago gives up speaking and 'seels' himself in silence *before* he is dead – 'Demand me nothing. What you know, you know./ From this time forth I never will speak word' (V, ii, 299–300); while the smothered Desdemona seems to speak *after* her death – 'Nobody – I myself. Farewell./Commend me to my kind lord. O. farewell!' (V, ii, 123–4). Ever courteous, unaccusing and forgiving, charitable and 'heavenly true' (V, ii, 135), Desdemona – and all she embodies and stands for – *outlasts* Iago.[1]

*

One way of thinking about *Othello* is to see the play as a sort of collision or intersection between a Renaissance heroic procession and a medieval Morality play. I will draw on the work of Philip Brockbank to explain this. As he says, *Othello* is 'at the confluence of several theatrical and literary traditions, moral, heroic, comic and domestic, and therefore, also, of the corresponding traditions of human values'.[2] In particular, alongside the Morality play there developed in Tudor times the heroic play. This genre was related to the festive procession such as often comprised a part of the Lord Mayor's midsummer shows – processions in which an African often figured prominently. 'The evidence is in the account books. They tell us that a black, or tawny, soldier-hero was a figure in festivals long before he reached the Tudor stage. The 1519 accounts include what seems to be the first reference to a popular African

[1]. The point is nicely made by Heilman. 'Whatever disasters it causes, wit fails in the end: it cuts itself off in a demonic silence before death, while witchcraft – love – speaks after death.' op.cit., p. 225.

[2]. Brockbank, op.cit., p. 198.

pageant which was to become a regular feature of the annual shows and carnivals... Two years later, the King of the Moors and sixty 'morians' appeared in another extravagant procession... we can attribute to him a distant political significance, as a festive representative of power and sexual potency in the early stages of Tudor empire.'[1] Out of such events developed the processional and pageant theatre of *Tamburlaine*, an important precursor to *Othello* to which the later play seems almost implicitly to refer. That, clearly, is where the figure of Othello comes from.

Iago emerges from the Mystery and Morality plays, in which figures called 'Youth' or 'Everyman' are tempted into sin and depravity by allegorical companions with names like 'Hypocrisy', 'Dissimulation', 'Fraud', 'Ambidexter' (Iago swears by double-faced Janus). Such figures are all related to the Morality devil and, like him, like Iago, enjoy what Brockbank calls his 'satanic privilege of intimacy with the audience.'[2] Iago, like the devil, comes forward and, with a slightly uncomfortable assumption of sympathy if not complicity says, in effect – watch me confuse, mislead, and then destroy this bombastic, gullible fool. The triumphal hero of the simple procession suddenly finds himself in a bewilderingly complex moral area which he cannot negotiate – and so, 'the warrior protagonist of the heroic play is exposed to the Vice of Morality, in the black comedy of a garrison town'. Shakespeare is thus testing 'the vitality of the heroic tradition and its associated declamatory style of poetry'.[3] And whatever else he achieves, Iago, as he promises, most certainly 'unpegs' Othello's 'music', reducing his proud martial rhetoric to obscene gibberish – 'Noses, ears, and lips?', 'goats and monkeys!' (IV, i, 43; IV, i, 263).

It is perfectly to Shakespeare's purpose that in his source (Cinthio's *Gli Hecatommithi*, 1565, which Shakespeare may have read in a French translation of 1584), the action is set in Cyprus, suspended as it were between northern civilized-

[1]. ibid., p. 200.
[2]. ibid., p. 201.
[3]. ibid., pp. 199, 203.

imperial Venice and southern barbarous-exotic Africa. (Iago calls the marriage between Othello and Desdemona 'a frail vow betwixt an erring barbarian and supersubtle Venetian' (I, iii, 352); as it transpires, the Venetians in this play are straightforward and honest; Othello 'errs' all right, but led by the 'supersubtle' Iago who is, significantly, *not* a Venetian and thus, effectively, an outsider – as Othello, much more obviously, also is.) Cyprus was of course the birthplace of Venus–Aphrodite and the site of Paphos, the reputedly libidinous ancient city sacred to the goddess. It should, not to put it too crudely, at least augur well for the honeymoon and the as yet unconsummated marriage. When Othello greets Desdemona with the words 'Honey, you shall be well desired in Cyprus' (II, 1, 202), one senses an anticipation of the sweet satisfactions of desire. In general there is a rather lubricious air about the whole place and, one way or another, sexual references are effectively constant. But sexual desire goes horribly wrong and turns into jealousy, nausea, madness, and violence. Venice and Africa mate, and then meet in Cyprus. But the mating does not work, and their representatives are destroyed.

Iago is a Morality devil, directing his theatricals to trap the unwary. But he is more complex than that. He is, as we learn from his first speech, a disaffected and resentful soldier who has been passed over for promotion. He expected, and felt he deserved, to receive the post of 'lieutenant'. But the job went to Cassio and Iago is still Othello's 'ancient'. This is important (*every* detail seems important in Shakespeare). An 'ancient' was a standard-bearer who would advance in front of the troops with the flag – a lieutenant would direct manoeuvres from behind. So when shortly after this, Iago explains to Roderigo that he must simulate loyalty to Othello, with these words:

> Though I do hate him as I do hell-pains,
> Yet, for necessity of present life,
> I must show out a flag and sign of love,
> Which is indeed but sign.
>
> (I, i, 151–4)

we should be particularly alerted. Iago is the one who shows the flags – any flags he chooses. He has made himself master of 'signs' which are indeed but signs – divorced from and unrelated to things. Anyone who has become used to relying on and following his flags (and *everyone* in the play keeps referring to him as 'honest Iago') is a potential victim of his acquired ability to 'show out the sign' – any sign.

Why does he hate Othello? In his last speech in Act II, scene ii, he seems to be turning over some reasons including the unlikely one that Othello may have cuckolded him – Coleridge felicitously called this 'the motive hunting of motiveless malignity'. Shakespeare – unerringly I feel – leaves this area vague and undecidable. As Iago himself says – 'What you know, you know.' And what you don't, you don't, and perhaps never can – for instance, what is the origin of that passion and energy for destructive evil which can erupt into the world through human agents. What *is* the whence and why of 'ruin's wasteful entrance'?

What we can say is that Iago is drawn to the idea of engendering – not new life; for such a sexual play it is curiously infertile – but 'the monstrous'. His relish is for negation and inversion – he likes to deepen darkness while pretending to bring light (on both nights, literally); he likes to introduce dirt into cleanliness and make white things 'grimy'; he enjoys administering poison while pretending to heal; he delights in causing madness while offering new mental clarifications. He is the flag-bearer to chaos and old night. He likes to reduce love to lust and when, to Roderigo, he says that before he would drown himself for love 'I would change my humanity with a baboon' (I, ii, 311), he indirectly reveals himself. For his special pleasure and intent *is* to transform men into beasts. (There are many references to animals in the play, most from the fouler end of the spectrum – monkeys, goats, dogs, toads, vipers.) When Othello says, too confidently, 'exchange me for a goat' (III, iii, 180) if I ever give in to jealousy, he is describing exactly what Iago is about to do to him, or effect in him. For Iago is a master of degenerative transformation – what we might call downward metamorphosis. Thus his supreme 'creative' act is the bringing forth of the monstrous:

> I have't! It is engendered! Hell and night
> Must bring this monstrous birth to the world's light.
>
> (I, iii, 394–5)

'Monster' derives from Latin *monstrum*, an omen portending the will of the gods, something supernatural, from *monere*, to warn. In being somehow 'out' of nature, 'the monstrous' is a strange category, or rather, it is that which threatens, disrupts and destroys categories, crossing and confusing taxonomic lines and confounding category differentiations. It is curiously related to tragedy, since one of the matters which tragedy explores is how or why or when does nature somehow engender and 'bring to birth' something seemingly 'unnatural', *anti*-nature. In Euripides' *Hippolytus*, a giant bull emerges from the sea to destroy Hippolytus. A bull from the *sea*? Monstrous! I shall have more to say about 'the monstrous' in connection with *King Lear*. But the emergence of the monstrous is crucial to *Othello*. There is a darkly ironic warning of what is to come when Othello, disturbed by the 'foul rout' which breaks out on the first night in Cyprus, says: ''Tis monstrous. Iago, who began't?' (II, iii, 216). Iago began it, of course, and he is even now beginning his monstrous midwifery. When he begins his inexplicit insinuations about Cassio and Desdemona, Othello again sails much closer to the truth than he can know, saying it is 'as if there were some monster in thy thought/Too hideous to be shown' (III, iii, 107–8). As indeed there is. Simulating shock that he might be not telling the truth, Iago feeds Othello the word; 'O monstrous world!' (III, iii, 374), and soon Othello is gulping down his obscene evocations – 'O monstrous! monstrous!' (III, iii, 424). The 'monster' is of course 'jealousy' – Emilia's definition cannot be bettered: 'It is a monster/Beget upon itself, born on itself.' Unnatural; but ruinously real. Once roused – once the unnatural beast is out of the sea – the ramifying consequences can be devastating, as the final 'tragic loading of this bed' (V, ii, 361) – murder and suicide – horribly demonstrate. Iago's hideous child has been delivered.

But why so quickly? Here we must address the notorious 'double-time' scheme of the play. There is a time gap between

Acts I and II to allow for the voyage to Cyprus, but thereafter the action indisputably takes place within two days, or rather two nights. As Bullough points out, this makes many statements almost incomprehensible – at least in terms of literal clock-time. Emilia says Iago 'hath a hundred times woo'd me to steal' Desdemona's handkerchief (III, iii, 292). When was that? Iago suggests to the credulous Othello that Desdemona is tired of her husband. After two days? He speaks of Cassio's and Desdemona's 'stolen hours of lust' (III, iii, 339). When can that have been? Bianca accuses Cassio of neglecting her for a week.[1] The crowning absurdity is Othello's pathetic and maddened cry 'Iago knows/That she with Cassio hath the act of shame/A thousand times committed' (V, ii, 207–9). Say, once a day for three years. But of course we are well past sanity and calendars by this time. In the source story, the action does indeed occur over some months. Shakespeare, who by now was – incontestably as I see it – in total, indeed awesome control over his medium, must have known what he was doing in thus impossibly conflating discrepant time schemes, so what was it? Arguments about ineptitude or carelessness (he never got round to intended revisions) hold no water. Shakespeare being Shakespeare can make us forget the clocks and accept both Long and Short time in the uninterruptedly accelerating tension and suspense of the drama. Bullough has an entirely acceptable explanation. 'Thus Shakespeare transcends external probabilities in a poetic vision of Iago's evil mind working with lightning rapidity to destroy the innocent, and of an agonized victim whose sense of past and present is increasingly confused under the stress of his jealousy.'[2] But in *two days*?

I think there is something else going on here. For a start, there is sufficient evidence to suggest that the marriage is not consummated. Othello himself says to Desdemona 'The profit's yet to come 'twixt me and you' (II, iii, 10). On the second night, Iago says 'He hath not yet made wanton the night with her' (II, ii, 16). When Othello goes to kill Desdemona the next night he says 'when I have pluck'd the rose, I cannot give it

[1]. op. cit., p. 229.
[2]. ibid., p. 231.

vital growth again' (V, ii, 13–14), which would seem to indicate that he has not yet 'pluck'd the rose' which would have been unambiguous enough for the Elizabethans. The interruptions of his two nights in bed with Desdemona are caused by street disturbances organized by Iago.[1] There is evidence that the interruptions are not entirely unwelcome. When the Duke of Venice tells Othello he must leave to fight the Turks, he uses an odd and rather unpleasant phrase – 'you must therefore be content to slubber the gloss of your new fortunes with this more stubborn and boisterous expedition' (I, ii, 223–5). To 'slubber' is to besmear, and 'slubbering the gloss' will be Iago's occupation. But Othello is happy to go, saying that he finds the 'steel couch of war' the softest 'bed of down'. 'I do agnize [i.e. know in myself]/A natural and prompt alacrity/I find in hardness' (I, iii, 228–30). When a Senator adds 'You must away tonight' Othello immediately and, one feels enthusiastically, replies – 'With all my heart' (I, iii, 273). *All* his heart? No part of it left for his new bride?

[1]. In his very interesting book, *Shakespeare's Festive World*, Cambridge University Press, 1991, François Laroque suggests that these raucous disturbances are linked to the old festive custom known as 'charivari' (or 'Skimmington riding') in which a couple were rudely woken in the night by some disturbance if the community disapproved of the marriage (it can be found in Thomas Hardy, *The Mayor of Casterbridge*). This makes Iago a sort of Lord of Misrule. 'Iago is the instigator of most of the popular traditions and scenarios evoked or indirectly suggested in the course of the play. He initiates a form of rough music, or charivari, in the dark streets of Venice to rouse Brabantio in the middle of the night; he engages in word-play and in a satirical portrait game with Desdemona in the tradition of Venetian *conversazione*, he sings merry drinking songs during the night of revels in Cyprus and possesses a whole repertoire of images of carnival customs. Iago ... conjures up popular games and folk traditions only to pervert them to his own ends' (p. 287). Laroque also reminds us, as does Bullough, that a well-known Spanish saint of the time was Sant Iago Matarmos – San James, the killer of Moors (taken as winning the battle of Clavijo against the Moors in the eleventh century). I don't think we need to look further for the source of the name for Shakespeare's Moor-killer.

Othello hardly seems an enthusiast for marriage. One of Iago's first questions to him is 'Are you fast married?' (I, ii, 10) and Othello, not quite giving a straight answer, goes on to say:

> For know, Iago,
> But that I love the gentle Desdemona,
> I would not my unhoused free condition
> Put into circumscription and confine
> For the sea's worth.
>
> (I, ii, 23–7)

Othello, the great soldier, is used to great distances, vast space; foreign parts and far-flung fighting-fields. He is certainly not prepared for circumscription, confinement, and being 'housed'. But he is married – so it is said – and thus 'housed'. This is a very domestic drama. And one thing it reveals is that, while Othello the great warrior can easily cope with storms at sea, he is, as we say, all at sea in a house. On the second day in Cyprus, after a few of Iago's insinuations he is saying 'Why did I marry?' (III, iii, 242) and:

> O curse of marriage,
> That we can call these delicate creatures ours,
> And not their appetites! I had rather be a toad
> And live upon the vapor of a dungeon
> Than keep a corner in the thing I love
> For others' uses.
>
> (III, iii, 267–71)

He speaks of Desdemona in terms of stone, 'monumental alabaster', snow – never as warm living flesh and blood, corporeal and penetrable. In the bedroom-murder scene, he kisses her as she is asleep and says, ominously enough – 'Be thus when thou art dead, and I will kill thee,/And love thee after' (V, ii, 18–19). Does this mean that he can *only* love her when she is asleep, stone, alabaster – dead?

When he enters the bedroom – in a rather trance-like, somnambulistic state – he is holding a torch and, looking at Desdemona, says:

> Put out the light, and then put out the light.
> If I quench thee, thou flaming minister,

> I can thy former light restore,
> Should I repent me ...
>
> (V, ii, 7–10)

he is of course addressing the torch, and goes on to say that if he puts out Desdemona's 'light' there will be nothing 'that can thy light relume'. Iago is Othello's 'flaming minister', constantly pretending to bring him 'illumination' as he leads him into ever-deeper darkness. *That* is the light he should have put out. But as it turns out, Othello, the peerless warrior, is curiously unable to kill his lowly 'ancient', even when he tries ('I bleed, sir, but not killed' – V, ii, 284). There is a touch of Satanic immortality about Iago. Can he *ever* be killed? Or is he, in his own evil way, another 'ancient of days'? Desdemona is true light and in smothering her, Othello simply, tragically, puts out the wrong light. Or does he?

'Yet I'll not shed her blood' (V, ii, 3) – these are Othello's words as he approaches his marriage bed for the third time. He is referring specifically to how he will kill Desdemona, but the words have, also, different implications. His wife is still a virgin and, not to put too fine a point on it, he *should* shed her blood (recall the practice of showing the blooded sheets after the first night of marriage – this is part of the suggestiveness of the red-spotted handkerchief which has 'magic in the web of it' and can subdue a husband 'entirely to her love' – II, iv, 60). But, if anything, Othello seems to dread the idea of the sexual act (he gives the impression that he regards copulation as something which loathsome toads do). We have seen his confident dismissal of the distractions of Cupid and heard of his 'prompt alacrity' for 'hardness'; heard, too, his rapid regret at having married. Part of him responds to the 'jewel' which is Desdemona, but not to the female, sexual body. His precipitate eagerness to trust and believe Iago's lubriciously vile, and quite incredible, scenarios – with a headlong speed which Shakespeare builds into the play at the risk of quotidian inconsistencies – reveal a positive *desire* to believe the false 'pageant' which holds him in 'false gaze'. Iago is indeed his reliable ensign, and (I want to suggest) in fact 'shows out' just the 'flags' which, by a profound and troubling paradox, a deep part of Othello wants to follow – certainly his late claim he was a man 'not easily jealous' who loved not wisely, but too well (V, ii, 341–2), is hardly justified by what we see in the play. What he 'loved' in Desdemona, remember, was the way she listened to his adventures and her 'pity' (I, iii, 167); it is not clear that he is, in fact, drawn to her sexually. I think there is quite a lot to Stanley Cavell's seemingly idiosyncratic contention that Othello, the immaculate soldier ('my perfect soul'), dreads sexual 'contamination'. 'I am claiming that we must understand Othello ... to want to believe Iago, to be trying, against his knowledge, to believe him. Othello's eager insistence on Iago's honesty, his eager slaking of his thirst for knowledge with that poison, is not a sign of his stupidity in the presence of poison but of his devouring need for it.'[1]

Let me try to make the point in another way by asking the seemingly foolish question – to whom *is* Othello 'fast married'? As we have seen, he does not actually answer Iago's question, and there is this very suggestive exchange in the second scene of the play:

Iago. He's married.
Cassio. To whom?
(*Enter Othello*.)
Iago. Marry, to – Come captain, will you go?

Shakespeare does nothing by accident, so why should he not have given Iago one or two words more before Othello's entrance – just a second to say 'Desdemona' or 'Brabantio's daughter'? I think it is because he wants to introduce just that element of doubt about Othello's marriage. He is married 'to –'. We neither see nor hear anything of Othello's actual marriage – the legitimating ritual – to Desdemona. What we *do* see in the decisive Act III, scene iii, in the course of which Othello effectively hands himself over to Iago – follows all his flags – is the two of them kneeling down together making what Othello calls 'a sacred vow'. In the course of the scene they exchange vows. Othello says: 'I am bound to thee for-

[1]. *Disowning Knowledge*, Cambridge University Press, 1987, p. 133.

ever'(212), and Iago says: 'I am your own forever'(476). I allow that a priest is absent and they are not in church, but there is much improvized law in this play, and this – I submit – is the 'marriage' we *do* see. Ocular proof.

I am not suggesting any sort of homosexual relationship. The tragedy of this play turns on the tragic incompatibility of the heroic and the domestic, the martial and the erotic (Othello prefers 'hardness' to 'honey'); Othello's 'occupation' is indeed 'gone', and in his new 'housed' situation he is so lost, so out of control, that he needs what he too often insists is his 'honest' Iago to show him the way, or – perhaps more desperately – the way out. That there is a curious closeness between Iago and Othello has, of course, been commented on. One of the most interesting essays on this relationship is by, sadly the late, Joel Fineman.[1] He sees Iago as Othello's motivator, as it were his first cause. He points to the two strange lines spoken by Iago in the first scene: 'Were I the Moor, I would not be Iago'(55) and 'I am not what I am'(62). If he is not what he is – *not* Iago – does it follow that somehow he *is* the Moor? Fineman's suggestion is that Iago claims that he is non-identical with himself 'and it is this principle – "I am not what I am" – . . . that, we can say, Iago, as complementary opposite of a less complicated Othello, introduces to or into Othello in the course of the play . . . we can think of Iago, because he is the motivator of Othello, as the inside of Othello, as a principle of disjunct being – "I am not what I am" – introduced into the smooth and simple existence of an Othello who, at least at the beginning, is whatever else he is, surely what he is.'[2] Certainly, Othello goes from being 'all in all sufficient' (IV, i, 265) – 'my perfect soul' – to what Fineman calls 'an empty shell of a hero'. After the murder and the realization of what he has done, Othello announces to the Venetian officials 'That's he that was Othello; Here I am' (V, ii, 280). Not exactly, 'I am not what I am' but certainly 'I am

[1]. 'The Sound of "O" in *Othello*: the Real of the Tragedy of Desire', in *The Subjectivity Effect in Western Literary Tradition*, MIT Press, 1991, pp. 143–64.

[2]. ibid., p. 148.

not what I *was*' – Iago has emptied him out; the hero is now hollow.

It is in this connection that Fineman draws attention to the unusual prevalence of the sound of 'O' in the play. It is a common enough exclamation, but it pervades this play as it does no other. It's in pretty well all the names. Not so surprising given they are Italians, you may say – but the name 'Othello' is Shakespeare's invention, and while there is a Thorello in Ben Jonson's *Every Man in his Humour*, Shakespeare clearly wants an 'O' at the beginning and end of his name. But more than that, characters use it as an exclamation at least one hundred times, by my counting. It would be otiose to list all the occurrences, but for an example – in the first scene of Act V it occurs twenty-two times. More notably, as Othello begins to be troubled by Emilia's vehement strictures ('O gull! O dolt! As ignorant as dirt!' – V, ii, 160–61), he falls on the bed crying – 'O! O! O!' (V, ii, 194), and when he is finally penetrated by the no longer deniable truth, one of his last cries is 'O Desdemon! Dead Desdemon; dead. O! O!' (V, ii, 278). (These triple O's have an extra terrible irony when Othello makes the wild cry that Desdemona and Cassio have 'the act of shame a thousand times committed' (V, ii, 209) – for a thousand is precisely 1 and three O's. O! O! O!) An O is a circle and a nought. As a circle it can symbolize perfection ('my perfect soul'); as a nought it signifies – nothing ('That's he that was Othello'). The tragedy is the spectacle of Othello being transformed from one to the other. At one point, as Iago is getting Othello more and more worked up, and bemused, Iago says to him:

> Marry patience;
> Or I shall say you're all in all in spleen,
> And nothing of a man.
>
> (IV, i, 91)

It is a veiled prediction – Iago will indeed serve to render Othello 'nothing of a man', though he has just enough of the heroic soldier left in him to pass judgement on the terrible zero he has become. O! O! O!

*

KING LEAR

'Now thou art an O without a figure' – this is the Fool, desperately trying to get Lear to realize the folly of what he has done: 'thou hast parted thy wit o' both sides and left nothing i' the middle . . . I am better than thou art now: I am a Fool, thou art nothing' (I, iv, 191–200). Under Iago's ministrations Othello became an 'O' in the course of the play. Lear makes himself 'nothing' at the start with no visible prompting or provocation. The play veritably starts with the eruption of, or into, nothingness and the word re-echoes throughout the opening scenes.

Cordelia. Nothing, my lord.
Lear. Nothing?
Cordelia. Nothing
Lear. Nothing will come of nothing.

(I, i, 90–93)

Lear repeats the word a number of times. Then Gloucester, very much a parallel figure for Lear, finds Edmund reading something. He asks him what it was.

Edmund. Nothing, my lord.
Gloucester. No? What needed then that terrible dispatch of it into your pocket? The quality of nothing hath not such need to hide itself. Let's see. Come, if it be nothing, I shall not need spectacles. (I, ii, 32–5)

The play will be preoccupied with problems of seeing and right vision, and given what is to happen to his eyes, his words carry a terrible proleptic irony. Shortly after, Lear is repeating himself to the Fool who asks him 'Can you make no use of nothing, Nuncle?' 'Why, no, boy. Nothing can be made out of nothing' (I, iv, 135–6). When Edgar, a little later, decides to disguise himself as Poor Tom he says 'Edgar I nothing am' (II, iii, 21). The word becomes increasingly ominous and it is as if we are watching the world of the play being infiltrated with 'nothingness' – indeed, actively serving to install it, a world literally an-*nihil*-ating itself. It is a spectacle almost to freeze you – a world turning, returning, itself to 'nothing'.

There was a well-known Elizabethan Morality play called

The Three Ladies of London (1584). The three ladies in question are – Conscience, Love, and Lucre, and they are variously beset and besought, importuned and rejected by characters such as – Dissimulation, Fraud, Simony, Simplicity, Usury, Hospitality, Sincerity, and so on. Lucre enjoys a good deal of success and boasts of turning Conscience out of house and home. In *King Lear*, too, we find many unjust banishings and harsh shuttings out. Sincerity has fallen on bad times for, as she complains, it is the flatterers who only love from the teeth forward who enjoy worldly success – and there could hardly be a better way to describe what Goneril and Regan are doing in their opening speeches to their father. Exactly like Cordelia, Sincerity prefers to 'see and say nothing' rather than attempt to match the dissimulators. Lucre's only gift to Sincerity is a Parsonage called St Nihil – and Nihil is nothing. It is Lear's gift to Cordelia. It becomes pretty well the gift to Lear's family, and of his realm to itself.

I am not arguing for a specific source for the play.[1] Rather, I want to draw attention to the importance of the exchanges in the opening scene. Cordelia who is indeed Sincere and has a Conscience can only 'see and say nothing' in the presence of so much Dissimulation and Fraud. But how has this situation come about? Like Othello, Lear asks for the wrong sort of evidence; asks disastrously the wrong questions. He asks for 'auricular assurance' of his daughters' love as Othello had

[1]. As I indicated, I do not intend to go into sources, but – briefly. There was an old folk tale in which a daughter tells her father that she loves him as much as salt. This makes him very angry until she explains that she means he is essential to her life. The story enters literature in the twelfth-century *History* of Geoffrey of Monmouth. In the sixteenth century it becomes part of British history and is told by John Higgins in the 1574 edition of *A Mirror for Magistrates*, by Warner in *Albion's England* (1586), by Holinshed, and by Spenser in Book II of *The Faerie Queen* (1590). Shakespeare probably knew all these. The most important thing to know, perhaps, is that in Holinshed Cordelia successfully restores her father to the throne and then succeeds him for five years – though she then commits suicide when imprisoned by her enemies. Only Shakespeare has Cordelia murdered.

asked for 'ocular proof' of his wife's unfaithfulness. But you can no more 'hear' love than you can 'see' honour. Worse, he asks in terms of quantity. 'Which of you shall we say doth love us most?' (I, i, 54). He hands himself over to rhetoric and easily manufactured hyperboles. In the matter of how many knights he can bring with him to his daughters' houses, when Goneril says to him 'disquantity your train' (I, iv, 255) she is in fact speaking his language. He is still trying to quantify love when Regan wants to reduce his train by another half: he turns to Goneril – 'Thy fifty yet doth double five-and twenty,/And thou art twice her love' (II, iv, 258–9). The sisters rapidly reduce his permitted train to zero. 'What need one?' says Regan, which provokes the searing response:

> O reason not the need! Our basest beggars
> Are in the poorest things superfluous.
> Allow not nature more than nature's needs,
> Man's life is cheap as beast's. Thou art a lady:
> If only to go warm were gorgeous,
> Why, nature needs not what thou gorgeous wear'st,
> Which scarcely keeps thee warm
>
> (II, iv, 264–9)

Many of the questions and preoccupations of the play are compacted in those lines, but let us return to the opening scene.

Lear's initial fault is exposed in Gloucester's opening words when he refers to 'the division of the kingdom' (I, i, 4). Almost immediately we see this made literal when Lear takes a map and divides the realm into three. It is a deed of horrifying irresponsibility and introduces 'division' into every unit of the society – family, court, realm. His explanation of what he is doing would have been even more shocking to the Elizabethans:

> Meantime we shall express our darker purpose.
> Give me the map there. Know that we have divided
> In three our kingdom; and 'tis our fast intent
> To shake all cares and business from our age,
> Conferring them on younger strengths, while we
> Unburthened crawl toward death ...

(Since now we will divest us both of rule,
Interest of territory, cares of state)

(I, i, 38–53)

By 'darker' he here means simply 'hidden' but it is an ominous word coming from a king, and, indeed, from this initial act there will spread a darkness over the realm until by the end 'all's cheerless, dark and deadly' (V, iii, 293). That a king, the great hub of the social wheel, the maintainer of unity and order, should suddenly express the wish to 'shake' off cares and 'crawl', like a child or a wounded animal, toward death, is almost terrifying if only because he should represent – indeed embody – stability, concord (not 'division'), the inexorable responsibilities involved in positions of power, and duties firmly discharged and unquestioningly upheld. He wants to keep the 'name' of king, but leave the 'execution' of his duties to others – a fatal attempt to divide word from thing. It is as though the linch-pin should withdraw itself from the wheel, the corner-stone rebel from its place in the structure of the church. No wonder the scene ends with a sense of dissolution and scattering. 'Kent *banished* thus? and France in choler *parted*?/And the king *gone* tonight?' (I, ii, 24–5 – emphasis added). The 'division' has started, initiating an atmosphere marked by rapid, furtive, untimely, and uncertain movement. The plotters turn up at odd times which surprise even themselves – 'out of season threading dark-eyed night'. Lear 'calls to horse, but will I know not whither'. The French army creeps into England 'on secret feet'. Gloucester and Kent grope around the heath looking for Lear. Everywhere there is a sense of midnight flight and fumbling which is either conspiratorial or desperate. All seems uncertain and unnerved. 'The images of revolt and flying off!' (II, iv, 88). Movement is no longer co-ordinated, harmonious, ceremonially managed; rather it is madly centrifugal – as though all things were being whirled off their right paths.

Shakespeare was clearly fascinated by what might happen if the great central maintaining principle of social order was withdrawn, or withdrew itself – he had tried the great experiment shortly before in *Measure for Measure*. It allows him to explore, dramatically, the question – what is human nature when it is, as it were, unchecked in all directions: when all the bonds have 'cracked' and the rats have bitten 'the holy cords atwain/Which are too intrince t'unloose' (II, ii, 76)? Lear's sudden abdication leaves a vacuum where there should be a majestic and irresistible principle of order, custom, and degree. And in that vacuum, the deep realities of human nature are afforded a dark arena in which to play themselves out. Majesty has fallen to folly, power has bowed to flattery, as Kent says – and indeed by the end of the play Lear will have bowed, fallen, knelt, and crawled in dead earnest. (It is a very sadistic play. People stumble, kneel, fall; are tripped, elbowed, shoved, kicked, and tortured. I will just note here that, in this play, it is the victims, the sufferers, the thrust-out and kicked-along, the blinded and maddened who, at intolerable cost, achieve true vision. By contrast, the perception of the evil characters seem to shrink progressively until by the end we have the image of Goneril and Regan 'squinting' at each other.) Wishing only to shake off his cares, shrug off his burdens, 'divest' himself of rule, Lear discovers that there is no stopping the divesting, and he will be stripped of his knights, his house, his clothes, his very reason – and finally of Cordelia. His terrible fate lies coiled and nascent in his own opening words.

'The King falls from the bias of nature,' says Gloucester (I, ii, 121). The last time Shakespeare used that metaphor was in *Twelfth Night* when Sebastian tells Olivia: 'So comes it, lady, you have mistook;/But nature to her bias drew in that' (V, i, 259–60). The metaphor is from bowling and Sebastian is saying that, although Olivia was mistaken when she married him – because of course she thought she was marrying Cesario – she has in fact swerved back to nature's proper course in marrying him, because Cesario is, of course, a woman – Viola. For her to have married a woman would have been to 'fall from the bias of nature'. To be sure, Lear has not contracted a homosexual marriage, but, more generally, the image suggests that, in nature, there is a right way for things to go, and a wrong way, and Lear has taken the wrong way. How nature may 'err from itself' (to take an image from *Othello*, III, iii, 227) is a matter to which I will return. But Lear has fallen from the 'bias of nature' by his division of the realm, his abdication, and – worst of all – his disastrous misjudgement of Cordelia. To Burgundy he says 'her price is fallen' (more quantification – Lear is assessing her in Iagoish money terms whereas, like Desdemona, she is a jewel), and dismisses her as 'little seeming substance' (I, i, 199–200). He describes her as *un*natural ('a wretch whom nature is ashamed/Almost t'acknowledge hers' – I, i, 214), strips her of her dowry, and strangers her with an oath. He is not only completely wrong, but has totally inverted true values – Cordelia is all substance and no seeming, and is (along with Kent and Edgar and, for the most part, Albany) the most steadfastly 'natural' character in the play (there are problems in such an assertion to which I will return). No wonder Kent says 'See better, Lear' (I, i, 160). Lear is going to have to travel a hard and painful road to learn to penetrate the seeming and mere show of things and discern true reality – 'the thing itself'. He will suffer greatly, indeed unendurably, before he draws back to 'the bias of nature'.

The King of France finds Lear's behaviour incredible, and finds it most strange that;

> The best, the dearest, should in this trice of time
> Commit a thing so monstrous to dismantle
> So many folds of favor . . .
>
> (I, i, 219–20)

When he learns of what her 'fault' consisted, he is happy to take her as she stands – metaphorically naked, like traditional pictures of truth. I will return to 'monstrous', but want here to concentrate on that phrase – 'dismantle so many folds of favor'. When Cordelia departs her last words are (to her sisters):

> The jewels of our father, with washed eyes
> Cordelia leaves you. I know you what you are . . .

More proleptic – by which I mean anticipatory – ironies. *Cordelia* is the 'jewel' of her father, and her 'washed eyes' and tears will be of extreme importance later in the play. Finally she says:

Time shall unfold what plighted cunning hides,
Who covers faults, at last shame them derides.

(I, i, 271–2, 282-3)

To this I must add the words of Isabella when she thinks she is not going to receive any justice at the hands of the Duke of Vienna (in *Measure for Measure*):

Then, O you blessed ministers above,
Keep me in patience, and with ripened time
Unfold the evil which is here wrapp'd up
In countenance.

(V, i, 115–18)

'Unfold' became a very important word for Shakespeare. It is one of the first verbs in *Hamlet*:

Barnado. Who's there?
Francisco. Nay, answer me. Stand and unfold yourself.

Thus the play opens, and it is a long 'unfolding' that is to come. In *Othello* it occurs at least four times. Desdemona says 'To my unfolding lend your prosperous ear' (I, iii, 245), and 'This honest creature doubtless/Sees and knows more, much more, than he unfolds' (III, iii, 242–3). Emilia, talking about her husband Iago, though she doesn't yet know it, says 'O heaven, that such companions thou'dst unfold,/And put in every honest hand a whip/To lash the rascals naked through the world' (IV, i, 141–3). Iago himself, expert folder, has a worry – 'the Moor may unfold me to him' (V, i, 21). Cunning is 'plighted' (pleated, enfolded); evil is 'wrapped up', and, ultimately, only 'ripe time' (also used in this play) can do the unfolding (the 'blessed ministers' are hardly to be relied on). This suggests that once evil has been released – made its 'wasteful entrance' – no human agent can arrest it, it must simply exhaust itself. In time. It is thus in this play where even Edmund cannot stop the murder of Cordelia he himself ordered. He is not – in time. Our acts get away from us. 'Unfolding' implies exposure, revealing, revelation, and, as we say, the story 'unfolds' in front of our eyes in the theatre. By the end of the play we too see them – all of them – 'what they are'.

But of course foldings and pleatings and wrappings directly evoke clothing and not for nothing are Goneril and Regan 'gourgeously' arrayed. There is much changing of clothes in the play. Edgar abandons his court clothes for a beggar's rags, then finally appears as a knight in armour. Cordelia dislikes Kent's necessary disguises. Lear himself sheds his crown, then his clothes, marks his uttermost descent into sheer nature by dressing in weeds, and is finally 'arrayed' in 'fresh garments' at Cordelia's command. There is a feeling that while clothes change, people do not – 'in nothing am I changed/But in my garments' says Edgar to his father (IV, vi, 8–9) – though people can certainly regress and degenerate. Clothes can indeed cover evil and cunning, but clothes are also the very mark of the human, and the 'folds of favor' can be the signs of an achieved and functioning civilization. This play 'dismantles' these folds as well, and in addition to exposing evil it lays bare the human body. Denudation is a deep theme of the play. Let us call it the spectacle and exploration of the 'disaccommodation' of man. Literally – the Fool warns Lear of the folly of having given away his crown, thus risking exposure. He calls him a 'shelled peascod' and he is contrasted with the oyster and snail who at least have the wisdom to carry their shells with them. In fury at the inhospitality of his daughters, Lear says 'I abjure all roofs, and choose/To wage against the enmity o' th' air' (II, iv, 207), and Act II ends with the sinisterly repeated order – 'Shut up your doors.' Directionless, Lear rushes wildly off into the heath where nature itself is at its most naked – 'For many miles about/There's scarce a bush' (II, iv, 300–301). Stripped of crown, palace and followers – his 'folds of favor' – Lear moves towards complete denudation. But the exposure brings the beginning of insight. When he tells the Fool to precede him into the hovel, he calls him 'You houseless poverty' and follows this by considering – perhaps for the first time – 'Poor naked wretches whereso'er you are', wondering

> How shall your houseless heads and unfed sides,
> Your looped and windowed raggedness, defend you
> From seasons such as these? *O, I have ta'en*
> *Too little care of this!*
>
> (III, iv, 30–33 – emphasis added)

Lear is becoming aware of basic, deprived conditions not thought about or cared for in the palace. But it is the sight of Edgar with his 'uncovered body' which provokes Lear to the final stripping.

Is man no more than this? . . . Thou art the thing itself; *unaccommodated man* is no more but such a poor, bare, forked animal as thou art. Off, off you lendings! Come, unbutton here. [Tearing off his clothes]
(III, iv, 105–11 – emphasis added)

The 'thing itself' was precisely what he could not see in the first scene, since he had put himself in the thrall of 'seeming'. Now we get the feeling that the terrible 'disaccommodation' which Lear has undergone has brought him – shatteringly – to true vision, even at the expense of what Edgar calls 'the safer sense' (i.e. sounder, saner – IV, vi, 81). Which is perhaps – in Lear's case – just what it costs. But in his 'madness', he breaks through to those piercing insights into and through the whole fabric of society – 'a dog's obeyed in office' (IV, vi, 160):

Through tattered clothes small vices do appear;
Robes and furred gowns hide all . . .
(IV, vi, 166–7)

Lear has been brought to see through *all* the pleats and wraps and folds. Well might Edgar say wonderingly – 'Reason in madness!' (IV, vi, 177).

France thinks Cordelia must have committed something 'monstrous' to 'dismantle so many folds of favor'. We shortly get an echo of this when Gloucester, too credulously accepting Edmund's account of Edgar's treachery, says 'He cannot be such a monster' (I, ii, 101). The word occurs quite frequently, but most importantly in Albany's rebukes to Goneril.

Thou changed and self-covered thing, for shame
Be-monster not thy feature.
(IV, ii, 62–3)

He calls her 'barbarous, degenerate' and says:

If that the heavens do not their visible spirits
Send quickly down to tame these vile offenses,

> It will come,
> Humanity must perforce prey on itself,
> Like monsters of the deep.
>
> (IV, ii, 46–50)

Heaven sends down no spirits, visible or invisible, in this play, and humanity – visibly – preys upon itself. Let me add this, from *Troilus and Cressida*:

> And appetite, a universal wolf,
> So doubly seconded with will and power,
> Must make perforce a universal prey,
> And last eat up himself.
>
> (I, iii, 121–4)

Just noting the recurrence of the word 'perforce', let us stay for a moment with the repeated word 'prey', usually used to refer to animals that hunt and kill other animals. The extraordinary proliferation of animal imagery and references to animals has often been noted. These references include – dog, cur, rats, monkeys, ant, eels, vulture, wolf, frog, toad, tadpole, newt, mice, foxes, cats, greyhound, worms, adders – this list is by no means exhaustive. The general feeling is that the human world is being rapidly taken over by animals – palaces seem to be repossessed by dogs and foxes and snakes and other low, mean, snapping and sliding animals. There is no sense of magnificent animal energy, rather of things that prowl and creep and slither – sharp-toothed yet devoid of valour and glamour. One of the horrors of the play is the sense of the fading away of the human while such animals scurry and leap and slip into the play from every side. But it is the humans who are reverting – degenerating – to animals. Goneril and Regan end up as 'adders' squinting at each other. Edmund turns out to be a 'foul-spotted toad'. The relapse, or regression, is, we feel, to some prior stage of evolution when things had but recently crawled out of the mud. These animals are not fine enough to be man's competitors; they are rather his mean ancestors. Yet how quickly they can repossess his world – how easily he can re-become them. So near is the ditch; so easy is the fall back into the slime. It is the copious listing of such encroaching and invading animals, or animalized humans, that gives such agonizing force to Lear's final complaint against the universe:

> Why should a dog, a horse, a rat, have life,
> And thou no breath at all. Thou'lt come no more,
> Never, never, never, never, never.
>
> (V, iii, 308–10)

That last line must be the most appalling in literature. This is a world in which rats retain all their mean, scurrying activity while Cordelia is hanged in lonely squalor by a paid murderer. And will come no more. This is unbearable. Who would want to see as well, or as much, as this?

It is, indeed, monstrous, and there are a number of people in the play who effectively regress to the condition of preying animals or, worse, 'be-monster' themselves. As I have indicated, the 'monstrous' is the non-natural, and we are again confronted in this play, as never before so horrifyingly, with the profound and insoluble problem of how nature can produce the unnatural – anti-nature. Kent points to the problem:

> It is the stars,
> The stars above us, govern our conditions;
> Else one self mate and make could not beget
> Such different issues.
>
> (IV, iii, 33–6)

Star-governed or not, how can Cordelia *and* Goneril and Regan issue from the same womb? (The play opens with the description of a pregnant belly – 'she grew round-wombed' – and the play will precipitate a deep exploration of just what the 'thick rotundity' of nature can bring forth.) Why should one daughter draw to the bias of nature and the others fall from it? And what *is* the bias of nature? This is what Albany says to Goneril:

> I fear your disposition:
> That nature which contemns its origin
> Cannot be bordered certain in itself;
> She that herself will sliver and disbranch
> From her material sap, perforce must wither
> And come to deadly use.
>
> (IV, ii, 31–6)

Again – *perforce*: by force, of necessity. It will happen whether we will it or not, with or without visible or invisible spirits, irrespective of the stars. This is the belief, or perhaps we should say – the hope. And note Albany's image. To 'sliver and disbranch' means to cut off from the main trunk, and introduces the idea that Goneril has perversely, unnaturally, stripped herself away from the true source of life. In her treatment of her father, she certainly 'contemns' her origin, and she *does* 'wither and came to deadly use'. She, in her turn, has despised Albany's 'milky gentleness', and here counters by calling him 'milk-livered man!' (IV, ii, 50). (In *Macbeth* we will hear of the 'milk of human kindness' – there is a 'great abatement of kindness' in *King Lear* – and the 'sweet milk of concord'.) Milk and sap evoke the nourishing, nurturing, generative and gentle aspects of nature. *Natural* nature. Evil is often rendered or figured as a state of desiccation in Shakespeare; conversely, there is a beneficent, life-promoting – milk and sap – force in nature which it is possible, indeed more natural, to remain attached to and keep in touch with. It is often associated with a benign moistness, and this is the importance of Cordelia's tears. They provoke an anonymous Gentleman to a description of astonishing beauty:

> You have seen
> Sunshine and rain at once: her smiles and tears
> Were like a better way: those happy smilets
> That played on her ripe lip seemed not to know
> What guests were in her eyes, which parted thence
> As pearls from diamonds dropped.
>
> (IV, iii, 18–24)

Rain, tears (and note that they are 'guests' in her eyes: when Cornwall and Regan put out Gloucester's eyes in his own house, among other things, they are hideously disfiguring and transgressing the sacred rules of hospitality and the guest–host relation, as Gloucester impotently complains); pearls, diamonds – here surely, irresistibly, are the true and enduring values. These are aligned with – spring from – the gentle and restorative virtues of nature – 'our foster-mother of nature is repose,' says the Doctor, indicating the nursing side of nature (IV, iv, 12) – which Cordelia invokes and summons as she seeks to cure and heal her mad father:

> All blest secrets
> All you unpublished virtues of the earth,
> Spring with my tears! be aidant and remediate
> In the good man's distress!
>
> (IV, iv, 15–18)

These tears are, indeed, 'holy water from her heavenly eyes' (IV, iii, 81). The 'unpublished virtues of the earth' may mean, specifically here, secret remedial herbs, but the words have an infinitely larger resonance. After all the predatory cruelty and viciousness we have witnessed, Cordelia's tears demonstrate and remind us that there *is* 'a better way'. The earth does have 'virtues' even if it does produce monsters. Cordelia is not an angel or a divinely appointed agent of redemption. She is – we must feel this – the truly, uncorrupted human: dutiful, kind, honest, 'heavenly true', respectful of her origin and all the bonds and obligations that branch from it – nature *most* natural. But she is murdered and Lear is on a 'wheel of fire' of mental anguish and dies of unsustainable grief. What of 'nature' now? It is not visibly 'aidant and remediate' – not at all. And it is *Shakespeare* who murders Cordelia, which is more than legend and chronicle ever did.[1]

When Albany hears Lear cursing Goneril with terrible rage, he asks – 'Now, gods that we adore, whereof comes this?'; to which Goneril replies – 'Never afflict yourself to know the cause' (I, iv, 297–8). Whereof comes a father's maddened rage; whereof comes a daughter's cruelty and ingratitude; whereof comes whatever it is that drives a man to pull out another man's eyes – whence 'ruin's wasteful entrance'? If we asked Iago such questions, we know what he would say, or rather what he wouldn't. Goneril's last words offer an eerie

[1]. Brockbank thinks Shakespeare does this to transform the play into a sacrifice: see '"Upon such sacrifices"...' op. cit., pp. 220–43. The case is powerfully argued but, finally, I cannot see it that way.

echo of Iago's, though unlike him she exits to commit suicide. Confronting her with one of her treacherous letters, Albany says 'read thine own evil... I perceive you know it'.

Goneril. Say, if I do, the laws are mine not thine:
Who can arraign me for't?
Albany. Most monstrous! O!
Knowst thou this paper?
Goneril. Ask me not what I know. (*Exit*.)
(V, iii, 160–63)

'Demand me nothing.' 'Never afflict yourself to know the cause.' 'The laws are mine.' Othello starts his long speech as he enters Desdemona's bedroom to kill her – 'It is the cause, it is the cause' ... he will not 'name' it, but his repetition of the word is immensely suggestive. 'Cause' has, at least, two senses. In natural science it is assumed that every 'effect' has a 'cause'. You cannot actually *see* causes – they have to be inferred or deduced. This way the laws of nature are discovered and established. The apple falls and the cause is gravity. Of course there is scope here for any number of problems, both scientific and philosophic. Causes may be multiple or untraceable: one cause is the effect of a prior cause, and so on. But the word was also used to refer to a matter (case, cause) which someone feels entitled to take to law. It could be that in his entranced invocations, Othello is hoping (asserting) that he has both natural and human law on his side. But we have seen how his legal improvizations are a gross travesty of the law. Lear improvizes a grotesque parody of a courtroom, in the farmhouse where Gloucester leads him from the heath.

I will arraign them straight.
[To Edgar] Come, sit thou here, most learned justice.
(III, vi, 21–2)

'Let us deal justly,' says Edgar, and Lear starts the proceedings. 'Arraign her first' (III, vi, 46) – meaning Goneril. Staying with the word 'arraign' for a moment, it is worth noting that it occurs in almost the last words of Goneril when she defies her husband, Albany: 'the laws are mine, not thine:/ Who can arraign me for't?' (V, iii, 160–61). To 'arraign' is to bring to trial, and her words suggest a complete collapse of the legal structure. How law legitimates itself is always potentially a problem – is it simply a way of rationalizing and preserving the status quo, with all its inequalities? Goneril reveals here that she recognizes no law except her own – adapting a good phrase of Melville's, we can say that her conscience has become simply 'a lawyer to her will'. She is beyond 'arraigning'. Lear himself moves to a perception of the manifold injustices concealed by 'law': 'see how yon justice rails upon yon simple thief. Hark in thine ear: change places, and, handy-dandy, which is the justice, which is the thief?' (I, vi, 154–6). Back to the farmhouse and the imaginary 'trial'. Having arraigned Goneril in the form of a 'joint stool', Lear moves on to Regan: 'Then let them anatomize Regan. See what breeds about her heart. Is there any cause in nature that makes these hard hearts?' (III, vi, 75–7).

One could see this as *the* question of the play. Is there a cause *in* nature for the effect which is Regan's hard heart. Or is the effect *itself* the cause – hearts are causes, and her heart is like that because it is like that. Chilling. Lear spends a lot of the play aiming his deranged anger at his daughters – as though they are to blame for everything. Like many tragic heroes (like Othello in this), Lear resists and fights against self-knowledge until almost the end, and, it must be remembered, it was Lear's initial actions which permitted, arguably encouraged, the *emergence* and release of evil, even if it was already latently there, 'wrapped up in countenance'. To that extent, *he* is responsible. Only after he has been exposed to a maximum of inner and outer buffeting can he kneel and say to Cordelia – 'I am a very foolish, fond old man' (IV, vii, 60). And then:

I know you do not love me; for your sisters
  Have, as I do remember, done me wrong.
  You have some cause, they have not.
Cordelia. No cause, no cause.

(IV, vii, 72–5)

The calm, generous gentleness of Cordelia's words awaken thoughts of a side of nature which has been systematically and brutally erased in the course of the play, but which is serenely above arguments about causes. It is the cause, it is the cause? No cause, no cause. It is the better way. Let them anatomize Cordelia. See what breeds about *her* heart. Is there any cause in nature that makes these gentle hearts? I think we have to give the Emilia answer. They are not ever gentle for the cause, but gentle for they're gentle.

Edmund, of course, despises law from the start – 'Fine word, "legitimate"' (I, ii, 18). Cornwall, determined to punish Gloucester, has an attitude to the law more like Goneril's.

> Though well we may not pass upon his life
> Without the form of justice, yet our power
> Shall do a court'sy to our wrath, which men
> May blame, but not control.
>
> (III, vii, 25–8)

This is another way of saying – 'the laws are mine'. He will twist the 'forms of justice' to satisfy his 'wrath', as he does in the horrifying improvized trial and torture scene that follows. There is a lot of anger in this play – Lear's rage, awesome in its excess, cosmic in its reach, as well as Cornwall's and Regan's sadistic wrath.

> To be in anger is impiety;
> But who is man that is not angry?
>
> (III, v, 57)

Thus Timon of Athens. And there is another kind of anger – call it righteous indignation – which must be seen as justified and part of the fully human. As Kent says: 'anger hath a privilege'. When Cornwall is bent on putting out Gloucester's eye, *a servant* – one of those usually voiceless, deferential, obedient appendages of the court – says:

> Hold your hand, my lord!
> I have served you ever since I was a child;
> But better service have I never done you
> Than now to bid you hold.
>
> (III, vii, 73–6)

Cornwall is incredulous at such insubordination, but the servant persists with the thrilling line – 'Nay, then, come on, and take the chance of anger' (II, vii, 80), and although

Regan stabs him in the back he has in fact killed Cornwall. The play starts with father turning against his child; then brother plots against brother; in due course husband and wife fall out (Albany and Goneril), and here the servant turns on his master. All the bonds are 'cracking'. But in this case it is a matter of the triumph of humanity over hierarchy. Evil has reached such a pitch that even the lowliest man – if he is still human – cannot stand idly by and watch. The cruelty of dukes can stir the anger of a serf. In a curious way, it is the hinge moment of the play. It occurs literally just about at mid-point, and in fact it marks the beginning of the end for the evil plotters. They have done much damage and will do more, but increasingly and in turn they 'come to deadly use'. Thus far, the tide of evil has gathered force and swept along unopposed. Now there is a physical reaction. Not words of horror but a deed of anger. And not by Albany, or Kent, or Edgar, but by an anonymous servant, a serf 'thrilled with remorse,/Opposed against the act' (V, ii, 723). That the agent who precipitates the turn, initiates the slow (too slow for Cordelia) self-correcting processes of nature, is part of the grim power of the play. Outraged reaction to, and taking preventative issue with evil, comes not from above, but from below, socially one of the lowest of the low.

This raises the question of whether there *is* anything or anyone above in this world. There are many references to divinities and the gods (always 'gods', generic and plural; there is no reference to 'God' as there is in *Macbeth*: there is no monotheism in this play[1]). We have invoked – Hecate, Apollo, Jupiter, Juno; we have 'heavens' with their 'visible spirits', 'the stars above', 'dearest gods', 'ever-gentle gods', Fortune, Jove, even 'fairies'. We are told 'the gods are just', 'the gods are clear' and pious references are made to 'gods that we adore'. When Albany hears of the servant's killing Cornwall his reaction is:

[1]. Not quite true. Lear says 'as if we were God's spies' (V, iii, 17). There is no knowing whether this was Shakespeare or the printer, but whoever capitalized the 'G', it is hardly evidence for an inchoate monotheism.

This shows you are above,
You justicers.
(IV, ii, 78–9)

'Thou, Nature, art my goddess' – Edmund's opening words, of course (I, ii, i). But when Lear curses his ungrateful daughters, he, too, divinizes Nature. 'Here, Nature, hear; dear Goddess hear' (I, iv, 282). What do these people believe? Are they pagans, pre-Christians, or what? (It is curiously hard to get a sense of the date and time of the action, even the place. No Elsinore, no Venice, no towns at all. In one of the oddest lines of the play the Fool says 'This prophecy Merlin shall make, for I live before his time' (III, ii, 95). It almost feels as though we are in pre-history.) Certainly, the very proliferation of divinities invoked makes it impossible to believe that these people live within any stable belief-system. There is a famous moment as the unbearable last scene comes to a climax:

Albany. The gods defend her!
(*Enter Lear, with Cordelia in his arms.*)

If these gods are 'justicers' it is of the most inscrutable sort. Russell Fraser wants to say – 'The Gods dispense justice. But they do not dispense poetic justice.'[1] He fastens on the fleeting presence of a vocabulary of 'redemption' in the play:

Thou hast one daughter
Who redeems nature from the general curse
Which twain have brought her to.
(IV, vi, 208–10)

The 'twain' could be Goneril and Regan – or Adam and Eve. Robert Heilman finds some of Lear's late speeches 'permeated with Christian feeling' – full of contrition, self-abasement, renunciation – and, in general, detects 'a pervading consciousness of deity . . . a largely unconscious, habitual reliance upon divine forces whose primacy is unquestioned'.[2] He points out

[1]. See *Shakespeare's Poetics in relation to King Lear*, Routledge, 1962, p. 30. This is an excellent study of the play.
[2]. See *This Great Stage*, Washington Press, 1963 – this is another magisterial study.

that Edmund, Goneril, Regan, Cornwall, and Oswald never invoke gods (unless as public gesture) and never pray; while Cordelia, Kent, Albany, Edgar – and Lear – all pray. But Stephen Greenblatt thinks that, although people may pray, the gods never answer – which perhaps means there are no gods *to* answer. '*King Lear* is haunted by a sense of rituals and beliefs that are no longer efficacious, that have been *emptied out*. The characters appeal again and again to the pagan gods, but the gods are utterly silent. Nothing answers to human questions but human voices . . .'[1] These are not entirely unreconcilable positions. There seems to be a good deal of vague, instinctive piety – conventional? desperate? – in the play, but there is certainly not the slightest hint of divine response or intervention. If anything, Albany might have said 'This shows you are *below*, you justicers' – nature does seem slowly to correct and re-regulate itself, and it is thus appropriate that the first agent in this process is a figure with the lowliest social status in the play. There is also, perhaps, what Frank Kermode calls 'a self-limiting factor in the nature of evil'. If it happens that evil finally withers and exhausts itself, and that a few of the good characters are left alive – just – then it happens 'per-force' and not per-Jove or Jupiter or any other spirits or, indeed, fairies. As for the Christian feeling in Lear's speeches to Cordelia as they are despatched to prison:

> We two alone shall sing like birds i'th'cage
> When thou dost ask me blessing, I'll kneel down
> And ask of thee forgiveness . . .
>
> Upon such sacrifices, my Cordelia,
> The gods themselves throw incense.
>
> (V, iii, 9–11, 20–21)

these speeches do indeed seem to catch a glimpse of a world of calm and love, secure beyond the reach of the devouring anarchy of the present. But when Kent was in the stocks, he uttered the unforgettable line – 'Nothing almost sees miracles/ But misery' (II, ii, 168–9), and I think we must regard Lear's

[1]. *Shakespearian Negotiations*, California Press, 1988, p. 119.

vision of a 'heaven' (or is it a nursery?) as a miracle *almost* seen. There are no 'miracles' in this play, and Cordelia is hanged.

And it was Shakespeare who made it happen. This made the play unpopular for long periods, particularly in the eighteenth century. Dr Johnson could not sit through the last scenes. It was even re-written, with a happy ending. By common consent, it is all but unbearable. As to why Shakespeare should wish to take or bring his audience to this extreme point, one can only speculate. At one point Regan says to Lear: 'O, sir, you are old,/Nature in you stands on the very verge/Of his confine' (II, iv, 145–7). When Edgar brings Gloucester to the cliff, he tells him 'you are now within a foot/ Of th'extreme verge' (IV, vi, 25–6). Dover cliffs are, in a sense, the 'extreme verge' of England; by extension, the extreme verge of the earth where it meets the sea, the element of flux and dissolution. Lear and Gloucester are indeed brought to the 'extreme verge' of all that living nature can bear, until, blessedly as we feel, they burst through the human 'confine'. I think Shakespeare wants to take us to that 'extreme verge'; to the point where, with Edgar, we feel 'I would not take this from report: it is,/And my heart breaks at it' (IV, vi, 143–4).

Except it is not, quite. When Edgar evokes for his father a vertiginous cliff with a monster standing at the top of it, we are watching Gloucester flopping and floundering about on a perfectly flat and empty stage. For his own purposes – to instil endurance – Edgar has conjured up a powerful 'image' of monsters and heights and depths. Which, we may say, is what Shakespeare, on a vaster scale, has done in *King Lear*. (A point also made by Greenblatt, albeit for a different purpose: 'Edgar does to Gloucester what the theatre usually does to the audience: he persuades his father to discount the evidence of his senses.'[1]) It is as if Shakespeare is giving us 'the thing itself' *and* reminding us that we are watching an 'image' of it. As Lear stoops over the dead Cordelia, there is the following exchange between Kent and Edgar:

Is this the promised end?
Or image of that horror?

[1]. op. cit., p. 118.

The promised end of the play – we are nearly there? Or the promised end of the world – many Elizabethans thought they were nearly *there*? There are many biblical echoes in the book and as well as Lear re-enacting, or re-experiencing, the tribulations of Job, Revelation and its account of the last days before final judgement is clearly in Shakespeare's mind. He is writing in a period when many people regarded the world's end as imminent, and an apocalyptic note is heard throughout the play. Although, at the end, Edgar and Albany are left to sustain 'the gored state' (V, ii, 322), there is no sense of restoration, restitution, let alone of regeneration. There is nothing 'redemptive' here: instead, we are confronted with what A. P. Rossiter used to call 'the alarmingness of the universe'. We have the sense of a few benumbed and cheerless survivors surrounded by the terrible harvest of the released chaos and evil of the play. Albany speaks of 'this great decay' (V, iii, 299), and it *is* possible to feel that we are witnessing something approaching the dark conclusion of things. Throughout, the play has seemed to be taking place in apocalyptic time rather than historical time. That we are also reminded that the whole play is an 'image' in no way diminishes its terrible power. It is one of the features of great tragedy – Nietzsche wrote eloquently of this in *Birth of Tragedy* – that by exacting a vision of the very worst that nature can do, tragedy, as theatre or ritual, sends out its audience back into life with renewed energy and reinforced psychic strength. *We* are the survivors. But, out of question, Shakespeare has taken us to the 'extreme verge' of what it is possible to endure in the theatre. When the howling Lear shows us the dead Cordelia, there seems to be no adequate or formulable response. Except possibly to snatch at a piece of the Fool's nonsense and say: 'So out went the candle, and we were left darkling' (I, iv, 223).

*

MACBETH

The candles go out in *Macbeth* as well. Act I ends with Macbeth having decided to 'do the deed' ('I am settled'). Act

II opens with Banquo and his son trying to find their way in the darkness round Macbeth's castle. Banquo remarks: 'There's husbandry in heaven./Their candles are all out' (II, i, 4–5). He is saying that the heavens are being frugal and not lighting up their candles – there are no stars to guide or illumine. (There is a slight displaced echo of the image in one of Macbeth's late speeches conveying a sense of terminal insentience and depletion – 'Out, out, brief candle!' (V, v, 23) where the candle is simply life itself.) The onset – summoned or suffered – of an ever-deepening darkness characterizes at least the first half of the play. As Macbeth feels the stirrings within himself of the murder he knows he is going to commit, he instinctively invokes the dark:

> Stars hide your fires;
> Let not light see my black and deep desires.
> (I, iv, 51–2)

The night of the murder of Duncan is 'unruly' ('the obscure bird/Clamored the livelong night' (II, iii, 61–2)) and the description by Ross points to the central question and struggle of the play:

> By the clock 'tis day,
> And yet dark night strangles the traveling lamp:
> Is't night's predominance or the day's shame,
> That darkness does the face of earth entomb,
> When living light should kiss it.
> (II, iv, 6–10)

We have the feeling that it is preternaturally dark and that the darkness is lasting an ominously long time. As though darkness itself had become a vicious agent in its own right, 'strangling' lights and lamps. The question 'Is't night's predominance or the day's shame' – is, in many ways, not only the central question of this play, but of tragedy itself. Whereof comes this? Is the light shamefully feebler than the dark? It is almost a Manichean worry. The possibility of 'night's predominance' is a nightmare indeed, and it is a possibility which tragedy must always at least canvass. Certainly, in this play Macbeth seems set on restoring or installing the empire of night. 'Come seeling night,' he says as he sets about planning the murder of Banquo and his son:

> Good things of day begin to droop and drowse,
> While night's black agents to their preys do rouse.
>
> (III, iii, 32–3)

Is it possible for those 'good things of day' to arouse themselves and resist 'night's black agents'? How? And if not – what then? We must feel the possibility of negative answers with growing alarm as the play unfolds. Almost exactly halfway through the play, Macbeth asks 'What is the night?' to which Lady Macbeth replies: 'Almost at odds with the morning, which is which' (III, iv, 128). 'At odds' – this means the morning and night are struggling with each other for supremacy. At this point it seems in the balance, the issue uncertain – 'which is which'. It certainly is a struggle and the morning is a long time in coming – we have yet to see Lady Macduff and her children murdered. Ross says, rather helplessly, to Lady Macduff:

> Things at their worst will cease, or else climb upward
> To what they were before.
>
> (IV, ii, 24–5)

Do we have to wait 'even till destruction sicken' (IV, i, 60) and evil exhausts itself? Until 'things' somehow restore themselves to some previous order – 'perforce'? Can the 'strangled' lamps be resurrected, reillumined? These are concerns raised by the play. When Malcolm affirms 'The night is long that never finds the day' we do feel that the dawn is slowly beginning to break. His conviction is the minimum assurance of the play. But the night has been long and the darkness deep.

The atmosphere of the first part of the play – perhaps two-thirds of it – is perfectly summarized in the marvellously succinct description of oncoming dusk – 'light thickens' (II, ii, 50). There is a pervasive sense of 'thickening': 'As thick as tale/Came post with post' (I, iii, 98), 'Come thick night,' says Lady Macbeth, so that 'heaven' may not 'peep through the blanket of the dark,/To cry "Hold, hold!"' (I, v, 54–5) – which, incidentally but crucially, is what the servant cried to Cornwall in *King Lear*. Lady Macbeth clearly articulates the what and why of her invocations:

> Make thick my blood,
> Stop up th'access and passage to remorse,
> That no compunctious visitings of nature
> Shake my fell purpose.
>
> (I, v, 44–7)

Appropriately, the Third Witch instructs: 'Make the gruel thick and slab' (i.e. viscous – IV, i, 32). This is an atmosphere in which it is becoming increasingly difficult to see things; in which the blood of human remorse and compunction is ceasing to flow, and nature itself seems almost to be thickening to a standstill. (In a famous essay, Thomas de Quincey interpreted the knocking on the gate in Act II as 'the pulses of life ... beginning to beat again'.) Yet – it is not so much of a paradox as it might seem – the play is marked by extraordinary haste. As I have said, this is both the shortest and the fastest of Shakespeare's tragedies. We speak of things coming 'thick and fast' and that is exactly right for this play. A lot of the speed is literal: from the beginning people seem in a tremendous hurry. 'What a haste looks through his eyes!' says Lennox as Ross rushes in with news of the death of Cawdor (I, ii, 46). Messengers keep coming – 'post with post' (I, iii, 98). Duncan, in his gratitude, says to Macbeth:

> thou are so before
> That swiftest wing of recompense is slow
> To overtake thee.
>
> (I, iv, 16–18)

There the 'overtaking' is metaphorical, but almost immediately it becomes literal:

> Our thane is coming.
> One of my fellows had the speed of him
> Who, almost dead for breath, had scarcely more
> Than would make his message ...
>
> (I, v, 35–8)

The King tries to reach Macbeth on the way to his castle:

> We coursed him at the heels, and had a purpose
> To be his purveyor: but he rides well,
> And his great love, sharp as his spur, hath holp him
> To his home before us.
>
> (I, vi, 21–4)

Indeed he does ride well. It seems that no one can either catch up or keep up with Macbeth. What his 'spur' is, we shall discover. It certainly is not 'love'. Macbeth's great problem and concern is whether, impossibly, he can outride himself. Something 'weird' (key word) is happening to time in this play. Macbeth sends letters to his wife about the prophecies of the 'weird sisters' and she tells him on his return:

> Thy letters have transported me beyond
> The ignorant present, and I feel now
> The future in an instant.
>
> (I, v, 57–9)

This unnatural displacement of the present by the future is the state that Macbeth, effectively, brings about in Scotland:

> good men's lives
> Expire before the flowers in their caps,
> Dying or ere they sicken.
>
> (IV, ii, 170–3)

Good men dying *before* they sicken? Something is ominously wrong with time.

When, shortly after encountering the witches, Macbeth hears Duncan establish succession to the crown on Malcolm, his immediate reaction is 'That is a step/On which I must fall down, or else o'erleap' (I, v, 49). At the end of his absolutely critical soliloquy at the start of Act I, scene vii, he says:

> I have no spur
> To prick the side of my intent, but only
> Vaulting ambition, which o'erleaps itself
> And falls on th' other –
>
> (I, vii, 25–8)

The other what? The other side, presumably. But the other side of *what*? Grammatically it should be 'itself', but how can anything jump over itself? Macbeth is accelerating dangerously, and at times it seems almost as if his *language* is trying to 'o'erleap itself'. The whole soliloquy is absolutely crucial and rather than quote it all I will attempt some summary of Macbeth's argument with himself. The opening words ('If it were done' etc.), whether or not deliberately, echo Christ's words to Judas Iscariot – the great betrayer. It could well be a conscious allusion. Macbeth knows exactly what his 'duties' are to his king and now that Duncan is in Macbeth's castle – 'he's here in double trust'. Macbeth is his kinsman, his subject, and now his host – all relationships and bonds which entail sacred duties, responsibilities, and obligations. The absolute reverse of Othello and Lear (and to some extent Hamlet), Macbeth sees with utmost clarity all the implications of the deed he is contemplating, and the precise nature of its evil. He recognizes Duncan's great 'virtues', and what would be 'the deep damnation of his taking off'. His language touches on the theological and he refers to 'angels trumpet-tongued' and 'heavens cherubin' who would damn and expose his 'horrid deed'. He has been saying to himself that if the 'assassination' could somehow catch and arrest ('trammel up') its own 'consequences'; if his murder ('surcease') could immediately stop anything that might follow (success); if, bluntly, 'this blow might be the be-all and end-all' – *if* all that, *then* we might risk it and never mind eternity and the after-life ('we'd *jump* the life to come' – emphasis added). *But* – and that's the point; there is a but:

> But in these cases
> We still have judgment here; that we but teach
> Bloody instructions, which, being taught, return
> To plague th'inventor

Macbeth's intelligence and conscience are, alike, still in good order here. He sees and recognizes the damnable nature of his meditated deed; the manifest goodness of the king; the inevitability of retribution; and the impossibility of blocking off, wrapping up, obliterating – try any metaphor – the consequences of a 'dreadful deed'. He comes to the morally and intellectually correct conclusion and resolution – 'We will proceed no further in this business.' (I will note in passing that 'business' is invariably used in Shakespeare to refer to more or less unscrupulous scheming – it is the Regan–Edmund word, Julius Caesar's word, and in this play it is both Lady Macbeth's – 'This night's great business' (I, v, 69) and Hecate's, engaged in 'great business' (III, v, 23). What is particularly frightening in this play is that within thirty lines of that eminently rational, sensible, honourable decision, Macbeth is saying – 'If we should fail?' (I, vii, 59). Disastrously, he has shifted his ground from – it is wrong to do this; to – do you think we can get away with it? There is an alarming haste in this swerve from nature. From now on, Macbeth will stake everything on speed.

'We still have judgment here . . .' What Macbeth is trying to do as he goes faster and faster, is perfectly summed up in one of his own phrases: he is trying to 'outrun the pauser, reason' (II, iii, 113). In an important article, Frances Fergusson showed that the whole movement and action of the play are summed up in that phrase.[1] The 'pauser' as I have said before, is that within us which gives us 'pause'; – conscience, reflection, reason, judgement. *Hamlet* is, effectively, one long pause, and it is very long. Macbeth is trying to get rid of that 'pause', trying to close the gap of conscience, to 'outrun' his own judgement – and his play is breathlessly short (almost exactly half the length of *Hamlet*). In connection with *Hamlet* I referred to Brutus' lines:

> Between the acting of a dreadful thing
> And the first motion, all the interim is
> Like a phantasma, or a hideous dream.

This is exactly Macbeth's experience – reality turns 'phantasmatic'. 'Are ye fantastical?' – to the witches; 'my thought, whose murder yet is but fantastical' – to himself. 'Is this a dagger which I see before me? . . . I have thee not, and yet I see thee still' (II, i, 33, 35). 'The time has been that . . . the man would die/And there an end; but now they rise again' (III, iv, 80–81) – as he sees Banquo's ghost. His world is rapidly

[1]. See *The Human Image in Dramatic Literature*, Doubleday Anchor, 1957, pp. 115–25.

becoming one in which it might well be said that 'nothing is, but what is not'. The 'interim' – and Macbeth uses the word (I, iv, 154) – has indeed become a 'hideous dream', and Macbeth becomes increasingly desperate to reduce it to nothing. He attempts to achieve this by speedy action. Let us take two quotations. After he has murdered 'the gracious Duncan' and thus, as with his customary clarity he realizes, given his 'eternal jewel' to the devil (Othello never arrives at such awful clearsightedness, for all his jewel-spangled talk), Macbeth follows the doomed logic to which he has committed himself: 'To be thus is nothing, but to be safely thus –' (III, i, 48). He arranges for Banquo and his son, Fleance, to be killed – the second of his 'secret murders'. With the death of these two, Macbeth expects to be 'perfect'. He uses the Othello word twice, albeit with a different intention from his forerunner (there is, perhaps, an added ironic resonance in view of the biblical injunction 'Be ye therefore perfect'). Fleance escapes and Macbeth realizes he is embarked on an endless course of 'blood' – he can only 'wade' deeper and deeper. He does not go into details with his wife:

> Strange things I have in head that will to hand,
> Which must be acted ere they may be scanned.
>
> (III, v, 40–41)

Note first the tenses and modes of the verbs: have, will, must, may – present, future, imperative – and subjunctive (scanning is to be foregone – or outrun). 'Scan' is the Hamlet word – it is what you do in the 'pause'; it is the enquiring, assessing mental activity which at once creates and occupies the 'interim'. And Macbeth wants to anticipate, pre-empt, and avoid it. Thus he intends to go straight from the 'first motion' ('things I have in head') to the 'acting of a dreadful thing' ('will to hand'). The trouble is he can never go quite fast enough. As he realizes when Macduff escapes to England:

> The flighty purpose never is o'ertook
> Unless the deed go with it. From this moment
> The very firstlings of my heart shall be
> The firstlings of my hand. And even now,
> To crown my thoughts with acts, be it thought and done . . .

This deed I'll do before this purpose cool ...

(IV, i, 145–9, 156)

He wants to bypass conscience and reflection entirely and translate impulse *immediately* into deed. This last is a recurring word in the play. Before the witches encounter Macbeth, the First Witch incants – 'I'll do, I'll do, and I'll do' (I, iii, 10). It is to become Macbeth's motto – almost his blazon. 'Words to the heat of deeds too cold breath gives./I go, and it is done' (II, i, 61–2). Language itself is, of course, the prime 'pauser' or instrument of pausing. While you are talking (or writing) about it, you are not *doing* it. Words defer. Thinking persists. 'These deeds must not be thought/After these ways,' says Lady Macbeth (II, ii, 32–3). *Deeds* must not be *thought* because then the risk is that 'function' (doing) will be 'smothered in surmise' (thinking). Lady Macbeth refers to 'thoughts which should indeed have died/With them they think on' (III, ii, 10–11) – but while kings may die, thoughts live on. 'I have done the deed,' announces Macbeth after killing the king. 'There shall be done a deed of dreadful note' (III, ii, 44), he promises, referring to the murder of Banquo. 'We are yet young in deed,' he says ominously to his wife, a little later (III, iv, 145) – implying there are many more deeds yet to be *done*. Thereafter, he seeks increasingly to live and move entirely in the realm of 'deeds' and lose himself (blot out the interim) in a life of unreflective action. Be it thoughtanddone – instantaneously, no gaps or pauses. He seeks a sort of all-at-once-ness, the future and the present constantaneous, the linear consequentiality of time annulled. But it is not *quite* possible. 'We still have judgments here' – by the end, Macbeth has effectively de-humanized himself and anaesthetized his conscience, but he still knows very precisely the values – the 'good things of day' – he has lost:

> And that which should accompany old age,
> As honor, love, obedience, troops of friends,
> I must not look to have ...
>
> (V, iii, 24–6)

But there is no going back, and he must go on doing the deed until his death. By contrast, Macduff says that unless he encounters Macbeth, he will sheathe his sword 'undeeded' – by this time that amazing neologism carries tremendous force.

Since Macbeth commits himself to an ever-accelerating life of action, we might consider one of his first reactions to the witches' prophecies:

> If chance will have me king, why, chance may crown me,
> Without my stir.
>
> (I, iii, 143–4)

In *Troilus and Cressida*, Ulysses has the line: 'Since things in motion sooner catch the eye/Than what stirs not' (II, iii, 182–3).

There is a strong Elizabethan feeling that virtue is associated with stillness (or slow, decorous movements). Think how little Desdemona and Cordelia actually 'stir'. Evil was much more likely to result from 'things in motion', particularly the sort of unappeasable motion of a Macbeth which creates a fearful world in which all those around him or under his sway can only 'float upon a wild and violent sea/Each way and move' (IV, ii, 21–2). It is in the context of this vortex of violent motion created by Macbeth that one must understand the long, slow, seemingly pointlessly protracted scene between Macduff and Malcolm in England. As Fergusson very aptly describes it; 'the scene is like a slow eddy on the edge of a swift current'.[1] As Malcolm explains, he cannot trust anything or anyone emerging from Macbeth's darkened Scotland – 'modest wisdom plucks me/From over-credulous haste' (IV, iii, 119–20). The play starts in 'haste' and seems to get ever vertiginously quicker. But here it is, laboriously, slowed down. The tide is beginning to turn.

'Know thyself' – this, surely, is one of the central, generative, admonitions in western culture. Most tragic heroes, from Oedipus on, have, for a variety of reasons, ever but slenderly known themselves, and when self-knowledge does finally break in, or through, it is invariably at ruinous cost. Hamlet, with his extraordinary ranging mind, doesn't know whether he knows himself or not (it is part of his self-paralysing

[1]. ibid., p. 124.

intelligence). It is a moot point whether Othello ever *really* comes to know himself as, in his last speech, he embarks on an exotic flight in which self-condemnation is richly mixed with self-exculpation. Lear spends much of the play furiously fending off self-knowledge (always the daughters, the daughters). It breaks in or through only when he is himself broken (or, arguably, the breaking in of it breaks him). And then Macbeth. Who knows himself – perfectly; all the way down, as we say. Perhaps only Shakespeare could have moved directly from a Lear to a Macbeth. For Macbeth embarks on an exactly contrary journey – *away* from self-knowledge. In the process, he engages, long before Rimbaud, on a systematic 'déréglement' of the senses. He seems to separate out what he calls 'each corporal agent' (I, vii, 80) and set them at odds with each other, involving them in a mutually estranging or antagonistic activity. Let 'the eye wink at the hand' (I, iv, 52): 'bear welcome in your eye/Your hand, your tongue' (I, v, 65–6) – that is Lady Macbeth, but at this point they are two of a kind); 'false face must hide what false heart doth know' (I, vii, 82); 'Mine eyes are made the fools o'th'other sense/Or else worth all the rest' (II, i, 44–5); 'Present him eminence with eye and tongue . . . And make our faces vizards to our hearts,/ Disguising what they are' (III, ii, 81, 84–5) – there are other examples of how he regards eyes, hands, heart, tongue as separable agents to whom he can issue contradictory instructions. When, at the start, Duncan declares 'There's no art/To find the mind's construction in the face' (I, iv, 11–12) he unwittingly prepares us for the breathtaking feats of dissembling to be attempted by the Macbeths. After her initial bout of truly demonic energy, Lady Macbeth simply cracks up, and recedes into madness and suicide. Macbeth soldiers on, as we may quite accurately say, but his senses are in sore disarray – they are, to use Menteith's supremely apt word, 'pestered':

Who then shall blame
His pestered senses to recoil and start,
When all that is within him does condemn
Itself for being there?

(V, ii, 21–4)

The words bear pondering – how can such internal chaos and insurrection come about? It is all the result of Macbeth's attempt knowingly to extinguish self-knowledge – an undertaking perhaps as impossible as jumping over yourself. The most telling line in the whole play is:

> To know my deed, 'twere best not know myself.
> (II, ii, 72)

Macbeth is the tragedy of man who goes to all lengths to o'erleap himself, outrun himself, *not* know himself. It proves both impossible and utterly disastrous – and not for him alone.

Such an attempt at achieving complete self-alienation, self-estrangment, is strange indeed, and 'strange' is one of the operative words of the play – the play opens with 'strange images of death' and I will return to them. The whole thing is overseen (precipitated?) by the *weird* sisters, and we had better look at them more closely. 'Weird' comes from Old English 'wyrd' – fate, destiny; also 'werde' – death. But also from 'weorthan' and German 'werden' – to become. And also old Latin 'uortere' (or 'vertere') – to turn. Thus, in the word 'weird' we have, in the words of Ann Lecercle, 'a becoming that is a turning, a turning back, a reversal, a becoming that is a negation of becoming, epitomized in the chiasmus of the liminal proposition of the play, "Fair is foul, and foul is fair."'[1] She maintains that 'It is no exaggeration to say that the entire structure of the work is contained in the word "weird" and the perverse circularity that informs it.' But what is the, as they say, ontological status of the 'weird sisters'? Supernatural solicitors? They are clearly meant to be *there* for the people in the play – Banquo sees them as well as Macbeth (by contrast only Macbeth sees Banquo's ghost). For the contemporary audience and King James, reputedly watching the play at its first performance, they would *not* have been simply 'fantastical'. Here we do need some details about the antecedents and sources of the play; for, as Bullough helpfully reminds us – 'Of course Shakespeare could have invented everything, but he

[1]. In a brilliant article entitled 'Mannerist *Macbeth*' in *Miroirs de L'Être*, Toulouse, 1988.

never liked to do that, preferring always to remake suitable existing material.'[1]

In 1605, when King James visited Oxford, he was greeted by three Sibyls as the descendant of Banquo. This was part of the Stuart political legitimating myth, which sought to provide the Stuarts with a proper ancestry, stretching back through Banquo to the first king, Kenneth Macalpine. On this occasion a debate was conducted on 'whether the imagination can produce real effects'. With the accession of James to the throne, there was a surge of interest in Scottish history. Bullough tells us that the story of Macbeth and Duncan goes back to the early eleventh century, when Scotland had largely been unified and the ideas of nationality and kingship were gradually developing. After killing Duncan, by all accounts a young and unsatisfactory king, Macbeth, though a cruel man, reigned successfully, and in many ways well, for *seventeen years*. Shakespeare collapses those years into what must be a matter of weeks ('haste') and makes Duncan old and venerable (thus, the deeper the damnation of his 'taking off'). In 1527, the *Scotorum Historiae* of Hector Boethius (Boece) was published, translated in 1536. This was Holinshed's main source, as Holinshed was Shakespeare's. In Boece Macbeth and Banquo meet three women referred to as 'thre weird sisteris or wiches' and 'wiches' are mentioned several times. Also referred to is Macbeth's 'innative cruelty'. In Holinshed, Banquo is involved in the murder of Duncan – Shakespeare decides to *contrast* the two men, starting with their instinctively different reaction to the witches. Holinshed also refers to 'weird sisters' and their prophecies, and 'witches' (and even 'wizzards') and Shakespeare combines these with the fantastic hags of current folk-lore and witch-hunts.

In 1597, James VI had published a book called *Daemonologie* in which he inveighed against witches and those who consulted them. Indeed, Bullough reminds us, his first Parliament passed an Act 'against Conjuration, Witchcraft, and dealing with evil and wicked spirits'. The King was much concerned

[1]. op. cit., p. 448. All the material that follows concerning sources is from the same volume, pp. 423–527.

with the existence and operations of demonic powers. He was also concerned about regicides. In the play 'the references to traitors and equivocation were obviously to the trials after the Gunpowder Plot, and especially to that of Father Garnet (March 1606), who after many of his denials had been countered, "fell into a large Discourse of defending *Equivocations*, with many weak and frivolous Distinctions".'[1] ('Equivocation' was a Jesuit device by which a prisoner under interrogation might pervert the truth in order to avoid self-accusation.) When the Porter, 'porter of hell gate', imagines he is admitting people to the infernal regions of the damned – as, in a sense, he is – and says: 'Faith, here's an equivocator, that would swear in both the scales against either scale; who committed treason enough for God's sake, yet could not equivocate to heaven. O, come in, equivocator' (II, iii, 8–12) – there is a contemporary reference which the audience would have recognized. However, as he continues and goes on to talk about the effects of 'drink', his words begin to 'swarm upon' Macbeth, albeit proleptically: 'Lechery, sir, it provokes and unprovokes; it provokes the desire, but it takes away from the performance: therefore much drink may be said to be an equivocator with lechery: it makes him and it mars him; it sets him on and takes him off; it persuades him and disheartens him; makes him stand to and not stand to; in conclusion, equivocates him in a sleep, and giving him the lie, leaves him (II, iii, 31–8). These last lines exactly describe the effect of the weird sisters' words – dangerous intoxicants? – upon Macbeth. They – the words – both make and mar him; set him on and take him off; persuade and dishearten him; give him the lie and leave him. Equivocate. To speak with equal and, by implication seemingly contradictory, voices. The play starts with the equivocations of the witches ('fair is foul'), and of the weather ('So foul and fair a day I have not seen' (I, iii, 38). Nature, and perhaps supernature, is speaking with a double voice. By the end of the play, Macbeth, with his customary lucidity and searing accuracy of formulation, realizes what has been happening:

[1]. ibid., p. 425.

I pull in resolution, and begin
To doubt the equivocation of the fiend
That lies like truth.

(V, v, 42–4)

This is when he hears that Birnam wood seems to be approaching his castle. When Macduff tells him of his non-birth (ripped from the womb), Macbeth knows what has been done to him:

And be these juggling fiends no more believed,
That palter with us in a double sense . . .

(V, viii, 19–20)

He has discovered from experience what Banquo suspected from the start:

But 'tis strange:
And oftentimes, to win us to our harm,
The instruments of darkness tell us truths,
Win us with honest trifles, to betray's
In deepest consequence.

(I, iii, 122–6)[1]

'Consequence' is something that Macbeth aspired to elude, outrun, block – 'trammel up'. What we watch are the 'consequences' of that impossible attempt.

But is everything the fault of 'the fiend'? Would Macbeth never have embarked on his bloody, treasonable, damnable course, if he had not been provoked or inflamed by the witches' ambiguous prophecies? Nothing in the play makes us feel this, but we must look at the weird sisters again. Whether Shakespeare believed in witches and the fiend, is both undiscoverable and irrelevant. Such beliefs were much in the air at the time and must have been even more so in eleventh-century

[1]. Frank Kermode very aptly compares Christ's accusation to Satan in Milton's *Paradise Regain'd*: 'That hath been thy craft,/By mixing somewhat true to vent more lies./But what have been thy answers, what but dark,/Ambiguous, and with double sense deluding? (I, 432–5: Riverside Shakespeare, p. 1308). Milton could, of course, have known Shakespeare's play – but this double-dealing, double-saying, is a traditional attribute of the devil.

Scotland. You don't have to believe in witches to believe in a people that believed in witches. Shakespeare's witches habitually speak equivocally, in riddling ambiguities and seeming contradictions – 'when the battle's lost and won' (I, i, 4); 'Lesser than Macbeth, and greater' (I, ii, 65). (This kind of equivocation – language doubling back on itself – infects other speakers: 'such welcome and unwelcome things at once,' says Macduff (IV, ii, 138); 'both more and less,' says Malcolm (V, v, 12), and so on). As figures, they are at once natural and unnatural, both in and out of nature – they 'look not like th'inhabitants o'th'earth,/And yet are on't,' as Banquo very accurately says (I, iii, 41–2). The edges or limits of 'nature' were ragged, or murky, or indeterminable for the Elizabethans. It was imperfectly ascertainable where nature left off, as it were (reached the limits of its confine), and something else began to hold sway. After all, from one point of view, Goneril and Regan are themselves 'weird sisters'. In *Macbeth* the weird sisters are, they embody, something equivocal in nature itself – whether to be classed as 'supernatural' or 'fiendish' hardly matters. They neither bewitch or enchant, compel or persuade, Macbeth.

They do not need to. Their words simply touch and release into action ('performance') the 'black and deep desires' he already harbours. It might be helpful here to think of what some classical scholars refer to as the phenomenon of 'double motivation' in Greek epic and tragedy. This refers to the undeniable fact that, in Homer, in Aeschylus, gods and goddesses are continuously interfering in human affairs with varying irresistible, or un-negatable, imperatives – compelling to action, or constraining to abstinence. At the same time, we never feel that the human agents are mere automata, puppets in the hands of this or that angry or partial god or goddess. Their actions, though directed by – whatever, from – wherever, are their own. They *are* what they *do*. Their deeds, or refrainings, are, as it were, exactly in line with the divine propulsions or forbiddings. What the gods dictate or decree is curiously an echo, an identification, a premonition, a revelation, of the 'black and deep desires' – or (less often) the enlightened and elevated aspirations – of the human actors whose doings they seem to oversee. And so it is with Macbeth and the witches. Their tantalizing predictions 'provoke' a desire which was already stirring. Their 'fog[gy] and filthy' words, at one and of a piece with the 'air' in which they move and from which they seem to emanate, simply serve to speed Macbeth along a path which, we are made to feel, he is determined, destined, doomed, to follow. He knows it is 'against the use of nature' (I, iii, 137), but he is going to do it anyway.

And even that perverse compulsion-decision is somehow within the realm of 'nature'. But 'tis strange. Weird.

'Strangeness' is everywhere, and the play starts with 'strange images of death' (I, iii, 97). We may say that it ends with a strange image of birth ('Macduff was from his mother's womb/Untimely ripped' – V, viii, 15–16), but, in truth, strange images of birth have from the start been co-present with strange images of death, clinging together and, for a period, choking their art. I am here alluding to the Captain's account of Macbeth's victory in battle which, after the opening chorus by the three witches, effectively opens the play. The first words spoken (after the witches) form a question:

What bloody man is this?

at this point it is the bleeding Captain, but in due course it will be Macbeth ('steeped in blood'), and that opening question becomes the question of the whole play – what bloody man is *that*? The Captain makes his bloody entry and I will just note here that a baby enters the world covered in blood. I hope the relevance of this will become clear. We need the Captain's opening speech:

Doubtful it stood,
As two spent swimmers, that do cling together
And choke their art. The merciless Macdonwald –
Worthy to be a rebel for to that
The multiplying villainies of nature
Do swarm upon him – from Western Isles
Of kerns and gallowglasses is supplied;
And Fortune, on his damned quarrel smiling,

> Showed like a rebel's whore: but all's too weak:
> For brave Macbeth – well he deserves that name –
> Disdaining Fortune, with his brandished steel,
> Which smoked with bloody execution,
> Like valor's minion carved out his passage
> Till he fac'd the slave;
> Which nev'r shook hands, nor bade farewell to him,
> Till he unseamed him from the nave to th'chops,
> And fixed his head upon our battlements.
>
> (I, ii, 8–23)

I will come back to the importance of 'doubtful it stood' – it hangs over most of the play. The opening image seems strange in the context of war – spent swimmers clinging together suggests exhausted lovers rather more than entangled warriors ('spend', of course, was used by the Elizabethans to refer to orgasm). But lovers who 'choke their art' while clinging together suggest a barren, self-destructive sexuality (to be succinctly expressed by Lady Macbeth later in the play when she says bleakly: 'Noughts had, all's spent,/Where our desire is got without content' – II, ii, 4–5). Fortune is a 'whore' while Macbeth, incongruously, is a 'minion', a pampered favourite. In a speech shortly following he becomes 'Bellona's bride-groom' (I, ii, 54). Bellona is the goddess of War, and we can say at once that there is, from the start, some perverse mixing (stirring together we might say, in view of the witcherly activities obtaining) of the sexual and the lethal. Venus contending with Mars is a familiar Renaissance image, and Shakespeare elsewhere can show unusually close connections or similarities between the marital and the martial, as in the wonderfully erotic scene in *Antony and Cleopatra* in which armour becomes a site and adjunct of *amour*. In that play, the mixing makes for 'fairness': in Macbeth, it tends to 'foulness'. In the brilliant article I have referred to, Ann Lecercle comments: 'If foul is fair and fair is foul, battle is brothel and brothel battle.'[1] After the 'spent swimmers', we have 'the multiplying villainies of nature do swarm upon him'. *Swarm.* It

[1]. op. cit. Our readings of the play coincide, but I certainly owe some of the following points to this arresting article.

is an incredibly powerful image. Bees swarm, and they swarm back to the Queen Bee in the hive. But the bees have become 'villainies' and the honey has turned to foulness. Something has gone wrong with nature's fecundity. (Lady Macbeth violently renounces all maternal feeling, while it is Hecate who has 'o'erteemed loins'.) The 'swarm' will shift from Macdonwald to his killer. And note the manner of his killing. Macbeth 'carve[s] out his passage – there is a hint of the birth passage there – and then 'unseam[s]' the 'slave', from the navel upwards. This is pure, slaughterous violence, but it must have been a somewhat similar process and action when Macduff was 'ripped' from the womb. Only that was for the birth of life. Macbeth is delivering death into the world – and will continue to do so. The Captain's next speech serves to extend this feeling of strange births:

> As whence the sun 'gins his reflection
> Shipwracking storms and direful thunders break,
> So from that spring whence comfort seemed to come
> Discomfort swells.
>
> (II, ii, 25–8)

The witches plan shipwrecks: nature is pregnant – swelling – with 'discomfort'. (This will shortly be echoed when Macbeth says in an aside: 'Two truths are told,/As happy prologues to the *swelling* act/Of the imperial theme' (I, iii, 17–19 – emphasis added). The deed will shortly reach its term.) At the end of his scene, the Captain is fainting and gasps – 'my gashes cry for help'. It could, in a horribly distorted form, be the cry of a woman about to give birth. 'Gash' is a crucial word, and it anticipates a truly monstrous birth. There are hints of strange or aborted births throughout. When Macbeth writes to his wife, he refers to her as 'dearest partner of greatness' (he repeats the word) and Lady Macbeth is instantly 'great' with a deed that bleeds rather than a child which 'sucks'. One of the ingredients of the witches' cauldron is 'Finger of birth-strangled babe/Ditch delivered by a drab' (IV, i, 30–31), and for their second apparition for Macbeth's benefit, they bring forth (from the cauldron?) 'a Bloody Child' (IV, i, 77). As Duncan approaches Macbeth's castle, he thinks it is a 'pleasant seat' and that the air is 'gentle' (I, vi, 1–3). Banquo responds by saying that, indeed, 'heaven's breath/Smells wooingly here' and that the 'martlet' (martin) has 'made his pendent and procreant cradle/Where they most breed' (I, vi, 8–9). The proleptic ironies are dark. There is to be no wooing, no breeding, no 'procreant cradle' in this play (unless we feel that 'pity, like a newborn babe' does finally emerge). Macbeth has married murder, and the child is Death. He transforms Scotland into a country which 'cannot/Be called our mother but our grave' (IV, ii, 16). Lady Macbeth 'unsex[es]' herself.

The most important description of this perverted or inverted birthing is provided by Macbeth when he justifies his killing of the murdered king's servants:

> Here lay Duncan,
> His silver skin laced with his golden blood,
> And his gashed stabs look like a breach in nature
> For ruin's wasteful entrance: there, the murderers,
> Steeped in the colors of their trade, their daggers
> Unmannerly breeched with gore.
>
> (II, iii, 113–18)

I have quoted this passage before, but now it must be more closely considered in the context I have been suggesting. The beautiful, the precious, the delicate (indeed the artistic) – silver 'laced' with gold – quickly gives way to the crude, the 'unmannerly', the gory. Fair turns into, turns out to be, foul. The sacred (suggestion of a sacred relic) degrades to the gross (suggestion of breeches). The body is 'gashed' as though it had, it was, 'a breach in nature' which could certainly suggest the entrance to the womb (a 'breach birth' is a difficult birth which often requires a Caesarian section, a 'ripping' or 'unseaming'). But what issues forth from this womb-wound is 'ruin', its entrance into the world 'wasteful'. Weird. A 'breach' is a break, a breaking, a breakage, and at this point nature itself seems to be broken. 'Breach', and 'breeched'. When things start to go wrong, begin to turn and swerve, Shakespeare likes to use apparently very different, even opposite, words which are very close in spelling and almost homophones. We have encountered seeing/seeling, and in this play there is surcease/success; highly/holily; but most importantly – breach/breech. 'Breech'd with gore' suggests the daggers have been clothed in trousers of blood (to 'breech' a boy was to take him out of petticoats and put him into 'breeches'). 'Breech' comes from Latin *braca* which means, as the OED puts it, 'doubtful, double'. This, of course, is perfect for Shakespeare's play (it is entirely irrelevant to what extent he may consciously have intended it). '*Doubtful* it stood,' said the Captain: '*double, double*, toil and trouble,' say the witches (IV, i, 35). Through the 'breach' in nature, a very active 'ruin' has been born (Macbeth is at once bloody parent, butcher-midwife, and child Ruin himself); and this is ushering in a 'breech'd' world – breeched 'with gore' and also with doubt and doubleness. It will take another 'unnatural' child – 'none of woman born' (IV, i, 80) – to confront, contest, and deliver *out* of the world, a child as monstrous as this.

Once again, we have witnessed nature awesomely – strangely, weirdly – engendering unnature. ''Tis unnatural/Even like the deed that's done,' says the Old Man of the strange climatic and animal disturbances which take place during the night of Duncan's murder (I, iv, 10–11). 'Unnatural deeds/Do breed unnatural troubles,' says the Doctor, commenting on the 'great perturbation in nature' manifest in Lady Macbeth's strange sleep-walking activities (V, i, 10, 75). He is the second doctor to appear in the play (it is, I think, the only play by Shakespeare to feature *two* doctors), and certainly the state of Scotland needs some drastic, if not miraculous, medicining and healing. The first doctor appears in the scene in England, in which he describes the royal ritual of curing the king's 'evil' (scrofula – but, in this play, the word seems fittingly generic for the disease spread by Macbeth):

> There are a crew of wretched souls
> That stay his cure: their malady convinces
> The great assay of art; but at this touch,
> Such sanctity hath heaven given his hand,
> They presently amend.
>
> (IV, iii, 141–5)

This, of course, adumbrates and forefigures the aid which the

King of England will afford Malcolm as he embarks on his mission to restore to health the 'wretched souls' – his subjects – who 'stay his cure', and rid Scotland of its 'malady'. We should note that the English King is said to be 'full of grace', and his 'healing benediction' ('put on with holy prayers') deemed 'miraculous' (IV, iii, 159, 154, 147). In *King Lear* we were shown an image of the 'promised end', and at the murder of Duncan, Macduff says 'see/The great doom's image!' which means much the same thing (II, iii, 80). But whereas *King Lear* takes place in a miasma of uncertainty concerning what – if anything – obtains or operates in the supernatural world, in *Macbeth* there are unmistakable references to, and an assured belief in, a religious (and effectively Christian) order. From his vocabulary, it is clear that Macbeth believes in 'God', 'the devil', 'heaven' and 'hell', and the 'soul' ('Death of thy soul!' he shouts to the servant who brings him news of the approaching army – the words are terribly self-applicable – V, iii, 16). Lennox articulates what seems to be a general belief in, as well as a yearning for, 'angels' and 'blessings' ('Some holy angel/ Fly to the court of England . . . that a swift blessing/May soon return to this our suffering country' – III, vi, 45–8). And Malcolm gives voice, in the darkest hour, to a belief that, somehow 'grace' remains itself and must persist:

> Angels are bright still, though the brightest fell:
> Though all things foul would wear the brows of grace,
> Yet grace must still look so.
>
> (IV, iii, 22–4)

In his last speech, heralding the restoration of the health and order of the land, he promises;

> what needful else
> That calls upon us, by the grace of Grace
> We will perform in measure, time, and place . . .
>
> (V, viii, 71–3)

'By the grace of Grace' – has Macbeth finally been defeated by divine intervention? Macbeth certainly becomes 'devilish Macbeth' and his 'fall' is as certain as Lucifer's. Yet though we are aware of an, at times almost despairing, faith ('the substance of things hoped for, the evidence of things not seen'), I do not think we sense the operation of divine retribution. I think we are aware of the working of natural cycles and rhythms – dawn must come *sometime* (anyone who lived through World War II will readily recognize the atmosphere of *Macbeth*); and once again, there is a sense of the unfolding and ripening of time. 'Time and the hour runs through the roughest day,' says Macbeth with his usual self-condemning accuracy (I, iii, 147). Thanks to him the day, or rather the night, is rough indeed. But time is running and at last runs through until, at the end, Macduff, holding Macbeth's head (an echo of what Macbeth did to Macdonwald at the start – more doubling), can proclaim – 'The time is free.'

Then again, there is certainly the intimation that 'destruction sicken[s]' of its own proceedings and, somehow, runs into the sand. But human agency is crucial and indispensable. Doctors and doctoring kings certainly help. But the crucial thing is, I think, again 'anger'. Macduff never explains – 'why in that rawness left you wife and child' (IV, iii, 26), and Lady Macduff's complaint that 'His flight was madness . . . the flight/So sins against all reason' (IV, ii, 3, 14–15) has always seemed to me unanswerable – certainly unanswered. But the slaughter of his family provides a motivation which serves to sharpen and shape him into the man who can confront Macbeth ('con*front*ing' is important: it is what Macbeth does to the first Thane of Cawdor as he kills him (I, ii, 55); young Siward receives his mortal wounds 'on the front' – V, vii, 47). Malcolm exhorts him in these terms:

> Be this the whetstone of your sword. Let grief
> Convert to anger; blunt not the heart, enrage it.
> (IV, iii, 228–9)

Grief converting to anger perhaps runs parallel to night 'converting' to day. If things can turn ('vert') awry, they can, in time, turn back ('convert') to some (temporarily) lost or destroyed natural ordering and harmony. Perhaps by the grace of Grace: certainly with the aid of energy summoned up and directed by the enraged heart. The habitually 'undeedful' Macduff is the man to do the one indisputably necessary deed of ridding the world of Macbeth. Be it registered, grieved over, thought through, angered about, and then – in due time – *done*. This is the powerfully restorative, reconstitutive feeling at the conclusion of the last of Shakespeare's great tragedies. But the evil has been evil indeed.

*

These four plays were written one after the other in the relatively short period of 1598 to 1606.

It beggars belief.

King's College, Cambridge — Tony Tanner

SELECT BIBLIOGRAPHY

BIOGRAPHY

The standard biography is now Samuel Schoenbaum, *William Shakespeare: A Documentary Life*, Oxford University Press, Oxford, 1975. A shortened version of this excellent volume was published in 1977. For those interested in Shakespearian mythology, Schoenbaum has also produced *Shakespeare's Lives*, Clarendon Press, Oxford, 1970, a witty dissection of the myriad theories concerning the playwright's identity and the authorship of the plays. Rather in the same vein is Anthony Burgess, *Shakespeare*, Penguin, London, 1972, a lively introduction to the presumed facts of the poet's life, enhanced by novelistic licence.

BIBLIOGRAPHY

Among the vast quantity of Shakespeare criticism it is probably only useful to list texts which are both outstanding and easily available. This I do below. For further information the serious student may consult the bibliographies of works listed. There are also three major journals which record the flow of critical work: The *Shakespeare Quarterly*; and the *Shakespeare Survey* and *Shakespeare Studies* which are published annually.

CRITICISM

The two indispensable Shakespearian critics are Johnson and Coleridge. Their dispersed comments are collected in *Samuel Johnson on Shakespeare*, ed., H. R. Woodhuysen, Penguin, London, 1989, and S. T. Coleridge, *Shakespearian Criticism*, two vols., Everyman's Library, London, 1960.

Among distinguished older commentaries which still have a great deal to offer are A. C. Bradley, *Shakespearian Tragedy*, Macmillan, London, 1904; Lily B. Campbell, *Shakespeare's Tragic Heroes: Slaves of Passion*, Cambridge University Press, Cambridge 1930; H. B. Charlton, *Shakespearian Tragedy*, Cambridge University Press, Cambridge, 1948; G. W. Knight's, *The Wheel of Fire*, Methuen, London, 1930; and Harley Granville-Barker, *Prefaces to Shakespeare*, two vols., Batsford, London, 1958. All contain detailed commentary on individual plays and discussion of Shakespeare's theatrical art, though Bradley concentrates on character study and Barker on dramaturgy, while the others pay more attention to themes, imagery and structure. All five grapple in different ways with the perplexing question of whether Shakespeare can be said to have a consistent practice and an implicit theory of tragedy – issues also addressed by more recent commentators, including Kenneth Muir, *Shakespeare and the Tragic Pattern*, Longman, London, 1958, and *William Shakespeare: The Great Tragedies*, Longman, London, 1961; Ruth Nevgo, *Tragic Form in Shakespeare*, Princeton University Press, Princeton, N.J., 1972; J. V. Cunningham, *Woe or Wonder: The Emotional Effect of Shakespearian Tragedy*, University of Denver Press, Denver, 1951; Maynard Mack, *Killing the King: Three Studies in Shakespeare's Tragic Structure*, Yale University Press, New Haven, 1973; and Irving Ribner, *Patterns in Shakespearian Tragedy*, Methuen, London, 1960.

John Holloway, *The Story of the Night: Studies in Shakespearian Tragedy*, Routledge, London, 1967; and John Lawlor, *The Tragic Sense in Shakespeare*, Chatto & Windus, London, 1960, both comment on the plays severally and together. N. M. Proser, *The Heroic Image in Five Shakespearian Tragedies*, Princeton University Press, Princeton, N.J., 1965, pursues the evolution of a single crucial image; P. N. Siegel considers the political context in *Shakespearian Tragedy and the Elizabethan Compromise*, New York University Press, New York, 1957; while William Rosen, *Shakespeare and the Craft of Tragedy*, Harvard University Press, Cambridge, Mass., 1960 and V. K. Whitaker, *The Mirror Up To Nature: The Technique of Shakespeare's Tragedies*, Huntingdon Library, San Marino, California, 1965, offer detailed examinations of the playwright's artistry with reference to contemporary writers.

Three innovative views can be found in Northrop Frye, *Fools of Time: Studies in Shakespearian Tragedy*, University of Toronto Press, Toronto, 1967; Jonathon Dollimore, *Radical Tragedy*, Harvester, Brighton, 1984; and Stephen Greenblatt, *Shakespearian Negotiations*, Clarendon, Oxford, 1988. Dollimore is a Cultural Materialist who wants to situate Shakespeare in the economic and political circumstances of his time; Greenblatt is a New Historicist who weaves the plays into a complex tapestry of contemporary texts and events; while Frye writes against the background of his own theory of Archetypes.

On particular plays the following texts may be found useful:

Hamlet
John Dover Wilson's *What Happens in Hamlet*, Cambridge University Press, Cambridge, 1935, is still an illuminating detailed exposition of the play and a stimulating discussion of the play by a great scholar.

The fruits of his scholarly researches into the text can be found in *The Manuscript of Shakespeare's 'Hamlet' and the problems of its Transmission*, Cambridge University Press, Cambridge, 1963.

Fredson Bowers, *Elizabethan Revenge Tragedy*, Princeton University Press, Princeton, N.J., 1940, situates the play in a familiar contemporary genre, as does E. A. Prosser in *Hamlet and Revenge*, Stanford University Press, Stanford, California, 1967.

On the question of the play's meaning, Harry Levin, *The Question of Hamlet*, Oxford University Press, New York, 1959; and Peter Alexander, *Hamlet: Father and Son*, Clarendon, Oxford, 1955, both probe the celebrated question of Hamlet's motivation and the complex tangle of relationships within the play in the context of modern psychology. In *The 'Hamlet' of Shakespeare's Audience*, Duke, North Carolina, 1938, J. W. Draper approaches the play from the other perspective, attempting to reconstruct its initial reception. Among shorter pieces, T. S. Eliot's celebrated essay on the play, reprinted in *Selected Essays*, Faber, London, 1961, is still well worth reading.

The Cambridge *Shakespeare Survey 9*, Cambridge University Press, Cambridge, 1956, is devoted to *Hamlet*, as are John Jump, *Hamlet: A Casebook*, Macmillan, London, 1969; and Nigel Alexander, *Poison, Play and Duel: A Study of Hamlet*, Routledge, London, 1971.

King Lear

Nicholas Brooke, *Shakespeare: 'King Lear'*, Edward Arnold, London, 1963, is an excellent close study of the text, as is R. B. Heilman, *This Great Stage: Image and Structure in King Lear*, University of Washington Press, Seattle, 1963. John Danby's *Shakespeare's Doctrine of Nature: A Study of 'King Lear'*, Faber, London, 1949, is a classic exploration of the play's wider philosophical context, and should be read with G. Wilson Knight, *The Wheel of Fire*, Methuen, London, 1930, still the most illuminating exposition of the play as dramatic poem. Among more recent studies, Russell Fraser, *Shakespeare's Poetic in Relation to 'King Lear'*, Routledge, London, 1962, is a penetrating examination of the play's place in Shakespeare's oeuvre. Among the huge quantity of essays on this play, some of the best are collected in *King Lear: A Casebook* edited by Frank Kermode, Macmillan, London, 1980; and *Aspects of 'King Lear'*, edited by Kenneth Muir and Stanley Wells, Cambridge University Press, Cambridge, 1982. Maynard Mack, *King Lear in Our Time*, Methuen, London, 1966, offers another conspectus of interpretations.

Othello
Shakespeare Survey 21, Cambridge University Press, Cambridge, 1968, is devoted to *Othello*, as is *Othello: A Casebook*, ed. John Wain, Macmillan, London, 1971. Both include essays covering the full range of relevant thematic topics and the Wain volume has an excellent introduction by the editor, surveying the history of *Othello* interpretation.

R. B. Heilman, *Magic in the Web: Action and Language in Othello*, Greenwood Press, Connecticut, 1977, offers a very detailed study of language and imagery, a topic on which there is also much useful commentary in Wolfgang Clemen, *The Development of Shakespeare's Imagery*, Harvard University Press, Cambridge, Mass., 1951.

Among recent criticism, Helen Gardner, *The Noble Moor*, Oxford University Press, London, 1956, is a magisterial essay by a respected scholar while E. A. J. Honigman provides a more up-to-date approach in *Shakespeare: Seven Tragedies*, Macmillan, London, 1976. Stephen Greenblatt's *Renaissance Self-Fashioning*, University of Chicago Press, Chicago, 1983, is an outstanding radical study of Shakespearian heroes.

Finally, there are two indispensable essays on the play by John Bayley and W. H. Auden, to be found in Bayley's *The Characters of Love*, Constable, London, 1960, and Auden's *The Dyer's Hand*, Faber, London, 1963.

Macbeth
There are several useful collections of critical essays on *Macbeth*. These include John Wain, ed., *Macbeth: A Casebook*, Macmillan, London, 1969; John Russell Brown, ed., *Focus on 'Macbeth'*, Routledge & Kegan Paul, London, 1982; and Kenneth Muir, ed., *Shakespeare Survey 19*, Cambridge University Press, Cambridge, 1966.

M. C. Bradbrook's fine 'The Sources of *Macbeth*' appears in *Shakespeare Survey 4*, Cambridge University Press, Cambridge, 1951, but perhaps the most celebrated single essay on the play is still L. C. Knights, 'How Many Children Had Lady Macbeth?', an attack on critical literalism reprinted in Knights, *Explorations*, Penguin, London, 1964. Knights develops his views in *Some Shakespearian Themes*, Stanford University Press, Stanford, 1960. More general discussions can be found in Maynard Mack Jr, *Killing The King*, Yale University Press, New Haven, 1973, and Henry N. Paul, *The Royal Play of Macbeth*, Macmillan, New York and London, 1950.

SELECT BIBLIOGRAPHY

BACKGROUND AND SOURCES

Shakespeare scholarship is massive and exhaustive, covering every imaginable aspect of the writer's work, life and times. Most editions of the text, including the Everyman Shakespeare, are now supplied with notes which are more than adequate for all normal purposes. However, those who wish to explore questions of Shakespearian language further may care to consult John Bartlett, *A New and Complete Concordance to Shakespeare*, Macmillan, New York, 1894, and C. T. Onions, *A Shakespeare Glossary*, Oxford University Press, London, 1911 (and frequently reprinted). Between them, these texts define and explain every single word Shakespeare uses, citing the places where they appear and exploring obsolete usages.

The thorny questions of textual transmission are covered in W. W. Greg's *The Shakespeare First Folio*, Oxford University Press, New York and London, 1955. This gives a detailed history of the first collected edition of the plays which appeared in 1623.

Finally, a word on sources. Most individual editions of the plays include a note on particular sources, together with extensive quotation. The most readily available and accessible general book on this matter is Kenneth Muir's *Shakespeare's Sources*, Methuen, London, 1957. Muir was one of the most distinguished scholar-critics of his time and his book throws fascinating light on the whole field of Shakespeare studies.

Even more comprehensive – though considerably more daunting – are the eight volumes of Geoffrey Bullough's *Narrative and Dramatic Sources of Shakespeare*, Routledge & Kegan Paul, London, and Columbia University Press, New York, 1957–1975.

CHRONOLOGY

DATE	AUTHOR'S LIFE	LITERARY CONTEXT
1564	Born in Stratford, Warwickshire, the eldest surviving son of John Shakespeare, glover and occasional dealer in wool, and Mary Arden, daughter of a prosperous farmer.	Birth of Christopher Marlowe.
1565	John Shakespeare elected Alderman of Stratford.	Clinthio: *Hecatommithi*. Edwards: *Damon and Pythias*.
1566	Birth of Shakespeare's brother Gilbert.	Gascoigne: *Supposes*.
1567		Udall: *Roister Doister*. Golding: *The Stories of Venus and Adonis and of Hermaphroditus and Salamcis*.
1568	His father is elected bailiff.	Gascoigne: *Jocasta*. Wilmot: *Tancred and Gismunda*. Second Edition of Vasari's *Lives of the Artists*.
1569	Probably starts attending the petty school attached to the King's New School in Stratford. Birth of his sister Joan.	
1570	His father involved in money-lending.	
1571	John Shakespeare is elected Chief Alderman and deputy to the new bailiff.	
1572		Whitgift's *Answer* to the 'Admonition' receives Cartwright's *Reply*, beginning the first literary debate between Anglicans and Puritans.
1573		Tasso: *Aminta*.
1574	Probably enters the Upper School (where studies include rhetoric, logic, the Latin poets, and a little Greek). Birth of his brother Richard.	

HISTORICAL EVENTS

Death of Michelangelo. Birth of Galileo.

Rebellion against Spain in the Netherlands. Birth of the actor Edward Alleyn.

Birth of the actor Richard Burbage.

Mary Stuart flees to England from Scotland.

Northern Rebellion.

Excommunication of Elizabeth. *Baïf's* Academy founded in Paris to promote poetry, music and dance.

Ridolfi Plot. Puritan 'Admonition' to Parliament.

Dutch rebels conquer Holland and Zeeland. Massacre of St Bartholomew's Day in Paris.

Accession of Henry III and new outbreak of civil war in France. First Catholic missionaries arrive in England from Douai. Earl of Leicester's Men obtain licence to perform within the City of London.

DATE	AUTHOR'S LIFE	LITERARY CONTEXT
1575		*Gammer Gurton's Needle* is printed.
1576		Castiglione's *The Book of the Courtier* banned by the Spanish Inquisition. George Gascoigne: *The Steel Glass*.
1577		John Northbrooke's attack in *Treatise wherein Dicing, Dancing, Vain Plays etc are reproved*.
1578	Shakespeare family fortunes are in decline, and John is having to sell off property to pay off his increasing debts.	Sidney writes *The Lady of May* and begins the 'Old' *Arcadia*. George Whetstone: *Promos and Cassandra*. John Lyly: *Euphues, the Anatomy of Wit*. Pierre de Ronsard, leader of the Pléiade, publishes his *Sonnets pour Hélène*. He is said to have exercised a considerable influence on the English sonnet-writers of the sixteenth century.
1579		Spenser: *The Shepherd's Calendar*. North: translation of Plutarch. Gossen: *The School of Abuse, and Pleasant Invective against Poets, Pipers, Players etc*.
1580	Birth of Shakespeare's brother Edmund.	Sidney: *Apologie for Poetrie*. Lodge: *Defense of Plays*.
1581		John Newton's translation of Seneca's *Ten Tragedies*. Barnaby Rich: *Apolonius and Silla*.
1582	Shakespeare marries Anne Hathaway, a local farmer's daughter, 7 or 8 years his senior, who is already pregnant with their first child.	Tasso: *Gerusalemme Liberata*. Watson: *Hekatompathia* (First sonnet sequence published in England). Whetstone: *Heptameron of Civil Discourses*. Sidney begins *Astrophel and Stella* and the 'New' *Arcadia*. Lope de Vega writing for the Corrals in Madrid.

CHRONOLOGY

HISTORICAL EVENTS

Kenilworth Revels.

Restricted by the City of London's order that no plays be performed within the City boundaries, James Burbage of The Earl of Leicester's Men builds The Theatre only just outside the boundaries in Shoreditch. The Blackfriars Theatre is built. End of civil war in France. Observatory of Uraniborg built for the Danish astronomer, Tycho Brahe. Death of Titian.
Drake's circumnavigation of the world. The Curtain Theatre built. Birth of Rubens.

First visit to England of the duc d'Alençon as a suitor to Elizabeth, provoking much opposition to a French match. The Corral de la Cruz built in Madrid.

Spanish conquest of Portugal. Jesuit mission arrives in England from Rome led by Edmund Campion and Parsons.
Stricter enforcement of treason laws and increased penalties on recusants. Campion captured and executed. Northern provinces of the Netherlands renounce their allegiance to Phillip II, and invite the duc d'Alençon to be their sovereign.
Sir Walter Ralegh established in the Queen's favour. The Corral del Principe built in Madrid.

DATE	AUTHOR'S LIFE	LITERARY CONTEXT
1583	Birth of their daughter Susanna.	
1583–4	The players' companies of the Earls of Essex, Oxford and Leicester perform in Stratford.	Giordarno Bruno visits England.
1584		Bruno publishes *La cena de le Ceneri* and *Spaccio della bestia trionfante*. Reginald Scott: *The Discovery of Witchcraft*.
1585	Birth of Shakespeare's twins Hamnet and Judith. The following years until 1592 are the 'Lost Years' for which no documentary records of his life survive, only legends such as the one of deer-stealing and flight from prosecution, and conjectures such as ones that he became a schoolmaster, travelled in Europe, or went to London to be an actor as early as the mid 1580s.	Death of Pierre de Ronsard. Bruno: *De gli eroici furori*, dedicated to Sidney.
1586		Timothy Bright: *A Treatise of Melancholy*.
1586–7	Five players' companies visit Stratford, including the Queen's, Essex's, Leicester's and Stafford's.	
1587		Holinshed: *Chronicles of England, Scotland and Ireland*. Marlowe: First part of *Tamburlaine the Great* acted. New edition of *The Mirror for Magistrates*.
1588		Marlowe: Second part of *Tamburlaine*. Thomas Kyd: *The Spanish Tragedy*. Lope de Vega, serving with the Armada, writes some of *The Beauty of Angelica*.

CHRONOLOGY

HISTORICAL EVENTS

First meeting of the Durham House Set led by Ralegh, Northumberland and Harriot, to promote mathematics, astronomy and navigation. Archbishop Whitgift leads more extreme anti-Puritan policy. Throckmorton plot, involving the Spanish ambassador.

Death of d'Alençon. Assassination of William of Orange. The Teatro Olimpico, Vicenza, built by Palladio.

England sends military aid to the Dutch rebels under the command of Leicester. Ralegh organizes the colonization of Virginia.

Babington plot. Death of Sir Philip Sidney. Rise of the Earl of Essex. Colonization of Munster.

Execution of Mary Stuart. Drake's raid on Cadiz.

Defeat of the Armada. Death of the Earl of Leicester. The first of the Puritan Marprelate Tracts published.

DATE	AUTHOR'S LIFE	LITERARY CONTEXT
1589	The earliest likely date at which Shakespeare began composition of his first play (1 *Henry VI*) when he would have been working as an actor at The Theatre, with Burbage's company.	Marlowe: *The Jew of Malta*. Thomas Nashe: *The Anatomy of Absurdity*. Richard Hakluyt: *Principal Navigations, Voyages and Discoveries of the English nation*.
1590	2 *Henry VI*, 3 *Henry VI*.	Spenser: first 3 books of *The Faerie Queen*. Publication of Sidney's 'New' *Arcadia*. Nashe: *An Almond for a Parrot*, one of the Marprelate Tracts. Greene: *Menaphon*. Guarina: *The Faithful Shepherd*.
1590–92	Performances of *Henry VI*, parts 2 and 3, *Titus* and *The Shrew* by the Earl of Pembroke's Men.	
1591	*Richard III* and *The Comedy of Errors* written.	Spenser's *Complaints* which includes his translation of fifteen of Joachim du Bellay's sonnets – du Bellay was a member of the Pléiade and responsible for its manifesto. Sir John Harington's translation of *Orlando Furioso*. Publication of Sidney's *Astrophel and Stella*.
1592	First recorded reference to Shakespeare as an actor and playwright in Greene's attack in *The Groatsworth of Wit* describing him as 'an upstart crow'.	Samuel Daniel: *Delia*. Marlowe's *Edward II* and *Doctor Faustus* performed. *Arden of Feversham* printed. Nashe: *Strange News*.
1592–4	*Titus Andronicus* written.	
1593	Publication of *Venus and Adonis*, dedicated to the Earl of Southampton. The *Sonnets* probably begun.	Marlowe: *Massacre of Paris*. *The Phoenix Nest*, miscellany of poems including ones by Ralegh, Lodge and Breton. Barnabe Barnes: *Parthenophil and Parthenope*. George Peele: *The Honour of the Garter*. Lodge: *Phillis*. Nashe: *Christ's Tears over Jerusalem*.
1593–4	*The Taming of the Shrew*; *The Two Gentlemen of Verona*.	

CHRONOLOGY

HISTORICAL EVENTS

Failure of the Portugal expedition. Henry III of France assassinated. English military aid sent to Henry of Navarre. Marlowe's tutor, Francis Ket, burned at the stake for atheism.

English government discovers and suppresses the Puritan printing press.

Earl of Essex given command of the English army in France. The last fight of the *Revenge* under Spanish attack.

Capture of Madre de Dios. Split in the main players' company. Shakespeare and Burbage's group remain at The Theatre, Alleyn's move to the Rose on Bankside. Plague in London: the theatres closed.

Marlowe arrested on blasphemy charges and murdered two weeks later. Kyd arrested for libel. Henry of Navarre converts to Catholicism in order to unite France.

DATE	AUTHOR'S LIFE	LITERARY CONTEXT
1593–6		John Donne writing his early poems, the Satires and Elegies.
1594	*The Rape of Lucrece* dedicated to his patron Southampton. *The Comedy of Errors* and *Titus Andronicus* performed at the Rose. Shakespeare established as one of the shareholders in his company, The Chamberlain's Men, which performs before the Queen during the Christmas festivities.	Daniel: *Cleopatra*. Spenser: *Amoretti* and *Epithalamion*. Drayton: *Idea's Mirror*. Nashe: *The Terrors of the Night*, *The Unfortunate Traveller*. Greene: *Friar Bacon and Friar Bungay*.
1594–5	*Love's Labor's Lost* and *Romeo and Juliet* written.	
1595	*Richard II*.	Daniel: *The First Four Books of the Civil Wars between the two houses of Lancaster and York*. Sidney: *Defence of Poesy* published. Ralegh: *The Discovery of the Empire of Guiana*.
1595–6	*A Midsummer Night's Dream*.	
1596	Death of his son, Hamnet. *The Merchant of Venice*. Shakespeare living in Bishopsgate ward. His father, John, is granted a coat of arms. *King John* written.	Lodge: *Wits Miserle*. First complete edition of Spenser's *Faerie Queen*.
1597	*Henry IV* Part 1. First performance of *The Merry Wives of Windsor*. Shakespeare's company now under the patronage of the new Lord Chamberlain, Hunsdon. In Stratford, Shakespeare buys New Place, the second largest house in the town, with its own orchards and vines.	John Donne writes 'The Storme' and 'The Calme'. Francis Bacon: first edition of *Essays*. Jonson and Nashe imprisoned for writing *The Isle of Dogs*.
1597–8	*Henry IV* Part 2.	
1598	*Much Ado About Nothing*. Shakespeare one of the 'principal comedians' with Richard Burbage, Heminge and Cordell in Jonson's *Every Man in his Humour*. For the second year, Shakespeare is listed as having failed to pay tax levied on all householders.	Publication of Sidney's *Works* and of Marlowe's *Hero and Leander* (together with Chapman's continuation). *Seven Books of the Iliads* (first of Chapman's Homeric translations). Meres: *Palladia Tamia*. New edition of Lodge's *Rosalynde*.

CHRONOLOGY

HISTORICAL EVENTS

Henry of Navarre accepted as King in Paris. Rebellion in Ireland. The London theatres re-open. The Swan Theatre is built. Ralegh accused of blasphemy.

France declares war on Spain. Failure of the Indies voyage and death of Hawkins. Ralegh's expedition to Guiana.

England joins France in the war against Spain. Death of Drake. Raid on Cadiz led by Essex. In long-standing power struggle with Essex, Robert Cecil is appointed Secretary of State.

Islands Voyage led by Essex and Ralegh. The government suppresses the *Isle of Dogs* at the Swan and closes the theatres. Despite the continued hostility of the City of London, they soon re-open. James Burbage builds the second Blackfriars Theatre. Death of James Burbage.

Peace between France and Spain. Death of Philip II. Tyrone defeats the English at Armagh. Essex appointed Lord Deputy of Ireland.

DATE	AUTHOR'S LIFE	LITERARY CONTEXT
1598 *cont.*		Lope de Vega: *La Arcadia*. James VI of Scotland: *The True Law of Free Monarchies*.
1599	*As You Like It*, *Henry V*, *Julius Caesar*. Shakespeare one of the shareholders in the Globe Theatre. He moves lodgings to Bankside. Publication of *The Passionate Pilgrim*, a miscellany of 20 poems, at least 5 by Shakespeare.	Jonson: *Every Man out of his Humour*. Dekker: *The Shoemaker's Holiday*. Sir John Hayward: *The First Part of the Life and Reign of King Henry IV*. Greene's translation of *Orlando Furioso*.
1600		'England's Helicon'.
1601	*Twelfth Night*. *Hamlet* (performed with Burbage as the Prince and Shakespeare as the Ghost). *The Phoenix and the Turtle*. The Lord Chamberlain's Men paid by one of Essex's followers to perform *Richard II* on the day before the rebellion. Death of John Shakespeare.	
1601–2	*Troilus and Cressida*.	
1602	Shakespeare buys more property in Stratford.	
1603–4	*All's Well That Ends Well*.	
1603	Shakespeare's company now under the patronage of King James. Shakespeare is one of the principal tragedians in Jonson's *Sejanus*.	Montaigne's *Essays* translated into English. Thomas Heywood: *A Woman Killed with Kindness*.
1604	Shakespeare known to be lodging in Silver Street with a Huguenot family called Mountjoy. *Othello*; first performance of *Measure for Measure*.	Chapman: *Bussy d'Ambois*. Marston: *The Malcontent*.
1604–5	Ten of his plays performed at court by the King's Men.	
1605	First performance of *King Lear* at the Globe, with Burbage as the King, and Robert Armin as the Fool. Shakespeare makes further investments in Stratford,	Cervantes: *Don Quixote* (part one). Bacon: *The Proficience and Advancement of Learning*. Jonson and Inigo Jones: *The Masque of Blackness*.

CHRONOLOGY

HISTORICAL EVENTS

The Burbage brothers, Richard and Cuthbert, pull down The Theatre and, with its timbers, build the Globe on Bankside. Essex's campaign fails in Ireland, and after returning without permission to court he is arrested. The government suppresses satirical writings, and burns pamphlets by Nashe and Harvey.

Essex released but still in disgrace. The Fortune Theatre built by Alleyn and Henslowe. Bruno executed for heresy by the Inquisition in Rome.
Essex's Rebellion. Essex and Southampton arrested, and the former executed. Spanish invasion of Ireland. Monopolies debates in Parliament.

Spanish troops defeated in Ireland.

Death of Elizabeth, and accession of James I. Ralegh imprisoned in the Tower. Plague in London. Sir Thomas Bodley re-founds the library of Oxford University.

Peace with Spain. Hampton Court Conference.

Gunpowder Plot.

DATE	AUTHOR'S LIFE	LITERARY CONTEXT
1605 *cont.*	buying a half interest in a lease of tithes.	Jonson and co-authors imprisoned for libellous references to the court in *Eastward Ho*.
1605–6		Jonson: *Volpone*.
1606	First performance of *Macbeth*.	John Ford's masque *Honour Triumphant*.
1607	*Antony and Cleopatra*. Susanna marries John Hall, a physician. Death of Shakespeare's brother Edmund, an actor.	Tourneur's *The Revenger's Tragedy* printed. Barnes: *The Devil's Charter*.
1607–8	*Timon of Athens*, *Coriolanus*, *Pericles*.	
1608	Shakespeare one of the shareholders in the Blackfriars Theatre. Death of his mother.	Lope de Vega: *Peribanez*. Beaumont and Fletcher: *Philaster*. Jonson and Jones: *The Masque of Beauty*. Donne writes *La Corona*. Twelve books of Homer's *Iliad* (Chapman's translation).
1609	Publication, probably unauthorized, of the quarto edition of the *Sonnets* and *A Lover's Complaint*.	Jonson and Jones: *The Masque of Queens*. Donne's 'The Expiration' printed; 'Liturgie' and 'On the Annunciation' written. Bacon: *De Sapientia Veterum*. Lope de Vega: *New Art of Writing Plays for the Theatre*.
1609–10	*Cymbeline*.	
1610		Donne: *Pseudo-Martyr* printed and *The First Anniversarie* written. Jonson: *The Alchemist*. Beaumont and Fletcher: *The Maid's Tragedy*.
1610–11	*The Winter's Tale*.	
1611	*The Tempest* performed in the Banqueting House, Whitehall. Simon Forman records seeing performances of *Macbeth*, *The Winter's Tale* and *Cymbeline*.	Beaumont and Fletcher: *A King and No King*, *The Knight of the Burning Pestle*. Tourneur: *The Atheist's Tragedy*. Jonson and Jones: *Masque of Oberon*. Authorized Version of the Bible. Sir John Davies: *The Scourge of Folly*.

CHRONOLOGY

HISTORICAL EVENTS

Monteverdi: *Orfeo*.
Bacon appointed Solicitor General.

Galileo's experiments with the telescope confirm the Copernican theory. Kepler draws up 'Laws of Planetary Motion'. Twelve-year Truce between Spain and Netherlands.

Galileo: *The Starry Messenger*. Assassination of Henry IV of France. Parliament submits the Petition of Grievances.

The Inquisition of Rome begins investigating Galileo.

DATE	AUTHOR'S LIFE	LITERARY CONTEXT
1611 *cont.*		Donne writes the *The Second Anniversarie* and a 'A Valediction: forbidding mourning'.
1612	Shakespeare appears as a witness in a Court of Requests case involving a dispute over a dowry owed by his former landlord, Mountjoy, to his son-in-law, Belott. Death of his brother Gilbert.	Webster: *The White Devil* printed. Tourneur: *The Nobleman.* Lope de Vega: *Fuente Ovejuna.*
1613	At a performance of his last play, *Henry VIII*, the Globe Theatre catches fire and is destroyed. As part of the court celebrations for the marriage of Princess Elizabeth, The King's Men perform 14 plays, including *Much Ado*, *Othello*, *The Winter's Tale* and *The Tempest.* Death of his brother Richard.	Sir Thomas Overbury: *The Wife.* Donne: 'Good Friday' and 'Epithalamion' on Princess Elizabeth's marriage. Cervantes: *Novelas ejemplares* – a collection of short stories.
1614	In Stratford, Shakespeare protects his property interests during a controversy over a threat to enclose the common fields.	Jonson: *Bartholomew Fair.* Webster: *The Duchess of Malfi.* Ralegh: *The History of the World.*
1615	The Warwick Assizes issue an order to prevent enclosures, which ends the dispute in Stratford.	Cervantes publishes 8 plays and *Don Quixote* (part two).
1616	Marriage of his daughter Judith to Thomas Quincy, a vintner, who a month later is tried for fornication with another woman whom he had made pregnant. Death of Shakespeare (23 April).	Jonson: *The Devil is an Ass.* Jonson publishes his *Works.*
1623	The players Heminge and Condell publish the plays of the First Folio.	

HISTORICAL EVENTS

Death of Henry, Prince of Wales.

Marriage of Princess Elizabeth to Frederick, Elector Palatine. Bacon appointed Attorney-General.

The second Globe and the Hope Theatre built.

Inquiry into the murder of Sir Thomas Overbury in the Tower implicates the wife of the King's favourite, Somerset.

Ralegh released from the Tower to lead an expedition to Guiana; on his return he is executed.

WILLIAM SHAKESPEARE

THE TRAGEDY OF HAMLET PRINCE OF DENMARK

Edited by Edward Hubler

[*Dramatis Personae*

CLAUDIUS, King of Denmark
HAMLET, son to the late, and nephew to the present, King
POLONIUS, Lord Chamberlain
HORATIO, friend to Hamlet
LAERTES, son to Polonius

VOLTEMAND, CORNELIUS, ROSENCRANTZ, GUILDENSTERN, OSRIC, A GENTLEMAN — courtiers

A PRIEST

MARCELLUS, BARNARDO — officers

FRANCISCO, a soldier
REYNALDO, servant to Polonius
PLAYERS
TWO CLOWNS, gravediggers
FORTINBRAS, Prince of Norway
A NORWEGIAN CAPTAIN
ENGLISH AMBASSADORS
GERTRUDE, Queen of Denmark, mother to Hamlet
OPHELIA, daughter to Polonius
GHOST OF HAMLET'S FATHER
LORDS, LADIES, OFFICERS, SOLDIERS, SAILORS, MESSENGERS, ATTENDANTS

Scene: Elsinore]

THE TRAGEDY OF HAMLET PRINCE OF DENMARK

ACT I

Scene I. [*A guard platform of the castle.*]

Enter Barnardo and Francisco, two sentinels.

BARNARDO Who's there?

FRANCISCO Nay, answer me. Stand and unfold yourself.

BARNARDO Long live the King!

FRANCISCO Barnardo?

BARNARDO He. 5

FRANCISCO You come most carefully upon your hour.

BARNARDO 'Tis now struck twelve. Get thee to bed, Francisco.

Text references are printed in bold type; the annotation follows in roman type.
I.i.2 unfold disclose **3 Long live the King** (perhaps a password, perhaps a greeting)

FRANCISCO For this relief much thanks. 'Tis bitter cold,
And I am sick at heart.

BARNARDO Have you had quiet guard?

10 FRANCISCO Not a mouse stirring.

BARNARDO Well, good night.
If you do meet Horatio and Marcellus,
The rivals of my watch, bid them make haste.

Enter Horatio and Marcellus.

FRANCISCO I think I hear them. Stand, ho! Who is there?

HORATIO Friends to this ground.

15 MARCELLUS And liegemen to the Dane.

FRANCISCO Give you good night.

MARCELLUS O, farewell, honest soldier.
Who hath relieved you?

FRANCISCO Barnardo hath my place.
Give you good night. *Exit Francisco.*

MARCELLUS Holla, Barnardo!

BARNARDO Say——
What, is Horatio there?

HORATIO A piece of him.

20 BARNARDO Welcome, Horatio. Welcome, good Marcellus.

MARCELLUS What, has this thing appeared again tonight?

BARNARDO I have seen nothing.

MARCELLUS Horatio says 'tis but our fantasy,
And will not let belief take hold of him
25 Touching this dreaded sight twice seen of us;
Therefore I have entreated him along
With us to watch the minutes of this night,
That, if again this apparition come,
He may approve our eyes and speak to it.

13 rivals partners **15 liegemen to the Dane** loyal subjects to the King of Denmark **16 Give you** God give you **29 approve** confirm

HORATIO Tush, tush, 'twill not appear.

BARNARDO Sit down awhile, 30
And let us once again assail your ears,
That are so fortified against our story,
What we have two nights seen.

HORATIO Well, sit we down,
And let us hear Barnardo speak of this.

BARNARDO Last night of all, 35
When yond same star that's westward from the pole
Had made his course t'illume that part of heaven
Where now it burns, Marcellus and myself,
The bell then beating one——

Enter Ghost.

MARCELLUS Peace, break thee off. Look where it comes again. 40

BARNARDO In the same figure like the king that's dead.

MARCELLUS Thou art a scholar; speak to it, Horatio.

BARNARDO Looks 'a not like the king? Mark it, Horatio.

HORATIO Most like: it harrows me with fear and wonder.

BARNARDO It would be spoke to.

MARCELLUS Speak to it, Horatio. 45

HORATIO What art thou that usurp'st this time of night,
Together with that fair and warlike form
In which the majesty of buried Denmark
Did sometimes march? By heaven I charge thee, speak.

MARCELLUS It is offended.

BARNARDO See, it stalks away. 50

HORATIO Stay! Speak, speak. I charge thee, speak.

Exit Ghost.

36 pole polestar 48 buried Denmark the buried King of Denmark

MARCELLUS 'Tis gone and will not answer.

BARNARDO How now, Horatio? You tremble and look pale.
Is not this something more than fantasy?
55 What think you on't?

HORATIO Before my God, I might not this believe
Without the sensible and true avouch
Of mine own eyes.

MARCELLUS Is it not like the King?

HORATIO As thou art to thyself.
60 Such was the very armor he had on
When he the ambitious Norway combated:
So frowned he once, when, in an angry parle,
He smote the sledded Polacks on the ice.
'Tis strange.

MARCELLUS Thus twice before, and jump at this dead
65 hour,
With martial stalk hath he gone by our watch.

HORATIO In what particular thought to work I know not;
But, in the gross and scope of my opinion,
This bodes some strange eruption to our state.

MARCELLUS Good now, sit down, and tell me he that
70 knows,
Why this same strict and most observant watch
So nightly toils the subject of the land,
And why such daily cast of brazen cannon
And foreign mart for implements of war,

57 **sensible and true avouch** sensory and true proof 61 **Norway** King of Norway 62 **parle** parley 63 **sledded Polacks** Poles in sledges 65 **jump** just 68 **gross and scope** general drift 72 **toils the subject** makes the subjects toil 74 **mart** trading

Why such impress of shipwrights, whose sore task 75
Does not divide the Sunday from the week,
What might be toward that this sweaty haste
Doth make the night joint-laborer with the day?
Who is't that can inform me?

HORATIO That can I.
At least the whisper goes so: our last king, 80
Whose image even but now appeared to us,
Was, as you know, by Fortinbras of Norway,
Thereto pricked on by a most emulate pride,
Dared to the combat; in which our valiant Hamlet
(For so this side of our known world esteemed him) 85
Did slay this Fortinbras, who, by a sealed compact
Well ratified by law and heraldry,
Did forfeit, with his life, all those his lands
Which he stood seized of, to the conqueror;
Against the which a moiety competent 90
Was gagèd by our King, which had returned
To the inheritance of Fortinbras,
Had he been vanquisher, as, by the same comart
And carriage of the article designed,
His fell to Hamlet. Now, sir, young Fortinbras, 95
Of unimprovèd mettle hot and full,
Hath in the skirts of Norway here and there
Sharked up a list of lawless resolutes,
For food and diet, to some enterprise
That hath a stomach in't; which is no other, 100
As it doth well appear unto our state,
But to recover of us by strong hand
And terms compulsatory, those foresaid lands
So by his father lost; and this, I take it,
Is the main motive of our preparations, 105

75 impress forced service 77 **toward** in preparation 87 **law and heraldry** heraldic law (governing the combat) 89 **seized** possessed 90 **moiety competent** equal portion 91 **gagèd** engaged, pledged 93 **comart** agreement 94 **carriage of the article designed** import of the agreement drawn up 96 **unimprovèd** untried 97 **skirts** borders 98 **Sharked up** collected indiscriminately (as a shark gulps its prey) 98 **resolutes** desperadoes 100 **hath a stomach in't** i.e., requires courage

The source of this our watch, and the chief head
Of this posthaste and romage in the land.

BARNARDO I think it be no other but e'en so;
Well may it sort that this portentous figure
110 Comes armèd through our watch so like the King
That was and is the question of these wars.

HORATIO A mote it is to trouble the mind's eye:
In the most high and palmy state of Rome,
A little ere the mightiest Julius fell,
115 The graves stood tenantless, and the sheeted dead
Did squeak and gibber in the Roman streets;
As stars with trains of fire and dews of blood,
Disasters in the sun; and the moist star,
Upon whose influence Neptune's empire stands,
120 Was sick almost to doomsday with eclipse.
And even the like precurse of feared events,
As harbingers preceding still the fates
And prologue to the omen coming on,
Have heaven and earth together demonstrated
125 Unto our climatures and countrymen.

Enter Ghost.

But soft, behold, lo where it comes again!
I'll cross it, though it blast me.—Stay, illusion.

It spreads his arms.

If thou hast any sound or use of voice,
Speak to me.
130 If there be any good thing to be done
That may to thee do ease and grace to me,
Speak to me.
If thou art privy to thy country's fate,
Which happily foreknowing may avoid,

106 **head** fountainhead, origin 107 **romage** bustle 109 **sort** befit 116 **Did squeak . . . Roman streets** (the break in the sense which follows this line suggests that a line has dropped out) 118 **Disasters** threatening signs 118 **moist star** moon 121 **precurse** precursor, foreshadowing 122 **harbingers** forerunners 122 **still** always 123 **omen** calamity 125 **climatures** regions 127 **cross it** (1) cross its path, confront it (2) make the sign of the cross in front of it 127 s.d. **his** i.e., its, the ghost's (though possibly what is meant is that Horatio spreads his own arms, making a cross of himself) 134 **happily** haply, perhaps

O, speak! 135
Or if thou hast uphoarded in thy life
Extorted treasure in the womb of earth,
For which, they say, you spirits oft walk in death,

The cock crows.

Speak of it. Stay and speak. Stop it, Marcellus.

MARCELLUS Shall I strike at it with my partisan? 140

HORATIO Do, if it will not stand.

BARNARDO 'Tis here.

HORATIO 'Tis here.

MARCELLUS 'Tis gone. *Exit Ghost.*
We do it wrong, being so majestical,
To offer it the show of violence,
For it is as the air, invulnerable, 145
And our vain blows malicious mockery.

BARNARDO It was about to speak when the cock crew.

HORATIO And then it started, like a guilty thing
Upon a fearful summons. I have heard,
The cock, that is the trumpet to the morn, 150
Doth with his lofty and shrill-sounding throat
Awake the god of day, and at his warning,
Whether in sea or fire, in earth or air,
Th' extravagant and erring spirit hies
To his confine; and of the truth herein 155
This present object made probation.

MARCELLUS It faded on the crowing of the cock.
Some say that ever 'gainst that season comes
Wherein our Savior's birth is celebrated,
This bird of dawning singeth all night long, 160
And then, they say, no spirit dare stir abroad,
The nights are wholesome, then no planets strike,
No fairy takes, nor witch hath power to charm:
So hallowed and so gracious is that time.

HORATIO So have I heard and do in part believe it. 165

137 Extorted ill-won **140 partisan** pike (a long-handled weapon) **154 extravagant and erring** out of bounds and wandering **156 probation** proof **158 'gainst** just before **162 strike** exert an evil influence **163 takes** bewitches

But look, the morn in russet mantle clad
Walks o'er the dew of yon high eastward hill.
Break we our watch up, and by my advice
Let us impart what we have seen tonight
170 Unto young Hamlet, for upon my life
This spirit, dumb to us, will speak to him.
Do you consent we shall acquaint him with it,
As needful in our loves, fitting our duty?

MARCELLUS Let's do't, I pray, and I this morning know
175 Where we shall find him most convenient. *Exeunt.*

Scene II. [*The castle.*]

Flourish. Enter Claudius, King of Denmark, Gertrude the Queen, Councilors, Polonius and his son Laertes, Hamlet, cum aliis [*including Voltemand and Cornelius*].

KING Though yet of Hamlet our dear brother's death
The memory be green, and that it us befitted
To bear our hearts in grief, and our whole kingdom
To be contracted in one brow of woe,
5 Yet so far hath discretion fought with nature
That we with wisest sorrow think on him
Together with remembrance of ourselves.
Therefore our sometime sister, now our Queen,
Th' imperial jointress to this warlike state,
10 Have we, as 'twere, with a defeated joy,
With an auspicious and a dropping eye,
With mirth in funeral, and with dirge in marriage,
In equal scale weighing delight and dole,
Taken to wife. Nor have we herein barred
15 Your better wisdoms, which have freely gone

I.ii.s.d. **Flourish** fanfare of trumpets s.d. **cum aliis** with others (Latin) 8 **our sometime sister** my (the royal "we") former sister-in-law 9 **jointress** joint tenant, partner 11 **auspicious** joyful

With this affair along. For all, our thanks.
Now follows that you know young Fortinbras,
Holding a weak supposal of our worth,
Or thinking by our late dear brother's death
Our state to be disjoint and out of frame, 20
Colleaguèd with this dream of his advantage,
He hath not failed to pester us with message,
Importing the surrender of those lands
Lost by his father, with all bands of law,
To our most valiant brother. So much for him. 25
Now for ourself and for this time of meeting.
Thus much the business is: we have here writ
To Norway, uncle of young Fortinbras—
Who, impotent and bedrid, scarcely hears
Of this his nephew's purpose—to suppress 30
His further gait herein, in that the levies,
The lists, and full proportions are all made
Out of his subject; and we here dispatch
You, good Cornelius, and you, Voltemand,
For bearers of this greeting to old Norway, 35
Giving to you no further personal power
To business with the King, more than the scope
Of these delated articles allow.
Farewell, and let your haste commend your duty.

CORNELIUS, VOLTEMAND In that, and all things, will we
show our duty. 40

KING We doubt it nothing. Heartily farewell.
Exit Voltemand and Cornelius.
And now, Laertes, what's the news with you?
You told us of some suit. What is't, Laertes?
You cannot speak of reason to the Dane
And lose your voice. What wouldst thou beg, Laertes, 45
That shall not be my offer, not thy asking?
The head is not more native to the heart,

20 frame order 21 advantage superiority 31 gait proceeding 32 proportions supplies for war 33 Out of his subject i.e., out of old Norway's subjects and realm 38 delated articles detailed documents 45 lose your voice waste your breath 47 native related

The hand more instrumental to the mouth,
Than is the throne of Denmark to thy father.
What wouldst thou have, Laertes?

50 LAERTES My dread lord,
Your leave and favor to return to France,
From whence, though willingly I came to Denmark
To show my duty in your coronation,
Yet now I must confess, that duty done,
55 My thoughts and wishes bend again toward France
And bow them to your gracious leave and pardon.

KING Have you your father's leave? What says Polonius?

POLONIUS He hath, my lord, wrung from me my slow leave
By laborsome petition, and at last
60 Upon his will I sealed my hard consent.
I do beseech you give him leave to go.

KING Take thy fair hour, Laertes. Time be thine,
And thy best graces spend it at thy will.
But now, my cousin Hamlet, and my son——

HAMLET [*Aside*] A little more than kin, and less than
65 kind!

KING How is it that the clouds still hang on you?

HAMLET Not so, my lord. I am too much in the sun.

QUEEN Good Hamlet, cast thy nighted color off,
And let thine eye look like a friend on Denmark.
70 Do not forever with thy vailèd lids
Seek for thy noble father in the dust.
Thou know'st 'tis common; all that lives must die,
Passing through nature to eternity.

60 Upon his . . . hard consent to his desire I gave my reluctant consent **64 cousin** kinsman **65 kind** (pun on the meanings "kindly" and "natural"; though doubly related—more than kin—Hamlet asserts that he neither resembles Claudius in nature or feels kindly toward him) **67 sun** sunshine of royal favor (with a pun on "son") **70 vailèd** lowered

HAMLET Ay, madam, it is common.

QUEEN If it be,
Why seems it so particular with thee? 75

HAMLET Seems, madam? Nay, it is. I know not "seems."
'Tis not alone my inky cloak, good mother,
Nor customary suits of solemn black,
Nor windy suspiration of forced breath,
No, nor the fruitful river in the eye, 80
Nor the dejected havior of the visage,
Together with all forms, moods, shapes of grief,
That can denote me truly. These indeed seem,
For they are actions that a man might play,
But I have that within which passes show; 85
These but the trappings and the suits of woe.

KING 'Tis sweet and commendable in your nature, Hamlet,
To give these mourning duties to your father,
But you must know your father lost a father,
That father lost, lost his, and the survivor bound 90
In filial obligation for some term
To do obsequious sorrow. But to persever
In obstinate condolement is a course
Of impious stubbornness. 'Tis unmanly grief.
It shows a will most incorrect to heaven, 95
A heart unfortified, a mind impatient,
And understanding simple and unschooled.
For what we know must be and is as common
As any the most vulgar thing to sense,
Why should we in our peevish opposition 100
Take it to heart? Fie, 'tis a fault to heaven,
A fault against the dead, a fault to nature,
To reason most absurd, whose common theme
Is death of fathers, and who still hath cried,
From the first corse till he that died today, 105
"This must be so." We pray you throw to earth

74 **common** (1) universal (2) vulgar 79 **windy suspiration** heavy sighing 92 **obsequious** suitable to obsequies (funerals) 93 **condolement** mourning 99 **vulgar** common 105 **corse** corpse

This unprevailing woe, and think of us
As of a father, for let the world take note
You are the most immediate to our throne,
110 And with no less nobility of love
Than that which dearest father bears his son
Do I impart toward you. For your intent
In going back to school in Wittenberg,
It is most retrograde to our desire,
115 And we beseech you, bend you to remain
Here in the cheer and comfort of our eye,
Our chiefest courtier, cousin, and our son.

QUEEN Let not thy mother lose her prayers, Hamlet.
I pray thee stay with us, go not to Wittenberg.

120 HAMLET I shall in all my best obey you, madam.

KING Why, 'tis a loving and a fair reply.
Be as ourself in Denmark. Madam, come.
This gentle and unforced accord of Hamlet
Sits smiling to my heart, in grace whereof
125 No jocund health that Denmark drinks today,
But the great cannon to the clouds shall tell,
And the King's rouse the heaven shall bruit again,
Respeaking earthly thunder. Come away.

Flourish. Exeunt all but Hamlet.

HAMLET O that this too too sullied flesh would melt,
130 Thaw, and resolve itself into a dew,
Or that the Everlasting had not fixed
His canon 'gainst self-slaughter. O God, God,
How weary, stale, flat, and unprofitable
Seem to me all the uses of this world!
135 Fie on't, ah, fie, 'tis an unweeded garden
That grows to seed. Things rank and gross in nature
Possess it merely. That it should come to this:
But two months dead, nay, not so much, not two,

107 **unprevailing** unavailing 114 **retrograde** contrary 115 **bend you** incline 127 **rouse** deep drink 127 **bruit** announce noisily 129 **sullied** (Q2 has **sallied**, here modernized to **sullied**, which makes sense and is therefore given; but the Folio reading, **solid**, which fits better with **melt**, is quite possibly correct) 132 **canon** law 137 **merely** entirely

So excellent a king, that was to this
Hyperion to a satyr, so loving to my mother 140
That he might not beteem the winds of heaven
Visit her face too roughly. Heaven and earth,
Must I remember? Why, she would hang on him
As if increase of appetite had grown
By what it fed on; and yet within a month— 145
Let me not think on't; frailty, thy name is woman—
A little month, or ere those shoes were old
With which she followed my poor father's body
Like Niobe, all tears, why she, even she—
O God, a beast that wants discourse of reason 150
Would have mourned longer—married with my uncle,
My father's brother, but no more like my father
Than I to Hercules. Within a month,
Ere yet the salt of most unrighteous tears
Had left the flushing in her gallèd eyes, 155
She married. O, most wicked speed, to post
With such dexterity to incestuous sheets!
It is not, nor it cannot come to good.
But break my heart, for I must hold my tongue.

Enter Horatio, Marcellus, and Barnardo.

HORATIO Hail to your lordship!

HAMLET I am glad to see you well. 160
Horatio—or I do forget myself.

HORATIO The same, my lord, and your poor servant ever.

HAMLET Sir, my good friend, I'll change that name with you.
And what make you from Wittenberg, Horatio?
Marcellus. 165

140 Hyperion the sun god, a model of beauty **141 beteem** allow **149 Niobe** (a mother who wept profusely at the death of her children) **150 wants discourse of reason** lacks reasoning power **155 left the flushing** stopped reddening **156 post** hasten **157 incestuous** (canon law considered marriage with a deceased brother's widow to be incestuous) **163 change** exchange

MARCELLUS My good lord!

HAMLET I am very glad to see you. [*To Barnardo*]
Good even, sir.
But what, in faith, make you from Wittenberg?

HORATIO A truant disposition, good my lord.

170 HAMLET I would not hear your enemy say so,
Nor shall you do my ear that violence
To make it truster of your own report
Against yourself. I know you are no truant.
But what is your affair in Elsinore?
175 We'll teach you to drink deep ere you depart.

HORATIO My lord, I came to see your father's funeral.

HAMLET I prithee do not mock me, fellow student.
I think it was to see my mother's wedding.

HORATIO Indeed, my lord, it followed hard upon.

180 HAMLET Thrift, thrift, Horatio. The funeral baked
meats
Did coldly furnish forth the marriage tables.
Would I had met my dearest foe in heaven
Or ever I had seen that day, Horatio!
My father, methinks I see my father.

HORATIO Where, my lord?

185 HAMLET In my mind's eye, Horatio.

HORATIO I saw him once. 'A was a goodly king.

HAMLET 'A was a man, take him for all in all,
I shall not look upon his like again.

HORATIO My lord, I think I saw him yesternight.

190 HAMLET Saw? Who?

HORATIO My lord, the King your father.

HAMLET The King my father?

HORATIO Season your admiration for a while
With an attent ear till I may deliver
Upon the witness of these gentlemen

172 truster believer **182 dearest** most intensely felt **186 'A** he **192 Season your admiration** control your wonder

This marvel to you.

HAMLET For God's love let me hear! 195

HORATIO Two nights together had these gentlemen,
Marcellus and Barnardo, on their watch
In the dead waste and middle of the night
Been thus encountered. A figure like your father,
Armèd at point exactly, cap-a-pe, 200
Appears before them, and with solemn march
Goes slow and stately by them. Thrice he walked
By their oppressed and fear-surprisèd eyes,
Within his truncheon's length, whilst they, distilled
Almost to jelly with the act of fear, 205
Stand dumb and speak not to him. This to me
In dreadful secrecy impart they did,
And I with them the third night kept the watch,
Where, as they had delivered, both in time,
Form of the thing, each word made true and good, 210
The apparition comes. I knew your father.
These hands are not more like.

HAMLET But where was this?

MARCELLUS My lord, upon the platform where we watched.

HAMLET Did you not speak to it?

HORATIO My lord, I did;
But answer made it none. Yet once methought 215
It lifted up it head and did address
Itself to motion like as it would speak:
But even then the morning cock crew loud,
And at the sound it shrunk in haste away
And vanished from our sight.

HAMLET 'Tis very strange. 220

HORATIO As I do live, my honored lord, 'tis true,
And we did think it writ down in our duty
To let you know of it.

200 cap-a-pe head to foot **204 truncheon's length** space of a short staff **204 distilled** reduced **205 act** action **207 dreadful** terrified **216 it** its

HAMLET Indeed, indeed, sirs, but this troubles me.
Hold you the watch tonight?

225 ALL We do, my lord.

HAMLET Armed, say you?

ALL Armed, my lord.

HAMLET From top to toe?

ALL My lord, from head to foot.

HAMLET Then saw you not his face.

230 HORATIO O, yes, my lord. He wore his beaver up.

HAMLET What, looked he frowningly?

HORATIO A countenance more in sorrow than in anger.

HAMLET Pale or red?

HORATIO Nay, very pale.

HAMLET And fixed his eyes upon you?

HORATIO Most constantly.

235 HAMLET I would I had been there.

HORATIO It would have much amazed you.

HAMLET Very like, very like. Stayed it long?

HORATIO While one with moderate haste might tell a hundred.

BOTH Longer, longer.

HORATIO Not when I saw't.

240 HAMLET His beard was grizzled, no?

HORATIO It was as I have seen it in his life,
A sable silvered.

HAMLET I will watch tonight.
Perchance 'twill walk again.

HORATIO I warr'nt it will.

HAMLET If it assume my noble father's person,

230 beaver visor, face guard **238 tell** count **240 grizzled** gray **242 sable silvered** black mingled with white

I'll speak to it though hell itself should gape 245
And bid me hold my peace. I pray you all,
If you have hitherto concealed this sight,
Let it be tenable in your silence still,
And whatsomever else shall hap tonight,
Give it an understanding but no tongue; 250
I will requite your loves. So fare you well.
Upon the platform 'twixt eleven and twelve
I'll visit you.

ALL Our duty to your honor.

HAMLET Your loves, as mine to you. Farewell.

Exeunt [all but Hamlet].

My father's spirit—in arms? All is not well. 255
I doubt some foul play. Would the night were come!
Till then sit still, my soul. Foul deeds will rise,
Though all the earth o'erwhelm them, to men's eyes.

Exit.

Scene III. [*A room.*]

Enter Laertes and Ophelia, his sister.

LAERTES My necessaries are embarked. Farewell.
And, sister, as the winds give benefit
And convoy is assistant, do not sleep,
But let me hear from you.

OPHELIA. Do you doubt that?

LAERTES For Hamlet, and the trifling of his favor, 5
Hold it a fashion and a toy in blood,
A violet in the youth of primy nature,
Forward, not permanent, sweet, not lasting,
The perfume and suppliance of a minute,

248 tenable held 256 doubt suspect I.iii.3 convoy conveyance 6 toy idle fancy 7 primy springlike 8 forward premature 9 suppliance diversion

No more.

OPHELIA No more but so?

10 LAERTES Think it no more.

For nature crescent does not grow alone
In thews and bulk, but as this temple waxes,
The inward service of the mind and soul
Grows wide withal. Perhaps he loves you now,
15 And now no soil nor cautel doth besmirch
The virtue of his will; but you must fear,
His greatness weighed, his will is not his own.
For he himself is subject to his birth.
He may not, as unvalued persons do,
20 Carve for himself; for on his choice depends
The safety and health of this whole state;
And therefore must his choice be circumscribed
Unto the voice and yielding of that body
Whereof he is the head. Then if he says he loves you,
25 It fits your wisdom so far to believe it
As he in his particular act and place
May give his saying deed, which is no further
Than the main voice of Denmark goes withal.
Then weigh what loss your honor may sustain
30 If with too credent ear you list his songs,
Or lose your heart, or your chaste treasure open
To his unmastered importunity.
Fear it, Ophelia, fear it, my dear sister,
And keep you in the rear of your affection,
35 Out of the shot and danger of desire.
The chariest maid is prodigal enough
If she unmask her beauty to the moon.
Virtue itself scapes not calumnious strokes.
The canker galls the infants of the spring
40 Too oft before their buttons be disclosed,
And in the morn and liquid dew of youth
Contagious blastments are most imminent.

11 **crescent** growing 12 **thews** muscles and sinews 12 **temple** i.e., the body 15 **cautel** deceit 17 **greatness weighed** high rank considered 19 **unvalued** of low rank 30 **credent** credulous 39 **canker** cankerworm 40 **buttons** buds

Be wary then; best safety lies in fear;
Youth to itself rebels, though none else near.

OPHELIA I shall the effect of this good lesson keep 45
As watchman to my heart, but, good my brother,
Do not, as some ungracious pastors do,
Show me the steep and thorny way to heaven,
Whiles, like a puffed and reckless libertine,
Himself the primrose path of dalliance treads 50
And recks not his own rede.

Enter Polonius.

LAERTES O, fear me not.
I stay too long. But here my father comes.
A double blessing is a double grace;
Occasion smiles upon a second leave.

POLONIUS Yet here, Laertes? Aboard, aboard, for
shame! 55
The wind sits in the shoulder of your sail,
And you are stayed for. There—my blessing with thee,
And these few precepts in thy memory
Look thou character. Give thy thoughts no tongue,
Nor any unproportioned thought his act. 60
Be thou familiar, but by no means vulgar.
Those friends thou hast, and their adoption tried,
Grapple them unto thy soul with hoops of steel,
But do not dull thy palm with entertainment
Of each new-hatched, unfledged courage. Beware 65
Of entrance to a quarrel; but being in,
Bear't that th' opposèd may beware of thee.
Give every man thine ear, but few thy voice;
Take each man's censure, but reserve thy judgment.
Costly thy habit as thy purse can buy, 70
But not expressed in fancy; rich, not gaudy,
For the apparel oft proclaims the man,
And they in France of the best rank and station

47 ungracious lacking grace 51 recks not his own rede does not heed his own advice 59 character inscribe 60 unproportioned unbalanced 65 courage gallant youth 69 censure opinion

Are of a most select and generous, chief in that.
75 Neither a borrower nor a lender be,
For loan oft loses both itself and friend,
And borrowing dulleth edge of husbandry.
This above all, to thine own self be true,
And it must follow, as the night the day,
80 Thou canst not then be false to any man.
Farewell. My blessing season this in thee!

LAERTES Most humbly do I take my leave, my lord.

POLONIUS The time invites you. Go, your servants tend.

LAERTES Farewell, Ophelia, and remember well
What I have said to you.

85 OPHELIA 'Tis in my memory locked,
And you yourself shall keep the key of it.

LAERTES Farewell. *Exit Laertes.*

POLONIUS What is't, Ophelia, he hath said to you?

OPHELIA So please you, something touching the Lord Hamlet.

90 POLONIUS Marry, well bethought.
'Tis told me he hath very oft of late
Given private time to you, and you yourself
Have of your audience been most free and bounteous.
If it be so—as so 'tis put on me,
95 And that in way of caution—I must tell you
You do not understand yourself so clearly
As it behooves my daughter and your honor.
What is between you? Give me up the truth.

OPHELIA He hath, my lord, of late made many tenders
100 Of his affection to me.

74 **Are of . . . in that** show their fine taste and their gentlemanly instincts more in that than in any other point of manners (Kittredge) 77 **husbandry** thrift 81 **season this** make fruitful this (advice) 83 **tend** attend 90 **Marry** (a light oath, from "By the Virgin Mary") 99 **tenders** offers (in line 103 it has the same meaning, but in line 106 Polonius speaks of **tenders** in the sense of counters or chips; in line 109 **Tend'ring** means "holding," and **tender** means "give," "present")

POLONIUS Affection pooh! You speak like a green girl,
Unsifted in such perilous circumstance.
Do you believe his tenders, as you call them?

OPHELIA I do not know, my lord, what I should think.

POLONIUS Marry, I will teach you. Think yourself a baby 105
That you have ta'en these tenders for true pay
Which are not sterling. Tender yourself more dearly,
Or (not to crack the wind of the poor phrase)
Tend'ring it thus you'll tender me a fool.

OPHELIA My lord, he hath importuned me with love 110
In honorable fashion.

POLONIUS Ay, fashion you may call it. Go to, go to.

OPHELIA And hath given countenance to his speech, my lord,
With almost all the holy vows of heaven.

POLONIUS Ay, springes to catch woodcocks. I do know, 115
When the blood burns, how prodigal the soul
Lends the tongue vows. These blazes, daughter,
Giving more light than heat, extinct in both,
Even in their promise, as it is a-making,
You must not take for fire. From this time 120
Be something scanter of your maiden presence.
Set your entreatments at a higher rate
Than a command to parley. For Lord Hamlet,
Believe so much in him that he is young,
And with a larger tether may he walk 125
Than may be given you. In few, Ophelia,
Do not believe his vows, for they are brokers,
Not of that dye which their investments show,
But mere implorators of unholy suits,
Breathing like sanctified and pious bonds, 130
The better to beguile. This is for all:

102 **Unsifted** untried 109 **tender me a fool** (1) present me with a fool (2) present me with a baby 115 **springes to catch woodcocks** snares to catch stupid birds 122 **entreatments** interviews 127 **brokers** procurers 128 **dye** i.e., kind 128 **investments** garments 129 **implorators** solicitors 130 **bonds** pledges

I would not, in plain terms, from this time forth
Have you so slander any moment leisure
As to give words or talk with the Lord Hamlet.
135 Look to't, I charge you. Come your ways.

OPHELIA I shall obey, my lord. *Exeunt.*

Scene IV. [*A guard platform.*]

Enter Hamlet, Horatio, and Marcellus.

HAMLET The air bites shrewdly; it is very cold.

HORATIO It is a nipping and an eager air.

HAMLET What hour now?

HORATIO I think it lacks of twelve.

MARCELLUS No, it is struck.

HORATIO Indeed? I heard it not. It then draws near the
5 season
Wherein the spirit held his wont to walk.

A flourish of trumpets, and two pieces go off.

What does this mean, my lord?

HAMLET The King doth wake tonight and takes his
rouse,
Keeps wassail, and the swagg'ring upspring reels,
10 And as he drains his draughts of Rhenish down
The kettledrum and trumpet thus bray out
The triumph of his pledge.

HORATIO Is it a custom?

133 **slander** disgrace I.iv.1 **shrewdly** bitterly 2 **eager** sharp 8 **wake** hold a revel by night 8 **takes his rouse** carouses 9 **upspring** (a dance) 10 **Rhenish** Rhine wine 12 **The triumph of his pledge** the achievement (of drinking a wine cup in one draught) of his toast

HAMLET Ay, marry, is't,
But to my mind, though I am native here
And to the manner born, it is a custom 15
More honored in the breach than the observance.
This heavy-headed revel east and west
Makes us traduced and taxed of other nations.
They clepe us drunkards and with swinish phrase
Soil our addition, and indeed it takes 20
From our achievements, though performed at height,
The pith and marrow of our attribute.
So oft it chances in particular men
That for some vicious mole of nature in them,
As in their birth, wherein they are not guilty, 25
(Since nature cannot choose his origin)
By the o'ergrowth of some complexion,
Oft breaking down the pales and forts of reason,
Or by some habit that too much o'erleavens
The form of plausive manners, that (these men, 30
Carrying, I say, the stamp of one defect,
Being nature's livery, or fortune's star)
Their virtues else, be they as pure as grace,
As infinite as man may undergo,
Shall in the general censure take corruption 35
From that particular fault. The dram of evil
Doth all the noble substance of a doubt,
To his own scandal.

Enter Ghost.

HORATIO Look, my lord, it comes.

HAMLET Angels and ministers of grace defend us!
Be thou a spirit of health or goblin damned, 40
Bring with thee airs from heaven or blasts from hell,
Be thy intents wicked or charitable,

18 **taxed of** blamed by 19 **clepe** call 20 **addition** reputation (literally, "title of honor") 22 **attribute** reputation 24 **mole** blemish 27 **complexion** natural disposition 28 **pales** enclosures 29 **o'er-leavens** mixes with, corrupts 30 **plausive** pleasing 32 **nature's livery, or fortune's star** nature's equipment (i.e., "innate"), or a person's destiny determined by the stars 35 **general censure** popular judgment 36–38 **The dram . . . own scandal** (though the drift is clear, there is no agreement as to the exact meaning of these lines) 40 **spirit of health** good spirit

Thou com'st in such a questionable shape
That I will speak to thee. I'll call thee Hamlet,
45 King, father, royal Dane. O, answer me!
Let me not burst in ignorance, but tell
Why thy canonized bones, hearsèd in death,
Have burst their cerements, why the sepulcher
Wherein we saw thee quietly interred
50 Hath oped his ponderous and marble jaws
To cast thee up again. What may this mean
That thou, dead corse, again in complete steel,
Revisits thus the glimpses of the moon,
Making night hideous, and we fools of nature
55 So horridly to shake our disposition
With thoughts beyond the reaches of our souls?
Say, why is this? Wherefore? What should we do?
Ghost beckons Hamlet.

HORATIO It beckons you to go away with it,
As if it some impartment did desire
To you alone.

60 MARCELLUS Look with what courteous action
It waves you to a more removèd ground.
But do not go with it.

HORATIO No, by no means.

HAMLET It will not speak. Then I will follow it.

HORATIO Do not, my lord.

HAMLET Why, what should be the fear?
65 I do not set my life at a pin's fee,
And for my soul, what can it do to that,
Being a thing immortal as itself?
It waves me forth again. I'll follow it.

HORATIO What if it tempt you toward the flood, my lord,
70 Or to the dreadful summit of the cliff

43 questionable (1) capable of discourse (2) dubious **47 canonized** buried according to the canon or ordinance of the church **48 cerements** waxed linen shroud **55 shake our disposition** disturb us **59 impartment** communication

That beetles o'er his base into the sea,
And there assume some other horrible form,
Which might deprive your sovereignty of reason
And draw you into madness? Think of it.
The very place puts toys of desperation, 75
Without more motive, into every brain
That looks so many fathoms to the sea
And hears it roar beneath.

HAMLET It waves me still.
Go on; I'll follow thee.

MARCELLUS You shall not go, my lord.

HAMLET Hold off your hands. 80

HORATIO Be ruled. You shall not go.

HAMLET My fate cries out
And makes each petty artere in this body
As hardy as the Nemean lion's nerve.
Still am I called! Unhand me, gentlemen.
By heaven, I'll make a ghost of him that lets me! 85
I say, away! Go on. I'll follow thee.

Exit Ghost, and Hamlet.

HORATIO He waxes desperate with imagination.

MARCELLUS Let's follow. 'Tis not fit thus to obey him.

HORATIO Have after! To what issue will this come?

MARCELLUS Something is rotten in the state of
Denmark. 90

HORATIO Heaven will direct it.

MARCELLUS Nay, let's follow him. *Exeunt.*

71 beetles juts out **73 deprive your sovereignty of reason** destroy the sovereignty of your reason **75 toys** whims, fancies **82 artere** artery **83 Nemean lion's nerve** sinews of the mythical lion slain by Hercules **85 lets** hinders

Scene V. [*The battlements.*]

Enter Ghost and Hamlet.

HAMLET Whither wilt thou lead me? Speak; I'll go no further.

GHOST Mark me.

HAMLET I will.

GHOST My hour is almost come,
When I to sulf'rous and tormenting flames
Must render up myself.

HAMLET Alas, poor ghost.

5 GHOST Pity me not, but lend thy serious hearing
To what I shall unfold.

HAMLET Speak. I am bound to hear.

GHOST So art thou to revenge, when thou shalt hear.

HAMLET What?

GHOST I am thy father's spirit,
10 Doomed for a certain term to walk the night,
And for the day confined to fast in fires,
Till the foul crimes done in my days of nature
Are burnt and purged away. But that I am forbid
To tell the secrets of my prison house,
15 I could a tale unfold whose lightest word
Would harrow up thy soul, freeze thy young blood,
Make thy two eyes like stars start from their spheres,
Thy knotted and combinèd locks to part,
And each particular hair to stand an end

I.v.12 **crimes** sins 17 **spheres** (in Ptolemaic astronomy, each planet was fixed in a hollow transparent shell concentric with the earth)

Like quills upon the fearful porpentine. 20
But this eternal blazon must not be
To ears of flesh and blood. List, list, O, list!
If thou didst ever thy dear father love——

HAMLET O God!

GHOST Revenge his foul and most unnatural murder. 25

HAMLET Murder?

GHOST Murder most foul, as in the best it is,
But this most foul, strange, and unnatural.

HAMLET Haste me to know't, that I, with wings as swift
As meditation or the thoughts of love, 30
May sweep to my revenge.

GHOST I find thee apt,
And duller shouldst thou be than the fat weed
That roots itself in ease on Lethe wharf,
Wouldst thou not stir in this. Now, Hamlet, hear.
'Tis given out that, sleeping in my orchard, 35
A serpent stung me. So the whole ear of Denmark
Is by a forgèd process of my death
Rankly abused. But know, thou noble youth,
The serpent that did sting thy father's life
Now wears his crown.

HAMLET O my prophetic soul! 40
My uncle?

GHOST Ay, that incestuous, that adulterate beast,
With witchcraft of his wits, with traitorous gifts—
O wicked wit and gifts, that have the power
So to seduce!—won to his shameful lust 45
The will of my most seeming-virtuous queen.
O Hamlet, what a falling-off was there,
From me, whose love was of that dignity
That it went hand in hand even with the vow
I made to her in marriage, and to decline 50

20 **fearful porpentine** timid porcupine 21 **eternal blazon** revelation of eternity 30 **meditation** thought 33 **Lethe wharf** bank of the river of forgetfulness in Hades 37 **forgèd process** false account 42 **adulterate** adulterous

Upon a wretch whose natural gifts were poor
To those of mine.
But virtue, as it never will be moved,
Though lewdness court it in a shape of heaven,
55 So lust, though to a radiant angel linked,
Will sate itself in a celestial bed
And prey on garbage.
But soft, methinks I scent the morning air;
Brief let me be. Sleeping within my orchard,
60 My custom always of the afternoon,
Upon my secure hour thy uncle stole
With juice of cursed hebona in a vial,
And in the porches of my ears did pour
The leperous distillment, whose effect
65 Holds such an enmity with blood of man
That swift as quicksilver it courses through
The natural gates and alleys of the body,
And with a sudden vigor it doth posset
And curd, like eager droppings into milk,
70 The thin and wholesome blood. So did it mine,
And a most instant tetter barked about
Most lazarlike with vile and loathsome crust
All my smooth body.
Thus was I, sleeping, by a brother's hand
75 Of life, of crown, of queen at once dispatched,
Cut off even in the blossoms of my sin,
Unhouseled, disappointed, unaneled,
No reck'ning made, but sent to my account
With all my imperfections on my head.
80 O, horrible! O, horrible! Most horrible!
If thou hast nature in thee, bear it not.
Let not the royal bed of Denmark be
A couch for luxury and damnèd incest.
But howsomever thou pursuest this act,
85 Taint not thy mind, nor let thy soul contrive

54 **lewdness** lust 61 **secure** unsuspecting 62 **hebona** a poisonous plant 68 **posset** curdle 69 **eager** acid 71 **tetter** scab 72 **lazarlike** leperlike 77 **Unhouseled, disappointed, unaneled** without the sacrament of communion, unabsolved, without extreme unction 83 **luxury** lust

Against thy mother aught. Leave her to heaven
And to those thorns that in her bosom lodge
To prick and sting her. Fare thee well at once.
The glowworm shows the matin to be near
And 'gins to pale his uneffectual fire. 90
Adieu, adieu, adieu. Remember me. *Exit.*

HAMLET O all you host of heaven! O earth! What else?
And shall I couple hell? O fie! Hold, hold, my heart,
And you, my sinews, grow not instant old,
But bear me stiffly up. Remember thee? 95
Ay, thou poor ghost, whiles memory holds a seat
In this distracted globe. Remember thee?
Yea, from the table of my memory
I'll wipe away all trivial fond records,
All saws of books, all forms, all pressures past 100
That youth and observation copied there,
And thy commandment all alone shall live
Within the book and volume of my brain,
Unmixed with baser matter. Yes, by heaven!
O most pernicious woman! 105
O villain, villain, smiling, damnèd villain!
My tables—meet it is I set it down
That one may smile, and smile, and be a villain.
At least I am sure it may be so in Denmark. [*Writes.*]
So, uncle, there you are. Now to my word: 110
It is "Adieu, adieu, remember me."
I have sworn't.

HORATIO AND MARCELLUS (*Within*) My lord, my lord!

Enter Horatio and Marcellus.

MARCELLUS Lord Hamlet!

HORATIO Heavens secure him!

HAMLET So be it!

MARCELLUS Illo, ho, ho, my lord! 115

HAMLET Hillo, ho, ho, boy! Come, bird, come.

89 matin morning **97 globe** i.e., his head **98 table** tablet, notebook **99 fond** foolish **100 saws** maxims **100 pressures** impressions **115 Illo, ho, ho** (falconer's call to his hawk)

MARCELLUS How is't, my noble lord?
HORATIO What news, my lord?
HAMLET O, wonderful!
HORATIO Good my lord, tell it.
HAMLET No, you will reveal it.
HORATIO Not I, my lord, by heaven.
120 MARCELLUS Nor I, my lord.
HAMLET How say you then? Would heart of man once think it?
But you'll be secret?
BOTH Ay, by heaven, my lord.
HAMLET There's never a villain dwelling in all Denmark
But he's an arrant knave.
HORATIO There needs no ghost, my lord, come from the
125 grave
To tell us this.
HAMLET Why, right, you are in the right;
And so, without more circumstance at all,
I hold it fit that we shake hands and part:
You, as your business and desire shall point you,
130 For every man hath business and desire
Such as it is, and for my own poor part,
Look you, I'll go pray.
HORATIO These are but wild and whirling words, my lord.
HAMLET I am sorry they offend you, heartily;
Yes, faith, heartily.
135 HORATIO There's no offense, my lord.
HAMLET Yes, by Saint Patrick, but there is, Horatio,
And much offense too. Touching this vision here,
It is an honest ghost, that let me tell you.
For your desire to know what is between us,
140 O'ermaster't as you may. And now, good friends,

127 circumstance details 138 honest ghost i.e., not a demon in his father's shape

As you are friends, scholars, and soldiers,
Give me one poor request.

HORATIO What is't, my lord? We will.

HAMLET Never make known what you have seen tonight.

BOTH My lord, we will not.

HAMLET Nay, but swear't.

HORATIO In faith, 145
My lord, not I.

MARCELLUS Nor I, my lord—in faith.

HAMLET Upon my sword.

MARCELLUS We have sworn, my lord, already.

HAMLET Indeed, upon my sword, indeed.

Ghost cries under the stage.

GHOST Swear.

HAMLET Ha, ha, boy, say'st thou so? Art thou there, truepenny? 150
Come on. You hear this fellow in the cellarage.
Consent to swear.

HORATIO Propose the oath, my lord.

HAMLET Never to speak of this that you have seen.
Swear by my sword.

GHOST [*Beneath*] Swear. 155

HAMLET *Hic et ubique?* Then we'll shift our ground;
Come hither, gentlemen,
And lay your hands again upon my sword.
Swear by my sword
Never to speak of this that you have heard. 160

GHOST [*Beneath*] Swear by his sword.

HAMLET Well said, old mole! Canst work i' th' earth so fast?
A worthy pioner! Once more remove, good friends.

150 truepenny honest fellow 156 Hic et ubique here and everywhere (Latin)
163 pioner digger of mines

HORATIO O day and night, but this is wondrous strange!

165 HAMLET And therefore as a stranger give it welcome.
There are more things in heaven and earth, Horatio,
Than are dreamt of in your philosophy.
But come:
Here as before, never, so help you mercy,
170 How strange or odd some'er I bear myself
(As I perchance hereafter shall think meet
To put an antic disposition on),
That you, at such times seeing me, never shall
With arms encumb'red thus, or this headshake,
175 Or by pronouncing of some doubtful phrase,
As "Well, well, we know," or "We could, an if we would,"
Or "If we list to speak," or "There be, an if they might,"
Or such ambiguous giving out, to note
That you know aught of me—this do swear,
180 So grace and mercy at your most need help you.

GHOST [*Beneath*] Swear. [*They swear.*]

HAMLET Rest, rest, perturbèd spirit. So, gentlemen,
With all my love I do commend me to you,
And what so poor a man as Hamlet is
185 May do t' express his love and friending to you,
God willing, shall not lack. Let us go in together,
And still your fingers on your lips, I pray.
The time is out of joint. O cursèd spite,
That ever I was born to set it right!
190 Nay, come, let's go together. *Exeunt.*

172 antic disposition fantastic behavior **174 encumb'red** folded **183 commend me** entrust myself

ACT II

Scene I. [*A room.*]

Enter old Polonius, with his man Reynaldo.

POLONIUS Give him this money and these notes, Reynaldo.

REYNALDO I will, my lord.

POLONIUS You shall do marvell's wisely, good Reynaldo,
Before you visit him, to make inquire
Of his behavior.

REYNALDO My lord, I did intend it. 5

POLONIUS Marry, well said, very well said. Look you sir,
Inquire me first what Danskers are in Paris,
And how, and who, what means, and where they keep,
What company, at what expense; and finding
By this encompassment and drift of question 10
That they do know my son, come you more nearer
Than your particular demands will touch it.
Take you as 'twere some distant knowledge of him,
As thus, "I know his father and his friends,
And in part him." Do you mark this, Reynaldo? 15

REYNALDO Ay, very well, my lord.

II.i.3 marvell's marvelous(ly) **7 Danskers** Danes **8 keep** dwell **10 encompassment** circling **12 demands** questions

POLONIUS "And in part him, but," you may say, "not well,
But if't be he I mean, he's very wild,
Addicted so and so." And there put on him
20 What forgeries you please; marry, none so rank
As may dishonor him—take heed of that—
But, sir, such wanton, wild, and usual slips
As are companions noted and most known
To youth and liberty.

REYNALDO As gaming, my lord.

POLONIUS Ay, or drinking, fencing, swearing, quarrel-
25 ing,
Drabbing. You may go so far.

REYNALDO My lord, that would dishonor him.

POLONIUS Faith, no, as you may season it in the charge.
You must not put another scandal on him,
30 That he is open to incontinency.
That's not my meaning. But breathe his faults so quaintly
That they may seem the taints of liberty,
The flash and outbreak of a fiery mind,
A savageness in unreclaimèd blood,
Of general assault.

35 REYNALDO But, my good lord——

POLONIUS Wherefore should you do this?

REYNALDO Ay, my lord,
I would know that.

POLONIUS Marry, sir, here's my drift,
And I believe it is a fetch of warrant.
You laying these slight sullies on my son
40 As 'twere a thing a little soiled i' th' working,
Mark you,
Your party in converse, him you would sound,

20 **forgeries** inventions 26 **Drabbing** wenching 30 **incontinency** habitual licentiousness 31 **quaintly** ingeniously, delicately 35 **Of general assault** common to all men 38 **fetch of warrant** justifiable device

Having ever seen in the prenominate crimes
The youth you breathe of guilty, be assured
He closes with you in this consequence: 45
"Good sir," or so, or "friend," or "gentleman"—
According to the phrase or the addition
Of man and country—

REYNALDO Very good, my lord.

POLONIUS And then, sir, does 'a this—'a does—
What was I about to say? By the mass, I was about 50
to say something! Where did I leave?

REYNALDO At "closes in the consequence," at "friend
or so," and "gentleman."

POLONIUS At "closes in the consequence"—Ay, marry!
He closes thus: "I know the gentleman; 55
I saw him yesterday, or t'other day,
Or then, or then, with such or such, and, as you say,
There was 'a gaming, there o'ertook in's rouse,
There falling out at tennis"; or perchance,
"I saw him enter such a house of sale," 60
Videlicet, a brothel, or so forth.
See you now—
Your bait of falsehood take this carp of truth,
And thus do we of wisdom and of reach,
With windlasses and with assays of bias, 65
By indirections find directions out.
So, by my former lecture and advice,
Shall you my son. You have me, have you not?

REYNALDO My lord, I have.

POLONIUS God bye ye, fare ye well.

REYNALDO Good my lord. 70

POLONIUS Observe his inclination in yourself.

43 Having ... crimes if he has ever seen in the aforementioned crimes 45 He closes ... this consequence he falls in with you in this conclusion 47 addition title 49 'a he 61 Videlicet namely 64 reach far-reaching awareness(?) 65 windlasses circuitous courses 65 assays of bias indirect attempts (metaphor from bowling; bias = curved course) 71 in yourself for yourself

REYNALDO I shall, my lord.

POLONIUS And let him ply his music.

REYNALDO Well, my lord.

POLONIUS Farewell. *Exit Reynaldo.*

Enter Ophelia.

How now, Ophelia, what's the matter?

75 OPHELIA O my lord, my lord, I have been so affrighted!

POLONIUS With what, i' th' name of God?

OPHELIA My lord, as I was sewing in my closet,
Lord Hamlet, with his doublet all unbraced,
No hat upon his head, his stockings fouled,
80 Ungartered, and down-gyvèd to his ankle,
Pale as his shirt, his knees knocking each other,
And with a look so piteous in purport,
As if he had been loosèd out of hell
To speak of horrors—he comes before me.

POLONIUS Mad for thy love?

85 OPHELIA My lord, I do not know,
But truly I do fear it.

POLONIUS What said he?

OPHELIA He took me by the wrist and held me hard;
Then goes he to the length of all his arm,
And with his other hand thus o'er his brow
90 He falls to such perusal of my face
As 'a would draw it. Long stayed he so.
At last, a little shaking of mine arm,
And thrice his head thus waving up and down,
He raised a sigh so piteous and profound
95 As it did seem to shatter all his bulk
And end his being. That done, he lets me go,
And, with his head over his shoulder turned,
He seemed to find his way without his eyes,

77 **closet** private room 78 **doublet all unbraced** jacket entirely unlaced
80 **down-gyvèd** hanging down like fetters 82 **purport** expression

For out o' doors he went without their helps,
And to the last bended their light on me. 100

POLONIUS Come, go with me. I will go seek the King.
This is the very ecstasy of love,
Whose violent property fordoes itself
And leads the will to desperate undertakings
As oft as any passions under heaven 105
That does afflict our natures. I am sorry.
What, have you given him any hard words of late?

OPHELIA No, my good lord; but as you did command,
I did repel his letters and denied
His access to me.

POLONIUS That hath made him mad. 110
I am sorry that with better heed and judgment
I had not quoted him. I feared he did but trifle
And meant to wrack thee; but beshrew my jealousy.
By heaven, it is as proper to our age
To cast beyond ourselves in our opinions 115
As it is common for the younger sort
To lack discretion. Come, go we to the King.
This must be known, which, being kept close, might
move
More grief to hide than hate to utter love.
Come. *Exeunt.* 120

102 ecstasy madness **103 property fordoes** quality destroys **112 quoted** noted **113 beshrew my jealousy** curse on my suspicions **114 proper** natural **115 To cast beyond ourselves** to be over-calculating **117–19 Come, go . . . utter love** (the general meaning is that while telling the King of Hamlet's love may anger the King, more grief would come from keeping it secret)

Scene II. [*The castle.*]

Flourish. Enter King and Queen, Rosencrantz, and Guildenstern [*with others*].

KING Welcome, dear Rosencrantz and Guildenstern.
Moreover that we much did long to see you,
The need we have to use you did provoke
Our hasty sending. Something have you heard
5 Of Hamlet's transformation: so call it,
Sith nor th' exterior nor the inward man
Resembles that it was. What it should be,
More than his father's death, that thus hath put him
So much from th' understanding of himself,
10 I cannot dream of. I entreat you both
That, being of so young days brought up with him,
And sith so neighbored to his youth and havior,
That you vouchsafe your rest here in our court
Some little time, so by your companies
15 To draw him on to pleasures, and to gather
So much as from occasion you may glean,
Whether aught to us unknown afflicts him thus,
That opened lies within our remedy.

QUEEN Good gentlemen, he hath much talked of you,
20 And sure I am, two men there is not living
To whom he more adheres. If it will please you
To show us so much gentry and good will
As to expend your time with us awhile
For the supply and profit of our hope,
25 Your visitation shall receive such thanks
As fits a king's remembrance.

ROSENCRANTZ Both your Majesties

II.ii.2 **Moreover that** beside the fact that 6 **Sith** since 11 **of so** from such 12 **youth and havior** behavior in his youth 13 **vouchsafe your rest** consent to remain 18 **opened** revealed 22 **gentry** courtesy

Might, by the sovereign power you have of us,
Put your dread pleasures more into command
Than to entreaty.

GUILDENSTERN But we both obey,
And here give up ourselves in the full bent 30
To lay our service freely at your feet,
To be commanded.

KING Thanks, Rosencrantz and gentle Guildenstern.

QUEEN Thanks, Guildenstern and gentle Rosencrantz.
And I beseech you instantly to visit 35
My too much changèd son. Go, some of you,
And bring these gentlemen where Hamlet is.

GUILDENSTERN Heavens make our presence and our practices
Pleasant and helpful to him!

QUEEN Ay, amen!

Exeunt Rosencrantz and Guildenstern [*with some Attendants*].

Enter Polonius.

POLONIUS Th' ambassadors from Norway, my good lord, 40
Are joyfully returned.

KING Thou still hast been the father of good news.

POLONIUS Have I, my lord? Assure you, my good liege,
I hold my duty, as I hold my soul,
Both to my God and to my gracious king; 45
And I do think, or else this brain of mine
Hunts not the trail of policy so sure
As it hath used to do, that I have found
The very cause of Hamlet's lunacy.

KING O, speak of that! That do I long to hear. 50

POLONIUS Give first admittance to th' ambassadors.
My news shall be the fruit to that great feast.

30 in the full bent entirely (the figure is of a bow bent to its capacity) **42 still** always **47 Hunts not . . . so sure** does not follow clues of political doings with such sureness

KING Thyself do grace to them and bring them in.
[*Exit Polonius.*]
He tells me, my dear Gertrude, he hath found
55 The head and source of all your son's distemper.

QUEEN I doubt it is no other but the main,
His father's death and our o'erhasty marriage.

KING Well, we shall sift him.

Enter Polonius, Voltemand, and Cornelius.

Welcome, my good friends.
Say, Voltemand, what from our brother Norway?

60 VOLTEMAND Most fair return of greetings and desires.
Upon our first, he sent out to suppress
His nephew's levies, which to him appeared
To be a preparation 'gainst the Polack;
But better looked into, he truly found
65 It was against your Highness, whereat grieved,
That so his sickness, age, and impotence
Was falsely borne in hand, sends out arrests
On Fortinbras; which he, in brief, obeys,
Receives rebuke from Norway, and in fine,
70 Makes vow before his uncle never more
To give th' assay of arms against your Majesty.
Whereon old Norway, overcome with joy,
Gives him threescore thousand crowns in annual fee
And his commission to employ those soldiers,
75 So levied as before, against the Polack,
With an entreaty, herein further shown,
[*Gives a paper.*]
That it might please you to give quiet pass
Through your dominions for this enterprise,
On such regards of safety and allowance
As therein are set down.

80 KING It likes us well;
And at our more considered time we'll read,
Answer, and think upon this business.

56 **doubt** suspect 56 **main** principal point 61 **first** first audience 67 **borne in hand** deceived 69 **in fine** finally 71 **assay** trial 79 **regards of safety and allowance** i.e., conditions 81 **considered time** time proper for considering

Meantime, we thank you for your well-took labor.
Go to your rest; at night we'll feast together.
Most welcome home! *Exeunt Ambassadors.*

POLONIUS This business is well ended. 85
My liege and madam, to expostulate
What majesty should be, what duty is,
Why day is day, night night, and time is time,
Were nothing but to waste night, day, and time.
Therefore, since brevity is the soul of wit, 90
And tediousness the limbs and outward flourishes,
I will be brief. Your noble son is mad.
Mad call I it, for, to define true madness,
What is't but to be nothing else but mad?
But let that go.

QUEEN More matter, with less art. 95

POLONIUS Madam, I swear I use no art at all.
That he's mad, 'tis true: 'tis true 'tis pity,
And pity 'tis 'tis true—a foolish figure.
But farewell it, for I will use no art.
Mad let us grant him then; and now remains 100
That we find out the cause of this effect,
Or rather say, the cause of this defect,
For this effect defective comes by cause.
Thus it remains, and the remainder thus.
Perpend. 105
I have a daughter: have, while she is mine,
Who in her duty and obedience, mark,
Hath given me this. Now gather, and surmise.
[*Reads*] *the letter.*
"To the celestial, and my soul's idol, the most beautified Ophelia"— 110
That's an ill phrase, a vile phrase; "beautified" is a vile phrase. But you shall hear. Thus:
"In her excellent white bosom, these, &c."

QUEEN Came this from Hamlet to her?

POLONIUS Good madam, stay awhile. I will be faithful. 115

86 expostulate discuss **90 wit** wisdom, understanding **98 figure** figure of rhetoric **105 Perpend** consider carefully

"Doubt thou the stars are fire,
Doubt that the sun doth move;
Doubt truth to be a liar,
But never doubt I love.

120 O dear Ophelia, I am ill at these numbers. I have not art to reckon my groans; but that I love thee best, O most best, believe it. Adieu.

Thine evermore, most dear lady, whilst this machine is to him, HAMLET."

125 This in obedience hath my daughter shown me,
And more above hath his solicitings,
As they fell out by time, by means, and place,
All given to mine ear.

KING But how hath she
Received his love?

POLONIUS What do you think of me?

130 KING As of a man faithful and honorable.

POLONIUS I would fain prove so. But what might you think,
When I had seen this hot love on the wing
(As I perceived it, I must tell you that,
Before my daughter told me), what might you,
135 Or my dear Majesty your Queen here, think,
If I had played the desk or table book,
Or given my heart a winking, mute and dumb,
Or looked upon this love with idle sight?
What might you think? No, I went round to work
140 And my young mistress thus I did bespeak:
"Lord Hamlet is a prince, out of thy star.
This must not be." And then I prescripts gave her,
That she should lock herself from his resort,
Admit no messengers, receive no tokens.
145 Which done, she took the fruits of my advice,
And he, repellèd, a short tale to make,

118 **Doubt** suspect 120 **ill at these numbers** unskilled in verses 124 **machine** complex device (here, his body) 126 **more above** in addition 136 **played the desk or table book** i.e., been a passive recipient of secrets 137 **winking** closing of the eyes 141 **star** sphere

Fell into a sadness, then into a fast,
Thence to a watch, thence into a weakness,
Thence to a lightness, and, by this declension,
Into the madness wherein now he raves, 150
And all we mourn for.

KING Do you think 'tis this?

QUEEN It may be, very like.

POLONIUS Hath there been such a time, I would fain know that,
That I have positively said " 'Tis so,"
When it proved otherwise?

KING Not that I know. 155

POLONIUS [*Pointing to this head and shoulder*] Take this from this, if this be otherwise.
If circumstances lead me, I will find
Where truth is hid, though it were hid indeed
Within the center.

KING How may we try it further?

POLONIUS You know sometimes he walks four hours together
Here in the lobby. 160

QUEEN So he does indeed.

POLONIUS At such a time I'll loose my daughter to him.
Be you and I behind an arras then.
Mark the encounter. If he love her not,
And be not from his reason fall'n thereon, 165
Let me be no assistant for a state
But keep a farm and carters.

KING We will try it.

Enter Hamlet reading on a book.

QUEEN But look where sadly the poor wretch comes reading.

POLONIUS Away, I do beseech you both, away.

Exit King and Queen.

148 watch wakefulness 149 lightness mental derangement 159 center center of the earth 163 arras tapestry hanging in front of a wall

170 I'll board him presently. O, give me leave.
How does my good Lord Hamlet?

HAMLET Well, God-a-mercy.

POLONIUS Do you know me, my lord?

HAMLET Excellent well. You are a fishmonger.

175 POLONIUS Not I, my lord.

HAMLET Then I would you were so honest a man.

POLONIUS Honest, my lord?

HAMLET Ay, sir. To be honest, as this world goes, is to be one man picked out of ten thousand.

180 POLONIUS That's very true, my lord.

HAMLET For if the sun breed maggots in a dead dog, being a good kissing carrion—— Have you a daughter?

POLONIUS I have, my lord.

185 HAMLET Let her not walk i' th' sun. Conception is a blessing, but as your daughter may conceive, friend, look to't.

POLONIUS [*Aside*] How say you by that? Still harping on my daughter. Yet he knew me not at first. 'A
190 said I was a fishmonger. 'A is far gone, far gone. And truly in my youth I suffered much extremity for love, very near this. I'll speak to him again.— What do you read, my lord?

HAMLET Words, words, words.

195 POLONIUS What is the matter, my lord?

HAMLET Between who?

POLONIUS I mean the matter that you read, my lord.

170 **board him presently** accost him at once 174 **fishmonger** dealer in fish (slang for a procurer) 182 **a good kissing carrion** (perhaps the meaning is "a good piece of flesh to kiss," but many editors emend **good** to **god**, taking the word to refer to the sun) 185 **Conception** (1) understanding (2) becoming pregnant 197 **matter** (Polonius means "subject matter," but Hamlet pretends to take the word in the sense of "quarrel")

HAMLET Slanders, sir; for the satirical rogue says here that old men have gray beards, that their faces are wrinkled, their eyes purging thick amber and plum-tree gum, and that they have a plentiful lack of wit, together with most weak hams. All which, sir, though I most powerfully and potently believe, yet I hold it not honesty to have it thus set down; for you yourself, sir, should be old as I am if, like a crab, you could go backward. 200 205

POLONIUS [*Aside*] Though this be madness, yet there is method in't. Will you walk out of the air, my lord?

HAMLET Into my grave.

POLONIUS Indeed, that's out of the air. [*Aside*] How pregnant sometimes his replies are! A happiness that often madness hits on, which reason and sanity could not so prosperously be delivered of. I will leave him and suddenly contrive the means of meeting between him and my daughter.—My lord, I will take my leave of you. 210 215

HAMLET You cannot take from me anything that I will more willingly part withal—except my life, except my life, except my life.

Enter Guildenstern and Rosencrantz.

POLONIUS Fare you well, my lord. 220

HAMLET These tedious old fools!

POLONIUS You go to seek the Lord Hamlet? There he is.

ROSENCRANTZ [*To Polonius*] God save you, sir!

[*Exit Polonius.*]

GUILDENSTERN My honored lord! 225

ROSENCRANTZ My most dear lord!

HAMLET My excellent good friends! How dost thou, Guildenstern? Ah, Rosencrantz! Good lads, how do you both?

204 honesty decency **211 pregnant** meaningful **211 happiness** apt turn of phrase

230 ROSENCRANTZ As the indifferent children of the earth.

GUILDENSTERN Happy in that we are not overhappy.
On Fortune's cap we are not the very button.

HAMLET Nor the soles of her shoe?

ROSENCRANTZ Neither, my lord.

235 HAMLET Then you live about her waist, or in the middle of her favors?

GUILDENSTERN Faith, her privates we.

HAMLET In the secret parts of Fortune? O, most true! She is a strumpet. What news?

240 ROSENCRANTZ None, my lord, but that the world's grown honest.

HAMLET Then is doomsday near. But your news is not true. Let me question more in particular. What have you, my good friends, deserved at the hands of
245 Fortune that she sends you to prison hither?

GUILDENSTERN Prison, my lord?

HAMLET Denmark's a prison.

ROSENCRANTZ Then is the world one.

HAMLET A goodly one, in which there are many
250 confines, wards, and dungeons, Denmark being one o' th' worst.

ROSENCRANTZ We think not so, my lord.

HAMLET Why, then 'tis none to you, for there is nothing either good or bad but thinking makes it so. To
255 me it is a prison.

ROSENCRANTZ Why then your ambition makes it one. 'Tis too narrow for your mind.

HAMLET O God, I could be bounded in a nutshell and count myself a king of infinite space, were it not
260 that I have bad dreams.

GUILDENSTERN Which dreams indeed are ambition, for

230 **indifferent** ordinary 237 **privates** ordinary men (with a pun on "private parts") 250 **wards** cells

the very substance of the ambitious is merely the shadow of a dream.

HAMLET A dream itself is but a shadow.

ROSENCRANTZ Truly, and I hold ambition of so airy and light a quality that it is but a shadow's shadow. 265

HAMLET Then are our beggars bodies, and our monarchs and outstretched heroes the beggars' shadows. Shall we to th' court? For, by my fay, I cannot reason. 270

BOTH We'll wait upon you.

HAMLET No such matter. I will not sort you with the rest of my servants, for, to speak to you like an honest man, I am most dreadfully attended. But in the beaten way of friendship, what make you at Elsinore? 275

ROSENCRANTZ To visit you, my lord; no other occasion.

HAMLET Beggar that I am, I am even poor in thanks, but I thank you; and sure, dear friends, my thanks are too dear a halfpenny. Were you not sent for? Is it your own inclining? Is it a free visitation? Come, come, deal justly with me. Come, come; nay, speak. 280

GUILDENSTERN What should we say, my lord?

HAMLET Why anything—but to th' purpose. You were sent for, and there is a kind of confession in your looks, which your modesties have not craft enough to color. I know the good King and Queen have sent for you. 285

ROSENCRANTZ To what end, my lord? 290

HAMLET That you must teach me. But let me conjure you by the rights of our fellowship, by the consonancy of our youth, by the obligation of our ever-

267–69 Then are ... beggars' shadows i.e., by your logic, beggars (lacking ambition) are substantial, and great men are elongated shadows **269 fay** faith **280 too dear a halfpenny** i.e., not worth a halfpenny

preserved love, and by what more dear a better
295 proposer can charge you withal, be even and direct
with me, whether you were sent for or no.

ROSENCRANTZ [*Aside to Guildenstern*] What say you?

HAMLET [*Aside*] Nay then, I have an eye of you.—If you
love me, hold not off.

300 GUILDENSTERN My lord, we were sent for.

HAMLET I will tell you why; so shall my anticipation
prevent your discovery, and your secrecy to the
King and Queen molt no feather. I have of late, but
wherefore I know not, lost all my mirth, forgone all
305 custom of exercises; and indeed, it goes so heavily
with my disposition that this goodly frame, the
earth, seems to me a sterile promontory; this most
excellent canopy, the air, look you, this brave
o'erhanging firmament, this majestical roof fretted
310 with golden fire: why, it appeareth nothing to me
but a foul and pestilent congregation of vapors.
What a piece of work is a man, how noble in reason,
how infinite in faculties, in form and moving how
express and admirable, in action how like an angel,
315 in apprehension how like a god: the beauty of the
world, the paragon of animals; and yet to me, what
is this quintessence of dust? Man delights not me;
nor woman neither, though by your smiling you
seem to say so.

320 ROSENCRANTZ My lord, there was no such stuff in my
thoughts.

HAMLET Why did ye laugh then, when I said "Man
delights not me"?

ROSENCRANTZ To think, my lord, if you delight not in
325 man, what lenten entertainment the players shall
receive from you. We coted them on the way, and
hither are they coming to offer you service.

302 prevent your discovery forestall your disclosure **309 fretted** adorned
314 express exact **325 lenten** meager **326 coted** overtook

HAMLET He that plays the king shall be welcome; his Majesty shall have tribute of me; the adventurous knight shall use his foil and target; the lover shall not sigh gratis; the humorous man shall end his part in peace; the clown shall make those laugh whose lungs are tickle o' th' sere; and the lady shall say her mind freely, or the blank verse shall halt for't. What players are they? 330 335

ROSENCRANTZ Even those you were wont to take such delight in, the tragedians of the city.

HAMLET How chances it they travel? Their residence, both in reputation and profit, was better both ways.

ROSENCRANTZ I think their inhibition comes by the means of the late innovation. 340

HAMLET Do they hold the same estimation they did when I was in the city? Are they so followed?

ROSENCRANTZ No indeed, are they not.

HAMLET How comes it? Do they grow rusty? 345

ROSENCRANTZ Nay, their endeavor keeps in the wonted pace, but there is, sir, an eyrie of children, little eyases, that cry out on the top of question and are most tyrannically clapped for't. These are now the fashion, and so berattle the common stages (so they call them) that many wearing rapiers are afraid of goosequills and dare scarce come thither. 350

HAMLET What, are they children? Who maintains 'em? How are they escoted? Will they pursue the

330 **target** shield 331 **humorous man** i.e., eccentric man (among stock characters in dramas were men dominated by a "humor" or odd trait) 333 **tickle o' th' sere** on hair trigger (sere = part of the gunlock) 334 or else 334 **halt** limp 340 **inhibition** hindrance 341 **innovation** (probably an allusion to the companies of child actors that had become popular and were offering serious competition to the adult actors) 347 **eyrie** nest 348 **eyases, that . . . of question** unfledged hawks that cry shrilly above others in matters of debate 349 **tyrannically** violently 350 **berattle the common stages** cry down the public theaters (with the adult acting companies) 352 **goosequills** pens (of satirists who ridicule the public theaters and their audiences) 354 **escoted** financially supported

355 quality no longer than they can sing? Will they not say afterwards, if they should grow themselves to common players (as it is most like, if their means are no better), their writers do them wrong to make them exclaim against their own succession?

360 ROSENCRANTZ Faith, there has been much to-do on both sides, and the nation holds it no sin to tarre them to controversy. There was, for a while, no money bid for argument unless the poet and the player went to cuffs in the question.

365 HAMLET Is't possible?

GUILDENSTERN O, there has been much throwing about of brains.

HAMLET Do the boys carry it away?

ROSENCRANTZ Ay, that they do, my lord—Hercules and
370 his load too.

HAMLET It is not very strange, for my uncle is King of Denmark, and those that would make mouths at him while my father lived give twenty, forty, fifty, a hundred ducats apiece for his picture in little.
375 'Sblood, there is something in this more than natural, if philosophy could find it out.

A flourish.

GUILDENSTERN There are the players.

HAMLET Gentlemen, you are welcome to Elsinore. Your hands, come then. Th' appurtenance of wel-
380 come is fashion and ceremony. Let me comply with you in this garb, lest my extent to the players (which I tell you must show fairly outwards) should more appear like entertainment than yours. You are welcome. But my uncle-father and aunt-mother are
385 deceived.

355 **quality** profession of acting 359 **succession** future 361 **tarre** incite 363 **argument** plot of a play 369–70 **Hercules and his load** i.e., the whole world (with a reference to the Globe Theatre, which had a sign that represented Hercules bearing the globe) 375 **'Sblood** by God's blood 380 **comply** be courteous 381 **garb** outward show 381 **extent** behavior

GUILDENSTERN In what, my dear lord?

HAMLET I am but mad north-northwest: when the wind is southerly I know hawk from a handsaw.

Enter Polonius.

POLONIUS Well be with you, gentlemen.

HAMLET Hark you, Guildenstern, and you too; at each ear a hearer. That great baby you see there is not yet out of his swaddling clouts. 390

ROSENCRANTZ Happily he is the second time come to them, for they say an old man is twice a child.

HAMLET I will prophesy he comes to tell me of the players. Mark it.—You say right, sir; a Monday morning, 'twas then indeed. 395

POLONIUS My lord, I have news to tell you.

HAMLET My lord, I have news to tell you. When Roscius was an actor in Rome—— 400

POLONIUS The actors are come hither, my lord.

HAMLET Buzz, buzz.

POLONIUS Upon my honor——

HAMLET Then came each actor on his ass——

POLONIUS The best actors in the world, either for tragedy, comedy, history, pastoral, pastoral-comical, historical-pastoral, tragical-historical, tragical-comical-historical-pastoral; scene individable, or poem unlimited. Seneca cannot be too heavy, nor Plautus too light. For the law of writ and the liberty, these are the only men. 405 410

387 **north-northwest** i.e., on one point of the compass only 388 **hawk from a handsaw** (**hawk** can refer not only to a bird but to a kind of pickax; **handsaw**—a carpenter's tool—may involve a similar pun on "hernshaw," a heron) 393 **Happily** perhaps 400 **Roscius** (a famous Roman comic actor) 402 **Buzz, buzz** (an interjection, perhaps indicating that the news is old) 408 **scene individable** plays observing the unities of time, place, and action 408–09 **poem unlimited** plays not restricted by the tenets of criticism 409 **Seneca** (Roman tragic dramatist) 410 **Plautus** (Roman comic dramatist) 410–11 **For the law of writ and the liberty** (perhaps "for sticking to the text and for improvising"; perhaps "for classical plays and for modern loosely written plays")

HAMLET O Jeptha, judge of Israel, what a treasure hadst thou!

POLONIUS What a treasure had he, my lord?

415 HAMLET Why,

"One fair daughter, and no more,
The which he lovèd passing well."

POLONIUS [*Aside*] Still on my daughter.

HAMLET Am I not i' th' right, old Jeptha?

420 POLONIUS If you call me Jeptha, my lord, I have a daughter that I love passing well.

HAMLET Nay, that follows not.

POLONIUS What follows then, my lord?

HAMLET Why,

425 "As by lot, God wot,"

and then, you know,

"It came to pass, as most like it was."

The first row of the pious chanson will show you more, for look where my abridgment comes.

Enter the Players.

430 You are welcome, masters, welcome, all. I am glad to see thee well. Welcome, good friends. O, old friend, why, thy face is valanced since I saw thee last. Com'st thou to beard me in Denmark? What, my young lady and mistress? By'r Lady, your 435 ladyship is nearer to heaven than when I saw you last by the altitude of a chopine. Pray God your voice, like a piece of uncurrent gold, be not cracked within the ring.—Masters, you are all welcome. We'll e'en to't like French falconers, fly at any-

412 **Jeptha, judge of Israel** (the title of a ballad on the Hebrew judge who sacrificed his daughter; see Judges 11) 428 **row of the pious chanson** stanza of the scriptural song 429 **abridgment** (1) i.e., entertainers, who abridge the time (2) interrupters 432 **valanced** fringed (with a beard) 434 **young lady** i.e., boy for female roles 436 **chopine** thick-soled shoe 437–38 **like a piece . . . the ring** (a coin was unfit for legal tender if a crack extended from the edge through the ring enclosing the monarch's head. Hamlet, punning on ring, refers to the change of voice that the boy actor will undergo)

thing we see. We'll have a speech straight. Come, give us a taste of your quality. Come, a passionate speech. 440

PLAYER What speech, my good lord?

HAMLET I heard thee speak me a speech once, but it was never acted, or if it was, not above once, for the play, I remember, pleased not the million; 'twas caviary to the general, but it was (as I received it, and others, whose judgments in such matters cried in the top of mine) an excellent play, well digested in the scenes, set down with as much modesty as cunning. I remember one said there were no sallets in the lines to make the matter savory; nor no matter in the phrase that might indict the author of affectation, but called it an honest method, as wholesome as sweet, and by very much more handsome than fine. One speech is't I chiefly loved. 'Twas Aeneas' tale to Dido, and thereabout of it especially when he speaks of Priam's slaughter. If it live in your memory, begin at this line—let me see, let me see: 445 450 455 460

"The rugged Pyrrhus, like th' Hyrcanian
beast——"

'Tis not so; it begins with Pyrrhus:

"The rugged Pyrrhus, he whose sable arms,
Black as his purpose, did the night resemble
When he lay couchèd in th' ominous horse, 465
Hath now this dread and black complexion
smeared
With heraldry more dismal. Head to foot
Now is he total gules, horridly tricked
With blood of fathers, mothers, daughters, sons,
Baked and impasted with the parching streets, 470

447 **caviary to the general** i.e., too choice for the multitude 449 **in the top of** overtopping 450–51 **modesty as cunning** restraint as art 452 **sallets** salads, spicy jests 455–56 **more handsome than fine** well-proportioned rather than ornamented 461 **Hyrcanian beast** i.e., tiger (Hyrcania was in Asia) 463 **sable** black 465 **ominous horse** i.e., wooden horse at the siege of Troy 467 **dismal** ill-omened 468 **total gules, horridly tricked** all red, horridly adorned 470 **impasted** encrusted

That lend a tyrannous and a damnèd light
To their lord's murder. Roasted in wrath and fire,
And thus o'ersizèd with coagulate gore,
With eyes like carbuncles, the hellish Pyrrhus
475 Old grandsire Priam seeks."
So, proceed you.

POLONIUS Fore God, my lord, well spoken, with good accent and good discretion.

PLAYER "Anon he finds him,
480 Striking too short at Greeks. His antique sword,
Rebellious to his arm, lies where it falls,
Repugnant to command. Unequal matched,
Pyrrhus at Priam drives, in rage strikes wide,
But with the whiff and wind of his fell sword
485 Th' unnervèd father falls. Then senseless Ilium,
Seeming to feel this blow, with flaming top
Stoops to his base, and with a hideous crash
Takes prisoner Pyrrhus' ear. For lo, his sword,
Which was declining on the milky head
490 Of reverend Priam, seemed i' th' air to stick.
So as a painted tyrant Pyrrhus stood,
And like a neutral to his will and matter
Did nothing.
But as we often see, against some storm,
495 A silence in the heavens, the rack stand still,
The bold winds speechless, and the orb below
As hush as death, anon the dreadful thunder
Doth rend the region, so after Pyrrhus' pause,
A rousèd vengeance sets him new awork,
500 And never did the Cyclops' hammers fall
On Mars's armor, forged for proof eterne,
With less remorse than Pyrrhus' bleeding sword
Now falls on Priam.
Out, out, thou strumpet Fortune! All you gods,
505 In general synod take away her power,

473 **o'ersizèd** smeared over 482 **Repugnant to command** disobedient 485 **senseless Ilium** insensate Troy 487 **Stoops to his base** collapses (his = its) 491 **painted tyrant** tyrant in a picture 492 **matter** task 494 **against** just before 495 **rack** clouds 501 **proof eterne** eternal endurance 505 **synod** council

Break all the spokes and fellies from her wheel,
And bowl the round nave down the hill of heaven,
As low as to the fiends."

POLONIUS This is too long.

HAMLET It shall to the barber's with your beard.— 510
Prithee say on. He's for a jig or a tale of bawdry, or he sleeps. Say on; come to Hecuba.

PLAYER "But who (ah woe!) had seen the mobled queen——"

HAMLET "The mobled queen"?

POLONIUS That's good. "Mobled queen" is good. 515

PLAYER "Run barefoot up and down, threat'ning the flames
With bisson rheum; a clout upon that head
Where late the diadem stood, and for a robe,
About her lank and all o'erteemèd loins,
A blanket in the alarm of fear caught up— 520
Who this had seen, with tongue in venom steeped
'Gainst Fortune's state would treason have pronounced.
But if the gods themselves did see her then,
When she saw Pyrrhus make malicious sport
In mincing with his sword her husband's limbs, 525
The instant burst of clamor that she made
(Unless things mortal move them not at all)
Would have made milch the burning eyes of heaven
And passion in the gods."

POLONIUS Look, whe'r he has not turned his color, 530
and has tears in's eyes. Prithee no more.

HAMLET 'Tis well. I'll have thee speak out the rest of this soon. Good my lord, will you see the players well bestowed? Do you hear? Let them be well

506 fellies rims **507 nave** hub **513 mobled** muffled **517 bisson rheum** blinding tears **517 clout** rag **519 o'erteemèd** exhausted with childbearing **528 milch** moist (literally, "milk-giving") **530 whe'r** whether **534 bestowed** housed

535 used, for they are the abstract and brief chronicles of the time. After your death you were better have a bad epitaph than their ill report while you live.

POLONIUS My lord, I will use them according to their desert.

540 HAMLET God's bodkin, man, much better! Use every man after his desert, and who shall scape whipping? Use them after your own honor and dignity. The less they deserve, the more merit is in your bounty. Take them in.

545 POLONIUS Come, sirs.

HAMLET Follow him, friends. We'll hear a play tomorrow. [*Aside to Player*] Dost thou hear me, old friend? Can you play *The Murder of Gonzago*?

PLAYER Ay, my lord.

550 HAMLET We'll ha't tomorrow night. You could for a need study a speech of some dozen or sixteen lines which I would set down and insert in't, could you not?

PLAYER Ay, my lord.

555 HAMLET Very well. Follow that lord, and look you mock him not. My good friends, I'll leave you till night. You are welcome to Elsinore.

Exeunt Polonius and Players.

ROSENCRANTZ Good my lord.

Exeunt [*Rosencrantz and Guildenstern*].

HAMLET Ay, so, God bye to you.—Now I am alone.
560 O, what a rogue and peasant slave am I!
Is it not monstrous that this player here,
But in a fiction, in a dream of passion,
Could force his soul so to his own conceit
That from her working all his visage wanned,
565 Tears in his eyes, distraction in his aspect,
A broken voice, and his whole function suiting

540 God's bodkin by God's little body **562 dream of passion** imaginary emotion **563 conceit** imagination **566 function** action

With forms to his conceit? And all for nothing!
For Hecuba!
What's Hecuba to him, or he to Hecuba,
That he should weep for her? What would he do 570
Had he the motive and the cue for passion
That I have? He would drown the stage with tears
And cleave the general ear with horrid speech,
Make mad the guilty and appall the free,
Confound the ignorant, and amaze indeed 575
The very faculties of eyes and ears.
Yet I,
A dull and muddy-mettled rascal, peak
Like John-a-dreams, unpregnant of my cause,
And can say nothing. No, not for a king, 580
Upon whose property and most dear life
A damned defeat was made. Am I a coward?
Who calls me villain? Breaks my pate across?
Plucks off my beard and blows it in my face?
Tweaks me by the nose? Gives me the lie i' th' throat 585
As deep as to the lungs? Who does me this?
Ha, 'swounds, I should take it, for it cannot be
But I am pigeon-livered and lack gall
To make oppression bitter, or ere this
I should ha' fatted all the region kites 590
With this slave's offal. Bloody, bawdy villain!
Remorseless, treacherous, lecherous, kindless villain!
O, vengeance!
Why, what an ass am I! This is most brave,
That I, the son of a dear father murdered, 595
Prompted to my revenge by heaven and hell,
Must, like a whore, unpack my heart with words
And fall a-cursing like a very drab,

567 **forms** bodily expressions 574 **appall the free** terrify (make pale?) the guiltless 578 **muddy-mettled** weak-spirited 578–79 **peak/Like John-a-dreams** mope like a dreamer 579 **unpregnant of** unquickened by 587 **'swounds** by God's wounds 588 **pigeon-livered** gentle as a dove 590 **region kites** kites (scavenger birds) of the sky 592 **kindless** unnatural 594 **brave** fine 598 **drab** prostitute

A stallion! Fie upon't, foh! About, my brains.
600 Hum——
I have heard that guilty creatures sitting at a play
Have by the very cunning of the scene
Been struck so to the soul that presently
They have proclaimed their malefactions.
605 For murder, though it have no tongue, will speak
With most miraculous organ. I'll have these players
Play something like the murder of my father
Before mine uncle. I'll observe his looks,
I'll tent him to the quick. If 'a do blench,
610 I know my course. The spirit that I have seen
May be a devil, and the devil hath power
T' assume a pleasing shape, yea, and perhaps
Out of my weakness and my melancholy,
As he is very potent with such spirits,
615 Abuses me to damn me. I'll have grounds
More relative than this. The play's the thing
Wherein I'll catch the conscience of the King. *Exit.*

599 **stallion** male prostitute (perhaps one should adopt the Folio reading, **scullion** = kitchen wench) 599 **About** to work 603 **presently** immediately 609 **tent** probe 609 **blench** flinch 616 **relative** (probably "pertinent," but possibly "able to be related plausibly")

ACT III

Scene I. [*The castle.*]

Enter King, Queen, Polonius, Ophelia, Rosencrantz, Guildenstern, Lords.

KING And can you by no drift of conference
Get from him why he puts on this confusion,
Grating so harshly all his days of quiet
With turbulent and dangerous lunacy?

ROSENCRANTZ He does confess he feels himself distracted, 5
But from what cause 'a will by no means speak.

GUILDENSTERN Nor do we find him forward to be sounded,
But with a crafty madness keeps aloof
When we would bring him on to some confession
Of his true state.

QUEEN Did he receive you well? 10

ROSENCRANTZ Most like a gentleman.

GUILDENSTERN But with much forcing of his disposition.

ROSENCRANTZ Niggard of question, but of our demands
Most free in his reply.

III.i.1 drift of conference management of conversation **7 forward to be sounded** willing to be questioned **12 forcing of his disposition** effort **13 Niggard of question** uninclined to talk

QUEEN Did you assay him
15 To any pastime?

ROSENCRANTZ Madam, it so fell out that certain players
We o'erraught on the way; of these we told him,
And there did seem in him a kind of joy
To hear of it. They are here about the court,
20 And, as I think, they have already order
This night to play before him.

POLONIUS 'Tis most true,
And he beseeched me to entreat your Majesties
To hear and see the matter.

KING With all my heart, and it doth much content me
25 To hear him so inclined.
Good gentlemen, give him a further edge
And drive his purpose into these delights.

ROSENCRANTZ We shall, my lord.

Exeunt Rosencrantz and Guildenstern.

KING Sweet Gertrude, leave us too,
For we have closely sent for Hamlet hither,
30 That he, as 'twere by accident, may here
Affront Ophelia.
Her father and myself (lawful espials)
Will so bestow ourselves that, seeing unseen,
We may of their encounter frankly judge
35 And gather by him, as he is behaved,
If't be th' affliction of his love or no
That thus he suffers for.

QUEEN I shall obey you.
And for your part, Ophelia, I do wish
That your good beauties be the happy cause
40 Of Hamlet's wildness. So shall I hope your virtues
Will bring him to his wonted way again,
To both your honors.

OPHELIA Madam, I wish it may.

[*Exit Queen.*]

14 assay tempt **17 o'erraught** overtook **29 closely** secretly **31 Affront** meet face to face **32 espials** spies

POLONIUS Ophelia, walk you here.—Gracious, so please you,
We will bestow ourselves. [*To Ophelia*] Read on this book,
That show of such an exercise may color 45
Your loneliness. We are oft to blame in this,
'Tis too much proved, that with devotion's visage
And pious action we do sugar o'er
The devil himself.

KING [*Aside*] O, 'tis too true.
How smart a lash that speech doth give my conscience! 50
The harlot's cheek, beautied with plast'ring art,
Is not more ugly to the thing that helps it
Than is my deed to my most painted word.
O heavy burden!

POLONIUS I hear him coming. Let's withdraw, my lord. 55
[*Exeunt King and Polonius.*]

Enter Hamlet.

HAMLET To be, or not to be: that is the question:
Whether 'tis nobler in the mind to suffer
The slings and arrows of outrageous fortune,
Or to take arms against a sea of troubles,
And by opposing end them. To die, to sleep— 60
No more—and by a sleep to say we end
The heartache, and the thousand natural shocks
That flesh is heir to! 'Tis a consummation
Devoutly to be wished. To die, to sleep—
To sleep—perchance to dream: ay, there's the rub, 65
For in that sleep of death what dreams may come
When we have shuffled off this mortal coil,
Must give us pause. There's the respect
That makes calamity of so long life:
For who would bear the whips and scorns of time, 70

45 **exercise may color** act of devotion may give a plausible hue to (the book is one of devotion) 65 **rub** impediment (obstruction to a bowler's ball) 67 **coil** (1) turmoil (2) a ring of rope (here the flesh encircling the soul) 68 **respect** consideration 69 **makes calamity of so long life** (1) makes calamity so long-lived (2) makes living so long a calamity

Th'oppressor's wrong, the proud man's contumely,
The pangs of despised love, the law's delay,
The insolence of office, and the spurns
That patient merit of th' unworthy takes,
75 When he himself might his quietus make
With a bare bodkin? Who would fardels bear,
To grunt and sweat under a weary life,
But that the dread of something after death,
The undiscovered country, from whose bourn
80 No traveler returns, puzzles the will,
And makes us rather bear those ills we have,
Than fly to others that we know not of?
Thus conscience does make cowards of us all,
And thus the native hue of resolution
85 Is sicklied o'er with the pale cast of thought,
And enterprises of great pitch and moment,
With this regard their currents turn awry,
And lose the name of action.—Soft you now,
The fair Ophelia!—Nymph, in thy orisons
Be all my sins remembered.

90 OPHELIA Good my lord,
How does your honor for this many a day?

HAMLET I humbly thank you; well, well, well.

OPHELIA My lord, I have remembrances of yours
That I have longèd long to redeliver.
I pray you now, receive them.

95 HAMLET No, not I,
I never gave you aught.

OPHELIA My honored lord, you know right well you did,
And with them words of so sweet breath composed
As made these things more rich. Their perfume lost,
100 Take these again, for to the noble mind

75 **quietus** full discharge (a legal term) 76 **bodkin** dagger 76 **fardels** burdens 79 **bourn** region 83 **conscience** self-consciousness, introspection 85 **cast** color 86 **pitch** height (a term from falconry) 87 **regard** consideration 89 **orisons** prayers

Rich gifts wax poor when givers prove unkind.
There, my lord.

HAMLET Ha, ha! Are you honest?

OPHELIA My lord?

HAMLET Are you fair? 105

OPHELIA What means your lordship?

HAMLET That if you be honest and fair, your honesty should admit no discourse to your beauty.

OPHELIA Could beauty, my lord, have better commerce than with honesty? 110

HAMLET Ay, truly; for the power of beauty will sooner transform honesty from what it is to a bawd than the force of honesty can translate beauty into his likeness. This was sometime a paradox, but now the time gives it proof. I did love you once. 115

OPHELIA Indeed, my lord, you made me believe so.

HAMLET You should not have believed me, for virtue cannot so inoculate our old stock but we shall relish of it. I loved you not.

OPHELIA I was the more deceived. 120

HAMLET Get thee to a nunnery. Why wouldst thou be a breeder of sinners? I am myself indifferent honest, but yet I could accuse me of such things that it were better my mother had not borne me: I am very proud, revengeful, ambitious, with more offenses at 125 my beck than I have thoughts to put them in, imagination to give them shape, or time to act them in. What should such fellows as I do crawling between earth and heaven? We are arrant knaves all; believe none of us. Go thy ways to a nunnery. 130 Where's your father?

103 **Are you honest** (1) are you modest (2) are you chaste (3) have you integrity 107–08 **your honesty . . . to your beauty** your modesty should permit no approach to your beauty 112 **bawd** procurer 118 **inoculate** graft 118–19 **relish of it** smack of it (our old sinful nature) 122 **indifferent honest** moderately virtuous 126 **beck** call

OPHELIA At home, my lord.

HAMLET Let the doors be shut upon him, that he may play the fool nowhere but in's own house. Farewell.

135 OPHELIA O help him, you sweet heavens!

HAMLET If thou dost marry, I'll give thee this plague for thy dowry: be thou as chaste as ice, as pure as snow, thou shalt not escape calumny. Get thee to a nunnery. Go, farewell. Or if thou wilt needs marry,
140 marry a fool, for wise men know well enough what monsters you make of them. To a nunnery, go, and quickly too. Farewell.

OPHELIA Heavenly powers, restore him!

HAMLET I have heard of your paintings, well enough.
145 God hath given you one face, and you make yourselves another. You jig and amble, and you lisp; you nickname God's creatures and make your wantonness your ignorance. Go to, I'll no more on't; it hath made me mad. I say we will have no
150 moe marriage. Those that are married already—all but one—shall live. The rest shall keep as they are. To a nunnery, go. *Exit.*

OPHELIA O what a noble mind is here o'erthrown!
The courtier's, soldier's, scholar's, eye, tongue, sword,
155 Th' expectancy and rose of the fair state,
The glass of fashion, and the mold of form,
Th' observed of all observers, quite, quite down!
And I, of ladies most deject and wretched,
That sucked the honey of his musicked vows,
160 Now see that noble and most sovereign reason
Like sweet bells jangled, out of time and harsh,
That unmatched form and feature of blown youth
Blasted with ecstasy. O, woe is me
T' have seen what I have seen, see what I see!

Enter King and Polonius.

141 monsters horned beasts, cuckolds **147–48 make your wantonness your ignorance** excuse your wanton speech by pretending ignorance **150 moe** more **155 expectancy and rose** i.e., fair hope **156 The glass . . . of form** the mirror of fashion, and the pattern of excellent behavior **162 blown** blooming **163 ecstasy** madness

KING Love? His affections do not that way tend, 165
Nor what he spake, though it lacked form a little,
Was not like madness. There's something in his soul
O'er which his melancholy sits on brood,
And I do doubt the hatch and the disclose
Will be some danger; which for to prevent, 170
I have in quick determination
Thus set it down: he shall with speed to England
For the demand of our neglected tribute.
Haply the seas, and the countries different,
With variable objects, shall expel 175
This something-settled matter in his heart,
Whereon his brains still beating puts him thus
From fashion of himself. What think you on't?

POLONIUS It shall do well. But yet do I believe
The origin and commencement of his grief 180
Sprung from neglected love. How now, Ophelia?
You need not tell us what Lord Hamlet said;
We heard it all. My lord, do as you please,
But if you hold it fit, after the play,
Let his queen mother all alone entreat him 185
To show his grief. Let her be round with him,
And I'll be placed, so please you, in the ear
Of all their conference. If she find him not,
To England send him, or confine him where
Your wisdom best shall think.

KING It shall be so. 190
Madness in great ones must not unwatched go.

Exeunt.

165 affections inclinations 169 doubt fear 176 something-settled somewhat settled 186 round blunt 188 find him not does not find him out

Scene II. [*The castle.*]

Enter Hamlet and three of the Players.

HAMLET Speak the speech, I pray you, as I pronounced it to you, trippingly on the tongue. But if you mouth it, as many of our players do, I had as lief the town crier spoke my lines. Nor do not saw the air too much
5 with your hand, thus, but use all gently, for in the very torrent, tempest, and (as I may say) whirlwind of your passion, you must acquire and beget a temperance that may give it smoothness. O, it offends me to the soul to hear a robustious periwig-pated
10 fellow tear a passion to tatters, to very rags, to split the ears of the goundlings, who for the most part are capable of nothing but inexplicable dumb shows and noise. I would have such a fellow whipped for o'erdoing Termagant. It out-herods
15 Herod. Pray you avoid it.

PLAYER I warrant your honor.

HAMLET Be not too tame neither, but let your own discretion be your tutor. Suit the action to the word, the word to the action, with this special observance, that
20 you o'erstep not the modesty of nature. For anything so o'erdone is from the purpose of playing, whose end, both at the first and now, was and is, to hold, as 'twere, the mirror up to nature; to show virtue her own feature, scorn her own image, and the very
25 age and body of the time his form and pressure.

III.ii.9 **robustious periwig-pated** boisterous wig-headed 11 **groundlings** those who stood in the pit of the theater (the poorest and presumably most ignorant of the audience) 12 **are capable of** are able to understand 12–13 **dumb shows** (it had been the fashion for actors to preface plays or parts of plays with silent mime) 14–15 **Termagant ... Herod** (boisterous characters in the old mystery plays) 21 **from** contrary to 25 **pressure** image, impress

Now, this overdone, or come tardy off, though it makes the unskillful laugh, cannot but make the judicious grieve, the censure of the which one must in your allowance o'erweigh a whole theater of others. O, there be players that I have seen play, 30 and heard others praise, and that highly (not to speak it profanely), that neither having th' accent of Christians, nor the gait of Christian, pagan, nor man, have so strutted and bellowed that I have thought some of Nature's journeymen had made 35 men, and not made them well, they imitated humanity so abominably.

PLAYER I hope we have reformed that indifferently with us, sir.

HAMLET O, reform it altogether! And let those that 40 play your clowns speak no more than is set down for them, for there be of them that will themselves laugh, to set on some quantity of barren spectators to laugh too, though in the meantime some necessary question of the play be then to be considered. That's 45 villainous and shows a most pitiful ambition in the fool that uses it. Go make you ready.

Exit Players.

Enter Polonius, Guildenstern, and Rosencrantz.

How now, my lord? Will the King hear this piece of work?

POLONIUS And the Queen too, and that presently. 50

HAMLET Bid the players make haste. *Exit Polonius.*
Will you two help to hasten them?

ROSENCRANTZ Ay, my lord. *Exeunt they two.*

HAMLET What, ho, Horatio!

Enter Horatio.

HORATIO Here, sweet lord, at your service. 55

HAMLET Horatio, thou art e'en as just a man

35 journeymen workers not yet masters of their craft 38 indifferently tolerably

As e'er my conversation coped withal.

HORATIO O, my dear lord——

HAMLET Nay, do not think I flatter.
For what advancement may I hope from thee,
60 That no revenue hast but thy good spirits
To feed and clothe thee? Why should the poor be flattered?
No, let the candied tongue lick absurd pomp,
And crook the pregnant hinges of the knee
Where thrift may follow fawning. Dost thou hear?
65 Since my dear soul was mistress of her choice
And could of men distinguish her election,
S' hath sealed thee for herself, for thou hast been
As one, in suff'ring all, that suffers nothing,
A man that Fortune's buffets and rewards
70 Hast ta'en with equal thanks; and blest are those
Whose blood and judgment are so well commeddled
That they are not a pipe for Fortune's finger
To sound what stop she please. Give me that man
That is not passion's slave, and I will wear him
75 In my heart's core, ay, in my heart of heart,
As I do thee. Something too much of this—
There is a play tonight before the King.
One scene of it comes near the circumstance
Which I have told thee, of my father's death.
80 I prithee, when thou seest that act afoot,
Even with the very comment of thy soul
Observe my uncle. If his occulted guilt
Do not itself unkennel in one speech,
It is a damnèd ghost that we have seen,
85 And my imaginations are as foul
As Vulcan's stithy. Give him heedful note,
For I mine eyes will rivet to his face,

57 **coped withal** met with 59 **advancement** promotion 62 **candied** sugared, flattering 63 **pregnant** (1) pliant (2) full of promise of good fortune 64 **thrift** profit 67 **S' hath sealed thee** she (the soul) has set a mark on you 71 **blood** passion 71 **commeddled** blended 81 **very comment** deepest wisdom 82 **occulted** hidden 86 **stithy** forge, smithy

And after we will both our judgments join
In censure of his seeming.

HORATIO Well, my lord.
If 'a steal aught the whilst this play is playing, 90
And scape detecting, I will pay the theft.

Enter Trumpets and Kettledrums, King, Queen, Polonius, Ophelia, Rosencrantz, Guildenstern, and other Lords attendant with his Guard carrying torches. Danish March. Sound a Flourish.

HAMLET They are coming to the play: I must be idle;
Get you a place.

KING How fares our cousin Hamlet?

HAMLET Excellent, i' faith, of the chameleon's dish; 95
I eat the air, promise-crammed; you cannot feed capons so.

KING I have nothing with this answer, Hamlet; these words are not mine.

HAMLET No, nor mine now. [*To Polonius*] My lord, you 100
played once i' th' university, you say?

POLONIUS That did I, my lord, and was accounted a good actor.

HAMLET What did you enact?

POLONIUS I did enact Julius Caesar. I was killed i' th' 105
Capitol; Brutus killed me.

HAMLET It was a brute part of him to kill so capital a calf there. Be the players ready?

ROSENCRANTZ Ay, my lord. They stay upon your patience. 110

QUEEN Come hither, my dear Hamlet, sit by me.

HAMLET No, good mother. Here's metal more attractive.

89 censure of his seeming judgment on his looks **92 be idle** play the fool **95 the chameleon's dish** air (on which chameleons were thought to live) **112–13 attractive** magnetic

POLONIUS [*To the King*] O ho! Do you mark that?

115 HAMLET Lady, shall I lie in your lap?

[*He lies at Ophelia's feet.*]

OPHELIA No, my lord.

HAMLET I mean, my head upon your lap?

OPHELIA Ay, my lord.

HAMLET Do you think I meant country matters?

120 OPHELIA I think nothing, my lord.

HAMLET That's a fair thought to lie between maids' legs.

OPHELIA What is, my lord?

HAMLET Nothing.

125 OPHELIA You are merry, my lord.

HAMLET Who, I?

OPHELIA Ay, my lord.

HAMLET O God, your only jig-maker! What should a man do but be merry? For look you how cheerfully
130 my mother looks, and my father died within's two hours.

OPHELIA Nay, 'tis twice two months, my lord.

HAMLET So long? Nay then, let the devil wear black, for I'll have a suit of sables. O heavens! Die two
135 months ago, and not forgotten yet? Then there's hope a great man's memory may outlive his life half a year. But, by'r Lady, 'a must build churches then, or else shall 'a suffer not thinking on, with the hobby-horse, whose epitaph is "For O, for O, the hobby-
140 horse is forgot!"

The trumpets sound. Dumb show follows:

119 **country matters** rustic doings (with a pun on the vulgar word for the pudendum) 128 **jig-maker** composer of songs and dances (often a Fool, who performed them) 134 **sables** (pun on "black" and "luxurious furs") 138–39 **hobbyhorse** mock horse worn by a performer in the morris dance

Enter a King and a Queen very lovingly, the Queen embracing him, and he her. She kneels; and makes show of protestation unto him. He takes her up, and declines his head upon her neck. He lies him down upon a bank of flowers. She, seeing him asleep, leaves him. Anon come in another man: takes off his crown, kisses it, pours poison in the sleeper's ears, and leaves him. The Queen returns, finds the King dead, makes passionate action. The poisoner, with some three or four, come in again, seem to condole with her. The dead body is carried away. The poisoner woos the Queen with gifts; she seems harsh awhile, but in the end accepts love.

Exeunt.

OPHELIA What means this, my lord?

HAMLET Marry, this is miching mallecho; it means mischief.

OPHELIA Belike this show imports the argument of the play. 145

Enter Prologue.

HAMLET We shall know by this fellow. The players cannot keep counsel; they'll tell all.

OPHELIA Will 'a tell us what this show meant?

HAMLET Ay, or any show that you will show him. Be not you ashamed to show, he'll not shame to tell you 150
what it means.

OPHELIA You are naught, you are naught; I'll mark the play.

PROLOGUE For us, and for our tragedy,
Here stooping to your clemency, 155
We beg your hearing patiently. [*Exit.*]

HAMLET Is this a prologue, or the posy of a ring?

OPHELIA 'Tis brief, my lord.

HAMLET As woman's love.

142 miching mallecho sneaking mischief **144 argument** plot **152 naught** wicked, improper **157 posy of a ring** motto inscribed in a ring

Enter [two Players as] King and Queen.

PLAYER KING Full thirty times hath Phoebus' cart gone
160 round
Neptune's salt wash and Tellus' orbèd ground,
And thirty dozen moons with borrowed sheen
About the world have times twelve thirties been,
Since love our hearts, and Hymen did our hands,
165 Unite commutual in most sacred bands.

PLAYER QUEEN So many journeys may the sun and
moon
Make us again count o'er ere love be done!
But woe is me, you are so sick of late,
So far from cheer and from your former state,
170 That I distrust you. Yet, though I distrust,
Discomfort you, my lord, it nothing must.
For women fear too much, even as they love,
And women's fear and love hold quantity,
In neither aught, or in extremity.
175 Now what my love is, proof hath made you know,
And as my love is sized, my fear is so.
Where love is great, the littlest doubts are fear;
Where little fears grow great, great love grows there.

PLAYER KING Faith, I must leave thee, love, and shortly
too;
180 My operant powers their functions leave to do:
And thou shalt live in this fair world behind,
Honored, beloved, and haply one as kind
For husband shalt thou——

PLAYER QUEEN O, confound the rest!
Such love must needs be treason in my breast.
185 In second husband let me be accurst!
None wed the second but who killed the first.

160 **Phoebus' cart** the sun's chariot 161 **Neptune's salt wash** the sea 161 **Tellus** Roman goddess of the earth 170 **distrust** am anxious about 173–74 **And women's . . . in extremity** (perhaps the idea is that women's anxiety is great or little in proportion to their love. The previous line, unrhymed, may be a false start that Shakespeare neglected to delete) 175 **proof** experience 180 **operant** active

HAMLET [*Aside*.] That's wormwood.

PLAYER QUEEN The instances that second marriage move
Are base respects of thrift, but none of love.
A second time I kill my husband dead 190
When second husband kisses me in bed.

PLAYER KING I do believe you think what now you speak,
But what we do determine oft we break.
Purpose is but the slave to memory,
Of violent birth, but poor validity, 195
Which now like fruit unripe sticks on the tree,
But fall unshaken when they mellow be.
Most necessary 'tis that we forget
To pay ourselves what to ourselves is debt.
What to ourselves in passion we propose, 200
The passion ending, doth the purpose lose.
The violence of either grief or joy
Their own enactures with themselves destroy:
Where joy most revels, grief doth most lament;
Grief joys, joy grieves, on slender accident. 205
This world is not for aye, nor 'tis not strange
That even our loves should with our fortunes change,
For 'tis a question left us yet to prove,
Whether love lead fortune, or else fortune love.
The great man down, you mark his favorite flies; 210
The poor advanced makes friends of enemies;
And hitherto doth love on fortune tend,
For who not needs shall never lack a friend;
And who in want a hollow friend doth try,
Directly seasons him his enemy. 215
But, orderly to end where I begun,
Our wills and fates do so contrary run
That our devices still are overthrown;
Our thoughts are ours, their ends none of our own.

187 **wormwood** a bitter herb 188 **instances** motives 188 **move** induce 189 **respects of thrift** considerations of profit 195 **validity** strength 203 **enactures** acts 215 **seasons him** ripens him into

220 So think thou wilt no second husband wed,
But die thy thoughts when thy first lord is dead.

PLAYER QUEEN Nor earth to me give food, nor heaven light,
Sport and repose lock from me day and night,
To desperation turn my trust and hope,
225 An anchor's cheer in prison be my scope,
Each opposite that blanks the face of joy
Meet what I would have well, and it destroy:
Both here and hence pursue me lasting strife,
If, once a widow, ever I be wife!

230 HAMLET If she should break it now!

PLAYER KING 'Tis deeply sworn. Sweet, leave me here awhile;
My spirits grow dull, and fain I would beguile
The tedious day with sleep.

PLAYER QUEEN Sleep rock thy brain,
[*He*] *sleeps.*
And never come mischance between us twain! *Exit.*

235 HAMLET Madam, how like you this play?

QUEEN The lady doth protest too much, methinks.

HAMLET O, but she'll keep her word.

KING Have you heard the argument? Is there no offense in't?

240 HAMLET No, no, they do but jest, poison in jest; no offense i' th' world.

KING What do you call the play?

HAMLET *The Mousetrap*. Marry, how? Tropically. This play is the image of a murder done in Vienna:
245 Gonzago is the Duke's name; his wife, Baptista. You shall see anon. 'Tis a knavish piece of work, but what of that? Your Majesty, and we that have free

225 anchor's anchorite's, hermit's **226 opposite that blanks** adverse thing that blanches **238 argument** plot **243 Tropically** figuratively (with a pun on "trap") **247 free** innocent

souls, it touches us not. Let the galled jade winch; our withers are unwrung.

Enter Lucianus.

This is one Lucianus, nephew to the King. 250

OPHELIA You are as good as a chorus, my lord.

HAMLET I could interpret between you and your love, if I could see the puppets dallying.

OPHELIA You are keen, my lord, you are keen.

HAMLET It would cost you a groaning to take off mine edge. 255

OPHELIA Still better, and worse.

HAMLET So you mistake your husbands.—Begin, murderer. Leave thy damnable faces and begin. Come, the croaking raven doth bellow for revenge. 260

LUCIANUS Thoughts black, hands apt, drugs fit, and time agreeing,
Confederate season, else no creature seeing,
Thou mixture rank, of midnight weeds collected,
With Hecate's ban thrice blasted, thrice infected,
Thy natural magic and dire property 265
On wholesome life usurps immediately.

Pours the poison in his ears.

HAMLET 'A poisons him i' th' garden for his estate. His name's Gonzago. The story is extant, and written in very choice Italian. You shall see anon how the murderer gets the love of Gonzago's wife. 270

OPHELIA The King rises.

HAMLET What, frighted with false fire?

QUEEN How fares my lord?

POLONIUS Give o'er the play.

248 galled jade winch chafed horse wince 252 interpret (like a showman explaining the action of puppets) 254 keen (1) sharp (2) sexually aroused 258 mistake err in taking 262 Confederate season the opportunity allied with me 264 Hecate's ban the curse of the goddess of sorcery 265 property nature 272 false fire blank discharge of firearms

275 KING Give me some light. Away!

POLONIUS Lights, lights, lights!

Exeunt all but Hamlet and Horatio.

HAMLET Why, let the strucken deer go weep,
The hart ungallèd play:
For some must watch, while some must sleep;
280 Thus runs the world away.
Would not this, sir, and a forest of feathers—if the rest of my fortunes turn Turk with me—with two Provincial roses on my razed shoes, get me a fellowship in a cry of players?

285 HORATIO Half a share.

HAMLET A whole one, I.
For thou dost know, O Damon dear,
This realm dismantled was
Of Jove himself; and now reigns here
290 A very, very—pajock.

HORATIO You might have rhymed.

HAMLET O good Horatio, I'll take the ghost's word for a thousand pound. Didst perceive?

HORATIO Very well, my lord.

295 HAMLET Upon the talk of poisoning?

HORATIO I did very well note him.

HAMLET Ah ha! Come, some music! Come, the recorders!
For if the King like not the comedy,
300 Why then, belike he likes it not, perdy.
Come, some music!

Enter Rosencrantz and Guildenstern.

GUILDENSTERN Good my lord, vouchsafe me a word with you.

281 **feathers** (plumes were sometimes part of a costume) 282 **turn Turk** i.e., go bad, treat me badly 283 **Provincial roses** rosettes like the roses of Provence (?) 283 **razed** ornamented with slashes 284 **cry** pack, company 290 **pajock** peacock 291 **You might have rhymed** i.e., rhymed "was" with "ass" 297–98 **recorders** flutelike instruments 300 **perdy** by God (French: **par dieu**)

HAMLET Sir, a whole history.

GUILDENSTERN The King, sir—— 305

HAMLET Ay, sir, what of him?

GUILDENSTERN Is in his retirement marvelous distemp'red.

HAMLET With drink, sir?

GUILDENSTERN No, my lord, with choler. 310

HAMLET Your wisdom should show itself more richer to signify this to the doctor, for for me to put him to his purgation would perhaps plunge him into more choler.

GUILDENSTERN Good my lord, put your discourse into 315 some frame, and start not so wildly from my affair.

HAMLET I am tame, sir; pronounce.

GUILDENSTERN The Queen, your mother, in most great affliction of spirit hath sent me to you.

HAMLET You are welcome. 320

GUILDENSTERN Nay, good my lord, this courtesy is not of the right breed. If it shall please you to make me a wholesome answer, I will do your mother's commandment; if not, your pardon and my return shall be the end of my business. 325

HAMLET Sir, I cannot.

ROSENCRANTZ What, my lord?

HAMLET Make you a wholesome answer; my wit's diseased. But, sir, such answer as I can make, you shall command, or rather, as you say, my mother. 330 Therefore no more, but to the matter. My mother, you say——

ROSENCRANTZ Then thus she says: your behavior hath struck her into amazement and admiration.

310 choler anger (but Hamlet pretends to take the word in its sense of "biliousness") 316 frame order, control 328 wholesome sane 334 admiration wonder

335 HAMLET O wonderful son, that can so stonish a mother! But is there no sequel at the heels of this mother's admiration? Impart.

ROSENCRANTZ She desires to speak with you in her closet ere you go to bed.

340 HAMLET We shall obey, were she ten times our mother. Have you any further trade with us?

ROSENCRANTZ My lord, you once did love me.

HAMLET And do still, by these pickers and stealers.

ROSENCRANTZ Good my lord, what is your cause of dis-
345 temper? You do surely bar the door upon your own liberty, if you deny your griefs to your friend.

HAMLET Sir, I lack advancement.

ROSENCRANTZ How can that be, when you have the voice of the King himself for your succession in
350 Denmark?

Enter the Players with recorders.

HAMLET Ay, sir, but "while the grass grows"—the proverb is something musty. O, the recorders. Let me see one. To withdraw with you—why do you go about to recover the wind of me as if you would
355 drive me into a toil?

GUILDENSTERN O my lord, if my duty be too bold, my love is too unmannerly.

HAMLET I do not well understand that. Will you play upon this pipe?

360 GUILDENSTERN My lord, I cannot.

HAMLET I pray you.

GUILDENSTERN Believe me, I cannot.

343 **pickers and stealers** i.e., hands (with reference to the prayer: "Keep my hands from picking and stealing") 347 **advancement** promotion 352 **proverb** ("While the grass groweth, the horse starveth") 353 **withdraw** speak in private 354 **recover the wind** get on the windward side (as in hunting) 355 **toil** snare 356–57 **if my duty . . . too unmannerly** i.e., if these questions seem rude, it is because my love for you leads me beyond good manners.

HAMLET I do beseech you.

GUILDENSTERN I know no touch of it, my lord.

HAMLET It is as easy as lying. Govern these ventages with your fingers and thumb, give it breath with your mouth, and it will discourse most eloquent music. Look you, these are the stops. 365

GUILDENSTERN But these cannot I command to any utt'rance of harmony; I have not the skill. 370

HAMLET Why, look you now, how unworthy a thing you make of me! You would play upon me; you would seem to know my stops; you would pluck out the heart of my mystery; you would sound me from my lowest note to the top of my compass; and there is much music, excellent voice, in this little organ, yet cannot you make it speak. 'Sblood, do you think I am easier to be played on than a pipe? Call me what instrument you will, though you can fret me, you cannot play upon me. 375 380

Enter Polonius.

God bless you, sir!

POLONIUS My lord, the Queen would speak with you, and presently.

HAMLET Do you see yonder cloud that's almost in shape of a camel? 385

POLONIUS By th' mass and 'tis, like a camel indeed.

HAMLET Methinks it is like a weasel.

POLONIUS It is backed like a weasel.

HAMLET Or like a whale.

POLONIUS Very like a whale. 390

HAMLET Then I will come to my mother by and by.

365 **ventages** vents, stops on a recorder 375 **compass** range of voice 377 **organ** i.e., the recorder 380 **fret** vex (with a pun alluding to the frets, or ridges, that guide the fingering on some instruments)

[*Aside*] They fool me to the top of my bent.—I will come by and by.

POLONIUS I will say so. *Exit.*

395 HAMLET "By and by" is easily said. Leave me, friends.
[*Exeunt all but Hamlet.*]
'Tis now the very witching time of night,
When churchyards yawn, and hell itself breathes out
Contagion to this world. Now could I drink hot blood
And do such bitter business as the day
400 Would quake to look on. Soft, now to my mother.
O heart, lose not thy nature; let not ever
The soul of Nero enter this firm bosom.
Let me be cruel, not unnatural;
I will speak daggers to her, but use none.
405 My tongue and soul in this be hypocrites:
How in my words somever she be shent,
To give them seals never, my soul, consent! *Exit.*

[Scene III. *The castle*]

Enter King, Rosencrantz, and Guildenstern.

KING I like him not, nor stands it safe with us
To let his madness range. Therefore prepare you.
I your commission will forthwith dispatch,
And he to England shall along with you.
5 The terms of our estate may not endure
Hazard so near's as doth hourly grow
Out of his brows.

GUILDENSTERN We will ourselves provide.

392 They fool ... my bent they compel me to play the fool to the limit of my capacity **393 by and by** very soon **402 Nero** (Roman emperor who had his mother murdered) **406 shent** rebuked **407 give them seals** confirm them with deeds **III.iii.5 terms** conditions **6 near's** near us

Most holy and religious fear it is
To keep those many many bodies safe
That live and feed upon your Majesty. 10

ROSENCRANTZ The single and peculiar life is bound
With all the strength and armor of the mind
To keep itself from noyance, but much more
That spirit upon whose weal depends and rests
The lives of many. The cess of majesty 15
Dies not alone, but like a gulf doth draw
What's near it with it; or it is a massy wheel
Fixed on the summit of the highest mount,
To whose huge spokes ten thousand lesser things
Are mortised and adjoined, which when it falls, 20
Each small annexment, petty consequence,
Attends the boist'rous ruin. Never alone
Did the King sigh, but with a general groan.

KING Arm you, I pray you, to this speedy voyage,
For we will fetters put about this fear, 25
Which now goes too free-footed.

ROSENCRANTZ We will haste us.

Exeunt Gentlemen.

Enter Polonius.

POLONIUS My lord, he's going to his mother's closet.
Behind the arras I'll convey myself
To hear the process. I'll warrant she'll tax him home,
And, as you said, and wisely was it said, 30
'Tis meet that some more audience than a mother,
Since nature makes them partial, should o'erhear
The speech of vantage. Fare you well, my liege.
I'll call upon you ere you go to bed
And tell you what I know.

KING Thanks, dear my lord. 35

Exit [Polonius].

11 **peculiar** individual, private 13 **noyance** injury 15 **cess of majesty** cessation (death) of a king 16 **gulf** whirlpool 22 **Attends** waits on, participates in 24 **Arm** prepare 27 **closet** private room 29 **process** proceedings 29 **tax him home** censure him sharply 33 **of vantage** from an advantageous place

O, my offense is rank, it smells to heaven;
It hath the primal eldest curse upon't,
A brother's murder. Pray can I not,
Though inclination be as sharp as will.
40 My stronger guilt defeats my strong intent,
And like a man to double business bound
I stand in pause where I shall first begin,
And both neglect. What if this cursèd hand
Were thicker than itself with brother's blood,
45 Is there not rain enough in the sweet heavens
To wash it white as snow? Whereto serves mercy
But to confront the visage of offense?
And what's in prayer but this twofold force,
To be forestallèd ere we come to fall,
50 Or pardoned being down? Then I'll look up.
My fault is past. But, O, what form of prayer
Can serve my turn? "Forgive me my foul murder"?
That cannot be, since I am still possessed
Of those effects for which I did the murder,
55 My crown, mine own ambition, and my queen.
May one be pardoned and retain th' offense?
In the corrupted currents of this world
Offense's gilded hand may shove by justice,
And oft 'tis seen the wicked prize itself
60 Buys out the law. But 'tis not so above.
There is no shuffling; there the action lies
In his true nature, and we ourselves compelled,
Even to the teeth and forehead of our faults,
To give in evidence. What then? What rests?
65 Try what repentance can. What can it not?
Yet what can it when one cannot repent?
O wretched state! O bosom black as death!
O limèd soul, that struggling to be free
Art more engaged! Help, angels! Make assay.
70 Bow, stubborn knees, and, heart with strings of steel,

37 **primal eldest curse** (curse of Cain, who killed Abel) 47 **confront** oppose 54 **effects** things gained 61 **shuffling** trickery 64 **rests** remains 68 **limèd** caught (as with birdlime, a sticky substance spread on boughs to snare birds) 69 **engaged** ensnared 69 **assay** an attempt

Be soft as sinews of the newborn babe.
All may be well. [*He kneels.*]

Enter Hamlet.

HAMLET Now might I do it pat, now 'a is a-praying,
And now I'll do't. And so 'a goes to heaven,
And so am I revenged. That would be scanned. 75
A villain kills my father, and for that
I, his sole son, do this same villain send
To heaven.
Why, this is hire and salary, not revenge.
'A took my father grossly, full of bread, 80
With all his crimes broad blown, as flush as May;
And how his audit stands, who knows save heaven?
But in our circumstance and course of thought,
'Tis heavy with him; and am I then revenged,
To take him in the purging of his soul, 85
When he is fit and seasoned for his passage?
No.
Up, sword, and know thou a more horrid hent.
When he is drunk asleep, or in his rage,
Or in th' incestuous pleasure of his bed, 90
At game a-swearing, or about some act
That has no relish of salvation in't—
Then trip him, that his heels may kick at heaven,
And that his soul may be as damned and black
As hell, whereto it goes. My mother stays. 95
This physic but prolongs thy sickly days. *Exit.*

KING [*Rises*] My words fly up, my thoughts remain below.
Words without thoughts never to heaven go. *Exit.*

75 would be scanned ought to be looked into **80 bread** i.e., worldly gratification **81 crimes broad blown** sins in full bloom **81 flush** vigorous **82 audit** account **88 hent** grasp (here, occasion for seizing) **92 relish** flavor **96 physic** (Claudius' purgation by prayer, as Hamlet thinks in line 85)

Scene IV. [*The Queen's closet.*]

Enter [Queen] Gertrude and Polonius.

POLONIUS 'A will come straight. Look you lay home to him.
Tell him his pranks have been too broad to bear with,
And that your Grace hath screened and stood between
Much heat and him. I'll silence me even here.
5 Pray you be round with him.

HAMLET (*Within*) Mother, Mother, Mother!

QUEEN I'll warrant you; fear me not. Withdraw; I hear him coming. [*Polonius hides behind the arras.*]

Enter Hamlet.

HAMLET Now, Mother, what's the matter?

10 QUEEN Hamlet, thou hast thy father much offended.

HAMLET Mother, you have my father much offended.

QUEEN Come, come, you answer with an idle tongue.

HAMLET Go, go, you question with a wicked tongue.

QUEEN Why, how now, Hamlet?

HAMLET What's the matter now?

QUEEN Have you forgot me?

15 HAMLET No, by the rood, not so!
You are the Queen, your husband's brother's wife,
And, would it were not so, you are my mother.

QUEEN Nay, then I'll set those to you that can speak.

HAMLET Come, come, and sit you down. You shall not budge.

III.iv.1 **lay home** thrust (rebuke) him sharply 2 **broad** unrestrained 12 **idle** foolish 15 **rood** cross

You go not till I set you up a glass 20
Where you may see the inmost part of you!

QUEEN What wilt thou do? Thou wilt not murder me?
Help, ho!

POLONIUS [*Behind*] What, ho! Help!

HAMLET [*Draws*] How now? A rat? Dead for a ducat,
dead! 25
[*Makes a pass through the arras and*] *kills Polonius.*

POLONIUS [*Behind*] O, I am slain!

QUEEN O me, what hast thou done?

HAMLET Nay, I know not. Is it the King?

QUEEN O, what a rash and bloody deed is this!

HAMLET A bloody deed—almost as bad, good Mother,
As kill a king, and marry with his brother. 30

QUEEN As kill a king?

HAMLET Ay, lady, it was my word.
[*Lifts up the arras and sees Polonius.*]
Thou wretched, rash, intruding fool, farewell!
I took thee for thy better. Take thy fortune.
Thou find'st to be too busy in some danger.—
Leave wringing of your hands. Peace, sit you down 35
And let me wring your heart, for so I shall
If it be made of penetrable stuff,
If damnèd custom have not brazed it so
That it be proof and bulwark against sense.

QUEEN What have I done that thou dar'st wag thy
tongue 40
In noise so rude against me?

HAMLET Such an act
That blurs the grace and blush of modesty,
Calls virtue hypocrite, takes off the rose
From the fair forehead of an innocent love,
And sets a blister there, makes marriage vows 45

20 glass mirror **38 brazed** hardened like brass **39 proof** armor **39 sense** feeling **45 sets a blister** brands (as a harlot)

As false as dicers' oaths. O, such a deed
As from the body of contraction plucks
The very soul, and sweet religion makes
A rhapsody of words! Heaven's face does glow
50 O'er this solidity and compound mass
With heated visage, as against the doom
Is thoughtsick at the act.

QUEEN Ay me, what act,
That roars so loud and thunders in the index?

HAMLET Look here upon this picture, and on this,
55 The counterfeit presentment of two brothers.
See what a grace was seated on this brow:
Hyperion's curls, the front of Jove himself,
An eye like Mars, to threaten and command,
A station like the herald Mercury
60 New lighted on a heaven-kissing hill—
A combination and a form indeed
Where every god did seem to set his seal
To give the world assurance of a man.
This was your husband. Look you now what follows.
65 Here is your husband, like a mildewed ear
Blasting his wholesome brother. Have you eyes?
Could you on this fair mountain leave to feed,
And batten on this moor? Ha! Have you eyes?
You cannot call it love, for at your age
70 The heyday in the blood is tame, it's humble,
And waits upon the judgment, and what judgment
Would step from this to this? Sense sure you have,
Else could you not have motion, but sure that sense
Is apoplexed, for madness would not err,
75 Nor sense to ecstasy was ne'er so thralled
But it reserved some quantity of choice

47 **contraction** marriage contract 49 **rhapsody** senseless string 49–52 **Heaven's face . . . the act** i.e., the face of heaven blushes over this earth (compounded of four elements), the face hot, as if Judgment Day were near, and it is thoughtsick at the act 53 **index** prologue 55 **counterfeit presentment** represented image 57 **front** forehead 59 **station** bearing 68 **batten** feed gluttonously 70 **heyday** excitement 72 **Sense** feeling 74 **apoplexed** paralyzed 75 **ecstasy** madness

To serve in such a difference. What devil was't
That thus hath cozened you at hoodman-blind?
Eyes without feeling, feeling without sight,
Ears without hands or eyes, smelling sans all, 80
Or but a sickly part of one true sense
Could not so mope.
O shame, where is thy blush? Rebellious hell,
If thou canst mutine in a matron's bones,
To flaming youth let virtue be as wax 85
And melt in her own fire. Proclaim no shame
When the compulsive ardor gives the charge,
Since frost itself as actively doth burn,
And reason panders will.

QUEEN O Hamlet, speak no more.
Thou turn'st mine eyes into my very soul, 90
And there I see such black and grainèd spots
As will not leave their tinct.

HAMLET Nay, but to live
In the rank sweat of an enseamèd bed,
Stewed in corruption, honeying and making love
Over the nasty sty——

QUEEN O, speak to me no more. 95
These words like daggers enter in my ears.
No more, sweet Hamlet.

HAMLET A murderer and a villain,
A slave that is not twentieth part the tithe
Of your precedent lord, a vice of kings,
A cutpurse of the empire and the rule, 100
That from a shelf the precious diadem stole
And put it in his pocket——

QUEEN No more.

78 cozened you at hoodman-blind cheated you at blindman's buff **80 sans** without **82 mope** be stupid **87 compulsive ardor** compelling passion **89 reason panders will** reason acts as a procurer for desire **91 grainèd** dyed in grain (fast dyed) **92 tinct** color **93 enseamèd** (perhaps "soaked in grease," i.e., sweaty; perhaps "much wrinkled") **98 tithe** tenth part **99 vice** (like the Vice, a fool and mischief-maker in the old morality plays)

Enter Ghost.

HAMLET A king of shreds and patches—
Save me and hover o'er me with your wings,
You heavenly guards! What would your gracious
105 figure?

QUEEN Alas, he's mad.

HAMLET Do you not come your tardy son to chide,
That, lapsed in time and passion, lets go by
Th' important acting of your dread command?
110 O, say!

GHOST Do not forget. This visitation
Is but to whet thy almost blunted purpose.
But look, amazement on thy mother sits.
O, step between her and her fighting soul!
115 Conceit in weakest bodies strongest works.
Speak to her, Hamlet.

HAMLET How is it with you, lady?

QUEEN Alas, how is't with you,
That you do bend your eye on vacancy,
And with th' incorporal air do hold discourse?
120 Forth at your eyes your spirits wildly peep,
And as the sleeping soldiers in th' alarm
Your bedded hair like life in excrements
Start up and stand an end. O gentle son,
Upon the heat and flame of thy distemper
125 Sprinkle cool patience. Whereon do you look?

HAMLET On him, on him! Look you, how pale he glares!
His form and cause conjoined, preaching to stones,
Would make them capable.—Do not look upon me,
Lest with this piteous action you convert
130 My stern effects. Then what I have to do
Will want true color; tears perchance for blood.

QUEEN To whom do you speak this?

115 **Conceit** imagination 119 **incorporal** bodiless 122 **bedded hair** hairs laid flat 122 **excrements** outgrowths (here, the hair) 123 **an end** on end 128 **capable** receptive 129–30 **convert/My stern effects** divert my stern deeds

HAMLET Do you see nothing there?

QUEEN Nothing at all; yet all that is I see.

HAMLET Nor did you nothing hear?

QUEEN No, nothing but ourselves.

HAMLET Why, look you there! Look how it steals away! 135
My father, in his habit as he lived!
Look where he goes even now out at the portal!
Exit Ghost.

QUEEN This is the very coinage of your brain.
This bodiless creation ecstasy
Is very cunning in.

HAMLET Ecstasy? 140
My pulse as yours doth temperately keep time
And makes as healthful music. It is not madness
That I have uttered. Bring me to the test,
And I the matter will reword, which madness
Would gambol from. Mother, for love of grace, 145
Lay not that flattering unction to your soul,
That not your trespass but my madness speaks.
It will but skin and film the ulcerous place
Whiles rank corruption, mining all within,
Infects unseen. Confess yourself to heaven, 150
Repent what's past, avoid what is to come,
And do not spread the compost on the weeds
To make them ranker. Forgive me this my virtue.
For in the fatness of these pursy times
Virtue itself of vice must pardon beg, 155
Yea, curb and woo for leave to do him good.

QUEEN O Hamlet, thou hast cleft my heart in twain.

HAMLET O, throw away the worser part of it,
And live the purer with the other half.
Good night—but go not to my uncle's bed. 160
Assume a virtue, if you have it not.

136 **habit** garment (Q1, though a "bad" quarto, is probably correct in saying that at line 102 the ghost enters "in his nightgown," i.e., dressing gown) 145 **gambol** start away 146 **unction** ointment 149 **mining** undermining 152 **compost** fertilizing substance 154 **pursy** bloated 156 **curb** bow low

That monster custom, who all sense doth eat,
Of habits devil, is angel yet in this,
That to the use of actions fair and good
165 He likewise gives a frock or livery
That aptly is put on. Refrain tonight,
And that shall lend a kind of easiness
To the next abstinence; the next more easy;
For use almost can change the stamp of nature,
170 And either the devil, or throw him out
With wondrous potency. Once more, good night,
And when you are desirous to be blest,
I'll blessing beg of you.—For this same lord,
I do repent; but heaven hath pleased it so,
175 To punish me with this, and this with me,
That I must be their scourge and minister.
I will bestow him and will answer well
The death I gave him. So again, good night.
I must be cruel only to be kind.
180 Thus bad begins, and worse remains behind.
One word more, good lady.

QUEEN What shall I do?

HAMLET Not this, by no means, that I bid you do:
Let the bloat King tempt you again to bed,
Pinch wanton on your cheek, call you his mouse,
185 And let him, for a pair of reechy kisses,
Or paddling in your neck with his damned fingers,
Make you to ravel all this matter out,
That I essentially am not in madness,
But mad in craft. 'Twere good you let him know,
190 For who that's but a queen, fair, sober, wise,
Would from a paddock, from a bat, a gib,
Such dear concernings hide? Who would do so?
No, in despite of sense and secrecy,

164 **use** practice 165 **livery** characteristic garment (punning on "habits" in line 163) 170 **either** (probably a word is missing after **either**; among suggestions are "master," "curb," and "house"; but possibly **either** is a verb meaning "make easier") 176 **their** i.e., the heavens' 177 **bestow** stow, lodge 185 **reechy** foul (literally "smoky") 187 **ravel** unravel, reveal 191 **paddock** toad 191 **gib** tomcat

Unpeg the basket on the house's top,
Let the birds fly, and like the famous ape, 195
To try conclusions, in the basket creep
And break your own neck down.

QUEEN Be thou assured, if words be made of breath,
And breath of life, I have no life to breathe
What thou hast said to me. 200

HAMLET I must to England; you know that?

QUEEN Alack,
I had forgot. 'Tis so concluded on.

HAMLET There's letters sealed, and my two school-
fellows,
Whom I will trust as I will adders fanged,
They bear the mandate; they must sweep my way 205
And marshal me to knavery. Let it work;
For 'tis the sport to have the enginer
Hoist with his own petar, and 't shall go hard
But I will delve one yard below their mines
And blow them at the moon. O, 'tis most sweet 210
When in one line two crafts directly meet.
This man shall set me packing:
I'll lug the guts into the neighbor room.
Mother, good night. Indeed, this counselor
Is now most still, most secret, and most grave, 215
Who was in life a foolish prating knave.
Come, sir, to draw toward an end with you.
Good night, Mother.

[*Exit the Queen. Then*] *exit Hamlet, tugging in Polonius.*

196 To try conclusions to make experiments **205 mandate** command **208 petar** bomb **211 crafts** (1) boats (2) acts of guile, crafty schemes

ACT IV

Scene I. [*The castle.*]

Enter King and Queen, with Rosencrantz and Guildenstern.

KING There's matter in these sighs. These profound heaves
You must translate; 'tis fit we understand them.
Where is your son?

QUEEN Bestow this place on us a little while.
[*Exeunt Rosencrantz and Guildenstern*]

5 Ah, mine own lord, what have I seen tonight!

KING What, Gertrude? How does Hamlet?

QUEEN Mad as the sea and wind when both contend
Which is the mightier. In his lawless fit,
Behind the arras hearing something stir,
10 Whips out his rapier, cries, "A rat, a rat!"
And in this brainish apprehension kills
The unseen good old man.

KING O heavy deed!
It had been so with us, had we been there.
His liberty is full of threats to all,
15 To you yourself, to us, to every one.
Alas, how shall this bloody deed be answered?
It will be laid to us, whose providence

IV.i.11 brainish apprehension mad imagination **17 providence** foresight

Should have kept short, restrained, and out of haunt
This mad young man. But so much was our love
We would not understand what was most fit, 20
But, like the owner of a foul disease,
To keep it from divulging, let it feed
Even on the pith of life. Where is he gone?

QUEEN To draw apart the body he hath killed;
O'er whom his very madness, like some ore 25
Among a mineral of metals base,
Shows itself pure. 'A weeps for what is done.

KING O Gertrude, come away!
The sun no sooner shall the mountains touch
But we will ship him hence, and this vile deed 30
We must with all our majesty and skill
Both countenance and excuse. Ho, Guildenstern!

Enter Rosencrantz and Guildenstern.

Friends both, go join you with some further aid:
Hamlet in madness hath Polonius slain,
And from his mother's closet hath he dragged him. 35
Go seek him out; speak fair, and bring the body
Into the chapel. I pray you haste in this.
[*Exeunt Rosencrantz and Guildenstern.*]
Come, Gertrude, we'll call up our wisest friends
And let them know both what we mean to do
And what's untimely done . . . 40
Whose whisper o'er the world's diameter,
As level as the cannon to his blank
Transports his poisoned shot, may miss our name
And hit the woundless air. O, come away!
My soul is full of discord and dismay. *Exeunt.* 45

18 out of haunt away from association with others **25–26 ore/Among a mineral** vein of gold in a mine **40 done . . .** (evidently something has dropped out of the text. Capell's conjecture, "So, haply slander," is usually printed) **42 blank** white center of a target **44 woundless** invulnerable

Scene II. [*The castle.*]

Enter Hamlet.

HAMLET Safely stowed.

GENTLEMEN (*Within*) Hamlet! Lord Hamlet!

HAMLET But soft, what noise? Who calls on Hamlet?
O, here they come.

Enter Rosencrantz and Guildenstern.

ROSENCRANTZ What have you done, my lord, with the
5 dead body?

HAMLET Compounded it with dust, whereto 'tis kin.

ROSENCRANTZ Tell us where 'tis, that we may take it
thence
And bear it to the chapel.

HAMLET Do not believe it.

10 ROSENCRANTZ Believe what?

HAMLET That I can keep your counsel and not mine own. Besides, to be demanded of a sponge, what replication should be made by the son of a king?

ROSENCRANTZ Take you me for a sponge, my lord?

15 HAMLET Ay, sir, that soaks up the King's countenance, his rewards, his authorities. But such officers do the King best service in the end. He keeps them, like an ape, in the corner of his jaw, first mouthed, to be last swallowed. When he needs what you have
20 gleaned, it is but squeezing you and, sponge, you shall be dry again.

ROSENCRANTZ I understand you not, my lord.

HAMLET I am glad of it: a knavish speech sleeps in a foolish ear.

IV.ii.12 **demanded of** questioned by 13 **replication** reply 15 **countenance** favor

ROSENCRANTZ My lord, you must tell us where the body is and go with us to the King. 25

HAMLET The body is with the King, but the King is not with the body. The King is a thing——

GUILDENSTERN A thing, my lord?

HAMLET Of nothing. Bring me to him. Hide fox, and all after. 30 *Exeunt.*

Scene III. [*The castle.*]

Enter King, and two or three.

KING I have sent to seek him and to find the body:
How dangerous is it that this man goes loose!
Yet must not we put the strong law on him:
He's loved of the distracted multitude,
Who like not in their judgment, but their eyes, 5
And where 'tis so, th' offender's scourge is weighed,
But never the offense. To bear all smooth and even,
This sudden sending him away must seem
Deliberate pause. Diseases desperate grown
By desperate appliance are relieved, 10
Or not at all.

Enter Rosencrantz, [*Guildenstern,*] *and all the rest.*

How now? What hath befall'n?

ROSENCRANTZ Where the dead body is bestowed, my lord,
We cannot get from him.

KING But where is he?

ROSENCRANTZ Without, my lord; guarded, to know your pleasure.

30–31 Hide fox, and all after (a cry in a game such as hide-and-seek; Hamlet runs from the stage) **IV.iii.4 distracted** bewildered, senseless **7 bear** carry out **9 pause** planning

KING Bring him before us.

15 ROSENCRANTZ Ho! Bring in the lord.

They enter.

KING Now, Hamlet, where's Polonius?

HAMLET At supper.

KING At supper? Where?

HAMLET Not where he eats, but where 'a is eaten. A
20 certain convocation of politic worms are e'en at
him. Your worm is your only emperor for diet. We
fat all creatures else to fat us, and we fat ourselves
for maggots. Your fat king and your lean beggar is
but variable service—two dishes, but to one table.
25 That's the end.

KING Alas, alas!

HAMLET A man may fish with the worm that hath eat of
a king, and eat of the fish that hath fed of that worm.

KING What dost thou mean by this?

30 HAMLET Nothing but to show you how a king may go a
progress through the guts of a beggar.

KING Where is Polonius?

HAMLET In heaven. Send thither to see. If your messenger
find him not there, seek him i' th' other
35 place yourself. But if indeed you find him not
within this month, you shall nose him as you go
up the stairs into the lobby.

KING [*To Attendants*] Go seek him there.

HAMLET 'A will stay till you come.

[*Exeunt Attendants.*]

40 KING Hamlet, this deed, for thine especial safety,
Which we do tender as we dearly grieve
For that which thou hast done, must send thee hence
With fiery quickness. Therefore prepare thyself.

20 **politic** statesmanlike, shrewd 24 **variable service** different courses
31 **progress** royal journey 41 **tender** hold dear

The bark is ready and the wind at help,
Th' associates tend, and everything is bent 45
For England.

HAMLET For England?

KING Ay, Hamlet.

HAMLET Good.

KING So is it, if thou knew'st our purposes.

HAMLET I see a cherub that sees them. But come, for England! Farewell, dear Mother.

KING Thy loving father, Hamlet. 50

HAMLET My mother—father and mother is man and wife, man and wife is one flesh, and so, my mother. Come, for England! *Exit.*

KING Follow him at foot; tempt him with speed aboard.
Delay it not; I'll have him hence tonight. 55
Away! For everything is sealed and done
That else leans on th' affair. Pray you make haste.
[*Exeunt all but the King.*]
And, England, if my love thou hold'st at aught—
As my great power thereof may give thee sense,
Since yet thy cicatrice looks raw and red 60
After the Danish sword, and thy free awe
Pays homage to us—thou mayst not coldly set
Our sovereign process, which imports at full
By letters congruing to that effect
The present death of Hamlet. Do it, England, 65
For like the hectic in my blood he rages,
And thou must cure me. Till I know 'tis done,
Howe'er my haps, my joys were ne'er begun.
Exit.

45 **tend** wait 48 **cherub** angel of knowledge 54 **at foot** closely 57 **leans** depends 60 **cicatrice** scar 61 **free awe** uncompelled submission 62–63 **coldly set/Our sovereign process** regard slightly our royal command 65 **present** instant 66 **hectic** fever 68 **haps** chances, fortunes

Scene IV. [*A plain in Denmark.*]

Enter Fortinbras with his Army over the stage.

FORTINBRAS Go, Captain, from me greet the Danish king.
Tell him that by his license Fortinbras
Craves the conveyance of a promised march
Over his kingdom. You know the rendezvous.
5 If that his Majesty would aught with us,
We shall express our duty in his eye;
And let him know so.

CAPTAIN I will do't, my lord.

FORTINBRAS Go softly on.

[*Exeunt all but the Captain.*]

Enter Hamlet, Rosencrantz, &c.

HAMLET Good sir, whose powers are these?

10 CAPTAIN They are of Norway, sir.

HAMLET How purposed, sir, I pray you?

CAPTAIN Against some part of Poland.

HAMLET Who commands them, sir?

CAPTAIN The nephew to old Norway, Fortinbras.

15 HAMLET Goes it against the main of Poland, sir,
Or for some frontier?

CAPTAIN Truly to speak, and with no addition,
We go to gain a little patch of ground
That hath in it no profit but the name.
20 To pay five ducats, five, I would not farm it,
Nor will it yield to Norway or the Pole
A ranker rate, should it be sold in fee.

IV.iv.3 **conveyance** escort for 6 **in his eye** before his eyes (i.e., in his presence) 8 **softly** slowly 9 **powers** forces 15 **main** main part 17 **with no addition** plainly 22 **ranker** higher 22 **in fee** outright

HAMLET Why, then the Polack never will defend it.

CAPTAIN Yes, it is already garrisoned.

HAMLET Two thousand souls and twenty thousand ducats 25
Will not debate the question of this straw.
This is th' imposthume of much wealth and peace,
That inward breaks, and shows no cause without
Why the man dies. I humbly thank you, sir.

CAPTAIN God bye you, sir. [*Exit.*]

ROSENCRANTZ Will't please you go, my lord? 30

HAMLET I'll be with you straight. Go a little before.
[*Exeunt all but Hamlet.*]
How all occasions do inform against me
And spur my dull revenge! What is a man,
If his chief good and market of his time
Be but to sleep and feed? A beast, no more. 35
Sure he that made us with such large discourse,
Looking before and after, gave us not
That capability and godlike reason
To fust in us unused. Now, whether it be
Bestial oblivion, or some craven scruple 40
Of thinking too precisely on th' event—
A thought which, quartered, hath but one part wisdom
And ever three parts coward—I do not know
Why yet I live to say, "This thing's to do,"
Sith I have cause, and will, and strength, and means 45
To do't. Examples gross as earth exhort me.
Witness this army of such mass and charge,
Led by a delicate and tender prince,
Whose spirit, with divine ambition puffed,
Makes mouths at the invisible event, 50
Exposing what is mortal and unsure

26 debate settle **27 imposthume** abscess, ulcer **34 market** profit **36 discourse** understanding **39 fust** grow moldy **40 oblivion** forgetfulness **41 event** outcome **46 gross** large, obvious **47 charge** expense **50 Makes mouths at the invisible event** makes scornful faces (is contemptuous of) the unseen outcome

To all that fortune, death, and danger dare,
Even for an eggshell. Rightly to be great
Is not to stir without great argument,
55 But greatly to find quarrel in a straw
When honor's at the stake. How stand I then,
That have a father killed, a mother stained,
Excitements of my reason and my blood,
And let all sleep, while to my shame I see
60 The imminent death of twenty thousand men
That for a fantasy and trick of fame
Go to their graves like beds, fight for a plot
Whereon the numbers cannot try the cause,
Which is not tomb enough and continent
65 To hide the slain? O, from this time forth,
My thoughts be bloody, or be nothing worth! *Exit.*

Scene V. [*The castle.*]

Enter Horatio, [Queen] Gertrude, and a Gentleman.

QUEEN I will not speak with her.

GENTLEMAN She is importunate, indeed distract.
Her mood will needs be pitied.

QUEEN What would she have?

GENTLEMAN She speaks much of her father, says she hears
There's tricks i' th' world, and hems, and beats her
5 heart,
Spurns enviously at straws, speaks things in doubt
That carry but half sense. Her speech is nothing,
Yet the unshapèd use of it doth move

54 **not** (the sense seems to require "not not") 54 **argument** reason 55 **greatly** i.e., nobly 58 **Excitements** incentives 61 **fantasy and trick of fame** illusion and trifle of reputation 64 **continent** receptacle, container IV.v.6 **Spurns enviously at straws** objects spitefully to insignificant matters 6 **in doubt** uncertainly

The hearers to collection; they yawn at it,
And botch the words up fit to their own thoughts, 10
Which, as her winks and nods and gestures yield them,
Indeed would make one think there might be thought,
Though nothing sure, yet much unhappily.

HORATIO 'Twere good she were spoken with, for she may strew
Dangerous conjectures in ill-breeding minds. 15

QUEEN Let her come in. [*Exit Gentleman.*]
[*Aside*] To my sick soul (as sin's true nature is)
Each toy seems prologue to some great amiss;
So full of artless jealousy is guilt
It spills itself in fearing to be spilt. 20

Enter Ophelia [*distracted.*]

OPHELIA Where is the beauteous majesty of Denmark?

QUEEN How now, Ophelia?

OPHELIA (*She sings.*) How should I your truelove know
From another one?
By his cockle hat and staff 25
And his sandal shoon.

QUEEN Alas, sweet lady, what imports this song?

OPHELIA Say you? Nay, pray you mark.
He is dead and gone, lady, (*Song*)
He is dead and gone; 30
At his head a grass-green turf,
At his heels a stone.
O, ho!

QUEEN Nay, but Ophelia——

OPHELIA Pray you mark. 35

8–9 Yet the . . . to collection i.e., yet the formless manner of it moves her listeners to gather up some sort of meaning **9 yawn** gape (?) **18 amiss** misfortune **19 artless jealousy** crude suspicion **20 spills** destroys **25 cockle hat** (a cockleshell on the hat was the sign of a pilgrim who had journeyed to shrines overseas. The association of lovers and pilgrims was a common one) **26 shoon** shoes

[*Sings.*] White his shroud as the mountain snow——
Enter King.

QUEEN Alas, look here, my lord.

OPHELIA Larded all with sweet flowers (*Song*)
Which bewept to the grave did not go
40 With truelove showers.

KING How do you, pretty lady?

OPHELIA Well, God dild you! They say the owl was a baker's daughter. Lord, we know what we are, but know not what we may be. God be at your table!

45 KING Conceit upon her father.

OPHELIA Pray let's have no words of this, but when they ask you what it means, say you this:
Tomorrow is Saint Valentine's day. (*Song*)
All in the morning betime,
50 And I a maid at your window,
To be your Valentine.

Then up he rose and donned his clothes
And dupped the chamber door,
Let in the maid, that out a maid
55 Never departed more.

KING Pretty Ophelia.

OPHELIA Indeed, la, without an oath, I'll make an end on't:
[*Sings.*] By Gis and by Saint Charity,
Alack, and fie for shame!
60 Young men will do't if they come to't,
By Cock, they are to blame.
Quoth she, "Before you tumbled me,
You promised me to wed."

38 **Larded** decorated 42 **dild** yield, i.e., reward 43 **baker's daughter** (an allusion to a tale of a baker's daughter who begrudged bread to Christ and was turned into an owl) 45 **Conceit** brooding 48 **Saint Valentine's day** Feb. 14 (the notion was that a bachelor would become the truelove of the first girl he saw on this day) 53 **dupped** opened (did up) 58 **Gis** (contraction of "Jesus") 61 **Cock** (1) God (2) phallus

He answers:
"So would I 'a' done, by yonder sun,
An thou hadst not come to my bed." 65

KING How long hath she been thus?

OPHELIA I hope all will be well. We must be patient, but I cannot choose but weep to think they would lay him i' th' cold ground. My brother shall know 70 of it; and so I thank you for your good counsel. Come, my coach! Good night, ladies, good night. Sweet ladies, good night, good night. *Exit.*

KING Follow her close; give her good watch, I pray you. *[Exit Horatio.]*
O, this is the poison of deep grief; it springs 75
All from her father's death—and now behold!
O Gertrude, Gertrude,
When sorrows come, they come not single spies,
But in battalions: first, her father slain;
Next, your son gone, and he most violent author 80
Of his own just remove; the people muddied,
Thick and unwholesome in their thoughts and whispers
For good Polonius' death, and we have done but greenly
In huggermugger to inter him; poor Ophelia
Divided from herself and her fair judgment, 85
Without the which we are pictures or mere beasts;
Last, and as much containing as all these,
Her brother is in secret come from France,
Feeds on his wonder, keeps himself in clouds,
And wants not buzzers to infect his ear 90
With pestilent speeches of his father's death,
Wherein necessity, of matter beggared,
Will nothing stick our person to arraign
In ear and ear. O my dear Gertrude, this,

81 **muddied** muddled 83 **greenly** foolishly 84 **huggermugger** secret haste 89 **wonder** suspicion 90 **wants not buzzers** does not lack talebearers 92 **of matter beggared** unprovided with facts 93 **Will nothing stick** will not hesitate

95 Like to a murd'ring piece, in many places
Gives me superfluous death. *A noise within.*

Enter a Messenger.

QUEEN Alack, what noise is this?

KING Attend, where are my Switzers? Let them guard the door.
What is the matter?

MESSENGER Save yourself, my lord.
The ocean, overpeering of his list,
100 Eats not the flats with more impiteous haste
Than young Laertes, in a riotous head,
O'erbears your officers. The rabble call him lord,
And, as the world were now but to begin,
Antiquity forgot, custom not known,
105 The ratifiers and props of every word,
They cry, "Choose we! Laertes shall be king!"
Caps, hands, and tongues applaud it to the clouds,
"Laertes shall be king! Laertes king!" *A noise within.*

QUEEN How cheerfully on the false trail they cry!
110 O, this is counter, you false Danish dogs!

Enter Laertes with others.

KING The doors are broke.

LAERTES Where is this king?—Sirs, stand you all without.

ALL No, let's come in.

LAERTES I pray you give me leave.

ALL We will, we will.

LAERTES I thank you. Keep the door. [*Exeunt his*
115 *Followers.*] O thou vile King,
Give me my father.

QUEEN Calmly, good Laertes.

95 **murd'ring piece** (a cannon that shot a kind of shrapnel) 97 **Switzers** Swiss guards 99 **list** shore 101 **in a riotous head** with a rebellious force 110 **counter** (a hound runs counter when he follows the scent backward from the prey)

LAERTES That drop of blood that's calm proclaims me bastard,
Cries cuckold to my father, brands the harlot
Even here between the chaste unsmirchèd brow
Of my true mother.

KING What is the cause, Laertes, 120
That thy rebellion looks so giantlike?
Let him go, Gertrude. Do not fear our person.
There's such divinity doth hedge a king
That treason can but peep to what it would,
Acts little of his will. Tell me, Laertes, 125
Why thou art thus incensed. Let him go, Gertrude.
Speak, man.

LAERTES Where is my father?

KING Dead.

QUEEN But not by him.

KING Let him demand his fill.

LAERTES How came he dead? I'll not be juggled with. 130
To hell allegiance, vows to the blackest devil,
Conscience and grace to the profoundest pit!
I dare damnation. To this point I stand,
That both the worlds I give to negligence,
Let come what comes, only I'll be revenged 135
Most throughly for my father.

KING Who shall stay you?

LAERTES My will, not all the world's.
And for my means, I'll husband them so well
They shall go far with little.

KING Good Laertes,
If you desire to know the certainty 140
Of your dear father, is't writ in your revenge
That swoopstake you will draw both friend and foe,
Winner and loser?

118 cuckold man whose wife is unfaithful **122 fear** fear for **124 peep to** i.e., look at from a distance **134 That both ... to negligence** i.e., I care not what may happen (to me) in this world or the next **138 husband them** use them economically **142 swoopstake** in a clean sweep

LAERTES None but his enemies.

KING Will you know them then?

LAERTES To his good friends thus wide I'll ope my
145 arms
And like the kind life-rend'ring pelican
Repast them with my blood.

KING Why, now you speak
Like a good child and a true gentleman.
That I am guiltless of your father's death,
150 And am most sensibly in grief for it,
It shall as level to your judgment 'pear
As day does to your eye.

A noise within: "Let her come in."

LAERTES How now? What noise is that?

Enter Ophelia.

O heat, dry up my brains; tears seven times salt
155 Burn out the sense and virtue of mine eye!
By heaven, thy madness shall be paid with weight
Till our scale turn the beam. O rose of May,
Dear maid, kind sister, sweet Ophelia!
O heavens, is't possible a young maid's wits
160 Should be as mortal as an old man's life?
Nature is fine in love, and where 'tis fine,
It sends some precious instance of itself
After the thing it loves.

OPHELIA They bore him barefaced on the bier (*Song*)
165 Hey non nony, nony, hey nony
And in his grave rained many a tear——
Fare you well, my dove!

LAERTES Hadst thou thy wits, and didst persuade
revenge,
It could not move thus.

170 OPHELIA You must sing "A-down a-down, and you call

146 **pelican** (thought to feed its young with its own blood) 147 **Repast** feed
150 **sensibly** acutely 155 **virtue** power 157 **turn the beam** weigh down the bar
(of the balance) 161 **fine** refined, delicate 162 **instance** sample

him a-down-a." O, how the wheel becomes it! It is the false steward, that stole his master's daughter.

LAERTES This nothing's more than matter.

OPHELIA There's rosemary, that's for remembrance. Pray you, love, remember. And there is pansies, that's for thoughts. 175

LAERTES A document in madness, thoughts and remembrance fitted.

OPHELIA There's fennel for you, and columbines. There's rue for you, and here's some for me. We may call it herb of grace o' Sundays. O, you must wear your rue with a difference. There's a daisy. I would give you some violets, but they withered all when my father died. They say 'a made a good end. 180
[*Sings*] For bonny sweet Robin is all my joy. 185

LAERTES Thought and affliction, passion, hell itself,
She turns to favor and to prettiness.

OPHELIA And will 'a not come again? (*Song*)
And will 'a not come again?
No, no, he is dead, 190
Go to thy deathbed,
He never will come again.

His beard was as white as snow,
All flaxen was his poll.
He is gone, he is gone, 195
And we cast away moan.
God 'a' mercy on his soul!
And of all Christian souls, I pray God. God bye you.
[*Exit*.]

171 **wheel** (of uncertain meaning, but probably a turn or dance of Ophelia's, rather than Fortune's wheel) 173 **This nothing's more than matter** this nonsense has more meaning than matters of consequence 177 **document** lesson 179 **fennel** (the distribution of flowers in the ensuing lines has symbolic meaning, but the meaning is disputed. Perhaps fennel, flattery; **columbines**, cuckoldry; **rue**, sorrow for Ophelia and repentance for the Queen; **daisy**, dissembling; **violets**, faithfulness. For other interpretations, see J. W. Lever in *Review of English Studies*, New Series 3 [1952], pp. 123-29) 187 **favor** charm, beauty 194 **All flaxen was his poll** white as flax was his head

LAERTES Do you see this, O God?

200 KING Laertes, I must commune with your grief,
Or you deny me right. Go but apart,
Make choice of whom your wisest friends you will,
And they shall hear and judge 'twixt you and me.
If by direct or by collateral hand
205 They find us touched, we will our kingdom give,
Our crown, our life, and all that we call ours,
To you in satisfaction; but if not,
Be you content to lend your patience to us,
And we shall jointly labor with your soul
To give it due content.

210 LAERTES Let this be so.
His means of death, his obscure funeral—
No trophy, sword, nor hatchment o'er his bones,
No noble rite nor formal ostentation—
Cry to be heard, as 'twere from heaven to earth,
That I must call't in question.

215 KING So you shall;
And where th' offense is, let the great ax fall.
I pray you go with me. *Exeunt.*

Scene VI. [*The castle.*]

Enter Horatio and others.

HORATIO What are they that would speak with me?

GENTLEMAN Seafaring men, sir. They say they have letters for you.

HORATIO Let them come in. [*Exit Attendant.*]
5 I do not know from what part of the world
I should be greeted, if not from Lord Hamlet.

204 collateral indirect 205 touched implicated 212 hatchment tablet bearing the coat of arms of the dead 213 ostentation ceremony

Enter Sailors.

SAILOR God bless you, sir.

HORATIO Let Him bless thee too.

SAILOR 'A shall, sir, an't please Him. There's a letter for you, sir—it came from th' ambassador that was bound for England—if your name be Horatio, as I am let to know it is. 10

HORATIO [*Reads the letter.*] "Horatio, when thou shalt have overlooked this, give these fellows some means to the King. They have letters for him. Ere we were two days old at sea, a pirate of very warlike appointment gave us chase. Finding ourselves too slow to sail, we put on a compelled valor, and in the grapple I boarded them. On the instant they got clear of our ship; so I alone became their prisoner. They have dealt with me like thieves of mercy, but they knew what they did: I am to do a good turn for them. Let the King have the letters I have sent, and repair thou to me with as much speed as thou wouldst fly death. I have words to speak in thine ear will make thee dumb; yet are they much too light for the bore of the matter. These good fellows will bring thee where I am. Rosencrantz and Guildenstern hold their course for England. Of them I have much to tell thee. Farewell. 15 20 25 30

He that thou knowest thine, HAMLET."

Come, I will give you way for these your letters,
And do't the speedier that you may direct me
To him from whom you brought them. *Exeunt.*

IV.vi.14 overlooked surveyed 17 appointment equipment 27 bore caliber (here, "importance")

Scene VII. [*The castle.*]

Enter King and Laertes.

KING Now must your conscience my acquittance seal,
And you must put me in your heart for friend,
Sith you have heard, and with a knowing ear,
That he which hath your noble father slain
Pursued my life.

5 LAERTES It well appears. But tell me
Why you proceeded not against these feats
So criminal and so capital in nature,
As by your safety, greatness, wisdom, all things else,
You mainly were stirred up.

KING O, for two special reasons,
10 Which may to you perhaps seem much unsinewed,
But yet to me they're strong. The Queen his mother
Lives almost by his looks, and for myself—
My virtue or my plague, be it either which—
She is so conjunctive to my life and soul,
15 That, as the star moves not but in his sphere,
I could not but by her. The other motive
Why to a public count I might not go
Is the great love the general gender bear him,
Who, dipping all his faults in their affection,
20 Would, like the spring that turneth wood to stone,
Convert his gyves to graces; so that my arrows,
Too slightly timbered for so loud a wind,
Would have reverted to my bow again,
And not where I had aimed them.

IV.vii.7 **capital** deserving death 9 **mainly** powerfully 10 **unsinewed** weak 14 **conjunctive** closely united 17 **count** reckoning 18 **general gender** common people 20 **spring that turneth wood to stone** (a spring in Shakespeare's county was so charged with lime that it would petrify wood placed in it) 21 **gyves** fetters 22 **timbered** shafted

LAERTES And so have I a noble father lost, 25
A sister driven into desp'rate terms,
Whose worth, if praises may go back again,
Stood challenger on mount of all the age
For her perfections. But my revenge will come.

KING Break not your sleeps for that. You must not think 30
That we are made of stuff so flat and dull
That we can let our beard be shook with danger,
And think it pastime. You shortly shall hear more.
I loved your father, and we love ourself,
And that, I hope, will teach you to imagine—— 35

Enter a Messenger with letters.

How now? What news?

MESSENGER Letters, my lord, from Hamlet:
These to your Majesty; this to the Queen.

KING From Hamlet? Who brought them?

MESSENGER Sailors, my lord, they say; I saw them not.
They were given me by Claudio; he received them 40
Of him that brought them.

KING Laertes, you shall hear them.—
Leave us. *Exit Messenger.*
[*Reads.*] "High and mighty, you shall know I am set naked on your kingdom. Tomorrow shall I beg leave to see your kingly eyes; when I shall (first 45 asking your pardon thereunto) recount the occasion of my sudden and more strange return.

HAMLET."

What should this mean? Are all the rest come back?
Or is it some abuse, and no such thing? 50

LAERTES Know you the hand?

KING 'Tis Hamlet's character. "Naked"!

26 terms conditions 27 go back again revert to what is past 44 naked destitute
50 abuse deception 51 character handwriting

And in a postscript here, he says "alone."
Can you devise me?

LAERTES I am lost in it, my lord. But let him come.
55 It warms the very sickness in my heart
That I shall live and tell him to his teeth,
"Thus did'st thou."

KING If it be so, Laertes
(As how should it be so? How otherwise?),
Will you be ruled by me?

LAERTES Ay, my lord,
60 So you will not o'errule me to a peace.

KING To thine own peace. If he be now returned,
As checking at his voyage, and that he means
No more to undertake it, I will work him
To an exploit now ripe in my device,
65 Under the which he shall not choose but fall;
And for his death no wind of blame shall breathe,
But even his mother shall uncharge the practice
And call it accident.

LAERTES My lord, I will be ruled;
The rather if you could devise it so
That I might be the organ.

70 KING It falls right.
You have been talked of since your travel much,
And that in Hamlet's hearing, for a quality
Wherein they say you shine. Your sum of parts
Did not together pluck such envy from him
75 As did that one, and that, in my regard,
Of the unworthiest siege.

LAERTES What part is that, my lord?

KING A very riband in the cap of youth,
Yet needful too, for youth no less becomes
The light and careless livery that it wears
80 Than settled age his sables and his weeds,
Importing health and graveness. Two months since

53 **devise** advise 62 **checking at** turning away from (a term in falconry) 67 **uncharge the practice** not charge the device with treachery 76 **siege** rank 80 **sables and his weeds** i.e., sober attire

Here was a gentleman of Normandy.
I have seen myself, and served against, the French,
And they can well on horseback, but this gallant
Had witchcraft in't. He grew unto his seat, 85
And to such wondrous doing brought his horse
As had he been incorpsed and deminatured
With the brave beast. So far he topped my thought
That I, in forgery of shapes and tricks,
Come short of what he did.

LAERTES A Norman was't? 90

KING A Norman.

LAERTES Upon my life, Lamord.

KING The very same.

LAERTES I know him well. He is the brooch indeed
And gem of all the nation.

KING He made confession of you, 95
And gave you such a masterly report,
For art and exercise in your defense,
And for your rapier most especial,
That he cried out 'twould be a sight indeed
If one could match you. The scrimers of their
nation 100
He swore had neither motion, guard, nor eye,
If you opposed them. Sir, this report of his
Did Hamlet so envenom with his envy
That he could nothing do but wish and beg
Your sudden coming o'er to play with you. 105
Now, out of this—

LAERTES What out of this, my lord?

KING Laertes, was your father dear to you?
Or are you like the painting of a sorrow,
A face without a heart?

LAERTES Why ask you this?

KING Not that I think you did not love your father, 110

84 can do 89 forgery invention 93 brooch ornament 95 confession report
100 scrimers fencers

But that I know love is begun by time,
And that I see, in passages of proof,
Time qualifies the spark and fire of it.
There lives within the very flame of love
115 A kind of wick or snuff that will abate it,
And nothing is at a like goodness still,
For goodness, growing to a plurisy,
Dies in his own too-much. That we would do
We should do when we would, for this "would" changes,
120 And hath abatements and delays as many
As there are tongues, are hands, are accidents,
And then this "should" is like a spendthrift sigh,
That hurts by easing. But to the quick of th' ulcer—
Hamlet comes back; what would you undertake
125 To show yourself in deed your father's son
More than in words?

LAERTES To cut his throat i' th' church!

KING No place indeed should murder sanctuarize;
Revenge should have no bounds. But, good Laertes,
Will you do this? Keep close within your chamber.
130 Hamlet returned shall know you are come home.
We'll put on those shall praise your excellence
And set a double varnish on the fame
The Frenchman gave you, bring you in fine together
And wager on your heads. He, being remiss,
135 Most generous, and free from all contriving,
Will not peruse the foils, so that with ease,
Or with a little shuffling, you may choose
A sword unbated, and, in a pass of practice,
Requite him for your father.

LAERTES I will do't,

112 passages of proof proved cases **113 qualifies** diminishes **115 snuff** residue of burnt wick (which dims the light) **116 still** always **117 plurisy** fullness, excess **122 spendthrift sigh** (sighing provides ease, but because it was thought to thin the blood and so shorten life it was spendthrift) **123 quick** sensitive flesh **127 Sanctuarize** protect **131 We'll put on those** we'll incite persons who **133 in fine** finally **138 unbated** not blunted **138 pass of practice** treacherous thrust.

And for that purpose I'll anoint my sword. 140
I bought an unction of a mountebank,
So mortal that, but dip a knife in it,
Where it draws blood, no cataplasm so rare,
Collected from all simples that have virtue
Under the moon, can save the thing from death 145
That is but scratched withal. I'll touch my point
With this contagion, that, if I gall him slightly,
It may be death.

KING Let's further think of this,
Weigh what convenience both of time and means
May fit us to our shape. If this should fail, 150
And that our drift look through our bad performance,
'Twere better not assayed. Therefore this project
Should have a back or second, that might hold
If this did blast in proof. Soft, let me see.
We'll make a solemn wager on your cunnings— 155
I ha't!
When in your motion you are hot and dry—
As make your bouts more violent to that end—
And that he calls for drink, I'll have prepared him
A chalice for the nonce, whereon but sipping, 160
If he by chance escape your venomed stuck,
Our purpose may hold there.—But stay, what noise?

Enter Queen.

QUEEN One woe doth tread upon another's heel.
So fast they follow. Your sister's drowned, Laertes.

LAERTES Drowned! O, where? 165

QUEEN There is a willow grows askant the brook,
That shows his hoar leaves in the glassy stream:
Therewith fantastic garlands did she make
Of crowflowers, nettles, daisies, and long purples,

141 **mountebank** quack 143 **cataplasm** poultice 144 **simplex** medicinal herbs 144 **virtue** power (to heal) 150 **shape** role 151 **drift look through** purpose show through 154 **blast in proof** burst (fail) in performance 160 **nonce** occasion 161 **stuck** thrust 166 **askant** aslant 167 **hoar** silver-gray 168 **Therewith** i.e., with willow twigs

170 That liberal shepherds give a grosser name,
But our cold maids do dead men's fingers call them.
There on the pendent boughs her crownet weeds
Clamb'ring to hang, an envious sliver broke,
When down her weedy trophies and herself
175 Fell in the weeping brook. Her clothes spread wide,
And mermaidlike awhile they bore her up,
Which time she chanted snatches of old lauds,
As one incapable of her own distress,
Or like a creature native and indued
180 Unto that element. But long it could not be
Till that her garments, heavy with their drink,
Pulled the poor wretch from her melodious lay
To muddy death.

LAERTES Alas, then she is drowned?

QUEEN Drowned, drowned.

185 LAERTES Too much of water hast thou, poor Ophelia,
And therefore I forbid my tears; but yet
It is our trick; nature her custom holds,
Let shame say what it will: when these are gone,
The woman will be out. Adieu, my lord.
190 I have a speech o' fire, that fain would blaze,
But that this folly drowns it. *Exit.*

KING Let's follow, Gertrude.
How much I had to do to calm his rage!
Now fear I this will give it start again;
Therefore let's follow. *Exeunt.*

170 liberal free-spoken, coarse-mouthed **172 crownet** coronet **173 envious sliver** malicious branch **177 lauds** hymns **178 incapable** unaware **179 indued** in harmony with **187 trick** trait, way **189 woman** i.e., womanly part of me

ACT V

Scene I. [*A churchyard.*]

Enter two Clowns.

CLOWN Is she to be buried in Christian burial when she willfully seeks her own salvation?

OTHER I tell thee she is. Therefore make her grave straight. The crowner hath sate on her, and finds it Christian burial. 5

CLOWN How can that be, unless she drowned herself in her own defense?

OTHER Why, 'tis found so.

CLOWN It must be *se offendendo*; it cannot be else. For here lies the point: if I drown myself wittingly, 10 it argues an act, and an act hath three branches—it is to act, to do, to perform. Argal, she drowned herself wittingly.

OTHER Nay, but hear you, Goodman Delver.

CLOWN Give me leave. Here lies the water—good. 15 Here stands the man—good. If the man go to this water and drown himself, it is, will he nill he, he goes; mark you that. But if the water come to him and drown him, he drowns not himself. Argal, he

V.i.s.d. **Clowns** rustics 4 **straight** straightway 4 **crowner** coroner 9 **se offendendo** (blunder for *se defendendo*, a legal term meaning "in self-defense") 12 **Argal** (blunder for Latin *ergo*, "therefore") 17 **will he nill he** will he or will he not (whether he will or will not)

20 that is not guilty of his own death, shortens not his own life.

OTHER But is this law?

CLOWN Ay marry, is't—crowner's quest law.

OTHER Will you ha' the truth on't? If this had not been
25 a gentlewoman, she should have been buried out o' Christian burial.

CLOWN Why, there thou say'st. And the more pity that great folk should have count'nance in this world to drown or hang themselves more than their
30 even-Christen. Come, my spade. There is no ancient gentlemen but gard'ners, ditchers, and grave-makers. They hold up Adam's profession.

OTHER Was he a gentleman?

CLOWN 'A was the first that ever bore arms.

35 OTHER Why, he had none.

CLOWN What, art a heathen? How dost thou understand the Scripture? The Scripture says Adam digged. Could he dig without arms? I'll put another question to thee. If thou answerest me not to the
40 purpose, confess thyself——

OTHER Go to.

CLOWN What is he that builds stronger than either the mason, the shipwright, or the carpenter?

OTHER The gallowsmaker, for that frame outlives a
45 thousand tenants.

CLOWN I like thy wit well, in good faith. The gallows does well. But how does it well? It does well to those that do ill. Now thou dost ill to say the gallows is built stronger than the church. Argal, the gallows
50 may do well to thee. To't again, come.

OTHER Who builds stronger than a mason, a shipwright, or a carpenter?

23 **quest** inquest 28 **count'nance** privilege 30 **even-Christen** fellow Christian 32 **hold up** keep up 34 **bore arms** had a coat of arms (the sign of a gentleman)

CLOWN Ay, tell me that, and unyoke.

OTHER Marry, now I can tell.

CLOWN To't. 55

OTHER Mass, I cannot tell.

Enter Hamlet and Horatio afar off.

CLOWN Cudgel thy brains no more about it, for your dull ass will not mend his pace with beating. And when you are asked this question next, say "a grave-maker." The houses he makes last till doomsday. 60 Go, get thee in, and fetch me a stoup of liquor.

[*Exit Other Clown.*]

In youth when I did love, did love, (*Song*)
Methought it was very sweet
To contract—O—the time for—a—my behove,
O, methought there—a—was nothing—a—meet. 65

HAMLET Has this fellow no feeling of his business? 'A sings in gravemaking.

HORATIO Custom hath made it in him a property of easiness.

HAMLET 'Tis e'en so. The hand of little employment 70 hath the daintier sense.

CLOWN But age with his stealing steps (*Song*)
Hath clawed me in his clutch,
And hath shipped me into the land,
As if I had never been such. 75

[*Throws up a skull.*]

HAMLET That skull had a tongue in it, and could sing once. How the knave jowls it to the ground, as if 'twere Cain's jawbone, that did the first murder! This might be the pate of a politician, which this

53 **unyoke** i.e., stop work for the day 56 **Mass** by the mass 61 **stoup** tankard 64 **behove** advantage 68–69 **in him a property of easiness** easy for him 71 **hath the daintier sense** is more sensitive (because it is not calloused) 77 **jowls** hurls

80 ass now o'erreaches, one that would circumvent God, might it not?

HORATIO It might, my lord.

HAMLET Or of a courtier, which could say "Good morrow, sweet lord! How dost thou, sweet lord?"
85 This might be my Lord Such-a-one, that praised my Lord Such-a-one's horse when 'a went to beg it, might it not?

HORATIO Ay, my lord.

HAMLET Why, e'en so, and now my Lady Worm's,
90 chapless, and knocked about the mazzard with a sexton's spade. Here's fine revolution, an we had the trick to see't. Did these bones cost no more the breeding but to play at loggets with them? Mine ache to think on't.

95 CLOWN A pickax and a spade, a spade, (*Song*)
For and a shrouding sheet;
O, a pit of clay for to be made
For such a guest is meet.

[*Throws up another skull.*]

HAMLET There's another. Why may not that be the
100 skull of a lawyer? Where be his quiddities now, his quillities, his cases, his tenures, and his tricks? Why does he suffer this mad knave now to knock him about the sconce with a dirty shovel, and will not tell him of his action of battery? Hum! This
105 fellow might be in's time a great buyer of land, with his statutes, his recognizances, his fines, his double vouchers, his recoveries. Is this the fine of his fines, and the recovery of his recoveries, to have his fine pate full of fine dirt? Will his vouchers vouch him

80 **o'erreaches** (1) reaches over (2) has the advantage over 90 **chapless** lacking the lower jaw 90 **mazzard** head 93 **loggets** (a game in which small pieces of wood were thrown at an object) 100 **quiddities** subtle arguments (from Latin **quidditas**, "whatness") 101 **quillities** fine distinctions 101 **tenures** legal means of holding land 103 **sconce** head 106 **his statutes, his recognizances, his fines** his documents giving a creditor control of a debtor's land, his bonds of surety, his documents changing an entailed estate into fee simple (unrestricted ownership) 107 **fine** end

no more of his purchases, and double ones too, than the length and breadth of a pair of indentures? The very conveyances of his lands will scarcely lie in this box, and must th' inheritor himself have no more, ha? 110

HORATIO Not a jot more, my lord. 115

HAMLET Is not parchment made of sheepskins?

HORATIO Ay, my lord, and of calveskins too.

HAMLET They are sheep and calves which seek out assurance in that. I will speak to this fellow. Whose grave's this, sirrah? 120

CLOWN Mine, sir.
[*Sings.*] O, a pit of clay for to be made
For such a guest is meet.

HAMLET I think it be thine indeed, for thou liest in't.

CLOWN You lie out on't, sir, and therefore 'tis not yours. For my part, I do not lie in't, yet it is mine. 125

HAMLET Thou dost lie in't, to be in't and say it is thine. 'Tis for the dead, not for the quick; therefore thou liest.

CLOWN 'Tis a quick lie, sir; 'twill away again from me to you. 130

HAMLET What man dost thou dig it for?

CLOWN For no man, sir.

HAMLET What woman then?

CLOWN For none neither. 135

HAMLET Who is to be buried in't?

CLOWN One that was a woman, sir; but, rest her soul, she's dead.

HAMLET How absolute the knave is! We must speak by the card, or equivocation will undo us. By the 140

111 **indentures** contracts 112 **conveyances** legal documents for the transference of land 119 **assurance** safety 128 **quick** living 139 **absolute** positive, decided 139–40 **by the card** by the compass card, i.e., exactly 140 **equivocation** ambiguity

Lord, Horatio, this three years I have took note of it, the age is grown so picked that the toe of the peasant comes so near the heel of the courtier he galls his kibe. How long hast thou been a grave-
145 maker?

CLOWN Of all the days i' th' year, I came to't that day that our last king Hamlet overcame Fortinbras.

HAMLET How long is that since?

CLOWN Cannot you tell that? Every fool can tell that. It
150 was that very day that young Hamlet was born—he that is mad, and sent into England.

HAMLET Ay, marry, why was he sent into England?

CLOWN Why, because 'a was mad. 'A shall recover his wits there; or, if 'a do not, 'tis no great matter there.

155 HAMLET Why?

CLOWN 'Twill not be seen in him there. There the men are as mad as he.

HAMLET How came he mad?

CLOWN Very strangely, they say.

160 HAMLET How strangely?

CLOWN Faith, e'en with losing his wits.

HAMLET Upon what ground?

CLOWN Why, here in Denmark. I have been sexton here, man and boy, thirty years.

165 HAMLET How long will a man lie i' th' earth ere he rot?

CLOWN Faith, if 'a be not rotten before 'a die (as we have many pocky corses nowadays that will scarce hold the laying in), 'a will last you some eight year or nine year. A tanner will last you nine year.

170 HAMLET Why he, more than another?

CLOWN Why, sir, his hide is so tanned with his trade

142 picked refined 144 kibe sore on the back of the heel 167 pocky corses bodies of persons who had been infected with the pox (syphilis)

that 'a will keep out water a great while, and your water is a sore decayer of your whoreson dead body. Here's a skull now hath lien you i' th' earth three and twenty years. 175

HAMLET Whose was it?

CLOWN A whoreson mad fellow's it was. Whose do you think it was?

HAMLET Nay, I know not.

CLOWN A pestilence on him for a mad rogue! 'A poured 180 a flagon of Rhenish on my head once. This same skull, sir, was, sir, Yorick's skull, and King's jester.

HAMLET This?

CLOWN E'en that.

HAMLET Let me see. [*Takes the skull.*] Alas, poor 185 Yorick! I knew him, Horatio, a fellow of infinite jest, of most excellent fancy. He hath borne me on his back a thousand times. And now how abhorred in my imagination it is! My gorge rises at it. Here hung those lips that I have kissed I know not how 190 oft. Where be your gibes now? Your gambols, your songs, your flashes of merriment that were wont to set the table on a roar? Not one now to mock your own grinning? Quite chapfall'n? Now get you to my lady's chamber, and tell her, let her paint an inch 195 thick, to this favor she must come. Make her laugh at that. Prithee, Horatio, tell me one thing.

HORATIO What's that, my lord?

HAMLET Dost thou think Alexander looked o' this fashion i' th' earth? 200

HORATIO E'en so.

HAMLET And smelt so? Pah! [*Puts down the skull.*]

HORATIO E'en so, my lord.

194 chapfall'n (1) down in the mouth (2) jawless 196 favor facial appearance

HAMLET To what base uses we may return, Horatio!
205 Why may not imagination trace the noble dust of Alexander till 'a find it stopping a bunghole?

HORATIO 'Twere to consider too curiously, to consider so.

HAMLET No, faith, not a jot, but to follow him thither
210 with modesty enough, and likelihood to lead it; as thus: Alexander died, Alexander was buried, Alexander returneth to dust; the dust is earth; of earth we make loam; and why of that loam whereto he was converted might they not stop a beer barrel?
215 Imperious Caesar, dead and turned to clay,
Might stop a hole to keep the wind away.
O, that that earth which kept the world in awe
Should patch a wall t' expel the winter's flaw!
But soft, but soft awhile! Here comes the King.

Enter King, Queen, Laertes, and a coffin, with Lords attendant [*and a Doctor of Divinity*].

220 The Queen, the courtiers. Who is this they follow?
And with such maimèd rites? This doth betoken
The corse they follow did with desp'rate hand
Fordo it own life. 'Twas of some estate.
Couch we awhile, and mark. [*Retires with Horatio*.]

LAERTES What ceremony else?

225 HAMLET That is Laertes,
A very noble youth. Mark.

LAERTES What ceremony else?

DOCTOR Her obsequies have been as far enlarged
As we have warranty. Her death was doubtful,
230 And, but that great command o'ersways the order,
She should in ground unsanctified been lodged
Till the last trumpet. For charitable prayers,

207 **curiously** minutely 210 **with modesty enough** without exaggeration
218 **flaw** gust 221 **maimèd** incomplete 223 **Fordo it** destroy its
223 **estate** high rank 224 **Couch** hide 229 **doubtful** suspicious

Shards, flints, and pebbles should be thrown on her.
Yet here she is allowed her virgin crants,
Her maiden strewments, and the bringing home 235
Of bell and burial.

LAERTES Must there no more be done?

DOCTOR No more be done.
We should profane the service of the dead
To sing a requiem and such rest to her
As to peace-parted souls.

LAERTES Lay her i' th' earth, 240
And from her fair and unpolluted flesh
May violets spring! I tell thee, churlish priest,
A minist'ring angel shall my sister be
When thou liest howling!

HAMLET What, the fair Ophelia?

QUEEN Sweets to the sweet! Farewell. 245
[*Scatters flowers.*]
I hoped thou shouldst have been my Hamlet's wife.
I thought thy bride bed to have decked, sweet maid,
And not have strewed thy grave.

LAERTES O, treble woe
Fall ten times treble on that cursèd head
Whose wicked deed thy most ingenious sense 250
Deprived thee of! Hold off the earth awhile,
Till I have caught her once more in mine arms.
Leaps in the grave.
Now pile your dust upon the quick and dead
Till of this flat a mountain you have made
T'o'ertop old Pelion or the skyish head 255
Of blue Olympus.

HAMLET [*Coming forward*] What is he whose grief

233 **Shards** broken pieces of pottery 234 **crants** garlands 235 **strewments** i.e., of flowers 250 **most ingenious sense** finely endowed mind 255 **Pelion** (according to classical legend, giants in their fight with the gods sought to reach heaven by piling Mount Pelion and Mount Ossa on Mount Olympus)

Bears such an emphasis, whose phrase of sorrow
Conjures the wand'ring stars, and makes them
stand
Like wonder-wounded hearers? This is I,
Hamlet the Dane.

260 LAERTES The devil take thy soul!
[*Grapples with him.*]

HAMLET Thou pray'st not well.
I prithee take thy fingers from my throat,
For, though I am not splenitive and rash,
Yet have I in me something dangerous,
265 Which let thy wisdom fear. Hold off thy hand.

KING Pluck them asunder.

QUEEN Hamlet, Hamlet!

ALL Gentlemen!

HORATIO Good my lord, be quiet.
[*Attendants part them.*]

HAMLET Why, I will fight with him upon this theme
Until my eyelids will no longer wag.

270 QUEEN O my son, what theme?

HAMLET I loved Ophelia. Forty thousand brothers
Could not with all their quantity of love
Make up my sum. What wilt thou do for her?

KING O, he is mad, Laertes.

275 QUEEN For love of God forbear him.

HAMLET 'Swounds, show me what thou't do.
Woo't weep? Woo't fight? Woo't fast? Woo't tear
thyself?
Woo't drink up eisel? Eat a crocodile?

258 wand'ring stars planets 260 s.d. **Grapples with him** (Q1, a bad quarto, presumably reporting a version that toured, has a previous direction saying "Hamlet leaps in after Laertes." Possibly he does so, somewhat hysterically. But such a direction—absent from the two good texts, Q2 and F—makes Hamlet the aggressor, somewhat contradicting his next speech. Perhaps Laertes leaps out of the grave to attack Hamlet) 263 **splenitive** fiery (the spleen was thought to be the seat of anger) 278 **eisel** vinegar

I'll do't. Dost thou come here to whine?
To outface me with leaping in her grave? 280
Be buried quick with her, and so will I.
And if thou prate of mountains, let them throw
Millions of acres on us, till our ground,
Singeing his pate against the burning zone,
Make Ossa like a wart! Nay, an thou'lt mouth, 285
I'll rant as well as thou.

QUEEN This is mere madness;
And thus a while the fit will work on him.
Anon, as patient as the female dove
When that her golden couplets are disclosed,
His silence will sit drooping.

HAMLET Hear you, sir. 290
What is the reason that you use me thus?
I loved you ever. But it is no matter.
Let Hercules himself do what he may,
The cat will mew, and dog will have his day.

KING I pray thee, good Horatio, wait upon him. 295

Exit Hamlet and Horatio.

[*To Laertes*] Strengthen your patience in our last night's speech.
We'll put the matter to the present push.
Good Gertrude, set some watch over your son.
This grave shall have a living monument.
An hour of quiet shortly shall we see; 300
Till then in patience our proceeding be. *Exeunt.*

284 burning zone sun's orbit **289 golden couplets are disclosed** (the dove lays two eggs, and the newly hatched [disclosed] young are covered with golden down) **297 present push** immediate test **299 living** lasting (with perhaps also a reference to the plot against Hamlet's life)

Scene II. [*The castle.*]

Enter Hamlet and Horatio.

HAMLET So much for this, sir; now shall you see the other.
You do remember all the circumstance?

HORATIO Remember it, my lord!

HAMLET Sir, in my heart there was a kind of fighting
5 That would not let me sleep. Methought I lay
Worse than the mutines in the bilboes. Rashly
(And praised be rashness for it) let us know,
Our indiscretion sometime serves us well
When our deep plots do pall, and that should learn us
10 There's a divinity that shapes our ends,
Rough-hew them how we will.

HORATIO That is most certain.

HAMLET Up from my cabin.
My sea gown scarfed about me, in the dark
Groped I to find out them, had my desire,
15 Fingered their packet, and in fine withdrew
To mine own room again, making so bold,
My fears forgetting manners, to unseal
Their grand commission; where I found, Horatio——
Ah, royal knavery!—an exact command,
20 Larded with many several sorts of reasons,
Importing Denmark's health, and England's too,
With, ho, such bugs and goblins in my life,
That on the supervise, no leisure bated,
No, not to stay the grinding of the ax,

V.ii.6 **mutines in the bilboes** mutineers in fetters 9 **pall** fail 15 **Fingered** stole 15 **in fine** finally 20 **Larded** enriched 22 **such bugs and goblins in my life** such bugbears and imagined terrors if I were allowed to live 23 **supervise** reading 23 **leisure bated** delay allowed

My head should be struck off.

HORATIO Is't possible? 25

HAMLET Here's the commission; read it at more leisure.
But wilt thou hear now how I did proceed?

HORATIO I beseech you.

HAMLET Being thus benetted round with villains,
Or I could make a prologue to my brains, 30
They had begun the play. I sat me down,
Devised a new commission, wrote it fair.
I once did hold it, as our statists do,
A baseness to write fair, and labored much
How to forget that learning, but, sir, now 35
It did me yeoman's service. Wilt thou know
Th' effect of what I wrote?

HORATIO Ay, good my lord.

HAMLET An earnest conjuration from the King,
As England was his faithful tributary,
As love between them like the palm might flourish, 40
As peace should still her wheaten garland wear
And stand a comma 'tween their amities,
And many suchlike as's of great charge,
That on the view and knowing of these contents,
Without debatement further, more or less, 45
He should those bearers put to sudden death,
Not shriving time allowed.

HORATIO How was this sealed?

HAMLET Why, even in that was heaven ordinant.
I had my father's signet in my purse,
Which was the model of that Danish seal, 50
Folded the writ up in the form of th' other,
Subscribed it, gave't th' impression, placed it safely,
The changeling never known. Now, the next day
Was our sea fight, and what to this was sequent
Thou knowest already. 55

30 Or ere **33** statists statesmen **34** fair clearly **37** effect purport **42** comma link **43** great charge (1) serious exhortation (2) heavy burden (punning on as's and "asses") **47** shriving absolution **48** ordinant ruling **50** model counterpart

HORATIO So Guildenstern and Rosencrantz go to't.

HAMLET Why, man, they did make love to this employment.
They are not near my conscience; their defeat
Does by their own insinuation grow.
60 'Tis dangerous when the baser nature comes
Between the pass and fell incensèd points
Of mighty opposites.

HORATIO Why, what a king is this!

HAMLET Does it not, think thee, stand me now upon—
He that hath killed my king, and whored my mother,
65 Popped in between th' election and my hopes,
Thrown out his angle for my proper life,
And with such coz'nage—is't not perfect conscience
To quit him with this arm? And is't not to be damned
To let this canker of our nature come
70 In further evil?

HORATIO It must be shortly known to him from England
What is the issue of the business there.

HAMLET It will be short; the interim's mine,
And a man's life's no more than to say "one."
75 But I am very sorry, good Horatio,
That to Laertes I forgot myself,
For by the image of my cause I see
The portraiture of his. I'll court his favors.
But sure the bravery of his grief did put me
Into a tow'ring passion.

80 HORATIO Peace, who comes here?

Enter young Osric, a courtier.

OSRIC Your lordship is right welcome back to Denmark.

59 insinuation meddling 61 pass thrust 61 fell cruel 63 stand me now upon become incumbent upon me 63 election (the Danish monarchy was elective) 66 angle fishing line 66 my proper life my own life 67 coz'nage trickery 68 quit pay back 79 bravery bravado

HAMLET I humbly thank you, sir. [*Aside to Horatio*] Dost know this waterfly?

HORATIO [*Aside to Hamlet*] No, my good lord.

HAMLET [*Aside to Horatio*] Thy state is the more gracious, for 'tis a vice to know him. He hath much land, and fertile. Let a beast be lord of beasts, and his crib shall stand at the king's mess. 'Tis a chough, but, as I say, spacious in the possession of dirt. 85 90

OSRIC Sweet lord, if your lordship were at leisure, I should impart a thing to you from his Majesty.

HAMLET I will receive it, sir, with all diligence of spirit. Put your bonnet to his right use. 'Tis for the head.

OSRIC I thank your lordship, it is very hot. 95

HAMLET No, believe me, 'tis very cold; the wind is northerly.

OSRIC It is indifferent cold, my lord, indeed.

HAMLET But yet methinks it is very sultry and hot for my complexion. 100

OSRIC Exceedingly, my lord; it is very sultry, as 'twere —I cannot tell how. But, my lord, his Majesty bade me signify to you that 'a has laid a great wager on your head. Sir, this is the matter——

HAMLET I beseech you remember. 105

[*Hamlet moves him to put on his hat.*]

OSRIC Nay, good my lord; for my ease, in good faith. Sir, here is newly come to court Laertes—believe me, an absolute gentleman, full of most excellent differences, of very soft society and great showing. Indeed, to speak feelingly of him, he is the card or calendar of gentry; for you shall find in him the continent of what part a gentleman would see. 110

88 mess table **89 chough** jackdaw (here, chatterer) **89 spacious** well off **100 complexion** temperament **109 differences** distinguishing characteristics **110 feelingly** justly **110 card** chart **112 continent** summary

HAMLET Sir, his definement suffers no perdition in you, though, I know, to divide him inventorially
115 would dozy th' arithmetic of memory, and yet but yaw neither in respect of his quick sail. But, in the verity of extolment, I take him to be a soul of great article, and his infusion of such dearth and rareness as, to make true diction of him, his semblable
120 is his mirror, and who else would trace him, his umbrage, nothing more.

OSRIC Your lordship speaks most infallibly of him.

HAMLET The concernancy, sir? Why do we wrap the gentleman in our more rawer breath?

125 OSRIC Sir?

HORATIO Is't not possible to understand in another tongue? You will to't, sir, really.

HAMLET What imports the nomination of this gentleman?

130 OSRIC Of Laertes?

HORATIO [*Aside to Hamlet*] His purse is empty already. All's golden words are spent.

HAMLET Of him, sir.

OSRIC I know you are not ignorant——

135 HAMLET I would you did, sir; yet, in faith, if you did, it would not much approve me. Well, sir?

OSRIC You are not ignorant of what excellence Laertes is——

HAMLET I dare not confess that, lest I should compare
140 with him in excellence; but to know a man well were to know himself.

113 **definement** description 113 **perdition** loss 115 **dozy** dizzy 115–16 **and yet . . . quick sail** i.e., and yet only stagger despite all (**yaw neither**) in trying to overtake his virtues 118 **article** (literally, "item," but here perhaps "traits" or "importance") 118 **infusion** essential quality 119 **diction** description 119 **semblable** likeness 120–21 **umbrage** shadow 123 **concernancy** meaning 127 **will to't** will get there 136 **approve** commend

OSRIC I mean, sir, for his weapon; but in the imputation laid on him by them, in his meed he's unfellowed.

HAMLET What's his weapon? 145

OSRIC Rapier and dagger.

HAMLET That's two of his weapons—but well.

OSRIC The King, sir, hath wagered with him six Barbary horses, against the which he has impawned, as I take it, six French rapiers and poniards, with 150 their assigns, as girdle, hangers, and so. Three of the carriages, in faith, are very dear to fancy, very responsive to the hilts, most delicate carriages, and of very liberal conceit.

HAMLET What call you the carriages? 155

HORATIO [*Aside to Hamlet*] I knew you must be edified by the margent ere you had done.

OSRIC The carriages, sir, are the hangers.

HAMLET The phrase would be more germane to the matter if we could carry a cannon by our sides. I 160 would it might be hangers till then. But on! Six Barbary horses against six French swords, their assigns, and three liberal-conceited carriages—that's the French bet against the Danish. Why is this all impawned, as you call it? 165

OSRIC The King, sir, hath laid, sir, that in a dozen passes between yourself and him he shall not exceed you three hits; he hath laid on twelve for nine, and it would come to immediate trial if your lordship would vouchsafe the answer. 170

HAMLET How if I answer no?

OSRIC I mean, my lord, the opposition of your person in trial.

142–43 imputation reputation **143 meed** merit **149 impawned** wagered **151 assigns** accompaniments **151 hangers** straps hanging the sword to the belt **152 carriages** (an affected word for hangers) **152–53 responsive** corresponding **154 liberal conceit** elaborate design **157 margent** i.e., marginal (explanatory) comment

HAMLET Sir, I will walk here in the hall. If it please
175 his Majesty, it is the breathing time of day with me. Let the foils be brought, the gentleman willing, and the King hold his purpose, I will win for him an I can; if not, I will gain nothing but my shame and the odd hits.

180 OSRIC Shall I deliver you e'en so?

HAMLET To this effect, sir, after what flourish your nature will.

OSRIC I commend my duty to your lordship.

HAMLET Yours, yours. [*Exit Osric*.] He does well to
185 commend it himself; there are no tongues else for's turn.

HORATIO This lapwing runs away with the shell on his head.

HAMLET 'A did comply, sir, with his dug before 'a
190 sucked it. Thus has he, and many more of the same breed that I know the drossy age dotes on, only got the tune of the time and, out of an habit of encounter, a kind of yeasty collection, which carries them through and through the most fanned
195 and winnowed opinions; and do but blow them to their trial, the bubbles are out.

Enter a Lord.

LORD My lord, his Majesty commended him to you by young Osric, who brings back to him that you attend him in the hall. He sends to know if your
200 pleasure hold to play with Laertes, or that you will take longer time.

HAMLET I am constant to my purposes; they follow the

175 **breathing time of day with me** time when I take exercise 187 **lapwing** (the new-hatched lapwing was thought to run around with half its shell on its head) 189 **'A did comply, sir, with his dug** he was ceremoniously polite to his mother's breast 192–93 **out of an habit of encounter** out of his own superficial way of meeting and conversing with people 193 **yeasty** frothy 196 **the bubbles are out** i.e., they are blown away (the reference is to the "yeasty collection")

King's pleasure. If his fitness speaks, mine is ready; now or whensoever, provided I be so able as now.

LORD The King and Queen and all are coming down. 205

HAMLET In happy time.

LORD The Queen desires you to use some gentle entertainment to Laertes before you fall to play.

HAMLET She well instructs me. [*Exit Lord.*]

HORATIO You will lose this wager, my lord. 210

HAMLET I do not think so. Since he went into France I have been in continual practice. I shall win at the odds. But thou wouldst not think how ill all's here about my heart. But it is no matter.

HORATIO Nay, good my lord—— 215

HAMLET It is but foolery, but it is such a kind of gain-giving as would perhaps trouble a woman.

HORATIO If your mind dislike anything, obey it. I will forestall their repair hither and say you are not fit.

HAMLET Not a whit, we defy augury. There is special 220 providence in the fall of a sparrow. If it be now, 'tis not to come; if it be not to come, it will be now; if it be not now, yet it will come. The readiness is all. Since no man of aught he leaves knows, what is't to leave betimes? Let be. 225

A table prepared. [*Enter*] *Trumpets, Drums, and Officers with cushions; King, Queen,* [*Osric,*] *and all the State,* [*with*] *foils, daggers,* [*and stoups of wine borne in*]; *and Laertes.*

KING Come, Hamlet, come, and take this hand from me.

[*The King puts Laertes' hand into Hamlet's.*]

207–08 to use some gentle entertainment to be courteous **217 gain-giving** misgiving **221 the fall of a sparrow** (cf. Matthew 10:29 "Are not two sparrows sold for a farthing? and one of them shall not fall on the ground without your Father") **225 betimes** early

HAMLET Give me your pardon, sir. I have done you wrong,
But pardon't, as you are a gentleman.
This presence knows, and you must needs have heard,
230 How I am punished with a sore distraction.
What I have done
That might your nature, honor, and exception
Roughly awake, I here proclaim was madness.
Was't Hamlet wronged Laertes? Never Hamlet.
235 If Hamlet from himself be ta'en away,
And when he's not himself does wrong Laertes,
Then Hamlet does it not, Hamlet denies it.
Who does it then? His madness. If't be so,
Hamlet is of the faction that is wronged;
240 His madness is poor Hamlet's enemy.
Sir, in this audience,
Let my disclaiming from a purposed evil
Free me so far in your most generous thoughts
That I have shot my arrow o'er the house
And hurt my brother.

245 LAERTES I am satisfied in nature,
Whose motive in this case should stir me most
To my revenge. But in my terms of honor
I stand aloof, and will no reconcilement
Till by some elder masters of known honor
250 I have a voice and precedent of peace
To keep my name ungored. But till that time
I do receive your offered love like love,
And will not wrong it.

HAMLET I embrace it freely,
And will this brother's wager frankly play.
Give us the foils. Come on.

255 LAERTES Come, one for me.

HAMLET I'll be your foil, Laertes. In mine ignorance

229 presence royal assembly **232 exception** disapproval **239 faction** party, side **250 voice and precedent** authoritative opinion justified by precedent **256 foil** (1) blunt sword (2) background (of metallic leaf) for a jewel

Your skill shall, like a star i' the darkest night,
Stick fiery off indeed.

LAERTES You mock me, sir.

HAMLET No, by this hand.

KING Give them the foils, young Osric. Cousin Hamlet, 260
You know the wager?

HAMLET Very well, my lord.
Your grace has laid the odds o' th' weaker side.

KING I do not fear it, I have seen you both;
But since he is bettered, we have therefore odds.

LAERTES This is too heavy; let me see another. 265

HAMLET This likes me well. These foils have all a length?

Prepare to play.

OSRIC Ay, my good lord.

KING Set me the stoups of wine upon that table.
If Hamlet give the first or second hit,
Or quit in answer of the third exchange, 270
Let all the battlements their ordnance fire.
The King shall drink to Hamlet's better breath,
And in the cup an union shall he throw
Richer than that which four successive kings
In Denmark's crown have worn. Give me the cups, 275
And let the kettle to the trumpet speak,
The trumpet to the cannoneer without,
The cannons to the heavens, the heaven to earth,
"Now the King drinks to Hamlet." Come, begin.

Trumpets the while.

And you, the judges, bear a wary eye. 280

HAMLET Come on, sir.

LAERTES Come, my lord. *They play.*

HAMLET One.

LAERTES No.

258 **Stick fiery off** stand out brilliantly 264 **bettered** has improved (in France) 270 **quit** repay, hit back 273 **union** pearl 276 **kettle** kettledrum

HAMLET Judgment?

OSRIC A hit, a very palpable hit.

Drum, trumpets, and shot. Flourish; a piece goes off.

LAERTES Well, again.

KING Stay, give me drink. Hamlet, this pearl is thine.
Here's to thy health. Give him the cup.

285 HAMLET I'll play this bout first; set it by awhile.
Come. [*They play.*] Another hit. What say you?

LAERTES A touch, a touch; I do confess't.

KING Our son shall win.

QUEEN He's fat, and scant of breath.
Here, Hamlet, take my napkin, rub thy brows.
290 The Queen carouses to thy fortune, Hamlet.

HAMLET Good madam!

KING Gertrude, do not drink.

QUEEN I will, my lord; I pray you pardon me. [*Drinks.*]

KING [*Aside*] It is the poisoned cup; it is too late.

HAMLET I dare not drink yet, madam—by and by.

295 QUEEN Come, let me wipe thy face.

LAERTES My lord, I'll hit him now.

KING I do not think't.

LAERTES [*Aside*] And yet it is almost against my conscience.

HAMLET Come for the third, Laertes. You do but dally.
I pray you pass with your best violence;
300 I am sure you make a wanton of me.

LAERTES Say you so? Come on. [*They*] *play.*

OSRIC Nothing neither way.

LAERTES Have at you now!

In scuffling they change rapiers, [*and both are wounded*].

288 fat (1) sweaty (2) out of training 300 wanton spoiled child

KING Part them. They are incensed.

HAMLET Nay, come—again! *[The Queen falls.]*

OSRIC Look to the Queen there, ho!

HORATIO They bleed on both sides. How is it, my lord? 305

OSRIC How is't, Laertes?

LAERTES Why, as a woodcock to mine own springe, Osric.
I am justly killed with mine own treachery.

HAMLET How does the Queen?

KING She sounds to see them bleed.

QUEEN No, no, the drink, the drink! O my dear Hamlet! 310
The drink, the drink! I am poisoned. *[Dies.]*

HAMLET O villainy! Ho! Let the door be locked.
Treachery! Seek it out. *[Laertes falls.]*

LAERTES It is here, Hamlet. Hamlet, thou art slain;
No med'cine in the world can do thee good. 315
In thee there is not half an hour's life.
The treacherous instrument is in thy hand,
Unbated and envenomed. The foul practice
Hath turned itself on me. Lo, here I lie,
Never to rise again. Thy mother's poisoned. 320
I can no more. The King, the King's to blame.

HAMLET The point envenomed too?
Then, venom, to thy work. *Hurts the King.*

ALL Treason! Treason!

KING O, yet defend me, friends. I am but hurt. 325

HAMLET Here, thou incestuous, murd'rous, damnèd Dane,
Drink off this potion. Is thy union here?
Follow my mother. *King dies.*

LAERTES He is justly served.

307 springe snare **309 sounds** swoons **318 practice** deception

It is a poison tempered by himself.
330 Exchange forgiveness with me, noble Hamlet.
Mine and my father's death come not upon thee,
Nor thine on me! *Dies.*

HAMLET Heaven make thee free of it! I follow thee.
I am dead, Horatio. Wretched Queen, adieu!
335 You that look pale and tremble at this chance,
That are but mutes or audience to this act,
Had I but time (as this fell sergeant, Death,
Is strict in his arrest) O, I could tell you—
But let it be. Horatio, I am dead;
340 Thou livest; report me and my cause aright
To the unsatisfied.

HORATIO Never believe it.
I am more an antique Roman than a Dane.
Here's yet some liquor left.

HAMLET As th' art a man,
Give me the cup. Let go. By heaven, I'll ha't!
345 O God, Horatio, what a wounded name,
Things standing thus unknown, shall live behind me!
If thou didst ever hold me in thy heart,
Absent thee from felicity awhile,
And in this harsh world draw thy breath in pain,
To tell my story. *A march afar off.* [*Exit Osric.*]
350 What warlike noise is this?

Enter Osric.

OSRIC Young Fortinbras, with conquest come from Poland,
To th' ambassadors of England gives
This warlike volley.

HAMLET O, I die, Horatio!
The potent poison quite o'ercrows my spirit.
355 I cannot live to hear the news from England,

329 **tempered** mixed 336 **mutes** performers who have no words to speak 337 **fell sergeant** dread sheriff's officer 341 **unsatisfied** uninformed 342 **antique Roman** (with reference to the old Roman fashion of suicide) 348 **felicity** i.e., the felicity of death 354 **o'ercrows** overpowers (as a triumphant cock crows over its weak opponent)

But I do prophesy th' election lights
On Fortinbras. He has my dying voice.
So tell him, with th' occurrents, more and less,
Which have solicited—the rest is silence. *Dies.*

HORATIO Now cracks a noble heart. Good night, sweet
Prince, 360
And flights of angels sing thee to thy rest.
[*March within.*]
Why does the drum come hither?

Enter Fortinbras, with the Ambassadors with Drum, Colors, and Attendants.

FORTINBRAS Where is this sight?

HORATIO What is it you would see?
If aught of woe or wonder, cease your search.

FORTINBRAS This quarry cries on havoc. O proud
Death, 365
What feast is toward in thine eternal cell
That thou so many princes at a shot
So bloodily hast struck?

AMBASSADOR The sight is dismal;
And our affairs from England come too late.
The ears are senseless that should give us hearing 370
To tell him his commandment is fulfilled,
That Rosencrantz and Guildenstern are dead.
Where should we have our thanks?

HORATIO Not from his mouth,
Had it th' ability of life to thank you.
He never gave commandment for their death. 375
But since, so jump upon this bloody question,
You from the Polack wars, and you from England,
Are here arrived, give order that these bodies
High on a stage be placèd to the view,
And let me speak to th' yet unknowing world 380
How these things came about. So shall you hear

358 **occurrents** occurrences 359 **solicited** incited 365 **quarry** heap of slain bodies 365 **cries on havoc** proclaims general slaughter 366 **toward** in preparation 373 **his** (Claudius') 376 **jump** precisely 379 **stage** platform

Of carnal, bloody, and unnatural acts,
Of accidental judgments, casual slaughters,
Of deaths put on by cunning and forced cause,
385 And, in this upshot, purposes mistook
Fall'n on th' inventors' heads. All this can I
Truly deliver.

FORTINBRAS Let us haste to hear it,
And call the noblest to the audience.
For me, with sorrow I embrace my fortune.
390 I have some rights of memory in this kingdom,
Which now to claim my vantage doth invite me.

HORATIO Of that I shall have also cause to speak,
And from his mouth whose voice will draw on more.
But let this same be presently performed,
Even while men's minds are wild, lest more mischance
395 On plots and errors happen.

FORTINBRAS Let four captains
Bear Hamlet like a soldier to the stage,
For he was likely, had he been put on,
To have proved most royal; and for his passage
400 The soldiers' music and the rite of war
Speak loudly for him.
Take up the bodies. Such a sight as this
Becomes the field, but here shows much amiss.
Go, bid the soldiers shoot.

Exeunt marching; after the which a peal of ordnance are shot off.

FINIS

383 **casual** not humanly planned, chance 390 **rights of memory** remembered claims 393 **voice will draw on** vote will influence 396 **On** on top of 398 **put on** advanced (to the throne) 399 **passage** death 403 **field** battlefield

Textual Note

SHAKESPEARE'S *Hamlet* comes to us in three versions. The first of them, known as the First Quarto, was published in 1603 by N. L. [Nicholas Ling] and John Trundell, who advertised it on the title page as having been played "by his Highness Servants in the City of London, as also in the two universities of Cambridge and Oxford, and elsewhere." This was a pirated edition, published without the consent of the owners, and Shakespeare had nothing to do with it. In the preceding year an attempt had been made to forestall just such a venture. On July 26, 1602, James Roberts, a printer friendly to Shakespeare's company, had entered in the Stationers' Register "A book called the Revenge of Hamlet Prince of Denmark as it was lately acted by the Lord Chamberlain his Servants." This was intended to serve as a kind of copyright. It should be said in passing that "his Highness Servants" were the King's Men and that the Chamberlain's Men became the King's Men on May 19, 1603, when James I took Shakespeare's company under his direct protection.

The copy which Ling and Trundell sent to the printer was an extraordinary hodgepodge, so that the First Quarto gives us a very poor notion of Shakespeare's play. How this copy came into being has been the subject of much investigation, but there is little agreement. In general there are three schools of thought: (1) the First Quarto is a badly reported version of *Hamlet* as Shakespeare wrote it once and for all; (2) it is a badly reported version of an early draft of Shakespeare's play; and (3) it was expanded from some actor's parts of an early version of the play. This last seems most likely, since some of the lines, notably those of Marcellus, are accurate, other passages are partially correct, and still others are sheer invention. All three levels are to be found in the soliloquy beginning "To be or not to be."

To be or not to be, ay there's the point,
To die, to sleep, is that all? Ay all:

No, to sleep, to dream, ay marry there it goes,
For in that dream of death, when we awake,
And borne before an everlasting judge,
From whence no passenger ever returned,
The undiscovered country, at whose sight
The happy smile, and the accursed damned.
But for this, the joyful hope of this,
Who'd bear the scorns and flattery of the world,
Scorned by the right rich, the rich cursed of the poor?
The widow being oppressed, the orphan wronged,
The taste of hunger, or a tyrant's reign,
And thousand more calamities besides,
To grunt and sweat under this weary life,
When that he may his full quietus make,
With a bare bodkin, who would this endure,
But for a hope of something after death?
Which pulses the brain, and doth confound the sense,
Which makes us rather bear those evils we have,
Than fly to others that we know not of.
Ay that, O this conscience makes cowards of us all,
Lady in thy orisons, be all my sins rememb'red

It is clear that there is a hand other than Shakespeare's in this. That the First Quarto is a debased version of an early version of the play is suggested by, most notably, changes in names. Why should Polonius, for instance, become Corambis if the copy were based on the version Shakespeare wrote once and for all?

It was not considered good business to publish a play while it was still popular in the theater, for it could then be acted in the provinces by other than its owners, reducing the public for the play when Shakespeare's company took it on tour. This being so, the publication of the First Quarto had done Shakespeare a double injury: the play was in print, and it misrepresented its author. Shakespeare had some leisure at this time, the theaters being closed because of the plague from March 1603 to April 1604. We may suppose that he decided to revise the play and have it printed. In any case, another edition of *Hamlet* appeared in 1604. The title page seems designed to tell the public that this is the genuine article: "The Tragical History of Hamlet, Prince of Denmark. By William Shakespeare. Newly imprinted and enlarged to almost as much again as it was, according to the true and perfect copy." The statement is literally true. The Second Quarto is almost twice as long as the First Quarto, and although it lacks some passages preserved in the First Folio, the Second Quarto is the fullest and best version of the play.

The third version of *Hamlet* is to be found in the First Folio, 1623, the collected edition of Shakespeare's plays made by his friends and associates in the theater, John Heminges and Henry Condell. Here the text is based on the acting version of the play. The Folio gives us some ninety lines not found in the Second Quarto. These include two passages of considerable length, II.ii.243–74 and II.ii.345–70, but the Folio does not give us some two hundred lines found in the Second Quarto. These are mostly reflective passages, including Hamlet's last soliloquy, "How all occasions do inform against me." As befits an acting version, the Folio stage directions are more numerous and frequently are fuller. Modern editions are made by collation of the Second Quarto and the First Folio and are therefore longer than either of them.

Because the Second Quarto is the longest version, giving us more of the play as Shakespeare conceived it than either of the others, it serves as the basic version for this text. Unfortunately the printers of it often worked carelessly. Words and phrases are omitted, there are plain misreadings of Shakespeare's manuscript, speeches are sometimes wrongly assigned. It was therefore necessary to turn to the First Folio for many readings. Neither the First Quarto nor the Second Quarto is divided into acts or scenes; the Folio indicates only the following: I.i, I.ii, I.iii, II, II.ii. The present edition, to allow for easy reference, follows the traditional divisions of the Globe edition, placing them (as well as indications of locale) in brackets to indicate that they are editorial, not authorial. Punctuation and spelling are modernized (*and* is given as *an* when it means "if"), obvious typographical errors are corrected, abbreviations are expanded, speech prefixes are regularized and the positions of stage directions are slightly altered where necessary. Other departures from the Second Quarto are listed below. First is given the adopted reading, in bold, and then the Second Quarto's reading, in roman. The vast majority of these adopted readings are from the Folio; if an adopted reading is not from the Folio, the fact is indicated by a bracketed remark explaining, for example, that it is drawn from the First Quarto [Q1] or the Second Folio [F2] or an editor's conjecture [ed].

I.i.16 **soldier** souldiers 63 **Polacks** [F has "Pollax"] pollax 68 **my** mine 73 **why** with 73 **cast** cost 88 **those** these 91 **returned** returne 94 **designed** [F2] design 112 **mote** [ed] moth 121 **feared** [ed] feare 138 **you** your 140 **at it** it 142 s.d. **Exit Ghost** [Q2 omits]

I.ii.1 s.d. **Councilors** [ed] Counsaile: as 41 s.d. **Exit Voltemand and Cornelius** [Q2 omits] 58 **He hath** Hath 67 **so** so much 77 **good** coold 82 **shapes** [ed; F has "shewes"] chapes 96 **a mind** or minde 132 **self-slaughter** seale slaughter 133 **weary** wary 137 **to this** thus 143 **would** should 149 **even she** [Q2 omits] 175 **to drink deep** for to drinke 178 **to see** to 209 **Where, as** [ed] Whereas 224 **Indeed, indeed, sirs** Indeede Sirs 237 **Very like, very like** Very like 238 **hundred** hundreth 257 **foul** fonde

I.iii.3 **convoy is** conuay in 12 **bulk** bulkes 18 **For he himself is subject to his birth** [Q2 omits] 49 **like a** a 68 **thine** thy 74 **Are** Or 75 **be** boy 76 **loan** loue 83 **invites** inuests 109 **Tend'ring** [Q1] Wrong [F has "Roaming"] 115 **springes** springs 123 **parley** parle 125 **tether** tider 131 **beguile** beguide

I.iv.1 **shrewdly** shroudly 2 **a nipping** nipping 6 s.d. **go** [ed] goes 19 **clepe** [ed] clip 27 **the** [ed] their 33 **Their** [ed] His 36 **evil** [ed] eale 57 s.d. **Ghost beckons Hamlet** Beckins 69 **my lord** my 70 **summit** [ed] somnet [F has "sonnet"] 82 **artere** [ed] arture [F has "artire"] 87 **imagination** imagion

I.v.47 **what a** what 55 **lust** but 56 **sate** sort 64 **leperous** leaprous 68 **posset** possesse 91 s.d. **Exit** [Q2 omits] 95 **stiffly** swiftly 113 **Horatio and Marcellus (Within)** Enter Horatio and Marcellus [Q2 gives the speech to Horatio] 116 **bird** and 122 **heaven, my lord** heauen 132 **Look you, I'll** I will 170 **some'er** [ed] so mere [F has "so ere"]

II.i. s.d. **Reynaldo** or two 28 **Faith, no** Fayth 38 **warrant** wit 39 **sullies** sallies 40 **i' th'** with 52–53 **at "friend or so," and "gentleman"** [Q2 omits] 112 **quoted** coted

II.ii.43 **Assure you** I assure 57 **o'erhasty** hastie 58 s.d. **Enter Polonius, Voltemand, and Cornelius** Enter Embassadors 90 **since brevity** breuitie 108 s.d. **the letter** [Q2 omits, but has "letter" at side of line 116] 126 **above** about 137 **winking** working 143 **his** her 148 **watch** wath 149 **a lightness** lightnes 151 **'tis** this this 167 s.d. **Enter Hamlet reading on a book** Enter Hamlet 190 **far gone, far gone** far gone 205 **you yourself** your selfe 205 **should be** shall growe 212 **sanity** sanctity 214–15 **and suddenly . . . between him** [Q2 omits] 217 **will** will not 227 **excellent** extent 231 **overhappy** euer happy 232 **cap** lap 240 **but that** but the 243–74 **Let me question . . . dreadfully attended**

[Q2 omits] **278 even** euer **285 Why anything** Any thing **312 a piece** peece **318 woman** women **329 of me** on me **332–33 the clown . . . o' th' sere** [from F, but F has "tickled a" for "tickle o' "; Q2 omits] **334 blank** black **345–70 Hamlet. How comes . . . load too** [Q2 omits] **350 berattle** [ed; F has "be-ratled"; Q2 omits] **357 most like** [ed; F has "like most"; Q2 omits] **381 lest my** let me **407–08 tragical-historical, tragical-comical-historical-pastoral** [Q2 omits] **434 By'r Lady** by lady **439 French falconers** friendly Fankners **454 affectation** affection **457 tale** talke **467 heraldry** heraldy **485 Then senseless Ilium** [Q2 omits] **492 And like** Like **506 fellies** [ed] follies **515 Mobled queen is good** [F has "Inobled" for "Mobled"; Q2 omits] **525 husband's** husband **530 whe'r** [ed] where **550–51 a need** neede **551 or sixteen lines** lines, or sixteene lines **556 till** tell **564 his visage** the visage **569 to Hecuba** to her **571 the cue** that **590 ha' fatted** [F has "have fatted"] a fatted **593 O, vengeance** [Q2 omits] **595 father** [Q4; Q2 and F omit] **611 devil, and the devil** deale, and the deale

III.i.**32–33 myself (lawful espials) Will** myself Wee'le **46 loneliness** lowliness **55 Let's withdraw** with-draw **83 cowards of us all** cowards **85 sicklied** sickled **92 well, well, well** well **107 your honesty** you **121 to a nunnery** a Nunry **129 knaves all** knaues **139 Go, farewell,** farewell **146 lisp** list **148 your ignorance** ignorance **155 expectancy** expectation **160 that** what **162 feature** stature **164** [Q2 concludes the line with a stage direction, "Exit"] **191 unwatched** vnmatcht

III.ii.**1 pronounced** pronound **24 own feature** feature **28 the which** which **31 praise** praysd **39 us, sir** vs **47 s.d. Exit Players** [Q2 omits] **51 s.d. Exit Polonius** [Q2 omits] **54 ho** [F has "hoa"] howe **91 detecting** detected **91 s.d. Rosencrantz . . . Flourish** [Q2 omits] **117–18 Hamlet. I mean . . . my lord** [Q2 omits] **140 s.d. sound** [ed] sounds **140 s.d. very lovingly** [Q2 omits] **140 s.d. She kneels . . . unto him** [Q2 omits] **140 s.d. Exeunt** [Q2 omits] **142 is miching** munching **147 keep counsel** keepe **161 ground** the ground **169 your** our **174 In neither** Eyther none, in neither **175 love** Lord **196 like** the **205 Grief joys** Greefe ioy **225 An** [ed] And **229 a I** be a **233 s.d. sleeps** [Q2 omits] **234 s.d. Exit** Exeunt **262 Confederate** Considerat **264 infected** inuected **266 s.d. Pours the poison in his ears** [Q2 omits] **272 Hamlet. What . . . fire** [Q2 omits] **282–83 two Provincial** prouinciall **316 start** stare **325 my business** busines **366 and thumb** & the vmber **375 the top of my** my **379 you can** you **394–95 Polonius . . . friends** Leaue me friends. I will, say so. By and by is easily said **397 breathes** breakes **399 bitter business as the day** buisnes as the bitter day **404 daggers** dagger

III.iii.**19 huge** hough **22 ruin** raine **23 with** a **50 pardoned** pardon **58 shove** showe **73 pat** but **79 hire and salary** base and silly

III.iv.**5–6 with him . . . Mother, Mother, Mother** [Q2 omits] **7 warrant** wait **21 inmost** most **23 ho** [F has "hoa"] how **25 s.d. kills Polonius** [Q2 omits] **53 That roars . . . index** [Q2 gives to Hamlet] **60 heaven-kissing** heaue, a kissing **89 panders** pardons **90 mine eyes into my very soul** my very eyes into my soule **91 grainèd** greeued **92 will not** will **98 tithe** kyth **140 Ecstasy** [Q2 omits] **144 And I** And **159 live** leaue **166 Refrain tonight** to refraine night **180 Thus** This **187 ravel** rouell **216 foolish** most foolish **218 s.d. exit Hamlet, tugging in Polonius** Exit

TEXTUAL NOTE

IV.i.35 dragged dreg'd

IV.ii.1 s.d. Enter Hamlet Enter Hamlet, Rosencraus, and others **2 Gentlemen. (Within) Hamlet! Lord Hamlet!** [Q2 omits] **4 s.d. Enter Rosencrantz and Guildenstern** [Q2 omits] **6 Compounded** Compound **18 ape** apple **30–31 Hide fox, and all after** [Q2 omits]

IV.iii.15 Ho [F has "Hoa"] How **43 With fiery quickness** [Q2 omits] **52 and** so **68 were ne'er begun** will nere begin

IV.v.16 Queen [Q2 gives line 16 as part of the previous speech] **20 s.d. Enter Ophelia distracted** Enter Ophelia [placed after line 16] **39 grave** ground **42 God** good **52 clothes** close **57 Indeed, la** Indeede **73 s.d. Exit** [Q2 omits] **82 in their** in **89 his** this **96 Queen. Alack, what noise is this** [Q2 omits] **97 are** is **106 They** The **142 swoopstake** [ed] soopstake **152 s.d. Let her come in** [Q2 gives to Laertes[**157 Till** Tell **160 an old** a poore **161–63 Nature . . . loves** [Q2 omits] **165 Hey . . . hey nony** [Q2 omits] **181 O, you must** you may **186 affliction** afflictions **194 All flaxen** Flaxen **198 Christian souls, I pray God** Christians soules **199 see this** this

IV.vi.9 an't and **23 good turn** turne **27 bore** bord **31 He** So **32 give you** you

IV.vii.6 proceeded proceede **14 conjunctive** concliue **20 Would** Worke **22 loud a wind** loued Arm'd **24 And** But **24 had** haue **36 How now . . . Hamlet** [Q2 omits] **42 s.d. Exit Messenger** [Q2 omits] **46 your pardon** you pardon **47 and more strange return** returne **48 Hamlet** [Q2 omits] **56 shall live** liue **62 checking** the King **88 my** me **115 wick** [ed] weeke **119 changes** change **122 spendthrift** [ed] spend thirfts **125 in deed** [ed] indeede **134 on** ore **138 pass** pace **140 for that** for **156 ha't** hate **159 prepared** prefard **167 hoar** horry **171 cold** cull-cold

V.i.9 se offendendo so offended **12 Argall** or all **35–38 Other. Why . . . without arms** [Q2 omits] **44 that frame** that **56 s.d. Enter Hamlet and Horatio afar off** Enter Hamlet and Horatio [Q2 places after line 65] **61 stoup** soope **71 daintier** dintier **90 mazzard** massene **107–08 Is this . . . recoveries** [Q2 omits] **109 his vouchers** vouchers **110 double ones** doubles **122 O** or **123 For such a guest is meet** [Q2 omits] **144–45 a gravemaker** Graue-maker **146 all the days** the dayes **167 corses now-a-days** corses **174–75 three and twenty** 23 **185 Let me see** [Q2 omits] **187 borne** bore **195 chamber** table **210–11 as thus** [Q2 omits] **218 winter's** waters **219 s.d. Enter King . . . Lords attendant** Enter K. Q. Laertes and the corse **233 Shards,** flints Flints **248 treble** double **252 s.d. Leaps in the grave** [Q2 omits] **263 and rash** rash **279 Dost thou** doost **287 thus** this **300 shortly** thirtie **301 Till** Tell

V.ii.5 Methought my thought **6 bilboes** bilbo **17 unseal** vnfold **19 Ah** [ed; F has "Oh"] A **43 as's** [F has "assis"] as sir **52 Subscribed** Subcribe **57 Why, man . . . employment** [Q2 omits] **68–80 To quit . . . comes here** [Q2 omits] **78 court** [ed; F has "count"; Q2 omits] **80 s.d. Young Osric** [Q2 omits] **81 Osric** [Q2 prints "Cour" consistently as the speech prefix] **83 humbly** humble **94 Put your** your **99 sultry** sully **99 for** or **102 But, my** my **108 gentleman** [ed] gentlemen **110 feelingly** [ed] sellingly **142 his weapon** [ed] this weapon **151 hangers** [ed] hanger **158 carriages** carriage **161 might be** be **164–65 all impawned, as** all **180 e'en so** so **184 Yours, yours. He** Yours **189 did comply** did **193 yeasty** histy **194 fanned** [ed; F has "fond"] prophane

TEXTUAL NOTE

195 **winnowed** trennowed 208 **to Laertes** [ed] Laertes 210 **lose this wager** loose 213 **But thou** thou 217 **gaingiving** gamgiuing 221 **If it be now** if it be 223 **will come** well come 241 **Sir, in this audience** [Q2 omits] 251 **keep my** my 251 **till** all 254 **Come on** [Q2 omits] 264 **bettered** better 266 **s.d. Prepare to play** [Q2 omits] 273 **union** Vnice 281 **s.d. They play** [Q2 omits] 287 **A touch, a touch** [Q omits] 301 **s.d. play** [Q omits] 303 **s.d. In scuffling they change rapiers** [Q2 omits] 304 **ho** [F has "hoa"] howe 312 **Ho** [ed] how 314 **Hamlet. Hamlet** Hamlet 317 **thy** my 323 **s.d. Hurts the King** [Q2 omits] 326 **murd'rous, damnèd** damned 327 **thy union** the Onixe 328 **s.d. King dies** [Q2 omits] 332 **s.d. Dies** [Q2 omits] 346 **live** I leaue 359 **Dies** [Q2 omits] 362 **s.d. with Drum, Colors, and Attendants** [Q2 omits] 380 **th' yet** yet 384 **forced** for no 393 **on** no 400 **rite** [ed; F has "rites"] right 404 **s.d. marching . . . shot off** [Q2 omits]

WILLIAM SHAKESPEARE

THE TRAGEDY OF OTHELLO THE MOOR OF VENICE

Edited by Alvin Kernan

[*Dramatis Personae*

OTHELLO, the Moor
BRABANTIO, father to Desdemona
CASSIO, an honorable lieutenant
IAGO, a villain
RODERIGO, a gulled gentleman
DUKE OF VENICE
SENATORS
MONTANO, Governor of Cyprus
GENTLEMAN OF CYPRUS
LODOVICO and GRATIANO, two noble Venetians
SAILORS
CLOWN
DESDEMONA, wife to Othello
EMILIA, wife to Iago
BIANCA, a courtesan
MESSENGER, HERALD, OFFICERS, GENTLEMEN, MUSICIANS, ATTENDANTS

Scene: Venice and Cyprus]

THE TRAGEDY OF OTHELLO

ACT I

Scene I. [*Venice. A street.*]

Enter Roderigo and Iago.

RODERIGO Tush! Never tell me? I take it much unkindly
That thou, Iago, who hast had my purse
As if the strings were thine, shouldst know of this.

IAGO 'Sblood, but you'll not hear me! If ever I did dream
Of such a matter, abhor me.

RODERIGO Thou told'st me 5
Thou didst hold him in thy hate.

IAGO Despise me
If I do not. Three great ones of the city,
In personal suit to make me his lieutenant,
Off-capped to him; and, by the faith of man,
I know my price; I am worth no worse a place. 10
But he, as loving his own pride and purposes,
Evades them with a bombast circumstance,

Text references are printed in **bold** type; the annotation follows in roman type.
I.i.4 **'Sblood** by God's blood 9 **Off-capped** doffed their caps—as a mark of respect
12 **bombast circumstance** stuffed, roundabout speech

Horribly stuffed with epithets of war;
Nonsuits my mediators. For, "Certes," says he,
"I have already chose my officer." And what was
15 he?
Forsooth, a great arithmetician,
One Michael Cassio, a Florentine,
(A fellow almost damned in a fair wife)
That never set a squadron in the field,
20 Nor the division of a battle knows
More than a spinster; unless the bookish theoric,
Wherein the tonguèd consuls can propose
As masterly as he. Mere prattle without practice
Is all his soldiership. But he, sir, had th' election;
25 And I, of whom his eyes had seen the proof
At Rhodes, at Cyprus, and on other grounds
Christian and heathen, must be belee'd and calmed
By debitor and creditor. This counter-caster,
He, in good time, must his lieutenant be,
And I—God bless the mark!—his Moorship's an-
30 cient.

RODERIGO By heaven, I rather would have been his hangman.

IAGO Why, there's no remedy. 'Tis the curse of service:
Preferment goes by letter and affection,
And not by old gradation, where each second
35 Stood heir to th' first. Now, sir, be judge yourself,
Whether I in any just term am affined
To love the Moor.

RODERIGO I would not follow him then.

14 **Nonsuits** rejects 16 **arithmetician** theorist (rather than practical) 18 **A . . . wife** (a much-disputed passage, which is probably best taken as a general sneer at Cassio as a dandy and a ladies' man. But in the story from which Shakespeare took his plot the counterpart of Cassio is married, and it may be that at the beginning of the play Shakespeare had decided to keep him married but later changed his mind) 22 **tonguèd** eloquent 28 **counter-caster** i.e., a bookkeeper who **casts** (reckons up) figures on a **counter** (abacus) 30 **ancient** standard-bearer; an underofficer 33 **letter and affection** recommendations (from men of power) and personal preference 34 **old gradation** seniority 36 **affined** bound

IAGO O, sir, content you.
I follow him to serve my turn upon him.
We cannot all be masters, nor all masters 40
Cannot be truly followed. You shall mark
Many a duteous and knee-crooking knave
That, doting on his own obsequious bondage,
Wears out his time, much like his master's ass,
For naught but provender; and when he's old, cashiered. 45
Whip me such honest knaves! Others there are
Who, trimmed in forms and visages of duty,
Keep yet their hearts attending on themselves,
And, throwing but shows of service on their lords,
Do well thrive by them, and when they have lined their coats, 50
Do themselves homage. These fellows have some soul;
And such a one do I profess myself. For, sir,
It is as sure as you are Roderigo,
Were I the Moor, I would not be Iago.
In following him, I follow but myself. 55
Heaven is my judge, not I for love and duty,
But seeming so, for my peculiar end;
For when my outward action doth demonstrate
The native act and figure of my heart
In complement extern, 'tis not long after 60
But I will wear my heart upon my sleeve
For daws to peck at; I am not what I am.

RODERIGO What a full fortune does the thick-lips owe
If he can carry't thus!

IAGO Call up her father,
Rouse him. Make after him, poison his delight, 65
Proclaim him in the streets, incense her kinsmen,
And though he in a fertile climate dwell,
Plague him with flies; though that his joy be joy,

42 knee-crooking bowing 57 peculiar personal 59 native natural, innate
60 complement extern outward appearances 63 owe own

Yet throw such chances of vexation on't
70 As it may lose some color.

RODERIGO Here is her father's house. I'll call aloud.

IAGO Do, with like timorous accent and dire yell
As when, by night and negligence, the fire
Is spied in populous cities.

RODERIGO What, ho, Brabantio! Signior Brabantio,
75 ho!

IAGO Awake! What, ho, Brabantio! Thieves! Thieves!
Look to your house, your daughter, and your bags!
Thieves! Thieves!

Brabantio above [*at a window*].

BRABANTIO What is the reason of this terrible summons?
80 What is the matter there?

RODERIGO Signior, is all your family within?

IAGO Are your doors locked?

BRABANTIO Why, wherefore ask you this?

IAGO Zounds, sir, y'are robbed! For shame. Put on your gown!
Your heart is burst, you have lost half your soul.
85 Even now, now, very now, an old black ram
Is tupping your white ewe. Arise, arise!
Awake the snorting citizens with the bell,
Or else the devil will make a grandsire of you.
Arise, I say!

BRABANTIO What, have you lost your wits?

RODERIGO Most reverend signior, do you know my
90 voice?

BRABANTIO Not I. What are you?

72 timorous frightening **78 s.d. above** (i.e., on the small upper stage above and to the rear of the main platform stage, which resembled the projecting upper story of an Elizabethan house)

RODERIGO My name is Roderigo.

BRABANTIO The worser welcome!
I have charged thee not to haunt about my doors.
In honest plainness thou hast heard me say
My daughter is not for thee; and now, in madness, 95
Being full of supper and distemp'ring draughts,
Upon malicious knavery dost thou come
To start my quiet.

RODERIGO Sir, sir, sir——

BRABANTIO But thou must needs be sure
My spirits and my place have in their power 100
To make this bitter to thee.

RODERIGO Patience, good sir.

BRABANTIO What tell'st thou me of robbing? This is Venice;
My house is not a grange.

RODERIGO Most grave Brabantio,
In simple and pure soul I come to you.

IAGO Zounds, sir, you are one of those that will not 105
serve God if the devil bid you. Because we come
to do you service and you think we are ruffians,
you'll have your daughter covered with a Barbary
horse, you'll have your nephews neigh to you,
you'll have coursers for cousins, and gennets for 110
germans.

BRABANTIO What profane wretch art thou?

IAGO I am one, sir, that comes to tell you your daughter
and the Moor are making the beast with two backs.

BRABANTIO Thou art a villain.

IAGO You are—a senator. 115

BRABANTIO This thou shalt answer. I know thee, Roderigo.

96 distemp'ring draughts unsettling drinks **98 start** disrupt **100 place** rank, i.e., of senator **108 grange** isolated house **108 Barbary** Arabian, i.e., Moorish **109 nephews** i.e., grandsons **110 cousins** relations **110–11 gennets for germans** Spanish horses for blood relatives

RODERIGO Sir, I will answer anything. But I beseech
you,
If't be your pleasure and most wise consent,
As partly I find it is, that your fair daughter,
120 At this odd-even and dull watch o' th' night,
Transported, with no worse nor better guard
But with a knave of common hire, a gondolier,
To the gross clasps of a lascivious Moor—
If this be known to you, and your allowance,
125 We then have done you bold and saucy wrongs;
But if you know not this, my manners tell me
We have your wrong rebuke. Do not believe
That from the sense of all civility
I thus would play and trifle with your reverence.
130 Your daughter, if you have not given her leave,
I say again, hath made a gross revolt,
Tying her duty, beauty, wit, and fortunes
In an extravagant and wheeling stranger
Of here and everywhere. Straight satisfy yourself.
135 If she be in her chamber, or your house,
Let loose on me the justice of the state
For thus deluding you.

BRABANTIO Strike on the tinder, ho!
Give me a taper! Call up all my people!
This accident is not unlike my dream.
140 Belief of it oppresses me already.
Light, I say! Light! *Exit [above].*

IAGO Farewell, for I must leave you.
It seems not meet, nor wholesome to my place,
To be produced—as, if I stay, I shall—
Against the Moor. For I do know the State,
145 However this may gall him with some check,
Cannot with safety cast him; for he's embarked
With such loud reason to the Cyprus wars,

120 odd-even between night and morning **128 sense of all civility** feeling of what is proper **133 extravagant** vagrant, wandering (Othello is not Venetian and thus may be considered a wandering soldier of fortune) **139 accident** happening **145 check** restraint **146 cast** dismiss

Which even now stands in act, that for their souls
Another of his fathom they have none
To lead their business; in which regard, 150
Though I do hate him as I do hell-pains,
Yet, for necessity of present life,
I must show out a flag and sign of love,
Which is indeed but sign. That you shall surely find him,
Lead to the Sagittary the raisèd search; 155
And there will I be with him. So farewell. *Exit.*

Enter Brabantio [in his nightgown], with Servants and torches.

BRABANTIO It is too true an evil. Gone she is;
And what's to come of my despisèd time
Is naught but bitterness. Now, Roderigo,
Where didst thou see her?—O unhappy girl!— 160
With the Moor, say'st thou?–Who would be a father?—
How didst thou know 'twas she?—O, she deceives me
Past thought!—What said she to you? Get moe tapers!
Raise all my kindred!—Are they married, think you?

RODERIGO Truly I think they are. 165

BRABANTIO O heaven! How got she out? O treason of the blood!
Fathers, from hence trust not your daughters' minds
By what you see them act. Is there not charms
By which the property of youth and maidhood
May be abused? Have you not read, Roderigo, 170
Of some such thing?

RODERIGO Yes, sir, I have indeed.

BRABANTIO Call up my brother.—O, would you had had her!—

148 stands in act takes place 149 fathom ability 155 Sagittary (probably the name of an inn) 163 moe more 168 act do 169 property true nature

Some one way, some another.—Do you know
Where we may apprehend her and the Moor?

175 RODERIGO I think I can discover him, if you please
To get good guard and go along with me.

BRABANTIO Pray you lead on. At every house I'll call;
I may command at most.—Get weapons, ho!
And raise some special officers of might.—
180 On, good Roderigo; I will deserve your pains.
Exeunt.

Scene II. [*A street.*]

Enter Othello, Iago, Attendants with torches.

IAGO Though in the trade of war I have slain men,
Yet do I hold it very stuff o' th' conscience,
To do no contrived murder. I lack iniquity
Sometime to do me service. Nine or ten times
I had thought t' have yerked him here, under the
5 ribs.

OTHELLO 'Tis better as it is.

IAGO Nay, but he prated,
And spoke such scurvy and provoking terms
Against your honor, that with the little godliness
I have
I did full hard forbear him. But I pray you, sir,
10 Are you fast married? Be assured of this,
That the magnifico is much beloved,
And hath in his effect a voice potential
As double as the Duke's. He will divorce you,
Or put upon you what restraint or grievance

180 **deserve your pains** be worthy of (and reward) your efforts I.ii.2 **stuff** essence 5 **yerked** stabbed 11 **magnifico** nobleman 12–13 **hath . . . Duke's** i.e., can be as effective as the Duke

The law, with all his might to enforce it on, 15
Will give him cable.

OTHELLO Let him do his spite.
My services which I have done the Signiory
Shall out-tongue his complaints. 'Tis yet to know—
Which when I know that boasting is an honor
I shall promulgate—I fetch my life and being 20
From men of royal siege; and my demerits
May speak unbonneted to as proud a fortune
As this that I have reached. For know, Iago,
But that I love the gentle Desdemona,
I would not my unhousèd free condition 25
Put into circumscription and confine
For the seas' worth. But look, what lights come yond?

Enter Cassio, with [Officers and] torches.

IAGO Those are the raisèd father and his friends.
You were best go in.

OTHELLO Not I. I must be found.
My parts, my title, and my perfect soul 30
Shall manifest me rightly. Is it they?

IAGO By Janus, I think no.

OTHELLO The servants of the Duke? And my lieutenant?
The goodness of the night upon you, friends.
What is the news?

CASSIO The Duke does greet you, general; 35
And he requires your haste-posthaste appearance
Even on the instant.

OTHELLO What is the matter, think you?

CASSIO Something from Cyprus, as I may divine.
It is a business of some heat. The galleys

16 cable range, scope **17 Signiory** the rulers of Venice **18 yet to know** unknown as yet **21 siege** rank **21 demerits** deserts **22–23 May . . . reached,** i.e., are the equal of the family I have married into **25 unhousèd** unconfined **30 perfect soul** clear, unflawed conscience

40 Have sent a dozen sequent messengers
This very night at one another's heels,
And many of the consuls, raised and met,
Are at the Duke's already. You have been hotly called for.
When, being not at your lodging to be found,
45 The Senate hath sent about three several quests
To search you out.

OTHELLO 'Tis well I am found by you.
I will but spend a word here in the house,
And go with you. [*Exit.*]

CASSIO Ancient, what makes he here?

IAGO Faith, he tonight hath boarded a land carack.
50 If it prove lawful prize, he's made forever.

CASSIO I do not understand.

IAGO He's married.

CASSIO To who?

[*Enter Othello.*]

IAGO Marry, to—Come, captain, will you go?

OTHELLO Have with you.

CASSIO Here comes another troop to seek for you.

Enter Brabantio, Roderigo, with Officers and torches.

IAGO It is Brabantio. General, be advised.
He comes to bad intent.

55 OTHELLO Holla! Stand there!

RODERIGO Signior, it is the Moor.

BRABANTIO Down with him, thief!
[*They draw swords.*]

IAGO You, Roderigo? Come, sir, I am for you.

OTHELLO Keep up your bright swords, for the dew will rust them.

40 sequent successive **45 several** separate **49 carack** treasure ship **52 Marry** By Mary (an interjection)

Good signior, you shall more command with years
Than with your weapons. 60

BRABANTIO O thou foul thief, where hast thou stowed my daughter?
Damned as thou art, thou hast enchanted her!
For I'll refer me to all things of sense,
If she in chains of magic were not bound,
Whether a maid so tender, fair, and happy, 65
So opposite to marriage that she shunned
The wealthy, curlèd darlings of our nation,
Would ever have, t'incur a general mock,
Run from her guardage to the sooty bosom
Of such a thing as thou—to fear, not to delight. 70
Judge me the world if 'tis not gross in sense
That thou hast practiced on her with foul charms,
Abused her delicate youth with drugs or minerals
That weaken motion. I'll have't disputed on;
'Tis probable, and palpable to thinking. 75
I therefore apprehend and do attach thee
For an abuser of the world, a practicer
Of arts inhibited and out of warrant.
Lay hold upon him. If he do resist,
Subdue him at his peril.

OTHELLO Hold your hands, 80
Both you of my inclining and the rest.
Were it my cue to fight, I should have known it
Without a prompter. Whither will you that I go
To answer this your charge?

BRABANTIO To prison, till fit time
Of law and course of direct session 85
Call thee to answer.

OTHELLO What if I do obey?
How may the Duke be therewith satisfied,
Whose messengers are here about my side

63 refer . . . sense i.e., base (my argument) on all ordinary understanding of nature **68 general mock** public shame **71 gross in sense** obvious **72 practiced** used tricks **74 motion** thought, i.e., reason **76 attach** arrest **78 inhibited . . . warrant** prohibited and illegal (black magic)

Upon some present business of the state
To bring me to him?

90 OFFICER 'Tis true, most worthy signior.
The Duke's in council, and your noble self
I am sure is sent for.

BRABANTIO How? The Duke in council?
In this time of the night? Bring him away.
Mine's not an idle cause. The Duke himself,
95 Or any of my brothers of the state,
Cannot but feel this wrong as 'twere their own;
For if such actions may have passage free,
Bondslaves and pagans shall our statesmen be.
Exeunt.

Scene III. [*A council chamber.*]

Enter Duke, Senators, and Officers [*set at a table, with lights and Attendants*].

DUKE There's no composition in this news
That gives them credit.

FIRST SENATOR Indeed, they are disproportioned.
My letters say a hundred and seven galleys.

DUKE And mine a hundred forty.

SECOND SENATOR And mine two hundred.
5 But though they jump not on a just accompt—
As in these cases where the aim reports
'Tis oft with difference—yet do they all confirm
A Turkish fleet, and bearing up to Cyprus.

DUKE Nay, it is possible enough to judgment.
10 I do not so secure me in the error,

89 present immediate **95 brothers** i.e., the other senators **I.iii.1 composition** agreement **2 gives them credit** makes them believable **5 jump** agree **5 just accompt** exact counting **6 aim** approximation **9 to judgment** when carefully considered

But the main article I do approve
In fearful sense.

SAILOR (*Within*) What, ho! What, ho! What, ho!

Enter Sailor.

OFFICER A messenger from the galleys.

DUKE Now? What's the business?

SAILOR The Turkish preparation makes for Rhodes.
So was I bid report here to the State 15
By Signior Angelo.

DUKE How say you by this change?

FIRST SENATOR This cannot be
By no assay of reason. 'Tis a pageant
To keep us in false gaze. When we consider
Th' importancy of Cyprus to the Turk, 20
And let ourselves again but understand
That, as it more concerns the Turk than Rhodes,
So may he with more facile question bear it,
For that it stands not in such warlike brace,
But altogether lacks th' abilities 25
That Rhodes is dressed in. If we make thought of this,
We must not think the Turk is so unskillful
To leave that latest which concerns him first,
Neglecting an attempt of ease and gain
To wake and wage a danger profitless. 30

DUKE Nay, in all confidence he's not for Rhodes.

OFFICER Here is more news.

Enter a Messenger.

MESSENGER The Ottomites, a reverend and gracious,
Steering with due course toward the isle of Rhodes,
Have there injointed them with an after fleet. 35

10–12 I do . . . sense i.e., just because the numbers disagree in the reports, I do not doubt that the principal information (that the Turkish fleet is out) is fearfully true **18 pageant** show, pretense **19 in false gaze** looking the wrong way **23 facile question** easy struggle **24 warlike brace** "military posture" **35 after** following

FIRST SENATOR Ay, so I thought. How many, as you guess?

MESSENGER Of thirty sail; and now they do restem
Their backward course, bearing with frank appearance
Their purposes toward Cyprus. Signior Montano,
40 Your trusty and most valiant servitor,
With his free duty recommends you thus,
And prays you to believe him.

DUKE 'Tis certain then for Cyprus.
Marcus Luccicos, is not he in town?

45 FIRST SENATOR He's now in Florence.

DUKE Write from us to him; post-posthaste dispatch.

FIRST SENATOR Here comes Brabantio and the valiant Moor.

Enter Brabantio, Othello, Cassio, Iago, Roderigo, and Officers.

DUKE Valiant Othello, we must straight employ you
Against the general enemy Ottoman.
[*To Brabantio*] I did not see you. Welcome gentle
50 signior.
We lacked your counsel and your help tonight.

BRABANTIO So did I yours. Good your grace, pardon me.
Neither my place, nor aught I heard of business,
Hath raised me from my bed; nor doth the general care
55 Take hold on me; for my particular grief
Is of so floodgate and o'erbearing nature
That it engluts and swallows other sorrows,
And it is still itself.

DUKE Why, what's the matter?

BRABANTIO My daughter! O, my daughter!

41 **free duty** unlimited respect 41 **recommends** informs 48 **straight** at once
49 **general** universal

SENATORS Dead?

BRABANTIO Ay, to me.
She is abused, stol'n from me, and corrupted 60
By spells and medicines bought of mountebanks;
For nature so prepost'rously to err,
Being not deficient, blind, or lame of sense,
Sans witchcraft could not.

DUKE Whoe'er he be that in this foul proceeding 65
Hath thus beguiled your daughter of herself,
And you of her, the bloody book of law
You shall yourself read in the bitter letter
After your own sense; yea, though our proper son
Stood in your action.

BRABANTIO Humbly I thank your Grace. 70
Here is the man—this Moor, whom now, it seems,
Your special mandate for the state affairs
Hath hither brought.

ALL We are very sorry for't.

DUKE [*To Othello*] What in your own part can you say to this?

BRABANTIO Nothing, but this is so. 75

OTHELLO Most potent, grave, and reverend signiors,
My very noble and approved good masters,
That I have ta'en away this old man's daughter,
It is most true; true I have married her.
The very head and front of my offending 80
Hath this extent, no more. Rude am I in my speech,
And little blessed with the soft phrase of peace,
For since these arms of mine had seven years' pith
Till now some nine moons wasted, they have used
Their dearest action in the tented field; 85
And little of this great world can I speak

64 **Sans** without 69 **proper** own 70 **Stood in your action** were the accused in your suit 77 **approved** tested, proven by past performance 80 **head and front** extreme form (front = forehead) 83 **pith** strength 84 **wasted** past 85 **dearest** most important

More than pertains to feats of broils and battle;
And therefore little shall I grace my cause
In speaking for myself. Yet, by your gracious patience,
90 I will a round unvarnished tale deliver
Of my whole course of love—what drugs, what charms,
What conjuration, and what mighty magic,
For such proceeding I am charged withal,
I won his daughter—

BRABANTIO A maiden never bold,
95 Of spirit so still and quiet that her motion
Blushed at herself; and she, in spite of nature,
Of years, of country, credit, everything,
To fall in love with what she feared to look on!
It is a judgment maimed and most imperfect
100 That will confess perfection so could err
Against all rules of nature, and must be driven
To find out practices of cunning hell
Why this should be. I therefore vouch again
That with some mixtures pow'rful o'er the blood,
105 Or with some dram, conjured to this effect,
He wrought upon her.

DUKE To vouch this is no proof,
Without more wider and more overt test
Than these thin habits and poor likelihoods
Of modern seeming do prefer against him.

110 FIRST SENATOR But, Othello, speak.
Did you by indirect and forcèd courses
Subdue and poison this young maid's affections?
Or came it by request, and such fair question
As soul to soul affordeth?

OTHELLO I do beseech you,
115 Send for the lady to the Sagittary

90 round blunt **95–96 her motion/Blushed at herself** i.e., she was so modest that she blushed at every thought (and movement) **108 habits** clothing **109 modern** trivial **113 question** discussion

And let her speak of me before her father.
If you do find me foul in her report,
The trust, the office, I do hold of you
Not only take away, but let your sentence
Even fall upon my life.

DUKE Fetch Desdemona hither. 120

OTHELLO Ancient, conduct them; you best know the place.

[*Exit Iago, with two or three Attendants.*]

And till she come, as truly as to heaven
I do confess the vices of my blood,
So justly to your grave ears I'll present
How I did thrive in this fair lady's love, 125
And she in mine.

DUKE Say it, Othello.

OTHELLO Her father loved me; oft invited me;
Still questioned me the story of my life
From year to year, the battle, sieges, fortune
That I have passed. 130
I ran it through, even from my boyish days
To th' very moment that he bade me tell it.
Wherein I spoke of most disastrous chances,
Of moving accidents by flood and field,
Of hairbreadth scapes i' th' imminent deadly breach, 135
Of being taken by the insolent foe
And sold to slavery, of my redemption thence
And portance in my travel's history,
Wherein of anters vast and deserts idle,
Rough quarries, rocks, and hills whose heads touch heaven, 140
It was my hint to speak. Such was my process.
And of the Cannibals that each other eat,
The Anthropophagi, and men whose heads

128 Still regularly **135 imminent** threatening **138 portance** manner of acting
139 anters caves **139 idle** empty, sterile **143 Anthropophagi** man-eaters

Grew beneath their shoulders. These things to hear
145 Would Desdemona seriously incline;
But still the house affairs would draw her thence;
Which ever as she could with haste dispatch,
She'd come again, and with a greedy ear
Devour up my discourse. Which I observing,
150 Took once a pliant hour, and found good means
To draw from her a prayer of earnest heart
That I would all my pilgrimage dilate,
Whereof by parcels she had something heard,
But not intentively. I did consent,
155 And often did beguile her of her tears
When I did speak of some distressful stroke
That my youth suffered. My story being done,
She gave me for my pains a world of kisses.
She swore in faith 'twas strange, 'twas passing
strange;
160 'Twas pitiful, 'twas wondrous pitiful.
She wished she had not heard it; yet she wished
That heaven had made her such a man. She thanked
me,
And bade me, if I had a friend that loved her,
I should but teach him how to tell my story,
165 And that would woo her. Upon this hint I spake.
She loved me for the dangers I had passed,
And I loved her that she did pity them.
This only is the witchcraft I have used.
Here comes the lady. Let her witness it.

Enter Desdemona, Iago, Attendants.

170 DUKE I think this tale would win my daughter too.
Good Brabantio, take up this mangled matter at the
best.
Men do their broken weapons rather use
Than their bare hands.

152 dilate relate in full **154 intentively** at length and in sequence **159 passing** surpassing **171 Take . . . best** i.e., make the best of this disaster

BRABANTIO I pray you hear her speak.
If she confess that she was half the wooer,
Destruction on my head if my bad blame 175
Light on the man. Come hither, gentle mistress.
Do you perceive in all this noble company
Where most you owe obedience?

DESDEMONA My noble father,
I do perceive here a divided duty.
To you I am bound for life and education; 180
My life and education both do learn me
How to respect you. You are the lord of duty,
I am hitherto your daughter. But here's my husband,
And so much duty as my mother showed
To you, preferring you before her father, 185
So much I challenge that I may profess
Due to the Moor my lord.

BRABANTIO God be with you. I have done.
Please it your Grace, on to the state affairs.
I had rather to adopt a child than get it.
Come hither, Moor. 190
I here do give thee that with all my heart
Which, but thou hast already, with all my heart
I would keep from thee. For your sake, jewel,
I am glad at soul I have no other child,
For thy escape would teach me tyranny, 195
To hang clogs on them. I have done, my lord.

DUKE Let me speak like yourself and lay a sentence
Which, as a grise or step, may help these lovers.
When remedies are past, the griefs are ended
By seeing the worst, which late on hopes depended. 200
To mourn a mischief that is past and gone
Is the next way to draw new mischief on.
What cannot be preserved when fortune takes,

186 challenge claim as right **189 get** beget **193 For your sake** because of you **197 lay a sentence** provide a maxim **198 grise** step **200 late on hopes depended** was supported by hope (of a better outcome) until lately **202 next** closest, surest

Patience her injury a mock'ry makes.
The robbed that smiles, steals something from the
205 thief;
He robs himself that spends a bootless grief.

BRABANTIO So let the Turk of Cyprus us beguile:
We lose it not so long as we can smile.
He bears the sentence well that nothing bears
210 But the free comfort which from thence he hears;
But he bears both the sentence and the sorrow
That to pay grief must of poor patience borrow.
These sentences, to sugar, or to gall,
Being strong on both sides, are equivocal.
215 But words are words. I never yet did hear
That the bruisèd heart was piercèd through the ear.
I humbly beseech you, proceed to th' affairs of state.

DUKE The Turk with a most mighty preparation makes for Cyprus. Othello, the fortitude of the place is
220 best known to you; and though we have there a substitute of most allowed sufficiency, yet opinion, a more sovereign mistress of effects, throws a more safer voice on you. You must therefore be content to slubber the gloss of your new fortunes
225 with this more stubborn and boisterous expedition.

OTHELLO The tyrant Custom, most grave senators,
Hath made the flinty and steel couch of war
My thrice-driven bed of down. I do agnize
A natural and prompt alacrity
230 I find in hardness and do undertake
This present wars against the Ottomites.

206 **bootless** valueless 216 **piercèd** (some editors emend to **pieced**, i.e., "healed." But **pierced** makes good sense: Brabantio is saying in effect that his heart cannot be further hurt [pierced] by the indignity of the useless, conventional advice the Duke offers him. **Pierced** can also mean, however, "lanced" in the medical sense, and would then mean "treated") 219 **fortitude** fortification 221 **substitute** viceroy 221 **most allowed sufficiency** generally acknowledged capability 221–23 **opinion . . . you** i.e., the general opinion, which finally controls affairs, is that you would be the best man in this situation 224 **slubber** besmear 225 **stubborn and boisterous** rough and violent 228 **thrice-driven** i.e., softest 228 **agnize** know in myself

Most humbly, therefore, bending to your state,
I crave fit disposition for my wife,
Due reference of place, and exhibition,
With such accommodation and besort 235
As levels with her breeding.

DUKE Why, at her father's.

BRABANTIO I will not have it so.

OTHELLO Nor I.

DESDEMONA Nor would I there reside,
To put my father in impatient thoughts
By being in his eye. Most gracious Duke,
To my unfolding lend your prosperous ear, 240
And let me find a charter in your voice,
T'assist my simpleness.

DUKE What would you, Desdemona?

DESDEMONA That I love the Moor to live with him,
My downright violence, and storm of fortunes,
May trumpet to the world. My heart's subdued 245
Even to the very quality of my lord.
I saw Othello's visage in his mind,
And to his honors and his valiant parts
Did I my soul and fortunes consecrate.
So that, dear lords, if I be left behind, 250
A moth of peace, and he go to the war,
The rites for why I love him are bereft me,
And I a heavy interim shall support
By his dear absence. Let me go with him.

OTHELLO Let her have your voice. 255
Vouch with me, heaven, I therefore beg it not
To please the palate of my appetite,
Nor to comply with heat—the young affects

234 **exhibition** grant of funds 236 **levels with** is suitable to 240 **unfolding** explanation 240 **prosperous** favoring 241 **charter** permission 245–46 **My . . . lord** i.e., I have become one in nature and being with the man I married (therefore, I too would go to the wars like a soldier) 252 **rites** (may refer either to the marriage rites or to the rites, formalities, of war) 255 **voice** consent 258 **heat** lust 258 **affects** passions

In me defunct—and proper satisfaction;
260 But to be free and bounteous to her mind;
And heaven defend your good souls that you think
I will your serious and great business scant
When she is with me. No, when light-winged toys
Of feathered Cupid seel with wanton dullness
265 My speculative and officed instrument,
That my disports corrupt and taint my business,
Let housewives make a skillet of my helm,
And all indign and base adversities
Make head against my estimation!—

270 DUKE Be it as you shall privately determine,
Either for her stay or going. Th' affair cries haste,
And speed must answer it.

FIRST SENATOR You must away tonight.

OTHELLO With all my heart.

DUKE At nine i' th' morning here we'll meet again.
275 Othello, leave some officer behind,
And he shall our commission bring to you,
And such things else of quality and respect
As doth import you.

OTHELLO So please your grace, my ancient;
A man he is of honesty and trust.
280 To his conveyance I assign my wife,
With what else needful your good grace shall think
To be sent after me.

DUKE Let it be so.
Good night to every one. [*To Brabantio*] And, noble signior,
If virtue no delighted beauty lack,
285 Your son-in-law is far more fair than black.

FIRST SENATOR Adieu, brave Moor. Use Desdemona well.

259 proper satisfaction i.e., consummation of the marriage **261 defend** forbid **264 seel** sew up **264 wanton** lascivious **265 speculative . . . instrument** i.e., sight (and, by extension, the mind) **268 indign** unworthy **269 Make head** form an army, i.e., attack **269 estimation** reputation **284 delighted** delightful

BRABANTIO Look to her, Moor, if thou hast eyes to see:
She has deceived her father, and may thee.
[*Exeunt Duke, Senators, Officers, &c.*]

OTHELLO My life upon her faith! Honest Iago,
My Desdemona must I leave to thee. 290
I prithee let thy wife attend on her,
And bring them after in the best advantage.
Come, Desdemona. I have but an hour
Of love, of wordly matter, and direction
To spend with thee. We must obey the time. 295
Exit [*Moor with Desdemona*].

RODERIGO Iago?

IAGO What say'st thou, noble heart?

RODERIGO What will I do, think'st thou?

IAGO Why, go to bed and sleep.

RODERIGO I will incontinently drown myelf. 300

IAGO If thou dost, I shall never love thee after. Why, thou silly gentleman?

RODERIGO It is silliness to live when to live is torment; and then have we a prescription to die when death is our physician. 305

IAGO O villainous! I have looked upon the world for four times seven years, and since I could distinguish betwixt a benefit and an injury, I never found man that knew how to love himself. Ere I would say I would drown myself for the love of a guinea hen, 310 I would change my humanity with a baboon.

RODERIGO What should I do? I confess it is my shame to be so fond, but it is not in my virtue to amend it.

IAGO Virtue? A fig! 'Tis in ourselves that we are thus, or thus. Our bodies are our gardens, to the which 315 our wills are gardeners; so that if we will plant nettles or sow lettuce, set hyssop and weed up thyme,

292 advantage opportunity 300 incontinently at once 312 virtue strength (Roderigo is saying that his nature controls him)

supply it with one gender of herbs or distract it with many—either to have it sterile with idleness or
320 manured with industry—why, the power and corrigible authority of this lies in our wills. If the balance of our lives had not one scale of reason to poise another of sensuality, the blood and baseness of our natures would conduct us to most prepost'rous
325 conclusions. But we have reason to cool our raging motions, our carnal stings or unbitted lusts, whereof I take this that you call love to be a sect or scion.

RODERIGO It cannot be.

330 IAGO It is merely a lust of blood and a permission of the will. Come, be a man! Drown thyself? Drown cats and blind puppies! I have professed me thy friend, and I confess me knit to thy deserving with cables of perdurable toughness. I could never better
335 stead thee than now. Put money in thy purse. Follow thou the wars; defeat thy favor with an usurped beard. I say, put money in thy purse. It cannot be long that Desdemona should continue her love to the Moor. Put money in thy purse. Nor
340 he his to her. It was a violent commencement in her and thou shalt see an answerable sequestration—put but money in thy purse. These Moors are changeable in their wills—fill thy purse with money. The food that to him now is as luscious as
345 locusts shall be to him shortly as bitter as coloquintida. She must change for youth; when she is sated with his body, she will find the errors of her choice. Therefore, put money in thy purse. If thou wilt needs damn thyself, do it a more delicate way
350 than drowning. Make all the money thou canst. If

318 **distract** vary 320–21 **corrigible** corrective 325 **conclusions** ends 326 **unbitted** i.e., uncontrolled 327–28 **sect or scion** offshoot 335 **stead** serve 336 **defeat thy favor** disguise your face 337 **usurped** assumed 341 **answerable** similar 345 **locusts** (a sweet fruit) 345–46 **coloquintida** (a purgative derived from a bitter apple)

sanctimony and a frail vow betwixt an erring barbarian and supersubtle Venetian be not too hard for my wits, and all the tribe of hell, thou shalt enjoy her. Therefore, make money. A pox of drowning thyself, it is clean out of the way. Seek thou rather to be hanged in compassing thy joy than to be drowned and go without her. 355

RODERIGO Wilt thou be fast to my hopes, if I depend on the issue?

IAGO Thou art sure of me. Go, make money. I have told thee often, and I retell thee again and again, I hate the Moor. My cause is hearted; thine hath no less reason. Let us be conjunctive in our revenge against him. If thou canst cuckold him, thou dost thyself a pleasure, me a sport. There are many events in the womb of time, which will be delivered. Traverse, go, provide thy money! We will have more of this tomorrow. Adieu. 360 365

RODERIGO Where shall we meet i' th' morning?

IAGO At my lodging. 370

RODERIGO I'll be with thee betimes.

IAGO Go to, farewell. Do you hear, Roderigo?

RODERIGO I'll sell all my land. *Exit.*

IAGO Thus do I ever make my fool my purse;
For I mine own gained knowledge should profane 375
If I would time expend with such snipe
But for my sport and profit. I hate the Moor,
And it is thought abroad that 'twixt my sheets
H'as done my office. I know not if't be true,
But I, for mere suspicion in that kind, 380
Will do, as if for surety. He holds me well;
The better shall my purpose work on him.

351 **sanctimony** sacred bond (of marriage) 351 **erring** wandering
356 **compassing** encompassing, achieving 362 **hearted** deep-seated in the heart
363 **conjunctive** joined 375 **gained knowledge** i.e., practical, worldly wisdom
381 **surety** certainty

Cassio's a proper man. Let me see now:
To get his place, and to plume up my will
385 In double knavery. How? How? Let's see.
After some time, to abuse Othello's ears
That he is too familiar with his wife.
He hath a person and a smooth dispose
To be suspected—framed to make women false.
390 The Moor is of a free and open nature
That thinks men honest that but seem to be so;
And will as tenderly be led by th' nose
As asses are.
I have't! It is engendered! Hell and night
395 Must bring this monstrous birth to the world's light.
[*Exit*.]

383 **proper** handsome 384 **plume up my will** (many explanations have been offered for this crucial line, which in Q1 reads "make up my will." The general sense is something like "to make more proud and gratify my ego") 388 **dispose** manner 389 **framed** designed

ACT II

Scene I. [*Cyprus.*]

Enter Montano and two Gentlemen, [*one above*].

MONTANO What from the cape can you discern at sea?

FIRST GENTLEMAN Nothing at all, it is a high-wrought flood.
I cannot 'twixt the heaven and the main
Descry a sail.

MONTANO Methinks the wind hath spoke aloud at land; 5
A fuller blast ne'er shook our battlements.
If it hath ruffianed so upon the sea,
What ribs of oak, when mountains melt on them,
Can hold the mortise? What shall we hear of this?

SECOND GENTLEMAN A segregation of the Turkish fleet. 10
For do but stand upon the foaming shore,
The chidden billow seems to pelt the clouds;
The wind-shaked surge, with high and monstrous main,
Seems to cast water on the burning Bear
And quench the guards of th' ever-fixèd pole. 15

II.i. s.d. (the Folio arrangement of this scene requires that the First Gentleman stand above—on the upper stage—and act as a lookout reporting sights which cannot be seen by Montano standing below on the main stage) 10 **segregation** separation 13 **main** (both "ocean" and "strength") 14–15 **Seems ... pole** (the constellation Ursa Minor contains two stars which are the **guards**, or companions, of the **pole**, or North Star)

I never did like molestation view
On the enchafèd flood.

MONTANO If that the Turkish fleet
Be not ensheltered and embayed, they are drowned;
It is impossible to bear it out.

Enter a [third] Gentleman.

20 THIRD GENTLEMAN News, lads! Our wars are done.
The desperate tempest hath so banged the Turks
That their designment halts. A noble ship of Venice
Hath seen a grievous wrack and sufferance
On most part of their fleet.

MONTANO How? Is this true?

25 THIRD GENTLEMAN The ship is here put in,
A Veronesa; Michael Cassio,
Lieutenant to the warlike Moor Othello,
Is come on shore; the Moor himself at sea,
And is in full commission here for Cyprus.

30 MONTANO I am glad on't. 'Tis a worthy governor.

THIRD GENTLEMAN But this same Cassio, though he speak of comfort
Touching the Turkish loss, yet he looks sadly
And prays the Moor be safe, for they were parted
With foul and violent tempest.

MONTANO Pray heavens he be;
35 For I have served him, and the man commands
Like a full soldier. Let's to the seaside, ho!
As well to see the vessel that's come in
As to throw out our eyes for brave Othello,
Even till we make the main and th' aerial blue
An indistinct regard.

40 THIRD GENTLEMAN Come, let's do so;
For every minute is expectancy
Of more arrivancie.

23 sufferance damage **39–40 the main . . . regard** i.e., the sea and sky become indistinguishable **42 arrivancie** arrivals

Enter Cassio.

CASSIO Thanks, you the valiant of the warlike isle,
That so approve the Moor. O, let the heavens
Give him defense against the elements, 45
For I have lost him on a dangerous sea.

MONTANO Is he well shipped?

CASSIO His bark is stoutly timbered, and his pilot
Of very expert and approved allowance;
Therefore my hopes, not surfeited to death, 50
Stand in bold cure. (*Within*) A sail, a sail, a sail!

CASSIO What noise?

FIRST GENTLEMAN The town is empty; on the brow o' th' sea
Stand ranks of people, and they cry, "A sail!"

CASSIO My hopes do shape him for the governor. 55
[*A shot.*]

SECOND GENTLEMAN They do discharge their shot of courtesy:
Our friends at least.

CASSIO I pray you, sir, go forth
And give us truth who 'tis that is arrived.

SECOND GENTLEMAN I shall. *Exit.*

MONTANO But, good lieutenant, is your general wived? 60

CASSIO Most fortunately. He hath achieved a maid
That paragons description and wild fame;
One that excels the quirks of blazoning pens,
And in th' essential vesture of creation
Does tire the ingener.

44 **approve** ("honor" or, perhaps, "are as warlike and valiant as your governor") 49 **approved allowance** known and tested 50 **not surfeited to death** i.e., not so great as to be in danger 51 **Stand in bold cure** i.e., are likely to be restored 62 **paragons** exceeds 62 **wild fame** extravagant report 63 **quirks of blazoning pens** ingenuities of praising pens 64 **essential vesture of creation** i.e., essential human nature as given by the Creator 65 **tire the ingener** (a difficult line which probably means something like "outdo the human ability to imagine and picture")

Enter [Second] Gentleman.

65 How now? Who has put in?

SECOND GENTLEMAN 'Tis one Iago, ancient to the general.

CASSIO H'as had most favorable and happy speed:
Tempests themselves, high seas, and howling winds,
The guttered rocks and congregated sands,
70 Traitors ensteeped to enclog the guiltless keel,
As having sense of beauty, do omit
Their mortal natures, letting go safely by
The divine Desdemona.

MONTANO What is she?

CASSIO She that I spake of, our great captain's captain,
75 Left in the conduct of the bold Iago,
Whose footing here anticipates our thoughts
A se'nnight's speed. Great Jove, Othello guard,
And swell his sail with thine own pow'rful breath,
That he may bless this bay with his tall ship,
80 Make love's quick pants in Desdemona's arms,
Give renewed fire to our extincted spirits.

Enter Desdemona, Iago, Roderigo, and Emilia.

O, behold! The riches of the ship is come on shore!
You men of Cyprus, let her have your knees.
[*Kneeling.*]
Hail to thee, lady! and the grace of heaven,
85 Before, behind thee, and on every hand,
Enwheel thee round.

DESDEMONA I thank you, valiant Cassio.
What tidings can you tell of my lord?

CASSIO He is not yet arrived, nor know I aught
But that he's well and will be shortly here.

90 DESDEMONA O but I fear. How lost you company?

69 **guttered** jagged 69 **congregated** gathered 70 **ensteeped** submerged 71 **sense** awareness 72 **mortal** deadly 76 **footing** landing 77 **se'nnight's** week's 79 **tall** brave

CASSIO The great contention of sea and skies
Parted our fellowship. (*Within*) A sail, a sail!
[*A shot.*]
But hark. A sail!

SECOND GENTLEMAN They give this greeting to the citadel;
This likewise is a friend.

CASSIO See for the news. 95
[*Exit Gentleman.*]
Good ancient, you are welcome. [*To Emilia*] Welcome, mistress.
Let it not gall your patience, good Iago,
That I extend my manners. 'Tis my breeding
That gives me this bold show of courtesy. [*Kisses Emilia.*]

IAGO Sir, would she give you so much of her lips 100
As of her tongue she oft bestows on me,
You would have enough.

DESDEMONA Alas, she has no speech.

IAGO In faith, too much.
I find it still when I have leave to sleep.
Marry, before your ladyship, I grant, 105
She puts her tongue a little in her heart
And chides with thinking.

EMILIA You have little cause to say so.

IAGO Come on, come on! You are pictures out of door,
Bells in your parlors, wildcats in your kitchens,
Saints in your injuries, devils being offended, 110

98 extend stretch 98 breeding careful training in manners (Cassio is considerably more the polished gentleman than Iago, and aware of it) 104 still . . . sleep i.e., even when she allows me to sleep she continues to scold 105 before your ladyship in your presence 108 pictures models (of virtue) 110 in your injuries when you injure others

Players in your housewifery, and housewives in your beds.

DESDEMONA O, fie upon thee, slanderer!

IAGO Nay, it is true, or else I am a Turk:
You rise to play, and go to bed to work.

EMILIA You shall not write my praise.

115 IAGO No, let me not.

DESDEMONA What wouldst write of me, if thou shouldst praise me?

IAGO O gentle lady, do not put me to't,
For I am nothing if not critical.

DESDEMONA Come on, assay. There's one gone to the harbor?

IAGO Ay, madam.

120 DESDEMONA [*Aside*] I am not merry; but I do beguile
The thing I am by seeming otherwise.—
Come, how wouldst thou praise me?

IAGO I am about it; but indeed my invention
Comes from my pate as birdlime does from frieze—
125 It plucks out brains and all. But my Muse labors,
And thus she is delivered:
If she be fair and wise: fairness and wit,
The one's for use, the other useth it.

DESDEMONA Well praised. How if she be black and witty?

130 IAGO If she be black, and thereto have a wit,
She'll find a white that shall her blackness fit.

DESDEMONA Worse and worse!

111 **housewifery** (this word can mean "careful, economical household management," and Iago would then be accusing women of only pretending to be good housekeepers, while in bed they are either [1] economical of their favors, or more likely [2] serious and dedicated workers) 124 **birdlime** a sticky substance put on branches to catch birds 124 **frieze** rough cloth 127 **fair** light-complexioned 129 **black** brunette

EMILIA How if fair and foolish?

IAGO She never yet was foolish that was fair,
For even her folly helped her to an heir. 135

DESDEMONA These are old fond paradoxes to make fools laugh i' th' alehouse. What miserable praise hast thou for her that's foul and foolish?

IAGO There's none so foul, and foolish thereunto,
But does foul pranks which fair and wise ones do. 140

DESDEMONA O heavy ignorance. Thou praisest the worst best. But what praise couldst thou bestow on a deserving woman indeed—one that in the authority of her merit did justly put on the vouch of very malice itself? 145

IAGO She that was ever fair, and never proud;
Had tongue at will, and yet was never loud;
Never lacked gold, and yet went never gay;
Fled from her wish, and yet said "Now I may";
She that being angered, her revenge being nigh, 150
Bade her wrong stay, and her displeasure fly;
She that in wisdom never was so frail
To change the cod's head for the salmon's tail;
She that could think, and nev'r disclose her mind;
See suitors following, and not look behind: 155
She was a wight (if ever such wights were)—

DESDEMONA To do what?

IAGO To suckle fools and chronicle small beer.

DESDEMONA O most lame and impotent conclusion. Do not learn of him, Emilia, though he be thy hus- 160 band. How say you, Cassio? Is he not a most profane and liberal counselor?

136 **fond** foolish 143–45 **one . . . itself** i.e., a woman so honest and deserving that even malice would be forced to approve of her 153 **To . . . tail** i.e., to exchange something valuable for something useless 156 **wight** person 158 **chronicle small beer** i.e., keep household accounts (the most trivial of occupations in Iago's opinion) 162 **liberal** licentious

CASSIO He speaks home, madam. You may relish him more in the soldier than in the scholar. [*Takes Desdemona's hand.*]

165 IAGO [*Aside*] He takes her by the palm. Ay, well said, whisper! With as little a web as this will I ensnare as great a fly as Cassio. Ay, smile upon her, do! I will gyve thee in thine own courtship.—You say true; 'tis so, indeed!—If such tricks as these strip
170 you out of your lieutenantry, it had been better you had not kissed your three fingers so oft—which now again you are most apt to play the sir in. Very good! Well kissed! An excellent curtsy! 'Tis so, indeed. Yet again your fingers to your lips? Would
175 they were clyster pipes for your sake! [*Trumpets within.*] The Moor! I know his trumpet.

CASSIO 'Tis truly so.

DESDEMONA Let's meet him and receive him.

CASSIO Lo, where he comes.

Enter Othello and Attendants.

OTHELLO O my fair warrior!

180 DESDEMONA My dear Othello.

OTHELLO It gives me wonder great as my content
To see you here before me. O my soul's joy!
If after every tempest come such calms,
May the winds blow till they have wakened death.
185 And let the laboring bark climb hills of seas
Olympus-high, and duck again as low
As hell's from heaven. If it were now to die,
'Twere now to be most happy; for I fear
My soul hath her content so absolute
190 That not another comfort like to this
Succeeds in unknown fate.

163 **speaks home** thrusts deeply with his speech 163–64 **relish him more in** enjoy him more as 168 **gyve** bind 172 **the sir** the fashionable gentleman 173 **curtsy** courtesy, i.e., bow 175 **clyster pipes** enema tubes 176 **his trumpet** (great men had their own distinctive calls)

DESDEMONA The heavens forbid
But that our loves and comforts should increase
Even as our days do grow.

OTHELLO Amen to that, sweet powers!
I cannot speak enough of this content;
It stops me here [*touches his heart*]; it is too much of joy. 195
And this, and this, the greatest discords be [*They kiss.*]
That e'er our hearts shall make!

IAGO [*Aside*] O, you are well tuned now!
But I'll set down the pegs that make this music,
As honest as I am.

OTHELLO Come, let us to the castle.
News, friends! Our wars are done; the Turks are drowned. 200
How does my old acquaintance of this isle?
Honey, you shall be well desired in Cyprus;
I have found great love amongst them. O my sweet,
I prattle out of fashion, and I dote
In mine own comforts. I prithee, good Iago, 205
Go to the bay and disembark my coffers.
Bring thou the master to the citadel;
He is a good one, and his worthiness
Does challenge much respect. Come, Desdemona,
Once more well met at Cyprus. 210

Exit Othello and Desdemona [*and all but Iago and Roderigo*].

IAGO [*To an Attendant*] Do thou meet me presently at the harbor. [*To Roderigo*] Come hither. If thou be'st valiant (as they say base men being in love have then a nobility in their natures more than is native to them), list me. The lieutenant tonight 215 watches on the court of guard. First, I must tell thee this: Desdemona is directly in love with him.

RODERIGO With him? Why, 'tis not possible.

198 set down the pegs loosen the strings (to produce discord) **209 challenge** require, exact **216 court of guard** guardhouse

IAGO Lay thy finger thus [*puts his finger to his lips*],
220 and let thy soul be instructed. Mark me with what violence she first loved the Moor but for bragging and telling her fantastical lies. To love him still for prating? Let not thy discreet heart think it. Her eye must be fed. And what delight shall she have to
225 look on the devil? When the blood is made dull with the act of sport, there should be a game to inflame it and to give satiety a fresh appetite, loveliness in favor, sympathy in years, manners, and beauties; all which the Moor is defective in. Now for want of
230 these required conveniences, her delicate tenderness will find itself abused, begin to heave the gorge, disrelish and abhor the Moor. Very nature will instruct her in it and compel her to some second choice. Now, sir, this granted—as it is a most preg-
235 nant and unforced position—who stands so eminent in the degree of this fortune as Cassio does? A knave very voluble; no further conscionable than in putting on the mere form of civil and humane seeming for the better compass of his salt
240 and most hidden loose affection. Why, none! Why, none! A slipper and subtle knave, a finder of occasion, that has an eye can stamp and counterfeit advantages, though true advantage never present itself. A devilish knave. Besides, the knave is hand-
245 some, young, and hath all those requisites in him that folly and green minds look after. A pestilent complete knave, and the woman hath found him already.

RODERIGO I cannot believe that in her; she's full of
250 most blessed condition.

IAGO Blessed fig's-end! The wine she drinks is made of grapes. If she had been blessed, she would never

226 **game** sport (with the added sense of "gamey," "rank") 228 **favor** countenance, appearance 228 **sympathy in years** sameness of age 230 **conveniences** advantages 231–32 **heave the gorge** vomit 234–35 **pregnant** likely 237 **no further conscionable** having no more conscience 238–39 **humane** polite 239 **salt** lecherous 240 **loose** immoral 241 **slipper** slippery

have loved the Moor. Blessed pudding! Didst thou not see her paddle with the palm of his hand? Didst not mark that? 255

RODERIGO Yes, that I did; but that was but courtesy.

IAGO Lechery, by this hand! [*Extends his index finger.*] An index and obscure prologue to the history of lust and foul thoughts. They met so near with their lips that their breaths embraced together. Villainous 260 thoughts, Roderigo. When these mutualities so marshal the way, hard at hand comes the master and main exercise, th' incorporate conclusion: Pish! But, sir, be you ruled by me. I have brought you from Venice. Watch you tonight; for the command, 265 I'll lay't upon you. Cassio knows you not. I'll not be far from you. Do you find some occasion to anger Cassio, either by speaking too loud, or tainting his discipline, or from what other course you please which the time shall more favorably minister. 270

RODERIGO Well.

IAGO Sir, he's rash and very sudden in choler, and haply may strike at you. Provoke him that he may; for even out of that will I cause these of Cyprus to mutiny, whose qualification shall come into no true 275 taste again but by the displanting of Cassio. So shall you have a shorter journey to your desires by the means I shall then have to prefer them; and the impediment most profitably removed without the which there were no expectation of our prosperity. 280

RODERIGO I will do this if you can bring it to any opportunity.

IAGO I warrant thee. Meet me by and by at the citadel. I must fetch his necessaries ashore. Farewell.

RODERIGO Adieu. *Exit.* 285

IAGO That Cassio loves her, I do well believe 't;

258 index pointer **263 incorporate** carnal **268 tainting** discrediting **272 choler** anger **275–76 qualification . . . taste** i.e., appeasement will not be brought about (wine was "qualified" by adding water)

That she loves him, 'tis apt and of great credit.
The Moor, howbeit that I endure him not,
Is of a constant, loving, noble nature,
290 And I dare think he'll prove to Desdemona
A most dear husband. Now I do love her too;
Not out of absolute lust, though peradventure
I stand accountant for as great a sin,
But partly led to diet my revenge,
295 For that I do suspect the lusty Moor
Hath leaped into my seat; the thought whereof
Doth, like a poisonous mineral, gnaw my inwards;
And nothing can or shall content my soul
Till I am evened with him, wife for wife.
300 Or failing so, yet that I put the Moor
At least into a jealousy so strong
That judgment cannot cure. Which thing to do,
If this poor trash of Venice, whom I trace
For his quick hunting, stand the putting on,
305 I'll have our Michael Cassio on the hip,
Abuse him to the Moor in the right garb
(For I fear Cassio with my nightcap too),
Make the Moor thank me, love me, and reward me
For making him egregiously an ass
310 And practicing upon his peace and quiet,
Even to madness. 'Tis here, but yet confused:
Knavery's plain face is never seen till used. *Exit.*

291 dear expensive **292 out of absolute** absolutely out of **292 peradventure** perchance **294 diet** feed **303 trace** (most editors emend to "trash," meaning to hang weights on a dog to slow his hunting; but "trace" clearly means something like "put on the trace" or "set on the track") **306 right garb** i.e., "proper fashion" **310 practicing upon** scheming to destroy

Scene II. [*A street.*]

Enter Othello's Herald, with a proclamation.

HERALD It is Othello's pleasure, our noble and valiant general, that upon certain tidings now arrived importing the mere perdition of the Turkish fleet, every man put himself into triumph. Some to dance, some to make bonfires, each man to what sport and revels his addition leads him. For, besides these beneficial news, it is the celebration of his nuptial. So much was his pleasure should be proclaimed. All offices are open, and there is full liberty of feasting from this present hour of five till the bell have told eleven. Bless the isle of Cyprus and our noble general Othello! *Exit.*

Scene III. [*The citadel of Cyprus.*]

Enter Othello, Desdemona, Cassio, and Attendants.

OTHELLO Good Michael, look you to the guard tonight.
Let's teach ourselves that honorable stop,
Not to outsport discretion.

CASSIO Iago hath direction what to do;
But notwithstanding, with my personal eye
Will I look to't.

OTHELLO Iago is most honest.
Michael, good night. Tomorrow with your earliest
Let me have speech with you. [*To Desdemona*]
Come, my dear love,

II.ii.3 mere perdition absolute destruction 6 addition rank 9 offices kitchens and storerooms of food

The purchase made, the fruits are to ensue,
10 That profit's yet to come 'tween me and you.
Good night.

Exit [Othello with Desdemona and Attendants].

Enter Iago.

CASSIO Welcome, Iago. We must to the watch.

IAGO Not this hour, lieutenant; 'tis not yet ten o' th' clock. Our general cast us thus early for the love
15 of his Desdemona; who let us not therefore blame. He hath not yet made wanton the night with her, and she is sport for Jove.

CASSIO She's a most exquisite lady.

IAGO And, I'll warrant her, full of game.

20 CASSIO Indeed, she's a most fresh and delicate creature.

IAGO What an eye she has! Methinks it sounds a parley to provocation.

CASSIO An inviting eye; and yet methinks right modest.

IAGO And when she speaks, is it not an alarum to
25 love?

CASSIO She is indeed perfection.

IAGO Well, happiness to their sheets! Come, lieutenant, I have a stoup of wine, and here without are a brace of Cyprus gallants that would fain have a
30 measure to the health of black Othello.

CASSIO Not tonight, good Iago. I have very poor and unhappy brains for drinking; I could well wish courtesy would invent some other custom of entertainment.

35 IAGO O, they are our friends. But one cup! I'll drink for you.

CASSIO I have drunk but one cup tonight, and that was craftily qualified too; and behold what innovation

II.iii.14 cast dismissed **24 alarum** the call to action, "general quarters" **28 stoup** two-quart tankard **38 qualified** diluted

it makes here. I am unfortunate in the infirmity and
dare not task my weakness with any more. 40

IAGO What, man! 'Tis a night of revels, the gallants
desire it.

CASSIO Where are they?

IAGO Here, at the door. I pray you call them in.

CASSIO I'll do't, but it dislikes me. *Exit.* 45

IAGO If I can fasten but one cup upon him
With that which he hath drunk tonight already,
He'll be as full of quarrel and offense
As my young mistress' dog. Now, my sick fool
Roderigo,
Whom love hath turned almost the wrong side out, 50
To Desdemona hath tonight caroused
Potations pottle-deep; and he's to watch.
Three else of Cyprus, noble swelling spirits,
That hold their honors in a wary distance,
The very elements of this warlike isle, 55
Have I tonight flustered with flowing cups,
And they watch too. Now, 'mongst this flock of
drunkards
Am I to put our Cassio in some action
That may offend the isle. But here they come.

Enter Cassio, Montano, and Gentlemen.

If consequence do but approve my dream, 60
My boat sails freely, both with wind and stream.

CASSIO 'Fore God, they have given me a rouse already.

MONTANO Good faith, a little one; not past a pint, as
I am a soldier.

IAGO Some wine, ho! 65
[*Sings*] And let me the canakin clink, clink;
And let me the canakin clink.

52 pottle-deep to the bottom of the cup **53 else** others **54 hold . . . distance** are scrupulous in maintaining their honor **62 rouse** drink

A soldier's a man;
O man's life's but a span,
70 Why then, let a soldier drink.
Some wine, boys!

CASSIO 'Fore God, an excellent song!

IAGO I learned it in England, where indeed they are most potent in potting. Your Dane, your German,
75 and your swag-bellied Hollander—Drink, ho!—are nothing to your English.

CASSIO Is your Englishman so exquisite in his drinking?

IAGO Why, he drinks you with facility your Dane dead
80 drunk; he sweats not to overthrow your Almain; he gives your Hollander a vomit ere the next pottle can be filled.

CASSIO To the health of our general!

MONTANO I am for it, lieutenant, and I'll do you justice.

85 IAGO O sweet England!
[*Sings*] King Stephen was and a worthy peer;
His breeches cost him but a crown;
He held them sixpence all too dear,
With that he called the tailor lown.
90 He was a wight of high renown,
And thou art but of low degree:
'Tis pride that pulls the country down;
And take thine auld cloak about thee.
Some wine, ho!

95 CASSIO 'Fore God, this is a more exquisite song than the other.

IAGO Will you hear't again?

CASSIO No, for I hold him to be unworthy of his place that does those things. Well, God's above all; and
100 there be souls must be saved, and there be souls must not be saved.

75 swag-bellied hanging **77 exquisite** superb **89 lown** lout

IAGO It's true, good lieutenant.

CASSIO For mine own part—no offense to the general, nor any man of quality—I hope to be saved.

IAGO And so do I too, lieutenant. 105

CASSIO Ay, but, by your leave, not before me. The lieutenant is to be saved before the ancient. Let's have no more of this; let's to our affairs.—God forgive us our sins!—Gentlemen, let's look to our business. Do not think, gentlemen, I am drunk. This is my 110 ancient; this is my right hand, and this is my left. I am not drunk now. I can stand well enough, and I speak well enough.

GENTLEMEN Excellent well!

CASSIO Why, very well then. You must not think then 115 that I am drunk. *Exit.*

MONTANO To th' platform, masters. Come, let's set the watch.

IAGO You see this fellow that is gone before.
He's a soldier fit to stand by Caesar
And give direction; and do but see his vice. 120
'Tis to his virtue a just equinox,
The one as long as th' other. 'Tis pity of him.
I fear the trust Othello puts him in,
On some odd time of his infirmity,
Will shake this island.

MONTANO But is he often thus? 125

IAGO 'Tis evermore the prologue to his sleep:
He'll watch the horologe a double set
If drink rock not his cradle.

MONTANO It were well
The general were put in mind of it.
Perhaps he sees it not, or his good nature 130
Prizes the virtue that appears in Cassio
And looks not on his evils. Is not this true?

121 just equinox exact balance (of dark and light) **127 watch . . . set** stay awake twice around the clock

Enter Roderigo.

IAGO [*Aside*] How now, Roderigo?
I pray you after the lieutenant, go! [*Exit Roderigo.*]

135 MONTANO And 'tis great pity that the noble Moor
Should hazard such a place as his own second
With one of an ingraft infirmity.
It were an honest action to say so
To the Moor.

IAGO Not I, for this fair island!
140 I do love Cassio well and would do much
To cure him of this evil. (Help! Help! *Within.*)
But hark? What noise?

Enter Cassio, pursuing Roderigo.

CASSIO Zounds, you rogue! You rascal!

MONTANO What's the matter, lieutenant?

CASSIO A knave teach me my duty? I'll beat the knave
145 into a twiggen bottle.

RODERIGO Beat me?

CASSIO Dost thou prate, rogue? [*Strikes him.*]

MONTANO Nay, good lieutenant! I pray you, sir, hold your hand.
[*Stays him.*]

150 CASSIO Let me go, sir, or I'll knock you o'er the mazzard.

MONTANO Come, come, you're drunk!

CASSIO Drunk? [*They fight.*]

IAGO [*Aside to Roderigo*] Away, I say! Go out and
155 cry a mutiny!
[*Exit Roderigo.*]
Nay, good lieutenant. God's will, gentlemen!
Help, ho! Lieutenant. Sir. Montano.
Help, masters! Here's a goodly watch indeed!
[*A bell rung.*]

137 ingraft ingrained 145 twiggen wicker-covered 151 mazzard head

Who's that which rings the bell? Diablo, ho!
The town will rise. God's will, lieutenant, 160
You'll be ashamed forever.

Enter Othello and Attendants.

OTHELLO What is the matter here?

MONTANO Zounds, I bleed still. I am hurt to the death.
He dies. [*He and Cassio fight again.*]

OTHELLO Hold for your lives!

IAGO Hold, ho! Lieutenant. Sir. Montano. Gentlemen! 165
Have you forgot all place of sense and duty?
Hold! The general speaks to you. Hold, for shame!

OTHELLO Why, how now, ho? From whence ariseth this?
Are we turned Turks, and to ourselves do that
Which heaven hath forbid the Ottomites? 170
For Christian shame put by this barbarous brawl!
He that stirs next to carve for his own rage
Holds his soul light; he dies upon his motion.
Silence that dreadful bell! It frights the isle
From her propriety. What is the matter, masters? 175
Honest Iago, that looks dead with grieving,
Speak. Who began this? On thy love, I charge thee.

IAGO I do not know. Friends all, but now, even now,
In quarter and in terms like bride and groom
Devesting them for bed; and then, but now— 180
As if some planet had unwitted men—
Swords out, and tilting one at other's breasts
In opposition bloody. I cannot speak
Any beginning to this peevish odds,
And would in action glorious I had lost 185
Those legs that brought me to a part of it!

OTHELLO How comes it, Michael, you are thus forgot?

CASSIO I pray you pardon me; I cannot speak.

OTHELLO Worthy Montano, you were wont to be civil;
The gravity and stillness of your youth 190

170 heaven ... Ottomites i.e., by sending the storm which dispersed the Turks
173 Holds his soul light values his soul lightly **175 propriety** proper order
179 In quarter on duty **184 odds** quarrel

The world hath noted, and your name is great
In mouths of wisest censure. What's the matter
That you unlace your reputation thus
And spend your rich opinion for the name
195 Of a night-brawler? Give me answer to it.

MONTANO Worthy Othello, I am hurt to danger.
Your officer, Iago, can inform you,
While I spare speech, which something now offends
me,
Of all that I do know; nor know I aught
200 By me that's said or done amiss this night,
Unless self-charity be sometimes a vice,
And to defend ourselves it be a sin
When violence assails us.

OTHELLO Now, by heaven,
My blood begins my safer guides to rule,
205 And passion, having my best judgment collied,
Assays to lead the way. If I once stir
Or do but lift this arm, the best of you
Shall sink in my rebuke. Give me to know
How this foul rout began, who set it on;
210 And he that is approved in this offense,
Though he had twinned with me, both at a birth,
Shall lose me. What? In a town of war
Yet wild, the people's hearts brimful of fear,
To manage private and domestic quarrel?
215 In night, and on the court and guard of safety?
'Tis monstrous. Iago, who began't?

MONTANO If partially affined, or leagued in office,
Thou dost deliver more or less than truth,
Thou art no soldier.

IAGO Touch me not so near.
220 I had rather have this tongue cut from my mouth
Than it should do offense to Michael Cassio.

192 **censure** judgment 193 **unlace** undo (the term refers specifically to the dressing of a wild boar killed in the hunt) 194 **opinion** reputation 198 **offends** harms, hurts 205 **collied** darkened 214 **manage** conduct 217 **If . . . office** if you are partial because you are related ("affined") or the brother officer (of Cassio)

Yet I persuade myself to speak the truth
Shall nothing wrong him. This it is, general.
Montano and myself being in speech,
There comes a fellow crying out for help, 225
And Cassio following him with determined sword
To execute upon him. Sir, this gentleman
Steps in to Cassio and entreats his pause.
Myself the crying fellow did pursue,
Lest by his clamor—as it so fell out— 230
The town might fall in fright. He, swift of foot,
Outran my purpose; and I returned then rather
For that I heard the clink and fall of swords,
And Cassio high in oath; which till tonight
I ne'er might say before. When I came back— 235
For this was brief—I found them close together
At blow and thrust, even as again they were
When you yourself did part them.
More of this matter cannot I report;
But men are men; the best sometimes forget. 240
Though Cassio did some little wrong to him,
As men in rage strike those that wish them best,
Yet surely Cassio I believe received
From him that fled some strange indignity,
Which patience could not pass.

OTHELLO I know, Iago, 245
Thy honesty and love doth mince this matter,
Making it light to Cassio. Cassio, I love thee;
But never more be officer of mine.

Enter Desdemona, attended.

Look if my gentle love be not raised up.
I'll make thee an example.

DESDEMONA What is the matter? 250

OTHELLO All's well now, sweeting; come away to bed.
[*To Montano*] Sir, for your hurts, myself will be your surgeon.
Lead him off. [*Montano led off.*]

245 pass allow to pass **246 mince** cut up (i.e., tell only part of)

Iago, look with care about the town
255 And silence those whom this vile brawl distracted.
Come, Desdemona: 'tis the soldiers' life
To have their balmy slumbers waked with strife.

Exit [with all but Iago and Cassio].

IAGO What, are you hurt, lieutenant?

CASSIO Ay, past all surgery.

260 IAGO Marry, God forbid!

CASSIO Reputation, reputation, reputation! O, I have lost my reputation! I have lost the immortal part of myself, and what remains is bestial. My reputation, Iago, my reputation.

265 IAGO As I am an honest man, I had thought you had received some bodily wound. There is more sense in that than in reputation. Reputation is an idle and most false imposition, oft got without merit and lost without deserving. You have lost no reputation 270 at all unless you repute yourself such a loser. What, man, there are more ways to recover the general again. You are but now cast in his mood—a punishment more in policy than in malice—even so as one would beat his offenseless dog to affright 275 an imperious lion. Sue to him again, and he's yours.

CASSIO I will rather sue to be despised than to deceive so good a commander with so slight, so drunken, and so indiscreet an officer. Drunk! And speak parrot! And squabble! Swagger! Swear! and dis- 280 course fustian with one's own shadow! O thou invisible spirit of wine, if thou hast no name to be known by, let us call thee devil!

IAGO What was he that you followed with your sword? What had he done to you?

285 CASSIO I know not.

IAGO Is't possible?

266 sense physical feeling **268 imposition** external thing **272 cast in his mood** dismissed because of his anger **273 in policy** politically necessary **278–79 speak parrot** gabble without sense **279–80 discourse fustian** speak nonsense ("fustian" was a coarse cotton cloth used for stuffing)

CASSIO I remember a mass of things, but nothing distinctly: a quarrel, but nothing wherefore. O God, that men should put an enemy in their mouths to steal away their brains! that we should with joy, 290 pleasance, revel, and applause transform ourselves into beasts!

IAGO Why, but you are now well enough. How came you thus recovered?

CASSIO It hath pleased the devil drunkenness to give 295 place to the devil wrath. One unperfectness shows me another, to make me frankly despise myself.

IAGO Come, you are too severe a moraler. As the time, the place, and the condition of this country stands, I could heartily wish this had not befall'n; but since 300 it is as it is, mend it for your own good.

CASSIO I will ask him for my place again: he shall tell me I am a drunkard. Had I as many mouths as Hydra, such an answer would stop them all. To be now a sensible man, by and by a fool, and presently 305 a beast! O strange! Every inordinate cup is unblest, and the ingredient is a devil.

IAGO Come, come, good wine is a good familiar creature if it be well used. Exclaim no more against it. And, good lieutenent, I think you think I love 310 you.

CASSIO I have well approved it, sir. I drunk?

IAGO You or any man living may be drunk at a time, man. I tell you what you shall do. Our general's wife is now the general. I may say so in this respect, 315 for that he hath devoted and given up himself to the contemplation, mark, and devotement of her parts and graces. Confess yourself freely to her; importune her help to put you in your place again. She is of so free, so kind, so apt, so blessed a disposition she 320 holds it a vice in her goodness not to do more than

317 devotement of her parts devotion to her qualities

she is requested. This broken joint between you and her husband entreat her to splinter; and my fortunes against any lay worth naming, this crack
325 of your love shall grow stronger than it was before.

CASSIO You advise me well.

IAGO I protest, in the sincerity of love and honest kindness.

CASSIO I think it freely; and betimes in the morning I
330 will beseech the virtuous Desdemona to undertake for me. I am desperate of my fortunes if they check me.

IAGO You are in the right. Good night, lieutenant; I must to the watch.

335 CASSIO Good night, honest Iago. *Exit Cassio.*

IAGO And what's he then that says I play the villain,
When this advice is free I give, and honest,
Probal to thinking, and indeed the course
To win the Moor again? For 'tis most easy
340 Th' inclining Desdemona to subdue
In any honest suit; she's framed as fruitful
As the free elements. And then for her
To win the Moor—were't to renounce his baptism,
All seals and symbols of redeemèd sin—
345 His soul is so enfettered to her love
That she may make, unmake, do what she list,
Even as her appetite shall play the god
With his weak function. How am I then a villain
To counsel Cassio to this parallel course,
350 Directly to his good? Divinity of hell!
When devils will the blackest sins put on,
They do suggest at first with heavenly shows,
As I do now. For whiles this honest fool
Plies Desdemona to repair his fortune,
355 And she for him pleads strongly to the Moor,

323 **splinter** splint 324 **lay** wager 331 **check** repulse 337 **free** generous and open 338 **Probal** to provable by 340 **inclining** inclined (to be helpful) 341 **framed as fruitful** made as generous 342 **elements** i.e., basic nature 347 **appetite** liking 348 **function** thought 351 **put on** advance, further 352 **shows** appearances

I'll pour this pestilence into his ear:
That she repeals him for her body's lust;
And by how much she strives to do him good,
She shall undo her credit with the Moor.
So will I turn her virtue into pitch, 360
And out of her own goodness make the net
That shall enmesh them all. How now, Roderigo?

Enter Roderigo.

RODERIGO I do follow here in the chase, not like a hound that hunts, but one that fills up the cry. My money is almost spent; I have been tonight exceed- 365 ingly well cudgeled; and I think the issue will be, I shall have so much experience for my pains; and so, with no money at all, and a little more wit, return again to Venice.

IAGO How poor are they that have not patience! 370
What wound did ever heal but by degrees?
Thou know'st we work by wit, and not by witchcraft;
And wit depends on dilatory time.
Does't not go well? Cassio hath beaten thee,
And thou by that small hurt hath cashiered Cassio. 375
Though other things grow fair against the sun,
Yet fruits that blossom first will first be ripe.
Content thyself awhile. By the mass, 'tis morning!
Pleasure and action make the hours seem short.
Retire thee; go where thou art billeted. 380
Away, I say! Thou shalt know more hereafter.
Nay, get thee gone! *Exit Roderigo.*
Two things are to be done:
My wife must move for Cassio to her mistress;
I'll set her on;
Myself awhile to draw the Moor apart 385
And bring him jump when he may Cassio find
Soliciting his wife. Ay, that's the way!
Dull not device by coldness and delay. *Exit.*

357 repeals him asks for (Cassio's reinstatement) **364 fills up the cry** makes up one of the hunting pack, adding to the noise but not actually tracking **383 move** petition **385 awhile** at the same time **386 jump** at the precise moment and place

ACT III

Scene I. [*A street.*]

Enter Cassio [*and*] *Musicians.*

CASSIO Masters, play here. I will content your pains.
Something that's brief; and bid "Good morrow, general." [*They play.*]

[*Enter Clown.*]

CLOWN Why, masters, have your instruments been in Naples that they speak i' th' nose thus?

5 MUSICIAN How, sir, how?

CLOWN Are these, I pray you, wind instruments?

MUSICIAN Ay, marry, are they, sir.

CLOWN O, thereby hangs a tail.

MUSICIAN Whereby hangs a tale, sir?

10 CLOWN Marry, sir, by many a wind instrument that I know. But, masters, here's money for you; and the general so likes your music that he desires you, for love's sake, to make no more noise with it.

MUSICIAN Well, sir, we will not.

15 CLOWN If you have any music that may not be heard, to't again. But, as they say, to hear music the general does not greatly care.

III.i.1 content your pains reward your efforts **2 s.d. Clown** fool **4 Naples** (this may refer either to the Neapolitan nasal tone, or to syphilis—rife in Naples—which breaks down the nose)

MUSICIAN We have none such, sir.

CLOWN Then put up your pipes in your bag, for I'll away. Go, vanish into air, away! 20

Exit Musicians.

CASSIO Dost thou hear me, mine honest friend?

CLOWN No. I hear not your honest friend. I hear you.

CASSIO Prithee keep up thy quillets. There's a poor piece of gold for thee. If the gentlewoman that attends the general's wife be stirring, tell her there's 25 one Cassio entreats her a little favor of speech. Wilt thou do this?

CLOWN She is stirring, sir. If she will stir hither, I shall seem to notify unto her. *Exit Clown.*

Enter Iago.

CASSIO In happy time, Iago.

IAGO You have not been abed then? 30

CASSIO Why no, the day had broke before we parted.
I have made bold, Iago, to send in to your wife;
My suit to her is that she will to virtuous Desdemona
Procure me some access.

IAGO I'll send her to you presently,
And I'll devise a mean to draw the Moor 35
Out of the way, that your converse and business
May be more free.

CASSIO I humbly thank you for 't. *Exit [Iago].*
I never knew
A Florentine more kind and honest.

Enter Emilia.

EMILIA Good morrow, good lieutenant. I am sorry 40
For your displeasure; but all will sure be well.
The general and his wife are talking of it,

23 quillets puns 29 seem ... her (the Clown is mocking Cassio's overly elegant manner of speaking) 39 Florentine i.e., Iago is as kind as if he were from Cassio's home town, Florence 42 displeasure discomforting

And she speaks for you stoutly. The Moor replies
That he you hurt is of great fame in Cyprus
45 And great affinity, and that in wholesome wisdom
He might not but refuse you. But he protests he loves
you,
And needs no other suitor but his likings
To bring you in again.

CASSIO Yet I beseech you,
If you think fit, or that it may be done,
50 Give me advantage of some brief discourse
With Desdemona alone.

EMILIA Pray you come in.
I will bestow you where you shall have time
To speak your bosom freely.

CASSIO I am much bound to you.
[*Exeunt.*]

Scene II. [*The citadel.*]

Enter Othello, Iago, and Gentlemen.

OTHELLO These letters give, Iago, to the pilot
And by him do my duties to the Senate.
That done, I will be walking on the works;
Repair there to me.

IAGO Well, my good lord, I'll do't.

5 OTHELLO This fortification, gentlemen, shall we see't?

GENTLEMEN We'll wait upon your lordship. *Exeunt.*

45 affinity family **53 bosom** inmost thoughts **III.ii. 4 Repair** go

Scene III. [*The citadel.*]

Enter Desdemona, Cassio, and Emilia.

DESDEMONA Be thou assured, good Cassio, I will do
All my abilities in thy behalf.

EMILIA Good madam, do. I warrant it grieves my husband
As if the cause were his.

DESDEMONA O, that's an honest fellow. Do not doubt, Cassio, 5
But I will have my lord and you again
As friendly as you were.

CASSIO Bounteous madam,
Whatever shall become of Michael Cassio,
He's never anything but your true servant.

DESDEMONA I know't; I thank you. You do love my lord. 10
You have known him long, and be you well assured
He shall in strangeness stand no farther off
Than in a politic distance.

CASSIO Ay, but, lady,
That policy may either last so long,
Or feed upon such nice and waterish diet, 15
Or breed itself so out of circumstances,
That, I being absent, and my place supplied,
My general will forget my love and service.

DESDEMONA Do not doubt that; before Emilia here
I give thee warrant of thy place. Assure thee, 20
If I do vow a friendship, I'll perform it

III.iii. 12-13 **He ... distance** i.e., he shall act no more distant to you than is necessary for political reasons 15 **nice** trivial 16 **Or ... circumstances** i.e., or grow so on the basis of accidental happenings and political needs 17 **supplied** filled 19 **doubt** imagine

To the last article. My lord shall never rest;
I'll watch him tame and talk him out of patience;
His bed shall seem a school, his board a shrift;
25 I'll intermingle everything he does
With Cassio's suit. Therefore be merry, Cassio,
For thy solicitor shall rather die
Than give thy cause away.

Enter Othello and Iago [*at a distance*].

EMILIA Madam, here comes my lord.

30 CASSIO Madam, I'll take my leave.

DESDEMONA Why, stay, and hear me speak.

CASSIO Madam, not now. I am very ill at ease,
Unfit for mine own purposes.

DESDEMONA Well, do your discretion. *Exit Cassio.*

IAGO Ha! I like not that.

35 OTHELLO What dost thou say?

IAGO Nothing, my lord; or if—I know not what.

OTHELLO Was not that Cassio parted from my wife?

IAGO Cassio, my lord? No, sure, I cannot think it
That he would steal away so guilty-like,
Seeing your coming.

40 OTHELLO I do believe 'twas he.

DESDEMONA [*Coming to them*] How now, my lord?
I have been talking with a suitor here,
A man that languishes in your displeasure.

OTHELLO Who is't you mean?

DESDEMONA Why, your lieutenant, Cassio. Good my
45 lord,
If I have any grace or power to move you,
His present reconciliation take.
For if he be not one that truly loves you,

23 watch him tame (animals were tamed by being kept awake) 24 board a shrift table (seem) a confessional 47 present immediate

That errs in ignorance, and not in cunning,
I have no judgment in an honest face. 50
I prithee call him back.

OTHELLO Went he hence now?

DESDEMONA I' sooth so humbled
That he hath left part of his grief with me
To suffer with him. Good love, call him back.

OTHELLO Not now, sweet Desdemon; some other time. 55

DESDEMONA But shall't be shortly?

OTHELLO The sooner, sweet, for you.

DESDEMONA Shall't be tonight at supper?

OTHELLO No, not tonight.

DESDEMONA Tomorrow dinner then?

OTHELLO I shall not dine at home;
I meet the captains at the citadel.

DESDEMONA Why then, tomorrow night, on Tuesday morn, 60
On Tuesday noon, or night, on Wednesday morn.
I prithee name the time, but let it not
Exceed three days. In faith, he's penitent;
And yet his trespass, in our common reason
(Save that, they say, the wars must make example 65
Out of her best), is not almost a fault
T' incur a private check. When shall he come?
Tell me, Othello. I wonder in my soul
What you would ask me that I should deny
Or stand so mamm'ring on. What? Michael Cassio, 70
That came awooing with you, and so many a time,
When I have spoke of you dispraisingly,
Hath ta'en your part—to have so much to do
To bring him in? By'r Lady, I could do much—

OTHELLO Prithee no more. Let him come when he will! 75
I will deny thee nothing.

66–67 is ... check is almost not serious enough for a private rebuke (let alone a public disgrace) 70 mamm'ring hesitating

DESDEMONA Why, this is not a boon;
'Tis as I should entreat you wear your gloves,
Or feed on nourishing dishes, or keep you warm,
Or sue to you to do a peculiar profit
80 To your own person. Nay, when I have a suit
Wherein I mean to touch your love indeed,
It shall be full of poise and difficult weight,
And fearful to be granted.

OTHELLO I will deny thee nothing!
Whereon I do beseech thee grant me this,
85 To leave me but a little to myself.

DESDEMONA Shall I deny you? No. Farewell, my lord.

OTHELLO Farewell, my Desdemona: I'll come to thee straight.

DESDEMONA Emilia, come. Be as your fancies teach you;
Whate'er you be, I am obedient. *Exit [with Emilia].*

90 OTHELLO Excellent wretch! Perdition catch my soul
But I do love thee! And when I love thee not,
Chaos is come again.

IAGO My noble lord——

OTHELLO What dost thou say, Iago?

IAGO Did Michael Cassio, when you wooed my lady,
95 Know of your love?

OTHELLO He did, from first to last. Why dost thou ask?

IAGO But for a satisfaction of my thought,
No further harm.

OTHELLO Why of thy thought, Iago?

IAGO I did not think he had been acquainted with her.

100 OTHELLO O, yes, and went between us very oft.

IAGO Indeed?

OTHELLO Indeed? Ay, indeed! Discern'st thou aught in that?

79 **peculiar profit** particularly personal good 82 **poise** weight 87 **straight** at once 100 **between us** i.e., as messenger

Is he not honest?

IAGO Honest, my lord?

OTHELLO Honest? Ay, honest.

IAGO My lord, for aught I know.

OTHELLO What dost thou think?

IAGO Think, my lord?

OTHELLO Think, my lord? 105

By heaven, thou echoest me,
As if there were some monster in thy thought
Too hideous to be shown. Thou dost mean something.
I heard thee say even now, thou lik'st not that,
When Cassio left my wife. What didst not like? 110
And when I told thee he was of my counsel
Of my whole course of wooing, thou cried'st "Indeed?"
And didst contract and purse thy brow together,
As if thou then hadst shut up in thy brain
Some horrible conceit. If thou dost love me, 115
Show me thy thought.

IAGO My lord, you know I love you.

OTHELLO I think thou dost;
And, for I know thou'rt full of love and honesty
And weigh'st thy words before thou giv'st them breath,
Therefore these stops of thine fright me the more; 120
For such things in a false disloyal knave
Are tricks of custom; but in a man that's just
They're close dilations, working from the heart
That passion cannot rule.

IAGO For Michael Cassio,
I dare be sworn, I think that he is honest. 125

OTHELLO I think so too.

111 of my counsel in my confidence 115 conceit thought 120 stops interruptions 122 of custom customary 123 close dilations expressions of hidden thoughts

IAGO Men should be what they seem;
Or those that be not, would they might seem none!

OTHELLO Certain, men should be what they seem.

IAGO Why then, I think Cassio's an honest man.

130 OTHELLO Nay, yet there's more in this.
I prithee speak to me as to thy thinkings,
As thou dost ruminate, and give thy worst of thoughts
The worst of words.

IAGO Good my lord, pardon me:
Though I am bound to every act of duty,
135 I am not bound to that all slaves are free to.
Utter my thoughts? Why, say they are vile and false,
As where's that palace whereinto foul things
Sometimes intrude not? Who has that breast so pure
But some uncleanly apprehensions
140 Keep leets and law days, and in sessions sit
With meditations lawful?

OTHELLO Thou dost conspire against thy friend, Iago,
If thou but think'st him wronged, and mak'st his ear
A stranger to thy thoughts.

IAGO I do beseech you——
145 Though I perchance am vicious in my guess
(As I confess it is my nature's plague
To spy into abuses, and of my jealousy
Shape faults that are not), that your wisdom
From one that so imperfectly conceits
150 Would take no notice, nor build yourself a trouble
Out of his scattering and unsure observance.
It were not for your quiet nor your good,
Nor for my manhood, honesty, and wisdom,
To let you know my thoughts.

OTHELLO What dost thou mean?

155 IAGO Good name in man and woman, dear my lord,
Is the immediate jewel of their souls.

140 leets and law days meetings of local courts

Who steals my purse steals trash; 'tis something, nothing;
'Twas mine, 'tis his, and has been slave to thousands;
But he that filches from me my good name
Robs me of that which not enriches him 160
And makes me poor indeed.

OTHELLO By heaven, I'll know thy thoughts!

IAGO You cannot, if my heart were in your hand;
Nor shall not whilst 'tis in my custody.

OTHELLO Ha!

IAGO O, beware, my lord, of jealousy! 165
It is the green-eyed monster, which doth mock
The meat it feeds on. That cuckold lives in bliss
Who, certain of his fate, loves not his wronger;
But O, what damnèd minutes tells he o'er
Who dotes, yet doubts—suspects, yet fondly loves! 170

OTHELLO O misery.

IAGO Poor and content is rich, and rich enough;
But riches fineless is as poor as winter
To him that ever fears he shall be poor.
Good God the souls of all my tribe defend 175
From jealousy!

OTHELLO Why? Why is this?
Think'st thou I'd make a life of jealousy,
To follow still the changes of the moon
With fresh suspicions? No! To be once in doubt
Is to be resolved. Exchange me for a goat 180
When I shall turn the business of my soul
To such exsufflicate and blown surmises,
Matching thy inference. 'Tis not to make me jealous
To say my wife is fair, feeds well, loves company,
Is free of speech, sings, plays, and dances; 185
Where virtue is, these are more virtuous.
Nor from mine own weak merits will I draw
The smallest fear or doubt of her revolt,

169 tells counts **170 fondly** foolishly **173 fineless** infinite **178 To follow still** to change always (as the phases of the moon) **182 exsufflicate and blown** inflated and flyblown

For she had eyes, and chose me. No, Iago;
190 I'll see before I doubt; when I doubt, prove;
And on the proof there is no more but this:
Away at once with love or jealousy!

IAGO I am glad of this; for now I shall have reason
To show the love and duty that I bear you
195 With franker spirit. Therefore, as I am bound,
Receive it from me. I speak not yet of proof.
Look to your wife; observe her well with Cassio;
Wear your eyes thus: not jealous nor secure.
I would not have your free and noble nature
200 Out of self-bounty be abused. Look to't.
I know our country disposition well:
In Venice they do let heaven see the pranks
They dare not show their husbands; their best conscience
Is not to leave't undone, but kept unknown.

205 OTHELLO Dost thou say so?

IAGO She did deceive her father, marrying you;
And when she seemed to shake and fear your looks,
She loved them most.

OTHELLO And so she did.

IAGO Why, go to then!
She that so young could give out such a seeming
210 To seel her father's eyes up close as oak—
He thought 'twas witchcraft. But I am much to blame.
I humbly do beseech you of your pardon
For too much loving you.

OTHELLO I am bound to thee forever.

IAGO I see this hath a little dashed your spirits.

OTHELLO Not a jot, not a jot.

215 IAGO Trust me, I fear it has.

200 **self-bounty** innate kindness (which attributes his own motives to others) 203–04 **their . . . unknown** i.e., their morality does not forbid adultery, but it does forbid being found out 210 **seel** hoodwink 210 **oak** (a close-grained wood)

I hope you will consider what is spoke
Comes from my love. But I do see y' are moved.
I am to pray you not to strain my speech
To grosser issues, nor to larger reach
Than to suspicion. 220

OTHELLO I will not.

IAGO Should you do so, my lord,
My speech should fall into such vile success
Which my thoughts aimed not. Cassio's my worthy friend—
My lord, I see y' are moved.

OTHELLO No, not much moved.
I do not think but Desdemona's honest. 225

IAGO Long live she so. And long live you to think so.

OTHELLO And yet, how nature erring from itself——

IAGO Ay, there's the point, as (to be bold with you)
Not to affect many proposèd matches
Of her own clime, complexion, and degree, 230
Whereto we see in all things nature tends—
Foh! one may smell in such a will most rank,
Foul disproportions, thoughts unnatural.
But, pardon me, I do not in position
Distinctly speak of her; though I may fear 235
Her will, recoiling to her better judgment,
May fall to match you with her country forms,
And happily repent.

OTHELLO Farewell, farewell!
If more thou dost perceive, let me know more.
Set on thy wife to observe. Leave me, Iago. 240

IAGO My lord, I take my leave. [*Going*.]

218 strain enlarge the meaning of **219 reach** meaning **230 degree** social station **231 in ... tends** i.e., all things in nature seek out their own kind **234 position** general argument **235 Distinctly** specifically **237 fall to match** happen to compare **237 country forms** i.e., the familiar appearances of her countrymen **238 happily** by chance

OTHELLO Why did I marry? This honest creature doubtless
Sees and knows more, much more, than he unfolds.

IAGO [*Returns.*] My lord, I would I might entreat your honor
245 To scan this thing no farther. Leave it to time.
Although 'tis fit that Cassio have his place,
For sure he fills it up with great ability,
Yet, if you please to hold him off awhile,
You shall by that perceive him and his means.
250 Note if your lady strain his entertainment
With any strong or vehement importunity;
Much will be seen in that. In the meantime
Let me be thought too busy in my fears
(As worthy cause I have to fear I am)
255 And hold her free, I do beseech your honor.

OTHELLO Fear not my government.

IAGO I once more take my leave.
Exit.

OTHELLO This fellow's of exceeding honesty,
And knows all qualities, with a learnèd spirit
Of human dealings. If I do prove her haggard,
260 Though that her jesses were my dear heartstrings,
I'd whistle her off and let her down the wind
To prey at fortune. Haply for I am black
And have not those soft parts of conversation
That chamberers have, or for I am declined
265 Into the vale of years—yet that's not much—
She's gone. I am abused, and my relief
Must be to loathe her. O curse of marriage,
That we can call these delicate creatures ours,
And not their appetites! I had rather be a toad

250 strain his entertainment urge strongly that he be reinstated **256 government** self-control **258 qualities** natures, types of people **259 haggard** a partly trained hawk which has gone wild again **260 jesses** straps which held the hawk's legs to the trainer's wrist **261 I'd . . . wind** I would release her (like an untamable hawk) and let her fly free **262 Haply for** it may be because **263 soft parts** gentle qualities and manners **264 chamberers** courtiers—or perhaps, accomplished seducers

And live upon the vapor of a dungeon 270
Than keep a corner in the thing I love
For others' uses. Yet 'tis the plague to great ones;
Prerogatived are they less than the base.
'Tis destiny unshunnable, like death.
Even then this forkèd plague is fated to us 275
When we do quicken. Look where she comes.

Enter Desdemona and Emilia.

If she be false, heaven mocked itself!
I'll not believe't.

DESDEMONA How now, my dear Othello?
Your dinner, and the generous islanders
By you invited, do attend your presence. 280

OTHELLO I am to blame.

DESDEMONA Why do you speak so faintly?
Are you not well?

OTHELLO I have a pain upon my forehead, here.

DESDEMONA Why, that's with watching; 'twill away again.
Let me but bind it hard, within this hour 285
It will be well.

OTHELLO Your napkin is too little;
[*He pushes the handkerchief away, and it falls.*]
Let it alone. Come, I'll go in with you.

DESDEMONA I am very sorry that you are not well.
Exit [*with Othello*].

EMILIA I am glad I have found this napkin;
This was her first remembrance from the Moor. 290
My wayward husband hath a hundred times
Wooed me to steal it; but she so loves the token

275 **forkèd** horned (the sign of the cuckold was horns) 276 **do quicken** are born 280 **attend** wait 283 **here** (he points to his imaginary horns) 286 **napkin** elaborately worked handkerchief 287 **it** (it makes a considerable difference in the interpretation of later events whether this "it" refers to Othello's forehead or to the handkerchief; nothing in the text makes the reference clear)

(For he conjured her she should ever keep it)
That she reserves it evermore about her
295 To kiss and talk to. I'll have the work ta'en out
And give't Iago. What he will do with it,
Heaven knows, not I; I nothing but to please his fantasy.

Enter Iago.

IAGO How now? What do you here alone?

EMILIA Do not you chide; I have a thing for you.

IAGO You have a thing for me? It is a common
300 thing——

EMILIA Ha?

IAGO To have a foolish wife.

EMILIA O, is that all? What will you give me now
For that same handkerchief?

IAGO What handkerchief?

305 EMILIA What handkerchief!
Why, that the Moor first gave to Desdemona,
That which so often you did bid me steal.

IAGO Hast stol'n it from her?

EMILIA No, but she let it drop by negligence,
310 And to th' advantage, I, being here, took't up.
Look, here 't is.

IAGO A good wench. Give it me.

EMILIA What will you do with't, that you have been so earnest
To have me filch it?

IAGO Why, what is that to you?
[*Takes it.*]

EMILIA If it be not for some purpose of import,
315 Give't me again. Poor lady, she'll run mad
When she shall lack it.

295 work ta'en out needlework copied 297 I nothing I wish nothing 297 fantasy fancy, whim 310 to th' advantage being lucky 314 import importance 316 lack miss

IAGO Be not acknown on't.
I have use for it. Go, leave me. *Exit Emilia.*
I will in Cassio's lodging lose this napkin
And let him find it. Trifles light as air
Are to the jealous confirmations strong 320
As proofs of Holy Writ. This may do something.
The Moor already changes with my poison:
Dangerous conceits are in their natures poisons,
Which at the first are scarce found to distaste,
But, with a little, act upon the blood, 325
Burn like the mines of sulfur. I did say so.

Enter Othello.

Look where he comes! Not poppy nor mandragora,
Nor all the drowsy syrups of the world,
Shall ever medicine thee to that sweet sleep
Which thou owedst yesterday.

OTHELLO Ha! ha! False to me? 330

IAGO Why, how now, general? No more of that.

OTHELLO Avaunt! be gone! Thou hast set me on the rack.
I swear 'tis better to be much abused
Than but to know't a little.

IAGO How now, my lord?

OTHELLO What sense had I of her stol'n hours of lust? 335
I saw't not, thought it not, it harmed not me;
I slept the next night well, fed well, was free and merry;
I found not Cassio's kisses on her lips.
He that is robbed, not wanting what is stol'n,
Let him not know't, and he's not robbed at all. 340

IAGO I am sorry to hear this.

316 Be not acknown on't forget you ever saw it **324 are scarce found to distaste** scarcely can be tasted **325 with a little** in a short time **327 poppy nor mandragora** (soporifics) **330 owedst** possessed **339 wanting** missing

OTHELLO I had been happy if the general camp,
Pioners and all, had tasted her sweet body,
So I had nothing known. O now, forever
345 Farewell the tranquil mind! Farewell content!
Farewell the plumèd troops, and the big wars
That makes ambition virtue! O, farewell!
Farewell the neighing steed and the shrill trump,
The spirit-stirring drum, th' ear-piercing fife,
350 The royal banner, and all quality,
Pride, pomp, and circumstance of glorious war!
And O you mortal engines whose rude throats
Th' immortal Jove's dread clamors counterfeit,
Farewell! Othello's occupation's gone!

355 IAGO Is't possible, my lord?

OTHELLO Villain, be sure thou prove my love a whore!
Be sure of it; give me the ocular proof;
Or, by the worth of mine eternal soul,
Thou hadst been better have been born a dog
Than answer my waked wrath!

360 IAGO Is't come to this?

OTHELLO Make me to see't; or at the least so prove it
That the probation bear no hinge nor loop
To hang a doubt on—or woe upon thy life!

IAGO My noble lord——

365 OTHELLO If thou dost slander her and torture me,
Never pray more; abandon all remorse;
On horror's head horrors accumulate;
Do deeds to make heaven weep, all earth amazed;
For nothing canst thou to damnation add
Greater than that.

370 IAGO O grace! O heaven forgive me!
Are you a man? Have you a soul or sense?
God b' wi' you! Take mine office. O wretched fool,
That lov'st to make thine honesty a vice!
O monstrous world! Take note, take note, O world,

343 **Pioners** (the basest manual laborers in the army, who dug trenches and mines)
351 **circumstance** pageantry 352 **mortal engines** lethal weapons, i.e., cannon
353 **clamors** i.e., thunder 362 **probation** proof

To be direct and honest is not safe. 375
I thank you for this profit, and from hence
I'll love no friend, sith love breeds such offense.

OTHELLO Nay, stay. Thou shouldst be honest.

IAGO I should be wise; for honesty's a fool
And loses that it works for.

OTHELLO By the world, 380
I think my wife be honest, and think she is not;
I think that thou art just, and think thou art not.
I'll have some proof. My name, that was as fresh
As Dian's visage, is now begrimed and black
As mine own face. If there be cords, or knives, 385
Poison, or fire, or suffocating streams,
I'll not endure it. Would I were satisfied!

IAGO I see you are eaten up with passion.
I do repent me that I put it to you.
You would be satisfied?

OTHELLO Would? Nay, and I will. 390

IAGO And may; but how? How satisfied, my lord?
Would you, the supervisor, grossly gape on?
Behold her topped?

OTHELLO Death and damnation! O!

IAGO It were a tedious difficulty, I think,
To bring them to that prospect. Damn them then, 395
If ever mortal eyes do see them bolster
More than their own! What then? How then?
What shall I say? Where's satisfaction?
It is impossible you should see this,
Were they as prime as goats, as hot as monkeys, 400
As salt as wolves in pride, and fools as gross
As ignorance made drunk. But yet, I say,

377 **sith** since 384 **Dian's** Diana's (goddess of the moon and of chastity) 392 **supervisor** onlooker 394 **tedious** hard to arrange 395 **prospect** sight (where they can be seen) 396 **bolster** go to bed 400-01 **prime, salt** lustful 401 **pride** heat

If imputation and strong circumstances
Which lead directly to the door of truth
405 Will give you satisfaction, you might have't.

OTHELLO Give me a living reason she's disloyal.

IAGO I do not like the office.
But sith I am entered in this cause so far,
Pricked to't by foolish honesty and love,
410 I will go on. I lay with Cassio lately,
And being troubled with a raging tooth,
I could not sleep.
There are a kind of men so loose of soul
That in their sleeps will mutter their affairs.
415 One of this kind is Cassio.
In sleep I heard him say, "Sweet Desdemona,
Let us be wary, let us hide our loves!"
And then, sir, would he gripe and wring my hand,
Cry "O sweet creature!" Then kiss me hard,
420 As if he plucked up kisses by the roots
That grew upon my lips; laid his leg o'er my thigh,
And sigh, and kiss, and then cry, "Cursèd fate
That gave thee to the Moor!"

OTHELLO O monstrous! monstrous!

IAGO Nay, this was but his dream.

425 OTHELLO But this denoted a foregone conclusion,
'Tis a shrewd doubt, though it be but a dream.

IAGO And this may help to thicken other proofs
That do demonstrate thinly.

OTHELLO I'll tear her all to pieces!

IAGO Nay, yet be wise. Yet we see nothing done;
430 She may be honest yet. Tell me but this:
Have you not sometimes seen a handkerchief
Spotted with strawberries in your wife's hand?

OTHELLO I gave her such a one; 'twas my first gift.

407 **office** duty 409 **Pricked** spurred 418 **gripe** seize 425 **foregone conclusion** consummated fact 426 **shrewd doubt** penetrating guess 428 **demonstrate** show, appear

IAGO I know not that; but such a handkerchief—
I am sure it was your wife's—did I today 435
See Cassio wipe his beard with.

OTHELLO If it be that——

IAGO If it be that, or any that was hers,
It speaks against her with the other proofs.

OTHELLO O, that the slave had forty thousand lives!
One is too poor, too weak for my revenge. 440
Now do I see 'tis true. Look here, Iago:
All my fond love thus do I blow to heaven.
'Tis gone.
Arise, black vengeance, from the hollow hell!
Yield up, O Love, thy crown and hearted throne 445
To tyrannous hate! Swell, bosom, with thy fraught,
For 'tis of aspics' tongues.

IAGO Yet be content.

OTHELLO O, blood, blood, blood!

IAGO Patience, I say. Your mind may change.

OTHELLO Never, Iago. Like to the Pontic Sea, 450
Whose icy current and compulsive course
Nev'r keeps retiring ebb, but keeps due on
To the Propontic and the Hellespont,
Even so my bloody thoughts, with violent pace,
Shall nev'r look back, nev'r ebb to humble love, 455
Till that a capable and wide revenge
Swallow them up. [*He kneels.*] Now, by yond
marble heaven,
In the due reverence of a sacred vow
I here engage my words.

IAGO Do not rise yet.
[*Iago kneels.*]
Witness, you ever-burning lights above, 460

445 **hearted** seated in the heart 446 **fraught** burden 447 **aspics'** asps' 447 **content** patient, quiet 450 **Pontic Sea** the Black Sea (famous for the strong and constant current with which it flows through the Bosporus into the Mediterranean, where the water level is lower) 456 **capable and wide** sufficient and far-reaching

You elements that clip us round about,
Witness that here Iago doth give up
The execution of his wit, hands, heart
To wronged Othello's service! Let him command,
465 And to obey shall be in me remorse,
What bloody business ever. [*They rise.*]

OTHELLO I greet thy love,
Not with vain thanks but with acceptance bounteous,
And will upon the instant put thee to't.
Within these three days let me hear thee say
470 That Cassio's not alive.

IAGO My friend is dead. 'Tis done at your request.
But let her live.

OTHELLO Damn her, lewd minx! O, damn her! Damn her!
Come, go with me apart. I will withdraw
To furnish me with some swift means of death
475 For the fair devil. Now art thou my lieutenant.

IAGO I am your own forever. *Exeunt.*

Scene IV. [*A street.*]

Enter Desdemona, Emilia, and Clown.

DESDEMONA Do you know, sirrah, where Lieutenant Cassio lies?

CLOWN I dare not say he lies anywhere.

DESDEMONA Why, man?

5 CLOWN He's a soldier, and for me to say a soldier lies, 'tis stabbing.

461 clip enfold **463 execution** workings, action **465 remorse** pity **466 ever** soever **467 bounteous** absolute **468 to't** i.e., to the work you have said you are prepared to do **II.iv.2 lies** lodges

DESDEMONA Go to. Where lodges he?

CLOWN To tell you where he lodges is to tell you where I lie.

DESDEMONA Can anything be made of this? 10

CLOWN I know not where he lodges, and for me to devise a lodging, and say he lies here or he lies there, were to lie in mine own throat.

DESDEMONA Can you enquire him out, and be edified by report? 15

CLOWN I will catechize the world for him; that is, make questions, and by them answer.

DESDEMONA Seek him, bid him come hither. Tell him I have moved my lord on his behalf and hope all will be well. 20

CLOWN To do this is within the compass of man's wit, and therefore I will attempt the doing it. *Exit Clown.*

DESDEMONA Where should I lose the handkerchief, Emilia?

EMILIA I know not, madam.

DESDEMONA Believe me, I had rather have lost my purse 25
Full of crusadoes. And but my noble Moor
Is true of mind, and made of no such baseness
As jealous creatures are, it were enough
To put him to ill thinking.

EMILIA Is he not jealous?

DESDEMONA Who? He? I think the sun where he was born 30
Drew all such humors from him.

EMILIA
Look where he comes.

13 **lie in mine own throat** (to lie in the throat is to lie absolutely and completely)
14 **edified** enlightened (Desdemona mocks the Clown's overly elaborate diction)
19 **moved** pleaded with 21 **compass** reach 23 **should** might 26 **crusadoes** Portuguese gold coins 31 **humors** characteristics

Enter Othello.

DESDEMONA I will not leave him now till Cassio
Be called to him. How is't with you, my lord?

OTHELLO Well, my good lady. [*Aside*] O, hardness to dissemble!—
How do you, Desdemona?

35 DESDEMONA Well, my good lord.

OTHELLO Give me your hand. This hand is moist, my lady.

DESDEMONA It hath felt no age nor known no sorrow.

OTHELLO This argues fruitfulness and liberal heart.
Hot, hot, and moist. This hand of yours requires
40 A sequester from liberty; fasting and prayer;
Much castigation; exercise devout;
For here's a young and sweating devil here
That commonly rebels. 'Tis a good hand,
A frank one.

DESDEMONA You may, indeed, say so;
45 For 'twas that hand that gave away my heart.

OTHELLO A liberal hand! The hearts of old gave hands,
But our new heraldry is hands, not hearts.

DESDEMONA I cannot speak of this. Come now, your promise!

OTHELLO What promise, chuck?

DESDEMONA I have sent to bid Cassio come speak with
50 you.

OTHELLO I have a salt and sorry rheum offends me.
Lend me thy handkerchief.

34 **hardness to dissemble** (Othello may refer here either to the difficulty he has in maintaining his appearance of composure, or to what he believes to be Desdemona's hardened hypocrisy) 36 **moist** (a moist, hot hand was taken as a sign of a lustful nature) 38 **argues** suggests 38 **liberal** free, open (but also with a suggestion of "licentious"; from here on in this scene Othello's words bear a double meaning, seeming to be normal but accusing Desdemona of being unfaithful) 40 **sequester** separation 47 **heraldry** heraldic symbolism 51 **a salt and sorry rheum** a heavy, running head cold

DESDEMONA Here, my lord.

OTHELLO That which I gave you.

DESDEMONA I have it not about me.

OTHELLO Not?

DESDEMONA No, indeed, my lord.

OTHELLO That's a fault.
That handkerchief 55
Did an Egyptian to my mother give.
She was a charmer, and could almost read
The thoughts of people. She told her, while she kept it
'Twould make her amiable and subdue my father
Entirely to her love; but if she lost it 60
Or made a gift of it, my father's eye
Should hold her loathèd, and his spirits should hunt
After new fancies. She, dying, gave it me,
And bid me, when my fate would have me wived,
To give it her. I did so; and take heed on't; 65
Make it a darling like your precious eye.
To lose't or give't away were such perdition
As nothing else could match.

DESDEMONA Is't possible?

OTHELLO 'Tis true. There's magic in the web of it.
A sibyl that had numbered in the world 70
The sun to course two hundred compasses,
In her prophetic fury sewed the work;
The worms were hallowed that did breed the silk,
And it was dyed in mummy which the skillful
Conserved of maidens' hearts.

DESDEMONA Indeed? Is't true? 75

OTHELLO Most veritable. Therefore look to't well.

DESDEMONA Then would to God that I had never seen't!

57 **charmer** magician 59 **amiable** desirable 69 **web** weaving 72 **prophetic fury** seized by the spirit and able to prophesy 74 **mummy** liquid drained from embalmed bodies

OTHELLO Ha! Wherefore?

DESDEMONA Why do you speak so startingly and rash?

80 OTHELLO Is't lost? Is't gone? Speak, is it out o' th' way?

DESDEMONA Heaven bless us!

OTHELLO Say you?

DESDEMONA It is not lost. But what an if it were?

OTHELLO How?

85 DESDEMONA I say it is not lost.

OTHELLO Fetch't, let me see't!

DESDEMONA Why, so I can; but I will not now.
This is a trick to put me from my suit:
Pray you let Cassio be received again.

90 OTHELLO Fetch me the handkerchief! My mind misgives.

DESDEMONA Come, come!
You'll never meet a more sufficient man——

OTHELLO The handkerchief!

DESDEMONA A man that all his time
Hath founded his good fortunes on your love,
95 Shared dangers with you——

OTHELLO The handkerchief!

DESDEMONA I'faith, you are to blame.

OTHELLO Away! *Exit Othello.*

EMILIA Is not this man jealous?

100 DESDEMONA I nev'r saw this before.
Sure there's some wonder in this handkerchief;
I am most unhappy in the loss of it.

EMILIA 'Tis not a year or two shows us a man.
They are all but stomachs, and we all but food;
105 They eat us hungerly, and when they are full,
They belch us.

92 **sufficient** complete, with all proper qualities

Enter Iago and Cassio.

Look you, Cassio and my husband.

IAGO There is no other way; 'tis she must do't.
And lo the happiness! Go and importune her.

DESDEMONA How now, good Cassio? What's the news with you?

CASSIO Madam, my former suit. I do beseech you 110
That by your virtuous means I may again
Exist, and be a member of his love
Whom I with all the office of my heart
Entirely honor. I would not be delayed.
If my offense be of such mortal kind 115
That nor my service past, nor present sorrows,
Nor purposed merit in futurity,
Can ransom me into his love again,
But to know so must be my benefit.
So shall I clothe me in a forced content, 120
And shut myself up in some other course
To fortune's alms.

DESDEMONA Alas, thrice-gentle Cassio,
My advocation is not now in tune.
My lord is not my lord; nor should I know him
Were he in favor as in humor altered. 125
So help me every spirit sanctified
As I have spoken for you all my best
And stood within the blank of his displeasure
For my free speech. You must awhile be patient.
What I can do I will; and more I will 130
Than for myself I dare. Let that suffice you.

IAGO Is my lord angry?

EMILIA He went hence but now,
And certainly in strange unquietness.

IAGO Can he be angry? I have seen the cannon
When it hath blown his ranks into the air 135
And, like the devil, from his very arm

113 office duty **119 benefit** good **123 advocation** advocacy **125 favor** countenance **128 blank** bull's-eye of a target

Puffed his own brother. And is he angry?
Something of moment then. I will go meet him.
There's matter in't indeed if he be angry.

DESDEMONA I prithee do so. *Exit* [*Iago*].

140 Something sure of state,
Either from Venice or some unhatched practice
Made demonstrable here in Cyprus to him,
Hath puddled his clear spirit; and in such cases
Men's natures wrangle with inferior things,
145 Though great ones are their object. 'Tis even so.
For let our finger ache, and it endues
Our other, healthful members even to a sense
Of pain. Nay, we must think men are not gods,
Nor of them look for such observancy
150 As fits the bridal. Beshrew me much, Emilia,
I was, unhandsome warrior as I am,
Arraigning his unkindness with my soul;
But now I find I had suborned the witness,
And he's indicted falsely.

EMILIA Pray heaven it be
155 State matters, as you think, and no conception
Nor no jealous toy concerning you.

DESDEMONA Alas the day! I never gave him cause.

EMILIA But jealous souls will not be answered so;
They are not ever jealous for the cause,
160 But jealous for they're jealous. It is a monster
Begot upon itself, born on itself.

DESDEMONA Heaven keep the monster from Othello's mind!

EMILIA Lady, amen.

DESDEMONA I will go seek him. Cassio, walk here about.
165 If I do find him fit, I'll move your suit
And seek to effect it to my uttermost.

138 moment importance **140 of state** state affairs **141 unhatched practice** undisclosed plot **143 puddled** muddied **148 endues** leads **156 toy** trifle **165 fit** receptive

CASSIO I humbly thank your ladyship.
Exit [*Desdemona with Emilia*].

Enter Bianca.

BIANCA Save you, friend Cassio!

CASSIO What make you from home?
How is't with you, my most fair Bianca?
I' faith, sweet love, I was coming to your house. 170

BIANCA And I was going to your lodging, Cassio.
What, keep a week away? Seven days and nights?
Eightscore eight hours? And lovers' absent hours
More tedious than the dial eightscore times?
O weary reck'ning.

CASSIO Pardon me, Bianca. 175
I have this while with leaden thoughts been pressed,
But I shall in a more continuate time
Strike off this score of absence. Sweet Bianca,
[*Gives her Desdemona's handkerchief.*]
Take me this work out.

BIANCA O Cassio, whence came this?
This is some token from a newer friend. 180
To the felt absence now I feel a cause.
Is't come to this? Well, well.

CASSIO Go to, woman!
Throw your vile guesses in the devil's teeth,
From whence you have them. You are jealous now
That this is from some mistress, some remembrance. 185
No, by my faith, Bianca.

BIANCA Why, whose is it?

CASSIO I know not neither; I found it in my chamber.
I like the work well; ere it be demanded,
As like enough it will, I would have it copied.
Take it and do't, and leave me for this time. 190

175 reck'ning addition **177 continuate** uninterrupted **178 Strike off this score** i.e., pay this bill (the score being the account of drinks kept in a tavern) **188 demanded** asked for (by the person who lost it)

BIANCA Leave you? Wherefore?

CASSIO I do attend here on the general
And think it no addition, nor my wish,
To have him see me womaned.

BIANCA Why, I pray you?

CASSIO Not that I love you not.

195 BIANCA But that you do not love me!
I pray you bring me on the way a little,
And say if I shall see you soon at night.

CASSIO 'Tis but a little way that I can bring you,
For I attend here; but I'll see you soon.

200 BIANCA 'Tis very good. I must be circumstanced.

Exeunt omnes.

196 bring accompany 200 circumstanced accept things as they are

ACT IV

Scene I. [*A street.*]

Enter Othello and Iago.

IAGO Will you think so?

OTHELLO Think so, Iago?

IAGO What,
To kiss in private?

OTHELLO An unauthorized kiss?

IAGO Or to be naked with her friend in bed
An hour or more, not meaning any harm?

OTHELLO Naked in bed, Iago, and not mean harm? 5
It is hypocrisy against the devil.
They that mean virtuously, and yet do so,
The devil their virtue tempts, and they tempt heaven.

IAGO If they do nothing, 'tis a venial slip.
But if I give my wife a handkerchief—— 10

OTHELLO What then?

IAGO Why, then 'tis hers, my lord; and being hers,
She may, I think, bestow't on any man.

OTHELLO She is protectress of her honor too.
May she give that? 15

IAGO Her honor is an essence that's not seen;
They have it very oft that have it not.
But for the handkerchief——

IV.i.2 unauthorized illicit

OTHELLO By heaven, I would most gladly have forgot it!
20 Thou said'st—O, it comes o'er my memory
As doth the raven o'er the infected house,
Boding to all—he had my handkerchief.

IAGO Ay, what of that?

OTHELLO That's not so good now.

IAGO What if I had said I had seen him do you wrong?
25 Or heard him say—as knaves be such abroad
Who having, by their own importunate suit,
Or voluntary dotage of some mistress,
Convincèd or supplied them, cannot choose
But they must blab——

OTHELLO Hath he said anything?

30 IAGO He hath, my lord; but be you well assured,
No more than he'll unswear.

OTHELLO What hath he said?

IAGO Why, that he did—I know not what he did.

OTHELLO What? what?

IAGO Lie——

OTHELLO With her?

35 IAGO With her, on her; what you will.

OTHELLO Lie with her? Lie on her?—We say lie on her when they belie her.—Lie with her! Zounds, that's fulsome. —Handkerchief—confessions—handkerchief!—To confess, and be hanged for his labor—
40 first to be hanged, and then to confess! I tremble at it. Nature would not invest herself in such shadowing passion without some instruction. It is not words that shakes me thus.—Pish! Noses, ears, and

21 raven (a harbinger of death) **25 abroad** i.e., in the world **27 voluntary dotage** weakness of the will **28 Convincèd or supplied** persuaded or gratified (the mistress) **38 fulsome** foul, repulsive **41–42 Nature ... instruction** i.e., my mind would not become so darkened (with anger) unless there were something in this (accusation); (it should be remembered that Othello believes in the workings of magic and supernatural forces)

lips? Is't possible?—Confess?—Handkerchief?—O
devil! *Falls in a trance.* 45

IAGO Work on.
My med'cine works! Thus credulous fools are caught,
And many worthy and chaste dames even thus,
All guiltless, meet reproach. What, ho! My lord!
My lord, I say! Othello!

Enter Cassio.

How now, Cassio? 50

CASSIO What's the matter?

IAGO My lord is fall'n into an epilepsy.
This is his second fit; he had one yesterday.

CASSIO Rub him about the temples.

IAGO The lethargy must have his quiet course. 55
If not, he foams at mouth, and by and by
Breaks out to savage madness. Look, he stirs.
Do you withdraw yourself a little while.
He will recover straight. When he is gone,
I would on great occasion speak with you. 60
[*Exit Cassio.*]
How is it, general? Have you not hurt your head?

OTHELLO Dost thou mock me?

IAGO I mock you not, by heaven.
Would you would bear your fortune like a man.

OTHELLO A hornèd man's a monster and a beast.

IAGO There's many a beast then in a populous city, 65
And many a civil monster.

OTHELLO Did he confess it?

IAGO Good, sir, be a man.
Think every bearded fellow that's but yoked
May draw with you. There's millions now alive

49 reproach shame **55 lethargy** coma **60 great occasion** very important matter **62 mock** (Othello takes Iago's comment as a reference to his horns—which it is) **66 civil** city-dwelling **69 draw** i.e., like the horned ox

70 That nightly lie in those unproper beds
Which they dare swear peculiar. Your case is better.
O, 'tis the spite of hell, the fiend's arch-mock,
To lip a wanton in a secure couch,
And to suppose her chaste. No, let me know;
75 And knowing what I am, I know what she shall be.

OTHELLO O, thou art wise! 'Tis certain.

IAGO Stand you awhile apart;
Confine yourself but in a patient list.
Whilst you were here, o'erwhelmèd with your grief—
A passion most unsuiting such a man—
80 Cassio came hither. I shifted him away
And laid good 'scuses upon your ecstasy;
Bade him anon return, and here speak with me;
The which he promised. Do but encave yourself
And mark the fleers, the gibes, and notable scorns
85 That dwell in every region of his face.
For I will make him tell the tale anew:
Where, how, how oft, how long ago, and when
He hath, and is again to cope your wife.
I say, but mark his gesture. Marry patience,
90 Or I shall say you're all in all in spleen,
And nothing of a man.

OTHELLO Dost thou hear, Iago?
I will be found most cunning in my patience;
But—dost thou hear?—most bloody.

IAGO That's not amiss;
But yet keep time in all. Will you withdraw?

[*Othello moves to one side, where his remarks are not audible to Cassio and Iago.*]

70 **unproper** i.e., not exclusively the husband's 71 **peculiar** their own alone 77 **a patient list** the bounds of patience 80 **shifted him away** got rid of him by a stratagem 81 **ecstasy** trance (the literal meaning, "outside oneself," bears on the meaning of the change Othello is undergoing) 83 **encave** hide 84 **fleers** mocking looks or speeches 84 **notable** obvious 90 **spleen** passion, particularly anger

Now will I question Cassio of Bianca, 95
A huswife that by selling her desires
Buys herself bread and cloth. It is a creature
That dotes on Cassio, as 'tis the strumpet's plague
To beguile many and be beguiled by one.
He, when he hears of her, cannot restrain 100
From the excess of laughter. Here he comes.

Enter Cassio.

As he shall smile, Othello shall go mad;
And his unbookish jealousy must conster
Poor Cassio's smiles, gestures, and light behaviors
Quite in the wrong. How do you, lieutenant? 105

CASSIO The worser that you give me the addition
Whose want even kills me.

IAGO Ply Desdemona well, and you are sure on't.
Now, if this suit lay in Bianca's power.
How quickly should you speed!

CASSIO Alas, poor caitiff! 110

OTHELLO Look how he laughs already!

IAGO I never knew woman love man so.

CASSIO Alas, poor rogue! I think, i' faith, she loves me.

OTHELLO Now he denies it faintly, and laughs it out.

IAGO Do you hear, Cassio?

OTHELLO Now he importunes him 115
To tell it o'er. Go to! Well said, well said!

IAGO She gives it out that you shall marry her.
Do you intend it?

CASSIO Ha, ha, ha!

OTHELLO Do ye triumph, Roman? Do you triumph? 120

CASSIO I marry? What, a customer? Prithee bear

96 **huswife** housewife (but with the special meaning here of "prostitute") 103 **unbookish** ignorant 103 **conster** construe 106 **addition** title 110 **caitiff** wretch 121 **customer** one who sells, a merchant (here, a prostitute)

some charity to my wit; do not think it so unwholesome. Ha, ha, ha!

OTHELLO So, so, so, so. They laugh that win.

125 IAGO Why, the cry goes that you marry her.

CASSIO Prithee, say true.

IAGO I am a very villain else.

OTHELLO Have you scored me? Well.

CASSIO This is the monkey's own giving out. She is
130 persuaded I will marry her out of her own love and
flattery, not out of my promise.

OTHELLO Iago beckons me; now he begins the story.
[*Othello moves close enough to hear.*]

CASSIO She was here even now; she haunts me in every
place. I was the other day talking on the sea bank
135 with certain Venetians, and thither comes the
bauble, and falls me thus about my neck——

OTHELLO Crying "O dear Cassio!" as it were. His gesture imports it.

CASSIO So hangs, and lolls, and weeps upon me; so
140 shakes and pulls me! Ha, ha, ha!

OTHELLO Now he tells how she plucked him to my
chamber. O, I see that nose of yours, but not that
dog I shall throw it to.

CASSIO Well, I must leave her company.

145 IAGO Before me! Look where she comes.

Enter Bianca.

CASSIO 'Tis such another fitchew! Marry a perfumed
one? What do you mean by this haunting of me?

BIANCA Let the devil and his dam haunt you! What did
you mean by that same handkerchief you gave me
150 even now? I was a fine fool to take it. I must take

128 **scored** marked, defaced 136 **bauble** plaything 145 **Before me!** (an exclamation of surprise) 146 **fitchew** polecat, i.e., strong-smelling creature

out the work? A likely piece of work that you should find it in your chamber and know not who left it there! This is some minx's token, and I must take out the work? There! [*She throws down the handkerchief.*] Give it your hobbyhorse. Wheresoever 155 you had it, I'll take out no work on't.

CASSIO How now, my sweet Bianca? How now? how now?

OTHELLO By heaven, that should be my handkerchief!

BIANCA If you'll come to supper tonight, you may; 160 if you will not, come when you are next prepared for. *Exit.*

IAGO After her, after her!

CASSIO Faith, I must; she'll rail in the streets else.

IAGO Will you sup there? 165

CASSIO Yes, I intend so.

IAGO Well, I may chance to see you, for I would very fain speak with you.

CASSIO Prithee come. Will you?

IAGO Go to, say no more. [*Exit Cassio.*] 170

OTHELLO [*Comes forward.*] How shall I murder him, Iago?

IAGO Did you perceive how he laughed at his vice?

OTHELLO O Iago!

IAGO And did you see the handkerchief? 175

OTHELLO Was that mine?

IAGO Yours, by this hand! And to see how he prizes the foolish woman your wife! She gave it him, and he hath giv'n it his whore.

OTHELLO I would have him nine years a-killing!—A 180 fine woman, a fair woman, a sweet woman?

155 hobbyhorse prostitute **161-62 next prepared for** next expected—i.e., never

IAGO Nay, you must forget that.

OTHELLO Ay, let her rot, and perish, and be damned tonight; for she shall not live. No, my heart is turned
185 to stone; I strike it, and it hurts my hand. O, the world hath not a sweeter creature! She might lie by an emperor's side and command him tasks.

IAGO Nay, that's not your way.

OTHELLO Hang her! I do but say what she is. So deli-
190 cate with her needle. An admirable musician. O, she will sing the savageness out of a bear! Of so high and plenteous wit and invention——

IAGO She's the worse for all this.

OTHELLO O, a thousand, a thousand times. And then,
195 of so gentle a condition?

IAGO Ay, too gentle.

OTHELLO Nay, that's certain. But yet the pity of it, Iago. O Iago, the pity of it, Iago.

IAGO If you are so fond over her iniquity, give her
200 patent to offend; for if it touch not you, it comes near nobody.

OTHELLO I will chop her into messes! Cuckold me!

IAGO O, 'tis foul in her.

OTHELLO With mine officer!

205 IAGO That's fouler.

OTHELLO Get me some poison, Iago, this night. I'll not expostulate with her, lest her body and beauty unprovide my mind again. This night, Iago!

IAGO Do it not with poison. Strangle her in her bed,
210 even the bed she hath contaminated.

OTHELLO Good, good! The justice of it pleases. Very good!

188 way proper course 192 invention imagination 195 gentle a condition (1) well born (2) of a gentle nature 200 touch affects 202 messes bits 207–08 unprovide my mind undo my resolution

IAGO And for Cassio, let me be his undertaker. You shall hear more by midnight.

OTHELLO Excellent good! [*A trumpet.*]
What trumpet is that same? 215

IAGO I warrant something from Venice.

Enter Lodovico, Desdemona, and Attendants.

'Tis Lodovico.
This comes from the Duke. See, your wife's with him.

LODOVICO God save you, worthy general.

OTHELLO With all my heart, sir.

LODOVICO The Duke and the senators of Venice greet you. [*Gives him a letter.*]

OTHELLO I kiss the instrument of their pleasures. 220
[*Opens the letter and reads.*]

DESDEMONA And what's the news, good cousin Lodovico?

IAGO I am very glad to see you, signior.
Welcome to Cyprus.

LODOVICO I thank you. How does Lieutenant Cassio?

IAGO Lives, sir.

DESDEMONA Cousin, there's fall'n between him and my lord 225
An unkind breach; but you shall make all well.

OTHELLO Are you sure of that?

DESDEMONA My lord?

OTHELLO [*Reads*] "This fail you not to do, as you will——"

LODOVICO He did not call; he's busy in the paper. 230
Is there division 'twixt my lord and Cassio?

213 **undertaker** (not "burier" but "one who undertakes to do something")
218 **With** i.e., I greet you with 226 **unkind** unnatural

DESDEMONA A most unhappy one. I would do much
T' atone them, for the love I bear to Cassio.

OTHELLO Fire and brimstone!

DESDEMONA My lord?

OTHELLO Are you wise?

DESDEMONA What, is he angry?

235 LODOVICO May be th' letter moved him;
For, as I think, they do command him home,
Deputing Cassio in his government.

DESDEMONA Trust me, I am glad on't.

OTHELLO Indeed?

DESDEMONA My lord?

OTHELLO I am glad to see you mad.

DESDEMONA. Why, sweet Othello——

240 OTHELLO Devil! [*Strikes her.*]

DESDEMONA. I have not deserved this.

LODOVICO My lord, this would not be believed in Venice,
Though I should swear I saw't. 'Tis very much.
Make her amends; she weeps.

OTHELLO O devil, devil!
245 If that the earth could teem with woman's tears,
Each drop she falls would prove a crocodile.
Out of my sight!

DESDEMONA I will not stay to offend you. [*Going.*]

LODOVICO Truly, an obedient lady.
I do beseech your lordship call her back.

OTHELLO Mistress!

DESDEMONA My lord?

250 OTHELLO What would you with her, sir?

233 atone reconcile **237 government** office **245 teem** conceive **246 falls** drops **246 crocodile** (the crocodile was supposed to shed false tears to lure its victims)

LODOVICO Who? I, my lord?

OTHELLO Ay! You did wish that I would make her turn.
Sir, she can turn, and turn, and yet go on
And turn again; and she can weep, sir, weep;
And she's obedient; as you say, obedient. 255
Very obedient. Proceed you in your tears.
Concerning this, sir—O well-painted passion!
I am commanded home.—Get you away;
I'll send for you anon.—Sir, I obey the mandate
And will return to Venice.—Hence, avaunt! 260
[*Exit Desdemona.*]
Cassio shall have my place. And, sir, tonight
I do entreat that we may sup together.
You are welcome, sir, to Cyprus.—Goats and monkeys! *Exit.*

LODOVICO Is this the noble Moor whom our full Senate
Call all in all sufficient? Is this the nature 265
Whom passion could not shake? whose solid virtue
The shot of accident nor dart of chance
Could neither graze nor pierce?

IAGO He is much changed.

LODOVICO Are his wits safe? Is he not light of brain?

IAGO He's that he is; I may not breathe my censure. 270
What he might be (if, what he might, he is not)
I would to heaven he were!

LODOVICO What, strike his wife?

IAGO Faith, that was not so well; yet would I knew
That stroke would prove the worst.

LODOVICO Is it his use?
Or did the letters work upon his blood 275
And new-create his fault?

IAGO Alas, alas!
It is not honesty in me to speak
What I have seen and known. You shall observe him,

274 use habit 275 blood passion

And his own courses will denote him so
280 That I may save my speech. Do but go after
And mark how he continues.

LODOVICO I am sorry that I am deceived in him.
Exeunt.

Scene II. [*The citadel.*]

Enter Othello and Emilia.

OTHELLO You have seen nothing then?

EMILIA Nor ever heard, nor ever did suspect.

OTHELLO Yes, you have seen Cassio and she together.

EMILIA But then I saw no harm, and then I heard
5 Each syllable that breath made up between them.

OTHELLO What, did they never whisper?

EMILIA Never, my lord.

OTHELLO Nor send you out o' th' way?

EMILIA Never.

OTHELLO To fetch her fan, her gloves, her mask, nor nothing?

10 EMILIA Never, my lord.

OTHELLO That's strange.

EMILIA I durst, my lord, to wager she is honest,
Lay down my soul at stake. If you think other,
Remove your thought. It doth abuse your bosom.
15 If any wretch have put this in your head,
Let heaven requite it with the serpent's curse,
For if she be not honest, chaste, and true,

279 courses actions IV.ii.5 **that breath made up** spoken 13 **at stake** as the wager 16 **serpent's curse** (God's curse on the serpent after the fall in Eden) 17 **honest** chaste

There's no man happy. The purest of their wives
Is foul as slander.

OTHELLO Bid her come hither. Go.

Exit Emilia.

She says enough; yet she's a simple bawd 20
That cannot say as much. This is a subtle whore,
A closet lock and key of villainous secrets,
And yet she'll kneel and pray; I have seen her do't.

Enter Desdemona and Emilia.

DESDEMONA My lord, what is your will?

OTHELLO Pray you, chuck, come hither.

DESDEMONA What is your pleasure?

OTHELLO Let me see your eyes. 25
Look in my face.

DESDEMONA What horrible fancy's this?

OTHELLO [*To Emilia*] Some of your function, mistress:
Leave procreants alone and shut the door;
Cough or cry hem if anybody come.
Your mystery, your mystery! Nay, dispatch! 30

Exit Emilia.

DESDEMONA Upon my knee, what doth your speech import?
I understand a fury in your words.

OTHELLO Why, what art thou?

DESDEMONA Your wife, my lord; your true
And loyal wife.

OTHELLO Come, swear it, damn thyself;
Lest, being like one of heaven, the devils themselves 35
Should fear to seize thee. Therefore be double-damned:
Swear thou art honest.

DESDEMONA Heaven doth truly know it.

20 bawd procuress **27 Some of your function** do your proper work (as the operator of a brothel) **30 mystery** trade **32 words** (Q1 adds to this line, "But not the words")

OTHELLO Heaven truly knows that thou art false as hell.

DESDEMONA To whom, my lord? With whom? How am I false?

40 OTHELLO Ah, Desdemon! Away! Away! Away!

DESDEMONA Alas the heavy day! Why do you weep?
Am I the motive of these tears, my lord?
If haply you my father do suspect
An instrument of this your calling back,
45 Lay not your blame on me. If you have lost him,
I have lost him too.

OTHELLO Had it pleased heaven
To try me with affliction, had they rained
All kinds of sores and shames on my bare head,
Steeped me in poverty to the very lips,
50 Given to captivity me and my utmost hopes,
I should have found in some place of my soul
A drop of patience. But, alas, to make me
The fixèd figure for the time of scorn
To point his slow and moving finger at.
55 Yet could I bear that too, well, very well.
But there where I have garnered up my heart,
Where either I must live or bear no life,
The fountain from the which my current runs
Or else dries up—to be discarded thence,
60 Or keep it as a cistern for foul toads
To knot and gender in—turn thy complexion there,
Patience, thou young and rose-lipped cherubin!
I here look grim as hell!

DESDEMONA I hope my noble lord esteems me honest.

65 OTHELLO O, ay, as summer flies are in the shambles,
That quicken even with blowing. O thou weed,

42 motive cause **43 haply** by chance **49 Steeped** submerged **53 The . . . scorn** the very image of scorn in our time **61 knot and gender** twist in bunches and procreate **61–63 turn . . . hell** (the rough sense would seem to be, "even Patience would grow pale, turn complexion, at Desdemona's perfidy, but that Othello looks grimly on") **65 shambles** abattoirs **66 quicken even with blowing** become impregnated as soon as they lay their eggs

Who art so lovely fair, and smell'st so sweet,
That the sense aches at thee, would thou hadst never
been born!

DESDEMONA Alas, what ignorant sin have I committed?

OTHELLO Was this fair paper, this most goodly book, 70
Made to write "whore" upon? What committed?
Committed? O thou public commoner,
I should make very forges of my cheeks
That would to cinders burn up modesty,
Did I but speak thy deeds. What committed? 75
Heaven stops the nose at it, and the moon winks;
The bawdy wind that kisses all it meets
Is hushed within the hollow mine of earth
And will not hear 't. What committed?

DESDEMONA By heaven, you do me wrong! 80

OTHELLO Are not you a strumpet?

DESDEMONA No, as I am a Christian!
If to preserve this vessel for my lord
From any other foul unlawful touch
Be not to be a strumpet, I am none.

OTHELLO What, not a whore?

DESDEMONA No, as I shall be saved! 85

OTHELLO Is't possible?

DESDEMONA O, heaven forgive us!

OTHELLO I cry you mercy then.
I took you for that cunning whore of Venice
That married with Othello. [*Calling*] You, mistress,

Enter Emilia.

That have the office opposite to Saint Peter 90
And keep the gate of hell! You, you, ay, you!
We have done our course; there's money for your
pains. [*Throws her some coins.*]

69 **ignorant** unknowing 72 **commoner** prostitute 76 **winks** closes its eyes (the moon was the symbol of chastity) 87 **cry you mercy** ask your pardon

I pray you turn the key and keep our counsel.

Exit.

EMILIA Alas, what does this gentleman conceive?

95 How do you, madam? How do you, my good lady?

DESDEMONA Faith, half asleep.

EMILIA Good madam, what's the matter with my lord?

DESDEMONA With who?

EMILIA Why, with my lord, madam.

DESDEMONA Who is thy lord?

100 EMILIA He that is yours, sweet lady.

DESDEMONA I have none. Do not talk to me, Emilia.
I cannot weep, nor answers have I none
But what should go by water. Prithee tonight
Lay on my bed my wedding sheets, remember;
And call thy husband hither.

105 EMILIA Here's a change indeed!

Exit.

DESDEMONA 'Tis meet I should be used so, very meet.
How have I been behaved, that he might stick
The small'st opinion on my least misuse?

Enter Iago and Emilia.

IAGO What is your pleasure, madam? How is't with you?

DESDEMONA I cannot tell. Those that do teach young
110 babes
Do it with gentle means and easy tasks.
He might have chid me so; for, in good faith,
I am a child to chiding.

IAGO What is the matter, lady?

EMILIA Alas, Iago, my lord hath so bewhored her,
115 Thrown such despite and heavy terms upon her
That true hearts cannot bear it.

103 water tears **107–08 stick ... misuse** base any doubt on my smallest fault
115 despite abuse

DESDEMONA Am I that name, Iago?

IAGO What name, fair lady?

DESDEMONA Such as she said my lord did say I was.

EMILIA He called her whore. A beggar in his drink
Could not have laid such terms upon his callet. 120

IAGO Why did he so?

DESDEMONA I do not know; I am sure I am none such.

IAGO Do not weep, do not weep. Alas the day.

EMILIA Hath she forsook so many noble matches,
Her father and her country, and her friends, 125
To be called whore? Would it not make one weep?

DESDEMONA It is my wretched fortune.

IAGO Beshrew him for 't!
How comes this trick upon him?

DESDEMONA Nay, heaven doth know.

EMILIA I will be hanged if some eternal villain,
Some busy and insinuating rogue, 130
Some cogging, cozening slave, to get some office,
Have not devised this slander. I will be hanged else.

IAGO Fie, there is no such man! It is impossible.

DESDEMONA If any such there be, heaven pardon him.

EMILIA A halter pardon him! And hell gnaw his bones! 135
Why should he call her whore? Who keeps her company?
What place? What time? What form? What likelihood?
The Moor's abused by some most villainous knave,
Some base notorious knave, some scurvy fellow.
O heavens, that such companions thou'dst unfold, 140
And put in every honest hand a whip
To lash the rascals naked through the world
Even from the east to th' west!

120 callet slut **127 Beshrew** curse **131 cogging** cheating **140 companions** fellows, rogues **140 unfold** disclose

IAGO Speak within door.

EMILIA O, fie upon them! Some such squire he was
145 That turned your wit the seamy side without
And made you to suspect me with the Moor.

IAGO You are a fool. Go to.

DESDEMONA Alas, Iago,
What shall I do to win my lord again?
Good friend, go to him, for, by this light of heaven,
150 I know not how I lost him. Here I kneel:
If e'er my will did trespass 'gainst his love
Either in discourse of thought or actual deed,
Or that mine eyes, mine ears, or any sense
Delighted them in any other form;
155 Or that I do not yet, and ever did,
And ever will (though he do shake me off
To beggarly divorcement) love him dearly,
Comfort forswear me. Unkindness may do much,
And his unkindness may defeat my life,
160 But never taint my love. I cannot say "whore."
It does abhor me now I speak the word;
To do the act that might the addition earn
Not the world's mass of vanity could make me.

IAGO I pray you be content. 'Tis but his humor.
165 The business of the state does him offense.

DESDEMONA If 'twere no other.

IAGO It is but so, I warrant.
[*Trumpets within.*]
Hark how these instruments summon to supper.
The messengers of Venice stay the meat.
Go in, and weep not. All things shall be well.
[*Exeunt Desdemona and Emilia.*]

Enter Roderigo.

170 How now, Roderigo?

143 within door more quietly and moderately **144 squire** (a term of contempt) **152 discourse of thought** thinking **159 defeat** destroy **164 humor** mood **168 stay the meat** await the meal

RODERIGO I do not find that thou deal'st justly with me.

IAGO What in the contrary?

RODERIGO Every day thou daff'st me with some device, Iago, and rather, as it seems to me now, keep'st from me all conveniency than suppliest me 175 with the least advantage of hope. I will indeed no longer endure it; nor am I yet persuaded to put up in peace what already I have foolishly suffered.

IAGO Will you hear me, Roderigo?

RODERIGO I have heard too much, and your words 180 and performances are no kin together.

IAGO You charge me most unjustly.

RODERIGO With naught but truth. I have wasted myself out of my means. The jewels you have had from me to deliver Desdemona would half have corrupted 185 a votarist. You have told me she hath received them, and returned me expectations and comforts of sudden respect and acquaintance; but I find none.

IAGO Well, go to; very well. 190

RODERIGO Very well? Go to? I cannot go to, man; nor 'tis not very well. Nay, I think it is scurvy, and begin to find myself fopped in it.

IAGO Very well.

RODERIGO I tell you 'tis not very well. I will make my- 195 self known to Desdemona. If she will return me my jewels, I will give over my suit and repent my unlawful solicitation. If not, assure yourself I will seek satisfaction of you.

IAGO You have said now? 200

RODERIGO Ay, and said nothing but what I protest intendment of doing.

173 daff'st put off 173-74 device scheme 175 conveniency what is needful 177 put up accept 186 votarist nun 188 sudden respect immediate consideration 193 fopped duped 201 protest aver

IAGO Why, now I see there's mettle in thee, and even from this instant do build on thee a better opinion
205 than ever before. Give me thy hand, Roderigo. Thou hast taken against me a most just exception; but yet I protest I have dealt most directly in thy affair.

RODERIGO It hath not appeared.

210 IAGO I grant indeed it hath not appeared, and your suspicion is not without wit and judgment. But, Roderigo, if thou hast that in thee indeed which I have greater reason to believe now than ever—I mean purpose, courage, and valor—this night show
215 it. If thou the next night following enjoy not Desdemona, take me from this world with treachery and devise engines for my life.

RODERIGO Well, what is it? Is it within reason and compass?

220 IAGO Sir, there is especial commission come from Venice to depute Cassio in Othello's place.

RODERIGO Is that true? Why, then Othello and Desdemona return again to Venice.

IAGO O, no; he goes into Mauritania and taketh away
225 with him the fair Desdemona, unless his abode be lingered here by some accident; wherein none can be so determinate as the removing of Cassio.

RODERIGO How do you mean, removing him?

IAGO Why, by making him uncapable of Othello's
230 place—knocking out his brains.

RODERIGO And that you would have me to do?

IAGO Ay, if you dare do yourself a profit and a right. He sups tonight with a harlotry, and thither will I go to him. He knows not yet of his honorable for-
235 tune. If you will watch his going thence, which I

203 mettle spirit **206 exception** objection **207 directly** straightforwardly **217 engines for** schemes against **219 compass** possibility **227 determinate** effective **233 harlotry** female

will fashion to fall out between twelve and one, you may take him at your pleasure. I will be near to second your attempt, and he shall fall between us. Come, stand not amazed at it, but go along with me. I will show you such a necessity in his death 240 that you shall think yourself bound to put it on him. It is now high supper time, and the night grows to waste. About it.

RODERIGO I will hear further reason for this.

IAGO And you shall be satisfied. *Exeunt.* 245

Scene III. [*The citadel.*]

Enter Othello, Lodovico, Desdemona, Emilia, and Attendants.

LODOVICO I do beseech you, sir, trouble yourself no further.

OTHELLO O, pardon me; 'twill do me good to walk.

LODOVICO Madam, good night. I humbly thank your ladyship.

DESDEMONA. Your honor is most welcome.

OTHELLO Will you walk, sir? O, Desdemona. 5

DESDEMONA My lord?

OTHELLO Get you to bed on th' instant; I will be returned forthwith. Dismiss your attendant there. Look't be done.

DESDEMONA I will, my lord. 10

Exit [*Othello, with Lodovico and Attendants*].

EMILIA How goes it now? He looks gentler than he did.

236 fall out occur **238 second** support

DESDEMONA He says he will return incontinent,
And hath commanded me to go to bed,
And bade me to dismiss you.

EMILIA Dismiss me?

15 DESDEMONA It was his bidding; therefore, good Emilia,
Give me my nightly wearing, and adieu.
We must not now displease him.

EMILIA I would you had never seen him!

DESDEMONA So would not I. My love doth so approve him
That even his stubbornness, his checks, his frowns— 20
Prithee unpin me—have grace and favor.

EMILIA I have laid these sheets you bade me on the bed.

DESDEMONA All's one. Good Father, how foolish are our minds!
If I do die before, prithee shroud me
In one of these same sheets.

25 EMILIA Come, come! You talk.

DESDEMONA My mother had a maid called Barbary.
She was in love; and he she loved proved mad
And did forsake her. She had a song of "Willow";
An old thing 'twas, but it expressed her fortune,
30 And she died singing it. That song tonight
Will not go from my mind; I have much to do
But to go hang my head all at one side
And sing it like poor Barbary. Prithee dispatch.

EMILIA Shall I go fetch your nightgown?

35 DESDEMONA No, unpin me here.
This Lodovico is a proper man.

EMILIA A very handsome man.

DESDEMONA He speaks well.

IV.iii.12 **incontinent** at once 20 **checks** rebukes 23 **All's one** no matter

EMILIA I know a lady in Venice would have walked barefoot to Palestine for a touch of his nether lip. 40

DESDEMONA [*Sings*]

"The poor soul sat singing by a sycamore tree,
Sing all a green willow;
Her hand on her bosom, her head on her knee,
Sing willow, willow, willow.
The fresh streams ran by her and murmured her moans; 45
Sing willow, willow, willow;
Her salt tears fell from her, and soft'ned the stones—
Sing willow, willow, willow—"
Lay by these. [*Give Emilia her clothes.*]
"Willow, Willow"—— 50
Prithee hie thee; he'll come anon.
"Sing all a green willow must be my garland.
Let nobody blame him; his scorn I approve"——
Nay, that's not next. Hark! Who is't that knocks?

EMILIA It is the wind. 55

DESDEMONA [*Sings*]

"I called my love false love; but what said he then?
Sing willow, willow, willow:
If I court moe women, you'll couch with moe men."
So, get thee gone; good night. Mine eyes do itch.
Doth that bode weeping?

EMILIA 'Tis neither here nor there. 60

DESDEMONA I have heard it said so. O, these men, these men.
Dost thou in conscience think, tell me, Emilia,
That there be women do abuse their husbands
In such gross kind?

EMILIA There be some such, no question.

51 hie hurry 51 anon at once 58 moe more

DESDEMONA Wouldst thou do such a deed for all the
65 world?

EMILIA Why, would not you?

DESDEMONA No, by this heavenly light!

EMILIA Nor I neither by this heavenly light.
I might do't as well i' th' dark.

DESDEMONA Wouldst thou do such a deed for all the
world?

70 EMILIA The world's a huge thing; it is a great price for
a small vice.

DESDEMONA In troth, I think thou wouldst not.

EMILIA In troth, I think I should; and undo't when I
had done. Marry, I would not do such a thing for
75 a joint-ring, nor for measures of lawn, nor for
gowns, petticoats, nor caps, nor any petty exhibition,
but for all the whole world? Why, who
would not make her husband a cuckold to make him
a monarch? I should venture purgatory for't.

80 DESDEMONA Beshrew me if I would do such a wrong
for the whole world.

EMILIA Why, the wrong is but a wrong i' th' world;
and having the world for your labor, 'tis a wrong
in your own world, and you might quickly make
85 it right.

DESDEMONA I do not think there is any such woman.

EMILIA Yes, a dozen; and as many to th' vantage as
would store the world they played for.
But I do think it is their husbands' faults
90 If wives do fall. Say that they slack their duties
And pour our treasures into foreign laps;
Or else break out in peevish jealousies,
Throwing restraint upon us; or say they strike us,

75 **joint-ring** (a ring with two interlocking halves) 75 **lawn** fine linen
76–77 **exhibition** payment 87–88 **to ... store** in addition as would fill 91
foreign alien, i.e., other than the wife

Or scant our former having in despite—
Why, we have galls; and though we have some grace, 95
Yet have we some revenge. Let husbands know
Their wives have sense like them. They see, and smell,
And have their palates both for sweet and sour,
As husbands have. What is it that they do
When they change us for others? Is it sport? 100
I think it is. And doth affection breed it?
I think it doth. Is't frailty that thus errs?
It is so too. And have not we affections?
Desires for sport? and frailty? as men have?
Then let them use us well; else let them know, 105
The ills we do, their ills instruct us so.

DESDEMONA Good night, good night. Heaven me such uses send,
Not to pick bad from bad, but by bad mend. *Exeunt.*

94 **scant ... despite** reduce, in spite, our household allowance (?) 100 **change** exchange 101 **affection** strong feeling, desire 106 **instruct us so** teach us to do likewise 107 **uses** practices

ACT V

Scene I. [*A street.*]

Enter Iago and Roderigo.

IAGO Here, stand behind this bulk; straight will he come.
Wear thy good rapier bare, and put it home.
Quick, quick! Fear nothing; I'll be at thy elbow.
It makes us, or it mars us, think on that,
5 And fix most firm thy resolution.

RODERIGO Be near at hand; I may miscarry in't.

IAGO Here, at thy hand. Be bold, and take thy stand.
[*Moves to one side.*]

RODERIGO I have no great devotion to the deed,
And yet he hath given me satisfying reasons.
10 'Tis but a man gone. Forth my sword! He dies!

IAGO I have rubbed this young quat almost to the sense,
And he grows angry. Now, whether he kill Cassio,
Or Cassio him, or each do kill the other,
Every way makes my gain. Live Roderigo,
15 He calls me to a restitution large
Of gold and jewels that I bobbed from him
As gifts to Desdemona.
It must not be. If Cassio do remain,

V.i.1 **bulk** projecting stall of a shop 11 **quat** pimple 11 **to the sense** raw
16 **bobbed** swindled

He hath a daily beauty in his life
That makes me ugly; and besides, the Moor 20
May unfold me to him; there stand I in much peril.
No, he must die. But so, I hear him coming.

Enter Cassio.

RODERIGO I know his gait. 'Tis he. Villain, thou diest!
[*Thrusts at Cassio.*]

CASSIO That thrust had been mine enemy indeed
But that my coat is better than thou know'st. 25
I will make proof of thine. [*Fights with Roderigo.*]

RODERIGO O, I am slain!

CASSIO I am maimed forever. Help, ho! Murder! Murder!

Enter Othello [to one side].

OTHELLO The voice of Cassio. Iago keeps his word.

RODERIGO O, villain that I am!

OTHELLO It is even so.

CASSIO O help, ho! Light! A surgeon! 30

OTHELLO 'Tis he. O brave Iago, honest and just,
That hast such noble sense of thy friend's wrong!
Thou teachest me. Minion, your dear lies dead,
And your unblest fate hies. Strumpet, I come.
Forth of my heart those charms, thine eyes, are blotted. 35
Thy bed, lust-stained, shall with lust's blood be spotted.

Exit Othello.

25 coat i.e., a mail shirt or bulletproof vest **26 slain** (most editors add here a stage direction which has Iago wounding Cassio in the leg from behind, but remaining unseen. However, nothing in the text requires this, and Cassio's wound can be given him in the fight with Roderigo, for presumably when Cassio attacks Roderigo the latter would not simply accept the thrust but would parry. Since Iago enters again at line 46, he must exit at some point after line 22) **33 Minion** hussy, i.e., Desdemona **34 unblest** unsanctified **34 hies** approaches swiftly

Enter Lodovico and Gratiano.

CASSIO What, ho? No watch? No passage? Murder! Murder!

GRATIANO 'Tis some mischance. The voice is very direful.

CASSIO O, help!

40 LODOVICO Hark!

RODERIGO O wretched villain!

LODOVICO Two or three groan. 'Tis heavy night.
These may be counterfeits. Let's think't unsafe
To come into the cry without more help.

45 RODERIGO Nobody come? Then shall I bleed to death.

LODOVICO Hark!

Enter Iago [*with a light*].

GRATIANO Here's one comes in his shirt, with light and weapons.

IAGO Who's there? Whose noise is this that cries on murder?

LODOVICO We do not know.

IAGO Do not you hear a cry?

CASSIO Here, here! For heaven's sake, help me!

50 IAGO What's the matter?

GRATIANO This is Othello's ancient, as I take it.

LODOVICO The same indeed, a very valiant fellow.

IAGO What are you here that cry so grievously?

CASSIO Iago? O, I am spoiled, undone by villains.
55 Give me some help.

IAGO O me, lieutenant! What villains have done this?

CASSIO I think that one of them is hereabout
And cannot make away.

37 **passage** passers-by

IAGO O treacherous villains!
[*To Lodovico and Gratiano*] What are you there?
Come in, and give some help.

RODERIGO O, help me there! 60

CASSIO That's one of them.

IAGO O murd'rous slave! O villain!
[*Stabs Roderigo*.]

RODERIGO O damned Iago! O inhuman dog!

IAGO Kill men i' th' dark?—Where be these bloody thieves?—
How silent is this town!—Ho! Murder! Murder!—
What may you be? Are you of good or evil? 65

LODOVICO As you shall prove us, praise us.

IAGO Signior Lodovico?

LODOVICO He, sir.

IAGO I cry you mercy. Here's Cassio hurt by villains.

GRATIANO Cassio? 70

IAGO How is't, brother?

CASSIO My leg is cut in two.

IAGO Marry, heaven forbid!
Light, gentlemen. I'll bind it with my shirt.

Enter Bianca.

BIANCA What is the matter, ho? Who is't that cried?

IAGO Who is't that cried? 75

BIANCA O my dear Cassio! My sweet Cassio!
O Cassio, Cassio, Cassio!

IAGO O notable strumpet!—Cassio, may you suspect
Who they should be that have thus mangled you?

CASSIO No. 80

GRATIANO I am sorry to find you thus. I have been to seek you.

IAGO Lend me a garter. So. O for a chair
To bear him easily hence.

BIANCA Alas, he faints! O Cassio, Cassio, Cassio!

85 IAGO Gentlemen all, I do suspect this trash
To be a party in this injury.—
Patience awhile, good Cassio.—Come, come.
Lend me a light. Know we this face or no?
Alas, my friend and my dear countryman
90 Roderigo? No.—Yes, sure.—Yes, 'tis Roderigo!

GRATIANO What, of Venice?

IAGO Even he, sir. Did you know him?

GRATIANO Know him? Ay.

IAGO Signior Gratiano? I cry your gentle pardon.
These bloody accidents must excuse my manners
That so neglected you.

95 GRATIANO I am glad to see you.

IAGO How do you, Cassio?—O, a chair, a chair!

GRATIANO Roderigo?

IAGO He, he, 'tis he! [*A chair brought in.*] O, that's well said; the chair.
Some good man bear him carefully from hence.
I'll fetch the general's surgeon. [*To Bianca*] For you,
100 mistress,
Save you your labor. [*To Cassio*] He that lies slain here, Cassio,
Was my dear friend. What malice was between you?

CASSIO None in the world; nor do I know the man.

IAGO What, look you pale?—O, bear him out o' th' air. [*Cassio is carried off.*]
Stay you, good gentlemen.—Look you pale, mis-
105 tress?
Do you perceive the gastness of her eye?
Nay, if you stare, we shall hear more anon.
Behold her well; I pray you look upon her.

98 well said well done **106 gastness** terror

Do you see, gentlemen? Nay, guiltiness will speak,
Though tongues were out of use. 110

[*Enter Emilia.*]

EMILIA Alas, what is the matter? What is the matter, husband?

IAGO Cassio hath here been set on in the dark
By Roderigo and fellows that are scaped.
He's almost slain, and Roderigo quite dead.

EMILIA Alas, good gentleman! Alas, good Cassio! 115

IAGO This is the fruits of whoring. Prithee, Emilia,
Go know of Cassio where he supped tonight.
[*To Bianca*] What, do you shake at that?

BIANCA He supped at my house; but I therefore shake not.

IAGO O, did he so? I charge you go with me. 120

EMILIA Oh fie upon thee, strumpet!

BIANCA I am no strumpet, but of life as honest
As you that thus abuse me.

EMILIA As I? Fie upon thee!

IAGO Kind gentlemen, let's go see poor Cassio dressed.
[*To Bianca*] Come, mistress, you must tell's another tale. 125
Emilia, run you to the citadel
And tell my lord and lady what hath happed.
[*Exit Emilia.*]
Will you go on afore? *Exeunt* [*all but Iago*].
This is the night
That either makes me or fordoes me quite. [*Exit.*]

110 tongues were out of use men no longer spoke 120 charge command
124 dressed bandaged 129 fordoes me quite completely ruins me

Scene II. [*Desdemona's chamber.*]

Enter Othello [*with a light*]*; and Desdemona in her bed.*

OTHELLO It is the cause, it is the cause, my soul.
Let me not name it to you, you chaste stars.
It is the cause. Yet I'll not shed her blood,
Nor scar that whiter skin of hers than snow,
5 And smooth as monumental alabaster.
Yet she must die, else she'll betray more men.
Put out the light, and then put out the light.
If I quench thee, thou flaming minister,
I can again thy former light restore,
10 Should I repent me; but once put out thy light,
Thou cunning'st pattern of excelling nature,
I know not where is that Promethean heat
That can thy light relume. When I have plucked the rose,
I cannot give it vital growth again;
15 It needs must wither. I'll smell thee on the tree.
[*He kisses her.*]
O balmy breath, that dost almost persuade
Justice to break her sword. One more, one more!
Be thus when thou art dead, and I will kill thee,
And love thee after. One more, and that's the last!
20 So sweet was ne'er so fatal. I must weep,
But they are cruel tears. This sorrow's heavenly;
It strikes where it doth love. She wakes.

DESDEMONA Who's there? Othello?

OTHELLO Ay, Desdemona.

V.ii.8 minister worker, servant **11 cunning'st** most intricate and skillfully wrought (by nature excelling itself) **12 Promethean heat** divine fire (Prometheus is the Titan who stole fire from heaven and gave it to man) **13 relume** relight **14 vital** living

DESDEMONA Will you come to bed, my lord?

OTHELLO Have you prayed tonight, Desdemon?

DESDEMONA Ay, my lord. 25

OTHELLO If you bethink yourself of any crime
Unreconciled as yet to heaven and grace,
Solicit for it straight.

DESDEMONA Alack, my lord, what may you mean by that?

OTHELLO Well, do it, and be brief; I will walk by. 30
I would not kill thy unpreparèd spirit.
No, heavens forfend! I would not kill thy soul.

DESDEMONA Talk you of killing?

OTHELLO Ay, I do.

DESDEMONA Then heaven
Have mercy on me!

OTHELLO Amen, with all my heart.

DESDEMONA If you say so, I hope you will not kill me. 35

OTHELLO Humh.

DESDEMONA And yet I fear you; for you're fatal then
When your eyes roll so. Why I should fear I know not,
Since guiltiness I know not; but yet I feel I fear.

OTHELLO Think on thy sins.

DESDEMONA They are loves I bear to you. 40

OTHELLO Ay, and for that thou diest.

DESDEMONA That death's unnatural that kills for loving.
Alas, why gnaw you so your nether lip?
Some bloody passion shakes your very frame.
These are portents; but yet I hope, I hope, 45
They do not point on me.

OTHELLO Peace and be still.

30 by nearby

DESDEMONA I will so. What's the matter?

OTHELLO That handkerchief which I so loved and gave thee,
Thou gav'st to Cassio.

DESDEMONA No, by my life and soul!
Send for the man and ask him.

50 OTHELLO Sweet soul, take heed,
Take heed of perjury; thou art on thy deathbed.

DESDEMONA Ay, but not yet to die.

OTHELLO Presently.
Therefore confess thee freely of thy sin,
For to deny each article with oath
55 Cannot remove nor choke the strong conception
That I do groan withal. Thou art to die.

DESDEMONA Then Lord have mercy on me.

OTHELLO I say, amen.

DESDEMONA And have you mercy too. I never did
Offend you in my life; never loved Cassio
60 But with such general warranty of heaven
As I might love. I never gave him token.

OTHELLO By heaven, I saw my handkerchief in's hand!
O perjured woman! thou dost stone my heart,
And mak'st me call what I intend to do
65 A murder, which I thought a sacrifice.
I saw the handkerchief.

DESDEMONA He found it then.
I never gave it him. Send for him hither.
Let him confess a truth.

OTHELLO He hath confessed.

DESDEMONA What, my lord?

OTHELLO That he hath used thee.

DESDEMONA How? Unlawfully?

52 Presently immediately **54 article** item (of the charge of adultery. Othello makes heavy use of legal terms in this scene) **60 warranty** allowance **63 stone** turn to stone

OTHELLO Ay. 70

DESDEMONA He will not say so.

OTHELLO No, his mouth is stopped.
Honest Iago hath ta'en order for't.

DESDEMONA O, my fear interprets. What, is he dead?

OTHELLO Had all his hairs been lives, my great revenge
Had stomach for them all. 75

DESDEMONA Alas, he is betrayed, and I undone!

OTHELLO Out, strumpet! Weep'st thou for him to my face?

DESDEMONA O, banish me, my lord, but kill me not!

OTHELLO Down, strumpet!

DESDEMONA Kill me tomorrow; let me live tonight! 80

OTHELLO Nay, if you strive——

DESDEMONA But half an hour!

OTHELLO Being done, there is no pause.

DESDEMONA But while I say one prayer!

OTHELLO It is too late
Smothers her.

Emilia at the door.

EMILIA [*Calls within.*] My lord, my lord! What, ho, my lord, my lord!

OTHELLO What noise is this? Not dead? Not yet quite dead? 85
I that am cruel am yet merciful;
I would not have thee linger in thy pain.
So, so.

EMILIA [*Within*] What, ho! My lord, my lord!

OTHELLO Who's there?

EMILIA [*Within*] O, good my lord, I would speak a word with you.

72 ta'en order for't made sure of it 75 stomach appetite

90 OTHELLO Yes, 'tis Emilia.—By and by.—She's dead.—
'Tis like she comes to speak of Cassio's death.
The noise was high. Ha! No more moving?
Still as the grave.—Shall she come in? Were't good?—
I think she stirs again. No.—What's best to do?
95 If she come in, she'll sure speak to my wife.
My wife! My wife! What wife? I have no wife.
O, insupportable! O heavy hour!
Methinks it should be now a huge eclipse
Of sun and moon, and that th' affrighted globe
Should yawn at alteration.

100 EMILIA [*Within*] I do beseech you
That I may speak with you, O good my lord!

OTHELLO I had forgot thee. O, come in, Emilia.
Soft, by and by.—Let me the curtains draw.—
[*Draws the bed hangings and then opens the door.*]
Where art thou?

Enter Emilia.

What's the matter with thee now?

105 EMILIA O my good lord, yonder's foul murders done!

OTHELLO What? Now?

EMILIA But now, my lord.

OTHELLO It is the very error of the moon.
She comes more nearer earth than she was wont
110 And makes men mad.

EMILIA Cassio, my lord, hath killed a young Venetian
Called Roderigo.

OTHELLO Roderigo killed?
And Cassio killed?

92 **high** loud (Q1 reads "here") 98–100 **Methinks . . . alteration** (the Elizabethans believed that great changes in human affairs were reflected by disorders in nature) 100 **yawn** gape open (as in an earthquake) 108 **error** wandering out of regular course (disorders in the heavens were believed by some to cause disorders on earth, as well as vice versa)

EMILIA No, Cassio is not killed.

OTHELLO Not Cassio killed? Then murder's out of tune,
And sweet revenge grows harsh. 115

DESDEMONA O, falsely, falsely murdered!

EMILIA O Lord! What cry is that?

OTHELLO That? What?

EMILIA Out and alas! that was my lady's voice.
Help! Help, ho! Help! O lady, speak again!
Sweet Desdemona! O sweet mistress, speak! 120

DESDEMONA A guiltless death I die.

EMILIA O, who hath done this deed?

DESDEMONA Nobody—I myself. Farewell.
Commend me to my kind lord. O, farewell!

[*She dies.*]

OTHELLO Why, how should she be murd'red?

EMILIA Alas, who knows? 125

OTHELLO You heard her say herself, it was not I.

EMILIA She said so. I must needs report the truth.

OTHELLO She's like a liar gone to burning hell!
'Twas I that killed her.

EMILIA O, the more angel she,
And you the blacker devil! 130

OTHELLO She turned to folly, and she was a whore.

EMILIA Thou dost belie her, and thou art a devil.

OTHELLO She was false as water.

EMILIA Thou art rash as fire to say
That she was false. O, she was heavenly true!

OTHELLO Cassio did top her. Ask thy husband else. 135
O, I were damned beneath all depth in hell
But that I did proceed upon just grounds
To this extremity. Thy husband knew it all.

EMILIA My husband?

OTHELLO Thy husband.

EMILIA That she was false to wedlock?

140 OTHELLO Ay, with Cassio. Had she been true,
If heaven would make me such another world
Of one entire and perfect chrysolite,
I'd not have sold her for it.

EMILIA My husband?

OTHELLO Ay, 'twas he that told me on her first.
145 An honest man he is, and hates the slime
That sticks on filthy deeds.

EMILIA My husband?

OTHELLO What needs this iterance? Woman, I say thy husband.

EMILIA O mistress, villainy hath made mocks with love!
My husband say she was false?

OTHELLO He, woman.
150 I say, thy husband. Dost understand the word?
My friend, thy husband; honest, honest Iago.

EMILIA If he say so, may his pernicious soul
Rot half a grain a day! He lies to th' heart.
She was too fond of her most filthy bargain.

155 OTHELLO Hah?

EMILIA Do thy worst.
This deed of thine is no more worthy heaven
Than thou wast worthy her.

OTHELLO Peace, you were best.

EMILIA Thou hast not half that pow'r to do me harm
160 As I have to be hurt. O gull! O dolt!
As ignorant as dirt! Thou hast done a deed—
[*Othello moves to draw his sword.*]
I care not for thy sword; I'll make thee known,
Though I lost twenty lives. Help! Help! Ho! Help!
The Moor hath killed my mistress! Murder! murder!

142 chrysolite topaz **158 Peace, you were best** i.e., you had better be silent

Enter Montano, Gratiano, and Iago [and Others].

MONTANO What is the matter? How now, general? 165

EMILIA O, are you come, Iago? You have done well,
That men must lay their murders on your neck.

GRATIANO What is the matter?

EMILIA Disprove this villain, if thou be'st a man.
He says thou told'st him that his wife was false. 170
I know thou didst not; thou'rt not such a villain.
Speak, for my heart is full.

IAGO I told him what I thought, and told no more
Than what he found himself was apt and true.

EMILIA But did you ever tell him she was false? 175

IAGO I did.

EMILIA You told a lie, an odious damnèd lie!
Upon my soul, a lie! A wicked lie!
She false with Cassio? Did you say with Cassio?

IAGO With Cassio, mistress. Go to, charm your
tongue. 180

EMILIA I will not charm my tongue; I am bound to
speak:
My mistress here lies murdered in her bed.

ALL O heavens forfend!

EMILIA And your reports have set the murder on.

OTHELLO Nay, stare not, masters. It is true indeed. 185

GRATIANO 'Tis a strange truth.

MONTANO O monstrous act!

EMILIA Villainy, villainy, villainy!
I think upon't—I think I smell't!—O villainy!
I thought so then.—I'll kill myself for grief.—
O villainy, villainy! 190

IAGO What, are you mad? I charge you get you home.

EMILIA Good gentlemen, let me have leave to speak.

180 charm control

'Tis proper I obey him, but not now.
Perchance, Iago, I will ne'er go home.

OTHELLO O! O! O! [*Falls on the bed.*]

195 EMILIA Nay, lay thee down and roar,
For thou hast killed the sweetest innocent
That e'er did lift up eye.

OTHELLO O, she was foul! [*Rises.*]
I scarce did know you, uncle. There lies your niece,
Whose breath, indeed, these hands have newly stopped.
200 I know this act shows horrible and grim.

GRATIANO Poor Desdemon! I am glad thy father's dead.
Thy match was mortal to him, and pure grief
Shore his old thread in twain. Did he live now,
This sight would make him do a desperate turn;
205 Yea, curse his better angel from his side,
And fall to reprobation.

OTHELLO 'Tis pitiful; but yet Iago knows
That she with Cassio hath the act of shame
A thousand times committed. Cassio confessed it;
210 And she did gratify his amorous works
With that recognizance and pledge of love,
Which I first gave her. I saw it in his hand.
It was a handkerchief, an antique token
My father gave my mother.

215 EMILIA O God! O heavenly God!

IAGO Zounds, hold your peace!

EMILIA 'Twill out, 'twill out! I peace?
No, I will speak as liberal as the north.
Let heaven and men and devils, let them all,
All, all, cry shame against me, yet I'll speak.

IAGO Be wise, and get you home.

220 EMILIA I will not.
[*Iago draws and threatens Emilia.*]

206 reprobation damnation 217 liberal as the north freely (and bitingly) as the north wind blows

GRATIANO Fie! Your sword upon a woman?

EMILIA O thou dull Moor, that handkerchief thou speak'st of
I found by fortune, and did give my husband;
For often with a solemn earnestness—
More than indeed belonged to such a trifle— 225
He begged of me to steal't.

IAGO Villainous whore!

EMILIA She give it Cassio? No, alas, I found it,
And I did give't my husband.

IAGO Filth, thou liest!

EMILIA By heaven, I do not, I do not, gentlemen.
O murd'rous coxcomb! What should such a fool 230
Do with so good a wife?

OTHELLO Are there no stones in heaven
But what serves for the thunder? Precious villain!
[*The Moor runs at Iago, but is disarmed by Montano. Iago kills his wife.*]

GRATIANO The woman falls. Sure he hath killed his wife.

EMILIA Ay, ay. O, lay me by my mistress' side.
[*Exit Iago.*]

GRATIANO He's gone, but his wife's killed. 235

MONTANO 'Tis a notorious villain. Take you this weapon,
Which I have recovered from the Moor.
Come, guard the door without. Let him not pass,
But kill him rather. I'll after that same villain,
For 'tis a damnèd slave.
Exit [*with all but Othello and Emilia*].

OTHELLO I am not valiant neither; 240
But every puny whipster gets my sword.
But why should honor outlive honesty?
Let it go all.

231 stones thunderbolts **236 notorious** out-and-out **241 puny whipster** small top-whipping boy (?)

EMILIA What did thy song bode, lady?
Hark, canst thou hear me? I will play the swan,
245 And die in music. [*Sings*] "Willow, willow, willow."
Moor, she was chaste. She loved thee, cruel Moor,
So come my soul to bliss as I speak true.
So speaking as I think, alas, I die. [*She dies.*]

OTHELLO I have another weapon in this chamber;
250 It was a sword of Spain, the ice-brook's temper.
O, here it is.—Uncle, I must come forth.

GRATIANO [*Within*] If thou attempt it, it will cost thee dear.
Thou hast no weapon, and perforce must suffer.

OTHELLO Look in upon me then and speak with me,
255 Or, naked as I am, I will assault thee.

[*Enter Gratiano.*]

GRATIANO What is the matter?

OTHELLO Behold, I have a weapon;
A better never did itself sustain
Upon a soldier's thigh. I have seen the day
That with this little arm and this good sword
260 I have made my way through more impediments
Than twenty times your stop. But O vain boast!
Who can control his fate? 'Tis not so now.
Be not afraid, though you do see me weaponed.
Here is my journey's end, here is my butt,
265 And very seamark of my utmost sail.
Do you go back dismayed? 'Tis a lost fear.
Man but a rush against Othello's breast,
And he retires. Where should Othello go?
Now, how dost thou look now? O ill-starred wench!
270 Pale as thy smock! When we shall meet at compt,
This look of thine will hurl my soul from heaven,
And fiends will snatch at it. Cold, cold, my girl?
Even like thy chastity.

264 butt target, stopping place **265 seamark of my utmost sail** marker of my farthest journey **267 Man but a rush** attack with only a reed **270 compt** Judgment Day

O cursèd, cursèd slave! Whip me, ye devils,
From the possession of this heavenly sight! 275
Blow me about in winds! roast me in sulfur!
Wash me in steep-down gulfs of liquid fire!
O Desdemon! Dead Desdemon; dead. O! O!

Enter Lodovico, Cassio, Montano, and Iago [as prisoner,] with Officers.

LODOVICO Where is this rash and most unfortunate man?

OTHELLO That's he that was Othello; here I am. 280

LODOVICO Where is that viper? Bring the villain forth.

OTHELLO I look down towards his feet—but that's a fable.
If that thou be'st a devil, I cannot kill thee.
[*Wounds Iago.*]

LODOVICO Wrench his sword from him.
[*Othello is disarmed.*]

IAGO I bleed, sir, but not killed.

OTHELLO I am not sorry neither. I'd have thee live; 285
For in my sense, 'tis happiness to die.

LODOVICO O thou Othello that was once so good,
Fall'n in the practice of a cursèd slave,
What shall be said to thee?

OTHELLO Why, anything:
An honorable murderer, if you will; 295
For naught I did in hate, but all in honor.

LODOVICO This wretch hath part confessed his villainy.
Did you and he consent in Cassio's death?

OTHELLO Ay.

CASSIO Dear general, I never gave you cause. 295

OTHELLO I do believe it, and I ask your pardon.
Will you, I pray, demand that demi-devil
Why he hath thus ensnared my soul and body?

275 the possession of being possessed by 282 towards his feet i.e., for his cloven hoofs 288 practice plotting

IAGO Demand me nothing. What you know, you know.
300 From this time forth I never will speak word.

LODOVICO What, not to pray?

GRATIANO Torments will ope your lips.

OTHELLO Well, thou dost best.

LODOVICO Sir, you shall understand what hath befall'n,
Which, as I think, you know not. Here is a letter
305 Found in the pocket of the slain Roderigo;
And here another. The one of them imports
The death of Cassio to be undertook
By Roderigo.

OTHELLO O villain!

CASSIO Most heathenish and most gross!

310 LODOVICO Now here's another discontented paper
Found in his pocket too; and this, it seems,
Roderigo mean t' have sent this damnèd villain;
But that, belike, Iago in the interim
Came in and satisfied him.

OTHELLO O thou pernicious caitiff!
315 How came you, Cassio, by that handkerchief
That was my wife's?

CASSIO I found it in my chamber;
And he himself confessed it but even now
That there he dropped it for a special purpose
Which wrought to his desire.

OTHELLO O fool! Fool! Fool!

320 CASSIO There is besides in Roderigo's letter,
How he upbraids Iago that he made him
Brave me upon the watch; whereon it came
That I was cast; and even but now he spake,
After long seeming dead—Iago hurt him,
325 Iago set him on.

LODOVICO You must forsake this room and go with us.
Your power and your command is taken off,
And Cassio rules in Cyprus. For this slave,

If there be any cunning cruelty
That can torment him much and hold him long, 330
It shall be his. You shall close prisoner rest
Till that the nature of your fault be known
To the Venetian state. Come, bring away.

OTHELLO Soft you, a word or two before you go.
I have done the state some service, and they know't. 335
No more of that. I pray you, in your letters,
When you shall these unlucky deeds relate,
Speak of me as I am. Nothing extenuate,
Nor set down aught in malice. Then must you speak
Of one that loved not wisely, but too well; 340
Of one not easily jealous, but, being wrought,
Perplexed in the extreme; of one whose hand,
Like the base Judean, threw a pearl away
Richer than all his tribe; of one whose subdued
eyes,
Albeit unusèd to the melting mood, 345
Drops tears as fast as the Arabian trees
Their med'cinable gum. Set you down this.
And say besides that in Aleppo once,
Where a malignant and a turbaned Turk
Beat a Venetian and traduced the state, 350
I took by th' throat the circumcisèd dog
And smote him—thus. [*He stabs himself.*]

LODOVICO O bloody period!

GRATIANO All that is spoke is marred.

OTHELLO I kissed thee ere I killed thee. No way but this,
Killing myself, to die upon a kiss. 355
[*He falls over Desdemona and dies.*]

CASSIO This did I fear, but thought he had no weapon;
For he was great of heart.

LODOVICO [*To Iago*] O Spartan dog,
More fell than anguish, hunger, or the sea!

343 **Judean** (most editors use the Q1 reading, "Indian," here, but F is clear; both readings point toward the infidel, the unbeliever) 353 **period** end 358 **fell** cruel

Look on the tragic loading of this bed.
360 This is thy work. The object poisons sight;
Let it be hid. [*Bed curtains drawn.*]
Gratiano, keep the house,
And seize upon the fortunes of the Moor,
For they succeed on you. To you, lord governor,
Remains the censure of this hellish villain,
365 The time, the place, the torture. O, enforce it!
Myself will straight aboard, and to the state
This heavy act with heavy heart relate. *Exeunt.*

FINIS

361 keep remain in

Textual Note

OTHELLO contains some of the most difficult editorial problems of any Shakespearean play. The play was entered in *The Stationer's Register* on 6 October, 1621, and printed in a quarto edition, Q1, by Thomas Walkley in 1622, some eighteen or nineteen years after it was first staged. More curiously, at the time that Walkley printed his quarto edition, the plans for printing the folio edition of Shakespeare's collected works were completed and printing was well along. The Folio, F, appeared in late 1623, and the text of *Othello* included in it differs considerably from Q1. A second quarto, Q2, was printed from F in 1630. The chief differences between the two major texts, Q1 and F, are: (1) There are 160 lines in F that are not in Q1; some of these omissions affect the sense in Q1, but others seem to be either intentional cuts in Q1 or additions in F. (2) There are a number of oaths in Q1 that are not in F; this fact can be interpreted in a number of ways, but all arguments go back to the prohibition in 1606 of swearing on stage—but apparently not in printed editions. (3) The stage directions in Q1 are much fuller than in F. (4) There are a large number of variant readings in the two texts, in single words, in phrases, and in lineation; where Q1, for example, reads "toged" (i.e., wearing a toga), F reads "tongued"; where Q1 reads "Worships," F reads "Moorships."

These may seem petty problems, but they present an editor with a series of most difficult questions about what to print at any given point where the two texts are in disagreement. The usual solution in the past has been for the editor to include all material in F and Q1, and where the two texts are in disagreement to select the reading he prefers. The result is what is known as an eclectic text. But modern bibliographical studies have demonstrated that it is possible to proceed, in some cases at least, in a more precise manner by examining the conflicting texts carefully in order to arrive at something like a reasonable judgment about their relative authority. Shakespearean bibliography has become a most elaborate affair, however, and in most cases it has become necessary to take the word of specialists on these matters. Unfortunately, in the case of *Othello* the experts are not in agreement, and none of their arguments has the ring of certainty. Here is, however, the most general opinion of how the two different texts came into being and how they are related.

After Shakespeare wrote the play, his original draft, usually termed "foul papers," was copied, around 1604, by a scribe and made into what is known as the "promptbook," the official copy of the play used in the theater as the basis for production. This promptbook was the property of the players' company, the King's Men in this case, and remained in their possession to be used, and perhaps revised, whenever they produced *Othello*. Being a repertory company they would present a play for a few performances, then drop it for a time, and then present it again when conditions seemed favorable. At some time around 1620, another copy was made of the original foul papers, or some later copy of them, and this served as the basis for the 1622 Quarto. Later, when the publishers of the Folio got around to printing *Othello*, they took a copy of Q1 and corrected it by the original promptbook, and this corrected copy was then given to the compositors who were setting type for F. There are genuine objections to this theory, the most telling raised by the most recent editor of the play, M. R. Ridley, in *The Arden Shakespeare* edition of *Othello*; but the theory does explain certain difficult facts, and most bibliographers seem to accept some version of it.

The end of this line of argument is to establish fairly reasonably the authority of the F text as being the closest either to what Shakespeare wrote originally or to the play as he finally left it after playhouse revisions. This agrees with what most scholars find in reading the two texts. Sir Walter Greg puts this common belief in the superiority of F in the strongest terms: "In the great majority of cases there can be no doubt that F has preserved the more Shakespearean reading." (*The Shakespeare First Folio*, Oxford, 1955, p. 365.) For practical purposes what this means is that where an F reading makes sense, then an editor has no choice but to accept it—even though he "likes" the Q reading better and would have used it if he had *written*, instead of only edited, the play. But while an editor may be aided and comforted by the bibliographers' decision that F is more authoritative than Q1, his problems are by no means solved. There are places where F does not make sense but Q1 does, places where F is deficient in some way and Q is clear and complete, and places where both fail to make sense or seem to point to a common failure to transcribe correctly their original. When this occurs an editor must try to understand how the trouble occurred and then fall back on his judgment. This will force him to try to reconstruct the original manuscript from which we are told Q and F both derive, and he must attempt to deduce the original reading which both scribes mangled or which the typesetters in the different printing houses misread or made a mistake in setting.

This editorial process is endlessly complicated, but the general basis of this edition is as follows: F is taken for the copy text and its readings are preserved wherever they make sense. Oaths and stage directions are, however, taken from Q1, since they were presumably part of the original manuscript, but were deleted by the promptbook transcriber to comply with the prohibition against swearing on stage and because the prompt copy did not require such elaborate stage directions as a reading version—somewhat contrary to common sense, this last, but the bibliographers insist upon it. Where mislineation occurs in F, but Q1 has it correctly, the Q1 lineation is used on the theory that it has a better chance of being the original than any hypothetical reconstruction of my own. Finally, when F and Q1 both produce nonsense, changes, based on the above theory about the transmission of the text and on the work of previous editors, have been made.

Where F is deficient, the reading adopted and printed in this text is given below first in bold; unless otherwise stated it is taken from Q1. The original F reading that has been changed follows in roman. Obvious typographical errors in F, expansions of abbreviations, spelling variants ("murder," "murther"), and changes in punctuation and lineation are not noted. The act and scene divisions are translated from Latin, and the division at II.iii is from the Globe edition rather than from F; otherwise the divisions of F and the Globe edition are identical. "The Names of the Actors," here printed at the beginning of the play, in F follows the play.

I.i.1 **Tush! Never** Never 4 **'Sblood, but** But 26 **other** others 27 **Christian** Christen'd 30 **God bless** blesse 63 **full** fall **thick-lips** Thicks-lips 83 **Zounds, sir** Sir 105 **Zounds, sir** Sir 111 **germans** Germaines 143 **produced** producted 151 **hell pains** (emendation) hell apines [hells paines Q1]

I.ii.33 **Duke** Dukes 37 **Even** enen 49 **carack** (emendation) Carract [Carrick Q1] 50 **he's made** he' made 57 **Come** Cme 67 **darlings** Deareling 74 **weaken** weakens 83 **Whither** Whether 86 **if I do** if do

I.iii.53 **nor** hor 74 **your** yonr 99 **maimed** main'd 106 **Duke** [F omits] 107 **overt test** oer Test 110 **First Senator** Sen. 122 **till** tell 138 **travel's** trauellours 140 **rocks, and hills** Rocks, Hills **heads** head 142 **other** others 146 **Thence** hence 154 **intentively** instinctively 203 **preserved** presern'd 227 **couch** (emendation) Coach [Cooch Q1] 229 **alacrity** Alacartie 259 **me** my [F and Q1] 273 **First Senator** Sen. 286 **First Senator** Sen. 321–22 **balance** braine 328 **scion** (emendation) Seyen [seyen Q1] 376 **snipe** snpe 379 **H'as** She ha's

II.i.9 **mortise** (emendation) morties [morties Q1] 33 **prays** praye 40 **Third Gentleman** Gent. 53 **First Gentleman** Gent. 56 **Second Gentleman** Gent. 59 **Second Gentleman** Gent. 65 **ingener** Ingeniuer 66 **Second Gentleman** Gent. 94 **Second Gentleman** Gent. 168 **gyve** (emendation) giue [catch Q1] 173 **an** and 175 **clyster** cluster 212 **hither** thither 242 **has** he's 261 **mutualities** mutabilities 299 **wife** wist 307 **nightcap** Night-Cape

II.iii.39 **unfortunate** infortunate 57 **to put** put to 61 **God** heauen 72 **God** Heauen 77 **Englishman** Englishmen 93 **thine** thy 95 **'Fore God** Why 99 **God's** heaven's 108 **god forgive** Forgiue 141 **Within . . . help** [F omits; Q1 reads "Helpe, helpe, within"] 142 **Zounds, you** You 156 **God's will** Alas 160 **God's will** Fie, fie 162 **Zounds, I** I 217 **leagued** (emendation) [league F and Q1] 260 **God** Heauen 274 **to** ro 288 **O God** Oh 343 **were 't** were to 362 **enmesh** en-mash 378 **By the mass** In troth

III.i.1 s.d. [F includes the Clown] 20 **Exeunt Musicians** Exit Mu. 25 **general's wife** Generall 30 **Cassio** [no speech ascription in F]

III.ii.6 **We'll** Well

III.iii.74 **By'r Lady** Trust me 94 **you** he 106 **By heaven** Alas 135 **free to** free 136 **vile** vild 139 **But some** Wherein 148 **Shape** (emendation) Shapes 162 **By heaven I'll** Ile 170 **fondly** (emendation) soundly [strongly Q1] 175 **God** heauen 182 **exsufflicate** (emendation) exufflicate (F and Q1) **blown** blowd 217 **my** your 222 **vile** vilde 248 **hold him** him 258 **qualities** Quantities 259 **human** humane 281 **to** too 335 **of** in 347 **make** makes 372 **b' wi'** buy 392 **supervisor** supervision 437 **that was** (Malone's emendation) it was [F and Q1]

III.iv.77 **God** Heauen 81 **Heaven** Blesse 97 **I'faith** In sooth 170 **I'faith** Indeed 186 **by my faith** in good troth

TEXTUAL NOTE

IV.i.21 infected infectious 37 Zounds, that's that's 79 unsuiting resulting 103 conster conserue 109 power dowre 113 i'faith indeed 124 win winnes 132 beckons becomes 164 Faith, I I 218 God save Save 248 an obedient obedient

IV.ii.16 requite requit 30 Nay May 48 kinds kind 154 in [Q2] or 168 stay stays

IV.iii.14 bade bid 51 hie high

V.i.1 bulk Barke 22 hear heard 34 hies highes 35 Forth For 50 heaven's heaven 104 out o' th' o' th'

V.ii.13 the rose thy Rose 35 say so say 57 Then Lord O Heauen 100 Should Did 116 O Lord Alas 126 heard heare 206 reprobation Reprobance 215 O God! O heavenly God O Heauen! Oh heauenly powres 216 Zounds Come

WILLIAM SHAKESPEARE

THE TRAGEDY OF KING LEAR

Edited by Russell Fraser

[*Dramatis Personae*

LEAR, King of Britain
KING OF FRANCE
DUKE OF BURGUNDY
DUKE OF CORNWALL, husband to Regan
DUKE OF ALBANY, husband to Goneril
DUKE OF KENT
EARL OF GLOUCESTER
EDGAR, son to Gloucester
EDMUND, bastard son to Gloucester
CURAN, a courtier
OSWALD, steward to Goneril
OLD MAN, tenant to Gloucester
DOCTOR
LEAR'S FOOL
A CAPTAIN, subordinate to Edmund
GENTLEMAN, attending on Cordelia
A HERALD
SERVANT OF CORNWALL
GONERIL, REGAN, CORDELIA — daughters to Lear
KNIGHTS attending on Lear, OFFICERS,
MESSENGERS, SOLDIERS, ATTENDANTS

Scene: Britain]

THE TRAGEDY OF KING LEAR

ACT I

Scene I. [*King Lear's palace.*]

Enter Kent, Gloucester, and Edmund.

KENT I thought the King had more affected the Duke of Albany than Cornwall.

GLOUCESTER It did always seem so to us; but now, in the division of the kingdom, it appears not which of the dukes he values most, for equalities are so weighed that curiosity in neither can make choice of either's moiety. 5

KENT Is not this your son, my lord?

GLOUCESTER His breeding, sir, hath been at my charge. I have so often blushed to acknowledge him that now I am brazed to't. 10

KENT I cannot conceive you.

GLOUCESTER Sir, this young fellow's mother could; whereupon she grew round-wombed, and had indeed, sir, a son for her cradle ere she had a husband for her bed. Do you smell a fault? 15

Footnotes are keyed to the text by line number. Text references are printed in **bold** type; the annotation follows in roman type.

I.i.1 **affected** loved 2 **Albany** Albanacte, whose domain extended "from the river Humber to the point of Caithness" (Holinshed) 5–7 **equalities ... moiety** i.e., shares are so balanced against one another that careful examination by neither can make him wish the other's portion 9 **breeding** upbringing 11 **brazed** made brazen, hardened 12 **conceive** understand (pun follows)

KENT I cannot wish the fault undone, the issue of it being so proper.

GLOUCESTER But I have a son, sir, by order of law,
20 some year elder than this, who yet is no dearer in my account: though this knave came something saucily to the world before he was sent for, yet was his mother fair, there was good sport at his making, and the whoreson must be acknowl-
25 edged. Do you know this noble gentleman, Edmund?

EDMUND No, my lord.

GLOUCESTER My Lord of Kent. Remember him hereafter as my honorable friend.

30 EDMUND My services to your lordship.

KENT I must love you, and sue to know you better.

EDMUND Sir, I shall study deserving.

GLOUCESTER He hath been out nine years, and away he shall again. The King is coming.

Sound a sennet. Enter one bearing a coronet, then King Lear, then the Dukes of Cornwall and Albany, next Goneril, Regan, Cordelia, and Attendants.

35 LEAR Attend the lords of France and Burgundy, Gloucester.

GLOUCESTER I shall, my lord. *Exit [with Edmund].*

LEAR Meantime we shall express our darker purpose.
Give me the map there. Know that we have divided
40 In three our kingdom; and 'tis our fast intent
To shake all cares and business from our age,
Conferring them on younger strengths, while we

17 **issue** result (child) 18 **proper** handsome 21 **account** estimation 21 **knave** fellow (without disapproval) 22 **saucily** (1) insolently (2) lasciviously 24 **whoreson** fellow (lit., son of a whore) 31 **sue** entreat 33 **out** away, abroad 34 s.d. **sennet** set of notes played on a trumpet, signalizing the entrance or departure of a procession 34 s.d. **coronet** small crown, intended for Cordelia 38 **darker purpose** hidden intention 40 **fast** fixed

Unburthened crawl toward death. Our son of Cornwall,
And you our no less loving son of Albany,
We have this hour a constant will to publish 45
Our daughters' several dowers, that future strife
May be prevented now. The Princes, France and Burgundy,
Great rivals in our youngest daughter's love,
Long in our court have made their amorous sojourn,
And here are to be answered. Tell me, my daughters 50
(Since now we will divest us both of rule,
Interest of territory, cares of state),
Which of you shall we say doth love us most,
That we our largest bounty may extend
Where nature doth with merit challenge. Goneril, 55
Our eldest-born, speak first.

GONERIL Sir, I love you more than word can wield the matter;
Dearer than eyesight, space and liberty;
Beyond what can be valued, rich or rare;
No less than life, with grace, health, beauty, honor; 60
As much as child e'er loved, or father found;
A love that makes breath poor, and speech unable:
Beyond all manner of so much I love you.

CORDELIA [*Aside*] What shall Cordelia speak? Love, and be silent.

LEAR Of all these bounds, even from this line to this, 65
With shadowy forests, and with champains riched,
With plenteous rivers, and wide-skirted meads,
We make thee lady. To thine and Albany's issues
Be this perpetual. What says our second daughter,

45 **constant will to publish** fixed intention to proclaim 46 **several** separate 47 **prevented** forestalled 52 **Interest** legal right 55 **nature . . . challenge** i.e., natural affection contends with desert for (or lays claim to) bounty 57 **wield** handle 58 **space** scope 62 **breath** language 62 **unable** impotent 63 **Beyond . . . much** beyond all these comparisons 66 **champains riched** enriched plains 67 **wide-skirted meads** extensive grasslands 68 **issues** descendants 69 **perpetual** in perpetuity

70 Our dearest Regan, wife of Cornwall? Speak.

REGAN I am made of that self mettle as my sister,
And prize me at her worth. In my true heart
I find she names my very deed of love;
Only she comes too short, that I profess
75 Myself an enemy to all other joys
Which the most precious square of sense professes,
And find I am alone felicitate
In your dear Highness' love.

CORDELIA [*Aside*] Then poor Cordelia!
And yet not so, since I am sure my love's
80 More ponderous than my tongue.

LEAR To thee and thine hereditary ever
Remain this ample third of our fair kingdom,
No less in space, validity, and pleasure
Than that conferred on Goneril. Now, our joy,
85 Although our last and least; to whose young love
The vines of France and milk of Burgundy
Strive to be interest; what can you say to draw
A third more opulent than your sisters? Speak.

CORDELIA Nothing, my lord.

90 LEAR Nothing?

CORDELIA Nothing.

LEAR Nothing will come of nothing. Speak again.

CORDELIA Unhappy that I am, I cannot heave
My heart into my mouth. I love your Majesty
95 According to my bond, no more nor less.

LEAR How, how, Cordelia? Mend your speech a little,
Lest you may mar your fortunes.

71 **self mettle** same material or temperament 72 **prize . . . worth** value me the same (imperative) 73 **my . . . love** what my love really is (a legalism) 74 **that** in that 76 **Which . . . professes** which the choicest estimate of sense avows 77 **felicitate** made happy 80 **ponderous** weighty 83 **validity** value 85 **least** youngest, smallest 86 **milk** i.e., pastures 87 **interest** closely connected, as interested parties 95 **bond** i.e., filial obligation

CORDELIA Good my lord,
You have begot me, bred me, loved me. I
Return those duties back as are right fit,
Obey you, love you, and most honor you. 100
Why have my sisters husbands, if they say
They love you all? Haply, when I shall wed,
That lord whose hand must take my plight shall carry
Half my love with him, half my care and duty.
Sure I shall never marry like my sisters, 105
To love my father all.

LEAR But goes thy heart with this?

CORDELIA Ay, my good lord.

LEAR So young, and so untender?

CORDELIA So young, my lord, and true.

LEAR Let it be so, thy truth then be thy dower! 110
For, by the sacred radiance of the sun,
The mysteries of Hecate and the night,
By all the operation of the orbs
From whom we do exist and cease to be,
Here I disclaim all my paternal care, 115
Propinquity and property of blood,
And as a stranger to my heart and me
Hold thee from this for ever. The barbarous Scythian,
Or he that makes his generation messes
To gorge his appetite, shall to my bosom 120
Be as well neighbored, pitied, and relieved,
As thou my sometime daughter.

KENT Good my liege——

LEAR Peace, Kent!

99 **Return . . . fit** i.e., am correspondingly dutiful 102 **Haply** perhaps 103 **plight** troth plight 112 **mysteries of Hecate** secret rites of Hecate (goddess of the infernal world, and of witchcraft) 113 **operation of the orbs** astrological influence 116 **Propinquity and property of blood** relationship and common blood 118 **Scythian** (type of the savage) 119 **makes his generation messes** eats his own offspring 122 **sometime** former

Come not between the Dragon and his wrath.
125 I loved her most, and thought to set my rest
On her kind nursery. Hence and avoid my sight!
So be my grave my peace, as here I give
Her father's heart from her! Call France. Who stirs?
Call Burgundy. Cornwall and Albany,
130 With my two daughters' dowers digest the third;
Let pride, which she calls plainness, marry her.
I do invest you jointly with my power,
Pre-eminence, and all the large effects
That troop with majesty. Ourself, by monthly course,
135 With reservation of an hundred knights,
By you to be sustained, shall our abode
Make with you by due turn. Only we shall retain
The name, and all th' addition to a king. The sway,
Revènue, execution of the rest,
140 Belovèd sons, be yours; which to confirm,
This coronet part between you.

KENT Royal Lear,
Whom I have ever honored as my king,
Loved as my father, as my master followed,
As my great patron thought on in my prayers——

LEAR The bow is bent and drawn; make from the
145 shaft.

KENT Let it fall rather, though the fork invade
The region of my heart. Be Kent unmannerly
When Lear is mad. What wouldst thou do, old man?
Think'st thou that duty shall have dread to speak

124 **Dragon** (1) heraldic device of Britain (2) emblem of ferocity 125 **set my rest** (1) stake my all (a term from the card game of primero) (2) find my rest 126 **nursery** care, nursing 130 **digest** absorb 131 **Let . . . her** i.e., let her pride be her dowry and gain her a husband 133–34 **effects/That troop with majesty** accompaniments that go with kingship 134 **Ourself** (the royal "we") 135 **reservation** the action of reserving a privilege (a legalism) 138 **addition** titles and honors 141 **coronet** (the crown which was to have been Cordelia's) 145 **make from the shaft** avoid the arrow 146 **fall** strike 146 **fork** forked head of the arrow

When power to flattery bows? To plainness honor's
bound 150
When majesty falls to folly. Reserve thy state,
And in thy best consideration check
This hideous rashness. Answer my life my
judgment,
Thy youngest daughter does not love thee least,
Nor are those empty-hearted whose low sounds 155
Reverb no hollowness.

LEAR Kent, on thy life, no more!

KENT My life I never held but as a pawn
To wage against thine enemies; nor fear to lose it,
Thy safety being motive.

LEAR Out of my sight!

KENT See better, Lear, and let me still remain 160
The true blank of thine eye.

LEAR Now by Apollo——

KENT Now by Apollo, King,
Thou swear'st thy gods in vain.

LEAR O vassal! Miscreant!
[*Laying his hand on his sword.*]

ALBANY, CORNWALL. Dear sir, forbear!

KENT Kill thy physician, and the fee bestow 165
Upon the foul disease. Revoke thy gift,
Or, whilst I can vent clamor from my throat,
I'll tell thee thou dost evil.

LEAR Hear me, recreant!
On thine allegiance, hear me!
That thou hast sought to make us break our vows, 170

151 **Reserve thy state** retain your kingly authority 152 **best consideration** most careful reflection 153 **Answer ... judgment** I will stake my life on my opinion 156 **Reverb** reverberate 156 **hollowness** (1) emptiness (2) insincerity 157 **pawn** stake in a wager 158 **wage** (1) wager (2) carry on war 159 **motive** moving cause 160 **still** always 161 **blank** the white spot in the center of the target (at which Lear should aim) 163 **vassal! Miscreant!** base wretch! Misbeliever! 167 **vent clamor** utter a cry 168 **recreant** traitor 169 **On thine allegiance** (to forswear, which is to commit high treason)

Which we durst never yet, and with strained pride
To come betwixt our sentence and our power,
Which nor our nature nor our place can bear,
Our potency made good, take thy reward.
175 Five days we do allot thee for provision
To shield thee from diseases of the world,
And on the sixth to turn thy hated back
Upon our kingdom. If, on the tenth day following,
Thy banished trunk be found in our dominions,
180 The moment is thy death. Away! By Jupiter,
This shall not be revoked.

KENT Fare thee well, King. Sith thus thou wilt appear,
Freedom lives hence, and banishment is here.
[*To Cordelia*] The gods to their dear shelter take thee, maid,
185 That justly think'st, and hath most rightly said.
[*To Regan and Goneril*] And your large speeches may your deeds approve,
That good effects may spring from words of love.
Thus Kent, O Princes, bids you all adieu;
He'll shape his old course in a country new. *Exit.*

Flourish. Enter Gloucester, with France and Burgundy; Attendants.

190 GLOUCESTER Here's France and Burgundy, my noble lord.

LEAR My Lord of Burgundy,
We first address toward you, who with this king
Hath rivaled for our daughter. What in the least
Will you require in present dower with her,
Or cease your quest of love?

195 BURGUNDY Most royal Majesty,
I crave no more than hath your Highness offered,

171 **strained** forced (and so excessive) 172 **sentence** judgment, decree 174 **Our potency made good** my royal authority being now asserted 175 **for provision** for making preparation 176 **diseases** troubles 179 **trunk** body 182 **Sith** since 186 **approve** prove true 187 **effects** results 189 **shape ... course** pursue his customary way 189 s.d. **Flourish** trumpet fanfare 194 **present** immediate

Nor will you tender less.

LEAR Right noble Burgundy,
When she was dear to us, we did hold her so;
But now her price is fallen. Sir, there she stands.
If aught within that little seeming substance, 200
Or all of it, with our displeasure pieced,
And nothing more, may fitly like your Grace,
She's there, and she is yours.

BURGUNDY I know no answer.

LEAR Will you, with those infirmities she owes,
Unfriended, new adopted to our hate, 205
Dow'red with our curse, and strangered with our oath,
Take her, or leave her?

BURGUNDY Pardon me, royal sir.
Election makes not up on such conditions.

LEAR Then leave her, sir; for, by the pow'r that made me,
I tell you all her wealth. [*To France.*] For you, great King, 210
I would not from your love make such a stray
To match you where I hate; therefore beseech you
T' avert your liking a more worthier way
Than on a wretch whom nature is ashamed
Almost t' acknowledge hers.

FRANCE This is most strange, 215
That she whom even but now was your best object,
The argument of your praise, balm of your age,
The best, the dearest, should in this trice of time
Commit a thing so monstrous to dismantle

197 **tender** offer 198 **dear** (1) beloved (2) valued at a high price 200 **little seeming substance** person who is (1) inconsiderable (2) outspoken 201 **pieced** added to it 202 **fitly like** please by its fitness 204 **owes** possesses 206 **strangered** made a stranger 208 **Election makes not up** no one can choose 211–12 **make such a stray/To** stray so far as to 212 **beseech** I beseech 213 **avert . . . way** turn your affections from her and bestow them on a better person 216 **best object** i.e., the one you loved most 217 **argument** subject 219 **dismantle** strip off

220 So many folds of favor. Sure her offense
Must be of such unnatural degree
That monsters it, or your fore-vouched affection
Fall into taint; which to believe of her
Must be a faith that reason without miracle
Should never plant in me.

225 CORDELIA I yet beseech your Majesty,
If for I want that glib and oily art
To speak and purpose not, since what I well intend
I'll do't before I speak, that you make known
It is no vicious blot, murder, or foulness,
230 No unchaste action or dishonored step,
That hath deprived me of your grace and favor;
But even for want of that for which I am richer,
A still-soliciting eye, and such a tongue
That I am glad I have not, though not to have it
Hath lost me in your liking.

235 LEAR Better thou
Hadst not been born than not t' have pleased me
better.

FRANCE Is it but this? A tardiness in nature
Which often leaves the history unspoke
That it intends to do. My Lord of Burgundy,
240 What say you to the lady? Love's not love
When it is mingled with regards that stands
Aloof from th' entire point. Will you have her?
She is herself a dowry.

BURGUNDY Royal King,
Give but that portion which yourself proposed,
245 And here I take Cordelia by the hand,
Duchess of Burgundy.

222 That monsters it as makes it monstrous, unnatural **222 fore-vouched** previously sworn **228 Fall into taint** must be taken as having been unjustified all along i.e., Cordelia was unworthy of your love from the first **224–25 reason . . . me** my reason would have to be supported by a miracle to make me believe **226 for** because **227 purpose not** not mean to do what I promise **233 still-soliciting** always begging **235 lost** ruined **237 tardiness in nature** natural reticence **238 leaves the history unspoke** does not announce the action **240 What say you** i.e., will you have **241 regards** considerations (the dowry) **241–42 stands . . . point** have nothing to do with the essential question (love)

LEAR Nothing. I have sworn. I am firm.

BURGUNDY I am sorry then you have so lost a father
That you must lose a husband.

CORDELIA Peace be with Burgundy.
Since that respects of fortune are his love, 250
I shall not be his wife.

FRANCE Fairest Cordelia, that art most rich being poor,
Most choice forsaken, and most loved despised,
Thee and thy virtues here I seize upon.
Be it lawful I take up what's cast away. 255
Gods, gods! 'Tis strange that from their cold'st neglect
My love should kindle to inflamed respect.
Thy dow'rless daughter, King, thrown to my chance,
Is Queen of us, of ours, and our fair France.
Not all the dukes of wat'rish Burgundy 260
Can buy this unprized precious maid of me.
Bid them farewell, Cordelia, though unkind.
Thou losest here, a better where to find.

LEAR Thou hast her, France; let her be thine, for we
Have no such daughter, nor shall ever see 265
That face of hers again. Therefore be gone,
Without our grace, our love, our benison.
Come, noble Burgundy.

Flourish. Exeunt [Lear, Burgundy, Cornwall, Albany, Gloucester, and Attendants].

FRANCE Bid farewell to your sisters.

CORDELIA The jewels of our father, with washed eyes 270
Cordelia leaves you. I know you what you are,

250 respects of fortune mercenary considerations **257 inflamed respect** more ardent affection **258 chance** lot **260 wat'rish** (1) with many rivers (2) weak, diluted **261 unprized precious** unappreciated by others, and yet precious **263 here ... where** in this place, in another place **267 benison** blessing **270 The jewels of our father** you creatures prized by our father **270 washed** (1) weeping (2) clear-sighted

And, like a sister, am most loath to call
Your faults as they are named. Love well our father.
To your professèd bosoms I commit him.
275 But yet, alas, stood I within his grace,
I would prefer him to a better place.
So farewell to you both.

REGAN Prescribe not us our duty.

GONERIL Let your study
Be to content your lord, who hath received you
280 At Fortune's alms. You have obedience scanted,
And well are worth the want that you have wanted.

CORDELIA Time shall unfold what plighted cunning hides,
Who covers faults, at last shame them derides.
Well may you prosper.

FRANCE Come, my fair Cordelia.

Exit France and Cordelia.

285 GONERIL Sister, it is not little I have to say of what most nearly appertains to us both. I think our father will hence tonight.

REGAN That's most certain, and with you; next month with us.

290 GONERIL You see how full of changes his age is. The observation we have made of it hath not been little. He always loved our sister most, and with what poor judgment he hath now cast her off appears too grossly.

295 REGAN 'Tis the infirmity of his age; yet he hath ever but slenderly known himself.

272 **like a sister** because I am a sister i.e., loyal, affectionate 273 **as they are named** i.e., by their right and ugly names 274 **professèd** pretending to love 276 **prefer** recommend 280 **At Fortune's alms** as a charitable bequest from Fortune (and so, by extension, as one beggared or cast down by Fortune) 280 **scanted** stinted 281 **worth . . . wanted** deserve to be denied, even as you have denied 282 **plighted** pleated, enfolded 283 **Who . . . derides** those who hide their evil are finally exposed and shamed ("He that hideth his sins, shall not prosper") 294 **grossly** obviously

GONERIL The best and soundest of his time hath been but rash; then must we look from his age to receive not alone the imperfections of long-ingrafted condition, but therewithal the unruly waywardness that infirm and choleric years bring with them. 300

REGAN Such unconstant starts are we like to have from him as this of Kent's banishment.

GONERIL There is further compliment of leave-taking between France and him. Pray you, let's hit together; if our father carry authority with such disposition as he bears, this last surrender of his will but offend us. 305

REGAN We shall further think of it. 310

GONERIL We must do something, and i' th' heat.

Exeunt.

Scene II. [*The Earl of Gloucester's castle.*]

Enter Edmund [*with a letter*].

EDMUND Thou, Nature, art my goddess; to thy law
My services are bound. Wherefore should I
Stand in the plague of custom, and permit
The curiosity of nations to deprive me,
For that I am some twelve or fourteen
moonshines 5

297 of his time period of his life up to now **299–300 long-ingrafted** implanted for a long time **300 condition** disposition **300 therewithal** with them **303 unconstant starts** impulsive whims **305 compliment** formal courtesy **306 hit** agree **307–8 carry . . . bears** continues, and in such frame of mind, to wield the sovereign power **308 last surrender** recent abdication **309 offend** vex **311 i' th' heat** while the iron is hot **I.ii. 1 Nature** (Edmund's conception of Nature accords with our description of a bastard as a natural child) **3 Stand . . . custom** respect hateful convention **4 curiosity** nice distinctions **5 For that** because **5 moonshines** months

Lag of a brother? Why bastard? Wherefore base?
When my dimensions are as well compact,
My mind as generous, and my shape as true,
As honest madam's issue? Why brand they us
10 With base? With baseness? Bastardy? Base? Base?
Who, in the lusty stealth of nature, take
More composition and fierce quality
Than doth, within a dull, stale, tired bed,
Go to th' creating a whole tribe of fops
15 Got 'tween asleep and wake? Well then,
Legitimate Edgar, I must have your land.
Our father's love is to the bastard Edmund
As to th' legitimate. Fine word, "legitimate."
Well, my legitimate, if this letter speed,
20 And my invention thrive, Edmund the base
Shall top th' legitimate. I grow, I prosper.
Now, gods, stand up for bastards.

Enter Gloucester.

GLOUCESTER Kent banished thus? and France in choler parted?
And the King gone tonight? prescribed his pow'r?
25 Confined to exhibition? All this done
Upon the gad? Edmund, how now? What news?

EDMUND So please your lordship, none.

GLOUCESTER Why so earnestly seek you to put up that letter?

30 EDMUND I know no news, my lord.

GLOUCESTER What paper were you reading?

EDMUND Nothing, my lord.

GLOUCESTER No? What needed then that terrible dispatch of it into your pocket? The quality of noth-

6 Lag of short of being (in age) **7 compact** framed **8 generous** gallant **9 honest** chaste **12 composition** completeness **12 fierce** energetic **14 fops** fools **15 Got** begot **19 speed** prosper **20 invention** plan **24 prescribed** limited **25 exhibition** an allowance or pension **26 Upon the gad** on the spur of the moment (as if pricked by a gad or goad) **28 put up** put away, conceal **33–34 terrible dispatch** hasty putting away

ing hath not such need to hide itself. Let's see. 35
Come, if it be nothing, I shall not need spectacles.

EDMUND I beseech you, sir, pardon me. It is a letter from my brother that I have not all o'er-read; and for so much as I have perused, I find it not fit for your o'erlooking. 40

GLOUCESTER Give me the letter, sir.

EDMUND I shall offend, either to detain or give it. The contents, as in part I understand them, are to blame.

GLOUCESTER Let's see, let's see. 45

EDMUND I hope, for my brother's justification, he wrote this but as an essay or taste of my virtue.

GLOUCESTER (*Reads*) "This policy and reverence of age makes the world bitter to the best of our times; keeps our fortunes from us till our oldness 50 cannot relish them. I begin to find an idle and fond bondage in the oppression of aged tyranny, who sways, not as it hath power, but as it is suffered. Come to me, that of this I may speak more. If our father would sleep till I waked him, you 55 should enjoy half his revenue for ever, and live the beloved of your brother, EDGAR."
Hum! Conspiracy? "Sleep till I waked him, you should enjoy half his revenue." My son Edgar! Had he a hand to write this? A heart and brain to 60 breed it in? When came you to this? Who brought it?

EDMUND It was not brought me, my lord; there's the cunning of it. I found it thrown in at the casement of my closet. 65

40 **o'erlooking** inspection 44 **to blame** blameworthy 47 **essay or taste** test 48 **policy and reverence** policy of reverencing (hendiadys) 49–50 **best of our times** best years of our lives (i.e., our youth) 51 **relish** enjoy 51–52 **idle and fond** foolish 53–54 **who ... suffered** which rules, not from its own strength, but from our allowance 56 **revenue** income 64–65 **casement of my closet** window of my room

GLOUCESTER You know the character to be your brother's?

EDMUND If the matter were good, my lord, I durst swear it were his; but in respect of that, I would
70 fain think it were not.

GLOUCESTER It is his.

EDMUND It is his hand, my lord; but I hope his heart is not in the contents.

GLOUCESTER Has he never before sounded you in this
75 business?

EDMUND Never, my lord. But I have heard him oft maintain it to be fit that, sons at perfect age, and fathers declined, the father should be as ward to the son, and the son manage his revenue.

80 GLOUCESTER O villain, villain! His very opinion in the letter. Abhorred villain, unnatural, detested, brutish villain; worse than brutish! Go, sirrah, seek him. I'll apprehend him. Abominable villain! Where is he?

85 EDMUND I do not well know, my lord. If it shall please you to suspend your indignation against my brother till you can derive from him better testimony of his intent, you should run a certain course; where, if you violently proceed against
90 him, mistaking his purpose, it would make a great gap in your own honor and shake in pieces the heart of his obedience. I dare pawn down my life for him that he hath writ this to feel my affection to your honor, and to no other pretense of
95 danger.

GLOUCESTER Think you so?

66 character handwriting **69 in respect of that** in view of what it is **70 fain** prefer to **74 sounded** sounded you out **77 perfect** mature **81 detested** detestable **82 sirrah** sir (familiar form of address) **88–89 run a certain course** i.e., proceed safely, know where you are going **91 gap** breach **92 pawn down** stake **93 feel** test **94–95 pretense of danger** dangerous purpose

EDMUND If your honor judge it meet, I will place you where you shall hear us confer of this, and by an auricular assurance have your satisfaction, and that without any further delay than this very evening. 100

GLOUCESTER He cannot be such a monster.

EDMUND Nor is not, sure.

GLOUCESTER To his father, that so tenderly and entirely loves him. Heaven and earth! Edmund, seek him out; wind me into him, I pray you; frame the business after your own wisdom. I would unstate myself to be in a due resolution. 105

EDMUND I will seek him, sir, presently; convey the business as I shall find means, and acquaint you withal. 110

GLOUCESTER These late eclipses in the sun and moon portend no good to us. Though the wisdom of Nature can reason it thus and thus, yet Nature finds itself scourged by the sequent effects. Love cools, friendship falls off, brothers divide. In cities, mutinies; in countries, discord; in palaces, treason; and the bond cracked 'twixt son and father. This villain of mine comes under the prediction, there's son against father; the King falls from bias of nature, there's father against child. We have seen the best of our time. Machinations, hollowness, treachery, and all ruinous disorders follow us disquietly to our graves. Find out this 115 120

97 meet fit **99 auricular assurance** proof heard with your own ears **106 wind me into him** insinuate yourself into his confidence for me **106 frame** manage **107–08 unstate ... resolution** forfeit my earldom to know the truth **109 presently** at once **109 convey** manage **111 withal** with it **112 late** recent **113–14 wisdom of Nature** scientific learning **114 reason** explain **114–15 yet ... effects** nonetheless our world is punished with subsequent disasters **116 falls off** revolts **117 mutinies** riots **119–20 This ... prediction** i.e., my son's villainous behavior is included in these portents, and bears them out **121 bias of nature** natural inclination (the metaphor is from the game of bowls) **122 best of our time** our best days **123 hollowness** insincerity **124 disquietly** unquietly

125 villain, Edmund; it shall lose thee nothing. Do it carefully. And the noble and true-hearted Kent banished; his offense, honesty. 'Tis strange.

Exit.

EDMUND This is the excellent foppery of the world, that when we are sick in fortune, often the surfeits
130 of our own behavior, we make guilty of our disasters the sun, the moon, and stars; as if we were villains on necessity; fools by heavenly compulsion; knaves, thieves, and treachers by spherical predominance; drunkards, liars, and adulterers by
135 an enforced obedience of planetary influence; and all that we are evil in, by a divine thrusting on. An admirable evasion of whoremaster man, to lay his goatish disposition on the charge of a star. My father compounded with my mother
140 under the Dragon's Tail, and my nativity was under Ursa Major, so that it follows I am rough and lecherous. Fut! I should have been that I am, had the maidenliest star in the firmament twinkled on my bastardizing. Edgar——

Enter Edgar.

145 and pat he comes, like the catastrophe of the old comedy. My cue is villainous melancholy, with a sigh like Tom o' Bedlam.—O, these eclipses do portend these divisions. Fa, sol, la, mi.

EDGAR How now, brother Edmund; what serious con-
150 templation are you in?

125 it ... nothing you will not lose by it **128 foppery** folly **129-30 often ... behavior** often caused by our own excesses **132 on** of **133-34 treachers ... predominance** traitors because of the ascendancy of a particular star at our birth **134-35 by ... influence** because we had to submit to the influence of our star **136 divine thrusting** on supernatural compulsion **137 whoremaster** lecherous **138 goatish** lascivious **139 compounded** (1) made terms (2) formed (a child) **140 Dragon's Tail** the constellation Draco **140 nativity** birthday **141 Ursa Major** the Great Bear **142 Fut!** 's foot (an impatient oath) **142 that** what **145 catastrophe** conclusion **146-47 My ... Bedlam** I must be doleful, like a lunatic beggar out of Bethlehem (Bedlam) Hospital, the London madhouse **148 Fa, sol, la, mi** (Edmund's humming of the musical notes is perhaps prompted by his use of the word "division," which describes a musical variation)

EDMUND I am thinking, brother, of a prediction I read this other day, what should follow these eclipses.

EDGAR Do you busy yourself with that?

EDMUND I promise you, the effects he writes of succeed unhappily: as of unnaturalness between the child and the parent, death, dearth, dissolutions of ancient amities, divisions in state, menaces and maledictions against King and nobles, needless diffidences, banishment of friends, dissipation of cohorts, nuptial breaches, and I know not what. 155 160

EDGAR How long have you been a sectary astronomical?

EDMUND Come, come, when saw you my father last?

EDGAR Why, the night gone by. 165

EDMUND Spake you with him?

EDGAR Ay, two hours together.

EDMUND Parted you in good terms? Found you no displeasure in him by word nor countenance?

EDGAR None at all. 170

EDMUND Bethink yourself wherein you may have offended him; and at my entreaty forbear his presence until some little time hath qualified the heat of his displeasure, which at this instant so rageth in him that with the mischief of your person it would scarcely allay. 175

EDGAR Some villain hath done me wrong.

EDMUND That's my fear. Brother I pray you have a continent forbearance till the speed of his rage goes slower; and, as I say, retire with me to my 180

155–56 succeed follow **157 unnaturalness** unkindness **158 amities** friendships **159–60 diffidences** distrusts **160–61 dissipation of cohorts** falling away of supporters **162–63 sectary astronomical** believer in astrology **169 countenance** expression **172–73 forbear his presence** keep away from him **173 qualified** lessened **175–76 with . . . allay** even an injury to you would not appease his anger **178–79 have a continent forbearance** be restrained and keep yourself withdrawn

lodging, from whence I will fitly bring you to hear my lord speak. Pray ye, go; there's my key. If you do stir abroad, go armed.

EDGAR Armed, brother?

185 EDMUND Brother, I advise you to the best. Go armed. I am no honest man if there be any good meaning toward you. I have told you what I have seen and heard; but faintly, nothing like the image and horror of it. Pray you, away.

190 EDGAR Shall I hear from you anon?

EDMUND I do serve you in this business.

Exit Edgar.

A credulous father, and a brother noble,
Whose nature is so far from doing harms
That he suspects none; on whose foolish honesty
195 My practices ride easy. I see the business.
Let me, if not by birth, have lands by wit.
All with me's meet that I can fashion fit. *Exit.*

Scene III. [*The Duke of Albany's palace.*]

Enter Goneril, and [*Oswald, her*] *Steward.*

GONERIL Did my father strike my gentleman for chiding of his Fool?

OSWALD Ay, madam.

GONERIL By day and night he wrongs me. Every hour
5 He flashes into one gross crime or other

181 fitly at a fit time **188–89 image and horror** true horrible picture **190 anon** in a little while **195 practices** plots **197 meet** proper **197 fashion fit** shape to my purpose **I.iii. 2 Fool** court jester **5 crime** offense

That sets us all at odds. I'll not endure it.
His knights grow riotous, and himself upbraids us
On every trifle. When he returns from hunting,
I will not speak with him. Say I am sick.
If you come slack of former services, 10
You shall do well; the fault of it I'll answer.
[*Horns within.*]

OSWALD He's coming, madam; I hear him.

GONERIL Put on what weary negligence you please,
You and your fellows. I'd have it come to question.
If he distaste it, let him to my sister, 15
Whose mind and mine I know in that are one,
Not to be overruled. Idle old man,
That still would manage those authorities
That he hath given away. Now, by my life,
Old fools are babes again, and must be used 20
With checks as flatteries, when they are seen
abused.
Remember what I have said.

OSWALD Well, madam.

GONERIL And let his knights have colder looks among
you.
What grows of it, no matter; advise your fellows so.
I would breed from hence occasions, and I shall, 25
That I may speak. I'll write straight to my sister
To hold my course. Go, prepare for dinner.
Exeunt.

7 riotous dissolute **10 come ... services** are less serviceable to him than formerly **11 answer** answer for **14 come to question** be discussed openly **15 distaste** dislike **17 Idle** foolish **21 With ... abused** with restraints as well as soothing words when they are misguided **25–26 breed ... speak** find in this opportunities for speaking out **26 straight** at once

Scene IV. [*A hall in the same.*]

Enter Kent [*disguised*].

KENT If but as well I other accents borrow
That can my speech defuse, my good intent
May carry through itself to that full issue
For which I razed my likeness. Now, banished Kent,
If thou canst serve where thou dost stand
5 condemned,
So may it come, thy master whom thou lov'st
Shall find thee full of labors.

Horns within. Enter Lear, [*Knights*] *and Attendants.*

LEAR Let me not stay a jot for dinner; go, get it ready. [*Exit an Attendant.*] How now, what art
10 thou?

KENT A man, sir.

LEAR What dost thou profess? What wouldst thou with us?

KENT I do profess to be no less than I seem, to
15 serve him truly that will put me in trust, to love him that is honest, to converse with him that is wise and says little, to fear judgment, to fight when I cannot choose, and to eat no fish.

I.iv. 2 **defuse** disguise 3 **full issue** perfect result 4 **razed my likeness** shaved off, disguised my natural appearance 6 **So may it come** so may it fall out 7 s.d. **within** offstage 8 **stay** wait 12 **What dost thou profess** what do you do 14 **profess** claim 17 **judgment** (by a heavenly or earthly judge) 18 **eat no fish** i.e., (1) I am no Catholic, but a loyal Protestant (2) I am no weakling (3) I use no prostitutes

LEAR What art thou?

KENT A very honest-hearted fellow, and as poor as the King. 20

LEAR If thou be'st as poor for a subject as he's for a king, thou art poor enough. What wouldst thou?

KENT Service.

LEAR Who wouldst thou serve? 25

KENT You.

LEAR Dost thou know me, fellow?

KENT No, sir, but you have that in your countenance which I would fain call master.

LEAR What's that? 30

KENT Authority.

LEAR What services canst thou do?

KENT I can keep honest counsel, ride, run, mar a curious tale in telling it, and deliver a plain message bluntly. That which ordinary men are fit for, I 35 am qualified in, and the best of me is diligence.

LEAR How old art thou?

KENT Not so young, sir, to love a woman for singing, nor so old to dote on her for anything. I have years on my back forty-eight. 40

LEAR Follow me; thou shalt serve me. If I like thee no worse after dinner, I will not part from thee yet. Dinner, ho, dinner! Where's my knave? my Fool? Go you and call my Fool hither.

[*Exit an Attendant*.]

Enter Oswald.

You, you, sirrah, where's my daughter? 45

OSWALD So please you—— *Exit.*

28 countenance bearing **29 fain** like to **33 honest counsel** honorable secrets **33–34 mar . . . it** i.e., I cannot speak like an affected courtier ("curious" = "elaborate," as against "plain") **43 knave** boy

LEAR What says the fellow there? Call the clotpoll back. [*Exit a Knight.*] Where's my Fool? Ho, I think the world's asleep.

[*Re-enter Knight.*]

50 How now? Where's that mongrel?

KNIGHT He says, my lord, your daughter is not well.

LEAR Why came not the slave back to me when I called him?

KNIGHT Sir, he answered me in the roundest manner,
55 he would not.

LEAR He would not?

KNIGHT My lord, I know not what the matter is; but to my judgment your Highness is not entertained with that ceremonious affection as you
60 were wont. There's a great abatement of kindness appears as well in the general dependants as in the Duke himself also and your daughter.

LEAR Ha? Say'st thou so?

KNIGHT I beseech you pardon me, my lord, if I be
65 mistaken; for my duty cannot be silent when I think your Highness wronged.

LEAR Thou but rememb'rest me of mine own conception. I have perceived a most faint neglect of late, which I have rather blamed as mine own
70 jealous curiosity than as a very pretense and purpose of unkindness. I will look further into't. But where's my Fool? I have not seen him this two days.

KNIGHT Since my young lady's going into France, sir,
75 the Fool hath much pined away.

LEAR No more of that; I have noted it well. Go you

47 **clotpoll** clodpoll, blockhead 54 **roundest** rudest 58–59 **entertained** treated 61 **dependants** servants 67 **rememb'rest** remindest 67–68 **conception** idea 68 **faint neglect** i.e., "weary negligence" (I.iii.13) 69–70 **mine own jealous curiosity** suspicious concern for my own dignity 70 **very pretense** actual intention

and tell my daughter I would speak with her. Go you, call hither my Fool. [*Exit an Attendant.*]

Enter Oswald.

O, you, sir, you! Come you hither, sir. Who am I, sir? 80

OSWALD My lady's father.

LEAR "My lady's father"? My lord's knave, you whoreson dog, you slave, you cur!

OSWALD I am none of these, my lord; I beseech your pardon. 85

LEAR Do you bandy looks with me, you rascal? [*Striking him.*]

OSWALD I'll not be strucken, my lord.

KENT Nor tripped neither, you base football player. [*Tripping up his heels.*]

LEAR I thank thee, fellow. Thou serv'st me, and I'll love thee. 90

KENT Come, sir, arise, away. I'll teach you differences. Away, away. If you will measure your lubber's length again, tarry; but away. Go to! Have you wisdom? So. [*Pushes Oswald out.*]

LEAR Now, my friendly knave, I thank thee. There's earnest of thy service. [*Giving Kent money.*] 95

Enter Fool.

FOOL Let me hire him too. Here's my coxcomb. [*Offering Kent his cap.*]

LEAR How now, my pretty knave? How dost thou?

FOOL Sirrah, you were best take my coxcomb.

KENT Why, Fool? 100

86 **bandy** exchange insolently (metaphor from tennis) 87 **strucken** struck 88 **football** (a low game played by idle boys to the scandal of sensible men) 91–92 **differences** (of rank) 92–93 **lubber's** lout's 93 **Go to** (expression of derisive incredulity) 93–94 **Have you wisdom** i.e., do you know what's good for you 94 **So** good 96 **earnest** money for services rendered 97 **coxcomb** professional fool's cap, shaped like a coxcomb 99 **you were best** you had better

FOOL Why? For taking one's part that's out of favor. Nay, an thou canst not smile as the wind sits, thou'lt catch cold shortly. There, take my coxcomb. Why, this fellow has banished two on's daughters,
105 and did the third a blessing against his will. If thou follow him, thou must needs wear my coxcomb. —How now, Nuncle? Would I had two coxcombs and two daughters.

LEAR Why, my boy?

110 FOOL If I gave them all my living, I'd keep my coxcombs myself. There's mine; beg another of thy daughters.

LEAR Take heed, sirrah—the whip.

FOOL Truth's a dog must to kennel; he must be
115 whipped out, when Lady the Brach may stand by th' fire and stink.

LEAR A pestilent gall to me.

FOOL Sirrah, I'll teach thee a speech.

LEAR Do.

120 FOOL Mark it, Nuncle.

Have more than thou showest,
Speak less than thou knowest,
Lend less than thou owest,
Ride more than thou goest,
125 Learn more than thou trowest,
Set less than thou throwest;
Leave thy drink and thy whore,
And keep in-a-door,
And thou shalt have more
130 Than two tens to a score.

KENT This is nothing, Fool.

102 an if **102 smile ... sits** ingratiate yourself with those in power **banish** alienated (by making them independent) **107 Nuncle** (contraction of "mine uncle") **110 living** property **115 Brach** bitch **117 gall** sore **123 owest** ownest **124 goest** walkest **125 trowest** knowest **126 Set ... throwest** bet less than you play for (get odds from your opponent) **129–30 have ... score** i.e., come away with more than you had (two tens, or twenty shillingts, make a score, or one pound)

FOOL Then 'tis like the breath of an unfeed lawyer—you gave me nothing for't. Can you make no use of nothing, Nuncle?

LEAR Why, no, boy. Nothing can be made out of nothing. 135

FOOL [*To Kent*] Prithee tell him, so much the rent of his land comes to; he will not believe a Fool.

LEAR A bitter Fool. 140

FOOL Dost thou know the difference, my boy, between a bitter Fool and a sweet one?

LEAR No, lad; teach me.

FOOL

That lord that counseled thee
To give away thy land, 145
Come place him here by me,
Do thou for him stand,
The sweet and bitter fool
Will presently appear;
The one in motely here, 150
The other found out there.

LEAR Dost thou call me fool, boy?

FOOL All thy other titles thou hast given away; that thou wast born with.

KENT This is not altogether fool, my lord. 155

FOOL No, faith; lords and great men will not let me. If I had a monopoly out, they would have part on't. And ladies too, they will not let me have all the fool to myself; they'll be snatching. Nuncle, give me an egg, and I'll give thee two crowns. 160

132 unfeed unpaid for **140 bitter** satirical **150 motley** the drab costume of the professional jester **151 found out** revealed **151 there** (the Fool points at Lear, as a fool in the grain) **156 let me** (have all the folly to myself) **157 monopoly** (James I gave great scandal by granting to his "snatching" courtiers royal patents to deal exclusively in some commodity)

LEAR What two crowns shall they be?

FOOL Why, after I have cut the egg i' th' middle and eat up the meat, the two crowns of the egg. When thou clovest thy crown i' th' middle and
165 gav'st away both parts, thou bor'st thine ass on thy back o'er the dirt. Thou hadst little wit in thy bald crown when thou gav'st thy golden one away. If I speak like myself in this, let him be whipped that first finds it so.
170 [*Singing*] Fools had ne'er less grace in a year,
For wise men are grown foppish,
And know not how their wits to wear,
Their manners are so apish.

LEAR When were you wont to be so full of songs,
175 sirrah?

FOOL I have used it, Nuncle, e'er since thou mad'st thy daughters thy mothers; for when thou gav'st them the rod, and put'st down thine own breeches,
[*Singing*] Then they for sudden joy did weep,
180 And I for sorrow sung,
That such a king should play bo-peep
And go the fools among.
Prithee, Nuncle, keep a schoolmaster that can teach thy Fool to lie. I would fain learn to lie.

185 LEAR And you lie, sirrah, we'll have you whipped.

FOOL I marvel what kin thou and thy daughters are. They'll have me whipped for speaking true; thou'lt have me whipped for lying; and sometimes I am whipped for holding my peace. I had rather be any
190 kind o' thing than a Fool, and yet I would not be

165–66 **bor'st . . . dirt** (like the foolish and unnatural countryman in Aesop's fable) 168 **like myself** like a Fool 168 **let him be whipped** i.e., let the man be whipped for a Fool who thinks my true saying to be foolish 170–73 **Fools . . . apish** i.e., fools were never in less favor than now, and the reason is that wise men, turning foolish, and not knowing how to use their intelligence, imitate the professional fools and so make them unnecessary 176 **used** practiced 181 **play bo-peep** (1) act like a child (2) blind himself 185 **And** if

thee, Nuncle: thou hast pared thy wit o' both sides and left nothing i' th' middle. Here comes one o' the parings.

Enter Goneril.

LEAR How now, daughter? What makes that frontlet on? Methinks you are too much of late i' th' frown. 195

FOOL Thou wast a pretty fellow when thou hadst no need to care for her frowning. Now thou art an O without a figure. I am better than thou art now: I am a Fool, thou art nothing. [*To Goneril.*] Yes, 200 forsooth, I will hold my tongue. So your face bids me, though you say nothing. Mum, mum,

He that keeps nor crust nor crum,
Weary of all, shall want some.

[*Pointing to Lear*] That's a shealed peascod. 205

GONERIL Not only, sir, this your all-licensed Fool,
But other of your insolent retinue
Do hourly carp and quarrel, breaking forth
In rank and not-to-be-endurèd riots. Sir,
I had thought by making this well known unto you 210
To have found a safe redress, but now grow
fearful,
By what yourself too late have spoke and done,
That you protect this course, and put it on
By your allowance; which if you should, the fault
Would not 'scape censure, nor the redresses sleep, 215
Which, in the tender of a wholesome weal,
Might in their working do you that offense,
Which else were shame, that then necessity
Will call discreet proceeding.

194 **frontlet** frown (lit., ornamental band) 199 **figure** digit, to give value to the cipher (Lear is a nought) 203 **crum** soft bread inside the loaf 204 **want** lack 205 **shealed peascod** empty pea pod 206 **all-licensed** privileged to take any liberties 207 **other** others 209 **rank** gross 211 **safe** sure 212 **too late** lately 213–14 **put . . . allowance** promote it by your approval 214 **allowance** approval 215 **redresses sleep** correction fail to follow 216 **tender of** desire for 216 **weal** state 217–19 **Might . . . proceeding** as I apply it, the correction might humiliate you; but the need to take action cancels what would otherwise be unfilial conduct in me

220 FOOL For you know, Nuncle,
The hedge-sparrow fed the cuckoo so long
That it had it head bit off by it young.
So out went the candle, and we were left darkling.

LEAR Are you our daughter?

225 GONERIL Come, sir,
I would you would make use of your good wisdom
Whereof I know you are fraught and put away
These dispositions which of late transport you
From what you rightly are.

230 FOOL May not an ass know when the cart draws the horse? Whoop, Jug, I love thee!

LEAR Does any here know me? This is not Lear.
Does Lear walk thus? Speak thus? Where are his eyes?
Either his notion weakens, or his discernings
235 Are lethargied—Ha! Waking? 'Tis not so.
Who is it that can tell me who I am?

FOOL Lear's shadow.

LEAR I would learn that; for, by the marks of sover-
240 eignty, knowledge, and reason, I should be false persuaded I had daughters.

FOOL Which they will make an obedient father.

LEAR Your name, fair gentlewoman?

GONERIL This admiration, sir, is much o' th' savor
Of other your new pranks. I do beseech you
245 To understand my purposes aright.
As you are old and reverend, should be wise.
Here do you keep a hundred knights and squires,

221 **cuckoo** (who lays its eggs in the nests of other birds) 222 **it** its 223 **darkling** in the dark 227 **fraught** endowed 228 **dispositions** moods 231 **Jug** Joan (? a quotation from a popular song) 234 **notion** understanding 234 **discernings** faculties 235 **lethargied** paralyzed 238–39 **marks of sovereignty** i.e., tokens that Lear is king, and hence father to his daughters 239 **false** falsely 241 **Which** whom (Lear) 243 **admiration** (affected) wonderment 243 **is much o' th' savor** smacks much 244 **other your** others of your

Men so disordered, so deboshed, and bold,
That this our court, infected with their manners,
Shows like a riotous inn. Epicurism and lust 250
Makes it more like a tavern or a brothel
Than a graced palace. The shame itself doth speak
For instant remedy. Be then desired
By her, that else will take the thing she begs,
A little to disquantity your train, 255
And the remainders that shall still depend,
To be such men as may besort your age,
Which know themselves, and you.

LEAR Darkness and devils!
Saddle my horses; call my train together.
Degenerate bastard, I'll not trouble thee: 260
Yet have I left a daughter.

GONERIL You strike my people, and your disordered rabble
Make servants of their betters.

Enter Albany.

LEAR Woe, that too late repents. O, sir, are you come?
Is it your will? Speak, sir. Prepare my horses. 265
Ingratitude! thou marble-hearted fiend,
More hideous when thou show'st thee in a child
Than the sea-monster.

ALBANY Pray, sir, be patient.

LEAR Detested kite, thou liest.
My train are men of choice and rarest parts, 270
That all particulars of duty know,
And, in the most exact regard, support
The worships of their name. O most small fault,

248 deboshed debauched **250 Shows** appears **250 Epicurism** riotous living **252 graced** dignified **253 desired** requested **255 disquantity your train** reduce the number of your dependents **256 remainders** those who remain **256 depend** attend on you **257 besort** befit **260 Degenerate** unnatural **269 kite** scavenging bird of prey **270 parts** accomplishments **272 exact regard** strict attention to detail **273 worships** honor

How ugly didst thou in Cordelia show!
Which, like an engine, wrenched my frame of
275 nature
From the fixed place; drew from my heart all love,
And added to the gall. O Lear, Lear, Lear!
Beat at this gate that let thy folly in [*Striking his head.*]
And thy dear judgment out. Go, go, my people.

280 ALBANY My lord, I am guiltless, as I am ignorant
Of what hath moved you.

LEAR It may be so, my lord.
Hear, Nature, hear; dear Goddess, hear:
Suspend thy purpose if thou didst intend
To make this creature fruitful.
285 Into her womb convey sterility.
Dry up in her the organs of increase,
And from her derogate body never spring
A babe to honor her. If she must teem,
Create her child of spleen, that it may live
290 And be a thwart disnatured torment to her.
Let it stamp wrinkles in her brow of youth,
With cadent tears fret channels in her cheeks,
Turn all her mother's pains and benefits
To laughter and contempt, that she may feel
295 How sharper than a serpent's tooth it is
To have a thankless child. Away, away! *Exit.*

ALBANY Now, gods that we adore, whereof comes this?

GONERIL Never afflict yourself to know the cause,
But let his disposition have that scope
300 As dotage gives it.

Enter Lear.

LEAR What, fifty of my followers at a clap?

275 engine destructive contrivance **274-76 wrenched . . . place** i.e., disordered my natural self **277 gall** bitterness **286 increase** childbearing **287 derogate** degraded **288 teem** conceive **289 spleen** ill humor **290 thwart disnatured** perverse unnatural **292 cadent** falling **292 fret** wear **293 benefits** the mother's beneficent care of her child **299 disposition** mood **300 As** that **301 at a clap** at one stroke

Within a fortnight?

ALBANY What's the matter, sir?

LEAR I'll tell thee [*To Goneril*] Life and death, I am ashamed
That thou hast power to shake my manhood thus!
That these hot tears, which break from me perforce, 305
Should make thee worth them. Blasts and fogs upon thee!
Th' untented woundings of a father's curse
Pierce every sense about thee! Old fond eyes,
Beweep this cause again, I'll pluck ye out
And cast you, with the waters that you loose, 310
To temper clay. Yea, is it come to this?
Ha! Let it be so. I have another daughter,
Who I am sure is kind and comfortable.
When she shall hear this of thee, with her nails
She'll flay thy wolvish visage. Thou shalt find 315
That I'll resume the shape which thou dost think
I have cast off for ever.

Exit [*Lear with Kent and Attendants*].

GONERIL Do you mark that?

ALBANY I cannot be so partial, Goneril,
To the great love I bear you——

GONERIL Pray you, content. What, Oswald, ho! 320
[*To the Fool*] You, sir, more knave than fool, after your master!

FOOL Nuncle Lear, Nuncle Lear, tarry. Take the Fool with thee.

304 **shake my manhood** i.e., with tears 305 **perforce** involuntarily, against my will 307 **untented woundings** wounds too deep to be probed with a tent (a roll of lint) 308 **fond** foolish 309 **Beweep** if you weep over 310 **loose** (1) let loose (2) lose, as of no avail 311 **temper** mix with and soften 313 **comfortable** ready to comfort 316 **shape** i.e., kingly role 318–19 **I cannot . . . you** i.e., even though my love inclines me to you, I must protest 322 **Fool** (1) the Fool himself (2) the epithet or character of "fool"

A fox, when one has caught her,
325 And such a daughter,
Should sure to the slaughter,
If my cap would buy a halter.
So the Fool follows after. *Exit.*

GONERIL This man hath had good counsel. A hundred knights!
330 'Tis politic and safe to let him keep
At point a hundred knights: yes, that on every dream,
Each buzz, each fancy, each complaint, dislike,
He may enguard his dotage with their pow'rs
And hold our lives in mercy. Oswald, I say!

ALBANY Well, you may fear too far.

335 GONERIL Safer than trust too far.
Let me still take away the harms I fear,
Not fear still to be taken. I know his heart.
What he hath uttered I have writ my sister.
If she sustain him and his hundred knights,
When I have showed th' unfitness——

Enter Oswald.

340 How now, Oswald?
What, have you writ that letter to my sister?

OSWALD Ay, madam.

GONERIL Take you some company, and away to horse.
Inform her full of my particular fear,
345 And thereto add such reasons of your own
As may compact it more. Get you gone,
And hasten your return. [*Exit Oswald.*] No, no, my lord,
This milky gentleness and course of yours,
Though I condemn not, yet under pardon,

327–28 **halter, after** pronounced "hauter," "auter" 330 **politic** good policy 331 **At point** armed 332 **buzz** rumor 333 **enguard** protect 334 **in mercy** at his mercy 337 **Not . . . taken** rather than remain fearful of being overtaken by them 343 **company** escort 344 **particular** own 346 **compact** strengthen 348 **milky . . . course** mild and gentle way (hendiadys) 349 **condemn not** condemn it not

You are much more attasked for want of wisdom 350
Than praised for harmful mildness.

ALBANY How far your eyes may pierce I cannot tell;
Striving to better, oft we mar what's well.

GONERIL Nay then——

ALBANY Well, well, th' event. *Exeunt* 355

Scene V. [*Court before the same.*]

Enter Lear, Kent, and Fool.

LEAR Go you before to Gloucester with these letters. Acquaint my daughter no further with anything you know than comes from her demand out of the letter. If your diligence be not speedy, I shall be there afore you. 5

KENT I will not sleep, my lord, till I have delivered your letter. *Exit.*

FOOL If a man's brains were in's heels, were't not in danger of kibes?

LEAR Ay, boy. 10

FOOL Then I prithee be merry. Thy wit shall not go slipshod.

LEAR Ha, ha, ha.

FOOL Shalt see thy other daughter will use thee kindly; for though she's as like this as a crab's 15 like an apple, yet I can tell what I can tell.

350 **attasked** taken to task, blamed 351 **harmful mildness** dangerous indulgence 355 **th' event** i.e., we'll see what happens I.v. 3–4 **than . . . letter** than her reading of the letter brings her to ask 8 **were't** i.e., the brains 9 **kibes** chilblains 11–12 **Thy . . . slipshod** your brains shall not go in slippers (because you have no brains to be protected from chilblains) 14 **Shalt** thou shalt 15 **kindly** (1) affectionately (2) after her kind or nature 15 **crab** crab apple

LEAR Why, what canst thou tell, my boy?

FOOL She will taste as like this as a crab does to a crab. Thou canst tell why one's nose stands i' th'
20 middle on's face?

LEAR No.

FOOL Why, to keep one's eyes of either side's nose, that what a man cannot smell out, he may spy into.

25 LEAR I did her wrong.

FOOL Canst tell how an oyster makes his shell?

LEAR No.

FOOL Nor I neither; but I can tell why a snail has a house.

30 LEAR Why?

FOOL Why, to put 's head in; not to give it away to his daughters, and leave his horns without a case.

LEAR I will forget my nature. So kind a father! Be my horses ready?

35 FOOL Thy asses are gone about 'em. The reason why the seven stars are no moe than seven is a pretty reason.

LEAR Because they are not eight.

FOOL Yes indeed. Thou wouldst make a good Fool.

40 LEAR To take't again perforce! Monster ingratitude!

FOOL If thou wert my Fool, Nuncle, I'd have thee beaten for being old before thy time.

LEAR How's that?

FOOL Thou shouldst not have been old till thou hadst
45 been wise.

20 **on's** of his 22 **of** on 32 **horns** (1) snail's horns (2) cuckold's horns 33 **nature** paternal instincts 36 **seven stars** the Pleiades 36 **moe** more 36 **pretty** apt 40 **To . . . perforce** (1) of Goneril, who has forcibly taken away Lear's privileges; or (2) of Lear, who meditates a forcible resumption of authority

LEAR O, let me not be mad, not mad, sweet heaven!
Keep me in temper; I would not be mad!

[*Enter Gentleman.*]

How now, are the horses ready?

GENTLEMAN Ready, my lord.

LEAR Come, boy. 50

FOOL She that's a maid now, and laughs at my departure,
Shall not be a maid long, unless things be cut shorter. *Exeunt.*

47 in temper sane **51–52 She . . . shorter** the maid who laughs, missing the tragic implications of this quarrel, will not have sense enough to preserve her virginity ("things" = penises)

ACT II

Scene I. [*The Earl of Gloucester's castle.*]

Enter Edmund and Curan, severally.

EDMUND Save thee, Curan.

CURAN And you, sir. I have been with your father, and given him notice that the Duke of Cornwall and Regan his duchess will be here with him this
5 night.

EDMUND How comes that?

CURAN Nay, I know not. You have heard of the news abroad? I mean the whispered ones, for they are yet but ear-kissing arguments.

10 EDMUND Not I. Pray you, what are they?

CURAN Have you heard of no likely wars toward, 'twixt the Dukes of Cornwall and Albany?

EDMUND Not a word.

CURAN You may do, then, in time. Fare you well,
15 sir. *Exit.*

EDMUND The Duke be here tonight? The better! best!

II.i.1 s.d. **severally** separately (from different entrances on stage) 1 **Save** God save 9 **ear-kissing arguments** subjects whispered in the ear 11 **likely** probable 11 **toward** impending 16 **The better** so much the better

This weaves itself perforce into my business.
My father hath set guard to take my brother,
And I have one thing of a queasy question
Which I must act. Briefness and Fortune, work! 20
Brother, a word; descend. Brother, I say!

Enter Edgar.

My father watches. O sir, fly this place.
Intelligence is given where you are hid.
You have now the good advantage of the night.
Have you not spoken 'gainst the Duke of Cornwall? 25
He's coming hither, now i' th' night, i' th' haste,
And Regan with him. Have you nothing said
Upon his party 'gainst the Duke of Albany?
Advise yourself.

EDGAR I am sure on't, not a word.

EDMUND I hear my father coming. Pardon me: 30
In cunning I must draw my sword upon you.
Draw, seem to defend yourself; now quit you well.
Yield! Come before my father! Light ho, here!
Fly, brother. Torches, torches!—So farewell.

Exit Edgar.

Some blood drawn on me would beget opinion 35

[*Wounds his arm*]

Of my more fierce endeavor. I have seen drunkards
Do more than this in sport. Father, father!
Stop, stop! No help?

Enter Gloucester, and Servants with torches.

GLOUCESTER Now, Edmund, where's the villain?

EDMUND Here stood he in the dark, his sharp sword out, 40
Mumbling of wicked charms, conjuring the moon
To stand auspicious mistress.

GLOUCESTER But where is he?

17 perforce necessarily 19 of a queasy question that requires delicate handling (to be "queasy" is to be on the point of vomiting) 20 Briefness speed 23 Intelligence information 26 i' th' haste in great haste 28 Upon his party censuring his enmity 29 Advise yourself reflect 29 on't of it 31 In cunning as a pretense 32 quit you acquit yourself 35 beget opinion create the impression

EDMUND Look, sir, I bleed.

GLOUCESTER Where is the villain, Edmund?

EDMUND Fled this way, sir, when by no means he could——

GLOUCESTER Pursue him, ho! Go after.

[*Exeunt some Servants.*]

45 By no means what?

EDMUND Persuade me to the murder of your lordship;
But that I told him the revenging gods
'Gainst parricides did all the thunder bend;
Spoke with how manifold and strong a bond
50 The child was bound to th' father. Sir, in fine,
Seeing how loathly opposite I stood
To his unnatural purpose, in fell motion
With his preparèd sword he charges home
My unprovided body, latched mine arm;
55 But when he saw my best alarumed spirits
Bold in the quarrel's right, roused to th' encounter,
Or whether gasted by the noise I made,
Full suddenly he fled.

GLOUCESTER Let him fly far.
Not in this land shall he remain uncaught;
60 And found—dispatch. The noble Duke my master,
My worthy arch and patron, comes tonight.
By his authority I will proclaim it,
That he which finds him shall deserve our thanks,
Bringing the murderous coward to the stake.
65 He that conceals him, death.

EDMUND When I dissuaded him from his intent,
And found him pight to do it, with curst speech
I threatened to discover him. He replied,

48 **bend** aim 50 **in fine** finally 51 **loathly opposite** bitterly opposed 52 **fell** deadly 52 **motion** thrust (a term from fencing) 54 **unprovided** unprotected 54 **latched** wounded (lanced) 55 **best alarumed** wholly aroused 56 **Bold ... right** confident in the rightness of my cause 57 **gasted** struck aghast 60 **dispatch** i.e., he will be killed 61 **arch** chief 65 **death** (the same elliptical form that characterizes "dispatch," 1.60) 67 **pight** determined 67 **curst** angry 68 **discover** expose

"Thou unpossessing bastard, dost thou think,
If I would stand against thee, would the reposal 70
Of any trust, virtue, or worth in thee
Make thy words faithed? No. What I should deny—
As this I would, ay, though thou didst produce
My very character—I'd turn it all
To thy suggestion, plot, and damnèd practice. 75
And thou must make a dullard of the world,
If they not thought the profits of my death
Were very pregnant and potential spirits
To make thee seek it."

GLOUCESTER O strange and fastened villain!
Would he deny his letter, said he? I never got him. 80

Tucket within.

Hark, the Duke's trumpets. I know not why he comes.
All ports I'll bar; the villain shall not 'scape;
The Duke must grant me that. Besides, his picture
I will send far and near, that all the kingdom
May have due note of him; and of my land, 85
Loyal and natural boy, I'll work the means
To make thee capable.

Enter Cornwall, Regan, and Attendants.

CORNWALL How now, my noble friend! Since I came hither,
Which I can call but now, I have heard strange news.

REGAN If it be true, all vengeance comes too short 90
Which can pursue th' offender. How dost, my lord?

GLOUCESTER O madam, my old heart is cracked, it's cracked.

69 **unpossessing** beggarly (landless) 70 **reposal** placing 72 **faithed** believed 74 **character** handwriting 75 **suggestion** instigation 75 **practice** device 76 **make . . . world** think everyone stupid 77 **not thought** did not think 78 **pregnant** teeming with incitement 78 **potential spirits** powerful evil spirits 79 **fastened** hardened 80 **got** begot 80 s.d. **Tucket** (Cornwall's special trumpet call) 82 **ports** exits, of whatever sort 86 **natural** (1) kind (filial) (2) illegitimate 87 **capable** able to inherit

REGAN What, did my father's godson seek your life?
He whom my father named, your Edgar?

95 GLOUCESTER O lady, lady, shame would have it hid.

REGAN Was he not companion with the riotous knights
That tended upon my father?

GLOUCESTER I know not, madam. 'Tis too bad, too bad.

EDMUND Yes, madam, he was of that consort.

100 REGAN No marvel then, though he were ill affected.
'Tis they have put him on the old man's death,
To have th' expense and waste of his revenues.
I have this present evening from my sister
Been well informed of them, and with such cautions
105 That, if they come to sojourn at my house,
I'll not be there.

CORNWALL Nor I, assure thee, Regan.
Edmund, I hear that you have shown your father
A childlike office.

EDMUND It was my duty, sir.

110 GLOUCESTER He did bewray his practice, and received
This hurt you see, striving to apprehend him.

CORNWALL Is he pursued?

GLOUCESTER Ay, my good lord.

CORNWALL If he be taken, he shall never more
Be feared of doing harm. Make your own purpose,
115 How in my strength you please. For you, Edmund,
Whose virtue and obedience doth this instant
So much commend itself, you shall be ours.
Natures of such deep trust we shall much need;
You we first seize on.

EDMUND I shall serve you, sir,
Truly, however else.

120 GLOUCESTER For him I thank your Grace.

99 consort company **100 ill affected** disposed to evil **101 put** set **102 expense and waste** squandering **108 childlike** filial **110 bewray his practice** disclose his plot **114 of doing** because he might do **114–15 Make . . . please** use my power freely, in carrying out your plans for his capture **116 virtue and obedience** virtuous obedience

CORNWALL You know not why we came to visit you?

REGAN Thus out of season, threading dark-eyed night.
Occasions, noble Gloucester, of some prize,
Wherein we must have use of your advice.
Our father he hath writ, so hath our sister, 125
Of differences, which I best thought it fit
To answer from our home. The several
messengers
From hence attend dispatch. Our good old friend,
Lay comforts to your bosom, and bestow
Your needful counsel to our businesses, 130
Which craves the instant use.

GLOUCESTER I serve you, madam.
Your Graces are right welcome.

Exeunt. Flourish.

Scene II. [*Before Gloucester's castle.*]

Enter Kent and Oswald, severally.

OSWALD Good dawning to thee, friend. Art of this house?

KENT Ay.

OSWALD Where may we set our horses?

KENT I' th' mire. 5

OSWALD Prithee, if thou lov'st me, tell me.

KENT I love thee not.

122 prize importance **125 differences** quarrels **125 which** (referring not to "differences," but to the letter Lear has written) **126 from** away from **127 attend dispatch** are waiting to be sent off **128 Lay . . . bosom** console yourself (about Edgar's supposed treason) **129 needful** needed **131 craves the instant use** demands immediate transaction II.ii. **1 dawning** (dawn is impending, but not yet arrived) **1-2 Art of this house** i.e., do you live here

OSWALD Why then, I care not for thee.

KENT If I had thee in Lipsbury Pinfold, I would make
10 thee care for me.

OSWALD Why dost thou use me thus? I know thee not.

KENT Fellow, I know thee.

OSWALD What dost thou know me for?

KENT A knave, a rascal, an eater of broken meats;
15 a base, proud, shallow, beggarly, three-suited,
hundred-pound, filthy worsted-stocking knave;
a lily-livered, action-taking, whoreson, glass-gazing,
superserviceable, finical rogue; one-trunk-inheriting
slave; one that wouldst be a bawd in
20 way of good service, and art nothing but the composition
of a knave, beggar, coward, pander, and
the son and heir of a mongrel bitch; one whom I
will beat into clamorous whining if thou deniest the
least syllable of thy addition.

25 OSWALD Why, what a monstrous fellow art thou, thus
to rail on one that is neither known of thee nor
knows thee!

KENT What a brazen-faced varlet art thou to deny
thou knowest me! Is it two days since I
30 tripped up thy heels and beat thee before the
King? [*Drawing his sword*] Draw, you rogue,
for though it be night, yet the moon shines. I'll
make a sop o' th' moonshine of you. You whoreson
cullionly barbermonger, draw!

9 **Lipsbury Pinfold** a pound or pen in which strayed animals are enclosed ("Lipsbury" may denote a particular place, or may be slang for "between my teeth") 14 **broken meats** scraps of food 15 **three-suited** (the wardrobe permitted to a servant or "knave") 16 **hundred-pound** (the extent of Oswald's wealth, and thus a sneer at his aspiring to gentility) 16 **worsted-stocking** (worn by servants) 17 **action-taking** one who refuses a fight and goes to law instead 17–18 **glass-gazing** conceited 18 **superserviceable** sycophantic, serving without principle. 18 **finical** overfastidious 18–19 **one-trunk-inheriting** possessing only a trunkful of goods 19–20 **bawd ... service** pimp, to please his master 20–21 **composition** compound 24 **addition** titles 33 **sop o' th' moonshine** i.e., Oswald will admit the moonlight, and so sop it up, through the open wounds Kent is preparing to give him 34 **cullionly barbermonger** base patron of hairdressers (effeminate man)

OSWALD Away, I have nothing to do with thee. 35

KENT Draw, you rascal. You come with letters against the King, and take Vanity the puppet's part against the royalty of her father. Draw, you rogue, or I'll so carbonado your shanks. Draw, you rascal. Come your ways! 40

OSWALD Help, ho! Murder! Help!

KENT Strike, you slave! Stand, rogue! Stand, you neat slave! Strike! [*Beating him*]

OSWALD Help, ho! Murder, murder!

Enter Edmund, with his rapier drawn, Cornwall, Regan, Gloucester, Servants.

EDMUND How now? What's the matter? Part! 45

KENT With you, goodman boy, if you please! Come, I'll flesh ye, come on, young master.

GLOUCESTER Weapons? Arms? What's the matter here?

CORNWALL Keep peace, upon your lives.
He dies that strikes again. What is the matter? 50

REGAN The messengers from our sister and the King.

CORNWALL What is your difference? Speak.

OSWALD I am scarce in breath, my lord.

KENT No marvel, you have so bestirred your valor. You cowardly rascal, nature disclaims in thee. A 55 tailor made thee.

CORNWALL Thou art a strange fellow. A tailor make a man?

KENT A tailor, sir. A stonecutter or a painter could

37 **Vanity the puppet's** Goneril, here identified with one of the personified characters in the morality plays, which were sometimes put on as puppet shows 39 **carbonado** cut across, like a piece of meat before cooking 40 **Come your ways** get along 42 **neat** (1) foppish (2) unmixed, as in "neat wine" 46 **With you** i.e., the quarrel is with you 46 **goodman boy** young man (peasants are "goodmen"; "boy" is a term of contempt) 47 **flesh** introduce to blood (term from hunting) 52 **difference** quarrel 54 **bestirred** exercised 55 **nature disclaims in thee** nature renounces any part in you 55–56 **A tailor made thee** (from the proverb "The tailor makes the man")

60 not have made him so ill, though they had been but two years o' th' trade.

CORNWALL Speak yet, how grew your quarrel?

OSWALD This ancient ruffian, sir, whose life I have spared at suit of his gray beard——

65 KENT Thou whoreson zed, thou unnecessary letter! My lord, if you will give me leave, I will tread this unbolted villain into mortar and daub the wall of a jakes with him. Spare my gray beard, you wagtail!

70 CORNWALL Peace, sirrah!
You beastly knave, know you no reverence?

KENT Yes, sir, but anger hath a privilege.

CORNWALL Why art thou angry?

KENT That such a slave as this should wear a sword,
Who wears no honesty. Such smiling rogues as
75 these,
Like rats, oft bite the holy cords atwain
Which are too intrince t' unloose; smooth
every passion
That in the natures of their lords rebel,
Being oil to fire, snow to the colder moods;
80 Renege, affirm, and turn their halcyon beaks
With every gale and vary of their masters,
Knowing naught, like dogs, but following.
A plague upon your epileptic visage!
Smile you my speeches, as I were a fool?

64 **at suit of** out of pity for 65 **zed** the letter Z, generally omitted in contemporary dictionaries 67 **unbolted** unsifted, i.e., altogether a villain 68 **jakes** privy 68–69 **wagtail** a bird that bobs its tail up and down, and thus suggests obsequiousness 71 **beastly** irrational 76 **holy cords** sacred bonds of affection (as between husbands and wives, parents and children) 77 **intrince** entangled, intricate 77 **smooth** appease 80 **Renege** deny 80 **halcyon beaks** (the halcyon or kingfisher serves here as a type of opportunist because, when hung up by the tail or neck, it was supposed to turn with the wind, like a weathervane) 81 **gale and vary** varying gale (hendiadys) 83 **epileptic** distorted by grinning 84 **Smile you** do you smile at

Goose, if I had you upon Sarum Plain, 85
I'd drive ye cackling home to Camelot.

CORNWALL What, art thou mad, old fellow?

GLOUCESTER How fell you out? Say that.

KENT No contraries hold more antipathy
Than I and such a knave. 90

CORNWALL Why dost thou call him knave? What is his fault?

KENT His countenance likes me not.

CORNWALL No more perchance does mine, nor his, nor hers.

KENT Sir, 'tis my occupation to be plain:
I have seen better faces in my time 95
Than stands on any shoulder that I see
Before me at this instant.

CORNWALL This is some fellow
Who, having been praised for bluntness, doth affect
A saucy roughness, and constrains the garb
Quite from his nature. He cannot flatter, he; 100
An honest mind and plain, he must speak truth.
And they will take it, so; if not, he's plain.
These kind of knaves I know, which in this plainness
Harbor more craft and more corrupter ends
Than twenty silly-ducking observants 105
That stretch their duties nicely.

KENT Sir, in good faith, in sincere verity,
Under th' allowance of your great aspect,
Whose influence, like the wreath of radiant fire

85 **Sarum Plain** Salisbury Plain 86 **Camelot** the residence of King Arthur (presumably a particular point, now lost, is intended here) 89 **contraries** opposites 92 **likes** pleases 99–100 **constrains . . . nature** forces the manner of candid speech to be a cloak, not for candor but for craft 102 **And** if 105 **silly-ducking observants** ridiculously obsequious attendants 106 **nicely** punctiliously 108 **allowance** approval 108 **aspect** (1) appearance (2) position of the heavenly bodies 109 **influence** astrological power

On flick'ring Phoebus' front——

110 CORNWALL What mean'st by this?

KENT To go out of my dialect, which you discommend so much. I know, sir, I am no flatterer. He that beguiled you in a plain accent was a plain knave, which, for my part, I will not be, though I should
115 win your displeasure to entreat me to't.

CORNWALL What was th' offense you gave him?

OSWALD I never gave him any.
It pleased the King his master very late
To strike at me, upon his misconstruction;
120 When he, compact, and flattering his displeasure,
Tripped me behind; being down, insulted, railed,
And put upon him such a deal of man
That worthied him, got praises of the King
For him attempting who was self-subdued;
125 And, in the fleshment of this dread exploit,
Drew on me here again.

KENT None of these rogues and cowards
But Ajax is their fool.

CORNWALL Fetch forth the stocks!
You stubborn ancient knave, you reverent
braggart,
We'll teach you.

KENT Sir, I am too old to learn.

110 **Phoebus' front** forehead of the sun 111 **dialect** customary manner of speaking 112 **He** i.e., the sort of candid-crafty man Cornwall has been describing 114–15 **though . . . to't** even if I were to succeed in bringing your graceless person ("displeasure" personified, and in lieu of the expected form, "your grace") to beg me to be a plain knave 118 **very late** recently 119 **misconstruction** misunderstanding 120 **compact** in league with the king 122 **put . . . man** pretended such manly behavior 123 **worthied him** made him seem heroic 124 **For . . . self-subdued** for attacking a man (Oswald) who offered no resistance 125 **fleshment** the bloodthirstiness excited by his first success or "fleshing" 126–27 **None . . . fool** i.e., cowardly rogues like Oswald always impose on fools like Cornwall (who is likened to Ajax: [1] the braggart Greek warrior [2] a jakes or privy) 128 **stubborn** rude 128 **reverent** old

Call not your stocks for me, I serve the King, 130
On whose employment I was sent to you.
You shall do small respect, show too bold malice
Against the grace and person of my master,
Stocking his messenger.

CORNWALL Fetch forth the stocks. As I have life and
honor, 135
There shall he sit till noon.

REGAN Till noon? Till night, my lord, and all night
too.

KENT Why, madam, if I were your father's dog,
You should not use me so.

REGAN Sir, being his knave, I will.

CORNWALL This is a fellow of the selfsame color 140
Our sister speaks of. Come, bring away the stocks.
Stocks brought out.

GLOUCESTER Let me beseech your Grace not to do so.
His fault is much, and the good King his master
Will check him for't. Your purposed low
correction
Is such as basest and contemnèd'st wretches 145
For pilf'rings and most common trespasses
Are punished with.
The King his master needs must take it ill
That he, so slightly valued in his messenger,
Should have him thus restrained.

CORNWALL I'll answer that. 150

REGAN My sister may receive it much more worse,
To have her gentleman abused, assaulted,
For following her affairs. Put in his legs.
[*Kent is put in the stocks.*]
Come, my good lord, away!
[*Exeunt all but Gloucester and Kent.*]

133 **grace and person** i.e., Lear as soveriegn and in his personal character 140 **color** kind 141 **away** out 144 **check** correct 144 **purposed** intended 145 **contemnèd'st** most despised 149 **slightly valued in** little honored in the person of 150 **answer** answer for

GLOUCESTER I am sorry for thee, friend. 'Tis the
155 Duke's pleasure,
Whose disposition all the world well knows
Will not be rubbed nor stopped. I'll entreat for
thee.

KENT Pray do not, sir. I have watched and traveled
hard.
Some time I shall sleep out, the rest I'll whistle.
160 A good man's fortune may grow out at heels.
Give you good morrow.

GLOUCESTER The Duke's to blame in this. 'Twill be
ill taken. *Exit.*

KENT Good King, that must approve the common
saw,
Thou out of Heaven's benediction com'st
165 To the warm sun.
Approach, thou beacon to this under globe,
That by thy comfortable beams I may
Peruse this letter. Nothing almost sees miracles
But misery. I know 'tis from Cordelia,
170 Who hath most fortunately been informed
Of my obscurèd course. And shall find time
From this enormous state, seeking to give
Losses their remedies. All weary and o'erwatched,
Take vantage, heavy eyes, not to behold
175 This shameful lodging. Fortune, good night;
Smile once more, turn thy wheel.

Sleeps.

156 **disposition** inclination 157 **rubbed** diverted (metaphor from the game of bowls) 158 **watched** gone without sleep 160 **A ... heels** even a good man may have bad fortune 161 **Give** God give 162 **taken** received 163 **approve** confirm 163 **saw** proverb 164–65 **Thou ... sun** i.e., Lear goes from better to worse, from Heaven's blessing or shelter to lack of shelter 166 **beacon ... globe** i.e., the sun, whose rising Kent anticipates 167 **comfortable** comforting 168–69 **Nothing ... misery** i.e., true perception belongs only to the wretched 171 **obscurèd** disguised 171–73 **shall ... remedies** (a possible reading: Cordelia, away from this monstrous state of things, will find occasion to right the wrongs we suffer) 174 **vantage** advantage (of sleep) 176 **turn thy wheel** i.e., so that Kent, who is at the bottom, may climb upward

[Scene III. *A wood.*]

Enter Edgar.

EDGAR I heard myself proclaimed,
And by the happy hollow of a tree
Escaped the hunt. No port is free, no place
That guard and most unusual vigilance
Does not attend my taking. Whiles I may 'scape, 5
I will preserve myself; and am bethought
To take the basest and most poorest shape
That ever penury, in contempt of man,
Brought near to beast; my face I'll grime with filth,
Blanket my loins, elf all my hairs in knots, 10
And with presented nakedness outface
The winds and persecutions of the sky.
The country gives me proof and precedent
Of Bedlam beggars, who, with roaring voices,
Strike in their numbed and mortified bare arms 15
Pins, wooden pricks, nails, sprigs of rosemary;
And with this horrible object, from low farms,
Poor pelting villages, sheepcotes, and mills,
Sometimes with lunatic bans, sometime with
prayers,
Enforce their charity. Poor Turlygod, Poor Tom, 20
That's something yet: Edgar I nothing am. *Exit.*

II.iii. 2 **happy** lucky 5 **attend my taking** watch to capture me 6 **am bethought** have decided 8-9 **penury . . . beast** poverty, to show how contemptible man is, reduced to the level of a beast 10 **Blanket** cover only with a blanket 10 **elf** tangle (into "elflocks," supposed to be caused by elves) 11 **presented** the show of 11 **outface** brave 13 **proof** example 14 **Bedlam** (see I.ii.r. 146-47) 15 **strike** stick 15 **mortified** not alive to pain 16 **pricks** skewers 17 **object** spectacle 17 **low** humble 18 **pelting** paltry 19 **bans** curses 20 **Poor . . . Tom** (Edgar recites the names a Bedlam beggar gives himself) 21 **That's . . . am** there's a chance for me in that I am no longer known for myself

[Scene IV. *Before Gloucester's castle. Kent in the stocks.*]

Enter Lear, Fool, and Gentleman.

LEAR 'Tis strange that they should so depart from home,
And not send back my messenger.

GENTLEMAN As I learned,
The night before there was no purpose in them
Of this remove.

KENT Hail to thee, noble master.

5 LEAR Ha!
Mak'st thou this shame thy pastime?

KENT No, my lord.

FOOL Ha, ha, he wears cruel garters. Horses are tied by the heads, dogs and bears by th' neck, monkeys by th' loins, and men by th' legs. When a man's over-
10 lusty at legs, then he wears wooden netherstocks.

LEAR What's he that hath so much thy place mistook
To set thee here?

KENT It is both he and she,
Your son and daughter.

LEAR No.

15 KENT Yes.

LEAR No, I say.

KENT I say yea.

II.iv. 3 **purpose** intention 4 **remove** 6 **Mak'st . . . pastime** i.e., are you doing this to amuse yourself 7 **cruel** (1) painful (2) "crewel," a worsted yarn used in garters 9–10 **overlusty at legs** (1) a vagabond (2) ? sexually promiscuous 10 **netherstocks** stockings (as opposed to knee breeches or upperstocks)

LEAR No, no, they would not.

KENT Yes, they have.

LEAR By Jupiter, I swear no! 20

KENT By Juno, I swear ay!

LEAR They durst not do't;
They could not, would not do't. 'Tis worse than murder
To do upon respect such violent outrage.
Resolve me with all modest haste which way
Thou mightst deserve or they impose this usage, 25
Coming from us.

KENT My lord, when at their home
I did commend your Highness' letters to them,
Ere I was risen from the place that showed
My duty kneeling, came there a reeking post,
Stewed in his haste, half breathless, panting forth 30
From Goneril his mistress salutations,
Delivered letters, spite of intermission,
Which presently they read; on whose contents
They summoned up their meiny, straight took horse,
Commanded me to follow and attend 35
The leisure of their answer, gave me cold looks,
And meeting here the other messenger,
Whose welcome I perceived had poisoned mine,
Being the very fellow which of late
Displayed so saucily against your Highness, 40
Having more man than wit about me, drew;
He raised the house, with loud and coward cries.
Your son and daughter found this trespass worth
The shame which here it suffers.

23 upon respect (1) on the respect due to the King (2) deliberately **24 Resolve** inform **24 modest** becoming **27 commend** deliver **29 reeking post** sweating messenger **30 stewed** steaming **32 spite of intermission** in spite of the interrupting of my business **33 presently** at once **33 on** on the strength of **34 meiny** retinue **40 Displayed** showed off **41 more man than wit** more manhood than sense **42 raised** aroused **43 worth** deserving

45 FOOL Winter's not gone yet, if the wild geese fly that way.

Fathers that wear rags
Do make their children blind,
But fathers that bear bags
50 Shall see their children kind.
Fortune, that arrant whore,
Ne'er turns the key to th' poor.

But for all this, thou shalt have as many dolors for thy daughters as thou canst tell in a year.

55 LEAR O, how this mother swells up toward my heart!
Hysterica passio, down, thou climbing sorrow,
Thy element's below. Where is this daughter?

KENT With the Earl, sir, here within.

LEAR Follow me not;
Stay here. *Exit.*

GENTLEMAN Made you no more offense but what you
60 speak of?

KENT None.
How chance the King comes with so small a number?

FOOL And thou hadst been set i' th' stocks for that question, thou'dst well deserved it.

65 KENT Why, Fool?

FOOL We'll set thee to school to an ant, to teach thee there's no laboring i' th' winter. All that follow

45–46 Winter's . . . way i.e., more trouble is to come, since Cornwall and Regan act so ("geese" is used contemptuously, as in Kent's quarrel with Oswald, II.ii.85–86) **48 blind** i.e., indifferent **49 bags** moneybags **52 turns the key** i.e., opens the door **53 dolors** (1) sorrows (2) dollars (English name for Spanish and German coins) **54 tell** (1) tell about (2) count **55–56 mother . . . Hysterica passio** hysteria, causing suffocation or choking **57 element** proper place **62 How chance** how does it happen that **68 And if** **66–67 Well . . . winter** (in the popular fable the ant, unlike the improvident grasshopper, anticipates the winter when none can labor by laying up provisions in the summer. Lear, trusting foolishly to summer days, finds himself unprovided for, and unable to provide, now that "winter" has come) their noses are led by their eyes but blind men, and there's not a nose among twenty but can smell him that's stinking. Let go thy hold when a great wheel runs down a hill, lest it break thy neck with following. But the great one that goes upward, let him draw thee after. When a wise man gives thee better counsel, give me mine again. I would have none but knaves follow it since a Fool gives it. 70 75

That sir, which serves and seeks for gain,
And follows but for form,
Will pack, when it begins to rain,
And leave thee in the storm. 80
But I will tarry; the Fool will stay,
And let the wise man fly.
The knave turns Fool that runs away,
The Fool no knave, perdy.

KENT Where learned you this, Fool? 85

FOOL Not i' th' stocks, fool.

Enter Lear and Gloucester.

LEAR Deny to speak with me? They are sick, they are weary,
They have traveled all the night? Mere fetches,
The images of revolt and flying off!
Fetch me a better answer.

GLOUCESTER My dear lord, 90
You know the fiery quality of the Duke,
How unremovable and fixed he is
In his own course.

LEAR Vengeance, plague, death, confusion!
Fiery? What quality? Why, Gloucester, Gloucester, 95
I'd speak with the Duke of Cornwall and his wife.

67–70 **All . . . stinking** i.e., all can smell out the decay of Lear's fortunes 78 **form** show 79 **pack** be off 83–84 **The . . . knave** i.e., the faithless man is the true fool, for wisdom requires fidelity. Lear's Fool, who remains faithful, is at least no knave 84 **perdy** by God (Fr. par Dieu) 87 **Deny** refuse 88 **fetches** subterfuges, acts of tacking (nautical metaphor) 89 **images** exact likenesses 89 **flying off** desertion 91 **quality** temperament

GLOUCESTER Well, my good lord, I have informed them so.

LEAR Informed them? Dost thou understand me, man?

GLOUCESTER Ay, my good lord.

LEAR The King would speak with Cornwall. The dear father
Would with his daughter speak, commands—tends
100 —service.
Are they informed of this? My breath and blood!
Fiery? The fiery Duke, tell the hot Duke that—
No, but not yet. May be he is not well.
Infirmity doth still neglect all office
Whereto our health is bound. We are not
105 ourselves
When nature, being oppressed, commands the mind
To suffer with the body. I'll forbear;
And am fallen out with my more headier will
To take the indisposed and sickly fit
For the sound man. [*Looking on Kent*] Death on
110 my state! Wherefore
Should he sit here? This act persuades me
That this remotion of the Duke and her
Is practice only. Give me my servant forth.
Go tell the Duke and's wife I'd speak with them!
Now, presently! Bid them come forth and hear
115 me,
Or at their chamber door I'll beat the drum
Till it cry sleep to death.

GLOUCESTER I would have all well betwixt you.

Exit.

100 tends attends (i.e., awaits); with, possibly, an ironic second meaning, "tenders," or "offers" **105 Whereto . . . bound** duties which we are required to perform, when in health **108 fallen out** angry **108 headier will** headlong inclination **110 state** royal condition **112 remotion** (1) removal (2) remaining aloof **113 practice** pretense **113 forth** i.e., out of the stocks **115 presently** at once **117 cry . . . death** follow sleep, like a cry or pack of hounds, until it kills it

LEAR O me, my heart, my rising heart! But down!

FOOL Cry to it, Nuncle, as the cockney did to the eels when she put 'em i' th' paste alive. She knapped 'em o' th' coxcombs with a stick and cried, "Down, wantons, down!" 'Twas her brother that, in pure kindness to his horse, buttered his hay. 120 125

Enter Cornwall, Regan, Gloucester, Servants.

LEAR Good morrow to you both.

CORNWALL Hail to your Grace.

Kent here set at liberty.

REGAN I am glad to see your Highness.

LEAR Regan, I think you are. I know what reason
I have to think so. If thou shouldst not be glad,
I would divorce me from thy mother's tomb, 130
Sepulchring an adultress. [*To Kent*] O, are you
free?
Some other time for that. Beloved Regan,
Thy sister's naught. O Regan, she hath tied
Sharp-toothed unkindness, like a vulture, here.

[*Points to his heart.*]

I can scarce speak to thee. Thou'lt not believe 135
With how depraved a quality—O Regan!

REGAN I pray you, sir, take patience. I have hope
You less know how to value her desert
Than she to scant her duty.

LEAR Say? how is that?

120 **cockney** Londoner (ignorant city dweller) 121 **paste** pastry pie 122 **knapped** rapped 122 **coxcombs** heads 123 **wantons** i.e., playful things (with a sexual implication) 125 **buttered his hay** i.e., the city dweller does from ignorance what the dishonest ostler does from craft: greases the hay the traveler has paid for, so that the horse will not eat 130–31 **divorce . . . adultress** i.e., repudiate your dead mother as having conceived you by another man 133 **naught** wicked 136 **quality** nature 137–39 **I . . . duty** (despite the double negative, the passage means, "I believe that you fail to give Goneril her due, rather than that she fails to fulfill her duty")

140 REGAN I cannot think my sister in the least
Would fail her obligation. If, sir, perchance
She have restrained the riots of your followers,
'Tis on such ground, and to such wholesome end,
As clears her from all blame.

LEAR My curses on her!

145 REGAN O, sir, you are old,
Nature in you stands on the very verge
Of his confine. You should be ruled, and led
By some discretion that discerns your state
Better than you yourself. Therefore I pray you
150 That to our sister you do make return,
Say you have wronged her.

LEAR Ask her forgiveness?
Do you but mark how this becomes the house:
"Dear daughter, I confess that I am old.

[*Kneeling*.]

Age is unnecessary. On my knees I beg
155 That you'll vouchsafe me raiment, bed, and food."

REGAN Good sir, no more. These are unsightly tricks.
Return you to my sister.

LEAR [*Rising*] Never, Regan.
She hath abated me of half my train,
Looked black upon me, struck me with her tongue,
160 Most serpentlike, upon the very heart.
All the stored vengeances of heaven fall
On her ingrateful top! Strike her young bones,
You taking airs, with lameness.

CORNWALL Fie, sir, fie!

LEAR You nimble lightnings, dart your blinding flames
165 Into her scornful eyes! Infect her beauty,

146–47 **Nature . . . confine** i.e., you are nearing the end of your life 148–49 **some . . . yourself** some discreet person who understands your condition more than you do 152 **becomes the house** suits my royal and paternal position 158 **abated** curtailed 162 **top** head 162 **young bones** (the reference may be to unborn children, rather than to Goneril herself) 163 **taking** infecting

You fen-sucked fogs, drawn by the pow'rful sun,
To fall and blister her pride.

REGAN O the blest gods!
So will you wish on me when the rash mood is on.

LEAR No, Regan, thou shalt never have my curse.
Thy tender-hefted nature shall not give 170
Thee o'er to harshness. Her eyes are fierce, but thine
Do comfort, and not burn. 'Tis not in thee
To grudge my pleasures, to cut off my train,
To bandy hasty words, to scant my sizes,
And, in conclusion, to oppose the bolt 175
Against my coming in. Thou better know'st
The offices of nature, bond of childhood,
Effects of courtesy, dues of gratitude.
Thy half o' th' kingdom hast thou not forgot,
Wherein I thee endowed.

REGAN Good sir, to th' purpose. 180

Tucket within.

LEAR Who put my man i' th' stocks?

CORNWALL What trumpet's that?

REGAN I know't—my sister's. This approves her letter,
That she would soon be here.

Enter Oswald.

Is your lady come?

LEAR This is a slave, whose easy borrowed pride
Dwells in the fickle grace of her he follows. 185
Out, varlet, from my sight.

CORNWALL What means your Grace?

166 **fen-sucked** drawn up from swamps by the sun 167 **fall and blister** fall upon and raise blisters 170 **tender-hefted** gently framed 174 **bandy** volley (metaphor from tennis) 174 **scant my sizes** reduce my allowances 175 **oppose the bolt** i.e., bar the door 177 **offices . . . childhood** natural duties, a child's duty to its parent 178 **Effects** manifestations 180 **to th' purpose** come to the point 182 **approves** confirms 184 **easy borrowed** (1) facile and taken from another (2) acquired without anything to back it up (like money borrowed without security) 185 **grace** favor 186 **varlet** base fellow

LEAR Who stocked my servant? Regan, I have good hope
Thou didst not know on't.

Enter Goneril.

Who comes here? O heavens!
If you do love old men, if your sweet sway
190 Allow obedience, if you yourselves are old,
Make it your cause. Send down, and take my part.
[*To Goneril*] Art not ashamed to look upon this beard?
O Regan, will you take her by the hand?

GONERIL Why not by th' hand, sir? How have I offended?
195 All's not offense that indiscretion finds
And dotage terms so.

LEAR O sides, you are too tough!
Will you yet hold? How came my man i' th' stocks?

CORNWALL I set him there, sir; but his own disorders
Deserved much less advancement.

LEAR You? Did you?

200 REGAN I pray you, father, being weak, seem so.
If till the expiration of your month
You will return and sojourn with my sister,
Dismissing half your train, come then to me.
I am now from home, and out of that provision
205 Which shall be needful for your entertainment.

LEAR Return to her, and fifty men dismissed?
No, rather I abjure all roofs, and choose
To wage against the enmity o' th' air,
To be a comrade with the wolf and owl,
210 Necessity's sharp pinch. Return with her?
Why, the hot-blooded France, that dowerless took

190 **Allow** approve of 191 **it** i.e., my cause 195 **finds** judges 196 **sides** breast 198 **disorders** misconduct 199 **advancement** promotion 200 **seem so** i.e., act weak 205 **entertainment** maintenance 208 **wage** fight 210 **Necessity's sharp pinch** (a summing up of the hard choice he has just announced) 211 **hot-blooded** passionate

Our youngest born, I could as well be brought
To knee his throne, and, squirelike, pension beg
To keep base life afoot. Return with her?
Persuade me rather to be slave and sumpter 215
To this detested groom. [*Pointing at Oswald.*]

GONERIL At your choice, sir.

LEAR I prithee, daughter, do not make me mad.
I will not trouble thee, my child; farewell.
We'll no more meet, no more see one another.
But yet thou art my flesh, my blood, my daughter, 220
Or rather a disease that's in my flesh,
Which I must needs call mine. Thou art a boil,
A plague-sore, or embossèd carbuncle
In my corrupted blood. But I'll not chide thee.
Let shame come when it will, I do not call it. 225
I do not bid the Thunder-bearer shoot,
Nor tell tales of thee to high-judging Jove.
Mend when thou canst, be better at thy leisure,
I can be patient, I can stay with Regan,
I and my hundred knights.

REGAN Not altogether so. 230
I looked not for you yet, nor am provided
For your fit welcome. Give ear, sir, to my sister,
For those that mingle reason with your passion
Must be content to think you old, and so—
But she knows what she does.

LEAR Is this well spoken? 235

REGAN I dare avouch it, sir. What, fifty followers?
Is it not well? What should you need of more?
Yea, or so many, sith that both charge and
danger
Speak 'gainst so great a number? How in one house

213 knee kneel before **213 squirelike** like a retainer **215 sumpter** pack horse **223 embossèd carbuncle** swollen boil **226 Thunder-bearer** i.e., Jupiter **227 high-judging** (1) supreme (2) judging from heaven **233 mingle . . . passion** i.e., consider your turbulent behavior coolly and reasonably **236 avouch** swear by **238 sith that** since **238 charge** expense

240 Should many people, under two commands,
Hold amity? 'Tis hard, almost impossible.

GONERIL Why might not you, my lord, receive attendance
From those that she calls servants, or from mine?

REGAN Why not, my lord? If then they chanced to slack ye,
245 We could control them. If you will come to me
(For now I spy a danger), I entreat you
To bring but five-and-twenty. To no more
Will I give place or notice.

LEAR I gave you all.

REGAN And in good time you gave it.

250 LEAR Made you my guardians, my depositaries,
But kept a reservation to be followed
With such a number. What, must I come to you
With five-and-twenty? Regan, said you so?

REGAN And speak't again, my lord. No more with me.

LEAR Those wicked creatures yet do look well-
255 favored
When others are more wicked; not being the worst
Stands in some rank of praise. [*To Goneril*] I'll go with thee.
Thy fifty yet doth double five-and-twenty,
And thou art twice her love.

GONERIL Hear me, my lord.
260 What need you five-and-twenty? ten? or five?
To follow in a house where twice so many
Have a command to tend you?

REGAN What need one?

LEAR O reason not the need! Our basest beggars

241 hold preserve **244 slack** neglect **248 notice** recognition **250 depositaries** trustees **251 reservation** condition **255 well-favored** handsome **256–57 not . . . praise** i.e., that Goneril is not so bad as Regan is one thing in her favor **259 her love** i.e., as loving as she **261 follow** attend on you **263 reason** scrutinize

Are in the poorest thing superfluous.
Allow not nature more than nature needs, 265
Man's life is cheap as beast's. Thou art a lady:
If only to go warm were gorgeous,
Why, nature needs not what thou gorgeous wear'st,
Which scarcely keeps thee warm. But, for true
need—
You heavens, give me that patience, patience I
need. 270
You see me here, you gods, a poor old man,
As full of grief as age, wretched in both.
If it be you that stirs these daughters' hearts
Against their father, fool me not so much
To bear it tamely; touch me with noble anger, 275
And let not women's weapons, water drops,
Stain my man's cheeks. No, you unnatural hags!
I will have such revenges on you both
That all the world shall—I will do such things—
What they are, yet I know not; but they shall be 280
The terrors of the earth. You think I'll weep.
No, I'll not weep.

Storm and tempest.

I have full cause of weeping, but this heart
Shall break into a hundred thousand flaws
Or ere I'll weep. O Fool, I shall go mad! 285

Exeunt Lear, Gloucester, Kent, and Fool.

CORNWALL Let us withdraw, 'twill be a storm.

REGAN This house is little; the old man and's people
Cannot be well bestowed.

GONERIL 'Tis his own blame; hath put himself from
rest
And must needs taste his folly. 290

264 Are . . . superfluous i.e., have some trifle not absolutely necessary **265 needs** i.e., to sustain life **267–69 If . . . warm** i.e., if to satisfy the need for warmth were to be gorgeous, you would not need the clothing you wear, which is worn more for beauty than warmth **274 fool** humiliate **275 To bear** as to make me bear **284 flaws** (1) pieces (2) cracks (3) gusts of passion **285 Or ere** before **288 bestowed** lodged **289 hath** he hath **289 rest** (1) place of residence (2) repose of mind

REGAN For his particular, I'll receive him gladly,
But not one follower.

GONERIL So am I purposed.
Where is my Lord of Gloucester?

CORNWALL Followed the old man forth.

Enter Gloucester.

He is returned.

GLOUCESTER The King is in high rage.

295 CORNWALL Whither is he going?

GLOUCESTER He calls to horse, but will I know not whither.

CORNWALL 'Tis best to give him way, he leads himself.

GONERIL My lord, entreat him by no means to stay.

GLOUCESTER Alack, the night comes on, and the high winds

300 Do sorely ruffle. For many miles about
There's scarce a bush.

REGAN O, sir, to willful men
The injuries that they themselves procure
Must be their schoolmasters. Shut up your doors.
He is attended with a desperate train,
305 And what they may incense him to, being apt
To have his ear abused, wisdom bids fear.

CORNWALL Shut up your doors, my lord; 'tis a wild night.
My Regan counsels well. Come out o' th' storm.

Exeunt.

291 his particular himself personally **292 purposed** determined **297 give . . . himself** let him go; he insists on his own way **300 ruffle** rage **305 incense** incite **305–06 being . . . abused** he being inclined to harken to bad counsel

ACT III

Scene I. [*A heath.*]

Storm still. Enter Kent and a Gentleman severally.

KENT Who's there besides foul weather?

GENTLEMAN One minded like the weather most unquietly.

KENT I know you. Where's the King?

GENTLEMAN Contending with the fretful elements;
Bids the wind blow the earth into the sea, 5
Or swell the curlèd waters 'bove the main,
That things might change, or cease; tears his white hair,
Which the impetuous blasts, with eyeless rage,
Catch in their fury, and make nothing of;
Strives in his little world of man to outscorn 10
The to-and-fro-conflicting wind and rain.
This night, wherein the cub-drawn bear would couch,
The lion, and the belly-pinchèd wolf
Keep their fur dry, unbonneted he runs,

III.i.s.d **still** continually 2 **minded . . . unquietly** disturbed in mind, like the weather 6 **main** land 7 **change** (1) be destroyed (2) be exchanged (i.e., turned upside down) (3) change for the better 8 **eyeless** (1) blind (2) invisible 10 **little world of man** (the microcosm, as opposed to the universe or macrocosm, which it copies in little) 12 **cub-drawn** sucked dry by her cubs, and so ravenously hungry 12 **couch** take shelter in its lair 13 **belly-pinchèd** starved 14 **unbonneted** hatless

And bids what will take all.

15 KENT But who is with him?

GENTLEMAN None but the Fool, who labors to outjest
His heart-struck injuries.

KENT Sir, I do know you,
And dare upon the warrant of my note
Commend a dear thing to you. There is division,
20 Although as yet the face of it is covered
With mutual cunning, 'twixt Albany and Cornwall;
Who have—as who have not, that their great stars
Throned and set high?—servants, who seem no less,
Which are to France the spies and speculations
25 Intelligent of our state. What hath been seen,
Either in snuffs and packings of the Dukes,
Or the hard rein which both of them hath borne
Against the old kind King, or something deeper,
Whereof, perchance, these are but furnishings—
30 But, true it is, from France there comes a power
Into this scattered kingdom, who already,
Wise in our negligence, have secret feet
In some of our best ports, and are at point
To show their open banner. Now to you:
35 If on my credit you dare build so far
To make your speed to Dover, you shall find
Some that will thank you, making just report
Of how unnatural and bemadding sorrow
The King hath cause to plain.
40 I am a gentleman of blood and breeding,

15 **take all** (like the reckless gambler, staking all he has left) 18 **warrant of my note** strength of what I have taken note (of you) 19 **Commend . . . thing** entrust important business 22 **that** whom 22–23 **stars/Throned** destinies have throned 23 **seem no less** seem to be so 24–25 **speculations/Intelligent** giving intelligence 26 **snuffs and packings** quarrels and plots 27 **hard . . . borne** close and cruel control they have exercised 29 **furnishings** excuses 30 **power** army 31 **scattered** disunited 33 **at point** ready 35 **If . . . build** if you can trust me, proceed 36 **To** as to 37 **making** for making 37 **just** accurate 38 **bemadding** maddening 39 **plain** complain of 40 **blood and breeding** noble family

And from some knowledge and assurance offer
This office to you.

GENTLEMAN I will talk further with you.

KENT No, do not.
For confirmation that I am much more
Than my out-wall, open this purse and take 45
What it contains. If you shall see Cordelia,
As fear not but you shall, show her this ring,
And she will tell you who that fellow is
That yet you do not know. Fie on this storm!
I will go seek the King. 50

GENTLEMAN Give me your hand. Have you no more to say?

KENT Few words, but, to effect, more than all yet:
That when we have found the King—in which your pain
That way, I'll this—he that first lights on him,
Holla the other. *Exeunt [severally].* 55

Scene II. [*Another part of the heath.*]

Storm still.

Enter Lear and Fool.

LEAR Blow, winds, and crack your cheeks. Rage, blow!
You cataracts and hurricanoes, spout
Till you have drenched our steeples, drowned the cocks.

41 **knowledge and assurance** sure and trustworthy information 42 **office** service (i.e., the trip to Dover) 45 **out-wall** superficial appearance 48 **fellow** companion 52 **to effect** in their importance 53 **pain** labor III.ii 2 **hurricanoes** waterspouts 3 **cocks** weathercocks

You sulph'rous and thought-executing fires,
5 Vaunt-couriers of oak-cleaving thunderbolts,
Singe my white head. And thou, all-shaking thunder,
Strike flat the thick rotundity o' th' world,
Crack Nature's molds, all germains spill at once,
That makes ingrateful man.

10 FOOL O Nuncle, court holy-water in a dry house is better than this rain water out o' door. Good Nuncle, in; ask thy daughters blessing. Here's a night pities neither wise man nor fools.

LEAR Rumble thy bellyful. Spit, fire. Spout, rain!
15 Nor rain, wind, thunder, fire are my daughters.
I tax not you, you elements, with unkindness.
I never gave you kingdom, called you children,
You owe me no subscription. Then let fall
Your horrible pleasure. Here I stand your slave,
20 A poor, infirm, weak, and despised old man.
But yet I call you servile ministers,
That will with two pernicious daughters join
Your high-engendered battles 'gainst a head
So old and white as this. O, ho! 'tis foul.

25 FOOL He that has a house to put 's head in has a good headpiece.

The codpiece that will house
Before the head has any,
The head and he shall louse:
30 So beggars marry many.
The man that makes his toe

4 **thought-executing** (1) doing execution as quick as thought (2) executing or carrying out the thought of him who hurls the lightning 5 **Vaunt-couriers** heralds, scouts who range before the main body of the army 7 **rotundity** i.e., not only the sphere of the globe, but the roundness of gestation (Delius) 8 **Nature's molds** the molds or forms in which men are made 8 **all germains spill** destroy the basic seeds of life 9 **ingrateful** ungrateful 10 **court holy-water** flattery 16 **tax** accuse 18 **subscription** allegiance, submission 19 **pleasure** will 21 **ministers** agents 23 **high-engendered battles** armies formed in the heavens 26 **headpiece** (1) helmet (2) brain 27 **codpiece** penis (lit., padding worn at the crotch of a man's hose) 29 **he** it 30 **many** i.e., lice 27-30 **The . . . many** i.e., the man who gratifies his sexual appetites before he has a roof over his head will end up a lousy beggar

What he his heart should make
Shall of a corn cry woe,
And turn his sleep to wake.
For there was never yet fair woman but she made mouths in a glass. 35

Enter Kent.

LEAR No, I will be the pattern of all patience,
I will say nothing.

KENT Who's there?

FOOL Marry, here's grace and a codpiece; that's a wise man and a fool. 40

KENT Alas, sir, are you here? Things that love night
Love not such nights as these. The wrathful skies
Gallow the very wanderers of the dark
And make them keep their caves. Since I was man, 45
Such sheets of fire, such bursts of horrid thunder,
Such groans of roaring wind and rain, I never
Remember to have heard. Man's nature cannot carry
Th' affliction nor the fear.

LEAR Let the great gods
That keep this dreadful pudder o'er our heads 50
Find out their enemies now. Tremble, thou wretch,
That hast within thee undivulgèd crimes
Unwhipped of justice. Hide thee, thou bloody hand,
Thou perjured, and thou simular of virtue

31–34 **The . . . wake** i.e., the man who, ignoring the fit order of things, elevates what is base above what is noble, will suffer for it as Lear has, in banishing Cordelia and enriching her sisters 35–36 **made mouths in a glass** posed before a mirror (irrelevant nonsense, except that it calls to mind the general theme of vanity and folly) 40 **Marry** by the Virgin Mary 40–41 **here's . . . fool** (Kent's question is answered: The King ("grace") is here, and the Fool—who customarily wears an exaggerated codpiece. But which is which is left ambiguous, since Lear has previously been called a codpiece) 44 **Gallow** frighten 45 **keep** remain inside 46 **horrid** horrible 48 **carry** endure 50 **pudder** turmoil 51 **Find . . . now** i.e., discover sinners by the terror they reveal 54 **perjured** perjurer 54 **simular** counterfeiter

55 That art incestuous. Caitiff, to pieces shake,
That under covert and convenient seeming
Has practiced on man's life. Close pent-up guilts,
Rive your concealing continents and cry
These dreadful summoners grace. I am a man
More sinned against than sinning.

60 KENT Alack, bareheaded?
Gracious my lord, hard by here is a hovel;
Some friendship will it lend you 'gainst the
tempest.
Repose you there, while I to this hard house
(More harder than the stones whereof 'tis raised,
65 Which even but now, demanding after you,
Denied me to come in) return, and force
Their scanted courtesy.

LEAR My wits begin to turn.
Come on, my boy. How dost, my boy? Art cold?
I am cold myself. Where is this straw, my fellow?
70 The art of our necessities is strange,
That can make vile things precious. Come, your
hovel.
Poor Fool and knave, I have one part in my heart
That's sorry yet for thee.

FOOL [*Singing*]
He that has and a little tiny wit,
75 With heigh-ho, the wind and the rain,
Must make content with his fortunes fit,
Though the rain it raineth every day.

LEAR True, my good boy. Come, bring us to this hovel.
Exit [*with Kent*].

55 **Caitiff** wretch 56 **seeming** hypocrisy 57 **practiced on** plotted against 57 **Close** hidden 58 **Rive** split open 58 **continents** containers 58–59 **cry . . . grace** beg mercy from the vengeful gods (here figured as officers who summoned a man charged with immorality before the ecclesiastical court) 61 **Gracious my lord** my gracious lord 65 **demanding after** asking for 67 **scanted** stinted 70 **art** magic powers of the alchemists, who sought to transmute base metals into precious 76 **Must . . . fit** must be satisfied with a fortune as tiny as his wit

FOOL This is a brave night to cool a courtesan. I'll speak a prophecy ere I go: 80

When priests are more in word than matter;
When brewers mar their malt with water;
When nobles are their tailors' tutors,
No heretics burned, but wenches' suitors;
When every case in law is right, 85
No squire in debt nor no poor knight;
When slanders do not live in tongues;
Nor cutpurses come not to throngs;
When usurers tell their gold i' th' field,
And bawds and whores do churches build, 90
Then shall the realm of Albion
Come to great confusion.
Then comes the time, who lives to see't,
That going shall be used with feet.

This prophecy Merlin shall make, for I live before 95
his time. *Exit.*

Scene III. [*Gloucester's castle.*]

Enter Gloucester and Edmund.

GLOUCESTER Alack, alack, Edmund, I like not this unnatural dealing. When I desired their leave that I might pity him, they took from me the use of mine

79 brave fine **81–84 When ... suitors** (the first four prophecies are fulfilled already, and hence "confusion" has come to England. The priest does not suit his action to his words. The brewer adulterates his beer. The nobleman is subservient to his tailor [i.e., cares only for fashion]. Religious heretics escape, and only those burn [i.e., suffer] who are afflicted with venereal disease) **89 tell ... field** count their money in the open **85–90 When ... build** (the last six prophecies, as they are Utopian, are meant ironically. They will never be fulfilled) **91 Albion** England **94 going ... feet** people will walk on their feet **95 Merlin** King Arthur's great magician who, according to Holinshed's *Chronicles*, lived later than Lear
II.iii. **3 pity** show pity to

own house, charged me on pain of perpetual dis-
5 pleasure neither to speak of him, entreat for him, or any way sustain him.

EDMUND Most savage and unnatural.

GLOUCESTER Go to; say you nothing. There is division between the Dukes, and a worse matter than that.
10 I have received a letter this night—'tis dangerous to be spoken—I have locked the letter in my closet. These injuries the King now bears will be revenged home; there is part of a power already footed; we must incline to the King. I will look
15 him and privily relieve him. Go you and maintain talk with the Duke, that my charity be not of him perceived. If he ask for me, I am ill and gone to bed. If I die for it, as no less is threatened me, the King my old master must be relieved. There is
20 strange things toward, Edmund; pray you be careful. *Exit.*

EDMUND This courtesy forbid thee shall the Duke
Instantly know, and of that letter too.
This seems a fair deserving, and must draw me
25 That which my father loses—no less than all.
The younger rises when the old doth fall.

Exit.

III.iii. 6 sustain care for **8 division** falling out **9 worse** more serious (i.e., the French invasion) **11 spoken** spoken of **12 closet** room **13 home** to the utmost **13 power** army **14 footed** landed **14 incline** to take the side of **14 look** search for **15 privily** secretly **16 of** by **20 toward** impending **22 courtesy forbid** kindness forbidden (i.e., to Lear) **24 fair deserving** an action deserving reward

Scene IV. [*The heath. Before a hovel.*]

Enter Lear, Kent, and Fool.

KENT Here is the place, my lord. Good my lord, enter.
The tyranny of the open night's too rough
For nature to endure.

Storm still.

LEAR Let me alone.

KENT Good my lord, enter here.

LEAR Wilt break my heart?

KENT I had rather break mine own. Good my lord, enter. 5

LEAR Thou think'st 'tis much that this contentious storm
Invades us to the skin: so 'tis to thee;
But where the greater malady is fixed,
The lesser is scarce felt. Thou'dst shun a bear;
But if thy flight lay toward the roaring sea, 10
Thou'dst meet the bear i' th' mouth. When the mind's free,
The body's delicate. The tempest in my mind
Doth from my senses take all feeling else,
Save what beats there. Filial ingratitude,
Is it not as this mouth should tear this hand 15
For lifting food to't? But I will punish home.
No, I will weep no more. In such a night
To shut me out! Pour on, I will endure.

III.iv 4 **break my heart** i.e., by shutting out the storm which distracts me from thinking 8 **fixed** lodged (in the mind) 11 **i' th' mouth** in the teeth 11 **free** i.e., from care 15 **as** as if 16 **home** to the utmost

In such a night as this! O Regan, Goneril,
Your old kind father, whose frank heart gave
20 all—
O, that way madness lies; let me shun that.
No more of that.

KENT Good my lord, enter here.

LEAR Prithee go in thyself; seek thine own ease.
This tempest will not give me leave to ponder
25 On things would hurt me more, but I'll go in.
[*To the Fool*] In, boy; go first. You houseless
poverty—
Nay, get thee in. I'll pray, and then I'll sleep.
Exit [*Fool*].
Poor naked wretches, wheresoe'er you are,
That bide the pelting of this pitiless storm,
30 How shall your houseless heads and unfed sides,
Your looped and windowed raggedness, defend
you
From seasons such as these? O, I have ta'en
Too little care of this! Take physic, pomp;
Expose thyself to feel what wretches feel,
35 That thou mayst shake the superflux to them,
And show the heavens more just.

EDGAR [*Within*] Fathom and half, fathom and half!
Poor Tom!

Enter Fool.

FOOL Come not in here, Nuncle, here's a spirit. Help
40 me, help me!

KENT Give me thy hand. Who's there?

FOOL A spirit, a spirit. He says his name's Poor Tom.

KENT What art thou that dost grumble there i' th'
straw?
Come forth.

20 **frank** liberal (magnanimous) 26 **houseless poverty** (the unsheltered poor, abstracted) 29 **bide** endure 31 **looped and windowed** full of holes 33 **Take physic, pomp** take medicine to cure yourselves, you great men 35 **superflux** superfluity 37 **Fathom and half** (Edgar, because of the downpour, pretends to take soundings)

Enter Edgar [disguised as a madman].

EDGAR Away! the foul fiend follows me. Through the sharp hawthorn blows the cold wind. Humh! Go to thy cold bed, and warm thee. 45

LEAR Didst thou give all to thy daughters? And art thou come to this?

EDGAR Who gives anything to Poor Tom? Whom the foul fiend hath led through fire and through flame, through ford and whirlpool, o'er bog and quagmire; that hath laid knives under his pillow and halters in his pew, set ratsbane by his porridge, made him proud of heart, to ride on a bay trotting horse over four-inched bridges, to course his own shadow for a traitor. Bless thy five wits, Tom's a-cold. O, do, de, do, de, do, de. Bless thee from whirlwinds, star-blasting, and taking. Do Poor Tom some charity, whom the foul fiend vexes. There could I have him now—and there—and there again—and there. 50 55 60

Storm still.

LEAR What, has his daughters brought him to this pass?
Couldst thou save nothing? Wouldst thou give 'em all?

FOOL Nay, he reserved a blanket, else we had been all shamed. 65

LEAR Now all the plagues that in the pendulous air
Hang fated o'er men's faults light on thy daughters!

45–46 **Through . . . wind** (a line from the ballad of "The Friar of Orders Gray") 46–47 **go . . . thee** (a reminiscence of *The Taming of the Shrew*, Induction, 1.10) 53–54 **knives . . . halters . . . ratsbane** (the fiend tempts Poor Tom to suicide) 54 **pew** gallery or balcony outside a window 54 **porridge** broth 55–56 **ride . . . bridges** i.e., risk his life 56 **course** chase 57 **for** as 57 **five wits** i.e., common wit, imagination, fantasy, estimation, memory 59 **star-blasting** the evil caused by malignant stars 59 **taking** pernicious influences 63 **pass** wretched condition 65 **blanket** i.e., to cover his nakedness 67 **pendulous** overhanging 68 **fated o'er** destined to punish

KENT He hath no daughters, sir.

LEAR Death, traitor; nothing could have subdued
70 nature
To such a lowness but his unkind daughters.
Is it the fashion that discarded fathers
Should have thus little mercy on their flesh?
Judicious punishment—'twas this flesh begot
75 Those pelican daughters.

EDGAR Pillicock sat on Pillicock Hill. Alow, alow, loo, loo!

FOOL This cold night will turn us all to fools and madmen.

80 EDGAR Take heed o' th' foul fiend; obey thy parents; keep thy word's justice; swear not; commit not with man's sworn spouse; set not thy sweet heart on proud array. Tom's a-cold.

LEAR What hast thou been?

85 EDGAR A servingman, proud in heart and mind; that curled my hair, wore gloves in my cap; served the lust of my mistress' heart, and did the act of darkness with her; swore as many oaths as I spake words, and broke them in the sweet face of 90 heaven. One that slept in the contriving of lust, and waked to do it. Wine loved I deeply, dice dearly; and in woman out-paramoured the Turk. False of heart, light of ear, bloody of hand; hog in sloth, fox in stealth, wolf in greediness, dog in 95 madness, lion in prey. Let not the creaking of shoes nor the rustling of silks betray thy poor

70 **subdued** reduced 73 **on** i.e., shown to 75 **pelican** (supposed to feed on its parent's blood) 76 **Pillicock . . . Hill** (probably quoted from a nursery rhyme, and suggested by "pelican." **Pillicock** is a term of endearment and the phallus) 76–77 **Alow . . . loo** (? a hunting call, or the refrain of the song) 81 **keep . . . justice** i.e., do not break thy word 81 **commit not** i.e., adultery 86 **gloves in my cap** i.e., as a pledge from his mistress 92 **out-paramoured the Turk** had more concubines than the Sultan 93 **light of ear** ready to hear flattery and slander 95 **prey** preying 95 **creaking** (deliberately cultivated, as fashionable)

heart to woman. Keep thy foot out of brothels, thy hand out of plackets, thy pen from lenders' books, and defy the foul fiend. Still through the hawthorn blows the cold wind; says suum, mun, nonny Dolphin my boy, boy, sessa! let him trot by. 100

Storm still.

LEAR Thou wert better in a grave than to answer with thy uncovered body this extremity of the skies. Is man no more than this? Consider him well. Thou ow'st the worm no silk, the beast no hide, the sheep no wool, the cat no perfume. Ha! here's three on's are sophisticated. Thou art the thing itself; unaccommodated man is no more but such a poor, bare, forked animal as thou art. Off, off, you lendings! Come, unbutton here. 105 110

[*Tearing off his clothes.*]

FOOL Prithee, Nuncle, be contented, 'tis a naughty night to swim in. Now a little fire in a wild field were like an old lecher's heart—a small spark, all the rest on's body, cold. Look, here comes a walking fire. 115

Enter Gloucester, with a torch.

EDGAR This is the foul fiend Flibbertigibbet. He begins at curfew, and walks till the first cock. He gives the web and the pin, squints the eye, and makes the harelip; mildews the white wheat, and hurts the poor creature of earth. 120

98 plackets openings in skirts **98–99 pen . . . books** i.e., do not enter your name in the moneylender's account book **100–01 suum, mun, nonny** the noise of the wind **101 Dolphin** the French Dauphin (identified by the English with the devil. Poor Tom is presumably quoting from a ballad) **101 sessa** an interjection: "Go on!" **103 answer** confront, bear the brunt of **104 extremity** extreme severity **106 ow'st** have taken from **107 cat** civet cat, whose glands yield perfume **108 on's** of us **108 sophisticated** adulterated, made artificial **109 unaccommodated** uncivilized **110 forked** i.e., two-legged **111 lendings** borrowed garments **112 naughty** wicked **113 wild** barren **117 Flibbertigibbet** (a figure from Elizabethan demonology **118 curfew**: 9 p.m. **118 first cock** midnight **119 web and the pin** cataract **119 squints** crosses **120 white** ripening

Swithold footed thrice the old;
He met the nightmare, and her nine fold;
Bid her alight
125 And her troth plight,
And aroint thee, witch, aroint thee!

KENT How fares your Grace?

LEAR What's he?

KENT Who's there? What is't you seek?

130 GLOUCESTER What are you there? Your names?

EDGAR Poor Tom, that eats the swimming frog, the toad, the todpole, the wall-newt and the water; that in the fury of his heart, when the foul fiend rages, eats cow-dung for sallets, swallows the old
135 rat and the ditch-dog, drinks the green mantle of the standing pool; who is whipped from tithing to tithing, and stocked, punished, and imprisoned; who hath had three suits to his back, six shirts to his body,
140 Horse to ride, and weapon to wear,
But mice and rats, and such small deer,
Have been Tom's food for seven long year.
Beware my follower! Peace, Smulkin, peace, thou fiend!

GLOUCESTER What, hath your Grace no better com-
145 pany?

EDGAR The Prince of Darkness is a gentleman.
Modo he's called, and Mahu.

122 Swithold . . . old Withold (an Anglo-Saxon saint who subdued demons) walked three times across the open country **123 nightmare** demon **123 fold** offspring **124 alight** i.e., from the horse she had possessed **125 her troth plight** pledge her word **126 aroint** be gone **132 todpole . . . water** tadpole, wall lizard, water newt **134 sallets** salads **135 ditch-dog** dead dog in a ditch **135 mantle** scum **136 standing** stagnant **136 tithing** a district comprising ten families **141–42 But . . . year** (adapted from a popular romance, "Bevis of Hampton") **141 deer** game **143 follower** familiar **143, 147 Smulkin, Modo, Mahu** (Elizabethan devils, from Samuel Harsnett's *Declaration* of 1603)

GLOUCESTER Our flesh and blood, my Lord, is grown so vile
That it doth hate what gets it.

EDGAR Poor Tom's a-cold. 150

GLOUCESTER Go in with me. My duty cannot suffer
T' obey in all your daughters' hard commands.
Though their injunction be to bar my doors
And let this tyrannous night take hold upon you,
Yet have I ventured to come seek you out, 155
And bring you where both fire and food is ready.

LEAR First let me talk with this philosopher.
What is the cause of thunder?

KENT Good my lord, take his offer; go into th' house.

LEAR I'll talk a word with this same learnèd Theban. 160
What is your study?

EDGAR How to prevent the fiend, and to kill vermin.

LEAR Let me ask you one word in private.

KENT Importune him once more to go, my lord.
His wits begin t' unsettle.

GLOUCESTER Canst thou blame him? 165

Storm still.

His daughters seek his death. Ah, that good Kent,
He said it would be thus, poor banished man!
Thou say'st the King grows mad—I'll tell thee, friend,
I am almost mad myself. I had a son,
Now outlawed from my blood; he sought my life 170
But lately, very late. I loved him, friend,
No father his son dearer. True to tell thee,
The grief hath crazed my wits. What a night's this!

149 **gets** begets 151 **suffer** permit me 160 **Theban** i.e., Greek philosopher 161 **study** particular scientific study 162 **prevent** balk 170 **outlawed from my blood** disowned and tainted, like a carbuncle in the corrupted blood 171 **late** recently

I do beseech your Grace——

LEAR O, cry you mercy, sir.

175 Noble philosopher, your company.

EDGAR Tom's a-cold.

GLOUCESTER In, fellow, there, into th' hovel; keep thee warm.

LEAR Come, let's in all.

KENT This way, my lord.

LEAR With him!
I will keep still with my philosopher.

KENT Good my lord, soothe him; let him take the
180 fellow.

GLOUCESTER Take him you on.

KENT Sirrah, come on; go along with us.

LEAR Come, good Athenian.

GLOUCESTER No words, no words! Hush.

185 EDGAR Child Rowland to the dark tower came;
His word was still, "Fie, foh, and fum,
I smell the blood of a British man." *Exeunt.*

174 **cry you mercy** I beg your pardon 180 **soothe** humor 181 **you on** with you 183 **Athenian** i.e., philosopher (like "Theban") 185 **Child . . . came** (? from a lost ballad; "child" = a candidate for knighthood; Rowland was Charlemagne's nephew, the hero of *The Song of Roland*) 186 **His . . . still** his motto was always 186–87 **Fie . . . man** (a deliberately absurd linking of the chivalric hero with the nursery tale of Jack the Giant-Killer)

Scene V. [*Gloucester's castle.*]

Enter Cornwall and Edmund.

CORNWALL I will have my revenge ere I depart his house.

EDMUND How, my lord, I may be censured, that nature thus gives way to loyalty, something fears me to think of. 5

CORNWALL I now perceive it was not altogether your brother's evil disposition made him seek his death; but a provoking merit, set a-work by a reprovable badness in himself.

EDMUND How malicious is my fortune that I must 10 repent to be just! This is the letter which he spoke of, which approves him an intelligent party to the advantages of France. O heavens, that his treason were not! or not I the detector!

CORNWALL Go with me to the Duchess. 15

EDMUND If the matter of this paper be certain, you have mighty business in hand.

CORNWALL True or false, it hath made thee Earl of Gloucester. Seek out where thy father is, that he may be ready for our apprehension. 20

EDMUND [*Aside.*] If I find him comforting the King, it will stuff his suspicion more fully.—I will persever in my course of loyalty, though the conflict be sore between that and my blood.

III.v.3 **censured** judged 4 **something fears** somewhat frightens 8–9 **a provoking . . . himself** a stimulating goodness in Edgar, brought into play by a blamable badness in Gloucester 12 **approves** proves 12 **intelligent party** (1) spy (2) well-informed person 13 **to the advantages** on behalf of 20 **apprehension** arrest 21 **comforting** supporting (a legalism) 28 **persever** persevere 24 **blood** natural feelings

25 CORNWALL I will lay trust upon thee, and thou shalt find a dearer father in my love. *Exeunt.*

Scene VI. [*A chamber in a farmhouse adjoining the castle.*]

Enter Kent and Gloucester.

GLOUCESTER Here is better than the open air; take it thankfully. I will piece out the comfort with what addition I can. I will not be long from you.

KENT All the power of his wits have given way to his
5 impatience. The gods reward your kindness.

Exit [*Gloucester*].

Enter Lear, Edgar, and Fool.

EDGAR Frateretto calls me, and tells me Nero is an angler in the lake of darkness. Pray, innocent, and beware the foul fiend.

FOOL Prithee, Nuncle, tell me whether a madman be a
10 gentleman or a yeoman.

LEAR A king, a king.

FOOL No, he's a yeoman that has a gentleman to his son; for he's a mad yeoman that sees his son a gentleman before him.

15 LEAR To have a thousand with red burning spits
Come hizzing in upon 'em—

25 lay trust upon (1) trust (2) advance **III.vi.5 impatience** raging **6 Frateretto** Elizabethan devil, from Harsnett's *Declaration* **6 Nero** (who is mentioned by Harsnett, and whose angling is reported by Chaucer in "The Monk's Tale") **7 innocent** fool **10 yeoman** farmer (just below a gentleman in rank. The Fool asks what class of man has most indulged his children, and thus been driven mad) **16 hizzing** hissing

EDGAR The foul fiend bites my back.

FOOL He's mad that trusts in the tameness of a wolf, a horse's health, a boy's love, or a whore's oath.

LEAR It shall be done; I will arraign them straight. 20
[*To Edgar*] Come, sit thou here, most learned justice.
[*To the Fool*] Thou, sapient sir, sit here. Now, you she-foxes——

EDGAR Look, where he stands and glares. Want'st thou eyes at trial, madam?
Come o'er the bourn, Bessy, to me. 25

FOOL Her boat hath a leak,
And she must not speak
Why she dares not come over to thee.

EDGAR The foul fiend haunts Poor Tom in the voice of a nightingale. Hoppedance cries in Tom's belly 30 for two white herring. Croak not, black angel; I have no food for thee.

KENT How do you, sir? Stand you not so amazed.
Will you lie down and rest upon the cushions?

LEAR I'll see their trial first. Bring in their evidence. 35
[*To Edgar*] Thou, robèd man of justice, take thy place.
[*To the Fool*] And thou, his yokefellow of equity,
Bench by his side. [*To Kent*] You are o' th' commission;
Sit you too.

EDGAR Let us deal justly. 40

20 **arraign** bring to trial 20 **straight** straightaway 21 **justice** justicer, judge 22 **sapient** wise 23 **he** i.e., a fiend 23–24 **Want'st . . . madam** (to Goneril) i.e., do you want eyes to look at you during your trial? The fiend serves that purpose 25 **bourn** brook (Edgar quotes from a popular ballad) 26–28 **Her . . . thee** (the Fool parodies the ballad) 30 **nightingale** i.e., the Fool's singing 30 **Hoppedance** Hoberdidance (another devil from Harsnett's *Declaration*) 31 **white herring** unsmoked (? as against the black and sulfurous devil) 31 **Croak** rumble (because his belly is empty) 33 **amazed** astonished 35 **evidence** the evidence of witnesses against them 37 **yokefellow of equity** partner in justice 38 **Bench** sit on the bench 38 **commission** those commissioned as king's justices

Sleepest or wakest thou, jolly shepherd?
Thy sheep be in the corn;
And for one blast of thy minikin mouth
Thy sheep shall take no harm.
45 Purr, the cat is gray.

LEAR Arraign her first. 'Tis Goneril, I here take my oath before this honorable assembly, she kicked the poor King her father.

FOOL Come hither, mistress. Is your name Goneril?

50 LEAR She cannot deny it.

FOOL Cry you mercy, I took you for a joint stool.

LEAR And here's another, whose warped looks proclaim
What store her heart is made on. Stop her there!
Arms, arms, sword, fire! Corruption in the place!
55 False justicer, why hast thou let her 'scape?

EDGAR Bless thy five wits!

KENT O pity! Sir, where is the patience now
That you so oft have boasted to retain?

EDGAR [*Aside*] My tears begin to take his part so much
60 They mar my counterfeiting.

LEAR The little dogs and all,
Tray, Blanch, and Sweetheart—see, they bark at me.

EDGAR Tom will throw his head at them. Avaunt, you curs.
Be thy mouth or black or white,

41–44 **Sleepest . . . harm** (probably quoted or adapted from an Elizabethan song) 42 **corn** wheat 43 **minikin** shrill 45 **gray** (devils were thought to assume the shape of a gray cat) 51 **Cry . . . joint stool** (proverbial and deliberately impudent apology for overlooking a person. A joint stool was a low stool made by a joiner, perhaps here a stage property to represent Goneril and in line 52, Regan. "Joint stool" can also suggest the judicial bench; hence Goneril may be identified by the Fool, ironically, with those in power, who judge) 53 **store** stuff 54 **Corruption . . . place** bribery in the court 60 **counterfeiting** i.e., feigned madness 64 **or . . . or** either . . . or

Tooth that poisons if it bite; 65
Mastiff, greyhound, mongrel grim,
Hound or spaniel, brach or lym,
Or bobtail tike, or trundle-tail—
Tom will make him weep and wail;
For, with throwing thus my head, 70
Dogs leaped the hatch, and all are fled.

Do, de, de, de. Sessa! Come, march to wakes and fairs and market towns. Poor Tom, thy horn is dry.

LEAR Then let them anatomize Regan. See what breeds 75 about her heart. Is there any cause in nature that make these hard hearts? [*To Edgar*] You, sir, I entertain for one of my hundred; only I do not like the fashion of your garments. You will say they are Persian; but let them be changed. 80

KENT Now, good my lord, lie here and rest awhile.

LEAR Make no noise, make no noise; draw the curtains.
So, so. We'll go to supper i' th' morning.

FOOL And I'll go to bed at noon.

Enter Gloucester.

GLOUCESTER Come hither, friend. Where is the King my master? 85

KENT Here, sir, but trouble him not; his wits are gone.

GLOUCESTER Good friend, I prithee take him in thy arms.

67 **brach** bitch 67 **lym** bloodhound (from the liam or leash with which he was led) 68 **bobtail ... trundle-tail** short-tailed or long-tailed cur 70 **throwing** jerking (as a hound lifts its head from the ground, the scent having been lost) 71 **leaped the hatch** leaped over the lower half of a divided door (i.e., left in a hurry) 72 **Sessa** be off 72 **wakes** feasts attending the dedication of a church 73 **horn** horn bottle which the Bedlam used in begging a drink (Edgar is suggesting that he is unable to play his role any longer) 75–76 **Then ... heart** i.e., if the Bedlam's horn is dry, let Regan, whose heart has become as hard as horn, be dissected 77 **make** (subjunctive) 78 **entertain** engage 78 **hundred** i.e., Lear's hundred knights 80 **Persian** gorgeous (ironically of Edgar's rags) 82 **curtains** (Lear imagines himself in bed) 84 **And ... noon** (the Fool's last words)

I have o'erheard a plot of death upon him.
There is a litter ready; lay him in't
And drive toward Dover, friend, where thou shalt
90 meet
Both welcome and protection. Take up thy master.
If thou shouldst dally half an hour, his life,
With thine and all that offer to defend him,
Stand in assurèd loss. Take up, take up,
95 And follow me, that will to some provision
Give thee quick conduct.

KENT Oppressèd nature sleeps.
This rest might yet have balmed thy broken
sinews,
Which, if convenience will not allow,
Stand in hard cure. [*To the Fool*] Come, help
to bear thy master.
Thou must not stay behind.

100 GLOUCESTER Come, come, away!
Exeunt [*all but Edgar*].

EDGAR When we our betters see bearing our woes,
We scarcely think our miseries our foes.
Who alone suffers suffers most i' th' mind,
Leaving free things and happy shows behind;
105 But then the mind much sufferance doth o'erskip
When grief hath mates, and bearing fellowship.
How light and portable my pain seems now,
When that which makes me bend makes the
King bow.
He childed as I fathered. Tom, away.
110 Mark the high noises, and thyself bewray
When false opinion, whose wrong thoughts defile
thee,

95 **provision** maintenance 96 **conduct** direction 97 **balmed thy broken sinews** soothed thy racked nerves 98 **convenience** fortunate occasion 99 **Stand . . . cure** will be hard to cure 102 **our foes** enemies peculiar to ourselves 104 **free** carefree 104 **shows** scenes 105 **sufferance** suffering 106 **bearing fellowship** suffering has company 107 **portable** able to be supported or endured 110 **Mark the high noises** observe the rumors of strife among those in power 110 **bewray** reveal 111 **wrong thoughts** misconceptions

In thy just proof repeals and reconciles thee.
What will hap more tonight, safe 'scape the King!
Lurk, lurk. [*Exit.*]

Scene VII. [*Gloucester's castle.*]

Enter Cornwall, Regan, Goneril, Edmund, and Servants.

CORNWALL [*To Goneril*] Post speedily to my Lord your husband; show him this letter. The army of France is landed. [*To Servants*] Seek out the traitor Gloucester. [*Exeunt some of the Servants.*]

REGAN Hang him instantly. 5

GONERIL Pluck out his eyes.

CORNWALL Leave him to my displeasure. Edmund, keep you our sister company. The revenges we are bound to take upon your traitorous father are not fit for your beholding. Advise the Duke where you 10 are going, to a most festinate preparation. We are bound to the like. Our posts shall be swift and intelligent betwixt us. Farewll, dear sister; farewell, my Lord of Gloucester.

Enter Oswald.

How now? Where's the King? 15

OSWALD My Lord of Gloucester hath conveyed him hence.

112 In ... thee on the manifesting of your innocence recalls you from outlawry and restores amity between you and your father 113 What ... more whatever else happens 114 Lurk hide III.vii.9 bound (1) forced (2) purposing to 11 festinate speedy 12 posts messengers 13 intelligent full of information 14 Lord of Gloucester i.e., Edmund, now elevated to the title

Some five or six and thirty of his knights,
Hot questrists after him, met him at gate;
Who, with some other of the lords dependants,
Are gone with him toward Dover, where they
20 boast
To have well-armèd friends.

CORNWALL Get horses for your mistress.

[*Exit Oswald.*]

GONERIL Farewell, sweet lord, and sister.

CORNWALL Edmund, farewell.

[*Exeunt Goneril and Edmund.*]

Go seek the traitor Gloucester,
Pinion him like a thief, bring him before us.

[*Exeunt other Servants.*]

25 Though well we may not pass upon his life
Without the form of justice, yet our power
Shall do a court'sy to our wrath, which men
May blame, but not control.

Enter Gloucester, brought in by two or three.

Who's there, the traitor?

REGAN Ingrateful fox, 'tis he.

30 CORNWALL Bind fast his corky arms.

GLOUCESTER What means your Graces? Good my friends, consider
You are my guests. Do me no foul play, friends.

CORNWALL Bind him, I say.

[*Servants bind him.*]

REGAN Hard, hard! O filthy traitor.

GLOUCESTER Unmerciful lady as you are, I'm none.

CORNWALL To this chair bind him. Villain, thou shalt
35 find——

18 questrists searchers **19 lords dependants** attendant lords (members of Lear's retinue) **25 pass upon** pass judgment on **27 do a court'sy to** indulge **30 corky** sapless (because old)

[*Regan plucks his beard.*]

GLOUCESTER By the kind gods, 'tis mostly ignobly done
To pluck me by the beard.

REGAN So white, and such a traitor?

GLOUCESTER Naughty lady,
These hairs which thou dost ravish from my chin
Will quicken and accuse thee. I am your host. 40
With robber's hands my hospitable favors
You should not ruffle thus. What will you do?

CORNWALL Come, sir, what letters had you late from France?

REGAN Be simple-answered, for we know the truth.

CORNWALL And what confederacy have you with the traitors 45
Late footed in the kingdom?

REGAN To whose hands you have sent the lunatic King:
Speak.

GLOUCESTER I have a letter guessingly set down,
Which came from one that's of a neutral heart,
And not from one opposed.

CORNWALL Cunning.

REGAN And false. 50

CORNWALL Where hast thou sent the King?

GLOUCESTER To Dover.

REGAN Wherefore to Dover? Wast thou not charged at peril——

CORNWALL Wherefore to Dover? Let him answer that.

35 s.d. **plucks his beard** (a deadly insult) 38 **Naughty** wicked 40 **quicken** come to life 41 **hospitable favors** face of your host 42 **ruffle** tear at violently 43 **late** recently 44 **simple-answered** straightforward in answering 48 **guessingly** without certain knowledge 53 **charged at peril** ordered under penalty

GLOUCESTER I am tied to th' stake, and I must stand
55 the course.

REGAN Wherefore to Dover?

GLOUCESTER Because I would not see thy cruel nails
Pluck out his poor old eyes; nor thy fierce sister
In his anointed flesh rash boarish fangs.
60 The sea, with such a storm as his bare head
In hell-black night endured, would have buoyed up
And quenched the stellèd fires.
Yet, poor old heart, he holp the heavens to rain.
If wolves had at thy gate howled that dearn time,
Thou shouldst have said, "Good porter, turn the
65 key."
All cruels else subscribe. But I shall see
The wingèd vengeance overtake such children.

CORNWALL See't shalt thou never. Fellows, hold the chair.
Upon these eyes of thine I'll set my foot.

GLOUCESTER He that will think to live till he be
70 old,
Give me some help.—O cruel! O you gods!

REGAN One side will mock another. Th' other too.

CORNWALL If you see vengeance——

FIRST SERVANT Hold your hand, my lord!
I have served you ever since I was a child;
75 But better service have I never done you
Than now to bid you hold.

REGAN How now, you dog?

FIRST SERVANT If you did wear a beard upon your chin,

55 **course** coursing (in which a relay of dogs baits a bull or bear tied in the pit) 59 **anointed** holy (because king) 59 **rash** strike with the tusk, like a boar 61 **buoyed** risen 62 **stellèd** (1) fixed (as opposed to the planets or wandering stars) (2) starry 63 **holp** helped 64 **dearn** dread 65 **turn the key** i.e., unlock the gate 66 **All cruels else subscribe** all cruel creatures but man are compassionate 67 **wingèd** (1) heavenly (2) swift 70 **will think** expects 72 **mock** make ridiculous (because of the contrast)

I'd shake it on this quarrel. What do you mean!

CORNWALL My villain!

Draw and fight.

FIRST SERVANT Nay, then, come on, and take the chance of anger. 80

REGAN Give me thy sword. A peasant stand up thus?

She takes a sword and runs at him behind, kills him.

FIRST SERVANT O, I am slain! my lord, you have one eye left
To see some mischief on him. O!

CORNWALL Lest it see more, prevent it. Out, vile jelly.
Where is thy luster now? 85

GLOUCESTER All dark and comfortless. Where's my son Edmund?
Edmund, enkindle all the sparks of nature
To quit this horrid act.

REGAN Out, treacherous villain,
Thou call'st on him that hates thee. It was he
That made the overture of thy treasons to us; 90
Who is too good to pity thee.

GLOUCESTER O my follies! Then Edgar was abused.
Kind gods, forgive me that, and prosper him.

REGAN Go thrust him out at gates, and let him smell
His way to Dover. *Exit [one] with Gloucester.*
How is't, my lord? How look you? 95

CORNWALL I have received a hurt. Follow me, lady.
Turn out that eyeless villain. Throw this slave
Upon the dunghill. Regan, I bleed apace.

78 **shake it** (an insult comparable to Regan's plucking of Gloucester's beard) 78 **What . . . mean** i.e., what terrible thing are you doing 79 **villain** serf (with a suggestion of the modern meaning) 83 **mischief** injury 87 **enkindle . . . nature** fan your natural feeling into flame 88 **quit** requite 90 **overture** disclosure 92 **abused** wronged 95 **How look you** how are you

Untimely comes this hurt. Give me your arm.

Exeunt.

100 SECOND SERVANT I'll never care what wickedness I do,
If this man come to good.

THIRD SERVANT If she live long,
And in the end meet the old course of death,
Women will all turn monsters.

SECOND SERVANT Let's follow the old Earl, and get the Bedlam
105 To lead him where he would. His roguish madness
Allows itself to anything.

THIRD SERVANT Go thou. I'll fetch some flax and whites of eggs
To apply to his bleeding face. Now heaven help him. [*Exeunt severally.*]

102 meet . . . death die the customary death of old age **105–6 His . . . anything** his lack of all self-control leaves him open to any suggestion

ACT IV

Scene I. [*The heath.*]

Enter Edgar.

EDGAR Yet better thus, and known to be contemned,
Than still contemned and flattered. To be worst,
The lowest and most dejected thing of fortune,
Stands still in esperance, lives not in fear:
The lamentable change is from the best, 5
The worst returns to laughter. Welcome then,
Thou unsubstantial air that I embrace!
The wretch that thou hast blown unto the worst
Owes nothing to thy blasts.

Enter Gloucester, led by an Old Man.

But who comes here?
My father, poorly led? World, world, O world! 10
But that thy strange mutations make us hate thee,
Life would not yield to age.

OLD MAN O, my good lord, I have been your tenant, and your father's tenant, these fourscore years.

GLOUCESTER Away, get thee away; good friend, be gone: 15

IV.i.1 **known to be contemned** conscious of being despised 3 **dejected** abased 4 **esperance** hope 6 **returns to laughter** changes for the better 9 **Owes** is in debt for 10 **poorly led** (1) led like a poor man, with only one attendant (2) led by a poor man 11–12 **But . . . age** we should not agree to grow old and hence die, except for the hateful mutability of life

Thy comforts can do me no good at all;
Thee they may hurt.

OLD MAN You cannot see your way.

GLOUCESTER I have no way and therefore want no eyes;
I stumbled when I saw. Full oft 'tis seen,
20 Our means secure us, and our mere defects
Prove our commodities. Oh, dear son Edgar,
The food of thy abusèd father's wrath!
Might I but live to see thee in my touch,
I'd say I had eyes again!

OLD MAN How now? Who's there?

EDGAR [*Aside*] O gods! Who is 't can say "I am at
25 the worst"?
I am worse than e'er I was.

OLD MAN 'Tis poor mad Tom.

EDGAR [*Aside*] And worse I may be yet: the worst is not
So long as we can say "This is the worst."

OLD MAN Fellow, where goest?

GLOUCESTER Is it a beggar-man?

30 OLD MAN Madman and beggar too.

GLOUCESTER He has some reason, else he could not beg.
I' th' last night's storm I such a fellow saw,
Which made me think a man a worm. My son
Came then into my mind, and yet my mind
Was then scarce friends with him. I have heard
35 more since.
As flies to wanton boys, are we to th' gods,

16 **comforts** ministrations 17 **hurt** injure 18 **want** require 20–21 **Our ... commodities** our resources make us overconfident, while our afflictions make for our advantage 22 **food** i.e., the object on which Gloucester's anger fed 22 **abusèd** deceived 23 **in** i.e., with, by means of 27–28 **the ... worst** so long as a man continues to suffer (i.e., is still alive), even greater suffering may await him 31 **reason** faculty of reasoning 36 **wanton** (1) playful (2) reckless

They kill us for their sport.

EDGAR [*Aside*] How should this be?

Bad is the trade that must play fool to sorrow,
Ang'ring itself and others. Bless thee, master!

GLOUCESTER Is that the naked fellow?

OLD MAN Ay, my lord. 40

GLOUCESTER Then, prithee, get thee gone: if for my sake
Thou wilt o'ertake us hence a mile or twain
I' th' way toward Dover, do it for ancient love,
And bring some covering for this naked soul,
Which I'll entreat to lead me.

OLD MAN Alack, sir, he is mad. 45

GLOUCESTER 'Tis the times' plague, when madmen lead the blind.
Do as I bid thee, or rather do thy pleasure;
Above the rest, be gone.

OLD MAN I'll bring him the best 'parel that I have,
Come on 't what will. *Exit.* 50

GLOUCESTER Sirrah, naked fellow——

EDGAR Poor Tom's a-cold [*Aside*] I cannot daub it further.

GLOUCESTER Come hither, fellow.

EDGAR [*Aside*] And yet I must.—Bless thy sweet eyes, they bleed. 55

GLOUCESTER Know'st thou the way to Dover?

EDGAR Both stile and gate, horse-way and footpath.
Poor Tom hath been scared out of his good wits.
Bless thee, good man's son, from the foul fiend!
Five fiends have been in Poor Tom at once; of lust, 60

37 **How should this be** i.e., how can this horror be? 39 **Ang'ring** offending 43 **ancient** (1) the love the Old Man feels, by virtue of his long tenancy (2) the love that formerly obtained between master and man 46 **times' plague** characteristic disorder of this time 47 **thy pleasure** as you like 48 **the rest** all 49 **'parel** apparel 52–53 **daub it** lay it on (figure from plastering mortar)

as Obidicut; Hobbididence, prince of dumbness; Mahu, of stealing; Modo, of murder; Flibbertigibbet, of mopping and mowing; who since possesses chambermaids and waiting-women. So,
65 bless thee, master!

GLOUCESTER Here, take this purse, thou whom the heavens' plagues
Have humbled to all strokes: that I am wretched
Makes thee the happier. Heavens, deal so still!
Let the superfluous and lust-dieted man,
70 That slaves your ordinance, that will not see
Because he does not feel, feel your pow'r quickly;
So distribution should undo excess,
And each man have enough. Dost thou know Dover?

EDGAR Ay, master.

GLOUCESTER There is a cliff whose high and bending
75 head
Looks fearfully in the confinèd deep:
Bring me but to the very brim of it,
And I'll repair the misery thou dost bear
With something rich about me: from that place
I shall no leading need.

80 EDGAR Give me thy arm:
Poor Tom shall lead thee. *Exeunt.*

61 **Obidicut** Hoberdicut, a devil (like the four that follow, from Harsnett's *Declaration*) 61–62 **dumbness** muteness (like the crimes and afflictions in the next lines, the result of diabolic possession) 63 **mopping and mowing** grimacing and making faces 67 **humbled to all strokes** brought so low as to bear anything humbly 69 **superfluous** possessed of superfluities 69 **lust-dieted** whose lust is gratified (like Gloucester's) 70 **slaves** (1) tramples, spurns like a slave (2) ? tears, rends (Old English *slaefan*) 70 **ordinance** law 72 **So . . . excess** then the man with too much wealth would distribute it among those with too little 75 **bending** overhanging 76 **fearfully** occasioning fear 76 **confinèd deep** the sea, hemmed in below

Scene II. [*Before the Duke of Albany's palace.*]

Enter Goneril and Edmund.

GONERIL Welcome, my lord: I marvel our mild husband
Not met us on the way.

Enter Oswald.

Now, where's your master?

OSWALD Madam, within; but never man so changed.
I told him of the army that was landed:
He smiled at it. I told him you were coming; 5
His answer was, "The worse." Of Gloucester's treachery,
And of the loyal service of his son
When I informed him, then he called me sot,
And told me I had turned the wrong side out:
What most he should dislike seems pleasant to him; 10
What like, offensive.

GONERIL [*To Edmund*] Then shall you go no further.
It is the cowish terror of his spirit,
That dares not undertake: he'll not feel wrongs,
Which tie him to an answer. Our wishes on the way
May prove effects. Back, Edmund, to my brother; 15
Hasten his musters and conduct his pow'rs.

IV.ii.2 **Not met** did not meet 8 **sot** fool 11 **What like** what he should like 12 **cowish** cowardly 13 **undertake** venture 14 **tie him to an answer** oblige him to retaliate 14–15 **Our . . . effects** our desires (that you might be my husband), as we journeyed here, may be fulfilled 16 **musters** collecting of troops 16 **conduct his pow'rs** lead his army

I must change names at home and give the distaff
Into my husband's hands. This trusty servant
Shall pass between us: ere long you are like to hear,
20 If you dare venture in your own behalf,
A mistress's command. Wear this; spare speech;

[*Giving a favor*]

Decline your head. This kiss, if it durst speak,
Would stretch thy spirits up into the air:
Conceive, and fare thee well.

EDMUND Yours in the ranks of death.

25 GONERIL My most dear Gloucester!

Exit [*Edmund*].

O, the difference of man and man!
To thee a woman's services are due:
My fool usurps my body.

OSWALD Madam, here comes my lord.

Exit.

Enter Albany.

GONERIL I have been worth the whistle.

ALBANY O Goneril!
30 You are not worth the dust which the rude wind
Blows in your face. I fear your disposition:
That nature which contemns its origin
Cannot be bordered certain in itself;
She that herself will sliver and disbranch

17 **change names** i.e., exchange the name of "mistress" for that of "master" 17 **distaff** spinning stick (wifely symbol) 21 **mistress's** lover's (and also, Albany having been disposed of, lady's or wife's) 22 **Decline your head** i.e., that Goneril may kiss him 24 **Conceive** understand (with a sexual implication, that includes "stretch thy spirits," 1. 23; and "death," 1. 25: "to die," meaning "to experience sexual intercourse") 28 **My fool usurps my body** my husband wrongfully enjoys me 29 **I . . . whistle** i.e., once you valued me (the proverb is implied, "It is a poor dog that is not worth the whistling") 31 **disposition** nature 32 **contemns** despises 33 **bordered . . . itself** kept within its normal bounds 34 **sliver and disbranch** cut off

From her material sap, perforce must wither 35
And come to deadly use.

GONERIL No more; the text is foolish.

ALBANY Wisdom and goodness to the vile seem vile:
Filths savor but themselves. What have you done?
Tigers, not daughters, what have you performed? 40
A father, and a gracious agèd man,
Whose reverence even the head-lugged bear
would lick,
Most barbarous, most degenerate, have you
madded.
Could my good brother suffer you to do it?
A man, a prince, by him so benefited! 45
If that the heavens do not their visible spirits
Send quickly down to tame these vile offenses,
It will come,
Humanity must perforce prey on itself,
Like monsters of the deep.

GONERIL Milk-livered man! 50
That bear'st a cheek for blows, a head for wrongs;
Who hast not in thy brows an eye discerning
Thine honor from thy suffering; that not know'st
Fools do those villains pity who are punished
Ere they have done their mischief. Where's thy
drum? 55
France spreads his banners in our noiseless
land,
With plumèd helm thy state begins to threat,

35 **material sap** essential and life-giving sustenance 36 **come to deadly use** i.e., be as a dead branch for the burning 37 **text** i.e., on which your sermon is based 39 **Filths savor but themselves** the filthy relish only the taste of filth 42 **head-lugged bear** bear-baited by the dogs, and hence enraged 43 **madded** made mad 46 **visible spirits** avenging spirits in material form 50 **Milk-livered** lily-livered (hence cowardly, the liver being regarded as the seat of courage) 52–53 **discerning . . . suffering** able to distinguish between insults that ought to be resented, and ordinary pain that is to be borne 54–55 **Fools . . . mischief** only fools are sorry for criminals whose intended criminality is prevented by punishment 56 **noiseless** i.e., the drum, signifying preparation for war, is silent 57 **helm** helmet 57 **thy . . . threat** France begins to threaten Albany's realm

Whilst thou, a moral fool, sits still and cries
"Alack, why does he so?"

ALBANY See thyself, devil!

60 Proper deformity seems not in the fiend
So horrid as in woman.

GONERIL O vain fool!

ALBANY Thou changèd and self-covered thing, for shame,
Be-monster not thy feature. Were 't my fitness
To let these hands obey my blood,
65 They are apt enough to dislocate and tear
Thy flesh and bones; howe'er thou art a fiend,
A woman's shape doth shield thee.

GONERIL Marry, your manhood mew——

Enter a Messenger.

ALBANY What news?

MESSENGER O, my good lord, the Duke of Cornwall's
70 dead,
Slain by his servant, going to put out
The other eye of Gloucester.

ALBANY Gloucester's eyes!

MESSENGER A servant that he bred, thrilled with remorse,
Opposed against the act, bending his sword
75 To his great master, who thereat enraged
Flew on him, and amongst them felled him dead,
But not without that harmful stroke which since

58 **moral** moralizing; but also with the implication that morality and folly are one 60 **Proper** (1) natural (to a fiend) (2) fair-appearing 62 **changèd and self-covered** i.e., transformed, by the contorting of her woman's face, on which appears the fiendish behavior she has allowed herself. (Goneril has disguised nature by wickedness) 63 **Be-monster not thy feature** do not change your appearance into a fiend's 63 **my fitness** appropriate for me 64 **blood** passion 66 **howe'er** but even if 68 **Marry** by the Virgin Mary 68 **your manhood mew** (1) coop up or confine your (pretended) manhood (2) molt or shed it, if that is what is supposed to "shield" me from you 71 **going to** as he was about to 73 **bred** reared 73 **thrilled with remorse** pierced by compassion 76 **amongst them felled** others assisting, they felled

Hath plucked him after.

ALBANY This shows you are above,
You justicers, that these our nether crimes
So speedily can venge. But, O poor Gloucester! 80
Lost he his other eye?

MESSENGER Both, both, my lord.
This letter, madam, craves a speedy answer;
'Tis from your sister.

GONERIL [*Aside*] One way I like this well;
But being widow, and my Gloucester with her,
May all the building in my fancy pluck 85
Upon my hateful life. Another way,
The news is not so tart.—I'll read, and answer.
Exit.

ALBANY Where was his son when they did take his eyes?

MESSENGER Come with my lady hither.

ALBANY He is not here.

MESSENGER No, my good lord; I met him back again. 90

ALBANY Knows he the wickedness?

MESSENGER Ay, my good lord; 'twas he informed against him,
And quit the house on purpose, that their punishment
Might have the freer course.

ALBANY Gloucester, I live
To thank thee for the love thou showed'st the King, 95
And to revenge thine eyes. Come hither, friend:
Tell me what more thou know'st. *Exeunt.*

78 plucked him after i.e., brought Cornwall to death with his servant 79 justicers judges 79 nether committed below (on earth) 80 venge avenge 82 craves demands 85–86 May . . . life these things (1.84) may send my future hopes, my castles in air, crashing down upon the hateful (married) life I lead now 86 Another way looked at another way 87 tart sour 90 back going back

[Scene III. *The French camp near Dover.*]

Enter Kent and a Gentleman.

KENT Why the King of France is so suddenly gone back, know you no reason?

GENTLEMAN Something he left imperfect in the state, which since his coming forth is thought of,
5 which imports to the kingdom so much fear and danger that his personal return was most required and necessary.

KENT Who hath he left behind him general?

GENTLEMAN The Marshal of France, Monsieur La Far.

10 KENT Did your letters pierce the queen to any demonstration of grief?

GENTLEMAN Ay, sir; she took them, read them in my presence,
And now and then an ample tear trilled down
Her delicate cheek: it seemed she was a queen
15 Over her passion, who most rebel-like
Sought to be king o'er her.

KENT O, then it moved her.

GENTLEMAN Not to a rage: patience and sorrow strove
Who should express her goodliest. You have seen
Sunshine and rain at once: her smiles and tears
20 Were like a better way: those happy smilets
That played on her ripe lip seemed not to know
What guests were in her eyes, which parted thence

IV.ii.3–4 **imperfect in the state** unsettled in his own kingdom 5 **imports** portends 10 **pierce** impel 13 **trilled** trickled 18 **Who ... goodliest** which should give her the most becoming expression 20 **Were like a better way** i.e., improved on that spectacle 20 **smilets** little smiles

As pearls from diamonds dropped. In brief,
Sorrow would be a rarity most belovèd,
If all could so become it.

KENT Made she no verbal question? 25

GENTLEMAN Faith, once or twice she heaved the name of "father"
Pantingly forth, as if it pressed her heart;
Cried "Sisters! Sisters! Shame of ladies! Sisters!
Kent! Father! Sisters! What, i' th' storm? i' th' night?
Let pity not be believed!" There she shook 30
The holy water from her heavenly eyes,
And clamor moistened: then away she started
To deal with grief alone.

KENT It is the stars,
The stars above us, govern our conditions;
Else one self mate and make could not beget 35
Such different issues. You spoke not with her since?

GENTLEMAN No.

KENT Was this before the King returned?

GENTLEMAN No, since.

KENT Well, sir, the poor distressèd Lear's i' th' town;
Who sometime in his better tune remembers 40
What we are come about, and by no means
Will yield to see his daughter.

GENTLEMAN Why, good sir?

KENT A sovereign shame so elbows him: his own unkindness

24–25 **Sorrow ...** it sorrow would be a coveted jewel if it became others as it does her 26 **heaved** expressed with difficulty 30 **Let pity not be believed** let it not be believed for pity 32 **clamor moistened** moistened clamor, i.e., mixed (and perhaps assuaged) her outcries with tears 34 **govern our conditions** determine what we are 35–36 **Else ... issues** otherwise the same husband and wife could not produce such different children 40 **better tune** composed, less jangled intervals 43 **sovereign** overpowering 43 **elbows** jogs his elbow i.e., reminds him

That stripped her from his benediction, turned her
45 To foreign casualties, gave her dear rights
To his dog-hearted daughters: these things sting
His mind so venomously that burning shame
Detains him from Cordelia.

GENTLEMAN Alack, poor gentleman!

KENT Of Albany's and Cornwall's powers you heard not?

50 GENTLEMAN 'Tis so; they are afoot.

KENT Well, sir, I'll bring you to our master Lear,
And leave you to attend him: some dear cause
Will in concealment wrap me up awhile;
When I am known aright, you shall not grieve
55 Lending me this acquaintance. I pray you, go
Along with me. [*Exeunt.*]

[Scene IV. *The same. A tent.*]

Enter, with drum and colors, Cordelia, Doctor, and Soldiers.

CORDELIA Alack, 'tis he: why, he was met even now
As mad as the vexed sea; singing aloud;
Crowned with rank femiter and furrow-weeds,
With hardocks, hemlock, nettles, cuckoo-flow'rs,
5 Darnel, and all the idle weeds that grow
In our sustaining corn. A century send forth;
Search every acre in the high-grown field,

45 **casualties** chances 50 **'Tis so** i.e., I have heard of them 52 **dear cause** important reason IV.iv. 3–5 **femiter . . . Darnel: femiter** fumitory, whose leaves and juice are bitter; **furrow-weeds** weeds that grow in the furrow, or plowed land; **hardocks** ? hoar or white docks, burdocks, harlocks; **hemlock** a poison; **nettles** plants which sting and burn; **cuckoo-flow'rs** identified with a plant employed to remedy diseases of the brain; **Darnel** tares, noisome weeds 6 **sustaining corn** life-maintaining wheat 6 **century** ? sentry; troop of a hundred soldiers

And bring him to our eye [*Exit an Officer.*] What
can man's wisdom
In the restoring his bereavèd sense?
He that helps him take all my outward worth. 10

DOCTOR There is means, madam:
Our foster-nurse of nature is repose,
The which he lacks: that to provoke in him,
Are many simples operative, whose power
Will close the eye of anguish.

CORDELIA All blest secrets, 15
All you unpublished virtues of the earth,
Spring with my tears! be aidant and remediate
In the good man's distress! Seek, seek for him,
Lest his ungoverned rage dissolve the life
That wants the means to lead it.

Enter Messenger.

MESSENGER News, madam; 20
The British pow'rs are marching hitherward.

CORDELIA 'Tis known before. Our preparation stands
In expectation of them. O dear father,
It is thy business that I go about;
Therefore great France 25
My mourning and importuned tears hath pitied.
No blown amibition doth our arms incite,
But love, dear love, and our aged father's right:
Soon may I hear and see him! *Exeunt.*

8 **What can man's wisdom** what can science accomplish 9 **bereavèd** impaired 10 **outward** material 12 **foster-nurse** fostering nurse 13 **provoke** induce 14 **simples operative** efficacious medicinal herbs 16 **unpublished virtues** i.e., secret remedial herbs 17 **remediate** remedial 20 **wants . . . it** i.e., lacks the reason to control the rage 25 **Therefore** because of that 26 **importuned** importunate 27 **blown** puffed up

[Scene V. *Gloucester's castle.*]

Enter Regan and Oswald.

REGAN But are my brother's pow'rs set forth?

OSWALD Ay, madam.

REGAN Himself in person there?

OSWALD Madam, with much ado:
Your sister is the better soldier.

REGAN Lord Edmund spake not with your lord at home?

5 OSWALD No, madam.

REGAN What might import my sister's letter to him?

OSWALD I know not, lady.

REGAN Faith, he is posted hence on serious matter.
It was great ignorance, Gloucester's eyes being out,
10 To let him live. Where he arrives he moves
All hearts against us: Edmund, I think, is gone,
In pity of his misery, to dispatch
His nighted life; moreover, to descry
The strength o' th' enemy.

OSWALD I must needs after him, madam, with my
15 letter.

REGAN Our troops set forth tomorrow: stay with us;
The ways are dangerous.

OSWALD I may not, madam:
My lady charged my duty in this business.

IV.v. 2 **ado** bother and persuasion 6 **import** purport, carry as its message 8 **is posted** has ridden speedily 9 **ignorance** folly 13 **nighted** (1) darkened, because blinded (2) benighted 18 **charged my duty** ordered me as a solemn duty

REGAN Why should she write to Edmund? Might not you
Transport her purposes by word? Belike, 20
Some things I know not what. I'll love thee much,
Let me unseal the letter.

OSWALD Madam, I had rather——

REGAN I know your lady does not love her husband;
I am sure of that: and at her late being here
She gave strange eliads and most speaking looks 25
To noble Edmund. I know you are of her bosom.

OSWALD I, madam?

REGAN I speak in understanding: y'are; I know 't:
Therefore I do advise you, take this note:
My lord is dead; Edmund and I have talked; 30
And more convenient is he for my hand
Than for your lady's: you may gather more.
If you do find him, pray you, give him this;
And when your mistress hears thus much from you,
I pray, desire her call her wisdom to her. 35
So, fare you well.
If you do chance to hear of that blind traitor,
Preferment falls on him that cuts him off.

OSWALD Would I could meet him, madam! I should show
What party I do follow.

REGAN Fare thee well. 40

Exeunt.

20 **Transport her purposes** convey her intentions 20 **Belike** probably 24 **late** recently 25 **eliads** amorous looks 26 **of her bosom** in her confidence 29 **take this note** take note of this 31 **convenient** fitting 32 **gather more** surmise more yourself 33 **this** this advice 35 **call** recall 38 **Preferment** promotion

[Scene VI. *Fields near Dover.*]

Enter Gloucester and Edgar.

GLOUCESTER When shall I come to th' top of that same hill?

EDGAR You do climb up it now. Look, how we labor.

GLOUCESTER Methinks the ground is even.

EDGAR Horrible steep.
Hark, do you hear the sea?

GLOUCESTER No, truly.

5 EDGAR Why then your other senses grow imperfect
By your eyes' anguish.

GLOUCESTER So may it be indeed.
Methinks thy voice is altered, and thou speak'st
In better phrase and matter than thou didst.

EDGAR Y'are much deceived: in nothing am I changed
But in my garments.

10 GLOUCESTER Methinks y'are better spoken.

EDGAR Come on, sir; here's the place: stand still. How fearful
And dizzy 'tis to cast one's eyes so low!
The crows and choughs that wing the midway air
Show scarce so gross as beetles. Half way down
15 Hangs one that gathers sampire, dreadful trade!
Methinks he seems no bigger than his head.
The fishermen that walk upon the beach
Appear like mice; and yond tall anchoring bark
Diminished to her cock; her cock, a buoy

IV.vi.6 **anguish** pain 13 **choughs** a kind of crow 13 **midway air** i.e., halfway down the cliff 14 **gross** large 15 **sampire** samphire, an aromatic herb associated with Dover Cliffs 18 **anchoring** anchored 19 **cock** cock-boat, a small boat usually towed behind the ship

Almost too small for sight. The murmuring surge 20
That on th' unnumb'red idle pebble chafes
Cannot be heard so high. I'll look no more,
Lest my brain turn and the deficient sight
Topple down headlong.

GLOUCESTER Set me where you stand.

EDGAR Give me your hand: you are now within a foot 25
Of th' extreme verge: for all beneath the moon
Would I not leap upright.

GLOUCESTER Let go my hand.
Here, friend, 's another purse; in it a jewel
Well worth a poor man's taking. Fairies and gods
Prosper it with thee! Go thou further off; 30
Bid me farewell, and let me hear thee going.

EDGAR Now fare ye well, good sir.

GLOUCESTER With all my heart.

EDGAR [*Aside*] Why I do trifle thus with his despair
Is done to cure it.

GLOUCESTER O you mighty gods!

He kneels.

This world I do renounce, and in your sights 35
Shake patiently my great affliction off:
If I could bear it longer and not fall
To quarrel with your great opposeless wills,
My snuff and loathèd part of nature should
Burn itself out. If Edgar live, O bless him! 40
Now, fellow, fare thee well.

He falls.

EDGAR Gone, sir, farewell.

21 **unnumb'red idle pebble** innumerable pebbles, moved to and fro by the waves to no purpose 23–24 **the deficient sight/Topple** my failing sight topple me 27 **upright** i.e., even up in the air, to say nothing of forward, over the cliff 29 **Fairies** (who are supposed to guard and multiply hidden treasure) 33–34 **Why . . . it** I play on his despair in order to cure it 37–38 **fall/To quarrel with** rebel against 38 **opposeless** not to be, and not capable of being, opposed 39 **snuff** the guttering (and stinking) wick of a burnt-out candle

And yet I know not how conceit may rob
The treasury of life, when life itself
Yields to the theft. Had he been where he thought,
45 By this had thought been past. Alive or dead?
Ho, you sir! friend! Hear you, sir! speak!
Thus might he pass indeed: yet he revives.
What are you, sir?

GLOUCESTER Away, and let me die.

EDGAR Hadst thou been aught but gossamer, feathers, air,
50 So many fathom down precipitating,
Thou'dst shivered like an egg: but thou dost breathe;
Hast heavy substance; bleed'st not; speak'st; art sound.
Ten masts at each make not the altitude
Which thou hast perpendicularly fell:
55 Thy life's a miracle. Speak yet again.

GLOUCESTER But have I fall'n, or no?

EDGAR From the dread summit of this chalky bourn.
Look up a-height; the shrill-gorged lark so far
Cannot be seen or heard: do but look up.

60 GLOUCESTER Alack, I have no eyes.
Is wretchedness deprived that benefit,
To end itself by death? 'Twas yet some comfort,
When misery could beguile the tyrant's rage
And frustrate his proud will.

EDGAR Give me your arm.
65 Up, so. How is 't? Feel you your legs? You stand.

GLOUCESTER Too well, too well.

EDGAR This is above all strangeness.
Upon the crown o' th' cliff, what thing was that

42 **how** but what 42 **conceit** imagination 44 **Yields to** allows 47 **pass** die 50 **precipitating** falling 53 **at each** one on top of the other 55 **life's** survival 57 **bourn** boundary 58 **a-height** on high 58 **gorged** throated, voiced 63 **beguile** cheat (i.e., by suicide) 65 **Feel you** have you any feeling in

Which parted from you?

GLOUCESTER A poor unfortunate beggar.

EDGAR As I stood here below, methought his eyes
Were two full moons; he had a thousand noses, 70
Horns whelked and waved like the enridgèd sea:
It was some fiend; therefore, thou happy father,
Think that the clearest gods, who make them honors
Of men's impossibilities, have preserved thee.

GLOUCESTER I do remember now: henceforth I'll bear 75
Affliction till it do cry out itself
"Enough, enough," and die. That thing you speak of,
I took it for a man; often 'twould say
"The fiend, the fiend"—he led me to that place.

EDGAR Bear free and patient thoughts.

Enter Lear [fantastically dressed with wild flowers].

But who comes here? 80
The safer sense will ne'er accommodate
His master thus.

LEAR No, they cannot touch me for coining; I am the King himself.

EDGAR O thou side-piercing sight! 85

LEAR Nature's above art in that respect. There's your press-money. That fellow handles his bow

71 **whelked** twisted 71 **enridgèd** i.e., furrowed into waves 72 **happy father** fortunate old man 73 **clearest** purest 73–74 **who . . . impossibilities** who cause themselves to be honored and revered by performing miracles of which men are incapable 80 **free** i.e., emancipated from grief and despair, which fetter the soul 81 **safer** sounder, saner 81 **accommodate** dress, adorn 83 **touch me for coining** arrest me for minting coins (the king's prerogative) 86 **Nature's . . . respect** i.e., a born king is superior to legal (and hence artificial) inhibition. There is also a glance here at the popular Renaissance debate, concerning the relative importance of nature (inspiration) and art (training) 87 **press-money** (paid to conscripted soldiers)

like a crow-keeper; draw me a clothier's yard. Look, look, a mouse! Peace, peace; this piece of
90 toasted cheese will do 't. There's my gauntlet; I'll prove it on a giant. Bring up the brown bills. O, well flown, bird! i' th' clout, i' th' clout; hewgh! Give the word.

EDGAR Sweet marjoram.

95 LEAR Pass.

GLOUCESTER I know that voice.

LEAR Ha! Goneril, with a white beard! They flattered me like a dog, and told me I had white hairs in my beard ere the black ones were there. To
100 say "ay" and "no" to everything that I said! "Ay" and "no" too was no good divinity. When the rain came to wet me once and the wind to make me chatter; when the thunder would not peace at my bidding; there I found 'em, there I smelt 'em
105 out. Go to, they are not men o' their words: they told me I was everything; 'tis a lie, I am not ague-proof.

GLOUCESTER The trick of that voice I do well remember: Is't not the king?

LEAR Ay, every inch a king.
110 When I do stare, see how the subject quakes.
I pardon that man's life. What was thy cause?

88 **crow-keeper** a farmer scaring away crows 88 **clothier's yard** (the standard English arrow was a cloth-yard long. Here the injunction is to draw the arrow back, like a powerful archer, a full yard to the ear) 90 **gauntlet** armored glove, thrown down as a challenge 91 **prove it on** maintain my challenge even against 91 **brown bills** halberds varnished to prevent rust (here the reference is to the soldiers who carry them) 92 **well flown** (falconer's cry; and perhaps a reference to the flight of the arrow) 92 **clout** the target shot at 92 **hewgh** ? imitating the whizzing of the arrow 93 **word** password 94 **Sweet marjoram** herb, used as a remedy for brain disease 98 **like a dog** as a dog flatters 98–99 **I . . . there** I was wise before I had even grown a beard 101 **no good divinity** (bad theology, because contrary to the Biblical saying [II Corinthians 1:18], "Our word toward you was not yea and nay." See also James 5:12 "But let your yea be yea, and your nay, nay; lest ye fall into condemnation"; and Matthew 5:36–37) 106–07 **ague-proof** secure against fever 108 **trick** intonation 111 **cause** offense

Adultery?
Thou shalt not die: die for adultery! No:
The wren goes to 't, and the small gilded fly
Does lecher in my sight. 115
Let copulation thrive; for Gloucester's bastard son
Was kinder to his father than my daughters
Got 'tween the lawful sheets.
To 't, luxury, pell-mell! for I lack soldiers.
Behold yond simp'ring dame, 120
Whose face between her forks presages snow,
That minces virtue and does shake the head
To hear of pleasure's name.
The fitchew, nor the soilèd horse, goes to 't
With a more riotous appetite. 125
Down from the waist they are Centaurs,
Though women all above:
But to the girdle do the gods inherit,
Beneath is all the fiend's.
There's hell, there's darkness, there is the sulphurous
pit, 130
Burning, scalding, stench, consumption; fie, fie, fie!
pah, pah! Give me an ounce of civet; good apothecary, sweeten my imagination: there's money for thee.

GLOUCESTER O, let me kiss that hand!

LEAR Let me wipe it first; it smells of mortality. 135

GLOUCESTER O ruined piece of nature! This great world
Shall so wear out to nought. Dost thou know me?

115 **lecher** copulate 118 **Got** begot 119 **luxury** lechery 119 **for . . . soldiers** i.e., ? (1) whom copulation will supply (2) and am therefore powerless 121 **Whose . . . snow** whose cold demeanor seems to promise chaste behavior ("forks": legs) 122 **minces** squeamishly pretends to 123 **pleasure's name** the very name of sexual pleasure 124 **fitchew** polecat (and slang for "prostitute") 124 **soilèd** put to pasture, and hence wanton with feeding 126 **Centaurs** lustful creatures, half man and half horse 128 **girdle** waist 128 **inherit** possess 132 **civet** perfume 135 **mortality** (1) death (2) existence 136–37 **This . . . nought** i.e., the universe (macrocosm) will decay to nothing in the same way as the little world of man (microcosm)

LEAR I remember thine eyes well enough. Dost thou squiny at me? No, do thy worst, blind Cupid; I'll
140 not love. Read thou this challenge; mark but the penning of it.

GLOUCESTER Were all thy letters suns, I could not see.

EDGAR I would not take this from report: it is,
And my heart breaks at it.

145 LEAR Read.

GLOUCESTER What, with the case of eyes?

LEAR O, ho, are you there with me? No eyes in your head, nor no money in your purse? Your eyes are in a heavy case, your purse in a light, yet you
150 see how this world goes.

GLOUCESTER I see it feelingly.

LEAR What, art mad? A man may see how this world goes with no eyes. Look with thine ears: see how yond justice rails upon yond simple thief. Hark,
155 in thine ear: change places, and, handy-dandy, which is the justice, which is the thief? Thou hast seen a farmer's dog bark at a beggar?

GLOUCESTER Ay, sir.

LEAR And the creature run from the cur? There thou
160 mightst behold the great image of authority: a dog's obeyed in office.
Thou rascal beadle, hold thy bloody hand!
Why dost thou lash that whore? Strip thy own
back;
Thou hotly lusts to use her in that kind

139 **squiny** squint, look sideways, like a prostitute 139 **blind Cupid** the sign hung before a brothel 140 **challenge** a reminiscence of ll. 89–90 143 **take** believe 146 **case** empty sockets 147 **are . . . me** is that what you tell me 149 **heavy case** sad plight (pun on l. 146) 149 **light** i.e., empty 151 **feelingly** (1) by touch (2) by feeling pain (3) with emotion 154 **simple** common, of low estate 155 **handy-dandy** i.e., choose, guess (after the children's game—"Handy-dandy, prickly prandy"—of choosing the right hand) 160 **image of authority** symbol revealing the true meaning of authority 160–61 **a . . . office** i.e., whoever has power is obeyed 162 **beadle** parish constable 164 **kind** i.e., sexual act

For which thou whip'st her. The usurer hangs the
cozener. 165
Through tattered clothes small vices do appear;
Robes and furred gowns hide all. Plate sin with
gold,
And the strong lance of justice hurtless breaks;
Arm it in rags, a pygmy's straw does pierce it.
None does offend, none, I say, none; I'll able
'em: 170
Take that of me, my friend, who have the power
To seal th' accuser's lips. Get thee glass eyes,
And, like a scurvy politician, seem
To see the things thou dost not. Now, now, now,
now.
Pull off my boots: harder, harder: so. 175

EDGAR O, matter and impertinency mixed!
Reason in madness!

LEAR If thou wilt weep my fortunes, take my eyes.
I know thee well enough; thy name is Gloucester:
Thou must be patient; we came crying hither: 180
Thou know'st, the first time that we smell the air
We wawl and cry. I will preach to thee: mark.

GLOUCESTER Alack, alack the day!

LEAR When we are born, we cry that we are come
To this great stage of fools. This' a good block. 185

164–65 **The usurer . . . cozener** i.e., the powerful moneylender, in his role as judge, puts to death the petty cheat 167 **Robes and furred gowns** (worn by a judge) 168 **hurtless** i.e., without hurting the sinner 170 **able** vouch for 171 **that** (the immunity just conferred) (l. 170) 172 **glass eyes** spectacles 173 **scurvy politician** vile politic man 176 **matter and impertinency** sense and nonsense 185 **This'** this is 185 **block** (various meanings have been suggested, for example, the stump of a tree, on which Lear is supposed to climb; a mounting-block, which suggests "horse" l. 187; a hat [which Lear or another must be made to wear], from the block on which a felt hat is molded, and which would suggest a "felt" l. 187. The proposal here is that "block" be taken to denote the quintain, whose function is to bear blows, "a mere lifeless block" [*As You Like It*. I.ii.263], an object shaped like a man and used for tilting practice. See also *Much Ado*, II.i.246–7, "she misused me past the endurance of a block!" and, in the same passage, the associated reference, "I stood like a man at a mark [target]" [l.253])

It were a delicate stratagem, to shoe
A troop of horse with felt: I'll put 't in proof;
And when I have stol'n upon these son-in-laws,
Then, kill, kill, kill, kill, kill, kill!

Enter a Gentleman [*with Attendants*].

190 GENTLEMAN O, here he is: lay hand upon him. Sir,
Your most dear daughter——

LEAR No rescue? What, a prisoner? I am even
The natural fool of fortune. Use me well;
You shall have ransom. Let me have surgeons;
I am cut to th' brains.

195 GENTLEMAN You shall have anything.

LEAR No seconds? all myself?
Why, this would make a man a man of salt,
To use his eyes for garden water-pots,
Ay, and laying autumn's dust.

200 GENTLEMAN Good sir——

LEAR I will die bravely, like a smug bridegroom. What!
I will be jovial: come, come; I am a king;
Masters, know you that?

GENTLEMAN You are a royal one, and we obey you.

205 LEAR Then there's life in 't. Come, and you get it, you shall get it by running. Sa, sa, sa, sa.

Exit [*running; Attendants follow*].

GENTLEMAN A sight most pitiful in the meanest wretch,
Past speaking of in a king! Thou hast one daughter
Who redeems nature from the general curse
210 Which twain have brought her to.

186 **delicate** subtle 187 **put't in proof** test it 193 **natural fool** born sport (with pun on "natural": "imbecile") 195 **cut** wounded 196 **seconds** supporters 197 **man of salt** i.e., all (salt) tears 201 **bravely** (1) smartly attired (2) courageously 201 **smug** spick and span 201 **bridegroom** whose "brave" sexual feats are picked up in the pun on "die" 205 **there's life in't** there's still hope 206 **Sa ... sa** hunting and rallying cry; also an interjection of defiance 209–10 **general ... to** (1) universal condemnation which Goneril and Regan have made for (2) damnation incurred by the original sin of Adam and Eve

EDGAR Hail, gentle sir.

GENTLEMAN Sir, speed you: what's your will?

EDGAR Do you hear aught, sir, of a battle toward?

GENTLEMAN Most sure and vulgar: every one hears that,
Which can distinguish sound.

EDGAR But, by your favor,
How near's the other army? 215

GENTLEMAN Near and on speedy foot; the main descry
Stands on the hourly thought.

EDGAR I thank you, sir: that's all.

GENTLEMAN Though that the Queen on special cause is here,
Her army is moved on.

EDGAR I thank you, sir.

Exit [Gentleman].

GLOUCESTER You ever-gentle gods, take my breath from me; 220
Let not my worser spirit tempt me again
To die before you please.

EDGAR Well pray you, father.

GLOUCESTER Now, good sir, what are you?

EDGAR A most poor man, made tame to fortune's blows;
Who, by the art of known and feeling sorrows, 225
Am pregnant to good pity. Give me your hand,
I'll lead you to some biding.

GLOUCESTER Hearty thanks;

211 gentle noble 211 speed God speed 212 toward impending 213 vulgar common knowledge 216–17 the . . . thought we expect to see the main body of the army any hour 221 worser spirit bad angel, evil side of my nature 224 tame submissive 225 art . . . sorrows instruction of sorrows painfully experienced 226 pregnant disposed 227 biding place of refuge

The bounty and the benison of heaven
To boot, and boot.

Enter Oswald.

OSWALD A proclaimed prize! Most happy!
230 That eyeless head of thine was first framed flesh
To raise my fortunes. Thou old unhappy traitor,
Briefly thyself remember: the sword is out
That must destroy thee.

GLOUCESTER Now let thy friendly hand
Put strength enough to 't.

[*Edgar interposes.*]

OSWALD Wherefore, bold peasant,
235 Dar'st thou support a published traitor? Hence!
Lest that th' infection of his fortune take
Like hold on thee. Let go his arm.

EDGAR Chill not let go, zir, without vurther 'casion.

OSWALD Let go, slave, or thou diest!

240 EDGAR Good gentleman, go your gait, and let poor volk pass. And chud ha' bin zwaggered out of my life, 'twould not ha' bin zo long as 'tis by a vortnight. Nay, come not near th' old man; keep out, che vor' ye, or I'se try whether your costard
245 or my ballow be the harder: chill be plain with out.

OSWALD Out, dunghill!

They fight.

228 **benison** blessing 229 **To boot, and boot** also, and in the highest degree 229 **proclaimed prize** i.e., one with a price on his head 229 **happy** fortunate (for Oswald) 230 **framed** created 232 **thyself remember** i.e., pray, think of your sins 233 **friendly** i.e., because it offers the death Gloucester covets 235 **published** proclaimed 238 **Chill . . .** (Edgar speaks in rustic dialect) 238 **Chill** I will 238 **vurther 'casion** further occasion 240 **gait** way 241 **volk** folk 241 **And chud ha' bin zwaggered** if I could have been swaggered 244 **Che vor' ye** I warrant you 244 **I'se** I shall 244 **costard** head (literally, "apple") 245 **ballow** cudgel

EDGAR Chill pick your teeth, zir: come; no matter vor your foins.

[*Oswald falls.*]

OSWALD Slave, thou hast slain me. Villain, take my purse: 250
If ever thou wilt thrive, bury my body,
And give the letters which thou find'st about me
To Edmund Earl of Gloucester; seek him out
Upon the English party. O, untimely death!
Death! 255

He dies.

EDGAR I know thee well. A serviceable villain,
As duteous to the vices of thy mistress
As badness would desire.

GLOUCESTER What, is he dead?

EDGAR Sit you down, father; rest you.
Let's see these pockets: the letters that he speaks of 260
May be my friends. He's dead; I am only sorry
He had no other deathsman. Let us see:
Leave, gentle wax; and, manners, blame us not:
To know our enemies' minds, we rip their hearts;
Their papers is more lawful. 265

Reads the letter.

"Let our reciprocal vows be remembered. You have many opportunities to cut him off: if your will want not, time and place will be fruitfully offered. There is nothing done, if he return the conqueror: then am I the prisoner, and his bed my 270 jail; from the loathed warmth whereof deliver me, and supply the place for your labor.

"Your—wife, so I would say—affectionate

248 Chill pick your teeth I will knock your teeth out **249 foins** thrusts **252 about** upon **254 party** side **256 serviceable** ready to be used **257 duteous** obedient **262 deathsman** executioner **263 Leave** by your leave **263 wax** (with which the letter is sealed) **265 Their papers** i.e., to rip their papers **267–68 if . . . not** if your desire (and lust) be not lacking **273 would** would like to

servant, and for you her own for venture,

275 'Goneril.' "

O indistinguished space of woman's will!
A plot upon her virtuous husband's life;
And the exchange my brother! Here in the sands
Thee I'll rake up, the post unsanctified
280 Of murderous lechers; and in the mature time,
With this ungracious paper strike the sight
Of the death-practiced Duke: for him 'tis well
That of thy death and business I can tell.

GLOUCESTER The King is mad: how stiff is my vile sense,
285 That I stand up, and have ingenious feeling
Of my huge sorrows! Better I were distract:
So should my thoughts be severed from my griefs,
And woes by wrong imaginations lose
The knowledge of themselves.

Drum afar off.

EDGAR Give me your hand:
290 Far off, methinks, I hear the beaten drum.
Come, father, I'll bestow you with a friend.

Exeunt.

Scene VII. [*A tent in the French camp.*]

Enter Cordelia, Kent, Doctor, and Gentleman.

CORDELIA O thou good Kent, how shall I live and work,

274 **and . . . venture** i.e., and one who holds you her own for venturing (Edmund had earlier been promised union by Goneril, "If you dare venture in your own behalf," IV.ii.20). 276 **indistinguished . . . will** unlimited range of woman's lust 278 **exchange** substitute 279 **rake up** cover up, bury 279 **post unsanctified** unholy messenger 280 **mature** ripe 281 **ungracious paper** wicked letter 281 **strike** blast 282 **death-practiced** whose death is plotted 284 **stiff** unbending 284 **vile sense** hateful capacity for feeling 285 **ingenious** conscious 286 **distract** distracted, mad 288 **wrong imaginations** delusions 291 **bestow** lodge

To match thy goodness? My life will be too short,
And every measure fail me.

KENT To be acknowledged, madam, is o'erpaid.
All my reports go with the modest truth, 5
Nor more nor clipped, but so.

CORDELIA Be better suited:
These weeds are memories of those worser hours:
I prithee, put them off.

KENT Pardon, dear madam;
Yet to be known shortens my made intent:
My boon I make it, that you know me not 10
Till time and I think meet.

CORDELIA Then be 't so, my good lord. [*To the Doctor.*] How does the King?

DOCTOR Madam, sleeps still.

CORDELIA O you kind gods!
Cure this great breach in his abusèd nature. 15
Th' untuned and jarring senses, O, wind up
Of this child-changèd father.

DOCTOR So please your Majesty
That we may wake the King: he hath slept long.

CORDELIA Be governed by your knowledge, and proceed
I' th' sway of your own will. Is he arrayed? 20

Enter Lear in a chair carried by Servants.

IV.vii. 5 **go** conform 6 **clipped** curtailed 6 **suited** attired 7 **weeds** clothes 7 **memories** reminders 9 **Yet . . . intent** to reveal myself just yet interferes with the plan I have made 10 **My boon I make it** I ask this reward 11 **meet** fitting 15 **abusèd** disturbed 16 **wind up** tune 17 **child-changèd** changed, deranged (and also, reduced to a child) by the cruelty of his children 20 **I' th' sway of** according to

GENTLEMAN Ay, madam; in the heaviness of sleep
We put fresh garments on him.

DOCTOR Be by, good madam, when we do awake him;
I doubt not of his temperance.

CORDELIA Very well.

DOCTOR Please you, draw near. Louder the music
25 there!

CORDELIA O my dear father, restoration hang
Thy medicine on my lips, and let this kiss
Repair those violent harms that my two sisters
Have in thy reverence made.

KENT Kind and dear Princess.

CORDELIA Had you not been their father, these white
30 flakes
Did challenge pity of them. Was this a face
To be opposed against the warring winds?
To stand against the deep dread-bolted thunder?
In the most terrible and nimble stroke
Of quick, cross lightning to watch—poor
35 perdu!—
With this thin helm? Mine enemy's dog,
Though he had bit me, should have stood that night
Against my fire; and wast thou fain, poor father,
To hovel thee with swine and rogues forlorn,
40 In short and musty straw? Alack, alack!
'Tis wonder that thy life and wits at once
Had not concluded all. He wakes; speak to him.

DOCTOR Madam, do you; 'tis fittest.

24 **temperance** sanity 29 **reverence** revered person 30 **flakes** hairs (in long strands) 31 **challenge** claim 33 **deep dread-bolted** deep-voiced and furnished with the dreadful thunderbolt 35 **cross** zigzag 35 **perdu** (1) sentry in a forlorn position (2) lost one 36 **helm** helmet (his scanty hair) 38 **fain** pleased 39 **rogues** vagabonds 40 **short** (when straw is freshly cut, it is long, and suitable for bedding, given its flexibility and crispness. As it is used, it becomes musty, shreds into pieces, is "short." In contemporary Maine usage, "short manure" refers to dung mixed with straw that has been broken up; "long manure" to dung mixed with coarse new straw) 42 **concluded all** come to a complete end

CORDELIA How does my royal lord? How fares your Majesty?

LEAR You do me wrong to take me out o' th' grave: 45
Thou art a soul in bliss; but I am bound
Upon a wheel of fire, that mine own tears
Do scald like molten lead.

CORDELIA Sir, do you know me?

LEAR You are a spirit, I know. Where did you die?

CORDELIA Still, still, far wide. 50

DOCTOR He's scarce awake: let him alone awhile.

LEAR Where have I been? Where am I? Fair daylight?
I am mightily abused. I should ev'n die with pity,
To see another thus. I know not what to say.
I will not swear these are my hands: let's see; 55
I feel this pin prick. Would I were assured
Of my condition.

CORDELIA O, look upon me, sir,
And hold your hand in benediction o'er me.
You must not kneel.

LEAR Pray, do not mock me:
I am a very foolish fond old man, 60
Fourscore and upward, not an hour more nor less;
And, to deal plainly,
I fear I am not in my perfect mind.
Methinks I should know you and know this man,
Yet I am doubtful; for I am mainly ignorant 65
What place this is, and all the skill I have
Remembers not these garments, nor I know not
Where I did lodge last night. Do not laugh at me,
For, as I am a man, I think this lady
To be my child Cordelia.

CORDELIA And so I am, I am. 70

LEAR Be your tears wet? Yes, faith. I pray, weep not.
If you have poison for me, I will drink it.

47 wheel of fire (torment associated by the Middle Ages with Hell, where Lear thinks he is) **50 wide** i.e., of the mark (of sanity) **53 abused** deluded **60 fond** in dotage **65 mainly** entirely

I know you do not love me; for your sisters
Have, as I do remember, done me wrong.
You have some cause, they have not.

75 CORDELIA No cause, no cause.

LEAR Am I in France?

KENT In your own kingdom, sir.

LEAR Do not abuse me.

DOCTOR Be comforted, good madam: the great rage,
You see, is killed in him: and yet it is danger
80 To make him even o'er the time he has lost.
Desire him to go in; trouble him no more
Till further settling.

CORDELIA Will 't please your Highness walk?

LEAR You must bear with me. Pray you now, forget
85 and forgive. I am old and foolish.

Exeunt. Mane[n]t Kent and Gentleman.

GENTLEMAN Holds it true, sir, that the Duke of Cornwall was so slain?

KENT Most certain, sir.

GENTLEMAN Who is conductor of his people?

90 KENT As 'tis said, the bastard son of Gloucester.

GENTLEMAN They say Edgar, his banished son, is with the Earl of Kent in Germany.

KENT Report is changeable. 'Tis time to look about; the powers of the kingdom approach apace.

95 GENTLEMAN The arbitrement is like to be bloody.
Fare you well, sir. *[Exit.]*

KENT My point and period will be thoroughly
wrought,
Or well or ill, as this day's battle's fought.

Exit.

77 **abuse** deceive 78 **rage** frenzy 80 **even o'er** smooth over by filling in; and hence, "recollect" 82 **settling** calming 83 **walk** (perhaps in the sense of "withdraw") 85 s.d. **Mane[n]t** remain 93 **Report is changeable** rumors are unreliable 94 **powers** armies 95 **arbitrement** deciding encounter 97 **My . . . wrought** the aim and end, the close of my life will be completely worked out

ACT V

Scene I. [*The British camp near Dover.*]

Enter, with drum and colors, Edmund, Regan, Gentlemen, and Soldiers.

EDMUND Know of the Duke if his last purpose hold,
Or whether since he is advised by aught
To change the course: he's full of alteration
And self-reproving: bring his constant pleasure.
[*To a Gentleman, who goes out.*]

REGAN Our sister's man is certainly miscarried. 5

EDMUND 'Tis to be doubted, madam.

REGAN Now, sweet lord,
You know the goodness I intend upon you:
Tell me, but truly, but then speak the truth,
Do you not love my sister?

EDMUND In honored love.

REGAN But have you never found my brother's way 10
To the forfended place?

EDMUND That thought abuses you.

V.i. 1 **Know** learn 1 **last purpose hold** most recent intention (to fight) be maintained 2 **advised** induced 4 **constant pleasure** fixed (final) decision 5 **miscarried** come to grief 6 **doubted** feared 9 **honored** honorable 11 **forfended** forbidden 11 **abuses** (1) deceives (2) demeans, is unworthy of

REGAN I am doubtful that you have been conjunct
And bosomed with her, as far as we call hers.

EDMUND No, by mine honor, madam.

15 REGAN I shall never endure her: dear my lord,
Be not familiar with her.

EDMUND Fear me not.—
She and the Duke her husband!

Enter, with drum and colors, Albany, Goneril [and] Soldiers.

GONERIL [*Aside*] I had rather lose the battle than that sister
Should loosen him and me.

20 ALBANY Our very loving sister, well be-met.
Sir, this I heard, the King is come to his daughter,
With others whom the rigor of our state
Forced to cry out. Where I could not be honest,
I never yet was valiant: for this business,
25 It touches us, as France invades our land,
Not bolds the King, with others, whom, I fear,
Most just and heavy causes make oppose.

EDMUND Sir, you speak nobly.

REGAN Why is this reasoned?

GONERIL Combine together 'gainst the enemy;
30 For these domestic and particular broils
Are not the question here.

ALBANY Let's then determine
With th' ancient of war on our proceeding.

EDMUND I shall attend you presently at your tent.

12–13 **I . . . hers** I fear that you have united with her intimately, in the fullest possible way 16 **Fear** distrust 19 **loosen** separate 20 **be-met** met 22 **rigor . . . state** tyranny of our government 23 **honest** honorable 25 **touches us, as** concerns me, only in that 26–27 **Not . . . oppose** and not in that France emboldens the King and others, who have been led, by real and serious grievances, to take up arms against us 28 **reasoned** argued 30 **particular broils** private quarrels 31 **question** issue 32 **th' ancient of war** experienced commanders

REGAN Sister, you'll go with us?

GONERIL No. 35

REGAN 'Tis most convenient; pray you, go with us.

GONERIL [*Aside*] O, ho, I know the riddle.—I will go.

Exeunt both the Armies. Enter Edgar [*disguised*].

EDGAR If e'er your Grace had speech with man so poor,
Hear me one word.

ALBANY [*To those going out*] I'll overtake you. [*To Edgar*] Speak.

Exeunt [*all but Albany and Edgar*].

EDGAR Before you fight the battle, ope this letter. 40
If you have victory, let the trumpet sound
For him that brought it: wretched though I seem,
I can produce a champion that will prove
What is avouchèd there. If you miscarry,
Your business of the world hath so an end, 45
And machination ceases. Fortune love you.

ALBANY Stay till I have read the letter.

EDGAR I was forbid it.
When time shall serve, let but the herald cry,
And I'll appear again.

ALBANY Why, fare thee well: I will o'erlook thy paper. *Exit* [*Edgar*]. 50

Enter Edmund.

EDMUND The enemy's in view: draw up your powers.
Here is the guess of their true strength and forces
By diligent discovery; but your haste

34 **us** me (rather than Edmund) 36 **convenient** fitting, desirable 37 **riddle** real reason (for Regan's curious request) 41–42 **sound/For** summon 48 **prove** i.e., by trial of combat 44 **avouchèd** maintained 45 **of** in 46 **machination** plotting 50 **o'erlook** read over 52 **guess** estimate 53 **By diligent discovery** obtained by careful reconnoitering

Is now urged on you.

ALBANY We will greet the time. *Exit.*

55 EDMUND To both these sisters have I sworn my love;
Each jealous of the other, as the stung
Are of the adder. Which of them shall I take?
Both? One? Or neither? Neither can be enjoyed,
If both remain alive: to take the widow
60 Exasperates, makes mad her sister Goneril;
And hardly shall I carry out my side,
Her husband being alive. Now then, we'll use
His countenance for the battle; which being done,
Let her who would be rid of him devise
65 His speedy taking off. As for the mercy
Which he intends to Lear and to Cordelia,
The battle done, and they within our power,
Shall never see his pardon; for my state
Stands on me to defend, not to debate. *Exit.*

Scene II. [*A field between the two camps.*]

Alarum within. Enter, with drum and colors, Lear, Cordelia, and Soldiers, over the stage; and exeunt.

Enter Edgar and Gloucester.

EDGAR Here, father, take the shadow of this tree
For your good host; pray that the right may thrive.
If ever I return to you again,
I'll bring you comfort.

GLOUCESTER Grace go with you, sir.
Exit [*Edgar*].

54 **greet** i.e., meet the demands of 56 **jealous** suspicious 61 **hardly** with difficulty 61 **carry . . . side** (1) satisfy my ambition (2) fulfill my bargain (with Goneril) 63 **countenance** authority 68–69 **for . . . debate** my position requires me to act, not to reason about right and wrong V.ii. s.d. **Alarum** a trumpet call to battle [1] **father** i.e., venerable old man (Edgar has not yet revealed his identity)

Alarum and retreat within. [Re-]enter Edgar.

EDGAR Away, old man; give me thy hand; away! 5
King Lear hath lost, he and his daughter ta'en:
Give me thy hand; come on.

GLOUCESTER No further, sir; a man may rot even here.

EDGAR What, in ill thoughts again? Men must endure
Their going hence, even as their coming hither: 10
Ripeness is all. Come on.

GLOUCESTER And that's true too.

Exeunt.

Scene III. [*The British camp near Dover.*]

Enter, in conquest, with drum and colors,
Edmund; Lear and Cordelia, as prisoners; Soldiers,
Captain.

EDMUND Some officers take them away: good guard,
Until their greater pleasures first be known
That are to censure them.

CORDELIA We are not the first
Who with best meaning have incurred the worst.
For thee, oppressèd King, I am cast down; 5
Myself could else out-frown false fortune's frown.
Shall we not see these daughters and these sisters?

LEAR No, no, no, no! Come, let's away to prison:
We two alone will sing like birds i' th' cage:
When thou dost ask me blessing, I'll kneel down 10
And ask of thee forgiveness: so we'll live,
And pray, and sing, and tell old tales, and laugh

4 s.d. **retreat** (signaled by a trumpet) 6 **ta'en** captured 11 **Ripeness** maturity, as of fruit that is ready to fall V.iii. 1 **good guard** let there be good guard 2 **their greater pleasures** the will of those in command, the great ones 3 **censure** pass judgment on 4 **meaning** intentions

At gilded butterflies, and hear poor rogues
Talk of court news; and we'll talk with them too,
15 Who loses and who wins, who's in, who's out;
And take upon's the mystery of things,
As if we were God's spies: and we'll wear out,
In a walled prison, packs and sects of great ones
That ebb and flow by th' moon.

EDMUND Take them away.

20 LEAR Upon such sacrifices, my Cordelia,
The gods themselves throw incense. Have I caught thee?
He that parts us shall bring a brand from heaven,
And fire us hence like foxes. Wipe thine eyes;
The good years shall devour them, flesh and fell,
Ere they shall make us weep. We'll see 'em starved
25 first.
Come. [*Exeunt Lear and Cordelia, guarded.*]

EDMUND Come hither, captain; hark.
Take thou this note: go follow them to prison:
One step I have advanced thee; if thou dost
30 As this instructs thee, thou dost make thy way
To noble fortunes: know thou this, that men
Are as the time is: to be tender-minded
Does not become a sword: thy great employment
Will not bear question; either say thou'lt do 't,
Or thrive by other means.

35 CAPTAIN I'll do 't, my lord.

13 **gilded butterflies** i.e., gorgeously attired courtiers, fluttering after nothing 16–17 **take . . . spies** profess to read the riddle of existence, as if endowed with divine omniscience 17 **wear out** outlast 18–19 **packs . . . moon** intriguing and partisan cliques of those in high station, whose fortunes change every month 20–21 **Upon . . . incense** i.e., the gods approve our renunciation of the world 22–23 **He . . . foxes** no human agency can separate us, but only divine interposition, as of a heavenly torch parting us like foxes who are driven from their place of refuge by fire and smoke 24 **good years** plague and pestilence ("undefined malefic power or agency," *N.E.D.*) 24 **them** i.e., the enemies of Lear and Cordelia 24 **fell** skin 32 **as the time is** i.e., absolutely determined by the exigencies of the moment 33 **become a sword** befit a soldier 34 **bear question** admit of discussion

EDMUND About it; and write happy when th' hast
done.
Mark; I say, instantly, and carry it so
As I have set it down.

CAPTAIN I cannot draw a cart, nor eat dried oats;
If it be man's work, I'll do't. *Exit Captain.* 40

Flourish. Enter Albany, Goneril, Regan [another Captain and] Soldiers.

ALBANY Sir, you have showed today your valiant
strain,
And fortune led you well: you have the captives
Who were the opposites of this day's strife:
I do require them of you, so to use them
As we shall find their merits and our safety 45
May equally determine.

EDMUND Sir, I thought it fit
To send the old and miserable King
To some retention and appointed guard;
Whose age had charms in it, whose title more,
To pluck the common bosom on his side, 50
And turn our impressed lances in our eyes
Which do command them. With him I sent the
Queen:
My reason all the same; and they are ready
Tomorrow, or at further space, t' appear
Where you shall hold your session. At this time 55
We sweat and bleed: the friend hath lost his friend;
And the best quarrels, in the heat, are cursed
By those that feel their sharpness.
The question of Cordelia and her father

36 **write happy** style yourself fortunate 37 **carry it so** manage the affair in exactly that manner (as if Cordelia had taken her own life) 41 **strain** (1) stock (2) character 43 **opposites of** opponents in 45 **merits** deserts 48 **retention . . . guard** confinement under duly appointed guard 49 **Whose** i.e., Lear's 50 **pluck . . . side** win the sympathy of the people to himself 51 **turn . . . eyes** turn our conscripted lancers against us 54 **further space** a later time 55 **session** trial 57–58 **the . . . sharpness** the worthiest causes may be judged badly by those who have been affected painfully by them, and whose passion has not yet cooled

Requires a fitter place.

60 ALBANY Sir, by your patience,
I hold you but a subject of this war,
Not as a brother.

REGAN That's as we list to grace him.
Methinks our pleasure might have been demanded,
Ere you had spoke so far. He led our powers,
65 Bore the commission of my place and person;
The which immediacy may well stand up
And call itself your brother.

GONERIL Not so hot:
In his own grace he doth exalt himself
More than in your addition.

REGAN In my rights,
70 By me invested, he compeers the best.

GONERIL That were the most, if he should husband you.

REGAN Jesters do oft prove prophets.

GONERIL Holla, holla!
That eye that told you so looked but a-squint.

REGAN Lady, I am not well; else I should answer
75 From a full-flowing stomach. General,
Take thou my soldiers, prisoners, patrimony;
Dispose of them, of me; the walls is thine:
Witness the world, that I create thee here
My lord, and master.

GONERIL Mean you to enjoy him?

80 ALBANY The let-alone lies not in your good will.

61 **subject of** subordinate in 62 **list to grace** wish to honor 65-67 **Bore ... brother** was authorized, as my deputy, to take command; his present status, as my immediate representative, entitles him to be considered your equal 69 **your addition** honors you have bestowed on him 70 **compeers** equals 71 **most** most complete investing in your rights 71 **husband you** become your husband 73 **a-squint** cross-eyed 75 **From ... stomach** angrily 76 **patrimony** inheritance 77 **walls is thine** i.e., Regan's person, which Edmund has stormed and won 80 **let-alone** power to prevent

EDMUND Nor in thine, lord.

ALBANY Half-blooded fellow, yes.

REGAN [*To Edmund*] Let the drum strike, and prove my title thine.

ALBANY Stay yet; hear reason. Edmund, I arrest thee
On capital treason; and in thy attaint
This gilded serpent [*pointing to Goneril*]. For your claim, fair sister, 85
I bar it in the interest of my wife.
'Tis she is subcontracted to this lord,
And I, her husband, contradict your banes.
If you will marry, make your loves to me;
My Lady is bespoke.

GONERIL An interlude! 90

ALBANY Thou art armed, Gloucester: let the trumpet sound:
If none appear to prove upon thy person
Thy heinous, manifest, and many treasons,
There is my pledge [*throwing down a glove*]: I'll make it on thy heart,
Ere I taste bread, thou art in nothing less 95
Than I have here proclaimed thee.

REGAN Sick, O, sick!

GONERIL [*Aside*] If not, I'll ne'er trust medicine.

EDMUND [*Throwing down a glove*] There's my exchange: what in the world he is
That names me traitor, villain-like he lies:
Call by the trumpet: he that dares approach, 100

81 **Half-blooded** bastard, and so only half noble 82 **prove ... thine** prove by combat your entitlement to my rights 84 **in thy attaint** as a sharer in the treason for which you are impeached 87 **subcontracted** pledged by a contract which is called into question by the existence of a previous contract (Goneril's marriage) 88 **contradict your banes** forbid your announced intention to marry (by citing the precontract) 89 **loves** love-suits 90 **bespoke** already pledged 90 **interlude** play 94 **pledge** gage 94 **make** prove 97 **medicine** poison 98 **exchange** (technical term, denoting the glove Edmund throws down) 99 **villain-like he lies** (the lie direct, a challenge to mortal combat) 100 **trumpet** trumpeter

On him, on you—who not?—I will maintain
My truth and honor firmly.

ALBANY A herald, ho!

EDMUND A herald, ho, a herald!

ALBANY Trust to thy single virtue; for thy soldiers,
105 All levied in my name, have in my name
Took their discharge.

REGAN My sickness grows upon me.

ALBANY She is not well; convey her to my tent.
[*Exit Regan, led.*]

Enter a Herald.

Come hither, herald. Let the trumpet sound—
And read out this.

110 CAPTAIN Sound, trumpet!

A trumpet sounds.

HERALD (*Reads.*) "If any man of quality or degree within the lists of the army will maintain upon Edmund, supposed Earl of Gloucester, that he is a manifold traitor, let him appear by the third sound
115 of the trumpet: he is bold in his defense."

EDMUND Sound!

First trumpet.

HERALD Again!

Second trumpet.

HERALD Again!

Third trumpet.

Trumpet answers within. Enter Edgar, at the third sound, armed, a trumpet before him.

ALBANY Ask him his purposes, why he appears
Upon this call o' th' trumpet.

120 HERALD What are you?

104 single virtue unaided valor **111 quality or degree** rank or position **112 lists** rolls **118 s.d. trumpet before him** trumpeter preceding him

Your name, your quality, and why you answer
This present summons?

EDGAR Know, my name is lost;
By treason's tooth bare-gnawn and canker-bit:
Yet am I noble as the adversary
I come to cope.

ALBANY Which is that adversary? 125

EDGAR What's he that speaks for Edmund, Earl of Gloucester?

EDMUND Himself: what say'st thou to him?

EDGAR Draw thy sword,
That if my speech offend a noble heart,
Thy arm may do thee justice: here is mine.
Behold it is my privilege, 130
The privilege of mine honors,
My oath, and my profession. I protest,
Maugre thy strength, place, youth, and eminence,
Despite thy victor sword and fire-new fortune,
Thy valor and thy heart, thou art a traitor, 135
False to thy gods, thy brother, and thy father,
Conspirant 'gainst this high illustrious prince,
And from th' extremest upward of thy head
To the descent and dust below thy foot,
A most toad-spotted traitor. Say thou "No," 140
This sword, this arm and my best spirits are bent
To prove upon thy heart, whereto I speak,
Thou liest.

EDMUND In wisdom I should ask thy name,
But since thy outside looks so fair and warlike,

121 **quality** rank 123 **canker-bit** eaten by the caterpillar 125 **cope** encounter 130–32 **it . . . profession** my knighthood entitles me to challenge you, and to have my challenge accepted 133 **Maugre** despite 134 **fire-new** fresh from the forge or mint 135 **heart** courage 137 **Conspirant** conspiring, a conspirator 138 **extremest upward** the very top 139 **the . . . foot** your lowest part (sole) and the dust beneath it 140 **toad-spotted traitor** spotted with treason (and hence venomous, as the toad is allegedly marked with spots that exude venom) 141 **bent** directed 142 **whereto I speak** (Edgar speaks from the heart, and speaks to the heart of Edmund) 148 **wisdom** prudence (since he is not obliged to fight with one of lesser rank)

And that thy tongue some say of breeding
145 breathes,
What safe and nicely I might well delay
By rule of knighthood, I disdain and spurn:
Back do I toss these treasons to thy head;
With the hell-hated lie o'erwhelm thy heart;
150 Which for they yet glance by and scarcely bruise,
This sword of mine shall give them instant way,
Where they shall rest for ever. Trumpets, speak!

Alarums. [They] fight. [Edmund falls.]

ALBANY Save him, save him!

GONERIL This is practice, Gloucester:
By th' law of war thou wast not bound to answer
155 An unknown opposite; thou art not vanquished,
But cozened and beguiled.

ALBANY Shut your mouth, dame,
Or with this paper shall I stop it. Hold, sir;
Thou worse than any name, read thine own evil.
No tearing, lady; I perceive you know it.

160 GONERIL Say, if I do, the laws are mine, not thine:
Who can arraign me for 't?

ALBANY Most monstrous! O!
Know'st thou this paper?

GONERIL Ask me not what I know.

Exit.

ALBANY Go after her; she's desperate; govern her.

EDMUND What you have charged me with, that have
I done;
165 And more, much more; the time will bring it out.
'Tis past, and so am I. But what art thou

145 **say** assay (i.e., touch, sign) 146 **safe and nicely** cautiously and punctiliously 146 **delay** i.e., avoid 148 **treasons** accusations of treason 149 **hell-hated** hated like hell 150–52 **Which . . . ever** which accusations of treason, since as yet they do no harm, even though I have hurled them back, I now thrust upon you still more forcibly, with my sword, so that they may remain with you permanently 153 **Save** spare 153 **practice** trickery 155 **opposite** opponent 157 **Hold, sir** (to Edmund: "Just a moment!") 158 **Thou** (probably Goneril) 163 **govern** control

That hast this fortune on me? If thou 'rt noble,
I do forgive thee.

EDGAR Let's exchange charity.
I am no less in blood than thou art, Edmund;
If more, the more th' hast wronged me. 170
My name is Edgar, and thy father's son.
The gods are just, and of our pleasant vices
Make instruments to plague us:
The dark and vicious place where thee he got
Cost him his eyes.

EDMUND Th' hast spoken right, 'tis true; 175
The wheel is come full circle; I am here.

ALBANY Methought thy very gait did prophesy
A royal nobleness: I must embrace thee:
Let sorrow split my heart, if ever I
Did hate thee or thy father!

EDGAR Worthy Prince, I know't. 180

ALBANY Where have you hid yourself?
How have you known the miseries of your father?

EDGAR By nursing them, my lord. List a brief tale;
And when 'tis told, O, that my heart would burst!
The bloody proclamation to escape 185
That followed me so near—O, our lives' sweetness,
That we the pain of death would hourly die
Rather than die at once!—taught me to shift
Into a madman's rags, t' assume a semblance
That very dogs disdained: and in this habit 190
Met I my father with his bleeding rings,
Their precious stones new lost; became his guide,
Led him, begged for him, saved him from despair;

167 **fortune on** victory over 168 **charity** forgiveness and love 169 **blood** lineage 170 **If more** if I am more noble (since legitimate) 172 **of our pleasant** out of our pleasurable 174 **place** i.e., the adulterous bed 174 **got** begot 176 **Wheel . . . here** i.e., Fortune's wheel, on which Edmund ascended, has now, in its downward turning, deposited him at the bottom, whence he began 177 **gait did prophesy** carriage did promise 180 **Worthy** honorable 185 **to escape** (my wish) to escape the sentence of death 186–88 **O . . . once** how sweet is life, that we choose to suffer death every hour rather than make an end at once 190 **habit** attire 191 **rings** sockets

Never—O fault!—revealed myself unto him,
195 Until some half-hour past, when I was armed,
Not sure, though hoping, of this good success,
I asked his blessing, and from first to last
Told him our pilgrimage. But his flawed heart—
Alack, too weak the conflict to support—
200 'Twixt two extremes of passion, joy and grief,
Burst smilingly.

EDMUND This speech of yours hath moved me,
And shall perchance do good: but speak you on;
You look as you had something more to say.

ALBANY If there be more, more woeful, hold it in;
205 For I am almost ready to dissolve,
Hearing of this.

EDGAR This would have seemed a period
To such as love not sorrow; but another,
To amplify too much, would make much more,
And top extremity.
210 Whilst I was big in clamor, came there in a man,
Who, having seen me in my worst estate,
Shunned my abhorred society; but then, finding
Who 'twas that so endured, with his strong arms
He fastened on my neck, and bellowed out
215 As he'd burst heaven; threw him on my father;
Told the most piteous tale of Lear and him
That ever ear received: which in recounting
His grief grew puissant, and the strings of life
Began to crack: twice then the trumpets sounded,
And there I left him tranced.

220 ALBANY But who was this?

EDGAR Kent, sir, the banished Kent; who in disguise
Followed his enemy king, and did him service
Improper for a slave.

198 our pilgrimage of our (purgatorial) journey **198 flawed** cracked **205 dissolve** i.e., into tears **206 period** limit **207–09 but . . . extremity** just one woe more, described too fully, would go beyond the extreme limit **210 big in clamor** loud in lamentation **211 estate** condition **212 abhorred** abhorrent **218 puissant** overmastering **220 tranced** insensible **222 enemy** hostile

Enter a Gentleman, with a bloody knife.

GENTLEMAN Help, help, O, help!

EDGAR What kind of help?

ALBANY Speak, man.

EDGAR What means this bloody knife?

GENTLEMAN 'Tis hot, it smokes; 225

It came even from the heart of—O, she's dead!

ALBANY Who dead? Speak, man.

GENTLEMAN Your lady, sir, your lady: and her sister

By her is poisoned; she confesses it.

EDMUND I was contracted to them both: all three 230

Now marry in an instant.

EDGAR Here comes Kent.

ALBANY Produce the bodies, be they alive or dead.

[*Exit Gentleman.*]

This judgment of the heavens, that makes us tremble,

Touches us not with pity.

Enter Kent.

O, is this he?

The time will not allow the compliment 235

Which very manners urges.

KENT I am come

To bid my king and master aye good night:

Is he not here?

ALBANY Great thing of us forgot!

Speak, Edmund, where's the King? and where's Cordelia?

Seest thou this object, Kent? 240

The bodies of Goneril and Regan are brought in.

KENT Alack, why thus?

225 **smokes** steams 230 **contracted** betrothed 231 **marry** i.e., unite in death 235 **compliment** ceremony 236 **very manners** ordinary civility 237 **aye** forever 238 **thing of** matter by 240 **object** sight (the bodies of Goneril and Regan)

EDMUND Yet Edmund was beloved:
The one the other poisoned for my sake,
And after slew herself.

ALBANY Even so. Cover their faces.

245 EDMUND I pant for life: some good I mean to do,
Despite of mine own nature. Quickly send,
Be brief in it, to th' castle; for my writ
Is on the life of Lear and on Cordelia:
Nay, send in time.

ALBANY Run, run, O, run!

250 EDGAR To who, my lord? Who has the office? Send
Thy token of reprieve.

EDMUND Well thought on: take my sword,
Give it the captain.

EDGAR Haste thee, for thy life.

[*Exit Messenger.*]

EDMUND He hath commission from thy wife and me
255 To hang Cordelia in the prison, and
To lay the blame upon her own despair,
That she fordid herself.

ALBANY The gods defend her! Bear him hence awhile.

[*Edmund is borne off.*]

Enter Lear, with Cordelia in his arms [*Gentleman, and others following*].

LEAR Howl, howl, howl, howl! O, you are men of stones:
260 Had I your tongues and eyes, I'd use them so
That heaven's vault should crack. She's gone for ever.
I know when one is dead and when one lives;
She's dead as earth. Lend me a looking-glass;
If that her breath will mist or stain the stone,
Why, then she lives.

241 Yet in spite of all **245 pant for life** gasp for breath **247 writ** command (ordering the execution) **250 office** commission **251 token of reprieve** sign that they are reprieved **257 fordid** destroyed **264 stone** i.e., the surface of the crystal looking glass

KENT Is this the promised end? 265

EDGAR Or image of that horror?

ALBANY Fall and cease.

LEAR This feather stirs; she lives. If it be so,
It is a chance which does redeem all sorrows
That ever I have felt.

KENT O my good master.

LEAR Prithee, away.

EDGAR 'Tis noble Kent, your friend. 270

LEAR A plague upon you, murderers, traitors all!
I might have saved her; now she's gone for ever.
Cordelia, Cordelia, stay a little. Ha,
What is 't thou say'st? Her voice was ever soft,
Gentle and low, an excellent thing in woman. 275
I killed the slave that was a-hanging thee.

GENTLEMAN 'Tis true, my lords, he did.

LEAR Did I not, fellow?
I have seen the day, with my good biting falchion
I would have made them skip: I am old now,
And these same crosses spoil me. Who are you? 280
Mine eyes are not o' th' best: I'll tell you straight.

KENT If Fortune brag of two she loved and hated,
One of them we behold.

LEAR This is a dull sight. Are you not Kent?

KENT The same,
Your servant Kent. Where is your servant Caius? 285

LEAR He's a good fellow, I can tell you that;
He'll strike, and quickly too: he's dead and rotten.

KENT No, my good lord; I am the very man.

265 promised end Doomsday **266 image** exact likeness **266 Fall and cease** i.e., let the heavens fall, and all things finish **268 redeem** make good **278 falchion** small curved sword **280 crosses** troubles **280 spoil me** i.e, my prowess as a swordsman **281 tell you straight** recognize you straightway **282 two** i.e., Lear, and some hypothetical second, who is also a prime example of Fortune's inconstancy ("loved and hated") **284 dull sight** (1) melancholy spectacle (2) faulty eyesight (Lear's own, clouded by weeping) **285 Caius** (Kent's name, in disguise)

LEAR I'll see that straight.

290 KENT That from your first of difference and decay
Have followed your sad steps.

LEAR You are welcome hither.

KENT Nor no man else: all's cheerless, dark and deadly.
Your eldest daughters have fordone themselves,
And desperately are dead.

LEAR Ay, so I think.

295 ALBANY He knows not what he says, and vain is it
That we present us to him.

EDGAR Very bootless.

Enter a Messenger.

MESSENGER Edmund is dead, my lord.

ALBANY That's but a trifle here.
You lords and noble friends, know our intent.
What comfort to this great decay may come
300 Shall be applied. For us, we will resign,
During the life of this old majesty,
To him our absolute power: [*To Edgar and Kent*] you, to your rights;
With boot, and such addition as your honors
Have more than merited. All friends shall taste
305 The wages of their virtue, and all foes
The cup of their deservings. O, see, see!

LEAR And my poor fool is hanged: no, no, no life?
Why should a dog, a horse, a rat, have life,

289 see that straight attend to that in a moment **290 your ... decay** beginning of your decline in fortune **292 Nor no man else** no, I am not welcome, nor is anyone else **293 fordone** destroyed **294 desperately** in despair **296 bootless** fruitless **299 What ... come** whatever aid may present itself to this great ruined man **300 us, we** (the royal "we") **303 boot** good measure **303 addition** additional titles and rights **307 fool** Cordelia ("fool" being a term of endearment. But it is perfectly possible to take the word as referring also to the Fool)

And thou no breath at all? Thou'lt come no more,
Never, never, never, never, never. 310
Pray you, undo this button. Thank you, sir.
Do you see this? Look on her. Look, her lips,
Look there, look there.

He dies.

EDGAR He faints. My lord, my lord!

KENT Break, heart; I prithee, break.

EDGAR Look up, my lord.

KENT Vex not his ghost: O, let him pass! He hates him 315
That would upon the rack of this tough world
Stretch him out longer.

EDGAR He is gone indeed.

KENT The wonder is he hath endured so long:
He but usurped his life.

ALBANY Bear them from hence. Our present business 320
Is general woe. [*To Kent and Edgar*] Friends of my soul, you twain,
Rule in this realm and the gored state sustain.

KENT I have a journey, sir, shortly to go;
My master calls me, I must not say no.

EDGAR The weight of this sad time we must obey, 325
Speak what we feel, not what we ought to say.
The oldest hath borne most: we that are young
Shall never see so much, nor live so long.

Exeunt, with a dead march.

FINIS

311 undo this button i.e., to ease the suffocation Lear feels 315 Vex . . . ghost do not trouble his departing spirit 316 rack instrument of torture, stretching the victim's joints to dislocation 317 longer (1) in time (2) in bodily length 319 usurped possessed beyond the allotted term 325 obey submit to

Textual Note

The earliest extant version of Shakespeare's *King Lear* is the First Quarto of 1608. This premier edition is known as the Pied Bull Quarto, after the sign which hung before the establishment of the printer. The title page reads as follows: "M. William Shak-speare: / HIS / True Chronicle Historie of the life and / death of King Lear and his three / Daughters. / *With the vnfortunate life of* Edgar, *sonne* / and heire to the Earle of Gloster, and his / sullen and assumed humor of / Tom of Bedlam: / *As it was played before the Kings Maiestie at Whitehall vpon* / S. Stephans *night in Christmas Hollidayes.* / By his Maiesties seruants playing vsually at the Gloabe / on the Bancke-side. / LONDON, / Printed for *Nathaniel Butter*, and are to be sold at his shop in *Pauls* / Church-yard at the signe of the Pide Bull neere / St. *Austin's* Gate. 1608." Twelve copies of the First Quarto survive. They are, however, in ten different states, because proofreading, and hence correcting, took place as the play was being printed. The instances (167 in all) in which these copies of Q1 differ one from another have been enumerated by contemporary scholarship.[1]

In 1619 appeared the Second Quarto, known as the N. Butter Quarto, and falsely dated in the same year as the first (the title page reads: "Printed for Nathaniel Butter. 1608"). The source of Q2 was apparently a copy of Q1 in which a number of sheets had been corrected.

Four years later *King Lear* was reprinted once more, this time in the first collection of Shakespeare's works, the First Folio of 1623. The source of the Folio text seems to have been, again, a corrected copy of Q1. The corrections in this copy, however, do not duplicate those in the presumptive source of Q2, but are at once more and less extensive. In some

[1] W. W. Greg, *The Variants in the First Quarto of "King Lear,"* London, 1940 (for 1939).

cases the Quarto which lies behind the Folio offers corrections not found in the source of Q2. In other cases, corrections incorporated in the course of Q2 are not included in the source of F1. The Folio text, moreover, omits some 300 lines found in the Quarto, and thus leads to the supposition that the copy used in preparing the Folio had been collated with the prompt book—a shorter, acting version of the play—in the possession of Shakespeare's company. The Folio text would seem, then, to stand in close relation to Shakespeare's play as it was actually performed. On the other hand, the Folio does include some 100 lines not found in the Quarto.

It is now very generally, though not unanimously, agreed that the Folio is superior to the Quarto, and ought to serve as the basis of any modern edition. The present text of *King Lear* is based, therefore, on the First Folio of 1623, except when the Folio is guilty of an obvious misprinting, or when it omits pertinent material found in the Quarto, or when its version seems to the editor so inferior to the Quarto version as to demand precedence for the latter, or when an emendation, even though perhaps unnecessary (like Edwards' "top th' legitimate"), has been canonized by use and wont.

In the preparation of this text, the spelling of Folio and Quarto has been modernized; punctuation and capitalization have been altered, when alteration seemed suitable; character designations have been expanded or clarified (F "Cor." becomes "Cordelia," F "Bastard" and "Steward" become "Edmund" and "Oswald"); contractions not affecting pronunciation have been eliminated (F "banish'd" becomes "banished"); necessary quotation marks (as in the reading of a letter) have been supplied; as have diacritical marks whenever a syllable that is normally unemphasized must be stressed (as in "oppressèd"). These changes are not recorded.

All other departures from the Folio appearing in this text are recorded here in bold type. Unless specifically noted, these departures derive in every case from the First Quarto [Q]. If some other source is levied on, such as the Second Quarto [Q2] or Second Folio [F2] or the conjecture of an editor (for example, [Theobald]), that source is given, within brackets, immediately after the reading. There follows next, in roman type, the Folio reading which has been superseded. If an editor's emendation has been preferred to both Folio and Quarto readings, the emendation, with its provenance, is followed by the Folio and Quarto readings it replaces.

Stage directions are not given lineation. Reference to them in these notes is determined, therefore, by the line of text they follow. If a stage direction occurs at the beginning of a scene, reference is to the line of text it precedes. On occasion, the stage direction in the present text represents a conflation of Folio and Quarto. In that case, both Folio and Quarto readings are set down in the notes. Stage directions and notations of place, printed within brackets, are, unless otherwise noted, substantially from the Globe edition. The list of Dramatis Personae, first given by Rowe, is taken also from the Globe edition.

I.i. **Act I. Scene I** Actus Primus. Scaena Prima 5 **equalities** qualities 34 s.d. **Sound ... Attendants** Sennet. Enter King Lear, Cornwall, Albany, Gonerill, Regan, Cordelia, and attendants [F] Sound a Sennet, Enter one bearing a Coronet, then Lear, then the Dukes of Albany, and Cornwall, next Gonerill, Regan, Cordelia, with followers [Q] 70 **speak** [F omits] 98 **loved me.** I loved me 99 **Return** I return 106 **To love my father all** [F omits] 112 **mysteries** [F2] miseries [F] mistress [Q] 157 **as a pawn** as pawn 158 **nor** nere [i.e., "ne'er"] 165 **the** thy 172 **sentence** sentences 176 **diseases** disasters 190 **Gloucester** Cor[delia] 208 **on** in 216 **best object** object 227 **well** will 235 **Better thou** better thou hadst 250 **respects of fortune** respect and Fortunes 268 s.d. **Lear ... Attendants** [Capell] Exit Lear and Burgundy [Q] 283 **shame them derides** with shame derides 291 **hath not been** hath been 299–300 **ingrafted** ingraffed 306 **let's hit** let us sit

I.ii. **Scene II** Scena Secunda 21 **top th'** [Edwards] to' th' [F] tooth' [Q] 103–05 **Edmund ... earth** [F omits] 142 **Fut** [F omits] 144 **Edgar** [F omits] 145 **and pat** [Steevens] Pat [F] and out [Q] 156–64 **as ... come** [F omits] 165 **Why, the** The 178 **brother** [F omits] 185 **Go armed** [F omits] 191 s.d. **Exit Edgar** Exit

I.iii. **Scene III** Scena Tertia 17–21 **Not ... abused** [F omits] 25–26 **I would ... speak** [F omits] 27 **Go, prepare** prepare

I.iv. **Scene IV** Scena Quarta 1 **well** will 51 **daughter** Daughters 100 **Fool** my Boy 115 **Lady the Brach** [Steevens] the Lady Brach [F] Ladie oth'e brach [Q] 144–59 **That ... snatching** [F omits] 158 **on't** [Q2] [F omits] an't [Q] 158 **ladies** [Q corrected] [F omits] lodes [Q uncorrected] 167 **crown** Crownes 182 **fools** Foole 195 **Methinks [F omits]** 222 **it had** it's had 225 **Come, Sir** [F omits] 234 **or his** his 237–41 **I ... father** [F omits] 264 **O ... come** [F omits] 298 **the cause** more of it 311 **Yea ... this** [F omits] 350 **You are** [F2] Your are [F] Y'are [Q] 350 **attasked for** [Q corrected: "attaskt"] at task for [F] alapt [Q uncorrected]

TEXTUAL NOTE

I.v. Scene V Scena Quinta 1 s.d. **Enter ... Fool** [Q2] Enter Lear, Kent, Gentleman, and Foole 17 **Why ... boy** What can'st tell Boy

II.i. **Act II. Scene I** Actus Secundus. Scena Prima 21 s.d. **Enter Edgar** [placed by Theobald] [F prints after l. 20] 55 **But** And 72 **I should** should I 73 **ay** [F omits] 80 **I ... him** [F omits] 80 s.d. **Tucket within** [placed by Malone] [F prints after l. 79] 81 **why** wher 89 **strange news** strangenesse

II.ii. **Scene II** Scena Secunda 23 **clamorous** [Q corrected] clamours [F] clamarous [Q uncorrected] 44 s.d. **Enter ... drawn** Enter Bastard, Cornewall, Regan, Gloster, Servants [F] Enter Edmund with his rapier drawne, Gloster the Duke and Dutchesse [Q] 77 **too** t' 80 **Renege** Revenge 81 **gale** gall 110 **flick'ring** [Pope: "flickering"] flicking [F] flitkering [Q] 125 **dread** dead 132 **respect** respects 141 s.d. **Stocks brought out** [placed by Dyce] [F prints after l. 139] [Q omits] 143–47 **His ... with** [F omits] 145 **contemnèd'st** [Capell] [F omits] contaned [Q uncorrected] temnest [Q corrected] 153 **For ... legs** [F omits] 154 **Come ... away** [F assigns to Cornwall] 154 **my good Lord** my Lord 154 s.d. **Exeunt ... Kent** Exit [F] [Q omits] 155 **Duke's** Duke 176 s.d. **Sleeps** [F omits]

II.iii. **Scene III** [Steevens] [F, Q omit] 4 **unusual** unusall 15 **mortified bare arms** mortified Armes 18 **sheepcotes** Sheeps-Cotes

II.iv.1 s.d. **Scene IV** [Steevens] [F, Q omit] 2 **messenger** Messengers 6 **thy** ahy 9 **man's** man 18–19 **No ... have** [F omits] 30 **panting** painting 33 **whose** those 61 **the** the the 75 **have** hause 86 s.d. **Enter ... Gloucester** [F prints after l. 84] 130 **mother's** Mother 167 **her pride** [F omits] 183 s.d. **Enter Oswald** [placed by Dyce] [F and Q print after l. 181] 185 **fickle** fickly 188 s.d. **Enter Goneril** [placed by Johnson] [F and Q print after l. 186] 282 s.d. **Storm and tempest** [F prints after l. 283] [Q omits] 285 s.d. **Exeunt ... Fool** [Q2] Exeunt [F] Exeunt Lear, Leister, Kent, and Foole [Q] 294 s.d. **Enter Gloucester** [F and Q print after l. 293]

III.i **Act III Scene 1** Actus Tertius. Scena Prima 7–14 **tears ... all** [F omits] 30–42 **But ... you** [F omits]

III.ii. **Scene II** Scena Secunda 3 **drowned** drown 71 **That** And 78 **True ... boy** True boy

III.iii. **Scene III** Scaena Tertia

III.iv. **Scene IV** Scena Quarta 7 **skin: so** [Rowe] skinso [F] skin, so [Q] 10 **thy** they 27 s.d. **Exit** [placed by Johnson] [F prints after l. 26] [Q omits] 38 s.d. **Enter Fool** [Duthie] Enter Edgar, and Foole [F, which prints after l.36] [Q omits] 44 s.d. **Enter Edgar** Enter Edgar, and Foole [F, which prints after l. 36] [Q omits] 46 **blows ... wind** blow the windes 47 **thy cold bed** thy bed 52 **ford** Sword 57 **Bless** Blisse 58 **Bless** blisse 63 **What, has** Ha's 91 **deeply** deerely 101 **sessa** [Malone] Sesey [F] caese [Q] cease [Q2] 116 s.d. **Enter ... torch** [F prints after l. 111] Enter Gloster [Q, which prints after l. 116] 117 **foul fiend Flibbertigibbet** foule Flibbertigibbet 118 **till ... cock** at first Cocke 138 **hath had** hath

III.v. **Scene V** Scena Quinta 13 **his** this 26 **dearer** deere

III.vi **Scene VI** Scena Sexta 5 s.d. **Exit** [placed by Capell] [F prints after l. 3] 17–55 **The ... 'scape** [F omits] 22 **Now** [Q2] [F omits] no [Q] 25 **bourn** [Capell] [F omits] broome [Q] 34 **cushions** [F omits] cushings [Q] 47 **she kicked** [Q2] [F omits] kicked [Q] 53 **made on** [Capell] [F omits] made an [Q] 67 **lym** [Hanmer]

Hym [F] him [Q] 68 **tike, or trundle** tight, or Troudle 72 **Sessa!** [Malone] sese [F] [Q omits] 84 s.d. **Enter Gloucester** [placed by Capell] [F prints after l. 80] 97–100 **Oppressèd ... behind** [F omits] 101–14 **When ... lurk** [F omits]

III.vii. **Scene VII** Scena Septima 21 s.d. **Exit Oswald** [Staunton] [F and Q omit] 23 s.d. **Exeunt ... Edmund** [Staunton] [F (Exit) and Q (Exit Gon. and Bast.) print after l. 22] 28 s.d. **Enter ... three** [Q, which prints after "traitor"] Enter Gloucester, and Servants [F, which prints as here after "control"] 59 **rash** sticke 64 **dearn** sterne 79 s.d. **Draw and fight** [F omits] 81 s.d. **She ... him** Killes him [F] Shee ... behind [Q] 100–108 **I'll ... him** [F omits] 100 **Second Servant** [Capell] [F omits] Servant [Q] 101 **Third Servant** [Capell] [F omits] 2 Servant [Q] 104 **Second Servant** [Capell] [F omits] 1 Ser. [Q] 105 **roguish** [Q2] [Q omits] 107 **Third Servant** [Capell] [F omits] 2 Ser. [Q] 108 s.d. **Exeunt severally** [F omits] Exit [Q]

IV.i. **Act IV Scene 1** Actus Quartus. Scena Prima 9 s.d. **led by an Old Man** [Q, which prints after l. 12] and an Old man [F, which places after l. 9, as here] 41 **Then, prithee, get thee gone** Get thee away 60–65 **Five ... master** [F omits] 62–63 **Flibbertigibbet** [Pope] Stiberdigebit [Q] 63 **mopping and mowing** [Theobald] Mobing, & Mohing [Q]

IV.ii. **Scene II** Scena Secunda 1 s.d. **Enter Goneril and Edmund** Enter Gonerill, Bastard, and Steward 2 s.d. [after "way"] **Enter Oswald** [placed by Theobald] [Q prints after "master," l.2] [F omits] 25 s.d. **Exit Edmund** [placed by Rowe] Exit [F, which prints after "death"] [Q omits] 28 s.d. **Exit** [F omits] Exit Stew. [Q] 31–50 **I ... deep** [F omits] 32 **its** ith [Q] 45 **benefited** [Q corrected] beniflicted [Q uncorrected] 47 **these** [Jennens; Heath conj.] the [Q uncorrected] this [Q corrected] 49 **Humanity** [Q corrected] Humanly [Q uncorrected] 53–59 **that ... so** [F omits] 56 **noiseless** [Q corrected] noystles [Q uncorrected] 57 **thy state begins to threat** [Jennens] thy slayer begin threats [Q uncorrected] thy state begins thereat [Q corrected] thy slaier begins threats [Q2] 58 **Whilst** [Q corrected] Whil's [Q uncorrected] 62–69 **Thou ... news** [F omits] 65 **dislocate** [Q3] dislecate [Qq.1,2] 68 **mew** [Q corrected] now [Q uncorrected] 68 s.d. **Enter a Messenger** [F prints after l. 61] Enter a Gentleman [Q, which prints after l. 69; and Q2, which prints after l. 68, as here] 75 **thereat enraged** threat-enrag'd 79 **justicers** [Q corrected] Iustices [F,Q] 87 s.d. **Exit** [F omits]

IV.iii. **Scene III** Scena Tertia [for Scene IV] 1 s.d. **Enter ... Gentleman** [F omits the entire scene] 12 **sir** [Theobald] say 17 **strove** [Pope] streme 21 **seemed** [Pope: "seem'd"] seeme 30 **believed** [Q2] beleeft 32 **moistened** [Capell] moystened her 56 **Exeunt** [Pope] Exit

IV.iv. **Scene IV** [Pope] Scena Tertia [F] [Q omits] 1 s.d. **Cordelia, Doctor, and Soldiers** Cordelia, Gentlemen, and Souldiours [F] Cordelia, Doctor and others [Q] 3 **femiter** Fenitar 6 **century** Centery 18 **distress** desires 28 **right** Rite

IV.v. **Scene V** [Pope] Scena Quarta [F] [Q omits] 39 **meet him** meet

IV.vi **Scene VI** [Pope] Scena Quinta [Q omits] 17 **walk** walk'd 34 s.d. **He kneels** [F omits] 41 s.d. **He falls** [F omits] 71 **whelked** wealk'd 71 **enridgèd** enraged 83 **coining** crying 97 **had white** had the white 166 **Through** Thorough **small** great 167 **Plate sin** [Theobald] Place sinnes [Q omits] 199 **Ay ... dust** [F omits] 200 **Good sir** [Q2] [F and Q omit] 206 s.d. **Exit ... follow** Exit [F] Exit King running [Q] 208 **one** a 244 **I'se** [Johnson; "Ise"] ice [F] ile [Q] 247 s.d. **They fight** [F omits] 255 s.d. **He dies** [F omits] 274 **and ... venture** [Q reads "Venter"] [F omits] [This line, from the First Quarto, is almost universally omitted from editions of the play] 276 **indistinguished** indinguish'd 289 s.d. **Drum afar off** [F prints after l. 287] A drum a farre off [Q, which prints as here]

IV.vii **Scene VII** Scaena Septima 1 s.d. **Enter ... Gentleman** Enter Cordelia, Kent, and Gentleman [F] Enter Cordelia, Kent, and Doctor [Q] 24 **doubt not** doubt 24-25 **Very ... there** [F omits] 32 **warring** iarring 33-36 **To ... helm** [F omits] 79-80 **and ... lost** [F omits] 85 s.d. **Exeunt ... Gentleman** Exeunt 86-98 **Holds ... fought** [F omits]

V.i. **Act V Scene I** Actus Quintus. Scena Prima 11-13 **That ... hers** [F omits] 16 **Fear me not** Feare not 18-19 **I ... me** [F omits] 23-28 **Where ... nobly** [F omits] 33 **I ... tent** [F omits] 36 **pray you** pray 39 s.d. **To those going out** [F and Q omit] **To Edgar** [F and Q omit] **Exeunt** [placed by Cambridge edition] [Q prints after "word," l. 39] [F omits] 46 **love** loues 50 s.d. **Exit** [placed by Dyce] [F and Q print after l. 49]

V.ii. **Scene II** Scena Secunda

V.iii. **Scene III** Scena Tertia 13 **hear poor rogues** heere (poore Rogues) [reference in F is to Lear and Cordelia] 26 s.d. **Exeunt ... guarded** Exit [F] [Q omits] 39-40 **I ... do't** [F omits] 40 s.d. **Exit Captain** [F prints after l. 38] [Q omits] 48 **and appointed guard** [Q corrected, and Q2] [F and Q omit] 55-60 **At ... place** [F omits] 56 **We** [Q corrected, and Q2] mee [Q] 58 **sharpness** [Q corrected, and Q2] sharpes [Q] 84 **attaint** arrest 85 **sister** Sisters 98 **he is** hes 103 **Edmund ... ho, a herald** [F omits] 108 s.d. **Enter a Herald** [placed by Hanmer] [F prints after l. 102] [Q omits] 110 **Sound, trumpet** [F omits] 110 s.d. **A trumpet sounds** [F prints after l. 109] [Q omits] trumpet [F2] Tumpet 116 **Sound** [F omits] 116 s.d. **First trumpet** [F prints after l. 115] [Q omits] 118 s.d. **Enter ... him** Enter Edgar armed [F] Enter Edgar at the third sound, a trumpet before him [Q] 137 **illustrious** illustirous 145 **some say** (some say) 152 s.d. **fight** Fights [F, which prints after l. 153, "him"] [Q omits] 162 **Ask ... know** [F gives to Edmund] 162 s.d. **Exit** [placed here by Q: "Exit. Gonorill"] [F prints after l. 161, "for't"] 206-23 **This ... slave** [F omits] 215 **him** [Theobald] me [Q] [F omits] 223 s.d. **Enter ... knife** Enter a Gentleman [F] Enter one with a bloudie knife [Q] 234 s.d. **Enter Kent** [placed by Q2] [F prints after l. 231, "Kent"] [Q prints after "allow" in l. 235] 240 s.d. **The ... in** Gonerill and Regans bodies brought out [F, which prints after l. 232] 253 s.d. **Exit Messenger** [Theobald] [F and Q omit] 259 **Howl, howl, howl, howl** Howle, howle, howle **you are** your are 279 **them** him 291 **You are** [Q2] Your are [F] You'r [Q] 296 s.d. **Enter a Messenger** [F, which prints after "him"] Enter Captaine [Q, placed as here]

WILLIAM SHAKESPEARE

THE TRAGEDY OF MACBETH

Edited by Sylvan Barnet

[*Dramatis Personae*

DUNCAN, King of Scotland

MALCOLM, CONALBAIN — his sons

MACBETH, BANQUO, MACDUFF, LENNOX, ROSS, MENTIETH, ANGUS, CAITHNESS — noblemen of Scotland

FLEANCE, son to Banquo

SIWARD, Earl of Northumberland, general of the English forces

YOUNG SIWARD, his son

SEYTON, an officer attending on Macbeth

SON OF MACDUFF

AN ENGLISH DOCTOR

A SCOTTISH DOCTOR

A PORTER

AN OLD MAN

THREE MURDERERS

LADY MACBETH

LADY MACDUFF

A GENTLEWOMAN attending on Lady Macbeth

HECATE

WITCHES

APPARITIONS

LORDS, OFFICERS, SOLDIERS, ATTENDANTS, and MESSENGERS

Scene: Scotland; England]

THE TRAGEDY OF MACBETH

ACT I

Scene I. [*An open place.*]

Thunder and lightning. Enter Three Witches.

FIRST WITCH When shall we three meet again?
In thunder, lightning, or in rain?

SECOND WITCH When the hurlyburly's done,
When the battle's lost and won.

THIRD WITCH That will be ere the set of sun. 5

FIRST WITCH Where the place?

SECOND WITCH Upon the heath.

THIRD WITCH There to meet with Macbeth.

FIRST WITCH I come, Graymalkin.

SECOND WITCH Paddock calls.

THIRD WITCH Anon!

ALL Fair is foul, and foul is fair. 10
Hover through the fog and filthy air.

Exeunt.

Footnotes are keyed to the text by line number. Text references are printed in **bold** type; the annotation follows in roman type.
I.i. 8 **Graymalkin** (the witch's attendant spirit, a gray cat) 9 **Paddock** toad
9 **Anon** at once

Scene II. [*A camp.*]

Alarum within. Enter King [*Duncan*], *Malcolm, Donalbain, Lennox, with Attendants, meeting a bleeding Captain.*

KING What bloody man is that? He can report,
As seemeth by his plight, of the revolt
The newest state.

MALCOLM This is the sergeant
Who like a good and hardy soldier fought
5 'Gainst my captivity. Hail, brave friend!
Say to the king the knowledge of the broil
As thou didst leave it.

CAPTAIN Doubtful it stood,
As two spent swimmers, that do cling together
And choke their art. The merciless Macdonwald—
10 Worthy to be a rebel for to that
The multiplying villainies of nature
Do swarm upon him—from the Western Isles
Of kerns and gallowglasses is supplied;
And Fortune, on his damnèd quarrel smiling,
15 Showed like a rebel's whore: but all's too weak:
For brave Macbeth—well he deserves that name—
Disdaining Fortune, with his brandished steel,
Which smoked with bloody execution,
Like valor's minion carved out his passage

I.ii. s.d. **Alarum within** trumpet call offstage 3 **sergeant** i.e., officer (he is called, perhaps with no inconsistency in Shakespeare's day, a captain in the s.d. and speech prefixes. **Sergeant** is trisyllabic) 6 **broil** quarrel 9 **choke their art** hamper each other's doings 12 **Western Isles** Hebrides 13 **Of kerns and gallowglasses** with lightly armed Irish foot soldiers and heavily armed ones 14 **damnèd quarrel** accursed cause 15 **Showed like a rebel's whore** i.e., falsely appeared to favor Macdonwald 19 **minion** (trisyllabic) favorite

Till he faced the slave; 20
Which nev'r shook hands, nor bade farewell to him,
Till he unseamed him from the nave to th' chops,
And fixed his head upon our battlements.

KING O valiant cousin! Worthy gentleman!

CAPTAIN As whence the sun 'gins his reflection 25
Shipwracking storms and direful thunders break,
So from that spring whence comfort seemed to come
Discomfort swells. Mark, King of Scotland, mark:
No sooner justice had, with valor armed,
Compelled these skipping kerns to trust their heels 30
But the Norweyan lord, surveying vantage,
With furbished arms and new supplies of men,
Began a fresh assault.

KING Dismayed not this
Our captains, Macbeth and Banquo?

CAPTAIN Yes;
As sparrows eagles, or the hare the lion. 35
If I say sooth, I must report they were
As cannons overcharged with double cracks;
So they doubly redoubled strokes upon the foe.
Except they meant to bathe in reeking wounds,
Or memorize another Golgotha, 40
I cannot tell—
But I am faint; my gashes cry for help.

KING So well thy words become thee as thy wounds;
They smack of honor both. Go get him surgeons.
[*Exit Captain, attended.*]

Enter Ross and Angus.

Who comes here?

22 nave to th' chops navel to the jaws **25 reflection** (four syllables; the ending—ion here and often elsewhere in the play—is disyllabic) **31 surveying vantage** seeing an opportunity **36 sooth** truth **37 cracks** explosives **39 Except** unless **40 memorize another Golgotha** make the place as memorable as Golgotha, "the place of the skull"

45 MALCOLM The worthy Thane of Ross.

LENNOX What a haste looks through his eyes! So should he look
That seems to speak things strange.

ROSS God save the king!

KING Whence cam'st thou, worthy Thane?

ROSS From Fife, great King;
Where the Norweyan banners flout the sky
50 And fan our people cold.
Norway himself, with terrible numbers,
Assisted by that most disloyal traitor
The Thane of Cawdor, began a dismal conflict;
Till that Bellona's bridegroom, lapped in proof,
55 Confronted him with self-comparisons,
Point against point, rebellious arm 'gainst arm,
Curbing his lavish spirit: and, to conclude,
The victory fell on us.

KING Great happiness!

ROSS That now
Sweno, the Norways' king, craves composition;
60 Nor would we deign him burial of his men
Till he disbursèd, at Saint Colme's Inch,
Ten thousand dollars to our general use.

KING No more that Thane of Cawdor shall deceive
Our bosom interest: go pronounce his present death,
65 And with his former title greet Macbeth.

ROSS I'll see it done.

KING What he hath lost, noble Macbeth hath won.

Exeunt.

45 **Thane** (a Scottish title of nobility) 47 **seems to** seems about to 51 **Norway** the King of Norway 58 **dismal** threatening 54 **Bellona's . . . proof** the mate of the goddess of war, clad in tested (proved) armor 55 **self-comparisons** counter-movements 57 **lavish** insolent 59 **composition** terms of peace 61 **Inch** island 62 **dollars** (Spanish and Dutch currency) 64 **Our bosom interest** my (plural of royalty) heart's trust 64 **present** immediate

Scene III. [*A heath.*]

Thunder. Enter the Three Witches.

FIRST WITCH Where hast thou been, sister?

SECOND WITCH Killing swine.

THIRD WITCH Sister, where thou?

FIRST WITCH A sailor's wife had chestnuts in her lap,
And mounched, and mounched, and mounched.
"Give me," quoth I. 5
"Aroint thee, witch!" the rump-fed ronyon cries.
Her husband's to Aleppo gone, master o' th' Tiger:
But in a sieve I'll thither sail,
And, like a rat without a tail,
I'll do, I'll do, and I'll do. 10

SECOND WITCH I'll give thee a wind.

FIRST WITCH Th' art kind.

THIRD WITCH And I another.

FIRST WITCH I myself have all the other;
And the very ports they blow, 15
All the quarters that they know
I' th' shipman's card.
I'll drain him dry as hay:
Sleep shall neither night nor day
Hang upon his penthouse lid; 20
He shall live a man forbid:
Weary sev'nights nine times nine
Shall he dwindle, peak, and pine:

I.iii. 6 **Aroint thee** begone 6 **rump-fed ronyon** fat-rumped scabby creature 15 **ports they blow** harbors to which the winds blow (?) 17 **card** compass card 20 **penthouse lid** eyelid (the figure is of a lean-to) 21 **forbid** cursed 23 **peak** waste away

Though his bark cannot be lost,
25 Yet it shall be tempest-tossed.
Look what I have.

SECOND WITCH Show me, show me.

FIRST WITCH Here I have a pilot's thumb,
Wracked as homeward he did come.

Drum within.

30 THIRD WITCH A drum, a drum!
Macbeth doth come.

ALL The weïrd sisters, hand in hand,
Posters of the sea and land,
Thus do go about, about:
35 Thrice to thine, and thrice to mine,
And thrice again, to make up nine.
Peace! The charm's wound up.

Enter Macbeth and Banquo.

MACBETH So foul and fair a day I have not seen.

BANQUO How far is 't called to Forres? What are these
40 So withered, and so wild in their attire,
That look not like th' inhabitants o' th' earth,
And yet are on 't? Live you, or are you aught
That man may question? You seem to understand me,
By each at once her choppy finger laying
45 Upon her skinny lips. You should be women,
And yet your beards forbid me to interpret
That you are so.

MACBETH Speak, if you can: what are you?

FIRST WITCH All hail, Macbeth! Hail to thee, Thane of Glamis!

SECOND WITCH All hail, Macbeth! Hail to thee, Thane of Cawdor!

32 **weïrd** destiny-serving (?) 33 **Posters** swift travelers 43 **question** talk to 44 **choppy** chapped

THIRD WITCH All hail, Macbeth, that shalt be King hereafter! 50

BANQUO Good sir, why do you start, and seem to fear
Things that do sound so fair? I' th' name of truth,
Are ye fantastical, or that indeed
Which outwardly ye show? My noble partner
You greet with present grace and great prediction 55
Of noble having and of royal hope,
That he seems rapt withal: to me you speak not.
If you can look into the seeds of time,
And say which grain will grow and which will not,
Speak then to me, who neither beg nor fear 60
Your favors nor your hate.

FIRST WITCH Hail!

SECOND WITCH Hail!

THIRD WITCH Hail!

FIRST WITCH Lesser than Macbeth, and greater. 65

SECOND WITCH Not so happy, yet much happier.

THIRD WITCH Thou shalt get kings, though thou be none.
So all hail, Macbeth and Banquo!

FIRST WITCH Banquo and Macbeth, all hail!

MACBETH Stay, you imperfect speakers, tell me more: 70
By Sinel's death I know I am Thane of Glamis;
But how of Cawdor? The Thane of Cawdor lives,
A prosperous gentleman; and to be King
Stands not within the prospect of belief,
No more than to be Cawdor. Say from whence 75
You owe this strange intelligence? Or why
Upon this blasted heath you stop our way

53 fantastical imaginary **55 grace** honor **56 having** possession **57 rapt withal** entranced by it **66 happy** fortunate **67 get** beget **70 imperfect** incomplete **71 Sinel** (Macbeth's father) **76 owe** own, have **76 intelligence** information

With such prophetic greeting? Speak, I charge
you.

Witches vanish.

BANQUO The earth hath bubbles as the water has,
80 And these are of them. Whither are they vanished?

MACBETH Into the air, and what seemed corporal
melted
As breath into the wind. Would they had stayed!

BANQUO Were such things here as we do speak about?
Or have we eaten on the insane root
85 That takes the reason prisoner?

MACBETH Your children shall be kings.

BANQUO You shall be King.

MACBETH And Thane of Cawdor too. Went it not so?

BANQUO To th' selfsame tune and words. Who's here?

Enter Ross and Angus.

ROSS The King hath happily received, Macbeth,
90 The news of thy success; and when he reads
Thy personal venture in the rebels' fight,
His wonders and his praises do contend
Which should be thine or his. Silenced with that,
In viewing o'er the rest o' th' selfsame day,
95 He finds thee in the stout Norweyan ranks,
Nothing afeard of what thyself didst make,
Strange images of death. As thick as tale
Came post with post, and every one did bear
Thy praises in his kingdom's great defense,
And poured them down before him.

100 ANGUS We are sent
To give thee, from our royal master, thanks;

81 **corporal** corporeal 84 **insane** insanity-producing 90 **reads** considers 92–93 **His wonders . . . his** i.e., Duncan's speechless admiration, appropriate to him, contends with his desire to praise you (?) 97–98 **As thick . . . post** as fast as could be counted came messenger after messenger

Only to herald thee into his sight,
Not pay thee.

ROSS And for an earnest of a greater honor,
He bade me, from him, call thee Thane of Cawdor; 105
In which addition, hail, most worthy Thane!
For it is thine.

BANQUO What, can the devil speak true?

MACBETH The Thane of Cawdor lives: why do you dress me
In borrowed robes?

ANGUS Who was the thane lives yet,
But under heavy judgment bears that life 110
Which he deserves to lose. Whether he was combined
With those of Norway, or did line the rebel
With hidden help and vantage, or that with both
He labored in his country's wrack, I know not;
But treasons capital, confessed and proved, 115
Have overthrown him.

MACBETH [*Aside*] Glamis, and Thane of Cawdor:
The greatest is behind. [*To Ross and Angus*] Thanks for your pains.
[*Aside to Banquo*] Do you not hope your children shall be kings,
When those that gave the Thane of Cawdor to me
Promised no less to them?

BANQUO [*Aside to Macbeth*] That, trusted home, 120
Might yet enkindle you unto the crown,
Besides the Thane of Cawdor. But 'tis strange:
And oftentimes, to win us to our harm,
The instruments of darkness tell us truths,
Win us with honest trifles, to betray's 125

104 earnest pledge 106 addition title 111 combined allied 112 line support 113 vantage opportunity 114 wrack ruin 117 behind i.e., to follow 120 home all the way

In deepest consequence.
Cousins, a word, I pray you.

MACBETH [*Aside*] Two truths are told,
As happy prologues to the swelling act
Of the imperial theme.—I thank you, gentlemen.—
130 [*Aside*] This supernatural soliciting
Cannot be ill, cannot be good. If ill,
Why hath it given me earnest of success,
Commencing in a truth? I am Thane of Cawdor:
If good, why do I yield to that suggestion
135 Whose horrid image doth unfix my hair
And make my seated heart knock at my ribs,
Against the use of nature? Present fears
Are less than horrible imaginings.
My thought, whose murder yet is but fantastical,
140 Shakes so my single state of man that function
Is smothered in surmise, and nothing is
But what is not.

BANQUO Look, how our partner's rapt.

MACBETH [*Aside*] If chance will have me King, why, chance may crown me,
Without my stir.

BANQUO New honors come upon him,
145 Like our strange garments, cleave not to their mold
But with the aid of use.

MACBETH [*Aside*] Come what come may,
Time and the hour runs through the roughest day.

BANQUO Worthy Macbeth, we stay upon your leisure.

MACBETH Give me your favor. My dull brain was wrought

126 In deepest consequence in the most significant sequel **127 Cousins** i.e., fellow noblemen **128 swelling** stately **130 soliciting** inviting **136 seated** fixed **137 Against the use of nature** contrary to my natural way **139 fantastical** imaginary **140 single** unaided, weak (or "entire"?) **145 strange** new **148 stay upon your leisure** await your convenience **149 favor** pardon

With things forgotten. Kind gentlemen, your pains 150
Are registered where every day I turn
The leaf to read them. Let us toward the King.
[*Aside to Banquo*] Think upon what hath
chanced, and at more time,
The interim having weighed it, let us speak
Our free hearts each to other.

BANQUO Very gladly. 155

MACBETH Till then, enough. Come, friends.

Exeunt.

Scene IV. [*Forres. The palace.*]

Flourish. Enter King [Duncan], Lennox, Malcolm, Donalbain, and Attendants.

KING Is execution done on Cawdor? Are not
Those in commission yet returned?

MALCOLM My liege,
They are not yet come back. But I have spoke
With one that saw him die, who did report
That very frankly he confessed his treasons, 5
Implored your Highness' pardon and set forth
A deep repentance: nothing in his life
Became him like the leaving it. He died
As one that had been studied in his death,
To throw away the dearest thing he owed 10
As 'twere a careless trifle.

154 **The interim having weighed it** i.e., when we have had time to think 155 **Our free hearts** our minds freely I.iv. s.d. **Flourish** fanfare 2 **in commission** i.e., commissioned to oversee the execution 9 **studied** rehearsed 10 **owed** owned 11 **careless** uncared-for

KING There's no art
To find the mind's construction in the face:
He was a gentleman on whom I built
An absolute trust.

Enter Macbeth, Banquo, Ross, and Angus.

O worthiest cousin!
15 The sin of my ingratitude even now
Was heavy on me: thou art so far before,
That swiftest wing of recompense is slow
To overtake thee. Would thou hadst less deserved,
That the proportion both of thanks and payment
20 Might have been mine! Only I have left to say,
More is thy due than more than all can pay.

MACBETH The service and the loyalty I owe,
In doing it, pays itself. Your Highness' part
Is to receive our duties: and our duties
25 Are to your throne and state, children and servants;
Which do but what they should, by doing every
thing
Safe toward your love and honor.

KING Welcome hither.
I have begun to plant thee, and will labor
To make thee full of growing. Noble Banquo,
30 That hast no less deserved, nor must be known
No less to have done so, let me enfold thee
And hold thee to my heart.

BANQUO There if I grow,
The harvest is your own.

KING My plenteous joys,
Wanton in fullness, seek to hide themselves
35 In drops of sorrow. Sons, kinsmen, thanes,
And you whose places are the nearest, know,
We will establish our estate upon
Our eldest, Malcolm, whom we name hereafter

19 proportion preponderance **23 pays itself** is its own reward **27 Safe toward** safeguarding (?) **34 Wanton** unrestrained **37 establish our estate** settle the succession

The Prince of Cumberland: which honor must
Not unaccompanied invest him only, 40
But signs of nobleness, like stars, shall shine
On all deservers. From hence to Inverness,
And bind us further to you.

MACBETH The rest is labor, which is not used for you.
I'll be myself the harbinger, and make joyful 45
The hearing of my wife with your approach;
So, humbly take my leave.

KING My worthy Cawdor!

MACBETH [*Aside*] The Prince of Cumberland! That is a step
On which I must fall down, or else o'erleap,
For in my way it lies. Stars, hide your fires; 50
Let not light see my black and deep desires:
The eye wink at the hand; yet let that be
Which the eye fears, when it is done, to see.

Exit.

KING True, worthy Banquo; he is full so valiant,
And in his commendations I am fed; 55
It is a banquet to me. Let's after him,
Whose care is gone before to bid us welcome.
It is a peerless kinsman. *Flourish. Exeunt.*

Scene V. [*Inverness. Macbeth's castle.*]

Enter Macbeth's wife, alone, with a letter.

LADY MACBETH [*Reads*] "They met me in the day of success; and I have learned by the perfect'st

44 The rest . . . you i.e., repose is laborious when not employed for you **52 wink at the hand** i.e., be blind to the hand's deed **55 his commendations** commendations of him

report they have more in them than mortal knowledge. When I burned in desire to question them
5 further, they made themselves air, into which they vanished. Whiles I stood rapt in the wonder of it, came missives from the King, who all-hailed me 'Thane of Cawdor'; by which title, before, these weïrd sisters saluted me, and referred me to the
10 coming on of time, with 'Hail, King that shalt be!' This have I thought good to deliver thee, my dearest partner of greatness, that thou mightst not lose the dues of rejoicing, by being ignorant of what greatness is promised thee. Lay it to thy heart,
15 and farewell."

Glamis thou art, and Cawdor, and shalt be
What thou art promised. Yet do I fear thy nature;
It is too full o' th' milk of human kindness
To catch the nearest way. Thou wouldst be great,
20 Art not without ambition, but without
The illness should attend it. What thou wouldst highly,
That wouldst thou holily; wouldst not play false,
And yet wouldst wrongly win. Thou'dst have, great Glamis,
That which cries "Thus thou must do" if thou have it;
25 And that which rather thou dost fear to do
Than wishest should be undone. Hie thee hither,
That I may pour my spirits in thine ear,
And chastise with the valor of my tongue
All that impedes thee from the golden round
30 Which fate and metaphysical aid doth seem
To have thee crowned withal.

Enter Messenger.

I.v. 7 **missives** messengers 11 **deliver thee** report to you 18 **milk of human kindness** i.e., gentle quality of human nature 21 **illness** wickedness 29 **round** crown 30 **metaphysical** supernatural 31 **withal** with

What is your tidings?

MESSENGER The King comes here tonight.

LADY MACBETH Thou'rt mad to say it!
Is not thy master with him, who, were 't so,
Would have informed for preparation?

MESSENGER So please you, it is true. Our thane is coming. 35
One of my fellows had the speed of him,
Who, almost dead for breath, had scarcely more
Than would make up his message.

LADY MACBETH Give him tending;
He brings great news. *Exit Messenger.*
The raven himself is hoarse
That croaks the fatal entrance of Duncan 40
Under my battlements. Come, you spirits
That tend on mortal thoughts, unsex me here,
And fill me, from the crown to the toe, top-full
Of direst cruelty! Make thick my blood,
Stop up th' access and passage to remorse, 45
That no compunctious visitings of nature
Shake my fell purpose, nor keep peace between
Th' effect and it! Come to my woman's breasts,
And take my milk for gall, you murd'ring ministers,
Wherever in your sightless substances 50
You wait on nature's mischief! Come, thick night,
And pall thee in the dunnest smoke of hell,
That my keen knife see not the wound it makes,
Nor heaven peep through the blanket of the dark,
To cry "Hold, hold!"

Enter Macbeth.

Great Glamis! Worthy Cawdor! 55
Greater than both, by the all-hail hereafter!

36 **had the speed of him** outdistanced him 42 **mortal** deadly 45 **remorse** compassion 46 **compunctious visitings of nature** natural feelings of compassion 47 **fell** savage 48 **effect** fulfillment 49 **for** in exchange for 49 **ministers** agents 50 **sightless** invisible 51 **wait on** assist 52 **pall** enshroud 52 **dunnest** darkest 56 **all-hail hereafter** the third all-hail (?) the all-hail of the future (?)

Thy letters have transported me beyond
This ignorant present, and I feel now
The future in the instant.

MACBETH My dearest love,
Duncan comes here tonight.

60 LADY MACBETH And when goes hence?

MACBETH Tomorrow, as he purposes.

LADY MACBETH O, never
Shall sun that morrow see!
Your face, my Thane, is as a book where men
May read strange matters. To beguile the time,
65 Look like the time; bear welcome in your eye,
Your hand, your tongue: look like th' innocent
flower,
But be the serpent under 't. He that's coming
Must be provided for: and you shall put
This night's great business into my dispatch;
70 Which shall to all our nights and days to come
Give solely sovereign sway and masterdom.

MACBETH We will speak further.

LADY MACBETH Only look up clear.
To alter favor ever is to fear.
Leave all the rest to me. *Exeunt.*

58 ignorant unknowing **59 instant** present **64 To beguile the time** i.e., to deceive people of the day **69 dispatch** management **72 look up clear** appear undisturbed **73 To alter . . . fear** to show a disturbed face is dangerous

Scene VI. [*Before Macbeth's castle.*]

Hautboys and torches. Enter King [*Duncan*], *Malcolm, Donalbain, Banquo, Lennox, Macduff, Ross, Angus, and Attendants.*

KING This castle hath a pleasant seat; the air
Nimbly and sweetly recommends itself
Unto our gentle senses.

BANQUO This guest of summer,
The temple-haunting martlet, does approve
By his loved mansionry that the heaven's breath 5
Smells wooingly here. No jutty, frieze,
Buttress, nor coign of vantage, but this bird
Hath made his pendent bed and procreant cradle.
Where they most breed and haunt, I have observed
The air is delicate.

Enter Lady [*Macbeth*].

KING See, see, our honored hostess! 10
The love that follows us sometime is our trouble,
Which still we thank as love. Herein I teach you
How you shall bid God 'ield us for your pains
And thank us for your trouble.

LADY MACBETH All our service
In every point twice done, and then done double, 15
Were poor and single business to contend
Against those honors deep and broad wherewith

I.vi. s.d. **Hautboys** oboes 1 **seat** site 3 **gentle** soothed 4 **temple-haunting martlet** martin (swift) nesting in churches 4 **approve** prove 5 **mansionry** nests 6 **jutty** projection 7 **coign of vantage** advantageous corner 8 **procreant** breeding 9 **haunt** visit 11–12 **The love . . . love** the love offered me sometimes inconveniences me, but still I value it as love 13 **'ield** reward 16 **single business** feeble service

Your Majesty loads our house: for those of old,
And the late dignities heaped up to them,
We rest your hermits.

20 KING Where's the Thane of Cawdor?
We coursed him at the heels, and had a purpose
To be his purveyor: but he rides well,
And his great love, sharp as his spur, hath holp
him
To his home before us. Fair and noble hostess,
We are your guest tonight.

25 LADY MACBETH Your servants ever
Have theirs, themselves, and what is theirs, in
compt,
To make their audit at your Highness' pleasure,
Still to return your own.

KING Give me your hand.
Conduct me to mine host: we love him highly,
30 And shall continue our graces towards him.
By your leave, hostess, *Exeunt.*

Scene VII. [*Macbeth's castle.*]

Hautboys. Torches. Enter a Sewer, and diverse
Servants with dishes and service over the stage.
Then enter Macbeth.

MACBETH If it were done when 'tis done, then 'twere
well
It were done quickly. If th' assassination

20 your hermits dependents bound to pray for you **21 coursed** pursued **22 purveyor** advance-supply officer **23 holp** helped **26 Have theirs . . . compt** have their dependents, themselves, and their possessions in trust **28 Still** always **I.vii. s.d. Sewer** chief butler **1 done** over and done with

Could trammel up the consequence, and catch,
With his surcease, success; that but this blow
Might be the be-all and the end-all—here, 5
But here, upon this bank and shoal of time,
We'd jump the life to come. But in these cases
We still have judgment here; that we but teach
Bloody instructions, which, being taught, return
To plague th' inventor: this even-handed justice 10
Commends th' ingredients of our poisoned
chalice
To our own lips. He's here in double trust:
First, as I am his kinsman and his subject,
Strong both against the deed; then, as his host,
Who should against his murderer shut the door, 15
Not bear the knife myself. Besides, this Duncan
Hath borne his faculties so meek, hath been
So clear in his great office, that his virtues
Will plead like angels trumpet-tongued against
The deep damnation of his taking-off; 20
And pity, like a naked newborn babe,
Striding the blast, or heaven's cherubin horsed
Upon the sightless couriers of the air,
Shall blow the horrid deed in every eye,
That tears shall drown the wind. I have no spur 25
To prick the sides of my intent, but only
Vaulting ambition, which o'erleaps itself
And falls on th' other——

Enter Lady [*Macbeth*].

How now! What news?

LADY MACBETH He has almost supped. Why have you left the chamber?

3 trammel up catch in a net **4 his surcease** Duncan's death (?) the consequence's cessation (?) **4 success** what follows **7 jump** risk **8 still** always **10 even-handed** impartial **11 Commends** offers **17 faculties** powers **18 clear** spotless **22 Striding** bestriding **23 sightless couriers** invisible coursers (i.e., the winds) **25 That** so that

MACBETH Hath he asked for me?

30 LADY MACBETH Know you not he has?

MACBETH We will proceed no further in this business:
He hath honored me of late, and I have bought
Golden opinions from all sorts of people,
Which would be worn now in their newest gloss,
Not cast aside so soon.

35 LADY MACBETH Was the hope drunk
Wherein you dressed yourself? Hath it slept since?
And wakes it now, to look so green and pale
At what it did so freely? From this time
Such I account thy love. Art thou afeard
40 To be the same in thine own act and valor
As thou art in desire? Wouldst thou have that
Which thou esteem'st the ornament of life,
And live a coward in thine own esteem,
Letting "I dare not" wait upon "I would,"
Like the poor cat i' th' adage?

45 MACBETH Prithee, peace!
I dare do all that may become a man;
Who dares do more is none.

LADY MACBETH What beast was 't then
That made you break this enterprise to me?
When you durst do it, then you were a man;
50 And to be more than what you were, you would
Be so much more the man. Nor time nor place
Did then adhere, and yet you would make both.
They have made themselves, and that their fitness now
Does unmake you. I have given suck, and know
55 How tender 'tis to love the babe that milks me:
I would, while it was smiling in my face,
Have plucked my nipple from his boneless gums,

32 bought acquired **37 green** sickly **44 wait upon** follow **45 cat** (who wants fish but fears to wet its paws) **48 break** broach **52 adhere** suit **53 that their** their very

And dashed the brains out, had I so sworn as you
Have done to this.

MACBETH If we should fail?

LADY MACBETH We fail?
But screw your courage to the sticking-place, 60
And we'll not fail. When Duncan is asleep—
Whereto the rather shall his day's hard journey
Soundly invite him—his two chamberlains
Will I with wine and wassail so convince,
That memory, the warder of the brain, 65
Shall be a fume, and the receipt of reason
A limbeck only: when in swinish sleep
Their drenchèd natures lies as in a death,
What cannot you and I perform upon
Th' unguarded Duncan, what not put upon 70
His spongy officers, who shall bear the guilt
Of our great quell?

MACBETH Bring forth men-children only;
For thy undaunted mettle should compose
Nothing but males. Will it not be received,
When we have marked with blood those sleepy two 75
Of his own chamber, and used their very daggers,
That they have done't?

LADY MACBETH Who dares receive it other,
As we shall make our griefs and clamor roar
Upon his death?

MACBETH I am settled, and bend up
Each corporal agent to this terrible feat. 80
Away, and mock the time with fairest show:
False face must hide what the false heart doth know.

Exeunt.

60 **But** only 60 **sticking place** notch (holding the bowstring of a taut crossbow) 64 **wassail** carousing 64 **convince** overpower 65 **warder** guard 66–67 **receipt . . . only** i.e., the receptacle (receipt), which should collect the distillate of thought—reason—will be a mere vessel (limbeck) of undistilled liquids 68 **lies** lie 71 **spongy** sodden 72 **quell** killing 73 **mettle** substance 77 **other** otherwise 81 **mock the time** beguile the world

ACT II

Scene I. [*Inverness. Court of Macbeth's castle.*]

Enter Banquo, and Fleance, with a torch before him.

BANQUO How goes the night, boy?

FLEANCE The moon is down; I have not heard the clock.

BANQUO And she goes down at twelve.

FLEANCE I take't, 'tis later, sir.

BANQUO Hold, take my sword. There's husbandry in heaven.

5 Their candles are all out. Take thee that too.
A heavy summons lies like lead upon me,
And yet I would not sleep. Merciful powers,
Restrain in me the cursèd thoughts that nature
Gives way to in repose!

Enter Macbeth, and a Servant with a torch.

Give me my sword!

10 Who's there?

MACBETH A friend.

BANQUO What, sir, not yet at rest? The King's a-bed:
He hath been in unusual pleasure, and
Sent forth great largess to your offices:
15 This diamond he greets your wife withal,
By the name of most kind hostess; and shut up
In measureless content.

II.i. 4 **husbandry** frugality 6 **summons** call (to sleep) 14 **largess to your offices** gifts to your servants' quarters 16 **shut up** concluded

MACBETH Being unprepared,
Our will became the servant to defect,
Which else should free have wrought.

BANQUO All's well.
I dreamt last night of the three weïrd sisters: 20
To you they have showed some truth.

MACBETH I think not of them.
Yet, when we can entreat an hour to serve,
We would spend it in some words upon that business,
If you would grant the time.

BANQUO At your kind'st leisure.

MACBETH If you shall cleave to my consent, when 'tis, 25
It shall make honor for you.

BANQUO So I lose none
In seeking to augment it, but still keep
My bosom franchised and allegiance clear,
I shall be counseled.

MACBETH Good repose the while!

BANQUO Thanks, sir. The like to you! 30

Exit Banquo [with Fleance].

MACBETH Go bid thy mistress, when my drink is ready,
She strike upon the bell. Get thee to bed.

Exit [Servant].

Is this a dagger which I see before me,
The handle toward my hand? Come, let me clutch thee.
I have thee not, and yet I see thee still. 35
Art thou not, fatal vision, sensible
To feeling as to sight, or art thou but
A dagger of the mind, a false creation,

18 **Our ... defect** our good will was hampered by our deficient preparations 25 **cleave... 'tis** join my cause, when the time comes 26 **So** provided that 28 **franchised** free (from guilt) 28 **clear** spotless 36 **sensible** perceptible

Proceeding from the heat-oppressèd brain?
40 I see thee yet, in form as palpable
As this which now I draw.
Thou marshal'st me the way that I was going;
And such an instrument I was to use.
Mine eyes are made the fools o' th' other senses,
45 Or else worth all the rest. I see thee still;
And on thy blade and dudgeon gouts of blood,
Which was not so before. There's no such thing.
It is the bloody business which informs
Thus to mine eyes. Now o'er the one half-world
50 Nature seems dead, and wicked dreams abuse
The curtained sleep; witchcraft celebrates
Pale Hecate's offerings; and withered murder,
Alarumed by his sentinel, the wolf,
Whose howl's his watch, thus with his stealthy pace,
55 With Tarquin's ravishing strides, towards his design
Moves like a ghost. Thou sure and firm-set earth,
Hear not my steps, which way they walk, for fear
Thy very stones prate of my whereabout,
And take the present horror from the time,
Which now suits with it. Whiles I threat, he
60 lives:
Words to the heat of deeds too cold breath gives.

A bell rings.

I go, and it is done: the bell invites me.
Hear it not, Duncan, for it is a knell
That summons thee to heaven, or to hell.

Exit.

46 **dudgeon** wooden hilt 46 **gouts** large drops 48 **informs** gives shape (?) 50 **abuse** deceive 52 **Hecate's offerings** offerings to Hecate (goddess of sorcery) 53 **Alarumed** called to action 55 **Tarquin** (Roman tyrant who ravished Lucrece) 59–60 **take . . . it** remove (by noise) the horrible silence attendant on this moment and suitable to it (?)

Scene II. [*Macbeth's castle.*]

Enter Lady [*Macbeth*].

LADY MACBETH That which hath made them drunk hath made me bold;
What hath quenched them hath given me fire. Hark! Peace!
It was the owl that shrieked, the fatal bellman,
Which gives the stern'st good-night. He is about it.
The doors are open, and the surfeited grooms 5
Do mock their charge with snores. I have drugged their possets,
That death and nature do contend about them,
Whether they live or die.

MACBETH [*Within*] Who's there? What, ho?

LADY MACBETH Alack, I am afraid they have awaked
And 'tis not done! Th' attempt and not the deed 10
Confounds us. Hark! I laid their daggers ready;
He could not miss 'em. Had he not resembled
My father as he slept, I had done't.

Enter Macbeth.

My husband!

MACBETH I have done the deed. Didst thou not hear a noise?

LADY MACBETH I heard the owl scream and the crickets cry. 15
Did not you speak?

MACBETH When?

II.ii. 3–4 **bellman . . . good-night** i.e., the owl's call, portending death, is like the town crier's call to a condemned man **6 possets** (bedtime drinks) **7 nature** natural vitality **11 Confounds** ruins

LADY MACBETH Now.

MACBETH As I descended?

LADY MACBETH Ay.

MACBETH Hark!
Who lies i' th' second chamber?

LADY MACBETH Donalbain.

20 MACBETH This is a sorry sight.

LADY MACBETH A foolish thought, to say a sorry sight.

MACBETH There's one did laugh in 's sleep, and one cried "Murder!"
That they did wake each other. I stood and heard them.
But they did say their prayers, and addressed them
Again to sleep.

25 LADY MACBETH There are two lodged together.

MACBETH One cried "God bless us!" and "Amen" the other,
As they had seen me with these hangman's hands:
List'ning their fear, I could not say "Amen,"
When they did say "God bless us!"

LADY MACBETH Consider it not so deeply.

MACBETH But wherefore could not I pronounce
30 "Amen"?
I had most need of blessing, and "Amen"
Stuck in my throat.

LADY MACBETH These deeds must not be thought
After these ways; so, it will make us mad.

MACBETH Methought I heard a voice cry "Sleep no more!
35 Macbeth does murder sleep"—the innocent sleep,
Sleep that knits up the raveled sleave of care,

20 sorry miserable **27 hangman's** executioner's (i.e., bloody) **36 knits up the raveled sleave** straightens out the tangled skein

The death of each day's life, sore labor's bath,
Balm of hurt minds, great nature's second course,
Chief nourisher in life's feast——

LADY MACBETH What do you mean?

MACBETH Still it cried "Sleep no more!" to all the
house: 40
"Glamis hath murdered sleep, and therefore
Cawdor
Shall sleep no more: Macbeth shall sleep no more."

LADY MACBETH Who was it that thus cried? Why,
worthy Thane,
You do unbend your noble strength, to think
So brainsickly of things. Go get some water, 45
And wash this filthy witness from your hand.
Why did you bring these daggers from the place?
They must lie there: go carry them, and smear
The sleepy grooms with blood.

MACBETH I'll go no more.
I am afraid to think what I have done; 50
Look on 't again I dare not.

LADY MACBETH Infirm of purpose!
Give me the daggers. The sleeping and the dead
Are but as pictures. 'Tis the eye of childhood
That fears a painted devil. If he do bleed,
I'll gild the faces of the grooms withal, 55
For it must seem their guilt.

Exit. Knock within.

MACBETH Whence is that knocking?
How is 't with me, when every noise appalls me?
What hands are here? Ha! They pluck out mine
eyes!
Will all great Neptune's ocean wash this blood
Clean from my hand? No; this my hand will rather 60

38 second course i.e., sleep (the less substantial first course is food) **44 unbend** relax **46 witness** evidence **54 painted** depicted **55 gild** paint

The multitudinous seas incarnadine,
Making the green one red.

Enter Lady [*Macbeth*].

LADY MACBETH My hands are of your color, but I shame
To wear a heart so white. (*Knock.*) I hear a knocking
65 At the south entry. Retire we to our chamber.
A little water clears us of this deed:
How easy is it then! Your constancy
Hath left you unattended. (*Knock.*) Hark! more knocking.
Get on your nightgown, lest occasion call us
70 And show us to be watchers. Be not lost
So poorly in your thoughts.

MACBETH To know my deed, 'twere best not know myself. (*Knock.*)
Wake Duncan with thy knocking! I would thou couldst! *Exeunt.*

Scene III. [*Macbeth's castle.*]

Enter a Porter. Knocking within.

PORTER Here's a knocking indeed! If a man were porter of hell gate, he should have old turning the key. (*Knock.*) Knock, knock, knock! Who's there,

61 incarnadine redden **62 the green one red** (perhaps "the green one" means "the ocean," but perhaps "one" here means "totally," "uniformly") **67–68 Your ... unattended** your firmness has deserted you **69 nightgown** dressing-gown **70 watchers** i.e., up late **71 poorly** weakly II.iii. **2 should have old** would certainly have plenty of

i' th' name of Beelzebub? Here's a farmer, that hanged himself on th' expectation of plenty. Come in time! Have napkins enow about you; here you'll sweat for 't. (*Knock.*) Knock, knock! Who's there, in th' other devil's name? Faith, here's an equivocator, that could swear in both the scales against either scale; who committed treason enough for God's sake, yet could not equivocate to heaven. O, come in, equivocator. (*Knock.*) Knock, knock, knock! Who's there? Faith, here's an English tailor come hither for stealing out of a French hose: come in, tailor. Here you may roast your goose. (*Knock.*) Knock, knock; never at quiet! What are you? But this place is too cold for hell. I'll devil-porter it no further. I had thought to have let in some of all professions that go the primrose way to th' everlasting bonfire. (*Knock.*) Anon, anon! [*Opens an entrance.*] I pray you, remember the porter.

Enter Macduff and Lennox.

MACDUFF Was it so late, friend, ere you went to bed,
That you do lie so late?

PORTER Faith, sir, we were carousing till the second cock: and drink, sir, is a great provoker of three things.

MACDUFF What three things does drink especially provoke?

PORTER Marry, sir, nose-painting, sleep, and urine. Lechery, sir, it provokes and unprovokes; it provokes the desire, but it takes away the performance: therefore much drink may be said to be an equivocator with lechery: it makes him and it mars

4–5 farmer ... plenty (the farmer hoarded so he could later sell high, but when it looked as though there would be a crop surplus he hanged himself) 6 enow enough 8–9 equivocator i.e., Jesuit (who allegedly employed deceptive speech to further God's ends) 14 French hose tight-fitting hose 15 goose pressing iron 25–26 second cock (about 3 a.m.)

35 him; it sets him on and it takes him off; it persuades him and disheartens him; makes him stand to and not stand to; in conclusion, equivocates him in a sleep, and giving him the lie, leaves him.

MACDUFF I believe drink gave thee the lie last night.

40 PORTER That it did, sir, i' the very throat on me: but I requited him for his lie, and, I think, being too strong for him, though he took up my legs sometime, yet I make a shift to cast him.

MACDUFF Is thy master stirring?

Enter Macbeth.

45 Our knocking has awaked him; here he comes.

LENNOX Good morrow, noble sir.

MACBETH Good morrow, both.

MACDUFF Is the king stirring, worthy Thane?

MACBETH Not yet.

MACDUFF He did command me to call timely on him:
I have almost slipped the hour.

MACBETH I'll bring you to him.

50 MACDUFF I know this is a joyful trouble to you;
But yet 'tis one.

MACBETH The labor we delight in physics pain.
This is the door.

MACDUFF I'll make so bold to call,
For 'tis my limited service.

Exit Macduff.

LENNOX Goes the king hence today?

55 MACBETH He does: he did appoint so.

39 **gave thee the lie** called you a liar (with a pun on "stretched you out") 43 **cast** (with a pun on "cast," meaning "vomit") 48 **timely** early 49 **slipped** let slip 52 **The labor ... pain** labor that gives us pleasure cures discomfort 54 **limited service** appointed duty

LENNOX The night has been unruly. Where we lay,
Our chimneys were blown down, and, as they say,
Lamentings heard i' th' air, strange screams of
death,
And prophesying with accents terrible
Of dire combustion and confused events 60
New hatched to th' woeful time: the obscure bird
Clamored the livelong night. Some say, the earth
Was feverous and did shake.

MACBETH 'Twas a rough night.

LENNOX My young remembrance cannot parallel
A fellow to it. 65

Enter Macduff.

MACDUFF O horror, horror, horror! Tongue nor heart
Cannot conceive nor name thee.

MACBETH and LENNOX What's the matter?

MACDUFF Confusion now hath made his masterpiece.
Most sacrilegious murder hath broke ope
The Lord's anointed temple, and stole thence 70
The life o' th' building.

MACBETH What is 't you say? The life?

LENNOX Mean you his Majesty?

MACDUFF Approach the chamber, and destroy your
sight
With a new Gorgon: do not bid me speak;
See, and then speak yourselves. Awake, awake! 75

Exeunt Macbeth and Lennox.

Ring the alarum bell. Murder and treason!
Banquo and Donalbain! Malcolm! Awake!
Shake off this downy sleep, death's counterfeit,
And look on death itself! Up, up, and see
The great doom's image! Malcolm! Banquo! 80

60 combustion tumult **61 obscure bird** bird of darkness, i.e., the owl **68 Confusion** destruction **74 Gorgon** (creature capable of turning beholders to stone) **78 counterfeit** imitation **80 great doom's image** likeness of Judgment Day

As from your graves rise up, and walk like sprites,
To countenance this horror. Ring the bell.

Bell rings. Enter Lady [Macbeth].

LADY MACBETH What's the business,
That such a hideous trumpet calls to parley
The sleepers of the house? Speak, speak!

85 MACDUFF O gentle lady,
'Tis not for you to hear what I can speak:
The repetition, in a woman's ear,
Would murder as it fell.

Enter Banquo.

O Banquo, Banquo!
Our royal master's murdered.

LADY MACBETH Woe, alas!
What, in our house?

90 BANQUO Too cruel anywhere.
Dear Duff, I prithee, contradict thyself,
And say it is not so.

Enter Macbeth, Lennox, and Ross.

MACBETH Had I but died an hour before this chance,
I had lived a blessèd time; for from this instant
95 There's nothing serious in mortality:
All is but toys. Renown and grace is dead,
The wine of life is drawn, and the mere lees
Is left this vault to brag of.

Enter Malcolm and Donalbain.

DONALBAIN What is amiss?

MACBETH You are, and do not know't.
100 The spring, the head, the fountain of your blood
Is stopped; the very source of it is stopped.

MACDUFF Your royal father's murdered.

81 sprites spirits **82 countenance** be in keeping with **87 repetition** report **95 serious in mortality** worthwhile in mortal life **96 toys** trifles **97 lees** dregs **98 vault** (1) wine vault (2) earth, with the sky as roof (?)

MALCOLM O, by whom?

LENNOX Those of his chamber, as it seemed, had done 't:
Their hands and faces were all badged with blood;
So were their daggers, which unwiped we found 105
Upon their pillows. They stared, and were distracted.
No man's life was to be trusted with them.

MACBETH O, yet I do repent me of my fury,
That I did kill them.

MACDUFF Wherefore did you so?

MACBETH Who can be wise, amazed, temp'rate and furious, 110
Loyal and neutral, in a moment? No man.
The expedition of my violent love
Outran the pauser, reason. Here lay Duncan,
His silver skin laced with his golden blood,
And his gashed stabs looked like a breach in nature 115
For ruin's wasteful entrance: there, the murderers,
Steeped in the colors of their trade, their daggers
Unmannerly breeched with gore. Who could refrain,
That had a heart to love, and in that heart
Courage to make 's love known?

LADY MACBETH Help me hence, ho! 120

MACDUFF Look to the lady.

MALCOLM [*Aside to Donalbain*] Why do we hold our tongues,
That most may claim this argument for ours?

DONALBAIN [*Aside to Malcolm*] What should be spoken here,
Where our fate, hid in an auger-hole,

104 **badged** marked 110 **amazed** bewildered 112 **expedition** haste 118 **Unmannerly breeched with gore** covered with unseemly breeches of blood 118 **refrain** check oneself 121 **Look to** look after 123 **That most . . . ours?** who are the most concerned with this topic 124 **auger-hole** i.e., unsuspected place

125 May rush, and seize us? Let's away:
Our tears are not yet brewed.

MALCOLM [*Aside to Donalbain*] Nor our strong sorrow
Upon the foot of motion.

BANQUO Look to the lady.

[*Lady Macbeth is carried out.*]

And when we have our naked frailties hid,
That suffer in exposure, let us meet
130 And question this most bloody piece of work,
To know it further. Fears and scruples shake us.
In the great hand of God I stand, and thence
Against the undivulged pretense I fight
Of treasonous malice.

MACDUFF And so do I.

ALL So all.

135 MACBETH Let's briefly put on manly readiness,
And meet i' th' hall together.

ALL Well contented.

Exeunt [*all but Malcolm and Donalbain*].

MALCOLM What will you do? Let's not consort with them.
To show an unfelt sorrow is an office
Which the false man does easy. I'll to England.

140 DONALBAIN To Ireland, I; our separated fortune
Shall keep us both the safer. Where we are
There's daggers in men's smiles; the near in blood,
The nearer bloody.

MALCOLM This murderous shaft that's shot
Hath not yet lighted, and our safest way

126–27 Our tears . . . motion i.e., we have not yet had time for tears nor to express our sorrows in action (?) **128 naked frailties hid** poor bodies clothed **130 question** discuss **181 scruples** suspicions **133 undivulged pretense** hidden purpose **135 briefly** quickly **138 office** function

Is to avoid the aim. Therefore to horse; 145
And let us not be dainty of leave-taking,
But shift away. There's warrant in that theft
Which steals itself when there's no mercy left.

Exeunt.

Scene IV. [*Outside Macbeth's castle.*]

Enter Ross with an Old Man.

OLD MAN Threescore and ten I can remember well:
Within the volume of which time I have seen
Hours dreadful and things strange, but this sore night
Hath trifled former knowings.

ROSS Ha, good father,
Thou seest the heavens, as troubled with man's act, 5
Threatens his bloody stage. By th' clock 'tis day,
And yet dark night strangles the traveling lamp:
Is 't night's predominance, or the day's shame,
That darkness does the face of earth entomb,
When living light should kiss it?

OLD MAN 'Tis unnatural, 10
Even like the deed that's done. On Tuesday last
A falcon, tow'ring in her pride of place,
Was by a mousing owl hawked at and killed.

ROSS And Duncan's horses—a thing most strange and certain—
Beauteous and swift, the minions of their race, 15

146 dainty of fussy about **147 warrant** justification **148 steals itself** steals oneself away II.iv. **3 sore** grievous **4 trifled former knowings** made trifles of former experiences **7 traveling lamp** i.e., the sun **8 predominance** astrological supremacy **12 tow'ring ... place** soaring at her summit **13 mousing** i.e., normally mouse-eating **15 minions** darlings

Turned wild in nature, broke their stalls, flung out,
Contending 'gainst obedience, as they would make
War with mankind.

OLD MAN 'Tis said they eat each other.

ROSS They did so, to th' amazement of mine eyes,
That looked upon 't.

Enter Macduff.

20 Here comes the good Macduff.
How goes the world, sir, now?

MACDUFF Why, see you not?

ROSS Is 't known who did this more than bloody deed?

MACDUFF Those that Macbeth hath slain.

ROSS Alas, the day!
What good could they pretend?

MACDUFF They were suborned:
25 Malcolm and Donalbain, the king's two sons,
Are stol'n away and fled, which puts upon them
Suspicion of the deed.

ROSS 'Gainst nature still.
Thriftless ambition, that will ravin up
Thine own life's means! Then 'tis most like
30 The sovereignty will fall upon Macbeth.

MACDUFF He is already named, and gone to Scone
To be invested.

ROSS Where is Duncan's body?

MACDUFF Carried to Colmekill,
The sacred storehouse of his predecessors
And guardian of their bones.

35 ROSS Will you to Scone?

MACDUFF No, cousin, I'll to Fife.

16 **flung out** lunged wildly 18 **eat** ate 24 **pretend** hope for 24 **suborned** bribed 28 **Thriftless** wasteful 28 **ravin up** greedily devour 31 **named** elected 32 **invested** installed as king

ROSS Well, I will thither.

MACDUFF Well, may you see things well done there.
Adieu,
Lest our old robes sit easier than our new!

ROSS Farewell, father.

OLD MAN God's benison go with you, and with those 40
That would make good of bad, and friends of foes!

Exeunt omnes.

40 benison blessing

ACT III

Scene I. [*Forres. The palace.*]

Enter Banquo.

BANQUO Thou hast it now: King, Cawdor, Glamis, all,
As the weïrd women promised, and I fear
Thou play'dst most foully for 't. Yet it was said
It should not stand in thy posterity,
5 But that myself should be the root and father
Of many kings. If there come truth from them—
As upon thee, Macbeth, their speeches shine—
Why, by the verities on thee made good,
May they not be my oracles as well
10 And set me up in hope? But hush, no more!

Sennet sounded. Enter Macbeth as King, Lady [Macbeth], Lennox, Ross, Lords, and Attendants.

MACBETH Here's our chief guest.

LADY MACBETH If he had been forgotten,
It had been as a gap in our great feast,
And all-thing unbecoming.

MACBETH Tonight we hold a solemn supper, sir,
And I'll request your presence.

15 BANQUO Let your Highness
Command upon me, to the which my duties

III.i. 4 **stand** continue s.d. **Sennet** trumpet call 13 **all-thing** altogether
14 **solemn** ceremonious

Are with a most indissoluble tie
For ever knit.

MACBETH Ride you this afternoon?

BANQUO Ay, my good lord.

MACBETH We should have else desired your good advice 20
(Which still hath been both grave and
prosperous)
In this day's council; but we'll take tomorrow.
Is 't far you ride?

BANQUO As far, my lord, as will fill up the time
'Twixt this and supper. Go not my horse the
better, 25
I must become a borrower of the night
For a dark hour or twain.

MACBETH Fail not our feast.

BANQUO My lord, I will not.

MACBETH We hear our bloody cousins are bestowed
In England and in Ireland, not confessing 30
Their cruel parricide, filling their hearers
With strange invention. But of that tomorrow,
When therewithal we shall have cause of state
Craving us jointly. Hie you to horse. Adieu,
Till you return at night. Goes Fleance with you? 35

BANQUO Ay, my good lord: our time does call upon 's.

MACBETH I wish your horses swift and sure of foot,
And so I do commend you to their backs.
Farewell. *Exit Banquo.*
Let every man be master of his time 40
Till seven at night. To make society
The sweeter welcome, we will keep ourself

21 still always **21 grave and prosperous** weighty and profitable **25 Go . . . better** unless my horse goes better than I expect **29 are bestowed** have taken refuge **32 invention** lies **33-34 cause . . . jointly** matters of state demanding our joint attention

Till supper-time alone. While then, God be with you!

Exeunt Lords [*and all but Macbeth and a Servant*].

Sirrah, a word with you: attend those men

45 Our pleasure?

ATTENDANT They are, my lord, without the palace gate.

MACBETH Bring them before us. *Exit Servant.*

To be thus is nothing, but to be safely thus—

Our fears in Banquo stick deep,

50 And in his royalty of nature reigns that

Which would be feared. 'Tis much he dares;

And, to that dauntless temper of his mind,

He hath a wisdom that doth guide his valor

To act in safety. There is none but he

55 Whose being I do fear: and under him

My genius is rebuked, as it is said

Mark Antony's was by Caesar. He chid the sisters,

When first they put the name of King upon me,

And bade them speak to him; then prophetlike

60 They hailed him father to a line of kings.

Upon my head they placed a fruitless crown

And put a barren scepter in my gripe,

Thence to be wrenched with an unlineal hand,

No son of mine succeeding. If 't be so,

65 For Banquo's issue have I filed my mind;

For them the gracious Duncan have I murdered;

Put rancors in the vessel of my peace

Only for them, and mine eternal jewel

Given to the common enemy of man,

70 To make them kings, the seeds of Banquo kings!

43 **While** until 44 **Sirrah** (common address to an inferior) 44 **attend** await 46 **without** outside 48 **but** unless 49 **in** about 51 **would** must 52 **to** added to 52 **temper** quality 56 **genius is rebuked** guardian spirit is cowed 62 **gripe** grasp 65 **filed** defiled 67 **rancors** bitter enmities 68 **eternal jewel** i.e., soul 69 **common enemy of man** i.e., the Devil

Rather than so, come, fate, into the list,
And champion me to th' utterance! Who's there?

Enter Servant and Two Murderers.

Now go to the door, and stay there till we call.

Exit Servant.

Was it not yesterday we spoke together?

MURDERERS It was, so please your Highness.

MACBETH Well then, now 75
Have you considered of my speeches? Know
That it was he in the times past, which held you
So under fortune, which you thought had been
Our innocent self; this I made good to you
In our last conference; passed in probation with you, 80
How you were born in hand, how crossed; the instruments,
Who wrought with them, and all things else that might
To half a soul and to a notion crazed
Say "Thus did Banquo."

FIRST MURDERER You made it known to us.

MACBETH I did so; and went further, which is now 85
Our point of second meeting. Do you find
Your patience so predominant in your nature,
That you can let this go? Are you so gospeled,
To pray for this good man and for his issue,
Whose heavy hand hath bowed you to the grave 90
And beggared yours for ever?

FIRST MURDERER We are men, my liege.

MACBETH Ay, in the catalogue ye go for men;

71 **list** lists 72 **champion me to th' utterance** fight against me to the death 77–78 **held . . . fortune** kept you from good fortune (?) 80 **passed in probation** reviewed the proofs 81 **borne in hand** deceived 81 **crossed** thwarted 81 **instruments** tools 83 **half a soul** a halfwit 83 **notion** mind 88 **gospeled** i.e., made meek by the gospel 92 **go for** pass as

As hounds and greyhounds, mongrels, spaniels,
curs,
Shoughs, water-rugs and demi-wolves, are clept
95 All by the name of dogs: the valued file
Distinguishes the swift, the slow, the subtle,
The housekeeper, the hunter, every one
According to the gift which bounteous nature
Hath in him closed, whereby he does receive
100 Particular addition, from the bill
That writes them all alike: and so of men.
Now if you have a station in the file,
Not i' th' worst rank of manhood, say 't,
And I will put that business in your bosoms
105 Whose execution takes your enemy off,
Grapples you to the heart and love of us,
Who wear our health but sickly in his life,
Which in his death were perfect.

SECOND MURDERER I am one, my liege,
Whom the vile blows and buffets of the world
110 Hath so incensed that I am reckless what
I do to spite the world.

FIRST MURDERER And I another
So weary with disasters, tugged with fortune,
That I would set my life on any chance,
To mend it or be rid on't.

MACBETH Both of you
Know Banquo was your enemy.

115 BOTH MURDERERS True, my lord.

MACBETH So is he mine, and in such bloody distance
That every minute of his being thrusts
Against my near'st of life: and though I could

94 **Shoughs, water-rugs** shaggy dogs, long-haired water dogs 94 **clept** called
95 **valued file** classification by valuable traits 97 **housekeeper** watchdog
99 **closed** enclosed 100 **Particular addition, from the bill** special distinction in opposition to the list 107 **wear . . . life** have only imperfect health while he lives
113 **set** risk 116 **distance** quarrel 118 **near'st of life** most vital spot

With barefaced power sweep him from my sight
And bid my will avouch it, yet I must not, 120
For certain friends that are both his and mine,
Whose loves I may not drop, but wail his fall
Who I myself struck down: and thence it is
That I to your assistance do make love,
Masking the business from the common eye 125
For sundry weighty reasons.

SECOND MURDERER We shall, my lord,
Perform what you command us.

FIRST MURDERER Though our lives——

MACBETH Your spirits shine through you. Within this hour at most
I will advise you where to plant yourselves,
Acquaint you with the perfect spy o' th' time, 130
The moment on 't; for 't must be done tonight,
And something from the palace; always thought
That I require a clearness: and with him—
To leave no rubs nor botches in the work—
Fleance his son, that keeps him company, 135
Whose absence is no less material to me
Than is his father's, must embrace the fate
Of that dark hour. Resolve yourselves apart:
I'll come to you anon.

MURDERERS We are resolved, my lord.

MACBETH I'll call upon you straight. Abide within. 140
It is concluded: Banquo, thy soul's flight,
If it find heaven, must find it out tonight. *Exeunt.*

120 **avouch** justify 121 **For** because of 122 **wail his fall** bewail his death 130 **perfect spy** exact information (?) (spy literally means "observation"; apparently Macbeth already has the Third Murderer in mind) 131 **on 't** of it 132 **something** some distance 132 **thought** remembered 133 **clearness** freedom from suspicion 134 **rubs** flaws 138 **Resolve yourselves apart** decide by yourself 140 **straight** immediately

Scene II. [*The palace.*]

Enter Macbeth's Lady and a Servant.

LADY MACBETH Is Banquo gone from court?

SERVANT Ay, madam, but returns again tonight.

LADY MACBETH Say to the King, I would attend his leisure
For a few words.

SERVANT Madam, I will. *Exit.*

LADY MACBETH Nought's had, all's spent,
5 Where our desire is got without content:
'Tis safer to be that which we destroy
Than by destruction dwell in doubtful joy.

Enter Macbeth.

How now, my lord! Why do you keep alone,
Of sorriest fancies your companions making,
Using those thoughts which should indeed have
10 died
With them they think on? Things without all remedy
Should be without regard: what's done is done.

MACBETH We have scorched the snake, not killed it:
She'll close and be herself, whilst our poor malice
15 Remains in danger of her former tooth.
But let the frame of things disjoint, both the worlds suffer,
Ere we will eat our meal in fear, and sleep
In the affliction of these terrible dreams

III.ii. 9 **sorriest** most despicable 11 **without** beyond 13 **scorched** slashed, scored 14 **close** heal 14 **poor malice** feeble enmity 16 **frame of things disjoint** universe collapse 16 **both the worlds** heaven and earth (?)

That shake us nightly: better be with the dead,
Whom we, to gain our peace, have sent to peace, 20
Than on the torture of the mind to lie
In restless ecstasy. Duncan is in his grave;
After life's fitful fever he sleeps well.
Treason has done his worst: nor steel, nor poison,
Malice domestic, foreign levy, nothing, 25
Can touch him further.

LADY MACBETH Come on.
Gentle my lord, sleek o'er your rugged looks;
Be bright and jovial among your guests tonight.

MACBETH So shall I, love; and so, I pray, be you:
Let your remembrance apply to Banquo; 30
Present him eminence, both with eye and tongue:
Unsafe the while, that we must lave
Our honors in these flattering streams
And make our faces vizards to our hearts,
Disguising what they are.

LADY MACBETH You must leave this. 35

MACBETH O, full of scorpions is my mind, dear wife!
Thou know'st that Banquo, and his Fleance, lives.

LADY MACBETH But in them nature's copy's not
eterne.

MACBETH There's comfort yet; they are assailable.
Then be thou jocund. Ere the bat hath flown 40
His cloistered flight, ere to black Hecate's summons
The shard-borne beetle with his drowsy hums
Hath rung night's yawning peal, there shall be done
A deed of dreadful note.

LADY MACBETH What's to be done?

21 **torture** i.e., rack 22 **ecstasy** frenzy 24 **his** its 25 **Malice domestic** civil war 27 **sleek** smooth 27 **rugged** furrowed 30 **Let . . . Banquo** focus your thoughts on Banquo 31 **Present him eminence** honor him 32 **Unsafe . . . lave** i.e., you and I are unsafe because we must dip 34 **vizards** masks 38 **nature's copy** nature's lease (?) imitation (i.e., a son) made by nature (?) 42 **shard-borne** borne on scaly wings (?) dung-bred (?)

MACBETH Be innocent of the knowledge, dearest
45 chuck,
Till thou applaud the deed. Come, seeling night,
Scarf up the tender eye of pitiful day,
And with thy bloody and invisible hand
Cancel and tear to pieces that great bond
50 Which keeps me pale! Light thickens, and the crow
Makes wing to th' rooky wood.
Good things of day begin to droop and drowse,
Whiles night's black agents to their preys do rouse.
Thou marvel'st at my words: but hold thee still;
55 Things bad begun make strong themselves by ill:
So, prithee, go with me. *Exeunt.*

Scene III. [*Near the palace.*]

Enter Three Murderers.

FIRST MURDERER But who did bid thee join with us?

THIRD MURDERER Macbeth.

SECOND MURDERER He needs not our mistrust; since he
delivers
Our offices and what we have to do
To the direction just.

FIRST MURDERER Then stand with us.
5 The west yet glimmers with some streaks of day.
Now spurs the lated traveler apace
To gain the timely inn, and near approaches
The subject of our watch.

45 **chuck** chick (a term of endearment) 46 **seeling** eye-closing 47 **Scarf up** blindfold 49 **bond** i.e., between Banquo and fate (?) Banquo's lease on life (?) Macbeth's link to humanity (?) 51 **rooky** full of rooks III.iii. 2-4 **He needs . . . just** we need not mistrust him (i.e., the Third Murderer) since he describes our duties according to our exact directions 6 **lated** belated

THIRD MURDERER Hark! I hear horses.

BANQUO (*Within*) Give us a light there, ho!

SECOND MURDERER Then 'tis he. The rest
That are within the note of expectation 10
Already are i' th' court.

FIRST MURDERER His horses go about.

THIRD MURDERER Almost a mile: but he does usually—
So all men do—from hence to th' palace gate
Make it their walk.

Enter Banquo and Fleance, with a torch.

SECOND MURDERER A light, a light!

THIRD MURDERER 'Tis he.

FIRST MURDERER Stand to 't. 15

BANQUO It will be rain tonight.

FIRST MURDERER Let it come down.

[*They set upon Banquo.*]

BANQUO O, treachery! Fly, good Fleance, fly, fly, fly!
[*Exit Fleance.*]
Thou mayst revenge. O slave! [*Dies.*]

THIRD MURDERER Who did strike out the light?

FIRST MURDERER Was 't not the way?

THIRD MURDERER There's but one down; the son is fled. 20

SECOND MURDERER We have lost best half of our affair.

FIRST MURDERER Well, let's away and say how much is
done. *Exeunt.*

10 within the note of expectation on the list of expected guests 19 way i.e., thing to do

Scene IV. [*The palace.*]

Banquet prepared. Enter Macbeth, Lady [*Macbeth*], *Ross, Lennox, Lords, and Attendants.*

MACBETH You know your own degrees; sit down:
At first and last, the hearty welcome.

LORDS Thanks to your Majesty.

MACBETH Ourself will mingle with society
5 And play the humble host.
Our hostess keeps her state, but in best time
We will require her welcome.

LADY MACBETH Pronounce it for me, sir, to all our friends,
For my heart speaks they are welcome.

Enter First Murderer.

MACBETH See, they encounter thee with their hearts'
10 thanks.
Both sides are even: here I'll sit i' th' midst:
Be large in mirth; anon we'll drink a measure
The table round. [*Goes to Murderer*] There's blood upon thy face.

MURDERER 'Tis Banquo's then.

15 MACBETH 'Tis better thee without than he within.
Is he dispatched?

MURDERER My lord, his throat is cut; that I did for him.

MACBETH Thou art the best o' th' cutthroats.

III.iv. 1 **degrees** ranks 4 **society** the company 6 **keeps her state** remains seated in her chair of state 7 **require** request 10 **encounter** meet 12 **measure** goblet 15 **thee without than he within** outside you than inside him

Yet he's good that did the like for Fleance;
If thou didst it, thou art the nonpareil. 20

MURDERER Most royal sir, Fleance is 'scaped.

MACBETH [*Aside*] Then comes my fit again: I had else been perfect,
Whole as the marble, founded as the rock,
As broad and general as the casing air:
But now I am cabined, cribbed, confined, bound in 25
To saucy doubts and fears.—But Banquo's safe?

MURDERER Ay, my good lord: safe in a ditch he bides,
With twenty trenchèd gashes on his head,
The least a death to nature.

MACBETH Thanks for that.
[*Aside*] There the grown serpent lies; the worm that's fled 30
Hath nature that in time will venom breed,
No teeth for th' present. Get thee gone. Tomorrow
We'll hear ourselves again. *Exit Murderer.*

LADY MACBETH My royal lord,
You do not give the cheer. The feast is sold
That is not often vouched, while 'tis a-making, 35
'Tis given with welcome. To feed were best at home;
From thence, the sauce to meat is ceremony;
Meeting were bare without it.

Enter the Ghost of Banquo, and sits in Macbeth's place.

MACBETH Sweet remembrancer!
Now good digestion wait on appetite,
And health on both!

23 **founded** firmly based 24 **broad . . . casing** unconfined as the surrounding 25 **cribbed** penned up 26 **saucy** insolent 28 **trenchèd** trenchlike 30 **worm** serpent 33 **hear ourselves** talk it over 34 **the cheer** a sense of cordiality 34–36 **The feast . . . home** i.e., the feast seems sold (not given) during which the host fails to welcome the guests. Mere eating is best done at home 37 **meat** food 38 **remembrancer** reminder

40 LENNOX May 't please your Highness sit.

MACBETH Here had we now our country's honor roofed,
Were the graced person of our Banquo present—
Who may I rather challenge for unkindness
Than pity for mischance!

ROSS His absence, sir,
45 Lays blame upon his promise. Please 't your Highness
To grace us with your royal company?

MACBETH The table's full.

LENNOX Here is a place reserved, sir.

MACBETH Where?

LENNOX Here, my good lord. What is 't that moves your Highness?

MACBETH Which of you have done this?

50 LORDS What, my good lord?

MACBETH Thou canst not say I did it. Never shake
Thy gory locks at me.

ROSS Gentlemen, rise, his Highness is not well.

LADY MACBETH Sit, worthy friends. My lord is often thus,
55 And hath been from his youth. Pray you, keep seat.
The fit is momentary; upon a thought
He will again be well. If much you note him,
You shall offend him and extend his passion.
Feed, and regard him not.—Are you a man?

60 MACBETH Ay, and a bold one, that dare look on that
Which might appall the devil.

LADY MACBETH O proper stuff!
This is the very painting of your fear.
This is the air-drawn dagger which, you said,

41 **our country's honor roofed** our noblity under one roof 43–44 **Who . . . mischance** whom I hope I may reprove because he is unkind rather than pity because he has encountered an accident 56 **upon a thought** as quick as thought 58 **extend his passion** lengthen his fit

Led you to Duncan. O, these flaws and starts,
Impostors to true fear, would well become 65
A woman's story at a winter's fire,
Authorized by her grandam. Shame itself!
Why do you make such faces? When all's done,
You look but on a stool.

MACBETH Prithee, see there!
Behold! Look! Lo! How say you? 70
Why, what care I? If thou canst nod, speak too.
If charnel houses and our graves must send
Those that we bury back, our monuments
Shall be the maws of kites. [*Exit Ghost*.]

LADY MACBETH What, quite unmanned in folly?

MACBETH If I stand here, I saw him.

LADY MACBETH Fie, for shame! 75

MACBETH Blood hath been shed ere now, i' th' olden time,
Ere humane statute purged the gentle weal;
Ay, and since too, murders have been performed
Too terrible for the ear. The times has been
That, when the brains were out, the man would die, 80
And there an end; but now they rise again,
With twenty mortal murders on their crowns,
And push us from our stools. This is more strange
Than such a murder is.

LADY MACBETH My worthy lord,
Your noble friends do lack you.

MACBETH I do forget. 85
Do not muse at me, my most worthy friends;
I have a strange infirmity, which is nothing
To those that know me. Come, love and health to all!

64 **flaws** gusts, outbursts 65 **to** compared with 67 **Authorized** vouched for 72 **charnel houses** vaults containing bones 73–74 **our . . . kites** our tombs shall be the bellies of rapacious birds 77 **purged the gentle weal** i.e., cleansed the state and made it gentle 82 **mortal murders on their crowns** deadly wounds on their heads

Then I'll sit down. Give me some wine, fill full.

Enter Ghost.

90 I drink to th' general joy o' th' whole table,
And to our dear friend Banquo, whom we miss;
Would he were here! To all and him we thirst,
And all to all.

LORDS Our duties, and the pledge.

MACBETH Avaunt! and quit my sight! Let the earth hide thee!

95 Thy bones are marrowless, thy blood is cold;
Thou hast no speculation in those eyes
Which thou dost glare with.

LADY MACBETH Think of this, good peers,
But as a thing of custom; 'tis no other.
Only it spoils the pleasure of the time.

100 MACBETH What man dare, I dare.
Approach thou like the rugged Russian bear,
The armed rhinoceros, or th' Hyrcan tiger;
Take any shape but that, and my firm nerves
Shall never tremble. Or be alive again,
105 And dare me to the desert with thy sword.
If trembling I inhabit then, protest me
The baby of a girl. Hence, horrible shadow!
Unreal mock'ry, hence! [*Exit Ghost.*]
Why, so: being gone,
I am a man again. Pray you, sit still.

LADY MACBETH You have displaced the mirth, broke the
110 good meeting,
With most admired disorder.

MACBETH Can such things be,
And overcome us like a summer's cloud,

92 **thirst** desire to drink 93 **all to all** everything to everybody (?) let everybody drink to everybody (?) 96 **speculation** sight 102 **Hyrcan** of Hyrcania (near the Caspian Sea) 103 **nerves** sinews 105 **the desert** a lonely place 106–07 **If . . . girl** if then I tremble, proclaim me a baby girl 111 **admired** amazing 112 **overcome us** come over us

Without our special wonder? You make me strange
Even to the disposition that I owe,
When now I think you can behold such sights, 115
And keep the natural ruby of your cheeks,
When mine is blanched with fear.

ROSS What sights, my lord?

LADY MACBETH I pray you, speak not: he grows worse and worse;
Question enrages him: at once, good night.
Stand not upon the order of your going, 120
But go at once.

LENNOX Good night; and better health
Attend his Majesty!

LADY MACBETH A kind good night to all!

Exeunt Lords.

MACBETH It will have blood, they say: blood will have blood.
Stones have been known to move and trees to speak;
Augures and understood relations have 125
By maggot-pies and choughs and rooks brought forth
The secret'st man of blood. What is the night?

LADY MACBETH Almost at odds with morning, which is which.

MACBETH How say'st thou, that Macduff denies his person
At our great bidding?

LADY MACBETH Did you send to him, sir? 130

MACBETH I hear it by the way, but I will send:

113-14 **You ... owe** i.e., you make me wonder what my nature is 120 **Stand ... going** do not insist on departing in your order of rank 125 **Augures and understood relations** auguries and comprehended reports 126 **By ... forth** by magpies, choughs, and rooks (telltale birds) revealed 127 **What is the night** what time of night is it 128 **at odds** striving 131 **by the way** incidentally

There's not a one of them but in his house
I keep a servant fee'd. I will tomorrow,
And betimes I will, to the weïrd sisters:
135 More shall they speak, for now I am bent to know
By the worst means the worst. For mine own good
All causes shall give way. I am in blood
Stepped in so far that, should I wade no more,
Returning were as tedious as go o'er.
140 Strange things I have in head that will to hand,
Which must be acted ere they may be scanned.

LADY MACBETH You lack the season of all natures, sleep.

MACBETH Come, we'll to sleep. My strange and self-abuse
Is the initiate fear that wants hard use.
145 Were are yet but young in deed. *Exeunt.*

Scene V. [*A Witches' haunt.*]

Thunder. Enter the Three Witches, meeting Hecate.

FIRST WITCH Why, how now, Hecate! you look angerly.

HECATE Have I not reason, beldams as you are,
Saucy and overbold? How did you dare
To trade and traffic with Macbeth
5 In riddles and affairs of death;

133 **fee'd** i.e., paid to spy 134 **betimes** quickly 135 **bent** determined 137 **causes** considerations 141 **may be scanned** can be examined 142 **season of all natures** seasoning (preservative) of all living creatures 143 **My strange and self-abuse** my strange delusion 144 **initiate . . . use** beginner's fear that lacks hardening practice III.v. 2 **beldams** hags

And I, the mistress of your charms,
The close contriver of all harms,
Was never called to bear my part,
Or show the glory of our art?
And, which is worse, all you have done 10
Hath been but for a wayward son,
Spiteful and wrathful; who, as others do,
Loves for his own ends, not for you.
But make amends now: get you gone,
And at the pit of Acheron 15
Meet me i' th' morning: thither he
Will come to know his destiny.
Your vessels and your spells provide,
Your charms and everything beside.
I am for th' air; this night I'll spend 20
Unto a dismal and a fatal end:
Great business must be wrought ere noon.
Upon the corner of the moon
There hangs a vap'rous drop profound;
I'll catch it ere it come to ground: 25
And that distilled by magic sleights
Shall raise such artificial sprites
As by the strength of their illusion
Shall draw him on to his confusion.
He shall spurn fate, scorn death, and bear 30
His hopes 'bove wisdom, grace, and fear:
And you all know security
Is mortals' chiefest enemy.

Music and a song.

Hark! I am called; my little spirit, see,
Sits in a foggy cloud and stays for me. [*Exit.*] 35

Sing within, "Come away, come away," *&c.*

FIRST WITCH Come, let's make haste; she'll soon be back again. *Exeunt.*

7 close contriver secret inventor **15 Acheron** (river of Hades) **14 profound** heavy **26 sleights** arts **27 artificial sprites** spirits created by magic arts (?) artful (cunning) spirits (?) **29 confusion** ruin **32 security** overconfidence

Scene VI. [*The palace.*]

Enter Lennox and another Lord.

LENNOX My former speeches have but hit your thoughts,
Which can interpret farther. Only I say
Things have been strangely borne. The gracious Duncan
Was pitied of Macbeth: marry, he was dead.
5 And the right-valiant Banquo walked too late;
Whom, you may say, if 't please you, Fleance killed,
For Fleance fled. Men must not walk too late.
Who cannot want the thought, how monstrous
It was for Malcolm and for Donalbain
10 To kill their gracious father? Damnèd fact!
How it did grieve Macbeth! Did he not straight,
In pious rage, the two delinquents tear,
That were the slaves of drink and thralls of sleep?
Was not that nobly done? Ay, and wisely too;
15 For 'twould have angered any heart alive
To hear the men deny 't. So that I say
He has borne all things well: and I do think
That, had he Duncan's sons under his key—
As, an 't please heaven, he shall not—they should find
20 What 'twere to kill a father. So should Fleance.
But, peace! for from broad words, and 'cause he failed
His presence at the tyrant's feast, I hear,

III.vi. 1 **My . . . thoughts** i.e., my recent words have only coincided with what you have in your mind 3 **borne** managed 8 **cannot want the thought** can fail to think 10 **fact** evil deed 13 **thralls** slaves 17 **borne** managed 19 **an 't** if it 21 **for from broad words** because of frank talk

Macduff lives in disgrace. Sir, can you tell
Where he bestows himself?

LORD The son of Duncan,
From whom this tyrant holds the due of birth, 25
Lives in the English court, and is received
Of the most pious Edward with such grace
That the malevolence of fortune nothing
Takes from his high respect. Thither Macduff
Is gone to pray the holy King, upon his aid 30
To wake Northumberland and warlike Siward;
That by the help of these, with Him above
To ratify the work, we may again
Give to our tables meat, sleep to our nights,
Free from our feasts and banquets bloody knives, 35
Do faithful homage and receive free honors:
All which we pine for now. And this report
Hath so exasperate the King that he
Prepares for some attempt of war.

LENNOX Sent he to Macduff?

LORD He did: and with an absolute "Sir, not I," 40
The cloudy messenger turns me his back,
And hums, as who should say "You'll rue the time
That clogs me with this answer."

LENNOX And that well might
Advise him to a caution, t' hold what distance
His wisdom can provide. Some holy angel 45
Fly to the court of England and unfold
His message ere he come, that a swift blessing
May soon return to this our suffering country
Under a hand accursed!

LORD I'll send my prayers with him.

Exeunt.

25 **due of birth** birthright 27 **Edward** Edward the Confessor (reigned 1042–1066) 28–29 **nothing . . . respect** does not diminish the high respect in which he is held 30 **upon his aid** to aid him (Malcolm) 31 **To wake Northumberland** i.e., to arouse the people in an English county near Scotland 36 **free** freely granted 41 **cloudy** disturbed 43 **clogs** burdens

ACT IV

Scene I. [*A Witches' haunt.*]

Thunder. Enter the Three Witches.

FIRST WITCH Thrice the brinded cat hath mewed.

SECOND WITCH Thrice and once the hedge-pig whined.

THIRD WITCH Harpier cries. 'Tis time, 'tis time.

FIRST WITCH Round about the caldron go:
5 In the poisoned entrails throw.
Toad, that under cold stone
Days and nights has thirty-one
Swelt'red venom sleeping got,
Boil thou first i' th' charmèd pot.

10 ALL Double, double, toil and trouble;
Fire burn and caldron bubble.

SECOND WITCH Fillet of a fenny snake,
In the caldron boil and bake;
Eye of newt and toe of frog,
15 Wool of bat and tongue of dog,
Adder's fork and blindworm's sting,
Lizard's leg and howlet's wing,

IV.i. 1 **brinded** brindled 2 **hedge-pig** hedgehog 3 **Harpier** (an attendant spirit, like Graymalkin and Paddock in I.i) 8 **Swelt'red venom sleeping got** venom sweated out while sleeping 12 **Fillet** slice 12 **fenny** from a swamp 16 **fork** forked tongue 16 **blindworm** (a legless lizard) 17 **howlet** owlet

For a charm of pow'rful trouble,
Like a hell-broth boil and bubble.

ALL Double, double, toil and trouble; 20
Fire burn and caldron bubble.

THIRD WITCH Scale of dragon, tooth of wolf,
Witch's mummy, maw and gulf
Of the ravined salt-sea shark,
Root of hemlock digged i' th' dark, 25
Liver of blaspheming Jew,
Gall of goat, and slips of yew
Slivered in the moon's eclipse,
Nose of Turk and Tartar's lips,
Finger of birth-strangled babe 30
Ditch-delivered by a drab,
Make the gruel thick and slab:
Add thereto a tiger's chaudron,
For th' ingredience of our caldron.

ALL Double, double, toil and trouble; 35
Fire burn and caldron bubble.

SECOND WITCH Cool it with a baboon's blood,
Then the charm is firm and good.

Enter Hecate and the other Three Witches.

HECATE O, well done! I commend your pains;
And every one shall share i' th' gains: 40
And now about the caldron sing,
Like elves and fairies in a ring,
Enchanting all that you put in.

Music and a song: "Black Spirits," &c.

[*Exeunt Hecate and the other Three Witches.*]

SECOND WITCH By the pricking of my thumbs,
Something wicked this way comes: 45
Open, locks,
Whoever knocks!

23 **Witch's mummy** mummified flesh of a witch 23 **maw and gulf** stomach and gullet 24 **ravined** ravenous 31 **Ditch-delivered by a drab** born in a ditch of a harlot 32 **slab** viscous 33 **chaudron** entrails

Enter Macbeth.

MACBETH How now, you secret, black, and midnight hags!
What is 't you do?

ALL A deed without a name.

50 MACBETH I conjure you, by that which you profess,
Howe'er you come to know it, answer me:
Though you untie the winds and let them fight
Against the churches: though the yesty waves
Confound and swallow navigation up;
55 Though bladed corn be lodged and trees blown down;
Though castles topple on their warders' heads;
Though palaces and pyramids do slope
Their heads to their foundations; though the treasure
Of nature's germens tumble all together,
60 Even till destruction sicken, answer me
To what I ask you.

FIRST WITCH Speak.

SECOND WITCH Demand.

THIRD WITCH We'll answer.

FIRST WITCH Say, if th' hadst rather hear it from our mouths,
Or from our masters?

MACBETH Call 'em, let me see 'em.

FIRST WITCH Pour in sow's blood, that hath eaten
65 Her nine farrow; grease that's sweaten
From the murderer's gibbet throw
Into the flame.

ALL Come, high or low,
Thyself and office deftly show!

53 yesty foamy **54 Confound** destroy **55 bladed corn be lodged** grain in the ear be beaten down **57 slope** bend **59 nature's germens** seeds of all life **60 sicken** i.e., sicken at its own work **65 farrow** young pigs **65 sweaten** sweated **68 office** function

Thunder. First Apparition: an Armed Head.

MACBETH Tell me, thou unknown power——

FIRST WITCH He knows thy thought:
Hear his speech, but say thou nought. 70

FIRST APPARITION Macbeth! Macbeth! Macbeth! Beware Macduff!
Beware the Thane of Fife. Dismiss me: enough.

He descends.

MACBETH Whate'er thou art, for thy good caution thanks:
Thou hast harped my fear aright. But one word more——

FIRST WITCH He will not be commanded. Here's another, 75
More potent than the first.

Thunder. Second Apparition: a Bloody Child.

SECOND APPARITION Macbeth! Macbeth! Macbeth!

MACBETH Had I three ears, I'd hear thee.

SECOND APPARITION Be bloody, bold, and resolute! Laugh to scorn
The pow'r of man, for none of woman born 80
Shall harm Macbeth. *Descends.*

MACBETH Then live, Macduff: what need I fear of thee?
But yet I'll make assurance double sure,
And take a bond of fate. Thou shalt not live;
That I may tell pale-hearted fear it lies, 85
And sleep in spite of thunder.

Thunder. Third Apparition: a Child Crowned, with a tree in his hand.

74 harped hit upon, struck the note of **84 take a bond of fate** get a guarantee from fate (i.e., he will kill Macduff and thus will compel fate to keep its word)

What is this,
That rises like the issue of a king,
And wears upon his baby-brow the round
And top of sovereignty?

ALL Listen, but speak not to 't.

THIRD APPARITION Be lion-mettled, proud, and take
90 no care
Who chafes, who frets, or where conspirers are:
Macbeth shall never vanquished be until
Great Birnam Wood to high Dunsinane Hill
Shall come against him. *Descends.*

MACBETH That will never be.
95 Who can impress the forest, bid the tree
Unfix his earth-bound root? Sweet bodements, good!
Rebellious dead, rise never, till the Wood
Of Birnam rise, and our high-placed Macbeth
Shall live the lease of nature, pay his breath
100 To time and mortal custom. Yet my heart
Throbs to know one thing. Tell me, if your art
Can tell so much: shall Banquo's issue ever
Reign in this kingdom?

ALL Seek to know no more.

MACBETH I will be satisfied. Deny me this,
105 And an eternal curse fall on you! Let me know.
Why sinks that caldron? And what noise is this?
Hautboys.

FIRST WITCH Show!

SECOND WITCH Show!

THIRD WITCH Show!

87 **issue** offspring 88–89 **round/And top of sovereignty** i.e., crown 95 **impress** conscript 96 **bodements** prophecies 97 **Rebellious dead** (perhaps a reference to Banquo; but perhaps a misprint for "rebellion's head") 99 **lease of nature** natural lifespan 100 **mortal custom** natural death 104 **satisfied** i.e., fully informed 106 **noise** music

ALL Show his eyes, and grieve his heart; 110
Come like shadows, so depart!

A show of eight Kings and Banquo, last [*King*] *with a glass in his hand.*

MACBETH Thou art too like a spirit of Banquo. Down!
Thy crown does sear mine eyelids. And thy hair,
Thou other gold-bound brow, is like the first.
A third is like the former. Filthy hags! 115
Why do you show me this? A fourth! Start, eyes!
What, will the line stretch out to th' crack of doom?
Another yet! A seventh! I'll see no more.
And yet the eighth appears, who bears a glass
Which shows me many more; and some I see 120
That twofold balls and treble scepters carry:
Horrible sight! Now I see 'tis true;
For the blood-boltered Banquo smiles upon me,
And points at them for his. What, is this so?

FIRST WITCH Ay, sir, all this is so. But why 125
Stands Macbeth thus amazedly?
Come, sisters, cheer we up his sprites,
And show the best of our delights:
I'll charm the air to give a sound,
While you perform your antic round, 130
That this great king may kindly say
Our duties did his welcome pay.

Music. The Witches dance, and vanish.

MACBETH Where are they? Gone? Let this pernicious hour
Stand aye accursèd in the calendar!
Come in, without there!

III. s.d. **glass** mirror 116 **Start** i.e., from the sockets 117 **crack of doom** blast (of a trumpet?) at doomsday 121 **twofold balls and treble scepters** (coronation emblems) 123 **blood-boltered** matted with blood 127 **sprites** spirits 130 **antic round** grotesque circular dance

Enter Lennox.

135 LENNOX What's your Grace's will?

MACBETH Saw you the weïrd sisters?

LENNOX No, my lord.

MACBETH Came they not by you?

LENNOX No indeed, my lord.

MACBETH Infected be the air whereon they ride.
And damned all those that trust them! I did hear
140 The galloping of horse. Who was 't came by?

LENNOX 'Tis two or three, my lord, that bring you word
Macduff is fled to England.

MACBETH Fled to England?

LENNOX Ay, my good lord.

MACBETH [*Aside*] Time, thou anticipat'st my dread exploits.
145 The flighty purpose never is o'ertook
Unless the deed go with it. From this moment
The very firstlings of my heart shall be
The firstlings of my hand. And even now,
To crown my thoughts with acts, be it thought and done:
150 The castle of Macduff I will surprise;
Seize upon Fife; give to th' edge o' th' sword
His wife, his babes, and all unfortunate souls
That trace him in his line. No boasting like a fool;
This deed I'll do before this purpose cool:
155 But no more sights!—Where are these gentlemen?
Come, bring me where they are. *Exeunt.*

140 **horse** horses (or "horsemen") 144 **anticipat'st** foretold 145-46 **The flighty . . . it** the fleeting plan is never fulfilled unless an action acccompanies it 147 **firstlings of my heart** i.e., first thoughts, impulses 150 **surprise** attack suddenly 153 **trace him in his line** are of his lineage

Scene II. [*Macduff's castle.*]

Enter Macduff's wife, her Son, and Ross.

LADY MACDUFF What had he done, to make him fly the land?

ROSS You must have patience, madam.

LADY MACDUFF He had none:
His flight was madness. When our actions do not,
Our fears do make us traitors.

ROSS You know not
Whether it was his wisdom or his fear.

LADY MACDUFF Wisdom! To leave his wife, to leave his babes,
His mansion and his titles, in a place
From whence himself does fly? He loves us not;
He wants the natural touch: for the poor wren,
The most diminutive of birds, will fight, 10
Her young ones in her nest, against the owl.
All is the fear and nothing is the love;
As little is the wisdom, where the flight
So runs against all reason.

ROSS My dearest coz,
I pray you, school yourself. But, for your husband, 15
He is noble, wise, judicious, and best knows
The fits o' th' season. I dare not speak much further:
But cruel are the times, when we are traitors
And do not know ourselves; when we hold rumor
From what we fear, yet know not what we fear, 20

IV.ii. 7 titles possessions **9 wants the natural touch** i.e., lacks natural affection for his wife and children **14 coz** cousin **15 school** control **17 fits o' th' season** disorders of the time **19–20 hold rumor/From what we fear** believe rumors because we fear

But float upon a wild and violent sea
Each way and move. I take my leave of you.
Shall not be long but I'll be here again.
Things at the worst will cease, or else climb upward
25 To what they were before. My pretty cousin,
Blessing upon you!

LADY MACDUFF Fathered he is, and yet he's fatherless.

ROSS I am so much a fool, should I stay longer,
It would be my disgrace and your discomfort.
I take my leave at once. *Exit Ross.*

30 LADY MACDUFF Sirrah, your father's dead:
And what will you do now? How will you live?

SON As birds do, mother.

LADY MACDUFF What, with worms and flies?

SON With what I get, I mean; and so do they.

LADY MACDUFF Poor bird! thou'dst never fear the net nor lime,
35 The pitfall nor the gin.

SON Why should I, mother? Poor birds they are not set for.
My father is not dead, for all your saying.

LADY MACDUFF Yes, he is dead: how wilt thou do for a father?

SON Nay, how will you do for a husband?

LADY MACDUFF Why, I can buy me twenty at any
40 market.

SON Then you'll buy 'em to sell again.

LADY MACDUFF Thou speak'st with all thy wit, and yet, i' faith,
With wit enough for thee.

24 cease i.e., cease worsening **29 It would be my disgrace** i.e., I would weep **30 Sirrah** (here an affectionate address to a child) **34 lime** bird-lime (smeared on branches to catch birds) **35 gin** trap **41 sell** betray **43 for thee** i.e., for a child

SON Was my father a traitor, mother?

LADY MACDUFF Ay, that he was. 45

SON What is a traitor?

LADY MACDUFF Why, one that swears and lies.

SON And be all traitors that do so?

LADY MACDUFF Every one that does so is a traitor, and must be hanged.

SON And must they all be hanged that swear and lie? 50

LADY MACDUFF Every one.

SON Who must hang them?

LADY MACDUFF Why, the honest men.

SON Then the liars and swearers are fools; for there are liars and swearers enow to beat the honest 55 men and hang up them.

LADY MACDUFF Now, God help thee, poor monkey! But how wilt thou do for a father?

SON If he were dead, you'd weep for him. If you would not, it were a good sign that I should quickly 60 have a new father.

LADY MACDUFF Poor prattler, how thou talk'st!

Enter a Messenger.

MESSENGER Bless you, fair dame! I am not to you known.
Though in your state of honor I am perfect.
I doubt some danger does approach you nearly: 65
If you will take a homely man's advice,
Be not found here; hence, with your little ones.
To fright you thus, methinks I am too savage;
To do worse to you were fell cruelty,
Which is too nigh your person. Heaven preserve you!

47 swears and lies i.e., takes an oath and breaks it **55 enow** enough **64 in . . . perfect** I am fully informed of your honorable rank **65 doubt** fear **66 homely** plain **69 fell** fierce

I dare abide no longer. *Exit Messenger.*

LADY MACDUFF Whither should I fly?
I have done no harm. But I remember now
I am in this earthly world, where to do harm
Is often laudable, to do good sometime
75 Accounted dangerous folly. Why then, alas,
Do I put up that womanly defense,
To say I have done no harm?—What are these faces?

Enter Murderers.

MURDERER Where is your husband?

LADY MACDUFF I hope, in no place so unsanctified
Where such as thou mayst find him.

80 MURDERER He's a traitor.

SON Thou li'st, thou shag-eared villain!

MURDERER What, you egg!

[*Stabbing him.*]

Young fry of treachery!

SON He has killed me, mother:
Run away, I pray you!

[*Dies.*]

Exit [*Lady Macduff*], *crying "Murder!"* [*followed by Murderers*].

Scene III. [*England. Before the King's palace.*]

Enter Malcolm and Macduff.

MALCOLM Let us seek out some desolate shade, and there
Weep our sad bosoms empty.

81 **shag-eared** hairy-eared (?), with shaggy hair hanging over the ears (?) 82 **fry** spawn

MACDUFF Let us rather
Hold fast the mortal sword, and like good men
Bestride our down-fall'n birthdom. Each new morn
New widows howl, new orphans cry, new sorrows 5
Strike heaven on the face, that it resounds
As if it felt with Scotland and yelled out
Like syllable of dolor.

MALCOLM What I believe, I'll wail;
What know, believe; and what I can redress,
As I shall find the time to friend, I will. 10
What you have spoke, it may be so perchance.
This tyrant, whose sole name blisters our tongues,
Was once thought honest: you have loved him well;
He hath not touched you yet. I am young; but something
You may deserve of him through me; and wisdom 15
To offer up a weak, poor, innocent lamb
T'appease an angry god.

MACDUFF I am not treacherous.

MALCOLM But Macbeth is.
A good and virtuous nature may recoil
In an imperial charge. But I shall crave your pardon; 20
That which you are, my thoughts cannot transpose:
Angels are bright still, though the brightest fell:
Though all things foul would wear the brows of grace
Yet grace must still look so.

IV.iii. 3 **mortal** deadly 4 **Bestride our down-fall'n birthdom** protectively stand over our native land 6 **that** so that 8 **Like syllable of dolor** similar sound of grief 10 **to friend** friendly, propitious 12 **sole** very 13 **honest** good 15 **deserve of him through me** i.e., earn by betraying me to Macbeth 15 **wisdom** it may be wise 19–20 **recoil/In** give way under 21 **transform** transform 22 **the brightest** i.e., Lucifer 23 **would wear** desire to wear 24 **so** i.e., like itself

MACDUFF I have lost my hopes.

MALCOLM Perchance even there where I did find my doubts.
25
Why in that rawness left you wife and child,
Those precious motives, those strong knots of love,
Without leave-taking? I pray you,
Let not my jealousies be your dishonors,
30 But mine own safeties. You may be rightly just
Whatever I shall think.

MACDUFF Bleed, bleed, poor country:
Great tyranny, lay thou thy basis sure,
For goodness dare not check thee: wear thou thy wrongs;
The title is affeered. Fare thee well, lord:
35 I would not be the villain that thou think'st
For the whole space that's in the tyrant's grasp
And the rich East to boot.

MALCOLM Be not offended:
I speak not as in absolute fear of you.
I think our country sinks beneath the yoke;
40 It weeps, it bleeds, and each new day a gash
Is added to her wounds. I think withal
There would be hands uplifted in my right;
And here from gracious England have I offer
Of goodly thousands: but, for all this,
45 When I shall tread upon the tyrant's head,
Or wear it on my sword, yet my poor country
Shall have more vices than it had before,
More suffer, and more sundry ways than ever,
By him that shall succeed.

MACDUFF What should he be?

MALCOLM It is myself I mean, in whom I know

26 **rawness** unprotected condition 29 **jealousies** suspicions 30 **rightly just** perfectly honorable 32 **basis** foundation 33 **check** restrain 34 **affeered** legally confirmed 41 **withal** moreover 42 **in my right** on behalf of my claim 43 **England** i.e., the King of England 44 **for** despite

All the particulars of vice so grafted
That, when they shall be opened, black Macbeth
Will seem as pure as snow, and the poor state
Esteem him as a lamb, being compared
With my confineless harms.

MACDUFF Not in the legions 55
Of horrid hell can come a devil more damned
In evils to top Macbeth.

MALCOLM I grant him bloody,
Luxurious, avaricious, false, deceitful,
Sudden, malicious, smacking of every sin
That has a name: but there's no bottom, none, 60
In my voluptuousness: your wives, your daughters,
Your matrons and your maids, could not fill up
The cistern of my lust, and my desire
All continent impediments would o'erbear,
That did oppose my will. Better Macbeth 65
Than such an one to reign.

MACDUFF Boundless intemperance
In nature is a tyranny; it hath been
Th' untimely emptying of the happy throne,
And fall of many kings. But fear not yet
To take upon you what is yours: you may 70
Convey your pleasures in a spacious plenty,
And yet seem cold, the time you may so hoodwink.
We have willing dames enough. There cannot be
That vulture in you, to devour so many
As will to greatness dedicate themselves, 75
Finding it so inclined.

MALCOLM With this there grows
In my most ill-composed affection such

51 **particulars** special kinds 51 **grafted** engrafted 52 **opened** in bloom, i.e., revealed 55 **confineless harms** unbounded evils 58 **Luxurious** lecherous 59 **Sudden** violent 61 **voluptuousness** lust 64 **continent** restraining 67 **In nature** in man's nature 71 **Convey** secretly manage 72 **time** age, i.e., people 77 **ill-composed affection** evilly compounded character

A stanchless avarice that, were I King,
I should cut off the nobles for their lands,
80 Desire his jewels and this other's house:
And my more-having would be as a sauce
To make me hunger more, that I should forge
Quarrels unjust against the good and loyal,
Destroying them for wealth.

MACDUFF This avarice
85 Sticks deeper, grows with more pernicious root
Than summer-seeming lust, and it hath been
The sword of our slain kings. Yet do not fear.
Scotland hath foisons to fill up your will
Of your mere own. All these are portable,
90 With other graces weighed.

MALCOLM But I have none: the king-becoming graces,
As justice, verity, temp'rance, stableness,
Bounty, perseverance, mercy, lowliness,
Devotion, patience, courage, fortitude,
95 I have no relish of them, but abound
In the division of each several crime,
Acting it many ways. Nay, had I pow'r, I should
Pour the sweet milk of concord into hell,
Uproar the universal peace, confound
All unity on earth.

100 MACDUFF O Scotland, Scotland!

MALCOLM If such a one be fit to govern, speak:
I am as I have spoken.

MACDUFF Fit to govern!
No, not to live. O nation miserable!
With an untitled tyrant bloody-sceptered,
105 When shalt thou see thy wholesome days again,

78 stanchless never-ending **86 summer-seeming** befitting summer, i.e., youthful (?) transitory (?) **87 sword of our slain kings** i.e., the cause of death to our kings **88–89 foisons . . . own** enough abundance of your own to satisfy your covetousness **89 portable** bearable **95 relish of** taste for (?) trace of (?) **96 division of each several crime** variations of each kind of crime **99 Uproar** put into a tumult

Since that the truest issue of thy throne
By his own interdiction stands accursed,
And does blaspheme his breed? Thy royal father
Was a most sainted king: the queen that bore thee,
Oft'ner upon her knees than on her feet, 110
Died every day she lived. Fare thee well!
These evils thou repeat'st upon thyself
Hath banished me from Scotland. O my breast,
Thy hope ends here!

MALCOLM Macduff, this noble passion,
Child of integrity, hath from my soul 115
Wiped the black scruples, reconciled my thoughts
To thy good truth and honor. Devilish Macbeth
By many of these trains hath sought to win me
Into his power; and modest wisdom plucks me
From over-credulous haste: but God above 120
Deal between thee and me! For even now
I put myself to thy direction, and
Unspeak mine own detraction; here abjure
The taints and blames I laid upon myself,
For strangers to my nature. I am yet 125
Unknown to woman, never was forsworn,
Scarcely have coveted what was mine own,
At no time broke my faith, would not betray
The devil to his fellow, and delight
No less in truth than life. My first false speaking 130
Was this upon myself. What I am truly,
Is thine and my poor country's to command:
Whither indeed, before thy here-approach,
Old Siward, with ten thousand warlike men,
Already at a point, was setting forth. 125
Now we'll together, and the chance of goodness
Be like our warranted quarrel! Why are you
silent?

107 interdiction curse, exclusion **108 breed** ancestry **111 Died** i.e., prepared for heaven **116 scruples** suspicions **118 trains** plots **119 modest wisdom** i.e., prudence **122 to** under **125 For** as **135 at a point** prepared **136–37 the chance ... quarrel** i.e., may our chance of success equal the justice of our cause

MACDUFF Such welcome and unwelcome things at once
'Tis hard to reconcile.

Enter a Doctor.

MALCOLM Well, more anon. Comes the King forth, I
140 pray you?

DOCTOR Ay, sir. There are a crew of wretched souls
That stay his cure: their malady convinces
The great assay of art; but at his touch,
Such sanctity hath heaven given his hand,
They presently amend.

145 MALCOLM I thank you, doctor.

Exit [*Doctor*].

MACDUFF What's the disease he means?

MALCOLM 'Tis called the evil:
A most miraculous work in this good King,
Which often since my here-remain in England
I have seen him do. How he solicits heaven,
150 Himself best knows: but strangely-visited people,
All swoll'n and ulcerous, pitiful to the eye,
The mere despair of surgery, he cures,
Hanging a golden stamp about their necks,
Put on with holy prayers: and 'tis spoken,
155 To the succeeding royalty he leaves
The healing benediction. With this strange virtue
He hath a heavenly gift of prophecy,
And sundry blessings hang about his throne
That speak him full of grace.

Enter Ross.

MACDUFF See, who comes here?

160 MALCOLM My countryman; but yet I know him not.

142 **stay** await 142–43 **convinces/The great assay of art** i.e. defies the efforts of medical science 145 **presently amend** immediately recover 146 **evil** (scrofula, called "the king's evil" because it could allegedly be cured by the king's touch) 150 **strangely-visited** oddly afflicted 152 **mere** utter 153 **stamp** coin 156 **virtue** power 159 **speak** proclaim

MACDUFF My ever gentle cousin, welcome hither.

MALCOLM I know him now: good God, betimes remove
The means that makes us strangers!

ROSS Sir, amen.

MACDUFF Stands Scotland where it did?

ROSS Alas, poor country!
Almost afraid to know itself! It cannot 165
Be called our mother but our grave, where nothing
But who knows nothing is once seen to smile;
Where sighs and groans, and shrieks that rent the air,
Are made, not marked; where violent sorrow seems
A modern ecstasy. The dead man's knell 170
Is there scarce asked for who, and good men's lives
Expire before the flowers in their caps,
Dying or ere they sicken.

MACDUFF O, relation
Too nice, and yet too true!

MALCOLM What's the newest grief?

ROSS That of an hour's age doth hiss the speaker; 175
Each minute teems a new one.

MACDUFF How does my wife?

ROSS Why, well.

MACDUFF And all my children?

ROSS Well too.

MACDUFF The tyrant has not battered at their peace?

ROSS No; they were well at peace when I did leave 'em.

161 gentle noble **162 betimes** quickly **166 nothing** no one **169 marked** noticed **170 modern ecstasy** i.e., ordinary emotion **173–74 relation/Too nice** tale too accurate **175 That . . . speaker** i.e., the report of the grief of an hour ago is hissed as stale news **176 teems** gives birth to

180 MACDUFF Be not a niggard of your speech: how goes 't?

ROSS When I came hither to transport the tidings,
Which I have heavily borne, there ran a rumor
Of many worthy fellows that were out;
Which was to my belief witnessed the rather,
185 For that I saw the tyrant's power afoot.
Now is the time of help. Your eye in Scotland
Would create soldiers, make our women fight,
To doff their dire distresses.

MALCOLM Be 't their comfort
We are coming thither. Gracious England hath
190 Lent us good Siward and ten thousand men;
An older and a better soldier none
That Christendom gives out.

ROSS Would I could answer
This comfort with the like! But I have words
That would be howled out in the desert air,
Where hearing should not latch them.

195 MACDUFF What concern they?
The general cause or is it a fee-grief
Due to some single breast?

ROSS No mind that's honest
But in it shares some woe, though the main part
Pertains to you alone.

MACDUFF If it be mine,
200 Keep it not from me, quickly let me have it.

ROSS Let not your ears despise my tongue for ever,
Which shall possess them with the heaviest sound
That ever yet they heard.

MACDUFF Humh! I guess at it.

ROSS Your castle is surprised; your wife and babes

182 **heavily** sadly 183 **out** i.e., up in arms 184 **witnessed** attested 185 **power** army 192 **gives out** reports 194 **would** should 195 **latch** catch 196–97 **fee-grief/Due to some single breast** i.e., a personal grief belonging to an individual 204 **surprised** suddenly attacked

Savagely slaughtered. To relate the manner, 205
Were, on the quarry of these murdered deer,
To add the death of you.

MALCOLM Merciful heaven!
What, man! Ne'er pull your hat upon your brows;
Give sorrow words. The grief that does not speak
Whispers the o'er-fraught heart, and bids it break. 210

MACDUFF My children too?

ROSS Wife, children, servants, all
That could be found.

MACDUFF And I must be from thence!
My wife killed too?

ROSS I have said.

MALCOLM Be comforted.
Let's make us med'cines of our great revenge,
To cure this deadly grief. 215

MACDUFF He has no children. All my pretty ones?
Did you say all? O hell-kite! All?
What, all my pretty chickens and their dam
At one fell swoop?

MALCOLM Dispute it like a man.

MACDUFF I shall do so; 220
But I must also feel it as a man.
I cannot but remember such things were,
That were most precious to me. Did heaven look on,
And would not take their part? Sinful Macduff,
They were all struck for thee! Naught that I am, 225
Not for their own demerits but for mine
Fell slaughter on their souls. Heaven rest them now!

MALCOLM Be this the whetstone of your sword. Let grief
Convert to anger; blunt not the heart, enrage it.

206 quarry heap of slaughtered game 210 Whispers the o'er-fraught heart whispers to the overburdened heart 217 hell-kite hellish bird of prey 220 Dispute counter 225 Naught wicked

230 MACDUFF O, I could play the woman with mine eyes,
And braggart with my tongue! But, gentle heavens,
Cut short all intermission; front to front
Bring thou this fiend of Scotland and myself;
Within my sword's length set him. If he 'scape,
Heaven forgive him too!

235 MALCOLM This time goes manly.
Come, go we to the King. Our power is ready;
Our lack is nothing but our leave. Macbeth
Is ripe for shaking, and the pow'rs above
Put on their instruments. Receive what cheer you
may.
240 The night is long that never finds the day. *Exeunt.*

232 intermission interval **232 front to front** forehead to forehead i.e., face to face **237 Our lack is nothing but our leave** i.e., we need only to take our leave i.e., we need only to take our leave **239 Put on their instruments** arm themselves (?) urge us, their agents, onward (?)

ACT V

Scene I. [*Dunsinane. In the castle.*]

Enter a Doctor of Physic and a Waiting-Gentlewoman.

DOCTOR I have two nights watched with you, but can perceive no truth in your report. When was it she last walked?

GENTLEWOMAN Since his Majesty went into the field, I have seen her rise from her bed, throw her night-gown upon her, unlock her closet, take forth paper, fold it, write upon 't, read it, afterwards seal it, and again return to bed; yet all this while in a most fast sleep. 5

DOCTOR A great perturbation in nature, to receive at once the benefit of sleep and do the effects of watching! In this slumb'ry agitation, besides her walking and other actual performances, what, at any time, have you heard her say? 10

GENTLEWOMAN That, sir, which I will not report after her. 15

DOCTOR You may to me, and 'tis most meet you should.

GENTLEWOMAN Neither to you nor anyone, having no witness to confirm my speech. 20

Enter Lady [*Macbeth*], *with a taper.*

V.i. 6 closet chest 11–12 effects of watching deeds of one awake 13 actual performance deeds 17 meet suitable

Lo you, here she comes! This is her very guise, and, upon my life, fast asleep! Observe her; stand close.

DOCTOR How came she by that light?

25 GENTLEWOMAN Why, it stood by her. She has light by her continually. 'Tis her command.

DOCTOR You see, her eyes are open.

GENTLEWOMAN Ay, but their sense are shut.

DOCTOR What is it she does now? Look, how she rubs

30 her hands.

GENTLEWOMAN It is an accustomed action with her, to seem thus washing her hands: I have known her continue in this a quarter of an hour.

LADY MACBETH Yet here's a spot.

35 DOCTOR Hark! she speaks. I will set down what comes from her, to satisfy my remembrance the more strongly.

LADY MACBETH Out, damned spot! Out, I say! One: two: why, then 'tis time to do 't. Hell is murky.

40 Fie, my lord, fie! A soldier, and afeard? What need we fear who knows it, when none can call our pow'r to accompt? Yet who would have thought the old man to have had so much blood in him?

DOCTOR Do you mark that?

45 LADY MACBETH The Thane of Fife had a wife. Where is she now? What, will these hands ne'er be clean? No more o' that, my lord, no more o' that! You mar all with this starting.

DOCTOR Go to, go to! You have known what you

50 should not.

GENTLEWOMAN She has spoke what she should not, I

21 guise custom **23 close** hidden **28 sense** i.e., powers of sight **36 satisfy** confirm **42 to accompt** into account **49 Go to** (an exclamation)

am sure of that. Heaven knows what she has known.

LADY MACBETH Here's the smell of the blood still. All the perfumes of Arabia will not sweeten this little hand. Oh, oh, oh! 55

DOCTOR What a sigh is there! The heart is sorely charged.

GENTLEWOMAN I would not have such a heart in my bosom for the dignity of the whole body.

DOCTOR Well, well, well—— 60

GENTLEWOMAN Pray God it be, sir.

DOCTOR This disease is beyond my practice. Yet I have known those which have walked in their sleep who have died holily in their beds.

LADY MACBETH Wash your hands; put on your night- 65 gown; look not so pale! I tell you again, Banquo's buried. He cannot come out on 's grave.

DOCTOR Even so?

LADY MACBETH To bed, to bed! There's knocking at the gate. Come, come, come, come, give me your 70 hand! What's done cannot be undone. To bed, to bed, to bed! *Exit Lady* [*Macbeth*].

DOCTOR Will she go now to bed?

GENTLEWOMAN Directly.

DOCTOR Foul whisp'rings are abroad. Unnatural deeds 75
Do breed unnatural troubles. Infected minds
To their deaf pillows will discharge their secrets.
More needs she the divine than the physician.
God, God forgive us all! Look after her;
Remove from her the means of all annoyance, 80
And still keep eyes upon her. So good night.

57 **charged** burdened 59 **dignity** worth, rank 62 **practice** professional skill 67 **on's** of his 80 **annoyance** injury 81 **still** continuously

My mind she has mated and amazed my sight:
I think, but dare not speak.

GENTLEWOMAN Good night, good doctor.

Exeunt.

Scene II

Drum and colors. Enter Menteith, Caithness, Angus, Lennox, Soldiers.

MENTEITH The English pow'r is near, led on by Malcolm,
His uncle Siward and the good Macduff.
Revenges burn in them; for their dear causes
Would to the bleeding and the grim alarm
Excite the mortified man.

5 ANGUS Near Birnam Wood
Shall we well meet them; that way are they coming.

CAITHNESS Who knows if Donalbain be with his brother?

LENNOX For certain, sir, he is not. I have a file
Of all the gentry: there is Siward's son,
10 And many unrough youths that even now
Protest their first of manhood.

MENTEITH What does the tyrant?

CAITHNESS Great Dunsinane he strongly fortifies.
Some say he's mad; others, that lesser hate him,
Do call it valiant fury: but, for certain,

82 mated baffled V.ii. **1 pow'r** army **3 dear** heartfelt **4–5 Would . . . man** i.e., would incite a dead man (or "a paralyzed man") to join the bloody and grim call to battle **8 file** list **10 unrough** i.e., beardless **11 Protest** assert

He cannot buckle his distempered cause 15
Within the belt of rule.

ANGUS Now does he feel
His secret murders sticking on his hands;
Now minutely revolts upbraid his faith-breach.
Those he commands move only in command,
Nothing in love. Now does he feel his title 20
Hang loose about him, like a giant's robe
Upon a dwarfish thief.

MENTEITH Who then shall blame
His pestered senses to recoil and start,
When all that is within him does condemn
Itself for being there?

CAITHNESS Well, march we on, 25
To give obedience where 'tis truly owed.
Meet we the med'cine of the sickly weal,
And with him pour we, in our country's purge,
Each drop of us.

LENNOX Or so much as it needs
To dew the sovereign flower and drown the
weeds. 30
Make we our march towards Birnam.

Exeunt, marching.

Scene III. [*Dunsinane. In the castle.*]

Enter Macbeth, Doctor, and Attendants.

MACBETH Bring me no more reports; let them fly all!
Till Birnam Wood remove to Dunsinane
I cannot taint with fear. What's the boy Malcolm?

15 **distempered** swollen by dropsy 16 **rule** self-control 18 **minutely revolts upbraid** rebellions every minute rebuke 23 **pestered** tormented 27 **med'cine** i.e., Malcolm 27 **weal** commonwealth 29 **Each drop of us** i.e., every last drop of our blood (?) 30 **dew** bedew, water (and thus make grow) 30 **sovereign** (1) royal (2) remedial V.iii. 3 **taint** become infected

Was he not born of woman? The spirits that know
All mortal consequences have pronounced me
5 thus:
"Fear not, Macbeth; no man that's born of woman
Shall e'er have power upon thee." Then fly, false
thanes,
And mingle with the English epicures.
The mind I sway by and the heart I bear.
10 Shall never sag with doubt nor shake with fear.

Enter Servant.

The devil damn thee black, thou cream-faced loon!
Where got'st thou that goose look?

SERVANT There is ten thousand——

MACBETH Geese, villain?

SERVANT Soldiers, sir.

MACBETH Go prick thy face and over-red thy fear,
15 Thou lily-livered boy. What soldiers, patch?
Death of thy soul! Those linen cheeks of thine
Are counselors to fear. What soldiers, whey-face?

SERVANT The English force, so please you.

MACBETH Take thy face hence. [*Exit Servant.*]
Seyton!—I am sick at heart,
20 When I behold—Seyton, I say!—This push
Will cheer me ever, or disseat me now.
I have lived long enough. My way of life
Is fall'n into the sear, the yellow leaf,
And that which should accompany old age,
25 As honor, love, obedience, troops of friends,
I must not look to have; but, in their stead,
Curses not loud but deep, mouth-honor, breath,
Which the poor heart would fain deny, and dare not.
Seyton!

5 **mortal consequences** future human events 9 **sway** move 11 **loon** fool 14 **over-red** cover with red 15 **patch** fool 16 **of** upon 16 **linen** i.e., pale 20 **push** effort 21 **disseat** i.e., unthrone (with wordplay on "cheer," pronounced "chair") 23 **sear** withered

Enter Seyton.

SEYTON What's your gracious pleasure?

MACBETH What news more? 30

SEYTON All is confirmed, my lord, which was reported.

MACBETH I'll fight, till from my bones my flesh be hacked.
Give me my armor.

SEYTON 'Tis not needed yet.

MACBETH I'll put it on.
Send out moe horses, skirr the country round. 35
Hang those that talk of fear. Give me mine armor.
How does your patient, doctor?

DOCTOR Not so sick, my lord,
As she is troubled with thick-coming fancies
That keep her from her rest.

MACBETH Cure her of that.
Canst thou not minister to a mind diseased, 40
Pluck from the memory a rooted sorrow,
Raze out the written troubles of the brain,
And with some sweet oblivious antidote
Cleanse the stuffed bosom of that perilous stuff
Which weighs upon the heart?

DOCTOR Therein the patient 45
Must minister to himself.

MACBETH Throw physic to the dogs, I'll none of it.
Come, put mine armor on. Give me my staff.
Seyton, send out.—Doctor, the thanes fly from me.—
Come, sir, dispatch. If thou couldst, doctor, cast 50
The water of my land, find her disease
And purge it to a sound and pristine health,
I would applaud thee to the very echo,

35 moe more 35 skirr scour 42 Raze out erase 43 oblivious causing forgetfulness 47 physic medical science 50 dispatch hurry 50–51 cast/The water analyze the urine

That should applaud again.—Pull 't off, I say.—
55 What rhubarb, senna, or what purgative drug,
Would scour these English hence? Hear'st thou of
them?

DOCTOR Ay, my good lord; your royal preparation
Makes us hear something.

MACBETH Bring it after me.
I will not be afraid of death and bane
60 Till Birnam Forest come to Dunsinane.

DOCTOR [*Aside*] Were I from Dunsinane away
and clear,
Profit again should hardly draw me here. *Exeunt.*

Scene IV. [*Country near Birnam Wood.*]

Drum and colors. Enter Malcolm, Siward, Macduff, Siward's Son, Menteith, Caithness, Angus, and Soldiers, marching.

MALCOLM Cousins, I hope the days are near at hand
That chambers will be safe.

MENTEITH We doubt it nothing.

SIWARD What wood is this before us?

MENTIETH The Wood of Birnam.

MALCOLM Let every soldier hew him down a bough
5 And bear 't before him. Thereby shall we shadow
The numbers of our host, and make discovery
Err in report of us.

SOLDIERS It shall be done.

58 it i.e., the armor **59 bane** destruction **V.iv. 2 That chambers will be safe** i.e., that a man will be safe in his bedroom **2 nothing** not at all **6 discovery** reconnaisance

SIWARD We learn no other but the confident tyrant
Keeps still in Dunsinane, and will endure
Our setting down before 't.

MALCOLM 'Tis his main hope, 10
For where there is advantage to be given
Both more and less have given him the revolt,
And none serve with him but constrainèd things
Whose hearts are absent too.

MACDUFF Let our just censures
Attend the true event, and put we on 15
Industrious soldiership.

SIWARD The time approaches,
That will with due decision make us know
What we shall say we have and what we owe.
Thoughts speculative their unsure hopes relate,
But certain issue strokes must arbitrate: 20
Towards which advance the war.

Exeunt, marching.

Scene V. [*Dunsinane. Within the castle.*]

Enter Macbeth, Seyton, and Soldiers, with drum and colors.

MACBETH Hang out our banners on the outward walls.
The cry is still "They come!" Our castle's strength
Will laugh a siege to scorn. Here let them lie
Till famine and the ague eat them up.
Were they not forced with those that should be
ours, 5

8 no other but nothing but that **9 endure** allow **11 advantage to be given** afforded an opportunity **12 more and less** high and low **14–15 just censures/ Attend the true event** true judgment await the actual outcome **18 owe** own (the contrast is between "what we shall say we have" and "what we shall really have") **20 certain issue strokes must arbitrate** the definite outcome must be decided by battle **21 war** army **V.v. 4 ague** fever **5 forced** reinforced

We might have met them dareful, beard to beard,
And beat them backward home.

A cry within of women.

What is that noise?

SEYTON It is the cry of women, my good lord. [*Exit.*]

MACBETH I have almost forgot the taste of fears:
10 The time has been, my senses would have cooled
To hear a night-shriek, and my fell of hair
Would at a dismal treatise rouse and stir
As life were in 't. I have supped full with horrors.
Direness, familiar to my slaughterous thoughts,
Cannot once start me.

[*Enter Seyton.*]

15 Wherefore was that cry?

SEYTON The Queen, my lord, is dead.

MACBETH She should have died hereafter;
There would have been a time for such a word.
Tomorrow, and tomorrow, and tomorrow
20 Creeps in this petty pace from day to day,
To the last syllable of recorded time;
And all our yesterdays have lighted fools
The way to dusty death. Out, out, brief candle!
Life's but a walking shadow, a poor player
25 That struts and frets his hour upon the stage
And then is heard no more. It is a tale
Told by an idiot, full of sound and fury
Signifying nothing.

Enter a Messenger.

Thou com'st to use thy tongue; thy story quickly!

30 MESSENGER Gracious my lord,
I should report that which I say I saw,
But know not how to do 't.

MACBETH Well, say, sir.

6 met them dareful i.e., met them in the battlefield boldly **11 fell** pelt **12 treatise** story **15 start** startle **17 should** inevitably would (?) **18 word** message

MESSENGER As I did stand my watch upon the hill,
I looked toward Birnam, and anon, methought,
The wood began to move.

MACBETH Liar and slave! 35

MESSENGER Let me endure your wrath, if 't be not so.
Within this three mile may you see it coming;
I say a moving grove.

MACBETH If thou speak'st false,
Upon the next tree shalt thou hang alive,
Till famine cling thee. If thy speech be sooth, 40
I care not if thou dost for me as much.
I pull in resolution, and begin
To doubt th' equivocation of the fiend
That lies like truth: "Fear not, till Birnam Wood
Do come to Dunsinane!" And now a wood 45
Comes toward Dunsinane. Arm, arm, and out!
If this which he avouches does appear,
There is nor flying hence nor tarrying here.
I 'gin to be aweary of the sun,
And wish th' estate o' th' world were now undone. 50
Ring the alarum bell! Blow wind, come wrack!
At least we'll die with harness on our back.

Exeunt.

Scene VI. [*Dunsinane. Before the castle.*]

Drum and colors. Enter Malcolm, Siward, Macduff, and their army, with boughs.

MALCOLM Now near enough. Your leavy screens throw down,
And show like those you are. You, worthy uncle,

40 **cling** wither 40 **sooth** truth 42 **pull in resolution** restrain confidence 43 **doubt** suspect 47 **avouches** asserts 50 **th' estate** the orderly condition 52 **harness** armor V.vi. 1 **leavy** leafy

Shall, with my cousin, your right noble son,
Lead our first battle. Worthy Macduff and we
5 Shall take upon 's what else remains to do,
According to our order.

SIWARD Fare you well.
Do we but find the tyrant's power tonight,
Let us be beaten, if we cannot fight.

MACDUFF Make all our trumpets speak; give them all breath,
10 Those clamorous harbingers of blood and death.

Exeunt. Alarums continued.

Scene VII. [*Another part of the field.*]

Enter Macbeth.

MACBETH They have tied me to a stake; I cannot fly,
But bearlike I must fight the course. What's he
That was not born of woman? Such a one
Am I to fear, or none.

Enter Young Siward.

YOUNG SIWARD What is thy name?

5 MACBETH Thou'lt be afraid to hear it.

YOUNG SIWARD No; though thou call'st thyself a hotter name
Than any is in hell.

MACBETH My name's Macbeth.

4 battle battalion **4 we** (Malcolm uses the royal "we") **6 order** plan **7 Do we** if we do **7 power** forces V.vii. **2 course** bout, round (he has in mind an attack of dogs or men upon a bear chained to a stake)

YOUNG SIWARD The devil himself could not pronounce a title
More hateful to mine ear.

MACBETH No, nor more fearful.

YOUNG SIWARD Thou liest, abhorrèd tyrant; with my sword 10
I'll prove the lie thou speak'st.

Fight, and Young Siward slain.

MACBETH Thou wast born of woman,
But swords I smile at, weapons laugh to scorn,
Brandished by man that's of a woman born.

Exit.

Alarums. Enter Macduff.

MACDUFF That way the noise is. Tyrant, show thy face!
If thou be'st slain and with no stroke of mine, 15
My wife and children's ghosts will haunt me still.
I cannot strike at wretched kerns, whose arms
Are hired to bear their staves. Either thou, Macbeth,
Or else my sword, with an unbattered edge,
I sheathe again undeeded. There thou shouldst be; 20
By this great clatter, one of the greatest note
Seems bruited. Let me find him, Fortune!
And more I beg not. *Exit. Alarums.*

Enter Malcolm and Siward.

SIWARD This way, my lord. The castle's gently rend'red:
The tyrant's people on both sides do fight;
The noble thanes do bravely in the war;
The day almost itself professes yours,
And little is to do.

17 kerns foot soldiers (contemptuous) **18 staves** spears **20 undeeded** i.e., having done nothing **22 bruited** reported **24 gently rend'red** surrendered without a struggle **27 itself professes** declares itself

MALCOLM We have met with foes
That strike beside us.

SIWARD Enter, sir, the castle.

Exeunt. Alarum.

[Scene VIII. *Another part of the field.*]

Enter Macbeth.

MACBETH Why should I play the Roman fool, and die
On mine own sword? Whiles I see lives, the gashes
Do better upon them.

Enter Macduff.

MACDUFF Turn, hell-hound, turn!

MACBETH Of all men else I have avoided thee.
5 But get thee back! My soul is too much charged
With blood of thine already.

MACDUFF I have no words:
My voice is in my sword, thou bloodier villain
Than terms can give thee out!

Fight. Alarum.

MACBETH Thou losest labor:
As easy mayst thou the intrenchant air
10 With thy keen sword impress as make me bleed:
Let fall thy blade on vulnerable crests;
I bear a charmèd life, which must not yield
To one of woman born.

29 beside us i.e., deliberately miss us (?) as our comrades (?) V.viii. **2 Whiles I see lives** so long as I see living men **5 charged** burdened **8 terms can give thee out** words can describe you **9 intrenchant** incapable of being cut **10 impress** make an impression on

MACDUFF Despair thy charm,
And let the angel whom thou still hast served
Tell thee, Macduff was from his mother's womb 15
Untimely ripped.

MACBETH Accursèd be that tongue that tells me so,
For it hath cowed my better part of man!
And be these juggling fiends no more believed,
That palter with us in a double sense; 20
That keep the word of promise to our ear,
And break it to our hope. I'll not fight with thee.

MACDUFF Then yield thee, coward,
And live to be the show and gaze o' th' time:
We'll have thee, as our rarer monsters are, 25
Painted upon a pole, and underwrit,
"Here may you see the tyrant."

MACBETH I will not yield,
To kiss the ground before young Malcolm's feet,
And to be baited with the rabble's curse.
Though Birnam Wood be come to Dunsinane, 30
And thou opposed, being of no woman born,
Yet I will try the last. Before my body
I throw my warlike shield. Lay on, Macduff;
And damned be him that first cries "Hold,
enough!" *Exeunt, fighting. Alarums.*

[Re-]enter fighting, and Macbeth slain. [Exit Macduff, with Macbeth.] Retreat and flourish. Enter, with drum and colors, Malcolm, Siward, Ross, Thanes, and Soldiers.

MALCOLM I would the friends we miss were safe
arrived. 35

SIWARD Some must go off; and yet, by these I see,
So great a day as this is cheaply bought.

13 **Despair** despair of 14 **angel** i.e., fallen angel, fiend 18 **better part of man** manly spirit 20 **palter** equivocate 24 **gaze o' th' time** spectacle of the age 25 **monsters** freaks 26 **Painted upon a pole** i.e., pictured on a banner set by a showman's booth 29 **baited** assailed (like a bear by dogs) 34s.d. **Retreat and flourish** trumpet call to withdraw, and fanfare 36 **go off** die (theatrical metaphor)

MALCOLM Macduff is missing, and your noble son.

ROSS Your son, my lord, has paid a soldier's debt:
40 He only lived but till he was a man;
The which no sooner had his prowess confirmed
In the unshrinking station where he fought,
But like a man he died.

SIWARD Then he is dead?

ROSS Ay, and brought off the field. Your cause of sorrow
45 Must not be measured by his worth, for then
It hath no end.

SIWARD Had he his hurts before?

ROSS Ay, on the front.

SIWARD Why then, God's soldier be he!
Had I as many sons as I have hairs,
I would not wish them to a fairer death:
And so his knell is knolled.

50 MALCOLM He's worth more sorrow,
And that I'll spend for him.

SIWARD He's worth no more:
They say he parted well and paid his score:
And so God be with him! Here comes newer comfort.

Enter Macduff, with Macbeth's head.

MACDUFF Hail, King! for so thou art: behold, where stands
55 Th'usurper's cursèd head. The time is free.
I see thee compassed with thy kingdom's pearl,
That speak my salutation in their minds,
Whose voices I desire aloud with mine:
Hail, King of Scotland!

ALL Hail, King of Scotland!

42 unshrinking station i.e., place at which he stood firmly **52 parted well and paid his score** departed well and settled his account **55 The time is free** the world is liberated **56 compassed** surrounded

Flourish.

MALCOLM We shall not spend a large expense of time 60
Before we reckon with your several loves,
And make us even with you. My thanes and
kinsmen,
Henceforth be earls, the first that ever Scotland
In such an honor named. What's more to do,
Which would be planted newly with the time— 65
As calling home our exiled friends abroad
That fled the snares of watchful tyranny,
Producing forth the cruel ministers
Of this dead butcher and his fiendlike queen,
Who, as 'tis thought, by self and violent hands 70
Took off her life—this, and what needful else
That calls upon us, by the grace of Grace
We will perform in measure, time, and place:
So thanks to all at once and to each one,
Whom we invite to see us crowned at Scone. 75

Flourish. Exeunt Omnes.

FINIS

61 **reckon with your several loves** reward the devotion of each of you 64–65 **What's more ... time** i.e., what else must be done which should be newly established in this age 68 **ministers** agents 70 **self and violent** her own violent 72 **calls upon us** demands my attention 73 **in measure, time and place** fittingly, at the appropriate time and place

Textual Note

Macbeth, never printed during Shakespeare's lifetime, was first printed in the Folio of 1623. The play is remarkably short, and it may be that there has been some cutting. That in I.v Lady Macbeth apparently proposes to kill Duncan, and that later in the play Macbeth kills him, is scarcely evidence that a scene had been lost, but the inconsistent stage directions concerning Macbeth's death (one calls for him to be slain on stage, another suggests he is both slain and decapitated off stage) indicate some sort of revision. Nevertheless, when one reads the account of Macbeth in Holinshed (Shakespeare's source) one does not feel that the play as it has come down to us omits anything of significance. If, as seems likely, the play was presented at court, its brevity may well be due to King James's known aversion to long plays. On the other hand, it is generally believed that Hecate is a non-Shakespearean addition to the play (she dominates III.v and has a few lines in IV.i), but the evidence is not conclusive, although the passages (along with IV.i.125–32) sound un-Shakespearean.

The present division into acts and scenes is that of the Folio except for V.viii, a division added by the Globe editors. The present edition silently modernizes spelling and punctuation, regularizes speech prefixes, and translates into English the Folio's Latin designations of act and scene. Other departures from the Folio are listed below. The reading of the present text is given first, in bold, and then the reading of the Folio (F) in roman.

I.i.9 **Second Witch . . . Anon** [F attributes to "All," as part of the ensuing speech]

I.ii.13 **gallowglasses** gallowgrosses 14 **quarrel** Quarry 26 **thunders break** Thunders 33–34 **Dismayed . . . Banquo** [one lin in F] 33–35 **Dismayed . . . lion** [three lines in F, ending: Banquoh, Eagles, Lyon] 42 **But . . . faint** [F gives to previous line] 46 **So . . . look** [F gives to next line] 59 **Sweno . . . king** [F gives to previous line]

TEXTUAL NOTE

I.iii.5 **Give . . . I** [F prints as a separate line]

32 **weïrd** weyward [also at I.v.9; II.i.20; "weyard" at III.i.2; III.iv.134; IV.i.136] 39 **Forres** Soris 78 **Speak . . . you** [F prints as a separate line] 81–82 **Into . . . stayed** [three lines in F, ending: corporall, Winde, stay'd] 98 **Came** can 108 **why . . . me** [F gives to next line] 111–14 **Which . . . not** [five lines in F, ending: loose, Norway, helpe, labour'd, not] 131 **If ill** [F gives to next line] 140–42 **Shakes . . . not** [F's lines end: Man, surmise, not] 143 **If . . . crown me** [two lines in F, ending: King, crown me] 149–53 **Give . . . time** [seven lines in F, ending: fauour, forgotten, registred, Leafe, them, vpon, time] 156 **Till . . . friends** [two lines in F, ending: enough, friends]

I.iv.1 **Are not** Or not [given in F to next line] 2–8 **My . . . died** [seven lines in F, ending: back, die, hee, Pardon, Repentance, him, dy'de] 23–27 **In . . . honor** [six lines in F, ending: selfe, Duties, State, should, Loue, Honor]

I.v.23–24 **And yet . . . have it** [three lines in F, ending: winne, cryes, haue it]

I.vi.1 **the air** [F gives to the next line] 4 **martlet** Barlet 9 **most** must 17–20 **Against . . . hermits** [F's lines end: broad, House, Dignities, Ermites]

I.vii.6 **shoal** Schoole [variant spelling] 47 **do** no 58 **as you** [F gives to next line]

II.i.4 **Hold . . . heaven** [two lines in F, ending: Sword, Heauen] 7–9 **And . . . repose** [F's endings: sleepe, thoughts, repose] 13–17 **He . . . content** [F's endings: Pleasure, Offices, withall, Hostesse, content] 25 **when 'tis** [F gives to next line] 55 **strides** sides 56 **sure** sowre 57 **way they** they may

II.ii.2–6 **What . . . possets** [6 lines in F, ending: fire, shriek'd, good-night, open, charge, Possets] 13 s.d. *Enter Macbeth* [F places after "die" in 1.8] 14 **I . . . noise** [two lines in F, ending: deed, noyse] 18–19 **Hark . . . chamber** [one line in F] 22–25 **There's . . . sleep** [F's endings: sleepe, other, Prayers, sleepe] 32 **Stuck . . . throat** [F gives to previous line] 64–65 **To wear . . . chamber** [three lines in F, ending: white, entry, Chamber] 68 **Hath . . . knocking** [two lines in F, ending: vnatended, knocking] 72–73 **To . . . couldst** [four lines in F, ending: deed, my selfe, knocking, could'st. The s.d. "Knock" appears after "deed"]

II.iii.25–27 **Faith . . . things** [two lines of verse in F, the second beginning "And"] 44 s.d. *Enter Macbeth* [F places after 1.43] 53–54 **I'll . . . service** [one line of prose in F] 56–63 **The night . . . shake** [10 lines in F, ending: vnruly, downe, Ayre, Death, terrible, Euents, time, Night, feuorous, shake] 66 **Tongue nor heart** [F gives to next line] 88–89 **O . . . murdered** [one line in F] 137–43 **What . . . bloody** [nine lines in F, ending: doe, them, Office, easie, England, I, safer, Smiles, bloody]

II.iv.14 **And . . . horses** [F prints as a separate line] 17 **make** [F gives to next line] 19 **They . . . so** [F prints as a separate line]

III.i.34–35 **Craving . . . with you** [three lines in F, ending: Horse, Night, you] 42–43 **The sweeter . . . you** [three lines in F, ending: welcome, alone, you] 72 **Who's there** [F prints as a separate line] 75–82 **Well . . . might** [ten lines in F, ending: then, speeches, past, fortune, selfe, conference, with you, crost, them, might] 85–91 **I . . . ever** [nine lines in F, ending: so, now, meeting, predominant,

TEXTUAL NOTE

goe, man, hand, begger'd, euer] 111 **I do** [F gives to previous line] 114–15 **Both ... enemy** [one line in F] 128 **Your ... most** [two lines in F, ending: you, most]

III.ii.16 **But ... suffer** [two lines in F, ending: dis-ioynt, suffer] 22 **Duncan ... grave** [F prints as a separate line] 43 **there ... done** [F gives to next line] 50 **and ... crow** [F gives to next line]

III.iii.9 **The rest** [F gives to next line] 17 **O ... fly, fly, fly** [two lines in F, the first ending: Trecherie] 21 **We ... affair** [two lines in F, ending: lost, Affaire]

III.iv.21–22 **Most ... perfect** [four lines in F, ending: Sir, scap'd, againe, perfect] 49 **Here ... Highness** [two lines in F, ending: Lord, Highness] 110 **broke ... meeting** [F gives to next line] 122 s.d. *Exeunt* Exit 123 **blood will have blood** [F prints as a separate line] 145 **in deed** indeed

III.v.36 **back again** [F prints as a separate line]

III.vi.1 **My ... thoughts** [two lines in F, ending: Speeches, Thoughts] 24 **son** Sonnes 38 **the** their

IV.i.46–47 **Open ... knocks** [one line in F] 59 **germens** Germaine 71 **Beware Macduff** [F prints as a separate line] 79 **Laugh to scorn** [F prints as a separate line] 86 **What is this** [F gives to next line] 93 **Dunsinane** Dunsmane 98 **Birnam** Byrnan [this F spelling, or with *i* for *y* or with a final *e*, occurs at V.ii.5, 31; V.iii.2, 60; V.iv.3; V.v.34, 44; V.viii.30] 119 **eighth** eight 133 **Let ... hour** [F prints as a separate line]

IV.ii.27 **Fathered ... fatherless** [two lines in F, ending: is, Father-lesse] IV.ii.34 **Poor bird** [F prints as a separate line] 36–43 **Why ... for thee** [ten lines in F, ending: Mother, for, saying, is dead, Father, Husband, Market, againe, wit, thee] 48–49 **Every ... hanged** [two lines of verse in F, ending: Traitor, hang'd] 57–58 [two lines of verse in F, ending: Monkie, Father] 77 **What ... faces** [F prints as a separate line]

IV.iii.4 **down-fall'n** downfall 15 **deserve** discerne 25 **where ... doubts** [F prints as a separate line] 102 **Fit to govern** [F gives to next line] 107 **accursed** accust 133 **thy** they 140 **I pray you** [F prints as a separate line] 173 **O relation** [F gives to next line] 211–12 **Wife ... found** [one line in F] 212–13 **And ... too** [one line in F]

V.iii.39 **Cure her** Cure 55 **senna** Cyme

V.vi.1 **Your ... down** [F prints as a separate line]

V.viii.54 **behold ... stands** [F prints as a separate line]

ABOUT THE INTRODUCER

TONY TANNER is Professor of English and American Literature in Cambridge University, and a Fellow of King's College. Previous publications include *The Reign of Wonder*, *City of Words*, *Adultery and the Novel*, and *Venice Desired*. He has also published studies of Jane Austen, Henry James, Saul Bellow and Thomas Pynchon.

TITLES IN EVERYMAN'S LIBRARY

CHINUA ACHEBE
Things Fall Apart

THE ARABIAN NIGHTS
(2 vols, tr. Husain Haddawy)

MARCUS AURELIUS
Meditations

JANE AUSTEN
Emma
Mansfield Park
Northanger Abbey
Persuasion
Pride and Prejudice
Sanditon and Other Stories
Sense and Sensibility

HONORÉ DE BALZAC
Cousin Bette
Eugénie Grandet
Old Goriot

SIMONE DE BEAUVOIR
The Second Sex

SAUL BELLOW
The Adventures of Augie March

WILLIAM BLAKE
Poems and Prophecies

JORGE LUIS BORGES
Ficciones

JAMES BOSWELL
The Life of Samuel Johnson

CHARLOTTE BRONTË
Jane Eyre
Villette

EMILY BRONTË
Wuthering Heights

MIKHAIL BULGAKOV
The Master and Margarita

SAMUEL BUTLER
The Way of all Flesh

ITALO CALVINO
If on a winter's night a traveler

ALBERT CAMUS
The Outsider

MIGUEL DE CERVANTES
Don Quixote

GEOFFREY CHAUCER
Canterbury Tales

ANTON CHEKHOV
My Life and Other Stories
The Steppe and Other Stories

KATE CHOPIN
The Awakening

CARL VON CLAUSEWITZ
On War

SAMUEL TAYLOR COLERIDGE
Poems

WILKIE COLLINS
The Moonstone
The Woman in White

JOSEPH CONRAD
Heart of Darkness
Lord Jim
Nostromo
The Secret Agent
Typhoon and Other Stories
Under Western Eyes
Victory

DANTE ALIGHIERI
The Divine Comedy

DANIEL DEFOE
Moll Flanders
Robinson Crusoe

CHARLES DICKENS
Bleak House
David Copperfield
Dombey and Son
Great Expectations
Hard Times
Little Dorrit
Martin Chuzzlewit
Nicholas Nickleby
The Old Curiosity Shop
Oliver Twist
Our Mutual Friend
The Pickwick Papers
A Tale of Two Cities

DENIS DIDEROT
Memoirs of a Nun

JOHN DONNE
The Complete English Poems

FYODOR DOSTOEVSKY
The Brothers Karamazov
Crime and Punishment

GEORGE ELIOT
Adam Bede
Middlemarch
The Mill on the Floss
Silas Marner

WILLIAM FAULKNER
The Sound and the Fury

HENRY FIELDING
Joseph Andrews and Shamela
Tom Jones

F. SCOTT FITZGERALD
The Great Gatsby
This Side of Paradise

GUSTAVE FLAUBERT
Madame Bovary

FORD MADOX FORD
The Good Soldier
Parade's End

E. M. FORSTER
Howards End
A Passage to India

ELIZABETH GASKELL
Mary Barton

EDWARD GIBBON
The Decline and Fall of the
Roman Empire
Vols 1 to 3: The Western Empire
Vols 4 to 6: The Eastern Empire

IVAN GONCHAROV
Oblomov

GÜNTER GRASS
The Tin Drum

GRAHAM GREENE
Brighton Rock
The Human Factor

THOMAS HARDY
Far From the Madding Crowd
Jude the Obscure
The Mayor of Casterbridge
The Return of the Native
Tess of the d'Urbervilles
The Woodlanders

JAROSLAV HAŠEK
The Good Soldier Švejk

NATHANIEL HAWTHORNE
The Scarlet Letter

JOSEPH HELLER
Catch-22

ERNEST HEMINGWAY
A Farewell to Arms
The Collected Stories

GEORGE HERBERT
The Complete English Works

HERODOTUS
The Histories

HINDU SCRIPTURES
(tr. R. C. Zaehner)

JAMES HOGG
Confessions of a Justified Sinner

HOMER
The Iliad
The Odyssey

VICTOR HUGO
Les Misérables

HENRY JAMES
The Awkward Age
The Bostonians
The Golden Bowl
The Portrait of a Lady
The Princess Casamassima
The Wings of the Dove

JAMES JOYCE
Dubliners
A Portrait of the Artist as
a Young Man
Ulysses

FRANZ KAFKA
Collected Stories
The Castle
The Trial

JOHN KEATS
The Poems

SØREN KIERKEGAARD
Fear and Trembling and
The Book on Adler

RUDYARD KIPLING
Collected Stories
Kim

THE KORAN
(tr. Marmaduke Pickthall)

CHODERLOS DE LACLOS
Les Liaisons dangereuses

GIUSEPPE TOMASI DI LAMPEDUSA
The Leopard

D. H. LAWRENCE
Collected Stories
The Rainbow
Sons and Lovers
Women in Love

MIKHAIL LERMONTOV
A Hero of Our Time

PRIMO LEVI
The Periodic Table

NICCOLÒ MACHIAVELLI
The Prince

THOMAS MANN
Buddenbrooks
Death in Venice and Other Stories
Doctor Faustus

KATHERINE MANSFIELD
The Garden Party and Other Stories

GABRIEL GARCÍA MÁRQUEZ
Love in the Time of Cholera
One Hundred Years of Solitude

ANDREW MARVELL
The Complete Poems

HERMAN MELVILLE
The Complete Shorter Fiction
Moby-Dick

JOHN STUART MILL
On Liberty and Utilitarianism

JOHN MILTON
The Complete English Poems

YUKIO MISHIMA
The Temple of the Golden Pavilion

MARY WORTLEY MONTAGU
Letters

THOMAS MORE
Utopia

TONI MORRISON
Song of Solomon

MURASAKI SHIKIBU
The Tale of Genji

VLADIMIR NABOKOV
Lolita
Pale Fire

V. S. NAIPAUL
A House for Mr Biswas

THE NEW TESTAMENT
(King James Version)

THE OLD TESTAMENT
(King James Version)

GEORGE ORWELL
Animal Farm
Nineteen Eighty-Four

THOMAS PAINE
Rights of Man and Common Sense

BORIS PASTERNAK
Doctor Zhivago

PLATO
The Republic

EDGAR ALLAN POE
The Complete Stories

ALEXANDER PUSHKIN
The Captain's Daughter and Other Stories

FRANÇOIS RABELAIS
Gargantua and Pantagruel

JOSEPH ROTH
The Radetzky March

JEAN-JACQUES ROUSSEAU
Confessions
The Social Contract and the Discourses

SALMAN RUSHDIE
Midnight's Children

WALTER SCOTT
Rob Roy

WILLIAM SHAKESPEARE
Comedies Vols 1 and 2
Histories Vols 1 and 2
Romances
Sonnets and Narrative Poems
Tragedies Vols 1 and 2

MARY SHELLEY
Frankenstein

ADAM SMITH
The Wealth of Nations

ALEXANDER SOLZHENITSYN
One Day in the Life of
Ivan Denisovich

SOPHOCLES
The Theban Plays

CHRISTINA STEAD
The Man Who Loved Children

JOHN STEINBECK
The Grapes of Wrath

STENDHAL
The Charterhouse of Parma
Scarlet and Black

LAURENCE STERNE
Tristram Shandy

ROBERT LOUIS STEVENSON
The Master of Ballantrae and
Weir of Hermiston
Dr Jekyll and Mr Hyde
and Other Stories

HARRIET BEECHER STOWE
Uncle Tom's Cabin

JONATHAN SWIFT
Gulliver's Travels

JUNICHIRŌ TANIZAKI
The Makioka Sisters

WILLIAM MAKEPEACE
THACKERAY
Vanity Fair

HENRY DAVID THOREAU
Walden

ALEXIS DE TOCQUEVILLE
Democracy in America

LEO TOLSTOY
Anna Karenina
Childhood, Boyhood and Youth
The Cossacks
War and Peace

ANTHONY TROLLOPE
Barchester Towers
Can You Forgive Her?
Doctor Thorne
The Eustace Diamonds
Framley Parsonage
The Last Chronicle of Barset
Phineas Finn
The Small House at Allington
The Warden

IVAN TURGENEV
Fathers and Children
First Love and Other Stories
A Sportsman's Notebook

MARK TWAIN
Tom Sawyer
and Huckleberry Finn

JOHN UPDIKE
Rabbit Angstrom

GIORGIO VASARI
Lives of the Painters, Sculptors and
Architects

VIRGIL
The Aeneid

VOLTAIRE
Candide and Other Stories

EVELYN WAUGH
The Complete Short Stories
Brideshead Revisited
Decline and Fall
The Sword of Honour Trilogy

EDITH WHARTON
The Age of Innocence
The Custom of the Country
The House of Mirth
The Reef

OSCAR WILDE
Plays, Prose Writings and Poems

MARY WOLLSTONECRAFT
A Vindication of the Rights of
Woman

VIRGINIA WOOLF
To the Lighthouse
Mrs Dalloway

W. B. YEATS
The Poems

ÉMILE ZOLA
Germinal

This book is set in EHRHARDT. The precise origin
of the typeface is unclear. Most of the founts were
probably cut by the Hungarian punch-cutter
Nicholas Kis for the Ehrhardt foundry
in Leipzig, where they were left
for sale in 1689. In 1938 the
Monotype foundry pro-
duced the modern
version.